Contemporary Retailing

WILLIAM H. BOLEN

Georgia Southern College

Contem

PRENTICE-HALL, INC., ENGLEWOOD CLIFFS, NEW JERSEY 07632

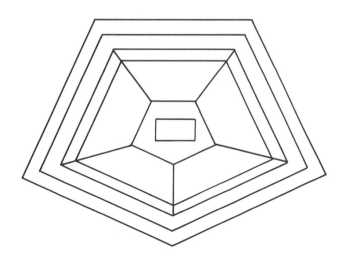

porary
Retailing

SECOND EDITION

Library of Congress Cataloging in Publication Data

Bolen, William H., (date)
    Contemporary retailing.

    Includes bibliographical references and index.
    1. Retail trade. 2. Marketing. 3. Merchandising.
I. Title.
HF5429.B595 1982   658.8'7   81-20964
ISBN 0-13-170266-1   AACR2

Contemporary Retailing, SECOND EDITION
WILLIAM H. BOLEN

Printed in the United States of America

10 9 8 7 6 5 4 3

Editorial/production supervision by Richard Laveglia
Interior design by Mark A. Binn and Richard Laveglia
Cover design by Mark A. Binn
Manufacturing Buyer: Ed O'Dougherty

ISBN 0-13-170266-1

Prentice-Hall International, Inc., *London*
Prentice-Hall of Australia Pty. Limited, *Sydney*
Prentice-Hall of Canada, Ltd., *Toronto*
Prentice-Hall of India Private Limited, *New Delhi*
Prentice-Hall of Japan, Inc., *Tokyo*
Prentice-Hall of Southeast Asia Pte. Ltd., *Singapore*
Whitehall Books Limited, *Wellington, New Zealand*

To Sheron, Bill, and Chuck

Contents

CHAPTER 6

Site Selection 90

CHAPTER 7

Store Design 114

CHAPTER 8

Store Organization 138

SECTION **IV** **Retail Personnel 287**

CHAPTER **16**

Staffing the Retail Store 289

CHAPTER **17**

Salesperson Development 313

CHAPTER **18**

Human Relations in Retailing 330

SECTION **V** **Retail Promotion 345**

CHAPTER **19**

Advertising 347

CHAPTER **20**

Sales Promotion 366

CHAPTER **21**

Retail Display 384

SECTION **VI** Customer Service 405

CHAPTER **22**

Retail Credit 407

CHAPTER **23**

Other Forms of Customer Service 428

SECTION VII Retail Control 449

CHAPTER 24

Retail Security 451

CHAPTER 25

Operations Control 473

SECTION VIII Retailing Applications and Trends 493

CHAPTER 26

Retailing Applications 495

APPENDIX **A**

Cases/Experiential Learning Exercises 527

APPENDIX **B**

Glossary of Retailing Terms 539

Index 555

Preface

Retailing is the summation of all activities which result in the offering for sale of goods and/or services to individuals and/or organizations for purposes of ultimate consumption. The purpose of *Contemporary Retailing* is to present this broad and complex subject in a manner that is easily understood. Emphasis is placed on practical applications for both small and large operations. A "how-to" approach is used along with a concise presentation of fundamental retail management concepts.

The above paragraph was used to introduce the First Edition of *Contemporary Retailing.* As evidenced by its success in the marketplace, what was said has proven to be true. Feedback from users has confirmed the fact that the book does present retailing in a concise, yet easy-to-understand manner. Given this foundation, it is the goal of the Second Edition of *Contemporary Retailing* to improve upon and expand the presentation of the subject of retailing. To accomplish this task, many changes have been made in the book. New diagrams have been added throughout the book to enhance learning. New topics from the ever-changing world of retailing have been included. Illustrations have been updated and more used to promote reader interest. A chapter on retail research has been added to underscore this important aspect of the retailer's job. Service retailing and nonstore retailing are also addressed in detail in the Second Edition as these topic areas grow in importance in today's world.

Another addition to the Second Edition is the conceptual model of retailing. Each section of the book opens with a visual presentation of the model that shows how that topic area fits into the overall subject of retailing. Section one, the outer framework of the conceptual model, deals with the foundations of retailing which include retailing history, retailing strategy (target market and retailing mix), guidelines for effective retailing, external retail restraints (laws, regulations, customs, unions, consumer behavior), and retailing research. Section two, store development, the next level in the model, examines those topics that pertain to a store's creation and continuing development. Subjects discussed include financial planning, site selection, store design, store organization, and planning for opening day. The third level of the retailing model consists of five areas of on-going retailing activity which must be strong for a store to be strong. These areas are merchandising, personnel, promotion, customer service, and control. Finally, the inner framework of the model includes applications and trends. Service and nonstore retailing are examined along with how retailing might be viewed in the years to come. As the various topics are studied, the new material builds on what has already been discussed. This building-block approach provides the reader with a more comprehensive view of the whole area of retailing. This approach should, therefore, enable the retailing student to better achieve the primary objective of this book—retailing knowledge.

The Second Edition of *Contemporary Retailing* has many unique features that help the reader while making the study of retailing more enjoyable. These include cases and experiential learning exercises, cartoons, diagrams, and numerous photographs and illustrations. A glossary of retailing terminology is also provided that serves as a quick reference source. Finally, unlike many other retailing texts, special attention is given to topics such as the definition of a target market, planning for opening day, franchising, merchandise distribution, research, human relations, display, customer service, fire and other forms of disaster, catalog and telephone selling, and retailing as a career.

One other aspect of this book must be mentioned. Every effort has been made throughout the pages of *Contemporary Retailing* to show fair treatment to both sexes and to reflect the fact that most any job in retailing can be performed by either sex. Throughout the book, numerous examples are used to reflect this situation. Retailing truly offers much opportunity regardless of the sex of the person.

No project of this magnitude can be accomplished without the assistance of many firms, organizations, and individuals. To the numerous retail firms, both large and small, who helped by providing insight, material, suggestions, illustrations, and encouragement (many are mentioned in the text or are shown in picture credits), a special thanks is due. Organizations like the National Retail Merchants Association were also very helpful. Their efforts are appreciated. Good reviewers also make for a better book. For their superb work, I express my thanks to Professor Richard Embertson, Western Michigan University; Professor Joe Ezell, Georgia Southern College; Professor Robert Fishco, Middlesex County College; Charles J. Meehan, Hudson Valley Community College; Professor Dorothy Rogers, New Hampshire College; and Professor Summer White, Massachusetts Bay Community College. Thanks are also given to the numerous users of the book who have passed on to me their ideas about how the book might be improved. Wherever possible, their ideas have been included in the Second Edition.

The many helpful people at Prentice-Hall deserve recognition for doing their usual good job of turning the manuscript into a finished product. Thanks are also due the retailing students at Georgia Southern College. Their ideas and suggestions from a student's perspective have been most helpful. Thanks are also expressed to Steve Thrift, Anne Harden, and Sue Oehlerking who aided me by working on the Second Edition in various ways. Finally, I acknowledge with gratitude the work of Delores Collins and Terrie Bennett. Their efforts proved invaluable to the success of the project.

As only those who have written books know, a book cannot be written without the understanding of one's family. For her understanding and assistance, both were of vital significance to the book, I dedicate this book to my wife, Sheron. My sons, Bill and Chuck, also get a note of thanks for their understanding. For this, I am dedicating the book to them as well.

William H. Bolen

Contemporary Retailing

Foundations of Retailing

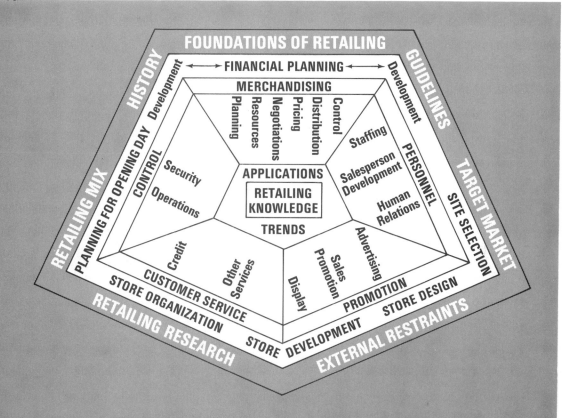

An overview of retailing, its relationship to marketing, the external restraints placed on the retail operation, and retailing research procedures are presented as a basis for the further, more in-depth study of retailing.

"Retailing: An Overview" presents a definition of the term, examines the evolution of the retail form of business operation, and studies the retailer's role in the marketing system as well as in the economy.

"Retailing: Its Relationship to Marketing" includes an analysis of the marketing concept, the target market, the retailing mix, and the various guidelines for effective retailing that should be pursued by a retailer.

"External Retail Restraints" contains an analysis of the impact of federal, state, and local regulations along with the effect of local custom, unions, and consumer behavior on the retail operation.

"Retailing Research" looks at the advantages and disadvantages of research as well as the procedures to follow in applying research to the retail situation.

CHAPTER 1

Retailing:
An Overview

Do you need a pair of shoes? Want a pizza? Does your car have a problem? No need to worry. Just go to the shoe store or the fast-food outlet or the repair shop. In other words, just go to a retailer.

Imagine, if you will, a world without retailers. Where would you buy the shoes? How would you know that the shoes were available? Would the shoes even be available without the ready market provided by retailers? Similar questions can be raised for an infinite number of other situations.

Retailing is an integral part of the way of life of most countries in the world. People have learned to take retailing for granted. Without it, life would certainly not be what it is today for most people.

RETAILING AND RETAILER DEFINED

Retailing is the summation of all activities that result in the offering for sale of goods and/or services to individuals and/or organizations for purposes of ultimate consumption. A retailer is a business firm whose predominant function is retailing.

The four parts of the retailing definition point out the true scope of the subject.

1. *Summation of all activities that result in the offering for sale.* This illustrates that retailing is more than just selling an item. It involves giving the item place utility by making it convenient to the customer. It includes giving credit and personal service by sales personnel. Advertising, buying of merchandise, and infinite other possibilities are involved in the term "activities."

   Under this definition, retailing does not require a store in a traditional sense. Activities may include selling door to door. Avon and Stanley Home Products have done so for years. It also includes selling by mail or by telephone as practiced by Spiegel and many other mail-order supply houses. It includes vending machines and even the street-corner vendor selling hot dogs from a pushcart. If the retailer selects properly and performs efficiently the various retailing activities, his or her chances of retail success are increased.

2. *Goods and/or services.* Some retailers do not sell goods in the physical sense. The TV Repair Shop may not sell television sets—only fix sets. The only product is service. The plumber may require nothing but his or her skill to correct a water problem. In this situation, service is offered the retail customer. In most situations, however, both goods and services are offered. The customer buys a dress that is altered by the store to fit the customer. The customer buys a set of tires and has them installed by the retailer. In varying degrees, both goods and services make up most retail transactions. Most customers buy some kind of service (e.g., sales assistance, credit, home delivery) when buying a product. In many cases, it is the service area that distinguishes one retailer from another or that gives that retailer a differential advantage over his or her competitors.

3. *Individuals and/or organizations.* Retailing is not limited to selling to individual customers. Firms, little and big, can also be retail customers. For example, a company may buy memo pads from an office supply store for use in the company's office. An organization may order flowers from a florist for use at a banquet. Retailers should take care not to overlook organizations as they seek potential customers.

4. *Purposes of ultimate consumption.* Ultimate consumption distinguishes retailing from intermediate marketing, which includes such things as industrial and institutional markets. For example, when the Ford Motor Company contracts with UniRoyal for tires to be placed on new cars, this is not retailing. The tires are being purchased for resale as part of a larger product—the new Ford. However, when a car owner buys new UniRoyal tires for his or her present car at a service center, retailing is in action. When a restaurant buys ketchup, this is institutional marketing. The ketchup being purchased will be used as part of the hamburger to be sold. On the other hand, if a customer buys a bottle of ketchup for *his or her own use* at a convenience store, then the product has been purchased for "purposes of ultimate consumption."

RETAILING'S ROLE IN THE MARKETING SYSTEM

To realize the role of retailing in the marketing system, it is necessary first to understand what is meant by the term—marketing system. A marketing system is the process of moving an idea from conception to ultimate consumption.

As noted in Figure 1-1, the system can take many forms from simple to complex depending upon the number of activities involved. For example, a new paper product may be produced by a manufacturer who will then use several wholesalers and distributors before the product reaches the small retailer and finally the consumer. On the other hand, a large retailer—Penney or Sears—may deal directly with the paper producer.

The retailer can influence the marketing system by successfully developing an idea. For example, the K mart Corporation in the 1960s developed its own idea of the discount K mart store. Although K mart (known as the S. S. Kresge Company at the time) did not have the first discount store, its impact on the marketing system led it to become the model for what discounting is all about.[1] The reader should note, from this example, that retailers have a direct influence on the marketing system. Ideas dealing with various services offered the customer, different store approaches (boutique, group of small stores in a mini-mall), and any other possibilities to which the customer will react favorably can have a positive impact on the marketing system.

Also, as shown in Figure 1-1, feedback is essential to the marketing system. At every stage of the way retailer, wholesaler, and producer alike are, or should be, listen-

Figure 1-1

Examples of marketing systems from a retailing viewpoint.

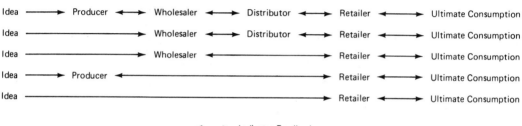

Figure 1-2

The sales floor of a retail store is visual proof that a store provides place utility, breaks bulk, and assumes the storage function while it brings the buyer and seller together.

(Courtesy of Venture Stores)

ing to what their customers want in the way of goods and services. Feedback is a necessary ingredient if the marketing system is to be responsive to the needs of the people within the system.

The role of retailing in the marketing system involves various functions—some of which are shown in Figure 1-2.

1. *Retailing brings buyer and product and/or service together.* By telling the buyer that such a product and/or service exist and by presenting that product in an environment that encourages the customer to buy.
2. *Retailing gives the product or service place utility.* By having the product or service in stock and/or available for the customer without excessive waiting for delivery.
3. *Retailing gives feedback to producer, wholesaler, and others.* By buying or not buying items for sale, a retailer tells the producer, in essence, what to produce. In other words, the retailer determines what he or she thinks customers will buy and buys from the producer accordingly.
4. *Retailing breaks bulk.* By buying in large quantities, the retailer is generally able to buy at a lower per unit cost, thereby making an item available to the customer at a more reasonable price. The retailer will also sell an item in an amount that is more practical for the customer than will the typical manufacturer. The store may buy 1,000 pounds of sugar but sell it to its customers in 1- and 5-pound bags.
5. *Retailing assumes storage function.* By receiving goods before their sale, retailers assist the distribution system by not requiring manufacturers to build enormous warehouse facilities. Retailing permits the merchandise to be stored for short periods near the point of sale. If this were not the case, distribution channels would break down com-

pletely during peak retailing periods such as the Christmas rush and be underutilized at other times of the year.

6. *Retailing assumes risk.* By assuming risk, retailing probably plays its most important role in the marketing system. Retailers buy merchandise before they sell it, thereby giving the manufacturer a more stable business operation. Retailers, in turn, assume risk by offering credit to customers. This action tends to level out business operations since customers no longer need to wait for payday to purchase items.

EVOLUTION OF RETAILING

Retailing has been an integral part of the marketing system for hundreds of years. The retail store or shop in some form or other has existed in every civilized land.[2] From the market square in ancient times to the shops of England in the 1500s to the nearly 2 million retail establishments in the United States today,[3] the evolution of retailing has reflected the evolution of society in a given location.

Trading Posts and Peddlers

The earliest forms of retailing in North America were trading posts and peddlers. When the Pilgrims came, they brought items that they traded for food with the Indians. Over time, a particular place would evolve into a trading post where settler and Indian alike would come to do business. As this area developed, the trading post often evolved into a general store that met the changing needs of the customers.

No one knows how far back in history peddlers go, but the word "emporium" is believed to owe its existence to them. The Greek word for merchant is *emporos*, which was formed from the prefix *en*, "in," and *porous*, "travel"; thus the first merchants were peddlers or hawkers who traveled about the country.[4] As was true in other countries, in the earliest stages of retail development in the United States, the peddler carried on his back the bare essentials to the outlying countryside. As an area developed, the peddler became a horseback peddler and then a wagon peddler with perhaps even a four- to six-horse rig. The wagon peddler was able to carry lace, fine cloth, and other nonessential notions to the housewife of the frontier. He was truly the first "traveling store."

General Store

As people gathered together in villages and towns, a great American institution was born. The general store, with its assortment of basic merchandise, a stove to sit around in winter, and a front porch to sit on during the warmer months, satisfied the needs of the customers of the day. The general store also began a service that has become an essential part of almost all retailing today. This service was the granting of credit to farmers during the year with repayment at harvest time. It helped to build customer loyalty and made the general store a necessary ingredient of small-town America. Many communities in existence today owe much to the general store of yesteryear that kept the town going by means of credit during a drought or other economic disaster.

Mail-Order Catalog

Another form of retailing that dates back to the 1800s is mail-order catalog retailing (see, for example, the catalog in Figure 1–3). The development of mail-order buying depended quite naturally on the development of a reliable delivery system by the Post Office. With the mail system established, Aaron Montgomery Ward rented a small shipping room in Chicago and put out a one-page price list—the first mail-order catalog—in August 1872. Early price lists offered bustles, wool socks, and even a back-gammon set for $1.00. A lady's ring was available for $3.00 and a "gent's cassimere coat" was $3.50.[5]

The other main catalog retailer of early days was the R. W. Sears Watch Company. In 1886, Richard W. Sears, a 23-year-old railroad station agent in Minnesota, started in business by arranging to sell by mail a consignment of watches misdirected to a local jeweler. From this beginning to 1924, the final year of exclusive mail operations, Sears increased sales to a level in excess of $220 million.[6]

Today, catalog purchasing is not restricted to the mail. Several retail units allow their shoppers to order from a catalog while they are in the store. An example of this operation is shown in Figure 1–4.

Department Store

Another development of the 1800s was the department store. The origin of the department store is hard to trace. In some cases, the store had its origin in a consolidation of several stores operated by as many individuals under one roof. Others say that the department store was "invented" by Aristide Boucicaut when he founded Bon Marché (French for "cheap" or "bargain") in Paris. Opened as a small piece-goods shop, it evolved into a department store sometime in the 1850s. Soon to be copied by American merchants such as A. T. Stewart, John Wanamaker, and others, Boucicaut introduced to the world such radical ideas as a "money-back guarantee" and high volume ÷ low margin = profit.[7]

From these early beginnings the department store has grown both in size and specialization. The department store today, with its complete assortment of goods and services, reflects the changing society in which it operates as it moves out of the central business district and changes its merchandise mix to meet new customer demands. With total sales in excess of $89 billion in 1979,[8] the department store form of retailing (Figure 1–5) is still viable in today's market.

Chain Store

The chain store, as a form of retailing, got its start in 1859 when the Great American Tea Company established the first chain. The first A&P (it was to become the Great Atlantic and Pacific Tea Company) units sold tea, spices, coffee, and a few other items. Other starting dates for selected chains still in existence are Woolworth in 1879, Kroger in 1882, S. H. Kress in 1896, K mart in 1897, Jewel Tea in 1899, and J. C. Penney in 1902.

For purposes of definition, a chain was defined originally as having two or more

Figure 1–3

An early example of mail-order catalog retailing.

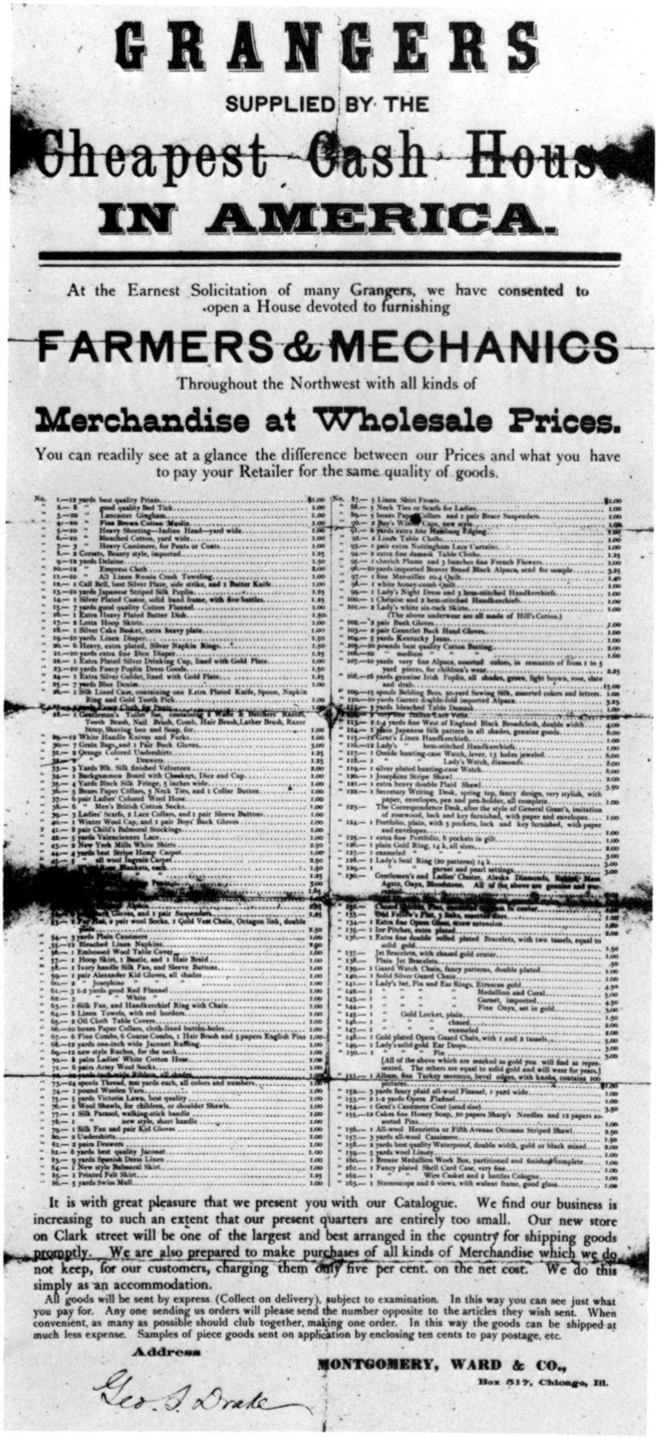

(Courtesy of Montgomery Ward.)

Figure 1-4

Today, the catalog has moved into the store. Many retail units have catalog order centers within the store itself.

(Courtesy of Sears, Roebuck and Co.)

Table 1-1

Chain store sales volume and percentage
of all retail sales, 1939–1979

Year	Sales Volume (billions)	Percentage of All Retail Sales
1979	$296.6	33.5%
1978	270.6	33.8
1976	199.6	31.1
1974	169.4	31.5
1972	137.7	30.7
1970	117.2	31.2
1968	94.2	27.7
1966	80.3	26.4
1964	68.3	26.1
1959	46.7	21.7
1954	31.7	18.7
1949	29.0	21.7
1944	16.2	23.1
1939	9.6	22.8

Sources: *Survey of Current Business,* Vols. 50–60, no. 6 (June 1970–1980); "1969 Business Statistics," 17th Biennial Supplement to the *Survey of Current Business,* 1969, p. 64.

Figure 1-5

Department store of today in a traditional downtown location.

(Courtesy of Carson Pirie Scott & Company)

units. The current definition as used by the U.S. Bureau of the Census defines a chain as having 11 or more retail stores. Sales for such units were $296.6 billion in 1979 in the United States, up from $270.6 billion in 1978.[9] As noted in Table 1-1, sales through chains are on the increase. In 1974, chains amassed $169.4 billion in sales as compared with $296.6 billion in 1979, an increase of over $127 billion or 75 percent over the 1974 sales level. Sales of merchandise in chains has also increased relative to all retail sales. As noted in Table 1-1, chains are getting an increasing share of total retail sales. It is also interesting to note that there are a significant number of stores who are doing a substantial volume. *Chain Store Age Executive* reports that, for 1979, 52 chains had annual sales in excess of $1 billion, whereas 315 organizations obtained a sales volume in excess of $100 million.[10]

Supermarket

A more recent innovation in retailing is the supermarket. After a beginning in the 1920s in southern California, the supermarket had reached the East Coast by the 1930s. The early supermarkets were not the attractive, bright, streamlined operations

Figure 1-6

Typical supermarket of today featuring a wide assortment of merchandise in an inviting shopping environment.

(Courtesy of Safeway.)

that are seen today (Figure 1–6). Instead, low prices, low-quality facilities, inexpensive fixtures, and little or no use of displays were the order of the day. Developing during the Great Depression, the supermarket of the 1930s was just what the consumer wanted. The supermarket of today is quite a change.

Using the definition of supermarket as provided by *Progressive Grocer*, a supermarket is any food store, chain or independent, doing $1 million or more in sales per year.[11] For 1979, there were 33,600 supermarkets or 19.9 percent of total grocery stores in the United States. These 33,600 stores had sales of $154.1 billion, which represents 77.3 percent of all grocery sales.[12] Graphs of these data are shown in Figure 1–7.

Discount Store

The discount store is perhaps the last major retail innovation to be established to date. At the end of World War II, some retail stores opened that offered major brand items at prices below the prevailing level. These stores were truly self-service with poor-quality facilities—certainly a far cry from the modern K mart or Woolco of today.

To better understand what is meant by the term discount store, *Discount Merchandiser* defines a discount store as a departmentalized retail establishment utilizing many self-service techniques to sell hard goods (refrigerators, television sets, etc.), health and beauty aids, apparel and other soft goods, and other general merchandise at uniquely low margins. It has a minimum annual volume of $500,000 and is at least 10,000 square feet in size.[13]

Figure 1-7

1979 Grocery store sales and number of stores by type of store.

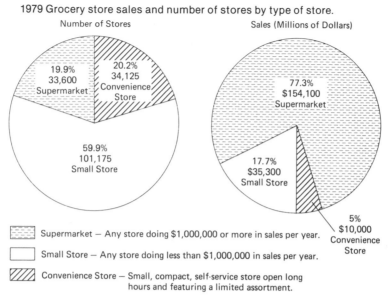

Number of Stores

Sales (Millions of Dollars)

19.9%
33,600
Supermarket

20.2%
34,125
Convenience
Store

59.9%
101,175
Small Store

77.3%
$154,100
Supermarket

17.7%
$35,300
Small Store

5%
$10,000
Convenience
Store

Supermarket — Any store doing $1,000,000 or more in sales per year.

Small Store — Any store doing less than $1,000,000 in sales per year.

Convenience Store — Small, compact, self-service store open long
hours and featuring a limited assortment.

(Source: "47th annual report of the grocery industry", *Progressive Grocer* Vol. 59 no. 4
(April 1980) pp. 46 and 50.)

In 1979, over 7,300 discount stores in operation in the United States registered sales in excess of $55 billion. The average store size was 81,554 square feet, whereas the average size new store was 73,876 square feet.[14] These figures demonstrate the trend toward smaller stores. Woolworth, in fact, is reducing the size of many of its existing Woolco units by 25,000 square feet. By the end of 1982, Woolworth will have reduced the size of 70 Woolco units at a per store saving of $130,000 in operating expenses.[15] Most major discounters continue to open stores in the 70,000- to 90,000-square-foot-size in major markets, but much of the growth of the industry is in the smaller markets, where 40,000- to 55,000-square-foot units are being built.

Other Retailing Institutions

In addition to the kinds of retail institutions already named, other types and variations of retail establishments merit the attention of the retailing student. These include specialty store, warehouse store, catalog showroom, combination store, and hypermarket.

Specialty Store. A specialty store is a store that centers its efforts on one merchandise line. Although it is usually identified with clothing, a specialty store may concentrate on paint, electronics, appliances, or fast food. One need look no further than the typical shopping mall to see numerous examples of specialty shops. In fact, the majority of the stores in a mall are of a specialty nature, be they concentrating on tobacco or earrings or whatever.

Warehouse Store. A warehouse store will carry a limited number of items while offering only a minimum level of service. Carpeting, building materials, home appliances, and home furnishings are popular product categories for this type of no-frills operation. Although not true in all cases, many are literally warehouses with none of the refinements usually considered to be a necessary part of a retail establishment. For example, a furniture warehouse store may have furniture on racks that go to the ceiling as opposed to room arrangements for display purposes. The end result is less expenses, which translates into higher profits even with lower prices.

Catalog Showroom. A type of retail mixture of mail-order buying and a warehouse store, the catalog showroom allows the customer to "shop" the catalog before coming to the store. At the store, customers will normally look at a "floor sample" of the item before writing up their own order or having a store employee do it for them. Customers then take their orders to a central receiving point to obtain the merchandise.

Combination Store. Warehouse and catalog stores both stress lower prices as a result of less variety, service, and the like. The combination store, however, offers the customer one-stop shopping and customer service. Typically a combination store is a two-store marriage between a drugstore and a supermarket or a drugstore and a discount store. In some cases, the two have literally been combined by removing the wall between them when one bought out the other. In other situations, they have been combined in concept as the store was developed. In most cases, what tends to identify the operation as a combination store is the fact that pharmaceuticals are an important part of the store's overall merchandising plan.

Hypermarket. When a discount store, supermarket, drugstore, and whatever else is desired by the marketplace are placed under one roof, the result is a hypermarket. The customer enters the store, gets a shopping cart, and places in that cart a camera, a fern plant, a dress, a shirt, a freshly baked pie, two cans of motor oil, a head of lettuce, and two small steaks. The customer then proceeds to the checkout and heads for home.

Kroger Sav-on and Safeway are two American users of the hypermarket concept. A European retailer, Carrefour, is credited by many as having been the first hypermarket retailer. The larger hypermarket retailer may have 50 checkouts up front, be 150,000 square feet in size, have parking for 3,000 cars, and do a sales volume in excess of $30 million per year. Needless to say, such stores must draw from a large population base. In times of high gasoline prices, it may cost the customer more to drive to the hypermarket if not located nearby, but the one-stop shopping offered by this retailing giant may result in savings to the customer if time, convenience, and other variables are considered.

Wheel of Retailing

A discussion of the evolution of retailing cannot be complete without a brief examination of the "wheel of retailing"—a concept put forth by Malcolm P. McNair.[16] The "wheel of retailing" (Figure 1–8) states that new types of retailers enter the market with

Figure 1-8

The wheel of retailing.

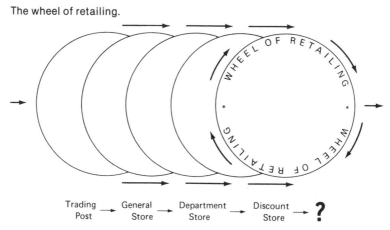

Trading Post → General Store → Department Store → Discount Store → **?**

low prices, low profit margins, low status, and little else to offer the consumer. Over time, the retailer becomes "fat." Higher costs necessitating higher margins, improved status, and many services for the customer make the retailer vulnerable to new retailers who can and are willing to operate at a lower-cost–lower-margin level. The wheel is continuous. The discount house has permanently altered the traditional department store; the "super" supermarkets are challenging the supermarket.[17] The self-service gas station is after the "service" station. Retailing is dynamic. The "wheel of retailing" is ever turning. Evidence of its progress is shown in Figure 1–9.

Retail Accordion

Another way to explain the evolutionary process of retailing is to view it not as a wheel but as an accordion. As stores develop, domination by general-line, wide-assortment retailers alternates with domination by specialized, narrow-line merchants.[18] The general store of the 1800s was replaced by the department store and then the specialty store for many types of merchandise. Now, the combination store and the hypermarket are on the scene, but so is the warehouse store. As is true with the "wheel of retailing," retailing today will yield examples that will "prove" the "retail accordion" to be a valid concept or will "disprove" it. It should be noted that the concept does appear to be valid if the proper time frame is applied and the analysis is made on the basis of a particular customer group. If too many generalizations are made, the accordion concept will lose its validity. As shown in Figure 1–10, the concept could prove to be valid in the grocery business if combination stores and hypermarkets become dominant in a market area. Of course, the only thing that appears certain is that, if the general-line merchant does dominate the market, there will come a time when the accordion effect will result in a return to the limited-line store. Retailing is truly evolutionary. It is also not opposed to repeating itself in terms of retail development.

Figure 1-9

Retailing is dynamic. The wheel of retailing never stops turning. As conditions change, stores must be prepared to change also.

Yesterday

Today

(Courtesy of Otasco, Oklahoma Tire & Supply Co.)

Figure 1-10

Retail Accordion.

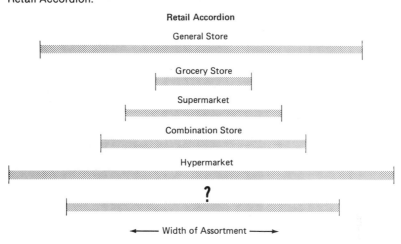

RETAILING AND THE ECONOMY

The significance of retailing to the economy of the United States can be shown best by the fact that total retail sales for the year 1979 were $886.0 billion, up $85.1 billion over 1978.[19] As noted in Table 1-2, every area of the retail industry experienced an increase over the previous year. A close examination of the data in the table will show some of the growth areas of the retail industry as well as some areas in which inflation has had an impact on sales data.

Looking back over the years, retail sales have increased significantly. As shown in Table 1-3, retail sales in 1939 were $42 billion. By 1949, sales had increased to $134 billion. In 1959, $215 billion in sales were recorded. A tremendous growth since 1959 had sales in 1969 totaling $352 billion. An even greater growth period covers the time span from 1969 to 1979. For that ten-year period, sales increased in the amount of $534 billion or more than double the amount of sales in 1969.[20]

Over the same period, employment in retailing rose from 4.7 million in 1939 to 8.2 million in 1959 to approximately 15 million in 1979 (Table 1-3). Of the 105 million people in the labor force in 1979,[21] approximately 15 percent were working in various forms of retailing. Not only does retailing bring buyer and merchandise together, it is a major employer in the economy as well, thereby giving many individuals the money to spend as customers.

When sales of $886 billion and 15 million jobs are added to the essential responsibility of retailers to bring the buyer and merchandise together for ultimate consumption, then retailing and the economy become one and the same. The economy as we know it today could not exist without retailing.

Table 1-2

Retail sales by type of business, 1978–1979 (billions of dollars)

Type of Business	1978	1979	Net Increase
Total	$800.9	$886.0	85.1
Durable goods stores[1]	281.5	308.2	26.7
Auto/home supply stores	14.2	16.4	2.2
Building materials and supply stores	31.6	35.1	3.5
Furniture, home furnishing stores	23.2	26.7	3.5
Hardware stores	7.2	9.0	1.8
Household appliance, radio, television	10.5	12.1	1.6
Motor vehicle dealers	153.9	161.3	7.4
Nondurable goods stores	519.4	577.9	58.5
Apparel and accessory stores[1]	39.4	43.0	3.6
Department stores	81.5	89.1	7.6
Drug and proprietary stores	24.8	27.2	2.4
Eating and drinking places	69.1	75.1	6.0
Food stores	180.0	191.3	11.3
Gasoline service stations	59.3	71.9	12.6
Liquor stores	13.8	15.6	1.8
Variety stores	7.4	7.9	0.5

[1]Includes data for items not shown separately.
Source: *Survey of Current Business,* Vol. 60, no. 6 (June 1980), p. S-10.

Table 1-3

Estimated retail trade: total sales and employment in the United States, selected years, 1939–1979

Year	Sales Not Seasonally Adjusted (millions of dollars)	Employment Seasonally Adjusted (thousands of people)
1979	$886,047	14,968
1978	800,890	14,542
1977	724,020	13,795
1976	642,507	13,431
1975	584,423	11,552
1974	537,782	12,751
1973	503,317	12,547
1972	448,379	11,765
1971	408,850	11,333
1970	375,527	11,098
1969	351,633	10,907
1964	261,870	8,971
1959	215,413	8,182
1954	169,135	7,496
1949	133,783	6,778
1944	70,208	5,296
1939	42,042	4,742

Sources: *Survey of Current Business,* Vols. 50-60, no. 6 (June 1970-1980); "1969 Business Statistics," 17th Biennial Supplement to the *Survey of Current Business,* 1969, pp. 58 and 71.

SUMMARY

Retailing is the summation of all activities that result in the offering for sale of goods and/or services to individuals and/or organizations for purposes of ultimate consumption. A business organization whose predominant function is retailing is referred to as a retailer. Retailing's role in the marketing system (the process of moving an idea from conception to ultimate consumption) is quite complex. Retailing must bring the buyer and product and/or service together. It must provide place utility as well as information feedback. In addition, retailing breaks bulk, stores the merchandise, and accepts risks.

The evolution of retailing has been going on for hundreds of years. In the last 200 years, retailing in North America has moved from the trading post to the general store to the mail-order catalog and department store up to more modern ideas such as the supermarket and discount house. Each new retail institution in the evolutionary process has been the result of retailing adapting to different conditions in the marketplace.

The role of retailing in the economy cannot be ignored. Sales have increased from $42 billion in 1939 to $886 billion in 1979. During the same period, employment in retailing went from 4.7 million to 15 million.

DISCUSSION QUESTIONS

1. Define retailing. Divide the definition into parts and explain these various parts.
2. Distinguish retailing from intermediate marketing. Cite examples.
3. Assume a world without retailing. Give examples of some of the problems you might encounter.
4. Define marketing system. Why is such a system important to a retailer?
5. Discuss the various tasks for which the retailer takes responsibility in the marketing system.
6. What is meant by the term evolution of retailing? Cite examples.
7. Discuss the "wheel of retailing." Is this a valid concept in retailing?
8. Retailing is not important in the economy today and it never has been. Comment on this statement.
9. Explain what is meant by the "retail accordion." Cite examples.
10. By means of a survey, ask ten people if we need retailing. Ask what it is and why we either need it or do not need it. Do you agree with what you found to be the results of your survey?

NOTES

[1] For a more in-depth discussion, see "Keeping up with Kresge," *Business Week*, 2353 (October 19, 1974), pp. 70 ff.

[2] For a discussion of the origin of retailing, see Paul H. Nystrom, *The Economics of Retailing* (New York: The Ronald Press Company, 1915), pp. 24 ff.

[3]U.S. Bureau of the Census, *Census of Retail Trade*, 1977 Area Series, United States, RC 77–A–52 (Washington, D.C.: U.S. Government Printing Office, 1979), p. 7.

[4]Copyright © 1979 by Robert Hendrickson. From the book *The Grand Emporiums*. Reprinted with permission of Stein and Day Publishers.

[5]Frank Latham, *1872–1972 A Century of Serving Consumers, The Story of Montgomery Ward* (Chicago: Montgomery Ward and Company, 1972), pp. 4–7.

[6]*The Story of Sears, Roebuck and Company* (New York: Fairchild Publications, Inc., 1961), p. 3.

[7]Robert Hendrickson, *The Grand Emporiums*, pp. 26–27.

[8]*Survey of Current Business*, Vol. 60, no. 6 (June 1980), p. S–10.

[9]*Survey of Current Business*, Vol. 60, no. 6 (June 1980).

[10]Reprinted by permission from *Chain Store Age Executive*, August 1980. © Copyright Lebhar-Friedman, Inc., 425 Park Avenue, New York, N.Y. 10022.

[11]"47th Annual Report of the Grocery Industry," *Progressive Grocer*, Vol. 59, no. 4 (April 1980), p. 50.

[12]Ibid., p. 46.

[13]"The True Look of the Discount Industry," *Discount Merchandiser*, Vol. 19, no. 5 (May 1979), p. 30.

[14]Reprinted by permission from *Chain Store Age Executive*, August 1980. © Copyright Lebhar-Friedman, Inc., 425 Park Avenue, New York, N.Y. 10022.

[15]Ibid., p. 60.

[16]For a complete discussion, see M. P. McNair, "Significant Trends and Developments in the Postwar Period," in *Competitive Distribution in a Free, High Level Economy and Its Implications for the University*, ed. A. B. Smith, by permission of the University of Pittsburgh Press, © 1957, pp. 1–25.

[17]"New Superstores Change Packaging, Increase Research Needs," *Marketing News*, Vol. 9, no. 7 (October 10, 1975), p. 1. Published by the American Marketing Association.

[18]Stanley C. Hollander, "Notes on the Retail Accordion," *Journal of Retailing*, Vol. 42, no. 2 (Summer 1966), pp. 29–40.

[19]*Survey of Current Business*, Vol. 60, no. 6 (June 1980), p. S–10.

[20]*Survey of Current Business*, Vols. 50–60, no. 6 (June 1970–1980); "1969 Business Statistics," 17th Biennial Supplement to the *Survey of Business Statistics*, 1969, p. 58.

[21]Ibid., p. 71.

CHAPTER 2

Retailing:
Its Relationship to Marketing

BROOM HILDA

Reprinted by permission of The Chicago Tribune-New York News
Syndicate, Inc.

"I just can't figure it out. I love my store. The merchandise is great. The location is great. The promotional effort is great. In fact, everything is just like I like it except for one thing—sales are lousy!" In examining this unhappy retailer's comments, note that there is no mention of the customer. Do customers love the store? Do they think the merchandise or the location or the promotional effort is great? The smart retailer will develop a store that is geared to meet the needs of customers, not store owners. Retailers must learn to think "customer."

To think "customer," the retailer must first have an understanding of marketing and the marketing concept. Knowledge of the target market and the marketing mix is also essential. Finally, guidelines for effective retailing should be developed and applied that will assist the retailer in the development and operation of the store. Each of these topic areas are examined in order to promote a better understanding of retailing's relationship to marketing (Figure 2–1).

MARKETING AND THE MARKETING CONCEPT

Retailing is part of marketing, but marketing is more than just retailing. Although difficult to define, marketing can be said to be the sum total of all business activities that result in the pricing, distribution, and promotion of products (goods, services, ideas) for the purpose of satisfying customers while obtaining a normal return (profit) on investment. From a retailing perspective, marketing is a very broad area. From the neighborhood garage sale to Sears, Roebuck and Company, retail operations are varied but the goals remain the same: *customer satisfaction* and *profit.*

To be successful in the long run, a firm cannot ignore the customer. Customer satisfaction is not a luxury in retailing, it is a requirement for success. With this idea in

Figure 2–1

Steps toward a successful retail operation.

Steps Toward Successful Retailing

mind, it is believed that every retail operation should adhere to the marketing concept, which is defined as a state of mind in a company that results in all planning, policies, procedures, and actions of the company being customer oriented.[1] The marketing concept is obviously not a tangible thing that can be studied, but it should become tangible as reflected in the various actions of the company that are taken to implement the concept. In other words, the retailer will make decisions based on the wants, needs, and desires of the customer, which are not necessarily the wishes of the retailer. For example, a retailer might open for business on Sunday even though the owner does not wish to do so because the market wants to shop on Sunday. Another retailer might add a line of clothes that are desired by the market even though the retailer has a personal dislike for the items. To aid the retailer in understanding the marketing concept, every effort should be made to understand what customers are buying—and market accordingly. Customers buy benefits; therefore, retailers should sell benefits. A fast-food store is not in the business of selling food—it is providing a service that will allow families to dine pleasantly and inexpensively in a minimum amount of time (Figure 2-2). A tire store is not in the business of selling tires—it is in the business of providing the customer safety. By thinking customer benefits, the retailer will make marketing decisions based upon the store's customer group. This thought process constitutes smart retailing.

As for profit, unless supported by an outside entity, a retail store cannot survive without a profit. No profit over time means no business. In some cases, a lack of profit may be caused by forces external to the firm such as a recession or a strike, but in most cases, lack of profit is a result of ineffective retail management. It is observed that profit should not be thought of as unethical. Normal profit is essential to the operation

Figure 2-2

The marketing concept in practice.

(Courtesy of Burger King Corporation)

of a business so that it can stay in existence to serve the customer. Customer satisfaction and profit are both essential to a retail business. The lack of either element means trouble for the retail store.

The target market for a retail operation is those customers on whom the store will place primary emphasis in developing a marketing program. For most retail operations, it would be incorrect to assume that the target market consists of all the residents of a town or a county. Such a target market determination would simply be a "motherhood and apple pie" market selection. To develop effectively a target market for a retail establishment, effort should be made to study the total market and to determine which segments of that market the retailer wishes to serve.

To assist the retailer in deciding on a target market, several variables should be considered.

Age

What is the age mix of the population in the area? How many people are 10 to 16, or 16 to 22, or whatever age groups are important for the type of store the retailer wishes to operate? If the retailer discovers that over 60 percent of the people in the target area are 50 years of age or older, the retailer should consider dropping any plans for a skating rink and develop instead a recreational center aimed at this large, older age group.

Income

How much money is available in the area? The retailer should be careful to examine the level of disposable income versus income and discretionary income versus disposable income to derive a true picture of spendable money. Income is the figure often given in published reports by various governmental agencies. But the figure does not indicate how much money a potential market may have to spend. Disposable income (after taxes) may be appropriate in examining the market for food and housing. Discretionary income, or income available after all essentials are taken care of (food, housing, etc.), is the figure most often desired in examining the income potential of a target market.

Education

The education level of a potential market reveals much about their interest in reading, travel, cooking, and many other aspects of life. Most stores would have difficulty in keying their marketing effort to various education levels such as the eighth-grade level and the college graduate level of customers at the same time. What would appeal to one might not appeal to the other.

Occupation

What a person does for a living affects that person as a consumer and affects as well his or her buying patterns. A person whose job calls for a coat and tie to be worn will normally have more clothes of this nature than will an individual whose occupation is that of a factory worker. A person whose occupation involves travel will usually eat more gourmet foods at home to match eating habits while on expense account.

Race, Religion, National Origin

The cultural background of the customer should be considered in determining how to best serve a market. Just as many products in recent years have become black oriented, many stores have done the same with their emphasis on this market through product selection and proper location. Another example of cultural orientation involves the common mistake of sending Christmas cards to all customers including those who are not Christians. By simply selecting a card that states "Season's Greetings" or "Happy Holidays" instead of one with religious overtones or even "Merry Christmas," no one in the market should be offended. Also, all countries do not have Santa Claus. If a portion of a potential market has other customs, these should be considered in determining how to best serve the market as a whole.

Place of Residence

Just as race or religion can influence marketing decisions, place of residence can have a bearing on the behavior of a target market. Urban customers tend to be more receptive to new products and stores than are their rural counterparts. Customers in the Northeast appear to be more conscious of new fashions than their southern and western cousins. The pace of living in the South tends to be slower than in the more northern parts of the nation thereby offering many more leisure-time retailing opportunities in the South.

Marital Status

How people live influences what they buy. Married couples are generally more interested in buying furniture than are single people. On the other hand, single people may eat out more often than their married counterparts. It is noted that people are staying single longer and that more people are living together outside of marriage. The singles market, for example, has opened up a retailing opportunity in rental furniture. Also, unmarried couples living together represent, from a retailing standpoint, just another married couple since they also will need all the items that are required to set up "housekeeping."

Sex

A clothing store whose projected target market is teenage girls obviously should locate in an area that contains females of the appropriate age level. Of course, if a store sells a product line that appeals to both sexes, the number of potential customers naturally will increase substantially. In many markets, barber shops and beauty parlors have changed to hair salons that cater to both males and females. Depending on the location, the change has been met with results that range from disaster to complete success.

Life-style

Another way of examining a potential target market is its life-style. Life-style is, in many ways, a summation of all those factors already mentioned as points to consider in determining a target market plus attitudes, activities, opinions, and interests. Life-style is what makes the teenager the fad-conscious person that he or she is regardless of the income or educational level of the parents. Life-style is what makes the older consumer more conservative in product choice even though money is generally more available to this age group. Some people belong to the "jet set" and some do not. Some people are devout churchgoers and some are not. Some people follow high school athletics and some do not. Why are such questions of life-style important to the retailer? Such knowledge enables the retailer to correctly make important decisions concerning the target market. For instance, a retailer whose customers follow high school athletics might wish to sponsor radio broadcasts of the games, or donate something to the school athletics program, or hire a football player from the school to help out in the store as a means of building traffic. None of these actions would be recommended if the customers' life-style did not include high school athletics.

Consumption Patterns

Does the retailer wish to concentrate on the heavy, medium, light, or nonuser of the goods and/or services to be offered by the store? For a store selling a new product, such as video cassettes, the choice is easy because most customers will be nonusers prior to the placement of the store in the market area. On the other hand, a pizza parlor will probably have more interest in the number of light, medium, and heavy users (consumers) of the product who live in the area. If the proposed target market is filled with nonusers of an established product such as pizza, the reason for the large number of nonusers should be determined before a pizza store is located in that market area.

Reasons for Purchase

"Why will customers come to my store?" Snob appeal, brand loyalty, store loyalty, and the desire to be different may all be reasons for buying at a particular store. A careful analysis of the target market can reveal what might attract a customer to a particular store and what might discourage customers. Having a thorough understanding of the reasons for purchase can be of great assistance to a retailer as the decision is made concerning how to position a store relative to the competition in the eyes of the customer.

Determination of Target Market

After having examined various aspects of his or her potential market, the retailer should begin the task of determining just who is or should be the target market. The use of a diagram such as the one illustrated in Figure 2–3 can help the retailer to put in writing the various judgments that have been made concerning the potential target market. At this point, the retailer should make every effort to also examine various competitors' target markets. Are competitors attempting to segment a market, or are they serving the broad "motherhood and apple pie" market? Being objective about a competitor's target customers is extremely difficult for some retailers. Objective efforts will, however, result in a more realistic appraisal of overall market conditions.

RETAILING MIX

As a retailer examines the potential target market and those of his or her competitors, an analysis also should be made of various retailing mixes that may be used or are presently being used by stores in the area.

The retailing mix of a store consists of all those elements that make the store the entity it is in the marketplace. It is important to note that a retail store will have a retail-

Figure 2-3

Variables that help to determine the target market.

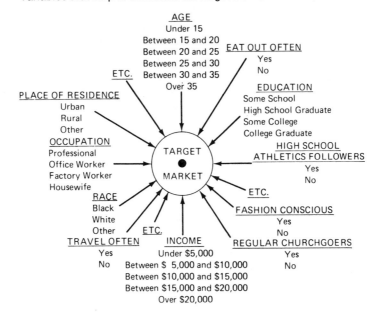

ing mix. The question is whether it is the best possible mix for the appropriate target market.

The five parts or "P's" of the retailing mix are *Product*, *Place*, *Promotion*, *Price*, and *Personality*. By developing the correct mixture of these five elements, the retail store will generally be successful given basic management know-how. The problem with the mix is the achievement of an appropriate balance of the five elements. If four elements are strong but the fifth is weak, then the whole retailing mix is weak. To illustrate, imagine, if you will, a scale with five arms (Figure 2–4). In the center is a weight representing the target market. Five counterweights representing the five "P's" are placed to balance the target market. If one or more of the five weights ("P's" of the mix) are too heavy or too light, the scale will be unbalanced and the target market may not be served efficiently. In many cases this target market may seek out another store. The retailer, then, must continuously juggle the retailing mix to keep it in balance with the target market. It is truly a dynamic concept.

The remainder of this book will examine these elements from many different viewpoints. For purposes of this discussion, the various parts of the retailing mix are now explained more fully.

Product

What items are carried in the store—what brands, sizes, colors, how many, and many other considerations. What services will be offered—home delivery, alterations, credit, interior decorating advice, and so on. Product consists of physical product, if any, plus the various other considerations that are wanted by the target market.

Place

Where is the store or where will it be? In what region of the country should it be located? What town? Should it stand alone or be in a shopping area? Should it be located in the central business district or in an outlying area? Should it be in a conventional shopping center or in a mall? Where should it be in the mall in relation to similar stores? The main stores? Is parking available at the site? Is the area safe particularly for nighttime operations? Is the site accessible to the target market?

Figure 2–4

Target market and retailing mix.

Promotion

Promotion consists of advertising, personal selling, and sales promotion. Promotional needs vary with the type of store and the target market it is attempting to reach. A 7–11 type of convenience store may advertise heavily to build traffic but require little personal selling effort in the store itself. A clothing store may, on the other hand, require a high level of personal selling to obtain a satisfied customer but require little in-store promotion through point-of-purchase displays as may be needed in a self-service store environment.

Price

Prices influence the target market in many ways. For one, customers tend to equate quality with price. The retailer should, therefore, guard against pricing too far below competition. Such efforts may result in scaring away customers rather than attracting more prospective buyers. Psychological pricing ($1.98 versus $2.00), price lines ($5.00 shirts, $10.00 shirts, $15.00 shirts, instead of 20 different prices between $5.00 and $15.00), and odd pricing (prices that force the salesclerk to make change and give an additional opportunity for suggestion selling) are three of many pricing alternatives for consideration by the retailer.

Personality

The personality or image of a retail store is an integral part of the retailing mix.[2] It differs from the other "P's," however, in that the other parts of the mix can be changed quite rapidly, but the personality of a store is a long-run concept that is learned by the customer over time. Just as the mention of the name K mart creates a picture of discount and savings, the name Neiman-Marcus engenders an image of high price, high quality, and status. Neither store would want or desire the personality of the other.

For purposes of definition, the personality of a store is the way in which the store is perceived by the customer. When the customer is away from the store, he or she recalls the store as a total unit and reacts in a positive or negative way to this memory. Personality is, therefore, the result of the total store and all its parts.

What makes or creates the image or personality of a store? Simply put—everything. Product, Price, Place, and Promotion are naturally integral parts of a store's Personality. The target market of the store itself helps to create the image. The attitude of store personnel can do much to generate a feeling of prestige or bargain basement. It is essential for the store to project an appropriate personality. A confused store image will result in confused customers—a most undesirable situation.

As the reader may have noted, the five parts of the retailing mix are highly integrated with each other and the target market. A retail manager should continually evaluate all aspects to ensure that all parts of the retailing mix are working in harmony with each other and with the target market. Strength in one element alone will not make a business successful (Figure 2–5).

Figure 2-5

From uniforms to buildings, the different elements of the retailing mix for this franchise chain are designed to meet the needs of its target market.

(Courtesy of KFC Corporation.)

GUIDELINES FOR EFFECTIVE RETAILING

As the retail strategy (target market and retailing mix) of the firm is developed and implemented, numerous decisions must be made that will have a significant impact on the firm. To assist the retailer in making these decisions, 26 guidelines are provided that, if followed, should play a significant role in the ultimate success of the retail operation (Figure 2–6). These guidelines are:

> *Define target market.* The retailer must learn to know his or her customers. As noted earlier in the chapter, most retailers do not actually sell to everyone. By defining the target market the retailer narrows his or her area of concern thereby permitting better concentration on fewer retail customers. By defining the market, the retailer may be able to effectively segment a market all to itself.

Figure 2-6

Guidelines for effective retailing.

Retailing Guidelines

Define Target Market
Understand Uncontrollable Factors
Conduct Appropriate Retail Research
Have Sound Financial Planning
Have Good Site Selection
Have A Good Store Design
Have A Good Management Organization
Have A Successful Opening Day
Make Use of Merchandise Planning
Select The Proper Merchandise Resources
Know The Terms of Sale
Use Pricing As A Merchandising Tool
Utilize Effective Means of Merchandise Distribution
Develop Procedures For Merchandise Control
Carefully Staff The Retail Store
Develop Creative Sales Personnel
Use Human Relations
Work For Effective Advertising
Work For Effective Sales Promotion
Work For Effective Retail Display
Work For Effective Retail Credit
Work For Effective Customer Service
Work For Effective Retail Security
Develop An Effective Accounting System
Develop A System Of Operations Control
Develop A Balance Between Customer Satisfaction And Profits

Understand uncontrollable factors. Retailers should be aware of the various federal, state, and local regulations under which they must operate. From consumer credit to advertising, controls are placed on the retailer. Local custom is also important as is consumer behavior. Unions must also be viewed as a possible uncontrollable factor.

Conduct appropriate retail research. By studying secondary data, many retailing questions can be answered. If secondary data are not available, answers may also be obtained by means of primary research (observation, survey, and experimentation). Many problems can be eliminated or minimized through appropriate retail research.

Have sound financial planning. Many retail failures can be attributed to poor financial planning. Without the guideline of sound planning, other guidelines of the retailer will never have a chance to be applied. In many cases, it is best to quantify the financial plans of the store. To work for a return on investment is acceptable, but to set an objective of 10 percent return on investment is better.

Have good site selection. A retail store out of place is a less than efficient operation. Is the store location correct for the target market? For the older store, have conditions changed that affect the desirability of the site? Optimum store location is a dynamic guideline. The retailer must continually examine the situation to determine if the guideline is being met.

Have a good store design. The design of the store—both exterior and interior— should be appropriate to the store's target market and store personality. Layout, colors, fixtures, atmosphere, and all other design components must be coordinated for optimum enhancement of this guideline.

Have a good management organization. Whether the store is large or small, the soundness of management is critical to the success of the firm. Well-thought-out store policies and procedures are essential to this guideline. A management that is receptive to change in order to meet different conditions is desirable.

Have a successful opening day. The store should get off to a good start by having a successful opening. From the time of its inception, all activites should be planned to climax on opening day. Opening a new store is an occasion for much free promotion in the media. Make use of it. A store that meets this guideline will not open without most people in the target market already knowing about it.

Make use of merchandise planning. To meet this guideline, the retailer should make every effort to estimate demand correctly. Assortment of merchandise, variety, breadth, and depth are also important considerations. By careful merchandise planning, greater sales should be the result.

Select the proper merchandise resources. Good suppliers are a real asset to a retailer. A careful analysis of each possible supplier should be made that will involve the study of such things as services rendered and reliability.

Know the terms of sale. The retailer can, in essence, make money by knowing the terms of sale and by knowing what terms to request from suppliers. For example, does the retailer obtain cash discounts? Regardless of federal laws to the contrary, many times the retailer will not receive the discount unless he or she requests it from the supplier. To achieve this guideline is to be informed.

Use pricing as a merchandising tool. Various pricing procedures (psychological prices, markups, and markdowns just to name several) should be used by the retailer to enhance the image of the store and its products. Pricing too far below or above the desired level can cause problems for the store. Pricing should be determined on the basis of what the merchandise is worth in the marketplace—not on the basis of what was paid for the item.

Utilize effective means of merchandise distribution. The retailer, in pursuing this guideline, should examine both external and internal distribution of merchandise. Having a knowledge of freight rates, how to handle claims, and understanding different methods of shipping is important. Internally, proper methods of merchandise receiving, storage, marking, rotation, and security are all important considerations.

Develop procedures for merchandise control. Merchandise control involves analysis of inventory by various procedures. Should inventory be taken on a perpetual or periodic basis? What role will electronic equipment play in merchandise control? These and other questions will be answered as the firm works to meet this guideline.

Select and place the staff of the retail store with care. The retail staff is the store to many customers. The retail staff must be carefully recruited, trained, and compensated if it is to represent the store in a desirable manner.

Develop creative sales personnel. Basic creative selling techniques should be explained to all personnel. How to close the sale, how to do suggestion selling, and how to not say "Can I help you?" should all be covered if this guideline is to be carried out.

Use human relations in dealing with personnel. Work to motivate personnel. Understand the role of status, resistance to change, and informal groups in the retail store. Remember—money is not everything to the retail employee.

Work for effective advertising. Know and understand the various media available. How to schedule and budget advertising for best results is important to the guideline as well as an understanding of the importance of continuous advertising as opposed to sporadic advertising.

Work for effective sales promotion. Effective use of contests, trading stamps, in-store demonstrations, and other traffic-building ideas do not just happen. Much effort will be required to meet the guideline.

Work for effective retail display. In meeting this guideline, it is important to note that effective displays do not necessarily mean more expensive displays. Careful selection of display items, display themes, and display safety and security are all important variables.

Work for effective retail credit. It goes without saying that most retail stores provide credit. The challenge lies in the use of credit to the advantage of the retail store. Having knowledge of credit and how to use it can be a differential advantage for a retailer in today's market.

Work for effective customer service. Customer service costs money, but it can be a real plus for the store. Home delivery, clothes alterations, and even restrooms are forms of customer service. To meet this guideline the retailer must examine the various services that can be offered and determine from these which ones should be offered by his or her store and in what form. The choices are infinite.

Work for effective retail security. Shoplifting, employee theft, bad checks, bad credit cards, and other problems of retail security should become areas of knowledge for the retailer. The retailer should then work on detection and prevention of these security problems. Failure to do so could result in heavy losses for the firm.

Develop an effective accounting system. The retailer should examine the pros and cons of the retail accounting system and the cost method of accounting. Having knowledge of these accounting methods will permit the retailer to meet this guideline of developing an accounting system that will best serve his or her needs.

Develop a system of operations control. The retail operator should establish various procedures of control to determine how the parts of the retail store are operating. Methods of analysis include examination of sales, performance analysis, and budget control of various kinds.

Develop a balance of customer satisfaction and profit. This guideline underscores the dual importance of these two variables. For the retailer to succeed, both parts of the guideline must be met. Whereas the other guidelines are more concrete in terms of attainment, this guideline is more a state of mind. The retailer must realize that, for the firm to succeed, satisfaction and profit must be in proper balance. Too much customer satisfaction may result in negative profit. In turn, too much profit may result in negative satisfaction and no sales.

The retail manager should work to meet the 26 guidelines as set forth here. To meet these guidelines successfully requires a full understanding of all aspects of retailing. The remainder of this book presents various information and data that will assist the reader in developing this understanding.

SUMMARY

The marketing concept is a state of mind in a company that results in all planning, policies, procedures, and actions of the company being customer oriented. To be customer oriented effectively requires the retailer to know who his or her target market customers are and to understand them in terms of age, income, education, occupation, race, place of residence, marital status, sex, life-style, consumption patterns, and reasons for purchase. As the retailer begins to learn the market he or she must put together a retailing mix (product, place, promotion, price, personality) that will best serve those target customers. To assist in this effort, the store operator should compile a list of guidelines for effective retailing or desired measures of performance for all aspects of the business that, if achieved, will enable the store to attain the desired retailing mix for the benefit of the target market.

DISCUSSION QUESTIONS

1. What is meant by the term marketing concept? How does it apply to retailing? Give examples.
2. You are considering opening a new store to sell clothing in your town. Conduct a target market analysis to determine the feasibility of opening such a store. Based on your analysis, define the particular market that you feel should be served by your store.
3. What is a retailing mix? Which part of the mix is the most important? Least important?
4. A retailer has no control over the personality or image of a store. Comment on this statement.
5. Select a retailer of your choice and determine how that store developed its retailing mix. Analyze the mix in use and provide suggestions as to how the mix might be improved.
6. Develop a list of retail guidelines for the operation of a store of your choice. Explain your reason for choosing each guideline.
7. The target market, retailing mix, and retailing guidelines are all important but are not of equal importance to a retailer. Which of the three is the most important and why?

NOTES

[1] For more discussion on the marketing concept, see Edward Cundiff, Richard Still, and Norman Govoni, *Fundamentals of Modern Marketing* (Englewood Cliffs, N.J.: Prentice-Hall, Inc., 1980), pp. 17–20, and Philip Kotler, *Principles of Marketing* (Englewood Cliffs, N.J.: Prentice-Hall, Inc., 1980), pp. 24–26.

[2] For an example of image research, see Leonard L. Berry, "The Components of Department Store Image, A Theoretical and Empirical Analysis," *Journal of Retailing*, Vol. 45, no. 1 (Spring, 1969), pp. 3–20.

CHAPTER 3

External Retail Restraints

Shoe

Reprinted by permission of The Chicago Tribune-New York News Syndicate, Inc.

The retailer in today's marketplace must decide from among almost infinite choices the best mix of retailing variables. This retailing mix must be selected in light of numerous restraints that are placed on the retailer by various sources (Figure 3–1). Restrictions from all levels of government put limits on retail activity. Customs in the area as well as union activity influence the retailer. Consumer behavior affects the retailer. The successful retailer must first become aware of the various restraints over which he or she has little or no control and, second, work to operate successfully within the limits caused by these restraints.

FEDERAL LAWS AND REGULATIONS

In examining the various retail restraints, the federal government is discussed first since many of the restrictions placed on retailing can be traced to actions at the federal level.[1] It is noted that, under the interpretation that retailers buy in interstate trade, all retailing is affected to varying degrees by federal laws and regulations. Some of the more significant federal laws and regulations are:

Sherman Antitrust Act (1890)

The Sherman Act states clearly that any conspiracy or combination involving restraint of trade is illegal. For the retailer, the Law means that Sears, Roebuck and J. C. Penney would more than likely not be permitted to merge or that a manufacturer of men's clothing may have to maintain a competitive market in the clothing field.

Figure 3–1

External restraints affect the retail operation.

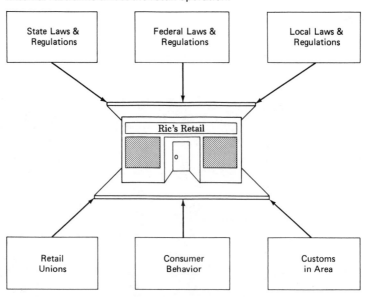

Another example is the practice where the operators of the laundries in a town meet and agree to charge a minimum of $2.00 for dry cleaning a garment. Such an agreement is in violation of the Act since it involves a conspiracy in restraint of trade.

Clayton Act (1914) and Robinson–Patman Act (1936)

These Acts deal with price discrimination. Simply stated, price differentials involving the same customer group must be justified. For the retailer, the problem is two sided. First, as a customer, is a fair price given to the retailer? For example, is the price differential between the large and small retailer simply a reflection of a quantity discount commensurate with a larger order by the larger retailer? This is legal. On the other hand, if the price differential is greater than can be justified by the economies of the large order, then price discrimination is found to exist.

The retailer should note that price discrimination can take many forms. It can show up, obviously, in the price of the merchandise itself, but it is more often reflected in quantity discounts, trade discounts (given for service rendered), and promotional allowances (given to promote the product). To protect itself against charges of discrimination, the manufacturer will, many times, run a "tombstone" ad (Figure 3–2) in major trade publications serving the particular retail market announcing that one or more allowances are available to qualified retailers. It is important for the retailer to

Figure 3–2

Example of a "tombstone" advertisement.

PROCTER & GAMBLE

NOTICE TO THE TRADE

ATTENTION STORE MANAGER:

We offer Cooperative Merchandising Agreements, promotion allowances and merchandising materials which are practical and usable by all retailers regardless of size.

Payments are made for newspaper or handbill featuring, display, and consumer directed promotion. Details are set forth in specific agreements. Proof of performance (e.g. tear sheets) and proof of delivery (jobber's invoice) are required for payment of allowance. Our merchandising materials consist of display material, newspaper mats and proofs etc.

If you would like to receive specific information on offers available to you, send your name, address and telephone number to Procter & Gamble, Box 162, Cincinnati, Ohio 45201. Please specify, if possible, the Division in whose brands you are interested.

Packaged Soap & Detergent Division
Toilet Goods Division
Paper Products Division
Food Products Division
Bar Soap & Household Cleaning
Products Division
Coffee Division

(Courtesy of Procter & Gamble.)

see these ads and to ask for the various discounts and allowances that are made available. These allowances can represent significant savings to the retailer.

Federal Trade Commission Act (1914) and Wheeler–Lea Amendment to Federal Trade Commission Act (1938)

Both of these Federal Acts deal with unfair methods of competition whereas the 1938 amendment goes further in placing special emphasis on unfair or deceptive advertising. In addition, the Federal Trade Commission Act set up the Federal Trade Commission, the main policing agency at the federal level as far as most retailers are concerned. It is the Federal Trade Commission that is involved when retailers violate almost any federal law or regulation involving anything from advertising to credit disclosure.

The Federal Trade Commission is also concerned with misrepresentation. For example, a retailer calls himself an importer. Is a substantial part of the goods carried in stock imported items? If not, such a statement may be injurious to competition. Is a chain of food retailers putting out statements that such and such a competitor is selling poor-quality merchandise at a higher price? If such statements are true, there is no problem. If such statements are not true, then competitors have a right to be protected.

Suppose that a store has a "cents-off" sale. The reduction price should be "cents-off" of existing prices in the area. It should not involve "cents-off" prices that have been inflated just for the sale. Also, if during the sale, items on sale are not carried in sufficient quantity to meet normal demand for such a sale and no quantity limit was established, the firm must provide rain checks for out-of-stock items as required by a Federal Trade Commission regulation.

One other area of interest is games of chance. The Federal Trade Commission has set forth regulations ensuring that contests offer all an equal chance of winning. Such action was taken after many contests and games were "structured" so as to ensure a good cross section of winners. From a marketing standpoint, a local winner enables the contest to have more interest. If customers know a winner, they will also come to the store and try to win. The result is more traffic for the store, which is a major objective of most retail games of chance. The problem was that a given store, for example, may have had only one winning card placed in the contest. If the winning card has already been given out, further customers were entering a contest with no chance of winning. Federal Trade Commission guidelines now prohibit the retailer from using a structured game unless the odds of winning are stated properly.

The Wheeler–Lea Amendment is known as the "Truth-in-Advertising Act." A retail ad must be noninjurious to competitors and customers alike. If a fast-food chain advertises that its hamburgers are cooked in a certain way, then they should be cooked in that manner. If an ad states that a retailer carries a certain product exclusively, then that should be the case. If a retailer runs an ad on television demonstrating the starting capability of a lawn mower and states that the ad is live, it must be. Another example dealing with Wheeler–Lea involves a major retailer who the Federal Trade Commission accused of using "bait" advertising. In this case, the retailer was ordered to cease all bait tactics, was required to include in all ads and to post in its stores throughout the period of promotion the statement, "Each of these advertised items is readily available for sale as advertised," and was required to have sufficient quantities of the advertised items available to meet reasonably anticipated demand.[2] It is significant to note that a retailer can still attempt to trade up a customer. The problem arises when the cheaper advertised item is not available when the customer chooses to buy it. In studying this external restraint, numerous other examples can also be cited. The main consideration for the retailer is that there is a federal statute that covers truthfulness in advertising when it involves the welfare of competitors or customers.

Consumer Credit Protection Act (1969)

The Consumer Credit Protection Act, usually referred to as Truth in Lending, calls for a disclosure of all credit terms to consumers in a uniform manner. Essentially all retail transactions are covered by the Law. The purpose of Truth in Lending is to permit customers to shop for credit just as the customer would shop for merchandise. In most cases, however, such shopping for credit has not taken place. One particular part of the Act that has affected many retailers deals with advertising. The Act requires disclosure of all credit terms in the ad if any credit information is given. No longer can the auto retailer run an advertisement that states "No money down—easy terms." Such an advertisement must include all credit terms including such things as annual interest rate, size of monthly payment, and number of monthly payments, or contain no credit information. For further discussion, see Chapter 22, on retail credit.

Federal Regulations Affecting Merchandise

Acts affecting retail merchandise include Fur Products Labeling Act (1951), Textile Fiber Products Identification Act (1958), and the Child Protection and Toy Safety Act (1969). These and similar Acts affect how the product can be labeled and sold, if allowed to be sold at all, at the retail level. Retailers should become aware of these Acts to ensure that merchandise bought for resale can be sold in the desired manner.

Fair Labor Standards Act (1938)

Of the many federal laws enacted, this Law probably has one of the greatest impacts on the day-to-day operation of the retail store. This Act, also referred to as the Federal Wage and Hour Law, provides for the setting of minimum wages and maximum hours with a provision for overtime compensation. As amended, the Law sets a wage floor per hour for all retail organizations having annual sales of $250,000 or more. The small store is, therefore, not subject to the minimum wage. Also exempt are stores owned and operated exclusively by one family with no other employees.

Civil Rights Acts (1960s)

The Civil Rights Acts require the retailer to operate in a nondiscriminatory manner. It is illegal to discriminate against a customer or employee because of sex, age, race, religion, or national origin. Customer discrimination for most retailers is somewhat a thing of the past. Employee discrimination in hiring, rate of compensation, rate of advancement, and working conditions is another matter. Much concern about employee discrimination is found to exist among retailers.

Other Federal Laws and Regulations

The list of other federal laws and regulations that affect the retail operation is much too long to be included here. Of equal importance is the fact that the list is forever changing. Fair Trade Laws have been a part of a discussion of federal regulations for many years. The U.S. Congress has now repealed such laws and other acts and regulations dealing with such things as credit rights for women and deceptive pricing are being added to the list. The retailer should be aware of the various federal rules and regulations affecting his or her operations. The retailer should also work for or against rules and regulations that will help or hinder his or her business. An informed retailer is generally a better retailer.

STATE LAWS AND REGULATIONS

Each state has many rules and regulations that complement federal law and cover those business establishments not covered by federal statute due to size, lack of interstate status, or other reasons. In addition, the individual states put before the retailer many unique laws and regulations that restrict the retailer from perhaps operating in a manner of optimum efficiency. Some of the more common state restraints are outlined in this section.

Unfair Practices Acts

These minimum markup laws that prohibit sales below cost are found in over half the states. Such laws state that loss leaders (items sold below cost to generate traffic) are illegal. The typical Unfair Practices Act will require a minimum 6 percent markup on an item but will allow a retailer to meet a competitor's lower legal price even if the resulting price is below the 6 percent level. It is noted that most items have markups that are greater than 6 percent. Therefore, the Laws are limited in their application from a practical standpoint.

Taxes

In almost every state, retailers are faced with taxes of many kinds. The greatest tax problem for most is that they must become tax collectors for the state by means of the state sales tax. Retailers must collect the tax and turn the funds over to the state. Not only is the actual tax collection a problem, but record keeping in a manner necessary to satisfy various state revenue agencies is also a necessity. Retailers must also train sales personnel to collect the proper tax. If insufficient funds are collected from the customers, the difference must be made up by the retailer.

Various other taxes such as a trading stamp tax or special taxes on certain items sold in the store (liquor, cigarettes, etc.) all result in the retailer having additional record keeping, additional expense, and higher take-home prices for the products and services offered by the store.

Blue Laws

These laws simply state that Sunday is a day of rest. Therefore, no retail activity other than the selling of necessities will be permitted. The problem with such laws is obviously the definition of necessity. Who determines what is a necessity? Most laws are written in such a confusing manner that they do not clearly define a necessity. Another problem with "blue laws" is the fact that enforcement is not uniform. In some communities the law is not enforced at all. In other communities, a drugstore will be permitted to sell anything whereas a variety store is forced to close. The retailer should be aware of the status of the Sunday closing ordinance in an area before going into a town. This information is especially important to the retailer who has a policy of Sunday sales.

Other State Laws and Regulations

The retailer is faced with numerous regulations at the state level that will place restraints on his or her business operation. For example, state law may prohibit the advertising of liquor or prescription prices. State law may require that a drugstore be partly owned by a pharmacist, or it may prohibit a medical doctor from owning a pharmacy. State laws may forbid the use of games of chance or set down particular procedures to follow if using such a game. Food establishments must follow state rules and regulations. A pet shop will have another set of regulations.

One very important job for every retailer is to determine which state regulations do pertain to his or her business and which do not. For multi-state operations, the task is made difficult by the vast number of complex and conflicting statutes among the several states. For simplicity of operation, the retailer might well want to develop methods of operation that will satisfy the several states collectively.

LOCAL LAWS AND REGULATIONS

As with state laws and regulations, local statutes can be numerous and complex, with much conflict between local governments. Some types of laws and regulations that usually are found to be of a restraining nature are now examined.

Zoning

The concept of zoning is good business. The difficulty comes when zoning is not applied equally to all. In many instances a firm may be denied a location for some dubious reason while in reality the only reason is competition. In such situations, zoning becomes an anti-new-business regulation. The area around a retail location is very important. From a retailing viewpoint, zoning should not be against new business.

Zoning should, however, call for consistency. If building styles and business types are similar in an area, as would be true under strong zoning regulations, all business in the area will benefit. What this may mean for a fast-food franchise, for example, is that the standard building design for the chain may not be permitted at a particular location because the standard design would not blend in with the local architecture. In these situations, some chains have taken the initiative to develop appropriate designs that will allow them to locate retail units in these zoned locations.

License

In most situations, a license is required to operate any kind of retail establishment. Business licenses are a source of revenue for most communities. A business license becomes a restraint when the question is raised as to whether the retailer can get a license and, if so, what it will cost. Like zoning, business licenses can be an anti-new-business device. An operating clothing store may be paying $200 for a license. A new store is asked to pay $500. A retailer should make every effort to determine what other similar stores are paying. Sometimes, calling the store something different on the license application can result in a cheaper license. For example, by calling a store a dress shop instead of a boutique, the fee may be less. It all depends on being an informed retailer.

Special licenses such as liquor or gasoline permits may place additional restraints on a retailer. A local ordinance may require that a store selling alcoholic beverages not be within 500 feet of a church or that a gasoline station be 1,000 feet from a school. A particular ordinance may require a three-year residency in the city before a license is issued to operate a pool hall, for example, thereby restraining all new firms from undertaking such activity.

Other Local Laws and Regulations

As is true at the federal and state level, local regulations contain many retail restraints. For example, the placing of a sign in front of the store may have to have city or county approval. The store building will generally have to meet the approval of the fire department before the building can be used. The store will usually be required to handle all waste in a prescribed manner. A particular kind of trash container may be required that is compatible with municipal trash collection equipment. Even the going out of business of a store is usually regulated. Many local governmental units have regulations that prevent stores from having an annual going-out-of-business sale. Fire sales are usually regulated in the same manner. As stated previously, the smart retailer knows the regulations. Ignorance can lead to costly mistakes.

RETAIL UNIONS

A definite restraint on retail management is retail unions. Wherever unions exist, retail management naturally loses much of its managerial flexibility. Retail unions have been around since the 1800s. In their earliest form, unions were referred to as "Early

Closing Societies" since much early activity centered around shorter hours. In the 1800s, a workday ran from 6 A.M. to 10 or 11 P.M. Sundays only required work from 6 A.M. until noon. Usually one of the clerks or the owner lived in the rooms above the store. If a customer knocked during hours other than store hours, the clerk was expected to open the shop and take care of the customer's needs. [3]

The largest union in retailing today is the United Food and Commercial Workers (UFCW) with a membership in excess of one million workers. This union, which is the result of the 1979 merger between the Retail Clerks International Association and the Amalgamated Meat Cutters, is a dominant force in the retail food industry and is working to represent more workers in other areas of retailing as well. [4] Local unions are also significant in particular geographic areas.

How do unions restrain management? The answer is "in many ways." [5]

Store Hours

In a union store, hours are no longer totally a management decision. Unions generally resist night hours. Sunday hours are also a point of difficulty.

Movement of Employees

Can a clerk be transferred from one department to another? In many union stores, the answer is "no." Can a clerk be transferred from one store to another? Again, such a transfer is a problem in a union operation.

Right to Discharge Employees

Contracts generally specify a probationary period (usually 90 days) before a person can become a union member. After the probationary period is over, it is quite difficult to discharge an employee. This restraint may force management to discharge some potentially good employees within the probationary period due to the risk involved in giving a marginal employee a longer trial employment period.

Seniority

Seniority is a basic management–union area of conflict. In slow times, unions want the most recently hired employee to be laid off. Management would generally prefer to base such decisions on ability. A positive point for seniority is that such a system may build employee loyalty. The older employee may remain with a company to benefit from the seniority system.

Restriction of Employee Duties

Unions are generally opposed to one classification of employees performing duties usually assigned to others because they feel that fewer employees will be needed if workers are permitted to perform multiple duties. In some cases, salespeople may not wheel stock to the selling floor since that is the job of the stockperson. Cash register checkers may not stock shelves during slow times. In turn, stock clerks may not assist cashiers during busy times of the day.

Resistance to Innovation

Unions generally oppose the use of scanning equipment in stores because scanners normally result in fewer checkout personnel as well as fewer stock clerks in those locations where individual shelf pricing is omitted. In addition, items that are delivered to the store that are prepacked, such as meat or produce, or prepriced, such as many soft goods, may meet union resistance.

What Should Be Done by Management

In many cases, retail management makes the mistake of ignoring the possibility of unionization until it is too late. A realistic wage and adequate working conditions will generally limit union growth. With so many part-time workers and secondary wage earners in the retail industry, adequate treatment of employees should restrict union activity. It is important to note that, if a store is involved in a union vote, care should be taken to follow up on the promises made to the workers to get them to vote against the union. It is an effective tool of union organization to go back to the workers and ask, "Where are the things that were promised by management?" If the promises are not kept, the second union election has a tendency to go in favor of the union.

It is not the intent of this section to infer that all unions are bad. In many cases, management and union have brought their different interests together for the good of the store. By their very nature, however, unions do restrict the retailer in the day-to-day operation of the store. A union contract is an external retail restraint.

CUSTOMS IN AREA OF OPERATION

A retailer must be concerned with the customs of the area in which the store operates. If not concerned, the retailer may make costly mistakes that could lead to financial disaster. One example to consider is Sunday operations. Regardless of any law, is the market ready to shop on Sunday? Will a store that opens on Sunday lose more business than it will gain? Another example is whether or not a grocery store should sell beer and wine. In many markets, the addition of beer and wine in a grocery store will discourage many shoppers. Naturally, it may attract others.

Many smaller communities have a custom of closing all businesses on Wednesday or Thursday afternoons. A store that tries to open on this particular afternoon may be met with verbal as well as printed attacks accusing the store of having no regard for its employees and the well-being of the town.

It may be the custom in a town for all merchants to support the local high school football program or community recreation program or whatever. To not do so may bring the wrath of many people in the town, which is doubly bad if these people also make up the store's target market.

Local custom as well as good business may require that a store hire local people to work in positions of responsibility in the store. Custom may also dictate that the manager or retail owner move to the town in which the store is located. The owner must also get involved in the local church, local civic club, and other local activities. Especially in small-town America, the retail operator who is "too good" to live in the community in which his or her store is located may lose many potential sales from people who will not buy from an "outsider."

Local customs and practices are an area that must not be overlooked. If a retailer decides to go against a custom for whatever the reason, that is certainly a retail management prerogative. It is noted that most problems are usually created when the retailer is ignorant of local customs. Customs do put restraints on the operation of the store. An informed retailer can make an intelligent decision as to whether or not to follow the custom. An uninformed retailer does not have that option.

CONSUMER BEHAVIOR

Consumer behavior places many restraints on the retailer. It is the retailer's task to sell goods and services to the consumer. To do so successfully requires an understanding of what makes the consumer buy or not buy. As the store operator develops the retailing mix, he or she is, or should be, concerned with how to better serve the customer. The retailer cannot change basic consumer behavior. It is the responsibility of the store operator to turn this limitation into a plus factor by developing an understanding of how customers think and what they want.

Consumer behavior may be defined as that behavior exhibited by people in planning, purchasing, and using economic goods and services.[6] Such behavior can be viewed from three different viewpoints (individual, group, and cultural). A better understanding of each should be of great assistance to the retailer (Figure 3–3).

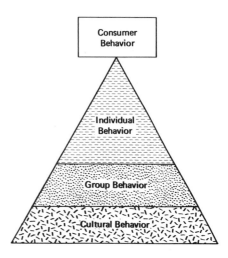

Figure 3–3

A customer's behavior is a function of various individual, group, and cultural considerations.

Motives, learning, attitudes, and perception all affect the behavior of an individual. Each merits a closer look.

Motives. A motive is something (need or desire) that causes a person to act.[7] Motives are generally thought to consist of a mixture of economical and psychosociological reasons why a certain action is taken. As noted in Figure 3–4, the mixture is determined on a continuum. For each consumer or consumer group, the point on the continuum can be different. For each situation, the point may be different. For purposes of definition, economic motives are concerned with quality of the product or service, price, and other rational considerations resulting in consumer action. Psychosociological motives are concerned with one's own emotions and with acceptance by one's own peers. Although these latter motives are many times referred to as irrational motives, they generally play the major role in consumer buying behavior.

Another way in which to view motives was developed by A. H. Maslow,[8] who divided behavior into a hierarchy of needs (Figure 3–5). Once the physiological or basic needs are satisfied, safety needs influence the individual. Once the safety needs are met, the need to belong becomes the driving force. As each need is satisfied, that particular need ceases to be a motivator.[9] Much of the retailing activity in the United States deals with customers who are at the third and fourth stages in Maslow's hierarchy of needs. Consumers want to be accepted. Therefore, the teenage girl tells her parents that she will "die" if she cannot have a particular bracelet. Her reason—"everyone else has one." The need to be accepted by the group by means of having this bracelet is very important to that particular customer. For the retailer, the need for the item should be observed and promoted to the market with profitable results.

The esteem need is also an important consumer motivator. Status and prestige are important to many people. By providing through various means such status or prestige, the retailer can attract customers to the store. Naturally, what constitutes status varies with the target market. Choosing the right symbols of status are important. For years, Neiman-Marcus has used status in its catalog to promote the store with legendary success. For other markets, the small intimate dress shop might be the "in" place. For the retailer, "in" places do not generally happen by accident. Careful study of the target market is required to determine what consumers want and desire. Much effort in selecting and pricing of the merchandise as well as promoting it will pay dividends for the retailer if such decisions are based on an understanding of consumer behavior.

Learning. It is also important for the retailer to understand how consumers learn (changes in responses and response tendencies due to the effects of experience[10]). For example, repeat business is vital to the success of a retail store. As consumers shop

Figure 3–4

Continuum of consumer behavior.

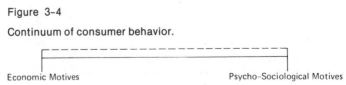

Economic Motives   Psycho-Sociological Motives

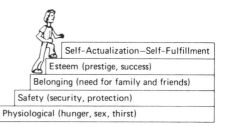

Figure 3-5

Hierarchy of needs.

in a particular store, they learn to like the store and everything about it. Their satisfaction with the store continues to grow. One day the customer experiences an unhappy situation in the store. Much of the earlier-learned satisfaction disappears. As Figure 3-6 illustrates, two successive negative shopping experiences may result in the customer being lost. Negative learning outweighs positive learning when compared on a one-to-one scale.

As the retailer studies consumer behavior, every effort should be made to discover the frequency with which negative shopping trips are occurring and why. Is the behavior of the salesclerks discouraging customers? Is the merchandise of poor quality? Is the store too cold or too hot? A complaint desk should be handy for the customer. Or complaint forms that can be filled out easily can be available. The retailer wants customers to learn nice things about the store. Bad situations must be detected and corrected. If enough customers have negative experiences, other potential customers will learn from them with the end result being no customers!

Attitudes.   A learned tendency to respond in a given manner to a particular situation is known as an attitude. As one study dealing with consumer attitudes toward discount stores[11] illustrates, consumer attitudes can be quite important. In the study, it was found that many higher socioeconomic shoppers would not buy some items such as handbags, men's dress shirts, men's dress slacks, and costume jewelry from discount stores because they thought their peers might find out where they purchased these items. On the other hand, they had little concern when buying sleepwear, toys, or cookwear from a discounter. By having knowledge of such consumer behavior, the retailer may be able to develop a more profitable merchandise mix for a given market situation. It is for just such a reason that a major department store will go to great effort to separate the regular store from the budget store. The retailer does not wish to confuse his or her various target markets.

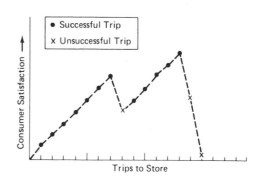

Figure 3-6

Cumulative customer satisfaction.

Perception.   Perception is defined as how one interprets a situation as a result of various stimuli. Do customers feel comfortable in the store? For the target market, the answer should be "yes." The customer should feel comfortable with the fixtures, merchandise, and employees. The store windows should also promote the correct perception as should the store's advertising.

Another aspect of perception deals with the tendency of some retailers to perceive that their own behavior is synonymous with the target market. Such a situation is particularly prevalent among small retailers. Many mistakes occur when such an assumption is made. Even if the retailer strongly believes that he or she understands the store's customers because he or she is one, every effort should be made to analyze consumer behavior as if such were not the case. The benefits should outweigh the effort required.

Group Behavior

The distinction between group behavior and individual behavior is difficult at best as these factors are related so closely. But if the retailer can understand how the "group" works and thinks, then individuals within the group may become customers. Two aspects of group behavior that are of special interest to retailers will be discussed: reference groups and opinion leaders.

Reference Groups.   People identify with groups relating to church, family, work, and other social situations. If a particular brand of shoes is desired by a teenage group, it will pay the retailer to carry the product and to inform that consumer group that the product is in stock. It is significant for the retailer to note that no other shoe will be satisfactory. For a different group, however, a different product such as imprinted T-shirts may be the thing. Whatever the reference group, they will establish norms of buying behavior for the individuals within the group.

Opinion Leaders.   Certain individuals exert a great influence over people in the marketplace. In many small towns, for example, the local preacher is a leader. If a retailer gets the preacher to buy a new suit with the new width lapels and a new width tie to go with it, others in the town will be in the store to buy new clothes as well. In some situations, retailers will even give the opinion leaders the merchandise because of their strong influence on the buying patterns of the market. Of course, the great difficulty lies with identifying the leaders. Unfortunately, there are no set rules available for this purpose. This activity must, by necessity, fall under the category of the art of retailing.

Cultural Behavior

Customs, which were discussed earlier, are somewhat a result of the culture of the market. Other considerations that merit discussion are social class and subcultures.

Social Class.   Social classes are relatively permanent and homogenous divisions in a society into which individuals or families sharing similar values, life-styles, interests, and behavior can be categorized.[12] Although much could be said about social class as it pertains to retailing, the contrast between "middle class" and "lower status" as developed by Martineau[13] will serve to illustrate its significance (Table 3–1). Using these data, the retailer who sells on credit to a "lower-status" customer should not be surprised if collection becomes a problem. These customers do not think in terms of the future. When making a purchase, the "lower-status" customer will seek assurances that it is the correct thing to do, whereas the "middle-class" customer will not feel that such assurances are necessary. Because more options are open to the "middle-class" customer, these customers will typically be less store loyal than will the "lower-status" customer with perceived limited options. These examples serve to illustrate that social class can have an influence on customer behavior.

Subcultures. Geography, religion, race, national origin, and almost anything else can result in the creation of a subculture. As mentioned earlier, small-town America is a culture different from that found in the "big" city. Particular stores might wish to cater to such a culture and locate in small towns across the country. In like manner, other retailers may choose to cater to black people or people of the Jewish faith or people from a particular group of countries. For example, a retailer in southern Florida may draw its target market from the Spanish-speaking community that is located there, whereas a store in California may choose to market itself to the Chinese subculture that is found in that geographic area.

SUMMARY

The retailer must operate within the framework of various restraints found in the marketplace. To do so requires an awareness of these restraints and an ability to

Table 3–1

Martineau's comparison of middle-class and lower-status groups

Middle Class	Lower Status
1. Pointed to the future	1. Pointed to the present and past
2. Viewpoint embraces a long expanse of time	2. Lives and thinks in a short expanse of time
3. Urban identification	3. Rural identification
4. Stresses rationality	4. Nonrational essentially
5. Well-structured sense of universe	5. Vague and unclear structuring of the world
6. Horizons not limited	6. Horizons sharply defined and limited
7. Greater sense of choice making	7. Limited sense of choice making
8. Self-confident	8. Lacks self-confidence
9. Immaterial and abstract in his thinking	9. Concrete and perceptive in his thinking
10. World tied to national happenings	10. World revolves around family and body

Source: Pierre Martineau, "Social Classes and Spending Behavior," *Journal of Marketing*, Vol. 23, no. 2 (October 1958), p. 129. Published by the American Marketing Association.

operate within them. First, federal laws ranging from the Sherman Antitrust Act to the Consumer Credit Protection Act set forth restrictions for the retailer to follow. The Fair Labor Standards Act and the Civil Rights Acts have a bearing on personnel policies. Other federal regulations involve everything from games of chance to truth in advertising. Second, the various states also restrict the retailer. Unfair Practices Acts, taxes, blue laws, and so on are factors that the retailer must consider. Third, zoning, licenses, and various regulations at the local level are also important. Even a firm that wants to go out of business will generally require a local government permit to do so. Fourth, unions also have a restricting impact. Store hours, movement of employees, and the right to discharge employees are among the areas in which unions influence a store's operation if the store is unionized. Fifth, customs in an area affect a retailer. Sunday operations, beer and wine sales, or not closing on a given weekday afternoon may be against local custom. Finally, consumer behavior influences the retailer. Individual, group, and cultural behavior will all have a bearing on numerous decisions affecting the store.

By being informed about the various external restraints placed upon the store, the retailer should be better able to cope with the controllable variables that are faced in day-to-day operations.

DISCUSSION QUESTIONS

1. What is meant by external restraints? Why is it important for a retailer to be aware of their existence?
2. Which is more important to the retailer—federal, state, or local restraints? Why?
3. Discuss various federal restraints on the retailer.
4. Discuss various state restraints on the retailer.
5. Discuss various local restraints on the retailer.
6. Why would retail management generally not be in favor of unions?
7. Why should a retailer be concerned with local custom?
8. Why is an understanding of consumer behavior important to a retailer?
9. Explain Maslow's hierarchy of needs. What use can a retailer make of the hierarchy?
10. Go to a retailer in your trade area and discuss with that person the various retail restraints that are presented in the chapter. Write a summary of your discussion.

NOTES

[1] For a more in-depth discussion, see Marshall C. Howard, "Government, the Retailer and the Consumer," *Journal of Retailing*, Vol. 48, no. 4 (Winter 1972–1973), pp. 48–62.

[2] "Sears, Roebuck and Company," *Federal Trade Commission Decisions*, Vol. 89 (1977), pp. 229–237.

[3] "Early Days of the RCIA," *It Pays to Belong* (Washington, D.C.: Retail Clerks International Association, 1968), p. 4.

[4] "Big New Retailing Union Eyes the Services," *Business Week*, 2575 (March 5, 1979), pp. 73–74.

[5] Discussion taken in part from Ronald D. Michman, "Union Impact on Retail Management," *Business Horizons*, Vol. 10, no. 1 (Spring 1967), pp. 79–84.

[6] Kenneth E. Runyon, *Consumer Behavior and the Practice of Marketing* (Columbus, Ohio: Charles E. Merrill Publishing Company, 1977), p. 29.

[7] By permission. From *Webster's New Collegiate Dictionary* © 1980 by G. & C. Merriam Co., Publishers of the Merriam-Webster Dictionaries.

[8] A. H. Maslow, "A Theory of Human Behavior," *Psychological Review*, Vol. 50, no. 4, 1943, pp. 370–396. Copyright 1943 by the American Psychological Association.

[9] Ibid.

[10] Carl E. Block and Kenneth J. Roering, *Essentials of Consumer Behavior* (Hinsdale, Ill.: The Dryden Press, 1976), p. 406.

[11] V. Kanti Prasad, "Socioeconomic Product Risk and Patronage Preferences of Retail Shoppers," *Journal of Marketing*, Vol. 39, no. 3 (July 1975), pp. 42–47. Published by the American Marketing Association.

[12] Adapted from James F. Engel, Roger D. Blackwell, and David T. Kollat, *Consumer Behavior*, 3rd ed. (Hinsdale, Ill.: The Dryden Press, 1978), p. 109.

[13] Pierre Martineau, "Social Classes and Spending Behavior," *Journal of Marketing*, Vol. 23, no. 2 (October 1958), p. 129. Published by the American Marketing Association.

CHAPTER 4

Retailing Research

"This research may not really be valid,
but the results look conclusive!"

How many people in the market area have a need for left-handed items? Is the proposed store location a place that will project the proper image? Is the store layout conducive to a strong sales effort throughout the store? As one of the foundations of retailing, retailing research can be utilized to help answer these questions. No matter how new or old the store might be, the retailer should consider research as a retailing tool.

In discussing this important aspect of retailing, a definition of research is important as is a brief look at the advantages and disadvantages that can result from it. Research procedures are then presented along with various applications as they pertain to retailing.

RESEARCH DEFINED

Marketing research is the systematic gathering, recording, and analyzing of data about problems relating to the marketing of goods and services.[1] Included in this definition is retailing research as well as many other research applications. When dealing specifically with retailing, research can be defined in a slightly different manner. Retailing research is the systematic gathering, recording, and analyzing of data pertaining to the retailer's target market and/or retailing mix (product, place, price, promotion, and personality).

All aspects of the retail environment are candidates for possible research. In terms of the target market, research can reveal the demographic makeup of the market area. Life-style factors as well as consumption preferences of the market can also be studied. In terms of product, research can attempt to determine if the merchandise assortment is correct for the store and if certain lines should be added or deleted. Next, place, or the second "P," is not only concerned with the placement of the store but also with the optimum location of items within the store. Price is also important for the retailer. What impact would a drop in price have on demand? Should the store use psychological pricing? Should the store place prices in advertisements for the store? Retailers need answers to questions such as these. The fourth element in the retailing mix—promotion—also involves many research questions. What media should the store use and what media plan should be adopted are just two questions for which research can help provide an answer for the retailer. Finally, the correct personality or image is crucial to a store's success. Determining what is the image of the store and what it should be are questions that should be addressed by every retailer with the aid of retailing research. These few examples are by no means all the ways in which research can be applied to retailing. Where needed, the retailer would be wise to apply research procedures whenever questions arise pertaining to the store's retail strategy (target market and retailing mix).

WHY RESEARCH?

What will be the benefits of the research versus the cost of the research? If a retailer chooses to use retailing research procedures in an effort to solve a problem, a commit-

Figure 4-1

What features do customers want in a product? The retailer can use retailing research to help answer this and many other questions about the store's target market and/or retailing mix. (Courtesy of Sears, Roebuck and Co.)

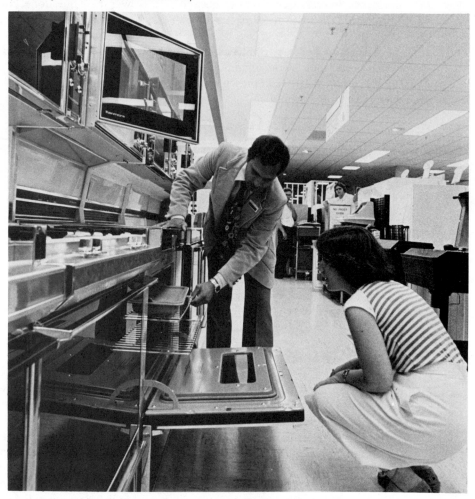

ment of time and money must be made. Is such a commitment worth it? Will the profitability of the store be increased in greater proportion than the cost of the research effort? These questions point out that there are both advantages and disadvantages to retailing research.

Advantages

If research reveals that the target market for the store does not exist in a particular market area, then a mistake will be avoided by not locating a store at that particular site. On the other hand, research may be used to discover those markets where the target market is located, thereby providing guidance for the location of the store. In addition to addressing specific research problems, research can also be used as a general planning tool. One of the greatest shortcomings of many retail stores is that no prior thought is given to whether the store location is appropriate or not. No consideration is given as to the appropriateness of the proposed store name. In these and other situations, little forethought is given before making a retail decision. By following a research procedure in addressing many questions, the retailer will be "forced" to plan, to think ahead, and to, perhaps, consider alternatives. These are the benefits of the retail research process.

Disadvantages

As mentioned, research costs both time and money. Even with the commitment of time and money, however, there is no guarantee that the research procedure will yield the "correct" answer. Research may indicate that customers want particular items to be carried by the store, yet these items do not move well when added to the assortment. Opinions change as do tastes and attitudes. Much research asks the customer what they will do or how they will react in a given situation. Actual behavior does not, however, always correlate with the research findings.

But even with the problems inherent in research, the retailer should give careful thought to using retailing research. Although the answers that are provided may not always be correct, research is still a decision-making tool. Careful application of research procedures can be of great benefit to the retailer so long as the limitations are understood as well as the benefits.

RESEARCH PROCEDURES

Problem definition, secondary data collection, primary data collection, data analysis, and data presentation and follow-up are the five major research steps that should be employed by a researcher when investigating the retailing situation (Figure 4–2). J. C. Penney has its own retailing research department. A large local store may hire an outside consultant. A small boutique owner may do all the research herself. No matter what the size of operation or the complexity of the task, however, the five basic elements of the research process should be followed and applied.[2] A discussion of these five steps is provided to promote understanding.

Problem Definition

Billy Bennett, the regional vice president for Golden Brothers, called a meeting of his district managers to announce that the Golden Brothers chain has a problem—"Sales are falling." His directive to his managers is to "do something about it!" But what can the district managers do about the situation? Nothing much can be done until it can be determined what is causing sales to fall. In other words, falling sales is the symptom. What the district managers need to know is the problem.

It should be emphasized that falling sales is certainly a "problem" for any store.

Figure 4-2

Research procedures.

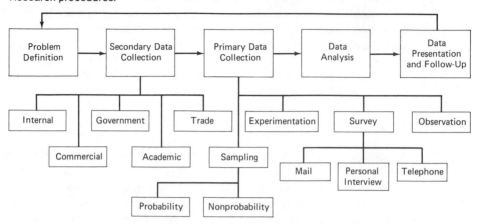

But to solve the "problem," a careful analysis should be made as to what is causing sales to fall. Once this fact is known, the remaining steps in the research procedure should be pursued as a means of solving the problem and implementing the solution. It is noted that the more precise the problem statement(s), the greater the probability that the remaining research steps will yield a workable solution.

Secondary Data Collection

In retailing, as in other areas of marketing, time is important. If a problem can be solved by using information that has already been collected, then the time, money, and effort needed to collect the data from scratch is saved by the firm. Against the time and cost advantages of secondary data must be weighed several disadvantages. One difficulty lies with the possibility that the secondary data are biased or otherwise slanted in favor of the organization that published the data. For example, should a retailer use Chamber of Commerce data for the purpose of analyzing a target market? Most Chambers of Commerce would not publish data that are unfavorable to their market area. What is published is usually correct. The problem rests with the facts that might have been left out that may be very pertinent for a given retailer.

Another problem rests with finding appropriate data. How old is the study? Many 1981 industry reports that are published in 1982 rely heavily on 1980 data. Of course, in retailing, where change is the only constant, a time lag in the data can be quite a problem. By the time facts become available on many fashion and fad items, the data are literally history.

A third problem with secondary data also concerns itself with finding appropriate data. In this case, however, the concern rests with whether the data as collected are pertinent to the retailer's target market. Also, if the study is pertinent, then was the sample used large enough to truly reflect the target market? Finally, if the sample appears to be also appropriate, then a judgment must be made as to the ethics of the data source. Were the data collected in the manner indicated in the methodology? Unfortunately, methodology and actual practice do not always agree. The researcher will have to make a judgment decision as to the reliability of the secondary data source.

Secondary data sources are numerous. While keeping in mind both the benefits and the potential problems, retailers should make themselves aware of the various sources of secondary data. These sources can be classified into five groups for purposes of discussion: internal, government, trade, academic, and commercial.

Internal. The most useful type of secondary data for most firms are the retailer's own internal data that are collected in the normal day-to-day operation of the firm. Selected internal data sources include:

Accounting reports	Point-of-sale (POS) scanning data
Credit sales reports	Salesperson performance reports
Inventory records	Want books/want slips
Sales return records	Customer complaint files

These data can yield much information for analysis purposes. They also may be current, which may not be so with other types of secondary data. Finally, a judgment can be made concerning their validity. If the store has a strong internal reporting system, then the retailer can use the information resulting from this system with confidence. Even if the system is not strong, however, the retailer should at least know the limitations inherent in the system, so that the resulting secondary data will be a known quantity in terms of its validity and reliability.

Government. When considering government, the various reports issued by the U.S. Department of Commerce are the first sources that come to the minds of most retailers. Some of these reports are:

Census of Retail Trade. Contains data on retail stores by type of store and location.

Census of Service Industries. Contains data on various service industries by type of business and location.

Census of Population. Contains demographic population data by state, SMSA, county, city, and smaller divisions.

Census of Housing. Contains housing data (type of dwelling, size of house, number of occupants, etc.) for areas as small as a city block in major cities. Maps are also available to complement the housing census.

Survey of Current Business. Provides numerous numerical data on all aspects of business. See Chapter 1 for several examples of the types of data to be found in the publication.

In addition to the Department of Commerce, other government (federal, state, local) sources include:

Vital records (births, deaths, marriages, etc.)
State sales tax collections
State industry and trade reports
Regional, state, and local planning and development commission reports
Business activity reports (number of building permits issued, number and type of business licenses purchased, etc.)

Federal reports, pamphlets, booklets, and other data are published in such numbers that a directory (*Monthly Catalog of United States Government Publications*) lists all the available information from the federal government published each month. A typical retailer would be surprised at how much useful information can be obtained from the various governmental agencies that generate secondary data. Moreover, much of the information is free or is obtainable for a nominal fee or is available for use in a library in the area that is a congressionally designated depository for U.S. government documents.

Although not indexed as well as federal data, state and local government data are also usually free or available for a small fee. A letter to various state and local agencies requesting data will usually provide the retailer with information as to what is available from these sources.

Trade. Trade associations and trade publications provide much information for the retailer. The National Retail Merchants Association (NRMA) is considered by most retailers to be the major trade association for all retailing, although it concentrates its efforts on the department store and specialty store aspects of the industry. Its *FOR (Financial and Operating Results) Report* and *MOR (Merchandising and Operating Results) Report* are two widely used sources of secondary data in retailing. The National Retail Hardware Association and the National Association of Retail Druggists are other examples of trade associations on the national level that provide useful secondary data. It should be noted that, in most states, state trade groups also provide data that can be of use to the retail operator.

Selected trade publications that contain useful secondary data on a regular basis are the following:

Advertising Age	*Merchandising*
Chain Store Age Executive	*Progressive Grocer*
Chain Store Age Supermarkets	*Retail and Distribution Management*
Discount Merchandiser	*Retail Week*
Hardware Retailing	*Stores*
Men's Wear	*Women's Wear Daily*

For retailers who choose not to subscribe to the appropriate trade publications, most are available in major city libraries as well as in the libraries of major academic institutions.

Academic. A secondary data source that is overlooked by many retailers is the academic community. Studies dealing with all aspects of retailing appear on a regular basis in academic journals such as:

Journal of Advertising	*Journal of Marketing Research*
Journal of Marketing	*Journal of Retailing*

and in the published proceedings of associations such as:

The American Marketing Association
The Southern Marketing Association
The Southwest Marketing Association

The increasing emphasis on retail research in the academic community can be illustrated best by the fact that the *Journal of Retailing* devoted its entire Spring 1980 issue to this topic. Also, the American Collegiate Retailing Association, an association of retailing educators, is becoming more cognizant of retail research and its possible use by retailers. With efforts such as these taking place, the future should find more useful secondary data from academic sources being made available to the retailer. As for its availability, like trade data, academic data can be purchased or are normally available through various city and academic libraries.

Commercial. In addition to the secondary sources already mentioned, data can also be obtained from various organizations for a fee. Two such commercial research firms are:

> *A. C. Nielsen.* Through its Retail Index Service, Nielsen provides data on a continuing basis for products sold in food stores and drugstores.
>
> *Selling Area-Marketing, Inc. (SAMI).* Provides information on the movement of goods to the retail outlet.

A check of various business directories will yield the names of firms that will provide secondary data of various kinds for a fee.

Primary Data Collection

If no secondary data are available that pertain to the problem or if the data are too old or are subject to question, then the retailer must decide if the problem is important enough to proceed further and collect primary data. If the answer is "yes," the data will then be collected by means of observation, survey, experimentation, or some combination thereof. It is also important to mention that most studies will not question all customers, suppliers, and so on. A sample will be taken that obviously will have a major impact on the data collected. Since the makeup of this sample is as important as the method of data collection, it will be discussed first.

Sampling. It would be impractical for the Federated Department Store chain to interview all its customers on the question of whether each store in the chain should retain its own name or change all names to Federated. The solution to this problem is sampling (probability or nonprobability). In a probability sample, each person in the sample population has an equal chance of selection. Examples of probability sampling include the simple random sample and the stratified random sample. In a stratified sample, the retail researcher develops a methodology that ensures that particular characteristics will be found in the sample. For example, if Safeway wishes to do a study on shopping behavior that compares Hispanic, Black, and Oriental customers, a simple random sample may yield 400 Hispanics, 175 Blacks, and 25 Orientals. Because the wide dispersion among the data cells will make data comparisons very difficult, the researcher may stratify the sample so that 200 in each category will be questioned. One other comment should be made concerning probability samples. Samples of this nature are much more costly and time consuming than are their nonprobability counterparts. But probability samples can be used to project the findings statistically to the population. This cannot technically be done with a nonprobability sample, although it is done by many firms.

As for nonprobability sampling, this is inexpensive, easy to obtain, and subject to error. A nonprobability sample relies heavily on the judgment of the researcher. In fact, one name for a nonprobability sample is a judgment sample. Other names include quota sample and convenience sample. An example of a nonprobability sampling procedure would be a retailer who wanted to question 300 people about where they shop for shoes. The person set up a table in a mall and asked whoever stopped at the table a series of questions. No effort was made to solicit respondents or to randomly pick the people to be questioned. This convenience sample could have been modified into a judgment sample if the retailer had made an effort to analyze approaching people and to ask people to participate whom he or she thought were representative of the target market. No matter what procedure is used, nonprobability sampling will still not yield as objective a group of respondents as will a probability sample. But it is less expensive and requires less time. In most cases, how to sample is viewed as a cost versus benefit question. One is better but the other is cheaper. The decision remains with the retailer.

Observation. "When a customer has the choice to go left or right in a store, which way will he or she go?" When asked this question, most customers do not really know the answer. A better solution is to watch customers as they enter the store and see which way they turn. The greatest advantage of observation is that the actions of people tell much when they are not placed in an artificial situation. But this advantage is also a major problem. Observation must wait for something to happen, but the retailer may not have the time to wait.

Survey. Because surveys do not wait for something to happen, they are much more popular than observation. Survey techniques (mail, personal interview, telephone) force the situation by asking questions that are designed to solicit appropriate responses. Naturally, much of the success of the survey method is dependent on the questions. If they are misleading or ambiguous, the data that results from such questions will have little value. A brief discussion follows on the three survey techniques.

Mail. Although a mail survey is an economical and convenient way in which to solicit data, the retailer should realize that many people will just not respond to a mail survey. At least two mailings of the questionnaire should be planned along with the use of a very positive cover letter and a means of returning the questionnaire postage free. Those who have a strong interest in the subject will respond to the mail questionnaire. The remainder, most likely the majority, will not.

Personal interview. For in-depth study, nothing can take the place of a personal interview. Face-to-face contact would be the most popular method of data collection were it not for its many problems that pertain to cost, time, interviewer bias, and the dangers associated with going door to door in some locations. An alternative used by many retailers is to invite the respondents to the store where interviews can be made on an individual basis or in a focus group setting. Although some fashion boards are strictly for public relations, others are used to solicit information on many aspects of the store's operation. Still other stores select a random sample of their customers for participation in an ongoing sample. In these cases, panel members are normally paid in cash or in merchandise for their assistance. Panels can be very enlightening if the retailer prepares properly for each session and is willing to listen.

Telephone. The telephone is a low-cost way in which to solicit data in a short time span. The retail researcher may use the telephone to determine if there is a need for a particular type of store in the area. Of course, if the target market for the store is lower income, typical customers may not have phones, and so a telephone survey would not yield the proper results. For the telephone to be a successful survey technique, the sample should be telephone users and the questions asked of them should be brief and to the point.

Experimentation. Any type of research that is not included elsewhere falls under the heading of experimentation. One possible application would be a retailer with two stores that sell to similar markets. The retailer might wish to test a new layout. To do so, the layout of one store would be changed while the other store would serve as a control store by keeping its layout as is. Under this methodology, it is assumed that the two stores are influenced by all variables equally. Therefore, the difference between the two stores in terms of performance will be assumed to be the result of the change in layout. The test market–control market procedure is quite popular in retail research and in other types of research as well.

Data Analysis

The data that are collected from secondary and/or primary sources must be checked for errors, compiled, and analyzed. Wherever possible, appropriate statistical procedures should be applied to aid in the study of the data. When the study is conducted by an outside source, the retailer should not hesitate to ask questions about the analysis. There is no such thing as a stupid question if the retailer does not understand the data.

Data Presentation and Follow-Up

Even if the data were analyzed by the retailer who collected the data and who will use the data, it is wise to write up the data for presentation to oneself. If, on the other hand, a retailer is presenting the findings of the study to the chain's buying committee, the presentation will naturally be written up and an elaborate visual presentation may also be prepared. In all situations, the research presentation should not just present the findings. Every effort should be made to determine what the findings mean. The findings should be clear. If the findings do not support the conclusions as strongly as they should, then, perhaps, more data are needed or more analysis is called for.

As for follow-up, it is wise for a retail firm that has spent money and time on the research effort to consider the findings and to follow through on the recommendations if such is the desire of management. In any event, a decision should be made on the research results before the entire study becomes dated due to procrastination. It is also helpful at times to follow up on research studies with additional study. For example, a store might conduct an annual survey of its target market that builds on or follows up on the findings of the previous studies. In addition, follow-up may point out the need for research in new areas. Follow-up can also be of great assistance in the formulation of the problem definition for a study that is similar to one that was conducted in the past. For retailers who understand research, it comes as no surprise that retailing research builds upon itself as the retailer continues to search for the best way to serve the market.

RESEARCH APPLICATIONS

Almost any area of the business can be examined with the aid of retailing research.[3] Projective techniques, ranking techniques, attitude techniques, and inquiry techniques are four particular research procedures that have numerous applications throughout the retail community. Each will be examined for the retailer.

Projective Techniques

One projective technique asks the respondent to assume the identity of someone else. As noted in Figure 4-3, instead of asking people what they thought about a sale at Foskey's, respondents are requested to write in what the "other" person would say in response to the question. Researchers feel that more truthful answers will be given using the projective technique as compared with asking people outright what their answers would be.

Another projective technique is a focus group. Group interviews or focus groups are used to solicit individual opinion as well as the effect of group interaction on that opinion. For example, a retailer may choose a focus group consisting of ten individuals who represent a cross section of the store's target market. The retailer would then call this group together to discuss the store's merchandise assortment, personnel, and so on. The group could be used on an irregular basis, or it might meet on a regular basis as some stores find desirable. Since most members of focus groups will be paid in cash and/or merchandise for their participation, the store should have these meetings well thought out. It can be a very expensive "gossip" session instead of a working session if management does not use a focus group wisely.

If the retailer is sincere in wanting to study why a shopper thinks in a particular way, then an in-depth interview may be utilized. The one-to-one meeting with the customer is aimed at determining his or her psychodynamic makeup. Although expensive, time consuming, and plagued with interviewer bias, it can be quite revealing. During the course of the interview, which may last an hour or longer, the interviewer may project customers into various situations to probe how they feel about the image of the store, its advertising, and numerous other areas of interest.

Figure 4–3

Projective technique.

Ranking Techniques

Respondents are shown two products. They are then asked, "If the store could carry only one of these products, which one should it be?" Two more products are then shown to the respondents and the same question is asked. By mixing up the products as the procedure continues, the end result will be a list of new products for the store ranked by customer preference. The same procedure can be used to evaluate the store's ads, display windows, and even salespeople.

Variations of the ranking technique may use a 1–10 grading scale or a −5 to +5 scale. In the second example, the respondent may be asked to rate various items that are carried by the store. A grade of −5 would mean to not carry the item, 0 means okay to carry or not carry the item, and +5 means to carry the item if at all possible.

Attitude Techniques

As noted in Chapter 3, an attitude is defined as a learned tendency to respond in a given manner to a particular situation. Based on this definition, it is not surprising to note that attitudes are hard to measure. But at the same time, most stores will face serious trouble if they ignore the attitudes of the target market. In most cases, it is smart retailing to attempt to find out what the target market thinks about the various aspects of the retail operation.

One technique that may be used to study attitudes is a Likert Scale. As illustrated in Figure 4–4, the Likert Scale provides the respondent with five choices for indicating his or her degree of agreement with each statement. By asking about numerous statements about the store, the summation of the respondents' answers provides an indication of the intensity of feeling that the respondents have about the store.

Another attitude measurement technique is the semantic differential. In Figure 4–5, a seven-point bipolar scale is used to measure positive or negative feelings about a store. Note that the questions when asked would be arranged so that all positive statements are not placed on the same end of the scale. This approach will encourage the respondent to read each series of statements before providing an answer. Once all respondents have provided answers, an attitude profile may be taken by plotting the median value for a statement or the mean or average value. Either technique has its followers who believe that their approach is the more appropriate. When plotting an overall profile, the statements should be arranged so that all positive statements appear on the same side as is shown in Figure 4–4. If more than one market segment is being tested, not only can a profile be provided but a contrasting profile can be given. For example, Foskey's may use the questionnaire in Figure 4–4 to study the attitudes of two groups: Foskey's regular customers and Foskey's inactive customers. The results of the study indicate that Foskey's inactive customers perceive a problem with the store's location. Promoting friendly service and better hours may increase some business but moving the store, encouraging catalog and phone sales and home delivery, or "selling" the current location to customers are three retailing options that should be given some thought as a result of the attitude study for Foskey's.

Before leaving the discussion of attitudes, it is significant to note that attitudes of customer groups do change over time. Some attitudes are entrenched and are slow to change, whereas others will change very rapidly. For a national retailer, it is important to remember that attitudes across the country are not the same on many issues. A particular merchandise assortment will be viewed with favor in one area and with disgust in another. Even with all the problems that are inherent in dealing with attitudes, the

Figure 4–4

Example of questionnaire using Likert scale.

	Strongly Disagree	Disagree	Neither Agree or Disagree	Agree	Strongly Agree
Foskey's has convenient hours					
Foskey's has friendly, courteous sales clerks					
Foskey's has reasonable prices					
Foskey's has a convenient location					

Figure 4–5

Customer profiles as provided by use of the semantic differential technique.

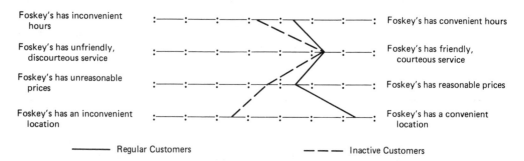

retailer is wise to attempt to study them carefully. After all, even one of the "P's" of the retailing mix is strongly associated with attitudes. If the retailer can project the proper image or personality of the store, success will be enhanced. To determine what the personality of the store is in the eyes of the customer requires attitude research.

Inquiry Techniques

Did the customer respond to the stimulus? The retailer runs an ad on the radio that directs the customer to call now and ask for Mr. Davis. The newspaper ad that is placed in the current paper also directs the customer to call now. The only difference is that the customer is directed to call and ask for Ms. Jenkins. The store has no employee by either name. Whoever answers the phone states that that "person" is not in and handles the call. As each call is received, a record is kept as to who was asked for. The end result may be that the $200 newspaper ad generated 14 calls while the $125 radio buy produced 37 calls. The result of the inquiry test is that, for that particular retailer at that particular time, radio is the more effective media to use for direct-response sales.

Inquiry techniques can be used for all types of advertising, especially direct mail. The advantage of this research procedure is that it measures customer reaction in the marketplace. No artificial stimulus is given. Inquiry measurements can be phone calls, walk-in traffic, and customer questions, just to name three possibilities. One other form of inquiry is sales. If the customer buys, it is obviously a positive inquiry. Of course, all inquiries do not result in sales. When they do not, the problem for the retailer is to determine why, since the reason for purchase may have little or nothing to do with the ad, product, sales aid, or whatever is the subject of the inquiry test currently being used by the retailer.

Other Applications

Specific research applications that were not addressed in this chapter because they are examined elsewhere in the book include store location, merchandise source selection, target market choice, and evaluation of customer service. In addition, research applications may also be informal in nature. A retailer can learn much by going on the sales floor and selling. Or by stopping a customer and asking that person what he or she thinks about a particular merchandise line. Or by inviting several customers to lunch where they will be asked about the assortment, advertising, and so on or about the store in general. Not only will such informal techniques build goodwill, but they can also be helpful if the retailer listens. Both formal and informal research are tools that can help the retailer to listen and learn.

SUMMARY

Retailing research is defined as the systematic gathering, recording, and analyzing of data pertaining to the retailer's target market and/or retailing mix (product, place, price, promotion, and personality). When deciding on whether to use research, the retailer must weigh the advantages against the disadvantages. Cost and time are two drawbacks; the assistance that it provides in planning is one of the pluses. Of course, to conduct research, the retailer should understand research procedures (problem definition; secondary data collection—internal, government, trade, academic, commercial; primary data collection—observation, survey, experimentation; data analysis; and data presentation and follow-up). These procedures may then be applied formally by using projective, ranking, attitude, inquiry, and/or other techniques, or they may be utilized on a more informal basis.

DISCUSSION QUESTIONS

1. To determine if retailers use research, select five retailers in your area and discuss with them the topic of retail research. Ascertain if they use research and, if so, what types.
2. List all the possible areas in retailing that might be aided by research. Be specific.
3. Derek May, owner of Derek's Dungeon, a pinball emporium in Chicago, feels that he needs to know more about his operation but is afraid of retailing research. He states, "I don't know anything about statistics or how to select a sample. With knowledge like that, I better not fool with research." How would you respond to his comment?
4. Explain the five-step research procedure as presented in the text by using a hypothetical research project for a retail store to illustrate each step in the process.
5. Develop an extensive list of secondary data sources for use by a retail store in your town. Classify the sources into the five categories: internal, government, trade, academic, commercial. Upon completion of the assignment, provide the retailer you have chosen with the list.
6. Explain the various techniques that can be used for primary data collection. Which one should the retailer use?
7. Using a sample of ten people, ask them what they think about a particular store in your town. Using another ten-person sample, ask the same question using the cartoon projective technique. Compare the responses you receive and write up an analysis.

8. For a store in your town, determine how people feel about certain aspects of the store. Explain your methodology and write up an analysis.
9. "It is better to ignore retailing research than to deviate from formal research procedures." Comment on this statement.
10. "Research costs too much for the small retailer to use. This is one retailing tool that is limited to Sears, K mart, and the other big operators." Comment on this statement.

NOTES

[1] Ralph S. Alexander and The Committee on Definitions of the American Marketing Association, *Marketing Definitions*, 1963, pp. 16–17. Published by the American Marketing Association.

[2] For additional information on research procedures see George E. Breen, *Do-It-Yourself Marketing Research* (New York: McGraw-Hill Book Company, 1977), and Gilbert A. Churchill, Jr., *Marketing Research: Methodological Foundations*, 2nd ed. (Hinsdale, Ill.: The Dryden Press, 1979). See also Robert Ferber, Paul Sheatsley, Anthony Turner, and Joseph Waksberg, *What Is a Survey?* (Washington, D.C.: American Statistical Association, 1980). Single copies available free from American Statistical Association, 806 Fifteenth Street, NW, Washington, D.C. 20005.

[3] For a discussion of how various stores are using marketing research, see Doreen Mangan, "Marketing Research Gaining as a New Retail Sales Tool," *Stores*, Vol. 61, no. 5 (May 1979), pp. 37–40. Copyright, National Retail Merchants Association, 1979.

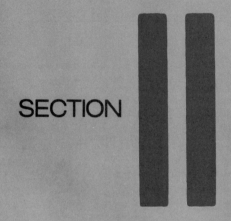

SECTION

Store

Development

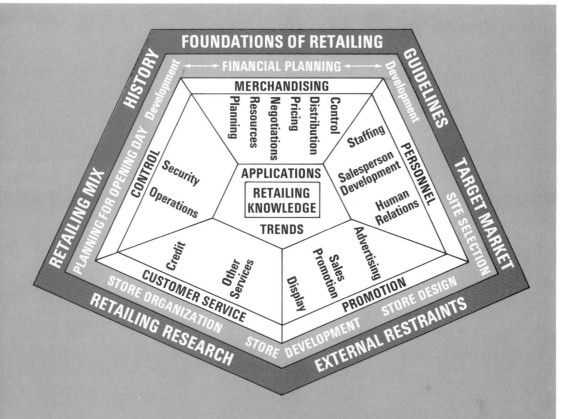

Financial planning, site selection, store design, store organization, and planning for opening day are all key elements in store development.

"Financial Planning" involves a discussion of the financial requirements for a store and, equally important, how to secure the financial resources to meet these requirements.

"Site Selection" examines techniques to determine the proper store location. Methods to aid the retailer in choosing the city, section of city, and actual site are presented.

"Store Design" deals with the development of the exterior and interior of the store. Signing, atmospherics, and layout are among the topics discussed.

"Store Organization" analyzes various management principles, formal organization structures, informal organizations, and objectives, policies, and procedures.

"Planning for Opening Day" develops a plan to ensure a good start for a store. Among the items presented are how to develop a press kit and how to build interest in the new store.

CHAPTER 5

Financial Planning

FRANK AND ERNIE

Reprinted by Permission. © 1977 NEA, Inc.

No matter whether the retail organization consists of numerous stores or just one, financial planning can lay the foundation for future success or future failure. When large store organizations fail, it is often said that the chain expanded faster than did its financial resources. Likewise, the lack of financial planning is the obvious cause for the failure of many small stores. The retailer, no matter what size, should never forget that financial planning is crucial to successful store development. This financial planning must also be done in conjunction with other planning (location, store design, managerial organization, and the opening itself) to ensure the most efficient utilization of resources and a sound foundation for the continuing operation of the business. The retailer must determine his or her financial requirements and, equally important, secure the financial resources to meet these needs. Planning involves examining the

1. Cost of new versus existing store
2. Cost of renting versus buying a building
3. Cost of fixtures
4. Cost of inventory
5. Cost of preopening expenses
6. Cost of operation
7. Opportunity cost

After these and other costs that might be pertinent to a given situation are determined, the retailer must next plan for the acquisition of funds by various means. Possible sources include equity, business loans, trade credit, government agencies, and leasing arrangements. As planning is undertaken, a particular mix of financial resources should be determined that will assure the optimum mix of available funds. Another question entering into the consideration of financing is the cost versus benefit of a franchise. The franchise organization may provide know-how plus all the necessary funds for financing the total operation. The retailer should be able to answer in a positive way all questions raised by a franchise agreement before this type of agreement is considered. Regardless of the arrangement, however, the need for funds should never exceed what the sources are capable of providing (Figure 5–1). When it does, the retail store is in trouble.

DETERMINATION OF FINANCIAL NEEDS[1]

Before undertaking a retail venture, a retailer must make a concerted effort to determine the financial requirements of that particular venture. The question of financial need is essential to every retailer regardless of size. Whether it be Sears, A & P, or Aunt Matilda's Beauty Shop, the retailer must be concerned with financial planning.

Determination of financial need is a complex question. Some of the more common variables that affect the determination of need are presented for analysis.

Cost of New versus Existing Store

What is the cost of an existing store? What is the retailer really buying? Is an ongoing store cheaper than a new store at the same dollar amount? or vice versa? If a store is started from scratch, the retailer does not have to pay for the ill will of customers

Figure 5-1

In terms of financial planning, the need for funds should not exceed the capability of the sources of funds.

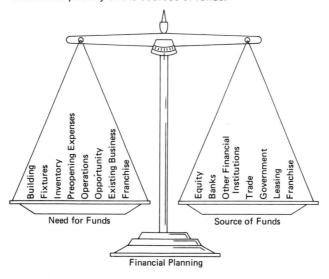

Need for Funds: Building, Fixtures, Inventory, Preopening Expenses, Operations, Opportunity, Existing Business, Franchise

Source of Funds: Equity, Banks, Other Financial Institutions, Trade, Government, Leasing, Franchise

Financial Planning

toward a previous owner. The retailer does not have to buy old merchandise, old fixtures, and old salesclerks who are set in their ways. In other words, the slate is clean. On the other side of the coin, if an ongoing store is purchased, it is very likely that the total store as a package will be cheaper in dollars than if it had to be started from scratch. Another consideration is the established clientele. If a store has an established target market of the type the new retailer will wish to have, such an established market makes the store have great value to the buyer. A word of caution is important at this point. Is the target market loyal to the store or the owner? For example, a major grocery chain in the Northeast purchased a successful bakery located near one of its retail outlets. The seller of the bakery, who had worked in the bakery but did no cooking, moved to Florida. The cook remained on the job. As well as quality can be measured, quality also remained the same. The only obvious changes were a new owner and lower sales volume. As business continued to deteriorate, the grocery chain became concerned and began to study the market. The results of the analysis disclosed that customers had been buying from the previous owner for many years. During this time, the owner had developed a personal relationship with his customers. He knew them by name. He sold to them on credit with no interest charges. He and his staff would work late on a rush order. The grocery chain discovered that customers did not believe that the new owners would provide such services or that they even cooked as well. Customers did not realize that the previous owner had not been involved in cooking. Therefore, it was revealed that the factor that brought business and success to that bakery was the owner. With the owner removed from the business, the firm was a new entity. In this situation, the grocery chain would probably have been just as well off to start a bakery of its own rather than to have bought the one that was for sale.

Another factor to be considered is future plans of the owner. The buyer of a business should stipulate in the contract that the seller will not engage in business in the particular geographic area for a specified number of years. To obtain such a statement in the sales agreement will, many times, involve additional expense to the buyer. In most situations, the additional cost will be justified. As a general rule, the store should not be bought without such a stipulation.

Another important consideration to note at this point is the seller's desire to sell the store. If there are valid reasons for a quick sale, the price agreed upon could be much less than the asking price. The only rule to follow is to never tell the seller what is an acceptable price. The store may be acquired for less.

One final factor in whether to buy an existing store is the value of the accounts receivable and the inventory. Accounts receivable (the amount customers owe the store) if bought with the store should be discounted at least to the level shown in the following schedule:[2]

> *Current accounts are worth 100 cents on the dollar.*
> *Two months past due are worth 90 cents on the dollar.*
> *Six months past due are worth 67 cents on the dollar.*
> *One year past due are worth 45 cents on the dollar.*
> *Two years past due are worth 23 cents on the dollar.*
> *Three years past due are worth 15 cents on the dollar.*
> *Five years past due are worth 1 cent on the dollar.*

As for inventory, it should be valued at cost or market value, whichever is lower. The buyer must remember that what a previous owner paid for something is not as important as what the retailer can sell the item for or what it will cost to replace the item. More than one incident is known where merchandise was valued for sale purposes at original retail (for example, cost plus 40 percent). Unless the replacement value of the inventory has increased at least to that level since the original purchase, such an inventory value should not be used from the buyer's viewpoint. Variables to be discussed also assist in determining whether to start a new store or purchase an existing one.

Cost of Renting versus Buying a Building

Should a retailer buy a building or rent it? Renting a building generally involves a lease agreement of some type. Outright ownership may be an option. If the retailer chooses to locate in a shopping center or other controlled situation, ownership of the building may not be a choice.

What are the "costs" of building ownership? Obviously, the initial outlay for the building is significant. Taxes and insurance as well as upkeep on the structure are factors. For example, how old is the building? If it is 20 years old, it may be time to put a new roof on the structure. Such projected repairs can add greatly to the cost of the building. To examine ownership further, the depreciation of a building site over time can be expensive to the building owner. Of course, appreciation of value over time can also occur to the benefit of the retailer.

Will the building have to be modernized? If it will, then the expense of modernization should be figured in the cost. A factor to consider is that needed modernization will take place. Only through ownership of the building is the retailer assured the right to modernize as he or she wishes.

Given the various considerations for buying a building, why do so many retailers rent their selling space? One major factor is that many do not choose to be in the real estate business. With only a certain amount of resources, they prefer to have more capital to spend on merchandise and operations than to have it tied up in a building. Many large retailers will erect their building on the desired spot, then sell it to an insurance company or other private investor who will, in turn, lease it back to the retailer. In this way, the retail organization gets the store they want on the site they want but with no money tied up in real estate.

The cost of the lease is also a consideration. It is important to note that a lease is a point of negotiation. Generally speaking, the larger the retailer, the better the lease. In a major shopping mall, the main stores (Sears, Penney, Macy's, or a large regional retailer like Belk's) can obtain very favorable terms because these types of stores are required for the ultimate success of the mall or shopping center. The smaller shops, on the other hand, need the mall so they can locate between the big stores. In such situations, for example, the rent may run $750 or more per month for a small 300-square-foot store ($30 per square foot) plus the store must pay a percentage of all sales over $180,000—generally around 5 percent. (This is calculated as follows: 300 square feet x $30 = $9,000 ÷ 12 months = $750 minimum rent per month; $9,000 minimum annual rent ÷ 5% of sales = $180,000.) A store the size of Sears or Penney may pay much less than this $30 per square foot with probably a much smaller percentage on all sales over a given amount. If a retailer has any bargaining strength, one of the best times to use it is when the lease is being negotiated. Financial considerations are not the only terms subject to negotiation. The major stores in a center can influence location of stores, store hours, and even the date of the opening of a retail complex. One factor limiting the power of the major stores in lease negotiations is the Federal Trade Commission. If this commission finds that a store is making demands that will restrain competition—such as by insisting that the developer bar a certain store from the premises—then the FTC will probably issue a complaint against the offending store.

Most lease agreements today include a percentage plus guaranteed minimum monthly rent as noted. Other lease arrangements are the straight percentage and the flat amount of rent. Under the straight percentage of sales, the retailer pays more in good times than bad. With the flat rate, the retailer may face a real problem when sales are low. In comparing the three rental plans, it is easy to see why the percentage with guaranteed minimum rent is the most popular. It gives the landlord an insured income and provides incentive to keep the building up. For the retailer, rent is tied somewhat to prosperity but a smaller percentage of sales is usually taken out if he or she agrees to pay a minimum amount. Figure 5–2 illustrates the various relationships for the three lease plans for a hypothetical situation. The percentage of sales plus guaranteed minimum lease agreement is a compromise. Both the landlord and the retailer have given a little to develop an agreement that is more agreeable to both parties. These rental contracts are usually revised on a yearly basis to better reflect actual sales.

One additional factor in the buying or leasing decision is the landlord. Will the building be kept up? Will the landlord fix the building the way you want it to be done? The retailer must remember that if he or she fixes up someone else's building, even with the permission of the landlord, the improvements become part of the building. There is more than one incident on record where, after the retailer fixed up a building at his own

Figure 5-2

Effect of various rental agreements on monthly rental expense.

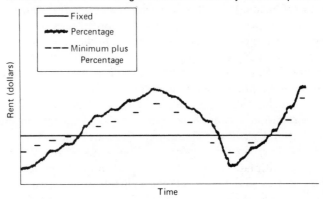

expense, the building owner raised the rent since the building had been improved. When the retailer got upset over the rent increase and decided to move out, he found that he could not tear out various improvements made and take them with him. The improvements were now part of the building. Before signing the lease, the retailer should get all conditions of all parties in writing. From a practical standpoint, it is also easier to get necessary work completed by the building owner before you move in, not afterward.

Cost of Fixtures

Fixtures are the various "furniture" items in a store that are used to make a store out of so many square feet of floor space (Figure 5-3). To determine what type of fixtures are needed, a proposed layout of the store will need to be developed as discussed in Chapter 7. Once the plan of the store is presented, the retailer should determine the cost of buying new fixtures to put in the store. The figure derived becomes the maximum value for determining cost of fixtures for the store.

To determine the cost of new fixtures is a very simple task. All the retailer need do is to contact various fixture manufacturers and request catalogs and price lists. Some of the leading manufacturers of store fixtures for general use are

Armstrong Store Fixture Corporation, Pittsburgh, Pennsylvania
Hussmann Store Equipment, Bridgeton, Missouri
Levin Fixture Corporation, Flushing, New York
Reflector Hardware Corporation, Melrose Park, Illinois
Self Serv Fixture Company, Dallas, Texas

These five companies do not make up the entire industry. Many companies specialize in fixtures for a particular type of store. A quick check of appropriate trade magazines in a subject area will usually show advertisements by these fixture suppliers.

Figure 5-3

Proper fixtures allow a retailer to display merchandise in an organized manner. Note the various types of fixtures that are being used in this store.

(Courtesy of K mart Corporation.)

With the availability and the cost of new fixtures known to the retailer, the owner can now shop for used store fixtures in an intelligent manner if he or she wishes to do so. On more than one occasion, a small retailer has paid more for used fixtures than he or she would have had to pay for new ones. The cause for such mistakes is ignorance. Shopping for used fixtures is like shopping for a used car. Most anything is available if the price is right. If the retailer does not need the fixtures immediately, a careful check of legitimate "going-out-of-business" sales may yield fixtures at a reasonable price. In major retail centers, firms specialize in used store fixtures. Stores that are changing their interiors may decide to buy new fixtures. The "old" fixtures in such stores are many times in excellent condition.

A third alternative is for the retailer to make his or her own fixtures. Many a shelf has been made of boards placed between concrete blocks or placed on a metal pipe frame. In this situation the cost of fixtures is held to a minimum, assuming that there is no charge for labor. The area of store fixtures is one place in which financial requirements can vary considerably based on what the retailer plans to do and where financial requirements can usually be cut to come nearer meeting available resources.

Cost of Inventory

How much inventory will the store require? What is the sales forecast for the store? The retailer who can determine what sales will be will generally have an accurate determination of inventory requirements. Knowledge of potential sales can be derived by observing retail activity in the area, by talking to other retailers, and by making use of available data on the area from governmental and other sources as discussed in Chapter 4.

Based on the sales forecast, the initial inventory of the store is determined and a value placed on the goods. By working with information provided by suppliers and product line representatives as well as personal knowledge and expertise, the retailer can derive the initial investment required for inventory purposes.

By having an estimate of sales and initial inventory requirements, the retailer is ready to determine the financial needs in terms of inventory:

Estimate annual sales to be $100,000
Estimate initial inventory at cost to be $20,000
Average planned gross margin = 40% (sales minus cost of goods sold) or
   (price of item minus cost of item)

Calculation of inventory requirements in dollars
Annual sales in dollars	$100,000
Gross margin in dollars	
($100,000 x 40%)	$ 40,000
Total inventory investment for year	$60,000
Initial inventory investment	$20,000
Inventory turnover for year	
($60,000 ÷ $20,000)	3

If the store is going to sell on credit, money to reinvest in inventory will be slow in reaching the store. Because a customer who buys in the first month of store operations may get the bill in the second month, and may wait 60 days to pay it, four months could easily lapse before payment is received. In the meantime, inventory is being depleted. As a result, at least six months of inventory should be provided for in the initial planning or $30,000 for inventory in the example given. An even higher amount should be considered if greater than normal bad-debt losses or other considerations are expected.

Cost of Preopening Expenses

The retailer has many expenses that are expended before the doors of the store are ever opened. Of particular importance to the small store owner is that most of these expenses are cash outlays rather than credit. In more than one situation, preopening expenses have led to retail failure because they were such a drain on the financial resources of a small business. The retailer had failed to realize the magnitude of such expenses. Some of the more common expenses are the following:

Business License.   A business license is required in most towns of any size. Depending on the type of business, cost may range from $5.00 to thousands of dollars.

In many small towns, the retailer may be able to get the license more cheaply by having a talk with the mayor or town or city clerk.

Utility Deposits.   A retail store generally needs a phone, electricity and water, and perhaps gas for heating purposes. Because the failure rate for retailers is so great during the first year or two of operation, most utilities require a deposit in an amount equaling at least two months' usage based on their estimates, not the retailer's. Even for a small store this could easily mean an electricity deposit of $500 before the electricity will be turned on. A $200 phone deposit would not be unusual in some areas. Similar amounts for water, gas, and other essential services can take much needed capital away. Of course, these fees are deposits that will generally be returned after the firm is established. Such knowledge does not, however, help the new retailer who is pressed for funds.

Incorporation.   Although all major chains are incorporated, not all retailers have a corporate form of organization (Figure 5-4). Because incorporation limits the liability of the individual retail owner, most retailers should look into the possibility of incorporating. To incorporate, however, costs money. Incorporation can easily cost $500 for a small store—a large sum for a financially tight firm.

Preopening Promotions.   As the date of the store opening nears, the retailer will usually want to saturate the market with various advertisements in the media. Once again, most media will require cash in advance from the new retailer. The media have written off as bad debts too many ads for a retailer who did not succeed.

Store Preparation Expense.   Someone must stock the shelves in the store with merchandise. Someone must even put the shelves in the store. Some painting may

Figure 5-4

Distribution of retail establishments and sales by legal form of organization, 1977.

Source: *1977 Census of Retail Trade* (Washington, D.C.: U.S. Department of Commerce, Bureau of the Census, 1977) p. 1-7

need to be done. The carpet may need to be cleaned after the store is completed. The sign in front of the store must be paid for before it is constructed. In terms of store preparation expense, each situation may involve different items on a never-ending list. Some areas can be reduced if time is not important. On the other hand, if the retailer is paying rent on a building, the store should be as productive as possible as quickly as possible. In this situation, 15 people may be hired with overtime no factor to get the store stocked without delay so it can open for business. A large store preparation expense would, in this case, be a sound investment.

Grand Opening Expense. The cost of the grand opening should be calculated to ensure that sufficient money will be available for the event. If a breakfast for dignitaries and the news media is held prior to the opening, the event will have to be budgeted. A cocktail party the night before the opening may also be held for VIPs. Off-duty police officers for crowd control, remote broadcast by a local radio station from the site, and even a small remembrance for the mayor who cut the ribbon are all expenses that, when added up, can result in a rather substantial cash outlay.

Cost of Operation

As noted in the discussion on inventory, actual dollars received from sales may be four to six months behind the actual sales transactions. It also takes time for the store to establish a clientele. For these and many other reasons, a store will not usually generate many cash dollars in the beginning. The retailer must realize this fact and plan for it in the initial financial plan. Each situation is, of course, different, but a general rule to follow is for the initial financial plan to cover the first six months of operation. The theory behind this rule is that, if the store has shown no financial promise after six months, serious decisions will have to be made concerning the future of the store. This would be particularly true for a clothing store or other types of establishments selling seasonal merchandise. In this case, the six months would represent one complete selling season.

In determining operating costs, the retailer should estimate on a monthly basis the various expenses that will be incurred, including rent, advertising, supplies, and salaries and wages. Utilities, insurance, taxes, interest, maintenance, and a miscellaneous or contingency amount must also be figured. The amount of contingency depends greatly on how well the other figures have been calculated. Even with careful calculations, the unexpected can happen. A contingency of 10 percent of the proposed budget would not be unreasonable for the average retailer. Once the retailer has determined the various out-of-pocket costs, the list of items should be added up to determine the amount of financing to be required for the period in question.

Opportunity Cost

One additional consideration for determining financial requirements is opportunity cost. This means how much money could the retailer make if he or she were doing something else besides operating this retail store. If a person resigned a $20,000-a-year position to go into retailing, the decision involves a $20,000 expenditure that must be, or should be, figured as a cost of doing business. The problems with opportunity costs are the intangible benefits of store ownership and being an independent business-person. How can a value be placed on these items to counter the $20,000 loss in so-called guaranteed income?

Opportunity cost can also be a factor for a major chain. For example, if the new store is going to cost the chain $250,000 in start-up expenses, could the chain take that money and obtain a greater return by remodeling existing units? Opportunity is a sub-jective matter, to be sure, but one that must be considered if the true cost of opening a business is to be determined.

SOURCES OF FUNDS

If a retailer has determined that $25,000 or $250,000 or any given amount is needed for initial operations, he or she has done more planning than many people who start a retail business. The fact that such planning has taken place will simplify the job of securing funds for the prospective business. Most lenders ask to see such plans when discussing a loan; thus, a well-thought-out plan of financial need can be a real plus in the retailer's favor. Big firms use such a plan; small firms should.

Possible sources of funds are almost unlimited for a given situation. Common sources are equity, banks, trade credit, governmental agencies, and leasing com-panies.

Equity

Almost all other sources of financing will require some equity financing on the part of the retailer. The reason for this is that, if a person believes enough in an idea to put his or her life savings into it or to borrow money for the business using his or her own house and other personal possessions as collateral, or if a chain will finance part of the undertaking itself, then chances of retail success will increase. Such a person or firm will or should have a higher degree of motivation than will a person or firm who has made no commitment to the business.

Many small retailers come up with equity by borrowing from friends and relatives on the side and then presenting these funds to other lenders as their equity. Such a source of funds may result in the highest possible "cost" for the retailer. The friend or relative who lent the money may have a friend who needs a job or, in some cases, the lender wants a job himself or herself, which could be even worse. "Friendly" lenders may attempt to influence the business in other ways. Since human nature is the way it is, the best policy for most retailers is to stay away from friends and relatives when in search of financial resources. If this is not possible, the retailer should be sure to put all friendly lending agreements in writing. It can help to reduce problems in the future.

Banks and Other Financial Institutions

One obvious source of funds is a bank, insurance company, or finance company. The retailer will face one of his or her first selling situations as the store is "sold" to the lending officer. With a sound store proposal, the retailer can shop around at the various financial institutions to see what lenders will provide. It may be that one lender will require 25 percent equity financing, whereas another will finance all but 15 percent of the need. It may be that one bank will lend the money just for 90 days, whereas another will require no payments on the loan for six months. One lender may also be willing to provide seasonal loans or may give a "line of credit" of substantial size to aid the retailer. A line of credit is a predetermined amount of money that a business firm can borrow from a lending institution without seeking additional approval from the lender. One other very important consideration is the interest rate. All interest rates are not the same. When seeking a $50,000 or $100,000 loan or even a $5 million loan, a fraction of a percentage difference on interest can be quite significant. The wise retailer will shop around for the best possible loan arrangement. Making the right decision here is literally like money in the bank.

Trade Credit

How much inventory will suppliers provide the retailer on credit? Can the store fixtures be bought now but paid for at a later time? Trade credit, if available, is definitely a source of funds. The lack of trade credit, in turn, is a financial hardship. For example, a small college bookstore found that it had to send a check to a book publisher before an order would be filled, thereby paying for merchandise before it was even received. Merchandise shipments were delayed because the checks had to clear before shipment. The result was that books were received by this store after the semester had started and the customers (students) had already secured books elsewhere. The delay resulted in lost sales, money tied up in inventory with no market, and a very difficult return situation as the merchandise had already been paid for. In most cases where return of merchandise was permitted, only credit was given against future purchases. Under this situation, unnecessary funds were tied up in inventory. Why? The store had no trade credit. With trade credit, the orders would have been processed quickly. Without credit, delays can be very costly.

The retailer who has no established trade credit should apply for this credit well in advance of the actual need. The problem is that most suppliers will want to know with whom the store already does business. If the retailer is new, naturally the store has done business with no one. In that case, the store will have to sell itself to suppliers and others in a position to provide such credit.

Even if a retailer has received many unsolicited catalogs of merchandise that imply that all that needs to be done is to complete the order blanks and return them, such is generally not the case. After an order is received, the time-consuming credit check will begin. For the retailer who needs merchandise, a credit check can be expensive and disheartening. The retailer should not be misled by such material sent out by various suppliers.

Equally as important as making sure that trade credit is established is making sure that those suppliers who do provide such credit are paid on time or even earlier. A positive track record will make more credit available to the firm. On the other hand, delays in payment of supplier accounts in the early days of a retail operation can mean almost certain financial disaster for the store.

Governmental Agencies

Many retailers can qualify for government-supported loans through the Small Business Administration (SBA) and other assistance programs. These programs generally require that a business must first apply to regular financial institutions before seeking governmental assistance. By law, for example, the SBA may not make a loan if a business can obtain a loan from some commercial or private source. In fact, in cities of over 200,000 population, a person must be turned down by two banks before applying for a SBA loan. The SBA can guarantee up to $500,000 or 90 percent, whichever is less, of a bank loan to a firm. When a bank is not willing to participate in that situation, the SBA may lend up to $150,000 on a direct basis, assuming that funds within the SBA are available. Such loans may be for up to 10 years. Exceptions include new construction, which may be financed for 20 years, and working capital loans (cash money to pay immediate expenses), which are usually limited to 6 years.

To secure a loan, the retailer must present to a lending institution his or her initial plans, as outlined earlier in the chapter, along with personal financial and background data on all the parties involved. If a direct loan is not possible, the retailer should ask the bank to make the loan under the SBA's Loan Guaranty Plan or to participate with the SBA in the loan. If the bank is interested in such an arrangement, it will contact the SBA and work out the details. If the bank is not interested and other financial institutions have similar reactions to the loan application, the retailer may then contact the SBA directly concerning a direct loan from that agency.

Leasing Companies

Leasing arrangements for various items in the store may be possible that will free money for other purposes as well as offer certain tax advantages to the retailer. Instead of buying cash registers at $500 or $5,000 apiece, why not lease them? Instead of being concerned about trade credit for buying fixtures, why not lease them? Instead of paying $100 now for a small display case, the cost may be just $20 for the first year. The retailer has gained $80 in current dollars for other purposes.

Various leasing arrangements are available. One possibility may include in the lease an option to buy. Another option may be to upgrade equipment over time at predetermined cost levels. The result is a store that remains modern and up-to-date in appearance.

There are, of course, two sides to the leasing question. If an item is purchased it belongs to the store for the next 20 years if the retailer wishes to use it that long. Under many basic leasing agreements, no equity or ownership on the part of the retailer ever occurs. Whether to lease or buy is an individual decision. The only certainty about leasing is that it provides more for the dollar in the short run than does any other form of financing. For many retailers, this fact alone makes leasing a very attractive alternative to other sources of funds.

Franchising is presented as a separate section because most franchises are unique from other forms of business in that much of the initial planning will generally be done by the franchising company for the retailer, not to mention the actual financing of the undertaking.[4]

Franchising as it is generally known today is a form of marketing or distribution in which a parent company customarily grants an individual or a relatively small company the right, or privilege, to do business in a prescribed manner over a certain period of time in a specified place. In 1979 there were 492,379 franchise establishments in operation in the United States, with approximately 82 percent of these being franchisee-owned (see Table 5-1). In terms of sales, all units collected $298,591 million, of which 85 percent came from franchisee-owned operations. As noted in the Table, the fastest-growing franchise area is real estate. This business group experienced a growth in sales of 65.5 percent and a 92.5 percent increase in number of establishments over the two-year period 1977-1979.[5]

To aid the reader in understanding the various kinds of franchise arrangements, the four main types of franchise systems are examined:

Type I: Manufacturer–retailer system. Type I franchise systems have long dominated the franchise field. Over half of all dollar sales in franchise units flow through manufacturer–retailer operations. Examples of this type of franchise are automobile makers and their dealers and oil companies and their retail outlets. Chevrolet, Ford, Texaco, Shell, Exxon, and International Harvester are all in this category.

Type II: Manufacturer–wholesaler system. A Type II franchise involves a form of organization that dates back to the 1800s. When Coca-Cola began operation in Atlanta, Georgia, it began to franchise its syrup to other individuals to bottle in their areas. Such a franchise requires the wholesaler to perform the distribution function for the manufacturer and to perhaps complete the transformation of the item into a consumer product. Examples of this franchise type besides Coca-Cola include Pepsi Cola, Seven-Up, Pabst Blue Ribbon, and various brands of tobacco products.

Type III: Wholesaler–retailer system. The common wholesaler–retailer franchise involves several areas of retailing such as hardware, drug, paint, furniture, and auto parts. Such a franchise allows the retailer to become part of a chain that enables the store to have identity on a broader scale than just that one store. Examples are Goodyear, Firestone, Western Auto, Rexall, Munford, Sherwin-Williams, Drexel, and American Parts. In many cases the customer may not know if he or she is dealing with a company store or a franchise. A company-owned Goodyear store and a franchise unit may be identical in appearance and operation. To many franchises this is a real advantage of the system. To others, it is felt to be a disadvantage since the retailer has no in-

Table 5-1

Franchising in the Economy, 1979[1]

Kinds of Franchised Business	Establishments (number)			Sales (thousands)			Percentage changes			
							1978–1979		1977–1979	
	Total	Company Owned	Franchisee Owned	Total	Company Owned	Franchisee Owned	Estab.	Sales	Estab.	Sales
Total, all franchising	492,379	89,367	403,012	$298,591,054	$44,492,347	$254,098,707	5.4%	8.8%	9.2%	17.8%
Automobile and truck dealers[2]	31,510	300	31,210	154,554,000	8,913,000	145,641,000	-0.3	8.2	-0.5	17.1
Automotive products and services[3]	53,367	4,895	48,472	7,953,914	2,550,479	5,403,435	5.2	14.1	9.5	22.1
Business aids and services	46,622	5,860	40,762	5,178,370	759,345	4,419,025	20.0	24.1	44.7	52.8
Accounting, credit, collection agencies, and general business systems	4,638	66	4,572	185,305	10,990	174,315	11.4	18.5	23.7	32.2
Employment services	4,400	1,063	3,337	1,311,422	489,671	821,751	15.5	22.4	29.0	46.4
Printing and copying services	2,687	166	2,521	253,289	16,104	237,185	18.2	20.4	39.4	39.5
Tax preparation services	8,793	4,271	4,522	270,661	145,760	124,901	1.8	12.6	4.2	27.7
Real estate[4]	22,045	154	21,891	2,860,644	44,990	2,815,654	33.8	27.3	92.5	65.5
Miscellaneous business services	4,059	140	3,919	297,049	51,830	245,219	16.3	20.0	24.7	29.0
Construction, home improvements, maintenance, and cleaning services	15,431	447	14,984	1,403,604	103,832	1,299,772	9.7	14.2	17.9	28.7
Convenience stores	16,268	10,553	5,715	5,229,444	2,945,785	2,283,659	7.0	10.7	15.0	21.1
Educational products and services	2,632	412	2,220	314,913	57,954	256,959	18.0	15.8	40.1	34.9
Fast-food restaurants (all types)	65,631	17,141	48,490	25,439,602	7,559,447	17,880,155	13.4	19.7	26.3	39.9
Gasoline service stations[2]	171,000	32,490	138,510	62,869,000	12,574,000	50,295,000	-0.8	5.5	-3.1	11.2
Hotels and motels	5,833	979	4,854	6,137,868	1,728,783	4,409,085	7.2	11.7	12.5	19.2
Campgrounds	1,085	22	1,063	117,147	6,707	110,440	2.1	4.9	2.6	7.6
Laundry and dry-cleaning services	3,059	72	2,987	298,485	14,645	283,840	5.3	16.7	10.5	30.2
Recreation, entertainment, and travel	5,082	86	4,996	334,544	33,802	300,742	10.3	17.8	19.0	39.6
Rental services (auto and truck)	7,574	1,918	5,656	2,530,678	1,478,310	1,052,368	5.3	10.3	10.0	20.2
Rental services (equipment)	1,611	155	1,456	235,081	78,986	156,095	8.3	10.6	13.4	22.3
Retailing (nonfood)	46,260	12,620	33,640	10,374,613	3,527,920	6,846,693	5.8	-3.5	10.8	0.4
Retailing (food other than convenience stores)	15,339	1,011	14,328	4,022,614	1,679,286	2,343,328	8.5	12.1	15.3	24.5
Soft drink bottlers[2,5]	2,025	70	1,955	11,270,000	383,000	10,887,000	-3.4	11.8	-5.6	24.6
Miscellaneous	2,050	336	1,714	327,177	97,066	230,111	16.3	19.2	9.6	-24.8

[1]1979 data estimated by respondents.
[2]Estimated by BDC based on Bureau of the Census and trade association data.
[3]Includes some establishments with significant sales of nonautomotive products such as household appliances, garden supplies, etc.
[4]Gross commissions.
[5]Includes soft drinks, fruit drinks, and ades; syrups, flavoring agents, and bases. Data do not include figures for independent private-label and contract-filler bottling companies that accounted for 24 percent in 1977, 23 percent in 1978, and 22 percent in 1979 of the value of shipments of the total industry.

Source: *Franchising in the Economy, 1977–1979* (Washington, D.C.: U.S. Department of Commerce, 1979), p. 34.

dependent identity. For example, if the customer becomes angry with Goodyear because he or she does not like the firm's blimp, that customer is also angry with the local Goodyear store, which may in reality be an independent operation.

Type IV: Trademark/trade name licensor–retailer system. The Type IV franchise system is what many people think of when they talk of franchises, Figure 5-5. Holiday Inn, Howard Johnson's, McDonald's, Kentucky Fried Chicken, Dunkin' Donuts, Burger King, Baskin-Robbins, Dairy Queen, Hertz, and H & R Block are all examples of the licensor franchise. Under this plan, the franchisor will offer a common trade name and standardized methods for successful operation of retail units.

In deciding whether to franchise or not, the retailer must assume a position that examines a franchise from a cost versus benefit standpoint. What will the retailer receive for the cash outlay and the reduction of independence that the typical franchise entails? Will managerial know-how be provided? An equally important concern stems from the question of whether managerial know-how from an outside source is needed for success. If it is not, why pay for it?

Another consideration is the relative importance to the market of transient customers. If the fried chicken restaurant is located on a major north–south highway, the traveler will stop if it looks familiar and they have heard of it. Put yourself in that

Figure 5-5

Franchises even sell products that interest the very young customer.

(Courtesy of Baskin-Robbins Ice Cream.)

hungry position. Kentucky Fried Chicken is on one corner and Aunt Jane's Chicken is on another. At which would you stop for dinner? What about the local folks?

A significant question is how much royalty do the franchisors take from the business? Dunkin' Donuts has a royalty fee of 4.9 percent of sales plus an advertising fee of 4 percent, whereas Insty-Prints collects 3 percent of gross sales and an additional 2 percent of sales for advertising purposes.[6] In addition to these typical royalty and advertising fees, most franchises also require a significant initial, usually nonrefundable, franchise fee. The cash outlay for the franchise is determined somewhat by whether or not the land and building are provided by the retailer or the franchisor. Many franchises require cash outlays in excess of $100,000, whereas others can be obtained for $15,000 or less.[7] Even with the franchisor financing the store to make it easier on the retailer, cost versus benefit should never be forgotten. Be sure that the target market will see benefits in the franchise. Be sure that the store could not function just as well as an independent store. While you may be inspired by the enthusiasm of the promotional brochures about the franchise, you should be sure that the data are correct—not hypothetical. Ask to visit that unit. Compare the printed facts with personal observation.

Also, remember that most franchise agreements are written in favor of the franchisor. Most agreements permit the franchisor to set up its own stores in the franchise holder's territory if it so desires. In addition, most agreements are for a limited time, so that the franchisor can simply take over a store at the end of, for example, the ten-year franchise period. In fact, the franchisee cannot even sell, in most cases, unless the sale is approved by the franchisor. The smart person will study the franchise agreement carefully as well as the franchise disclosure statements as required by the Federal Trade Commission. Only after considering *all* the facts should a retailer enter into a franchise agreement. Careful effort now can make tomorrow more enjoyable for the franchisee.

SHOULD I OPEN A STORE?

In answering this question, the individual should realistically balance financial need and financial capacity. In terms of the large chain, the question is not "should I go into business" but "should I expand the business by adding another unit?" In either case, inadequate financial capacity to get the new store started and underway can cause great hardship.

It is usually easier to obtain more funds in the beginning to start a business than it is to get a small amount and have to go back to the lender with hat in hand asking for more. In such a situation, the psychological attitude of the lender is generally not in the retailer's favor. The more successful retailer who has done his or her homework as shown by an accurate financial plan will obtain sufficient funds to begin with and not have to ask for more.

After all the planning is complete and financial capacity has been determined, the decision must be made to either proceed with the store or to put the plan on the shelf for consideration at some future time. If the decision is to not open the store, the remainder of this book becomes an academic exercise for that particular individual. On the other hand, if the answer is to proceed, then trade area, layout, merchandising, customer service, retail accounting, and all the other topics related to retailing take on added significance. Obviously, the remainder of this book assumes a "go" decision on the part of the retailer. Without these positive decisions there would be no such thing as retailing as we know it today.

SUMMARY

To begin a new retail venture successfully, care must be taken to determine the initial financial requirements for the store. Cost considerations involving fixtures, inventory, and operations as well as cost comparisons for a new versus an existing store or for buying versus renting a building should all be analyzed and dollar amounts determined. After financial need is determined, financial capacity is the next step. How much money can be raised through the use of equity, loans from financial and governmental agencies, trade credit, and leasing arrangements. An alternative to much of this planning may be a franchise in which much of the planning and financing will already be worked out by the franchisor. The retailer must be careful to weigh the cost of the franchise against the benefits that may be offered. After all plans are developed and all alternatives have been studied, the decision to go or not go into the new retail venture must be made. By careful planning such a decision will prove to be correctly determined.

DISCUSSION QUESTIONS

1. Why is financial planning important to a retailer?
2. The Mary Jane's clothing store is for sale. What factors concerning the store should a prospective buyer consider?
3. A building can be bought outright or leased by the retailer for one year with an option to renew for another year. What factors should be considered in making a decision in this situation.
4. In determining the cost of inventory in terms of financial need, John took the cost of inventory and added a 50 percent margin to each item. Comment on his approach to the problem.
5. Preopening expenses are important for a small store but are of no significance for a retailer like K mart or Woolworth's. Comment on this statement.
6. Discuss various methods of obtaining funds for a business.
7. Trade credit versus leasing, which is better?
8. "To franchise or not to franchise—that is the question." Comment on this statement.
9. Discuss franchising with a franchiseholder in your area. Ascertain how the franchise is set up. Is the franchiseholder satisfied with the arrangement? Why?
10. Select a retailer in the area and interview this person concerning going into business. Ask this person how he or she answered the question, "Should I open a store?"

[1] For further assistance in starting a business, see *Checklist for Going into Business*, Small Marketers Aid, No. 71 (Washington, D.C.: Small Business Administration, 1973); *Business Plan for Retailers*, Small Marketers Aid, No. 150 (Washington, D.C.: Small Business Administration, 1973); and *Thinking about Going into Business*, Small Marketers Aid, No. 170 (Washington, D.C.: Small Business Administration, 1979).

[2] Robert H. Cole, *Consumer and Commercial Credit Management* (Homewood, Ill.: Richard D. Irwin, Inc., 1972), p. 342.

[3] For further information, see *Business Loans from the SBA* (Washington, D.C.: Small Business Administration, 1980).

[4] The discussion in this section is taken in part from Charles L. Vaughn, *Franchising*, 2nd ed. (Lexington, Mass.: Lexington Books, D. C. Heath and Company, 1979), pp. 1–9.

[5] *Franchising in the Economy, 1977–1979* (Washington, D.C.: U.S. Department of Commerce, 1979), p. 34.

[6] Reprinted by permission of *The Wall Street Journal*, © Dow Jones & Company, Inc., 1980. All Rights Reserved.

[7] For information on many types of franchises, see Peter G. Norback and Craig T. Norback, *The Dow Jones–Irwin Guide to Franchises* (Homewood, Ill.: Dow Jones–Irwin, 1978).

CHAPTER 6

Site Selection

HEATHCLIFF

"THEY'VE OPENED A MALL!"

Reprinted by permission of McNaught Syndicate, Inc.

If Bill's Discount Store had the best prices within 500 miles for good-quality merchandise very much in demand, would Bill's be successful in attracting customers to the store? The answer to this question depends on the location of the store. If it is located on a small, sparsely inhabited island in the middle of the Pacific, lots of luck to Bill. If, on the other hand, it is located in a large shopping mall that attracts the kind of customer who normally shops at stores like Bill's, then his discount store is probably in very good shape. The example, although obviously exaggerated, points out a very important concept to the retail operator. The location of the store can be a critical factor in the success or failure of the retail operation.

Retail location, as a part of the retailing mix, should be dependent on the target market. Where are these target market customers and where do they wish to shop? In which town or city will they shop in sufficient numbers to merit placing a store in the area? In what part or section of the particular city or town will they be willing to shop to support a given store? At what particular site will they prefer the store to locate for maximum accessibility?

The questions of city, section of city, and actual site are interrelated (Figure 6-1). Answers to certain questions are dependent on other factors. For example, the choice of a certain part of town may depend on what particular sites are available. A particular site may be excellent from a physical standpoint but be located in an undesirable city. Although interrelated, the various considerations will be presented separately for discussion purposes. To make the final selection, however, the retail operator should make the choice in light of all the variables.[1]

Figure 6-1

The store location decision is multidimensional in scope.

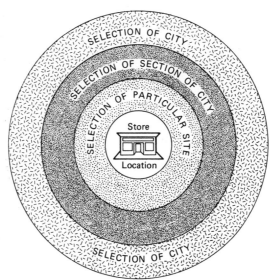

In determining the location of a store, the selection of the city is important enough to be analyzed even if the prospective retail owner already lives in a city or town and wants to place the store in that location. Such an analysis of the city may serve to reinforce the person's determination to open the store or present data that would indicate that the proposed city would not be desirable for such a store.

Possible considerations for analyzing a city are infinite. Variables that should be included on such a list are the following:

Trade-area analysis
Population size, characteristics, and trends
Retail trade potential
Stability and outlook for the community
Available services in the area
Legal restrictions
Labor market conditions
Unique factors in a particular community

An individual working with this list should guard against the idea that the list is all in-clusive or that trade-area analysis is most important since it is shown first on the list. The study of various cities for possible selection should be conducted in a manner that will obtain as much information as possible to help the retailer. Since the items given would be excellent sources of information, they are now presented in detail.

Trade-Area Analysis

A trade area can be defined as a geographically delineated region containing potential customers for whom there exists a probability greater than zero of their purchasing a given class of products and/or services offered for sale by a particular firm or by a par-ticular agglomeration of firms.[2] If the retailer knows what this trade area is for a retail store, he or she will have some idea as to the size of the market. Therefore, the purpose of trade-area analysis is to determine from what distance a town or city will attract customers. The city or town in which the store is located may have a census population of 20,000 yet have a drawing power of 120,000 people from a retailing viewpoint. It is this figure of 120,000 that is of interest to the retailer. The type of store is a considera-tion in determining if the 120,000 people should be included in the trade area for the store in question. For furniture stores or department stores that deal in shopping goods (items that consumers search out and compare), the large trade area will be realistic. A store selling milk or bread (convenience items) or a neighborhood drugstore will generally not be concerned with such large areas. In view of these considerations, the type of trade-area analysis is determined somewhat by the type of retail store under study.

For the shopping-goods store that expects to draw from outlying areas, a good starting point for determining trade area is Reilly's Law of Retail Gravitation.[3] The original law stated that two cities attract from an intermediate town in the vicinity of the breaking point approximately in direct proportion to the population of the two cities and in inverse proportion to the squares of the distances from these two cities to the intermediate town.

Reilly's original formula was

$$\frac{B_a}{B_b} = \left(\frac{P_a}{P_b}\right)\left(\frac{D_b}{D_a}\right)^2$$

Where B_a = Proportion of trade attracted by city A
B_b = Proportion of trade attracted by city B
P_a = Population of city A
P_b = Population of city B
D_a = Distance from intermediate town to city A
D_b = Distance from intermediate town to city B

To illustrate, Terrieville (1980 census of 12,316) is 40 miles from Decatur (1980 census of 38,743) and 25 miles from Jackson (1980 census of 29,014):

$$\frac{B_a}{B_b} = \left(\frac{38,743}{29,014}\right)\left(\frac{25}{40}\right)^2 = .52 \qquad \begin{array}{l} .52 \div 1.52 = 34\% \\ 1.00 \div 1.52 = 66\% \end{array}$$

Using the formula, the result is that Decatur attracts .52 times as much trade as Jackson or that Decatur receives 34 percent of the business leaving Terrieville whereas Jackson gets the remaining 66 percent leaving the area.

To go an additional step, it is possible to calculate the break-even point in miles between two towns. At what distance from a town are the customers likely to shop locally or go to another town? For this purpose, a second formula can be used with A being the larger town and B being the smaller town, such as Terrieville.

$$\frac{\text{Miles between A and B}}{1 + \sqrt{\dfrac{\text{Population of A}}{\text{Population of B}}}}$$

With this formula, the boundaries of the trade area can be determined.

Using the same example as before, the break-even point or trade-area boundary for Terrieville as compared with Decatur and Jackson would be as follows:

$$\frac{40}{1 + \sqrt{\dfrac{38,743}{12,316}}} = \begin{array}{c} \text{14 miles from} \\ \text{Terrieville} \\ \text{toward Decatur} \end{array}$$

$$\frac{25}{1 + \sqrt{\dfrac{29,014}{12,316}}} = \begin{array}{c} \text{10 miles from} \\ \text{Terrieville} \\ \text{toward Jackson} \end{array}$$

Because Reilly's Law assumes that the larger the town, the greater the pulling power, the break-even point is naturally nearer to Terrieville in both calculations.

Figure 6-2

Trade area determined by retail gravitation method.

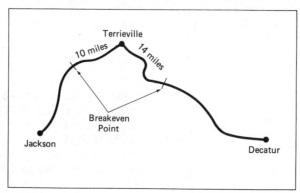

Using the calculations up to this point, it is determined that the trade area for Terrieville on two sides is as shown in Figure 6-2, with 66 percent of the trade leaving the area going to Jackson and 34 percent going to Decatur, assuming that no other towns in the area have retail drawing power.

Certain adjustments in the calculation of the trade area may be necessary to make the figures more realistic for a given situation. For example, if highway access to Decatur is excellent, the town may draw more business from Terrieville than it would otherwise. In this case, driving time in minutes might be substituted for land miles in the formula. Another possibility is to use retail sales volume of a city instead of population figures. The theory behind this idea is that population in and of itself may not always be directly related to retail pulling power. A practical note is also important in this discussion. To compare a small town such as Terrieville with New York City makes a mockery of the analysis. No analysis of this nature is worthwhile if the retailer does not use good judgment in the calculations.

An additional consideration in trade-area analysis involves analysis of auto tags in the area. Many states now put the county name or number on the auto tag. Traffic checks will reveal the number of cars from each town or county in the area that come to a given city. Care should be taken in college or military towns to make note of out-of-the-area cars that have local identification stickers on the vehicle. If such care is not taken, the tag analysis may reveal that the trade area for the city includes an area far too large to be realistic. In those locations in which city tags are used, analysis can also be used to study from which cities the customers are coming.

After the tag data have been collected, it may be decided that any county in which 500 cars were accounted for will be included in the trade area for the city. The 500 figure is a judgment decision on the part of the retailer; it, therefore, can be adjusted upward or downward as the situation warrants. Such a determination would then be plotted on the trade-area map.

Another variable to be analyzed is the origin of checkwriters and credit users in the area. An analysis of checks given at appropriate retail outlets will show where these customers are from. The same is true for credit card and charge account users. Once again, a determination is made as to how many checkwriters and credit users warrant inclusion in the trade area. If 100 is determined to be an appropriate figure, based on the data collected, then every area containing this amount of customer attraction will be plotted on the trade-area map.

Similar analysis can be conducted using records of the local credit bureau. Every area having substantial traffic coming to the town, as evidenced by credit bureau records, will be added to the map.

Another method of determining trade area is to run a contest or obtain entry forms of a recent contest run by a similar retailer in the area if the analysis is for a now nonexistent store. A plot on the trade-area map is made of where these entries said that they were from using a predetermined number of entries (e.g., 50 participants per county) as the decision rule for inclusion in the trade area. Such a method is very good since the customers who entered were in the city under study. One word of caution is in order if the data are to be used on a trade-area map. Some customers enter the same contest many times. A check of names to eliminate repeaters is important to keep the analysis somewhat realistic. Without such care, one shopper who happens to like contests can get the analysis out of proportion to reality.

One final plot on the map to be discussed is a shopper survey. For example, interviewers stop every third person on the street and ask them where they are from and what they are shopping for. Tabulation of that data will reveal where they are from and if they are shopping for the kinds of items offered, or to be offered, by the retail store in question.

After all the various methods of trade-area analysis are plotted on a trade-area map, the results of such an exercise will show the primary trade area for the store as well as the fringe or secondary trade area. For the existing store, trade-area analysis can be very enlightening to a retailer. The analysis as shown on the map in Figure 6–3 may reveal that the store is advertising to the wrong area or to too large an area. For the

Figure 6–3

Trade-area map. (Hypothetical plot for illustrative purposes.)

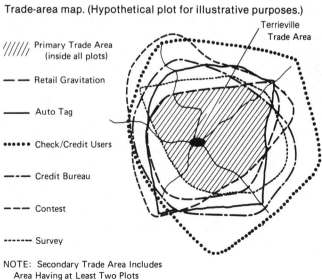

////// Primary Trade Area
(inside all plots)

— — Retail Gravitation

——— Auto Tag

••••• Check/Credit Users

—•— Credit Bureau

——— Contest

•••••• Survey

NOTE: Secondary Trade Area Includes
Area Having at Least Two Plots

prospective store the analysis may reveal that there are not sufficient prospective customers in the area to justify the establishment of the proposed store or that the area will support such a store.

Population Size, Characteristics, and Trends

The retailer should be concerned with the number of people in a prospective area and the characteristics of these people. For this purpose, the U.S. Bureau of the Census can provide much data, especially if the area under study is designated as a Standard Metropolitan Statistical Area (SMSA). An SMSA contains one city of 50,000 or more inhabitants or "twin cities" that have a combined population of at least 50,000. The SMSA includes the county of each central city or cities and adjacent counties that are found to be metropolitan in character and economically and socially integrated with the central city.

Besides census data, studies done by various governmental planning units and other bodies such as Chambers of Commerce and Bureaus of Business Research at various colleges and universities can be of assistance in studying the population. Of particular interest in many of the studies are the population trends revealed in the data. Is the area continuing to grow? Are certain age groups increasing or decreasing in size in the area? Is income rising? These and other questions that pertain to a target market when studied over time assist the retailer in learning about his or her potential target customers in each prospective market area.

Retail Trade Potential

Retail trade potential involves a study of the buying potential in an area and how existing stores are serving this potential. The buying potential of an area can be determined by various methods including the use of retail sales volume as reflected in sales tax collections and *Sales & Marketing Management's* Buying Power Index. Because these data are readily available for most governmental units (counties and cities), buying power can easily be determined on a relative basis for the various areas under investigation (see Figure 6–4).

As for the question of how existing stores are serving the retail potential of the area, the type of goods to be sold becomes a consideration. If the goods to be sold are shopping goods (furniture, housewares, clothing), then the new store will usually serve to complement the existing outlets to the benefit of all. If, on the other hand, the new service station is to join other service stations on the three corners of an intersection, these retailing activities can be said to be redundant. Another common example is the convenience stores (such as the 7–11 stores) across the street from each other or two supermarkets in the same shopping center. Projecting these examples to a city as a whole, an overstored city may make the new retailer face many unnecessary difficulties. Many competing stores offering the same services is inefficient retailing. On the other hand, many competing stores offering complementary services increase the pulling power of the retail trade area and make for more efficient retailing.

Another way to look at retail potential is by means of LaLonde's Index of Retail

Figure 6-4

Buying power index is a weighted average for each market's strength.

Weight of 3 For Percent of U.S. Retail Sales in county/city
Weight of 2 For Percent of U.S. Population in county/city
Weight of 5 For Percent of U.S. Effective Buying Income
(A Sales Management Calculation but similar to Disposable Income)
Buying Power Index = Total Weighted Percentage ÷ 10
Buyer Power Index for United States equals 100.0000

NEW HAMPSHIRE

N.H. COUNTIES CITIES	Met. Area Code	POPULATION 12/31/74 Total (thousands)	% Of U.S.	Households (thousands)	EBI 1974 Net Dollars ($000)	Median Hsld. EBI	% Hslds. by EBI Group (A) $0 – $2,999 A	(B) $3,000 – $4,999 B	(C) $5,000 – $7,999 C	(D) $8,000 – $9,999 D	(E) $10,000 – $14,999 E	(F) $15,000 and Over F	RETAIL SALES—1974 Total Retail Sales ($000)	% Of U.S.	Food ($000)	General Mdse. ($000)	Furnit.-Furnish.-Appl. ($000)	Auto-motive ($000)	Drug ($000)	Buying Power Index
Belknap		36.0	.0169	12.0	180,331	12,919	9.7	8.0	10.5	8.6	22.0	41.2	130,741	.0234	26,795	7,474	3,149	30,832	3,993	.0196
Carroll		21.7	.0102	7.8	84,912	9,417	13.7	10.0	17.2	12.7	25.3	21.1	90,081	.0161	19,471	5,416	2,266	13,459	1,044	.0112
Cheshire		57.1	.0269	18.4	248,832	12,074	9.2	6.6	12.3	10.0	27.8	34.1	162,788	.0291	43,977	15,268	5,500	26,138	5,203	.0268
Coos		34.1	.0160	11.3	125,511	10,094	13.4	9.9	14.8	11.2	28.5	22.2	80,077	.0143	23,434	4,823	2,810	16,173	1,607	.0139
Grafton		59.5	.0280	18.9	256,041	10,958	11.3	8.1	14.7	10.6	25.5	29.8	207,415	.0371	60,083	24,953	8,561	26,368	3,770	.0298
Hillsborough	161	246.3	.1159	78.9	1,118,259	13,078	9.7	6.6	10.7	8.0	24.8	40.2	737,820	.1320	167,321	125,281	27,897	144,045	18,029	.1199
Manchester		94.3	.0444	32.6	407,833	11,295	13.1	8.3	13.0	9.0	25.1	31.5	334,314	.0598	73,373	42,797	12,389	80,176	9,497	.0477
Nashua		64.4	.0303	20.7	311,961	13,999	7.7	5.7	9.6	7.1	25.3	44.6	243,166	.0435	53,100	49,938	11,250	48,827	4,242	.0351
Merrimack		89.7	.0422	28.8	406,441	12,284	9.3	7.3	12.4	9.0	25.6	36.4	217,364	.0389	44,392	19,380	8,378	47,637	5,340	.0409
Rockingham		158.0	.0743	49.5	726,766	13,490	7.7	5.8	10.6	8.5	24.9	42.5	513,907	.0920	121,663	82,782	21,285	84,480	7,211	.0796
Strafford		80.3	.0378	24.3	306,468	11,236	10.6	7.9	13.6	10.9	28.1	28.9	218,521	.0391	48,910	40,098	13,382	34,570	4,442	.0349
Sullivan		33.2	.0156	11.3	140,226	10,743	11.2	8.5	14.3	11.6	27.3	27.1	100,686	.0180	24,279	11,844	2,762	25,524	2,175	.0157
STATE TOTALS		815.9	.3838	261.2	3,593,787	12,259	9.8	7.1	12.1	9.3	25.6	36.1	2,459,400	.4400	580,325	337,319	95,990	449,226	52,814	.3923

Source: "Annual Survey of Buying Power", *Sales & Marketing Management*, Volume 115, No. 2 (July 21, 1975), p. D-67.

Saturation.[4] As shown, the index is a function of the number of consumers, number of retail stores, and per capita retail expenditures for an area. The formula states that

$$IRS = \frac{C \times RE}{RF}$$

Where IRS = Index of Retail Saturation
C = Number of consumers in area for product or service
RE = Retail expenditures per consumer for product or service
RF = Retail facilities (square feet) in area for product or service

Assume that the retailer uses the various techniques of retail research as discussed in Chapter 4 to determine that the market area for the store consists of 200,000 people with a per capita consumption level of $7.00 for the items carried in the particular type of store. If there are ten such stores in the area with an average size of 90,000 square feet, then the Index of Retail Saturation will be

$$IRS = \frac{200,000 \times \$7.00}{90,000 \times 10} = \$1.56$$

The $1.56 per square foot of selling space calculation tells the retailer that, if more than $1.56 per square foot is needed to break even, then the particular location is not satisfactory. Assuming that the *IRS* is greater than the break-even figure and more than one area is under study, everything else being equal, the retailer would favor that location with the highest *IRS*. In other words, the higher the *IRS* figure, the lower the saturation level in the market, thereby making the market more desirable from a retail potential standpoint.

Stability and Outlook for the Community

A prospective city for a store should be viewed for its stability and outlook for the future. In terms of stability, is the city in question a "one-horse" town? In other words, is the economic base for the town dependent on one industry or is it diversified? The more diversity the more stability since the economic base of the area will be better able to absorb a strike or a depression in a given industry if it can depend on nonaffected industries during such periods of crisis. Many examples exist of cities that have placed too much dependence on one industry. Seattle, Washington, for example, succeeds to the extent of the aircraft industry. Many small towns between New York and Florida depend on the tourist trade as their only predominant industry. The economic vulnerability of these cities and towns is seen when Boeing goes on strike or has a bad year in Seattle or when a new section of highway removes the tourist traffic from a town. Although the retailer will generally sell to a wide range of people in an area, much of their income will be tied, at least indirectly, to the industries in the town. With a limited number of industries in the area, the stability of the area will not be what it might. The retailer who plans to invest in a city by locating there should weigh very carefully any decision involving going into a one- or limited-industry community.

As for the outlook of the community, the retailer should attempt to determine if the community is growing. To determine this growth, the following items might be checked:

Public Utility Connections. For the past 12 months, how many electricity customers have been added to the lines? How many new phone subscribers have there been in the last year? In some cases, how many cable TV hookups have there been over time? Water connections are a good indication of activity in areas having public water. Sewer and gas connections can also reveal interesting statistics concerning the growth of the area.

Building Permits Issued. New construction in a community is a widely used barometer of growth. Knowing how many permits have been issued, the dollar amounts, and for what purpose can be quite revealing.

School Enrollments and Birth Records. How many children are in the schools in the area? In using the data, care should be taken to include various private schools in the market area. A study of enrollments over the past five years can show growth patterns for the community. Combining this data with birth records for the past five years will reveal the possible population patterns in the area for years to come.

Overall Progressiveness of the Community. Does it have adequate police and fire protection? For example, the level of fire protection can affect the insurance rates for the store. Is the cultural life of the community very active? If it is, there will be more jewelry sold by the proposed jewelry store for purposes of wearing to such cultural events. The community will affect the success of the store in many ways.

Available Services in the Area

What services are offered by the geographic area under study? Such a list of services will help to point out some positive points for the town while revealing some possible problem areas for the retailer should he or she choose that town. Some common services to examine are the following:

Consolidated Delivery Service. Does the retailer require the availability of a delivery service for an expected operation? If so, is a service available? Is the service reliable? What is its cost? What is the area served? How many times a week are deliveries made to a given section of the trade area? In some areas, the local cab company will perform the delivery function if requested. Whether it be the cab company or a delivery service, one other important variable is the appearance of the delivery person and the vehicle. If the person coming to the customer's house drives a truck that has not been washed in a year and the odor of the person implies that such is also the case for him, the retail store has not helped itself by using such a method of delivery from the store. To the customers, the store and delivery are one and the same. If the delivery person stinks—so does the store.

Credit Information Exchange. Is the town served by a credit bureau or other credit facility? If so, the retailer can have ready access to much needed information about customers from the first day of operation. If credit facilities are not available, extra effort and dollars will have to be expended to collect credit information on various prospective customers. Another factor is the quality of information available at the credit bureau. Is it a source of credit data or a gossip factory? If the latter is the case, the existence of a credit bureau in and of itself will mean little to the retailer.

Existence of Public Transportation. Is mass transit available that will bring the customers to the store? Do the customers use these facilities? In New York and Chicago the obvious answer is "yes." In small-town America, the response is "no." The problem areas as far as this question is concerned are the intermediate cities of 200,000–1,000,000 population. Such a city is large enough to have, for example, a bus company but not large enough to require people to use it to get around. As for the retailer, the consideration of this point is based mainly on whether the target market normally rides a mass transit vehicle or drives a car. If the target market is 65 and over, public transportation may be very important to the retailer. If the target group is 18–25, mass transit will generally not be a factor.

Media Availability. If the retailer plans to use daily newspaper ads to promote the store, it is essential that a daily newspaper be available for such purposes. In a similar vein, are radio, television, outdoor, and transit media available? Of additional concern is the quality of the media. Are the media of a type that reach the target market? Is there a choice of radio or TV stations or two or more newspapers to better serve the target group? Do the media offer data to assist the retailer in selecting the best choice of advertising vehicle? What is the quality of this data? Is it, at least, somewhat objective or is it strictly promotional material for the advertising supplier? Once the retailer moves into a town, the store must be promoted with the advertising resources available in the area. The time to examine the shortcomings of the media is before the location decision, not after the die is cast.

Nearness of Suppliers and Distributors. Everything else being equal, a location near major suppliers can be advantageous to the retailer. In that case, little or no inventory has to be carried by the store. The latest items will be available immediately. Transportation costs are minimal and delivery efficiency is high. To locate in a city because it is the location of a major supplier would be folly without considering other variables. In turn, to ignore this variable is poor retail management.

Legal Restrictions

As was noted in Chapter 3, legal restrictions can be numerous in a given community. The important point is that various cities and towns have different requirements for licensing, zoning, and various rules and regulations. Just as the trade area of town A should be compared with that of B, the legal restrictions found in town A should be compared with those of town B. The cost of the business license may vary from town to town. Does each town permit Sunday sales? Perhaps one city has a 1-cent local sales tax and the other does not. One community may permit mixed drinks to be served in the proposed restaurant whereas another community does not. Legal restrictions can be quite bothersome as well as expensive and time consuming to a new store in a town. In most cases the greatest difficulty is finding out about the restrictions and then meeting the various deadlines so that your store can open as planned.

Knowledge of restrictions is essential. If a regulation requires that you prepare all food on the premises for your new restaurant and you had planned to cook all pies and cakes at a different location, the sooner you find out about such a restriction the better. Because of such a restriction you may wish to locate elsewhere. Such a decision to seek another location is obviously more difficult after you have signed the lease or, even worse, opened for business.

Labor Market Conditions

As for the labor market, are there sufficient workers in the labor force who can and will work in retailing? Do these workers have the knowledge necessary to perform adequately? Both verbal and mathematical skills are essential for success.

In analyzing labor market conditions, the pool of available employees should be analyzed with particular attention to the part-time labor group. Are capable part-time people available? Housewives, wives of professional people, students, and people who desire to moonlight usually make good part-time employees.

Along with the number of prospective employees, what about the quality of these people? Are they dependable? punctual? Do they have an understanding of people? of business? What skills do they possess? Are they unionized? These and similar questions will serve to analyze the labor market conditions of the cities under analysis.

Where is such labor market information obtained by the retailer? One source of information is personal observation. Other possibilities include state employment agencies, various governmental planning and development commissions, Chambers of Commerce, and private (for a fee) consultants.

Unique Factors in a Particular Community

Aside from the items already mentioned, is there something that makes a town unique that in turn would be of advantage to the retailer? An annual arts festival would be of benefit to an art supply store. An active community recreation program would result in more athletic supplies being sold than would normally be the case for a sporting-goods store. The retailer seeks a town or community where an event or happening can be recognized for its retail potential and promoted accordingly. If town A has no unique selling points whereas town B has many possibilities, careful consideration should be given to town B while not ignoring other factors.

SELECTION OF SECTION OF CITY

In what part of town should the retailer locate the store? Should the store be in the central business district or in a suburban shopping center? Should the retailer seek out a cluster of other stores or seek a section of town where the store will be more isolated? In making this decision, the retailer should consider three factors:

1. Location of target market
2. Physical and psychological barriers to an area
3. Types of shopping situations

Location of Target Market

Without target customers, the store is obviously a failure. Do target customers live in the area of the proposed store? If not, do they pass the area at times when they would be shopping for the type of goods to be carried by the store? As a retailer, keep in mind that, although public transportation may be a factor, most customers, even in times of high gasoline costs, still prefer to use their own transportation vehicles. Therefore, the location of the target market is not as crucial as it might be otherwise. This factor would, of course, change drastically if gasoline rationing were ever implemented as a device for controlling fuel consumption.

Physical and Psychological Barriers to an Area

A given section of town may be cut off from a customer either physically or psychologically (Figure 6-5). For example, a section may not attract from all areas equally because a limited-access highway cuts through the area. A heavily congested

Figure 6-5

Barriers to an area.

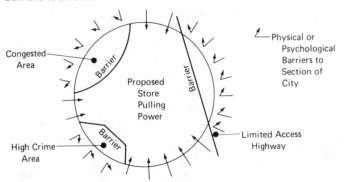

area near or in the section may reduce the attractiveness of the particular part of town. Both the limited-access highway and the congested area can also be psychological barriers to an area of town. The customer may be able to get around the congested area, for example, but chooses not to do so. Another example of psychological barriers is the feeling, whether true or not, that the particular section is in, or is near, a high crime area. If the customers believe that such is the case, many will stay away, particularly during hours of darkness.

Types of Shopping Situations

In examining the types of stores in the area, one important consideration is the kind of environment the new store will have in that section of town. Does the proposed area have shopping centers or malls? Isolated or free-standing locations? Store clusters or string streets? Or does the area include the central business district?

Central Business District. In viewing the central business district as a possible store location, the progressiveness of the area should be examined. Is the area undergoing dynamic growth or is it in a state of decay? Do the merchants work together or do they continuously fight each other? Do the stores in the area complement the proposed store or are the stores redundant? Is traffic a problem? Do customers consider parking a problem?

Many communities are undergoing downtown revitalization. Streets in the central business district are being closed, sidewalks removed. Trees and shrubbery are being planted (Figure 6–6). Renovations have worked in some communities but not in others. The hardships placed on merchants during these renovations is well documented. Some have failed during these periods as customers tend to stay away during construction. In deciding on a central business location under these circumstances, the cost of the proposed site will normally be cheaper before revitalization but better, obviously, for the retailer after revitalization.[5]

String Street. The string street gets its name from having a number of stores side by side along a street. Parking may be parallel or diagonal in front of the stores.

Figure 6-6

Downtown revitalization can take many forms such as this minipark in Boston.

(Courtesy of Filene's.)

String streets are generally found in older parts of town and/or on heavily traveled streets in the community. For those stores in a string street area, the market served generally travels that street anyway. Even the side of the street can be important for success in this area. A restaurant specializing in breakfast in a string location should be on the side of the street used most often for going to work. A fast-food restaurant or package shop should seek out an area on the homeward side of the street.

Store Cluster.   A cluster is a group of stores generally off by itself with off-street parking that normally serves a neighborhood. In a store cluster might be found a convenience store, laundromat, service station, and beauty or barber shop. If the neighborhood is appropriate a tennis or ice cream shop or similar store might also be included. If the store under consideration fits into a cluster arrangement, special care should be taken to determine which cluster or clusters the target customers now patronize.

Shopping Center or Mall.   To locate in a shopping center or mall may solve some problems for a retailer but may create other problems. Assuming that the shopping center is well managed, the area will have balanced tenancy—enough of one kind of store to attract traffic but not too many stores of the same type. For example, six shoe stores located in a large mall will complement each other since shoes are shopping goods. Six ice cream parlors in the same mall would be too many to survive. Adequate parking is also a characteristic advantage. The center should be designed so that stores are visible from the parking area. A customer who can see a store does not mind parking a good distance from it in a large parking lot.

The shopping center as it is thought of today is also a traffic generator. Such centers have two or more large stores—for example, Penney, Sears, and other national and regional chains, and large local operations—to draw the customer. These stores are located strategically so that customers must pass the other stores to go from one giant to another. It is not unusual in today's retailing environment to find 50 to 100 stores "living off" the several anchor stores in a shopping mall (Figure 6–7).

Another advantage of a shopping center is that it is generally modern in appearance. Such an atmosphere is in stark contrast to many other retail areas in a town.

Perhaps one of the strong arguments for a planned center is the "cooperation" of the merchants in working together on sales, special promotions, and community events. "Cooperation" is in quotes since such cooperation is usually specified in the contract. Without such a contract, cooperation becomes a problem. By working together to promote the center and their stores, the merchants gain a differential advantage over merchants in string street, cluster, and central business district locations that have traditionally not worked together on anything.

Disadvantages of a shopping center or mall accompany the very advantages that have just been discussed. To receive all the benefits of a well-planned and -operated mall is expensive. Cost of occupancy may run $30 or more a square foot. The fact that the store is in a center or mall may cause the store to lose some of its identity to meet the requirements of the center. How big can the sign be over the door? Are there restrictions on how the front of the building can look? The retailer may not be permitted to do as he or she pleases in a planned center.

Another disadvantage of shopping centers and malls is that they may not be well-planned and -managed. The wrong store mix, the wrong section of town, a weak merchant contract, and numerous other difficulties can cause a shopping center to fail or at least be less than 100 percent effective. It must be remembered that stores in shopping centers do fail. In deciding on a section of town, a shopping center should be studied just as carefully as the central area of the town. Neither location ensures success or guarantees failure. The overly optimistic attitude about large shopping malls being the cure for all retail problems should be guarded against by the realistic retailer. If for no other reason, this caution is warranted because of the expense involved in locating in a large mall.

To assist the retailer in thinking about a shopping center or mall location, a list of 35 checkpoints provided by John Mertes[6] can be used as a guide. The list in Figure 6–8 points out general areas of concern. The checkpoints should not be considered all inclusive.

Free-Standing Location. Some retailers choose to locate near shopping areas but do not want to be a physical part of the shopping center, mall, or the like. Discount stores have historically been the greatest users of this approach. The advantages of a free-standing location include retention of full control over the store's operation and no loss of store identity. A possible disadvantage may be the traffic congestion that is caused by nontarget market customers going to the mall or center adjacent to the site.

Isolated Location.   The retailer who wishes an isolated location will have to seek out a new area of town not already developed. The greatest advantage in the isolated place may be the cost of the land. Against this advantage can be put the resistance of people in that area of town who do not wish a retailer to come into their neighborhood. Another factor against the isolated site is the amount of advertising necessary to attract customers to the location. Will such expenses outweigh the cost benefit of the isolated spot?

In examining the various sections of town, the disadvantages and strong points of each must be studied. One helpful tool is to draw out each area under consideration and mark all complementary stores and all directly competing stores in each area. In addition, note should be made of target market location and psychological and physical barriers in relation to each area. When examining the various possibilities shown in Figure 6–9, the retailer can see exactly what the situation is in the town and then use this information as each particular site is examined.

SELECTION OF A PARTICULAR SITE

Each particular site will tend to have advantages and disadvantages that should be analyzed by the retailer. There may be more than one type of store situation available in the area that has been analyzed as the best for the store. There may even be a choice of sites within a particular store situation. For example, one site may be available on a string street or two sites may be available in a particular shopping center or mall. Several areas may be somewhat equal, thereby making the location decision rest primarily with the characteristics of each particular site. In any event, if all other factors point to a certain location but site evaluation of this location proves negative, a second look at the facts should be taken before choosing that particular site. The particular site may still be chosen as the best alternative, but site evaluation will or should make the retailer aware of the problems associated with the site.

In analyzing the individual sites, several factors should be considered.

History of the Site

Has there ever been a store at that location before? Was it successful? Why did it move? The previous retailer should be sought so that these and similar questions can be answered firsthand. Talking to other merchants in the area can also reveal interesting facts about the site. It should be noted that just because the last three retailers failed at a location does not imply that the new retailer will not succeed. Neither does previous

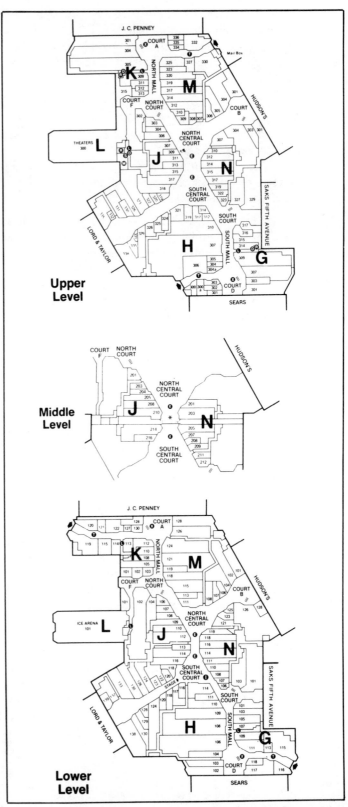

Figure 6-7

Fairlane Town Center, an example
of a regional shopping mall.

(Courtesy of the Taubman Company, Inc., Fairlane Town Center developer.)

Department Stores

J.C. Penney
Sears
Hudson's
Lord & Taylor
Saks Fifth Avenue

Women's Apparel

H-310 Alvin's
H-108 Winkelman's
H-106 Gantos
K-304 Arden's
G-301 Hartman's
K-305 Alberts
N-126 Marianne
M-121 Jean Nicole
N-310 Nawrot Pendleton Shop
G-307 Casual Corner
M-124 The Limited
N-314 Fashion Conspiracy
J-112 Alcove
M-319 Paul Harris
J-116 Foxmoor
J-208 Susie's Casuals
J-109 Ups & Downs
M-119 Merry Go Round
J-318 The Gap
M-102 County Seat
H-104 Just Pants
M-305 Today
J-113 Satisfaction
N-119 No Name
M-301 Brooks
J-335 August Max

Women's Specialty

M-310 Page Boy Maternity
G-107 The Tall Girls Shop
H-111 Size 5-7-9 Shop
N-107 Joan Bari
J-107 Donna Sacs
M-307 i Natural Cosmetics
J-204 National Uniforms
N-106 Parklane
H-305 Bernard Wigs
N-111 Wilson's
H-116 Merle Norman Cosmetics
K-102 Motherhood Maternity
J-313 Mason's
N-103 Woman's World Shops
H-321 Tannery West
H-109 Josephines Closet
H-138 Lane Bryant
J-114 Annis Furs
H-318 Tennis Lady

Women's Shoes

M-306 Joyce by Roberta
J-306 Naturalizer Shoes
M-108 Red Cross Shoes
K-309 Chandlers
N-121 The Wild Pair
M-118 Bakers
N-315 Shoe Revue
H-114 Sibleys Florsheim
H-118 Pappagallo
H-331 Sundance Shoes
J-203 Tall & Wide Shoes by Eastown
N-207 Chester

Fine & Costume Jewelry

N-307 Charles W. Warren Jeweler
M-111 Wright Kay Jewelers
G-111 Meyer Treasure Chest Stores
M-325 Shifrin Willens
G-101 J.B. Robinson Jewelers
J-303 DeRoy Ringsmiths
M-106 Corey's Jewel Box
N-322 Ad Libs
M-335 Torri Jewelry
N-211 Buck N' Ear
H-303 Engravers Point
K-312 Silver Brick Road
G-318 Black Starr & Frost

Men's Apparel

H-307 Hughes & Hatcher
N-304 Anton's
M-115 Chelsea
M-304 Fifth Avenue
N-310 Nawrot Pendleton Shop
J-307 J. Riggings
N-118 Silverman's
J-110 Proving Ground
N-317 Americana Club
M-102 County Seat
J-318 The Gap
H-104 Just Pants
G-109 Teen/Man
M-320 United Shirt
N-114 Oak Tree
J-210 Chess King
J-113 Satisfaction
J-126 Montee's
H-338 Outrigger

Men's Specialty

G-103 Gabes
N-111 Wilson's
M-317 Harry's Big & Tall
H-321 Tannery West
H-324 Custom Shop Shirtmakers
H-109 Napoleon's Closet
N-208 President Tuxedo

Men's Shoes

G-316 Bally of Switzerland
M-309 Shermans Florsheim
N-121 The Wild Pair
K-103 Vanguard
K-110 Father & Son
M-323 Thom McAn
H-114 Sibleys Florsheim
J-120 Johnston & Murphy
J-139 Bostonian
H-304 Flagg Brothers
N-207 Chester
H-326 Nunn Bush Brass Boot

Family & Children's Shoes

N-319 Stride Rite
N-209 Roots Natural Footwear
M-126 Kinney Shoes
H-103 Nobil Shoes
N-303 Playmakers
J-124 Footlocker

Children's Apparel

N-312 Youth Center
J-323 The Children's Place

Restaurants

G-115 The Magic Pan Creperie
M-330 Toll Gate
K-315 Olga's Kitchen
J-104 Broadway Deli
H-124 Bonanza
K-119 Burger King
H-306 Elias Brothers Big Boy
M-327 Happy Hero
K-114 Koney Island Inn
M-332 Friendly Restaurants
J-101 Jonathon B. Pub
K-122 Nanny's Soup Kettle

Food Specialty

N-125 Candy Hut
M-334 Cookie Factory
N-212 The Coffee Beanery
J-201 Tiffany's Bakery
G-118 Miami Bake Shoppe
K-112 Alpen Pantry
K-128 General Nutrition Center
K-127 Hot Sam
J-309 Fanny Farmer Candies
J-118 The Fudge Factory
H-117 Au Bon Pain
K-113 Piccadilly's
H-314 Godiva Chocolatier

Optical

K-130 Detroit Optometric Centers
H-302 Detroit Optometric Centers
H-325 Tuckerman Optical

Book Stores

N-327 B. Dalton Bookseller
J-130 Waldenbooks
J-304 The Childrens Bookmark

Records, Music & Electronic Specialties

M-312 Musicland
K-108 Anderson Music
N-201 Wurlitzer
J-216 Radio Shack
J-315 Schaak Electronics

Fabric Stores & Sewing

N-128 Singer
M-101 Showcase of Fine Fabrics

Home Furnishings

M-128 Homemaker Shops
N-301 Raimi's Curtains
G-117 Austin Galleries
N-123 Creations by Nature
J-319 Time and Clock
J-317 Ultima
N-205 Phone Center Store
J-311 Country Peddler
G-105 Yankee Peddler

Gifts, Cards, Flowers, Tobacco & Office Supply

H-102 Finger's
J-106 European Flower Markets
N-110 Fischer's Hallmark
M-314 Hugh Jarvis Gifts
N-323 Glass Gallery
K-311 Asian Bazaar
K-313 The Music Box Shop
N-116 Tuerkes
M-113 Wicks 'n' Sticks
H-329 Epitome
M-107 Hoffritz for Cutlery
M-308 Churchills
H-319 Franklin Mint
K-101 Gold Chest

Sporting Goods, Toys, Hobbies, Cameras, Luggage & Pets

G-309 Schneider's Sport Shops
N-108 Lobby Hobby
M-104 Kay Bee Toy & Hobby Shop
J-214 Hobby Center
G-303 Rug Crafters
J-102 Herman's World of Sporting Goods
K-120 Docktor Pet Center
M-336 One Hour Photo

Variety Stores

K-301 C.V.S.

Services

K-115 Hair Cut House
G-116 NBD Dearborn
G-113 Elliott Travel
J-108 York Photography Studios
J.C. Penney Automotive Center
Sears Automotive Center

Theaters & Entertainment

L-300 The Movies

Public Service Symbols
I. Information and stroller rental
T. Telephones
R. Restrooms
D. Drinking fountains
L. Lockers
X. Escalators
E. Elevators
S. Security
M. Management Offices

≡ — Stairs

*A.C.T. System located middle level

Ice Arena

L-101 Fairlane Ice Arena

Center Hours
Monday through Saturday -
10:00 a.m. to 9:00 p.m.
Sunday Noon to 5:00 p.m.

Special Holiday Hours
Monday through Saturday -
9:30 a.m. to 9:30 p.m.
Sunday 11:00 a.m. to 6:00 p.m.

Fairlane Town Center
Dearborn, Michigan 48126
Telephone
(313) 593-3330

50M 12-80

Figure 6-8

Checkpoints for evaluating shopping center locations.

1. Who is the shopping center developer?
2. How long has he been in the business of developing real estate?
3. What are his financial resources?
4. With whom has he arranged for the financing of the center?
5. What is his reputation for integrity?
6. Who performed the economic analysis? Does the report cover both favorable and unfavorable factors?
7. What experience has the economic consultant had?
8. Has an architectural firm been retained to plan the center?
9. Has the architect designed other centers? Have they been successful from a retailing standpoint?
10. Who will build the center? The developer? An experienced contractor? An inexperienced contractor?
11. Has the developer had experience with other centers?
12. What is, or will be, the quality of management for the center?
13. Will the management have merchandising and promotion experience? (Some developers are large retailers rather than real estate operators.)
14. What percent of the leases have been signed? Are they on a contingent basis?
15. Has every facet of the lease been carefully studied?
16. Is the ratio of parking area to selling area 3-to-1 or more?
17. Has sufficient space (400 feet) been assigned to each car?
18. Is the parking space designed so that the shopper does not walk more than 300 to 350 feet from the farthest spot to the store?
19. What is the angle of parking space? (Ninety degrees provides the best expacity and circulation.)
20. What is the planned or actual car turnover? (3.3 cars per parking space per day is the average.)
21. Is the number of total spaces adequate for the planned business volume? (Too many spaces make the center look dead; too few openly invite competition around the center.)
22. Does the parking scheme distribute the cars so as to favor no one area?
23. Is there an adequate number of ingress/egress roads in proper relationship with the arrangement of parking spaces?
24. For the larger centers, a ring road is preferable. Is this the case?
25. Is the site large enough for the type of center?
26. Is the size sufficiently dominant to forestall the construction of similar shopping centers nearby?
27. Is the center of regular shape? If not, does the location of the buildings minimize the disadvantage of the site's shape?
28. Is the site sufficiently deep? (A depth of at least 400 feet is preferred; if less, the center may look like a strip development.)
29. Is the site level? Is it on well-drained land?
30. Does the center face north and/or east?
31. Can the center be seen from a distance?
32. Are any structures, such as a service station, located in the parking area? (If so, do they impede the site's visibility?
33. Is the site a complete unit? (A road should not pass through the site.)
34. Are the buildings set far enough back on the site that the entire area may be seen?
35. Are all the stores readily accessible to each other, with none having an advantage?

success at the site guarantee anything. One point in favor of previous failures at the site is that the cost of the location may be lower to promote its use by retailers.

Traffic Flow

Does the target market pass the location? Is it accessible to customers? If the proposed store is in a shopping mall, is it directly between the anchor stores or off to the side? In Figure 6–10, location A, which will generally cost more, will usually have much more traffic flow than will location B. Traffic flow should be concerned, however, with target customers, not just traffic counts. If most of the target market customers who come to the mall pass location B as shown in the illustration, then location B for that situation would be more than adequate at the probable cheaper price. In fact, such a location in certain situations may be far more desirable. Other sites may have too much congestion and traffic, thereby making a particular target group shy away from the area.

Figure 6-9

Proposed sections of town.

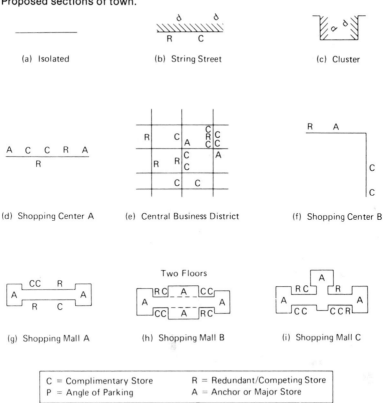

(a) Isolated

(b) String Street

(c) Cluster

(d) Shopping Center A

(e) Central Business District

(f) Shopping Center B

(g) Shopping Mall A

(h) Shopping Mall B

(i) Shopping Mall C

C = Complimentary Store   R = Redundant/Competing Store
P = Angle of Parking   A = Anchor or Major Store

Parking and Mass Transportation

Under area selection, parking and mass transportation were discussed in terms of adequacy of the service and facilities for the area. In particular site selection, the concern is parking in relation to the store. Is parking adequate in the immediate area of the store throughout the day? Does the bus stop in front of the store or nearby? As for parking, it may be sufficient during the day but not so at night due to a movie theater in the area. Or the reverse may be true due to office buildings in the vicinity. These causes of inadequate parking may be overshadowed by the benefits of having people drawn to the area. At this point, the number of available parking spaces per hour in the immediate area of the store is the concern. As for mass transit, the bus stop in front of the store can be great for the drugstore snack bar but not for an exclusive jewelry store. The question

Figure 6-10

Possible store locations in mall.

is—do the target customers ride the bus? Great location if the answer is "yes." Not so if the answer is "no."

Conditions of Immediate Area Around Store

Unless the retailer is large enough to dominate its own environment, a store should be concerned with the immediate area around it that is not under its control. Factors that affect the quality of the area surrounding a store include the following:

Vacant Stores and Buildings. Empty stores generate no traffic. They give an area a depressing appearance. Such buildings are almost never kept up, thereby becoming places where litter builds up. These situations can even be scary to the nighttime shopper, especially if they become places where local youths congregate. In other words, nothing positive can be said about vacant structures from a retailing viewpoint.

Smoke and Odors. Not only will smoke reduce the visibility of the store, but it may also prove to be irritating to customers and employees alike. As for odors, any odor is a bad odor. Even the smell of freshly baked bread, which is pleasing to almost anyone, can be a bad thing if every item bought at the dress shop smells like fresh bread from the bakery next door. Any business in the area that generates an odor of any kind should be studied carefully as to its effect on the proposed site.

Poor Walking Areas. The lack of sidewalks or poor sidewalks at a nonshopping center location can inhibit customer traffic. In addition, anything blocking traffic flow on a sidewalk is bothersome. For example, if an auto garage is located in the same block as a possible store site, the garage will normally restrict pedestrian flow by parking cars on the sidewalk in front of the garage with hoods raised, engines running, and lots of noise and fumes. Any type of activity that makes the customer choose the other side of the street to walk on is undesirable.

Hours of Operation in Area. Are the stores in the area open during the proposed store's planned time of operation? If the new store sells shopping goods, consideration of store hours in use is a must since such a store needs complementary stores to help generate business. A shoe store open on Friday night in an area where nothing else is open can be a very lonely place.

Location Clutter. Can customers approaching a shopping location see the store? A shopping center or mall, for example, may become hidden from view thanks to satellite structures such as banks and fast-food establishments that are built up around a location. This location problem is obvious if it already exists. If it does not exist, what the retailer should do is ascertain if such a situation could develop at a particular location over time. Where appropriate, the retailer should check zoning and/or contract restrictions that could have a bearing on this problem.

Growth Trends in the Area of the Site

Is the site under consideration in the growth pattern for the area or in the opposite direction? In many cities, the so-called main shopping street has shifted over the years. Good site selection makes an effort to interpret trends that will place the store location in the path of growth. By doing this, the site is acquired before its price increases. Care should be taken not to base location decisions on probabilities that lie too far into the future. The retailer must also operate profitably while waiting for the predicted growth to take place. By applying growth trends to the analysis, the optimum site is hopefully suitable for current use and will improve over time.

MAKING THE DECISION

After all the facts are in on various cities, sections of cities, and particular sites within sections, the decision must be made as to a given site. Some major firms will go a step further and use a computer to digest the various data using predetermined weights for variables of various kinds. Computer usage is not necessary in making a location decision. This equipment will tend, however, to assist the retailer in assimilating the data into a workable form.

With or without the aid of a computer, is there such a thing as an optimum location for a retail store? Such a site is possible, but, in most situations, one site will have both strong and weak points with the same true for a second or third location. In other words, site selection procedures are designed to gather the facts and place them before the retail decision maker. The final choice is up to the decision maker. No computer location model can or will replace this person. If a computer is needed to analyze the data, it should be remembered that the machine is making the location decision as it has been instructed to do. The actual decision maker is still the retailer.[7]

SUMMARY

The location of a store can be a critical factor in the success or failure of a retail operation. In what city should a retailer locate? To answer this question requires information on each town under consideration dealing with trade area, population size and characteristics, retail trade potential, stability and outlook for the community, available services in the area, legal restrictions, labor market conditions, and factors unique to each particular town. As for a decision concerning what section of town, accessibility of the target market, physical and psychological barriers, and types of available store situations such as shopping centers, malls, string streets, store clusters, isolated areas, or the central business district are all variables that should be analyzed. Particular site examination should include history of the site, traffic flow, availability of parking and mass transportation, the growth trends in area, and environmental conditions in the immediate vicinity of the proposed location. The choice of city, section of city, and particular site are interrelated. The decision maker must weigh the variables together to determine the best location. Computers are used many times to assist in the assimilation process. Location analysis gathers facts about various possible store locations. It does not make the selection. The retailer must make the final decision.

1. How would you develop a trade-area analysis for a shoe store in the town in which you live? How would a trade-area analysis differ for a convenience store in the same town? Using census and mileage data on towns in your area, calculate the trade area for one of the towns using Reilly's Law.
2. Sin City is 50 miles from Dullsville and 100 miles from Funville. The populations of the towns are as follows:

Dullsville	27,000
Funville	312,000
Sin City	243,000

   Using Reilly's Law, what is the break-even point in miles from Dullsville on the Sin City highway.
3. Why is retail potential an important consideration in the selection of a city in which to locate a store? In terms of retail potential, explain *IRS*.
4. Discuss various measures of stability and growth of a given community from a retailing viewpoint.
5. Develop a list of services that may be desirable to a retailer who is considering an area. Are some more important than others?
6. Explain what is meant by the term physical and psychological barriers in relation to selection of an area of a town in which to locate a store.
7. Discuss various "shopping situations" that may be found in a town. Discuss possible advantages and disadvantages of each.
8. In analyzing the immediate vicinity of a proposed store location, what are some factors that should be considered?
9. "The retailer decides on a town, then a section of town, and finally on the particular site within the chosen section." Comment on this statement.
10. Retail Merchandising Associates (RMA), the operator of a chain of shoe stores, is attempting to determine if it should locate a store in Morgan and/or Stewartville. Morgan contains a target market of 35,000 in the trade area and Stewartville has 100,000. In all its stores, RMA has found that the average purchase is $30 and that one out of ten people buys shoes in the particular market. In Morgan, the average size store is 2,000 square feet; in Stewartville, the average is 1,800 square feet. There are three shoe stores in Morgan and seven in Stewartville. Assuming that RMA requires $20 per square foot to break even, should the chain open a store in either town? Why?

[1] For more information on site selection, see Jac L. Goldstucker, Danny Bellenger, Thomas J. Stanley, and Ruth L. Otte, *New Developments in Retail Trade Area Analysis and Site Selection*, Research Monograph No. 78 (Atlanta: Georgia State University, 1978).

[2] David L. Huff, "Defining and Estimating a Trade Area," *Journal of Marketing*, Vol. 28, no. 3 (July 1964), p. 38. Published by the American Marketing Association.

[3] P. D. Converse, "New Laws of Retail Gravitation," *Journal of Marketing*, Vol. 14, no. 3 (October 1949), pp. 379–384. Published by the American Marketing Association.

[4] Bernard LaLonde, "The Logistics of Retail Location," in William D. Stevens, ed., *1961 Fall American Marketing Association Proceedings*. Published by the American Marketing Association.

[5] For one example of downtown revitalization, see Frederick C. Klein, "Chicago Pins Hopes of Downtown Revival on Big Shopping Mall," *The Wall Street Journal*, Vol. 195, no. 49 (March 11, 1980), pp. 1, 24.

[6] John Mertes, "Site Opportunities for the Small Retailer," *Journal of Retailing*, Vol. 39, no. 3 (Fall 1963), p. 44.

[7] For additional ideas on site selection, see Lewis A. Spalding, "Beating the Bushes for New Store Locations," *Stores*, Vol. 62, no. 10 (October 1980), pp. 30–35.

CHAPTER 7

Store Design

HEATHCLIFF

"YOUR DOG FOOD SECTION IS TWO FEET
LONGER THAN YOUR CAT FOOD SECTION."

Reprinted by permission of McNaught Syndicate, Inc.

Just as site selection works to obtain the best location for a store, store design attempts to make optimum use of that site in terms of both exterior and interior potential. The store is the package that contains the merchandise. Just as many product manufacturers spend as much or more effort on the package as they do on the actual product, the retailer should take special care in designing the store. If the package (the store) does not attract, entice, or at least interest the customer, the product (merchandise) will not sell. A good design helps to sell the product. A poor design will not.[1]

EXTERIOR DESIGN

As noted, store design falls into two areas: exterior design and interior design. Exterior design is examined first since the first visual impression is given by the store's exterior. Included for consideration under this topic are signing, marquee, type of entrance, windows, and overall appearance.

Signing

To be effective, the sign for the store must serve its identification function. It should identify the store by name and by type of store. The traditional balls on a pawn shop sign have identified this type of store for hundreds of years. In more recent times, the McDonald's golden arch or Kentucky Fried Chicken's red-and-white-striped bucket have signaled to the passing customer that "good food and fast service" are available.

The sign in front of the store (Figure 7–1) should contain the name of the store and

Figure 7–1

Exterior signing should be distinctive.

(Courtesy of Schwinn Bicycle Company.)

its logo (how store name is written or any symbols that will be used to identify the store). The name of the store is very important to its success. A high-fashion dress shop should not be called "Peggy's Fashion Shop." A better name would be "Paris Unlimited" or better still a French name. A high-class restaurant called "Bill's Beanery" or a budget shoe store named "Mademoiselle's Bootery" would have names inconsistent with their target market and type of operation. Consistency is also important with the logo. An antique shop should not have a modern logo. A shop for the teenaged girl may use a modernistic car for its logo to go with its name, "The Body Shop."

One last point to mention about the name is the question of naming the store after the owner or the store location. When considering the owner's name, is it easy to pronounce? Is it easy to remember? Does it promote a suitable picture for the store in the customer's mind? A medium-priced gift shop called "The Green Frog" is probably a better name than "Smith's Gift's." If the gifts are very expensive, just "Smith's" may be the better choice. If the store is named after its location, what happens when it moves or opens branch stores? The "39th Street Florist" loses the identity it has built up with customers when it has to move to 42nd Street. When the "Forest Way Appliance Center" opens a branch on Jones Avenue it becomes the "Forest Way Appliance Center on Jones Avenue." This can confuse customers. Therefore, special thought should be given to the choice of a name for a store. The impact of the decision should be considered beyond the importance of the name on the sign at present.

Marquee

Should a store have a canopy or other form of shelter over the front of the building? Such an addition will protect shoppers from the elements as well as the merchandise in the windows if windows are in use. The real problem with marquees is to make them an integral part of the building—not something that appears to be bolted on as an afterthought. Many are constructed of various metals that give the appearance of a makeshift arrangement made out of something designed for a carport. A poorly designed marquee can be a real eyesore to an otherwise attractive store front. One other factor is that the marquee should be high enough off the walk level so as to permit a sign under the marquee with at least an eight foot vertical clearance. A marquee that is too low can be a hazard to shoppers and a problem for the retailer (Figure 7–2).

Type of Entrance

What type of doors and entrance area should the store have? One good rule of thumb to follow is to have only one door if at all possible. Two or more entrances mean security problems and difficulty in developing an effective traffic pattern within the store. If necessary the store may have a door in the alley or the "back" of the store for access from parking areas in the rear. If a door is in the rear, it should never be viewed as the "back door." Every customer door should be considered as important as any other. In such cases, the back exterior should be as well planned as the traditional "front door."

In an interior mall location, the store can have the option of having no physical store front (Figure 7–3), with chain or glass doors used to close the store during hours of nonoperation. An open front gives the feeling of complete openness, which en-

Figure 7-2

A Marquee should be designed to look like part of the building. It should also be high enough to permit a sign to be placed under it without danger to the customer.

(Courtesy of Radio Shack.)

courages the shopper to come inside and look around. Many stores today do not take advantage of what an interior mall can offer in terms of openness. Care should be taken to design the store in that situation so that the customer can see in, or better still, go in.

In a nonmall location, a recessed front can attract people into the store just as an open front can attract customers in a mall. The recessed front will allow passers-by to look in the window without interfering with customer traffic (Figure 7–4). It is hoped that some of the window shoppers will enter the store. A recessed front is particularly helpful to a shoe store or other shopping-goods store because it gives more window area for display per store-front-foot. In addition, by having the door recessed, less congestion is created when the door is opened than if it opened into the pedestrian traffic area. The recessed front also gives weather protection when a marquee is not used. One drawback to a recessed front is that it will, by its nature, serve as a place that attracts litter blown in off the street. If a recessed entrance is planned, regular cleanup should also be planned.

Figure 7-3

Open-front stores invite the customer inside by showing more of the store and its merchandise to the passer-by.

(Courtesy of Athletic Attic.)

Another consideration when thinking about the type of entrance is energy loss. Each entrance for a store means a chance of heat or air conditioning loss. The way to overcome this problem is by means of an air lock for each door or by using revolving doors. Revolving doors do prevent energy loss, but they are a real problem for the handicapped shopper. An air lock (Figure 7–5) with automatic doors can solve the handicap problem but at the expense of valuable selling space. In areas where the climate is extreme—either hot or cold—the air lock will pay for the space it takes away from the productive sales floor in the form of reduced energy expense. In this time of high energy cost, an air lock for each entrance makes good sense for almost any store.

Display Windows

Windows are very important to shopping-goods stores; not as important to others. The retailer has three choices: no windows, closed-back windows, and no-back win-

Figure 7–4

Examples of recessed store entrances.

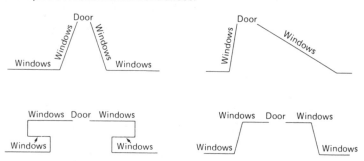

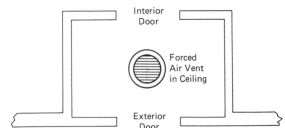

Figure 7-5

Air lock for store entrance.

dows. For some types of merchandise no windows might be appropriate such as for a high-fashion store that deals in originals. Another case for no windows is when the retailer does not plan to use the windows effectively. As discussed in Chapter 21, Retail Display, a poor display is generally worse than no display at all. If no effort is put into display, then the exterior of the building might be best designed without windows. That alternative may also be distinctive. With every other store having windows, the one without windows will stand out.

Closed-back windows form glass-enclosed display rooms for the presentation of merchandise. Nothing in the background distracts from the items on display. The interior wall behind the windows can also be used as any other wall in the store. The opposite is true for no-back windows (Figure 7–6). The interior of the store itself becomes

Figure 7-6

No-back windows provide light and let the customers see in or out.

(Courtesy of Lady Madonna Maternity Boutique.)

part of the display. Displays especially designed for the window shopper may or may not be used. In addition, the no-back window is good for security. These windows open up the store for observation. Finally, the windows put more natural light into the store thereby giving customers a more open feeling.

Overall Exterior Appearance

The overall exterior of a store must be tasteful and eye-catching, as well as functional, as is the store shown in Figure 7-1. In planning the exterior, several considerations are:[2]

1. *Size*—the building should convey the size of the business and the range of merchandise and services offered by the store.
2. *Permanence*—the exterior should project trust and dependability.
3. *Definition from its neighbors*—a unique exterior different from other firms on the block should be sought.
4. *Nature of merchandise and customer*—everything about the store should convey the message that the store is what that particular target market is searching for.
5. *Store character*—the exterior should convey the appropriate store personality.
6. *Regional or community characteristic*—for example, if the store is located in an historical area, the exterior should be in keeping with the character of the surrounding area.

An exception to these considerations is the stores of Best Products Company, a catalog merchandiser based in Richmond, Virginia. This firm uses exterior designs for some of its stores that resemble nothing else in retailing. For example, the Best Store in Sacramento, California, does not have a front entrance. Instead, it has a 45-ton "chunk" that is moved out of the way when the store opens to give a 14-foot gaping hole for an entrance. When the store closes at night, the "chunk" is moved back over the "entrance." Needless to say, customer reaction is mixed on whether they like this unique retail store exterior that opens up on a somewhat traditional catalog showroom. Although "structurally outrageous," as Best's president calls these stores, they do seem to attract attention and customers in the areas where they are located.[3]

INTERIOR DESIGN

First impressions are very important in retailing. Therefore, the quality of the exterior of a store is vital to such a business. Sales are generally made, however, in the store. Equal care should be taken to have the interior complement the exterior so the whole package will be rated as superior in the customer's mind. In interior design, atmospherics, layout patterns, merchandise groupings, and department location are all factors for review.

Atmospherics is defined as the conscious designing of space to create certain effects in buyers.[4] To create the correct atmosphere in a store is vital to the success of the business. Such an atmosphere is generally created through the use of the various senses—smell, sound, touch, and sight—to the benefit of the retailer (Figure 7-7).[5]

Smell.   The interior design of a candy store should have candy up front for the passer-by to smell. The design may even include fans to help distribute the pleasing odor. Another store may have perfume automatically dispensed into the air every few minutes in its cosmetic department. Just as appropriate odor is good, a wrong odor can be a problem. A store that smells of stale cigarette smoke or musty carpet will not be inviting to the customer. A fabric shop that smells of fabric dye may even cause an allergic reaction in some customers that will force them to leave the store. Also, what is good for one retailer may not be good for the store next door. A bakery puts out a doughnut fragrance that sells many products. The dress shop next door may suffer because customers do not want clothes that smell like doughnuts.

Sound.   Sound gives atmosphere to a store. A teen shop selling jeans plays rock music for its customers. Likewise, a high-fashion conservative store has quiet, restful background accompaniment. Music eliminates the "dead store" sound in a

Figure 7-7

The sights and sound of the Radio Shack layout help to create the right atmosphere in the store.

(Courtesy of Radio Shack.)

store. It has been found that when music is playing in a store and then shuts off, customers become quiet and uneasy. Every noise seems louder. Sales personnel also seem to get slower. When the music is turned back on everyone gets a psychological lift. This lift is believed to be so important that Muzak, a company that supplies music to stores and others, sets up its music with a break or silence every 15 minutes. The beat of the music is also increased during the 15-minute period as it builds to the short period of silence.

Music is very important for atmospheric consideration, but it is not the only important source of sound. The sound of popcorn popping sells popcorn. The sound as well as the sight of a flaming dessert being prepared in a restaurant sells desserts to others in the room. The sound of a wind chime or cuckoo clock sells these items. A demonstration stereo or CB radio operating for the customer or a person playing a $39 organ can be an attention-getter. Physical layout should consider the importance of sound by placing appropriate items where they can be heard.

Touch.   The layout of a store should encourage touching. Toys were meant to be played with. Magazines were created to read. The retail outlet that provides a place for children to play with toys that are for sale will probably sell more toys. A magazine rack with all books in cellophane wrappers will usually lose sales. One bookshop has paperback books on the wall from floor to ceiling—12 feet high. If the customer wants one high on the wall, he or she must ask for it. Many probably never bother to ask. In many antique shops and gift operations, a common sign discourages the customer from touching and perhaps buying. The secret to selling a new car is many times touch or getting the customer to try it out. Many clothes are also sold with touch as an important consideration. As a general rule, even with theft and damage a real possibility, a store should get the customer involved with the merchandise by means of touch. Any store design that discourages touch should be reconsidered.

Sight.   If one of the senses might be thought to be more important than the others in terms of store atmosphere, sight would be considered by most to be the most important. When the customer comes in the door, what is seen? To take the store from the top and work down, what does the ceiling look like? Is it exposed pipes or attractive ceiling tile? Is the ceiling cracking or in good repair? How high is the ceiling? If it is too high, has a crown molding been placed on the walls at about the eight-foot level with the ceiling color in a dark shade painted down to that molding to give the visual effect of a lower ceiling? A light-colored ceiling will give the opposite effect. Also, insulation can be added to the ceiling with certain types of ceiling treatments. Once again, a possible way to save energy dollars can be utilized by the retailer.

Is the signing in the store appropriate? Is it in keeping with the merchandise carried in the store? What about interior lighting? Is all lighting exposed fluorescent tubing or enclosed in fixtures? Are lighting levels different throughout the store or constant? Lighting needs generally vary within a store. The TV department needs less candlepower so that its sets will stand out when operating. A restaurant may also reduce its lighting level for the desired atmosphere. Such is not the case for Hardee's. Lighting can be used to set off interior signs and displays to best advantage, as, for example, pink lights over a meat counter in a food store to give the meat a good appearance. Although fluorescent tubes are the most efficient light source, most stores will find a combination of lighting equipment the best possible choice in terms of atmospherics. Also, a burned-out light does little for atmosphere. Keep lights in good repair for an image of an up-to-date, ongoing business (Figure 7–8).

Walls and floors also give color, shape, and personality to a retail design. Different colors mean different things to people.[6] By painting the walls with different shades and designs, each area of the store can take on a unique personality. As noted in Table 7–1, red gives an exciting and passionate impression. This color would be excellent for use in a night club or lounge. Yellow is excellent for almost any mass-market store situation since it is cheerful. For a high-fashion store seeking a peaceful, subdued atmosphere, blue and green would be good. For the bakery or food department, the image of cleanliness can be conveyed by using white. Different parts of the store can convey different images through the use of color treatments. Also, as shown in Table 7–1, colors can be used throughout the layout to convey the season of the year as well

Figure 7–8

Appropriate interior lighting, signing and ceiling, wall and floor treatments all help to visually set off a department.

(Courtesy of Venture Stores.)

Table 7-1

Modern American Color Associations

Color	General Appearance	Mental Associations	Direct Associations	Objective Impressions	Subjective Impressions
Red	Brilliant, intense, opaque, dry	Hot, fire, heat, blood	Danger, Christmas, Fourth of July, Saint Valentine's Day, Mother's Day	Passionate, exciting, fervid, active	Intensity, rage, rapacity, fierceness
Orange	Bright, luminous, glowing	Warm, metallic, autumnal	Halloween, Thanksgiving	Jovial, lively, energetic, forceful	Hilarity, exuberance, satiety
Yellow	Sunny, incandescent, radiant	Sunlight	Caution	Cheerful, inspiring, vital, celestial	High spirit, health
Green	Clear, moist	Cool, nature, water	Clear, St. Patrick's Day	Quieting, refreshing, peaceful, innocent	Ghastliness, disease, terror, guilt
Blue	Transparent, wet	Cold, sky, water, ice	Service, flag	Subduing, melancholy, sober	Gloom, fearfulness, furtiveness
Purple	Deep, soft, atmospheric	Cool, mist, dark, shadow	Mourning, Easter	Dignified, pompous, mournful, mystic	Loneliness, desperation
White	Spatial light	Cool, snow	Cleanliness, Mother's Day, flag	Pure, clean, frank, youthful	Brightness of spirit, normality
Black	Spatial darkness	Neutral, night, emptiness	Mourning	Funereal, ominous, deadly, depression	Negation of spirit, death

Source: Faber Birrens, *Color Psychology and Color Therapy* (New York: University Books, Inc., 1961), p. 143. Published by arrangement with Lyle Stuart.

(e.g., red for Christmas and St. Valentine's Day, orange for Hallowe'en and Thanksgiving, green for St. Patrick's Day). A layout may be developed that would permit certain wall panels, for example, to be changed to reflect the different color associations throughout the year.

As for floors, at one time a floor had to be a plain floor. Then tiles of various kinds were put into use. Now, carpet of a type that will hold up in a retail situation is available for consideration by the retailer. Not only is carpet pleasing to the eye and ear, it is also pleasing to the tired shopper's feet. Salesclerks also learn to appreciate it as they will usually not tire as quickly in a carpeted store.

In terms of walls and floors, flexibility is important. Permanent interior walls are not desirable. A store needs to change occasionally to create the image of progress and newness. One quick way in which to change the store's appearance is the movement of a flexible wall. Because floor designs may not be changed as often, care should be taken to always keep future possible changes in mind when making floor decisions.

In addition, the location of control panels, heating and air conditioning ducts and vents, outlets of various kinds, and pipes and other obstructions should be studied and adjusted if necessary before the carpets and walls are installed. As a general rule, it is always better to have too many outlets than not enough. Proper layout planning in the beginning will allow greater layout flexibility for atmospherics' sake in the future.

Layout Patterns

In deciding on the layout (the physical arrangement of fixtures) of the store, the opposite ends of the layout continuum are the grid pattern and the free-flow pattern. As observed in the grid pattern illustration (Figure 7–9), this design gets its name from the fact that all the counters and other fixtures are at right angles to each other, thereby forming a maze for the customer to move through. In a study conducted by *Progressive Grocer*, the direction of traffic flow in a grid layout, consisting of an odd number of single-length gondolas, was found to promote thorough shopping. The top three figures within the aisles, shown in Figure 7–9, show the percentage of shoppers passing down the aisles in different directions. The bottom three figures show the percentage of shoppers passing a given aisle or department, the percentage of total shoppers who buy, and the percentage of passers who buy.[7] Not only will the grid design provide a smooth and thorough traffic flow, such a layout will also give the most merchandise exposure per square foot of selling space. By its nature, little space is "wasted" on open areas. An attractive example of the grid design is shown in Figure 7–10.

The other extreme of layout design is the free-flow pattern. Free flow makes use of much open space while providing the shopper with many different choices in terms of direction. Just as the food store is the universal example for a grid pattern, a high-fashion dress shop or a dress boutique within a department store is the logical choice for a free-flow design. As noted in Figure 7–11, the customer is not put in a maze with the use of free flow. Colors, arrangement of counters, and floor treatments are all coordinated for the desired effect, but no effort is made to physically control the traffic flow. Figure 7–12 shows this arrangement in a women's clothing department.

In comparing the two layout plans, certain contrasts are noted. The grid pattern

Figure 7-9

Grid pattern layout.

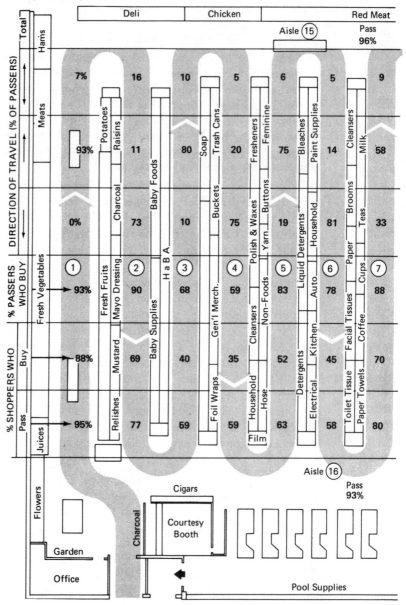

Source: "Consumer Behavior in a Supermarket," *Progressive Grocer*, Vol. 54, no. 10 (October 1975) pp. 56–57.

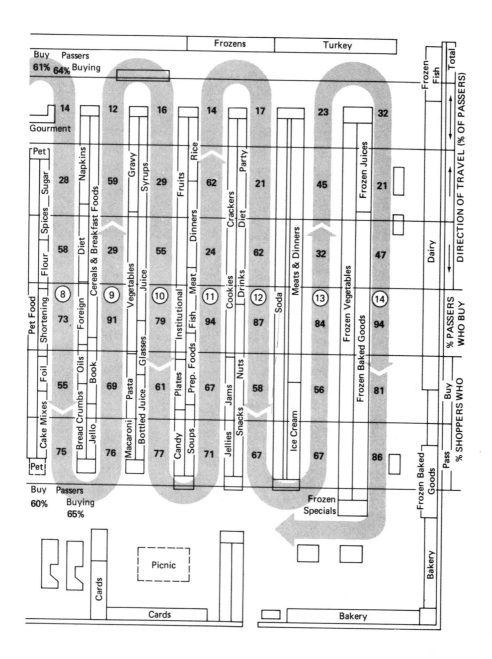

Figure 7-10

A type of grid layout is found in many stores besides a food store.

(Courtesy of Sears, Roebuck and Co.)

implies lower-priced, lower-quality goods through its "full" appearance. Many customers may be scared away by the wide-open spaces of the free-flow design. More merchandise and self-service are points in favor of the grid. Perceived crowding of customers becomes most pronounced when there is interference, for example, when shopping paths are obstructed.[8] This factor is generally not a problem in a free-flow

Figure 7-11

A free-flow layout.

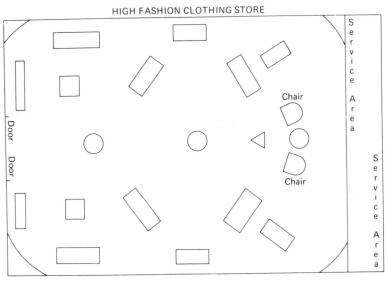

Figure 7-12

A free-flow layout.

(Courtesy of Filene's.)

layout. In other words, atmospherics once again are introduced. The physical layout of a store can and does create certain effects on buyers.

Not only is the placement of the fixtures (store furniture) important to a layout, but the fixtures themselves are important as well. Choice of fixtures is contingent on whether the store is self-service or store-service. Careful selection can result in the fixtures and the building "working together" for the desired effect. A hodgepodge effect can be the result if no thought is given to the layout when fixtures are purchased. This usually results in the purchase of too many fixtures and, consequently, means wasted dollars.

Merchandise Groupings

In developing a layout, where should the merchandise be placed? Several considerations are the following:

Generic. Place merchandise in terms of its common characteristics. The usual arrangement of produce, meat, frozen food, dairy, and dry goods in a supermarket is a generic layout.

Consumer Preference. Under this arrangement, layout should not be based on the physical differences of products or on shelf space or servicing requirements. The product group or cluster should be based on what the customer perceives it to be.[9] Ex-

Figure 7–13

All trend-setting fashion merchandise is gathered from all areas of the store and placed in the discovery shop for the benefit of the shopper.

(Courtesy of The Broadway.)

amples of this arrangement may be a gift department that has many physically different items such as cologne, playing cards, and candy; and a discovery shop that has unusual items from all over the store. The last is shown in Figure 7–13.

Target Market. Such a layout could result in the same item's being placed at several different places in the store. The most common example would be the high level of duplication of merchandise in a budget store and its "parent" store—many times located within the same building. For much of the merchandise, the only difference in the two locations is the price. Another example is sometimes found in a restaurant with two rooms. One room is nicer than the other. That room has higher prices. Each of the rooms serves a different market but with the same food.

Trade Practice. In many cases the layout is developed along the lines of layouts in use in similar stores, as that procedure provides a layout with which the customer will already be familiar. No effort is made to provide the store with any unique layout features under this plan.

Department Location

When the decision is made as to how to group the merchandise, the next consideration involves where to place each merchandise group within the layout. For an example of how one store places its departments, see Figure 7–14.

Value of Floor Space. One factor to examine is the value of the floor space. Using a 100 foot X 20 foot "gunbarrel" store as an example, the first 20 feet inside the front door may have up to five times more potential value to the store than the 20 feet at the back. Figure 7–15 illustrates this point. When the layout is designed, impulse items* as well as high-margin (high-profit) items should be placed near the front. On

* Impulse items are purchased without prior desire for a product. Most such items are considered inexpensive by the target market. An example is a college student who goes into a gift shop just to look around and comes out with what will be the hit of the next party—"a rubber chicken."

Figure 7-14

This layout provides maximum exposure for clothing and sportings goods. Main traffic aisles are shown by shaded lines. Map as shown is given to customers upon entering the store.

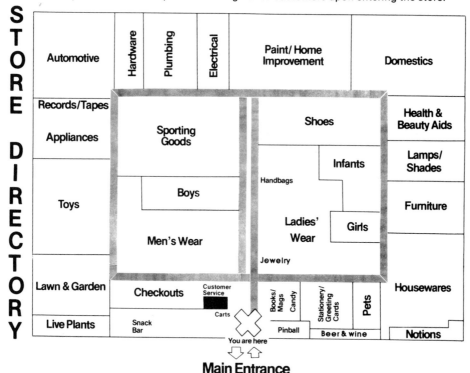

(Courtesy of Cook, United, Inc.)

the other hand, items that people seek out should be placed near the back to pull customer traffic in that direction.

    Sales Productivity.   In conjunction with the value of floor space, the sales productivity of each department should be considered. Estimated sales divided by the average amount of sales per square foot using trade data[10] for such a department will provide the figure. To include the value of floor space in the calculation simply involves determining the distance of the department from the store entrance. For the store mentioned earlier in the example, the department at the front should have up to five times more productivity per square foot than the department in the rear to be compared on an equal basis. The formula is presented on the following page.

Figure 7-15

Estimated percentage of potential customer exposure to merchandise.

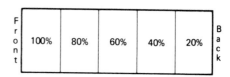

$$\text{Sales productivity} = \frac{\text{Estimated departmental sales}}{\text{Industry average sales per square foot in department} \times \text{floor value factor}}$$

$$\text{Floor value factor} = \frac{\text{Distance from entrance to back of store}}{\text{Distance from entrance to department}}$$

For the traditional productivity calculation, a floor factor of 1 can be used.

Adjustments in the calculations using a floor factor must be made for visual or other barriers that may alter a shopper's natural shopping procedure. It is also a problem when more than one door is in use. Two or more doors do not void the concept of the floor factor in conjunction with sales productivity. Calculations can be made for each door. Such figures do become quite subjective, however, when used in layout decisions.

Sales versus Nonsales Area. As the layout is developed, how much space should be allocated to activities other than direct selling effort? The tendency is to provide more space for nonselling activities on a percentage basis as the store becomes larger. Figures from the National Retail Merchants Association reflect this trend as shown for various sizes of specialty stores: [11]

Specialty Store with Sales of	Nonselling Space as a Percentage of Total Space	
	1974	1979
Under $1 million	19%	18%
$1 million to $5 million	24	24
Over $5 million	35	25

It is also significant that retailers are making an effort to reduce the amount of nonselling space in their stores. Although larger stores appear to be moving more aggressively in this direction, as shown in the NRMA data, it is felt that all stores will eventually follow this trend. Why? Less floor space for nonselling purposes is one way to make a store more productive with a given amount of space resources.

In developing the layout, care should be taken to develop a proper balance between selling and nonselling areas. Needless to say, when there is doubt, selling should outweigh nonselling activities. For definition purposes, the selling area includes the space occupied by selling departments, fitting rooms, forward stock areas, clerk aisles, and customer aisles between departments. Areas around vertical transportation and main traffic aisles are not considered part of the selling area. [12]

Fitting rooms, as a part of the selling area, should be designed so as to have only one entry and exit for the customer to use. This door should require the customer to reenter the sales floor—not go to the escalator, elevator, or exit. The room or rooms should also be placed where they can be supervised by the store personnel at all times while being convenient for the customer. Layout should not have the fitting rooms too private. No doors permitted—only curtains that are at least 18 inches off the floor. Rooms should also be completely separate from all storage areas. Careful placement of the fitting rooms in the layout will reduce many shoplifting problems for the store in the future. The retailer should also make an effort to make the fitting rooms attractive and part of the store. To prevent a possible accident, there should not be any exposed wiring or light bulbs. A nicely decorated room with adequate mirror and a place to sit down will eliminate the "outhouse" feeling that is given so often by fitting rooms.

Checkout positions must also be carefully placed in the store. The 100 foot x 20 foot store cited earlier must have a register position at or near the front of the store to ensure proper store security. In a larger store, register desks may fall within logical department areas. In a discount operation such as K mart, central cashiering may be used with spot registers in big-ticket and specialty departments. In developing a layout, adequate wiring and lighting must be provided at each possible register location.

In deciding on the number of registers or fitting rooms, waiting-line analysis can be conducted. This analysis requires the retailer to determine the estimated average length of time it takes to serve a customer and the estimated average length of time between customers coming up to the register, so as to ascertain the estimated waiting time for a customer to be served. [13] Although an oversimplification of waiting-line analysis is given here, this information can be useful in deciding on the number of registers. If customers have to wait too long, they may have an unsatisfactory learning experience as discussed in Chapter 3 and never shop again in that store. On the other hand, six registers unused 90 percent of the time is neither efficient nor practical.

Another layout consideration is the use of vertical transportation. Unless such transportation is provided, special thought should be given before going into a two-level operation. For many target groups, stairways are not adequate. The older customer, the young parents with a stroller, the pregnant woman, and lazy customers in general will not use stairs. If stair usage is necessary, they will go elsewhere. Elevators and escalators are now more common than ever before in retail stores of smaller sizes. Generally, elevators are for moving longer distances whereas escalators are better for the short haul. If room permits, the escalator is by far the best means of vertical transportation for most customers and retailers. It puts the customer up over the store so that he or she can see the whole area. Special displays and interior signing are many times designed for this customer (Figure 7–16).

The relatively new, glass-enclosed elevator can also achieve some of this effect if the physical setting is appropriate for such equipment. The greatest boon for the elevator has been the do-it-yourself model that has reduced the need for an operator. Such an invention may not have a silver lining. Many customers are afraid to ride in an automatic elevator by themselves. If elevators are used, they should be put to good use. Carpet samples and other displays may be put in the elevators. A store directory would also be helpful. Attractive but secure displays should greet the customer at every floor. As noted in the definition of selling area, the sales floor around the escalator or elevator is not thought to be very productive. Special care should be taken to make such areas of the store more profitable.

Restrooms and other customer facilities spell trouble for many retailers. In an effort to control shoplifting, some have placed restrooms outside the interior selling area

Figure 7-16

An escalator display.

(Courtesy of Sears, Roebuck and Co.)

so that customers will literally have to leave the store to use the facility. Water fountains, rest areas, and even eating facilities use up valuable selling space. Where should such items be put in a layout? Eating and rest areas are usually put in the "dead" areas of the store. Water fountains are placed near children's departments or walk areas frequently used by both customers and employees. The mother who takes Johnny to get that inevitable drink of water may see something to buy while at the drinking fountain. If she does not, Johnny will. Whether to have such nonmerchandise facilities in the layout is an important management decision. Once the decision is made in favor of these facilities, the task of selecting the best place for them must be undertaken. One last consideration is cleanliness of such facilities. A rest area with overflowing ash trays and a dirty floor is not inviting. A water fountain with chewing gum stuck in the drain says negative things to the customer. If the retailer is not going to keep *all* areas of the store clean, make this decision in the beginning so that the facilities can be removed from the layout.

Location of workrooms and storage areas should be studied carefully so as to promote the greatest efficiency among the employees. As noted in Leonard Konopa's article on work simplification in the *Journal of Retailing*, [14] careful placement of work areas can reduce the amount of time spent going to and from various tasks. Under such circumstances improved efficiency can result.

Mention has already been made of the importance of having the outside and inside of the store "work together" as a package. Many retailers in central business locations are redoing their store exteriors to conform to a master plan for the area. However, nothing is done to the interior. In that case, "beauty is only skin deep." Customers who are drawn to the attractive store are turned off when they go inside. Equally a problem is the interior remodeling that many people never see because they do not get by the terrible exterior.

The ideal approach is to carefully consider both the inside and outside appearance of the store (Figure 7–17).[15] Store design is like a motorcycle. If either tire is flat, it just will not go.

SUMMARY

Effective store design is essential to the success of a retail establishment. Without the proper exterior and interior for a given target market and merchandise mix, the store itself will be a hindrance to the retailer. As for the exterior of the store, signing and

Figure 7–17

Store design involves the consideration of both exterior and interior aspects of the store. A model sometimes helps to ensure that all the variables are coordinated for best effect.

(Courtesy of J. C. Penney Company)

choice of store name are vital. Decisions concerning the marquee, type of entrance, and display windows must be made. The image portrayed by the exterior should also be studied. As for the interior, atmospherics is the key. Proper use of the various senses can result in desirable surroundings for the customer. The extremes of grid and free flow in layout design and the infinite possibilities in between provide layout considerations for the retailer to examine. In addition, the questions of how to group merchandise (generic, consumer preference, target market, or trade practice) and how to locate departments (floor value, sales productivity, and sales versus nonsales) must be answered. In the nonsales areas, special care must be taken to keep such space (restrooms, workrooms, vertical transportation, etc.) at a minimum. Special effort should be made to insure that all the elements of interior and exterior design are coordinated. To be effective, the total store must have a well-thought-out and coordinated design.

DISCUSSION QUESTIONS

1. Which is more important—exterior design or interior design?
2. Give examples of good and bad store names. Explain the reasons for your choice.
3. Distinguish between the different choices for display windows. Which is better for a shopping-goods store? A convenience-goods store?
4. Define atmospherics. Give examples of its application to a retail situation.
5. How can a retailer use color for design purposes in a store?
6. Which is the better layout pattern—grid or free flow? Why?
7. Discuss various ways to group merchandise for layout purposes. Which method is the one you prefer? Why?
8. Using trade data for various retail departments, calculate sales productivity using floor value factors of three and one for a department with estimated sales of $100,000. How would a retailer use that information in developing a layout?
9. Where should fitting rooms and checkout areas be placed in a store? How many should the store have?
10. Vertical transportation is important to a store. What factors should be considered in choosing the means of moving customers from floor to floor?

NOTES

[1] For an in-depth discussion of store planning, see Charles S. Telchin and Seymour Helfant, *Planning Your Store for Maximum Sales and Profits* (New York: National Retail Merchants Association, 1969).

[2] William T. Snaith, "How Retailing Principles Affect Design," *Stores and Shopping Centers*, ed. James S. Hornbeck (New York: McGraw-Hill Book Company, 1962), p. 9.

[3] John L. Moore, "The Ruin, the Tilt and a Gaping Hole Are Luring Shoppers," *The Wall Street Journal*, Vol. 193, no. 40 (February 27, 1979), pp. 1, 20.

[4] Philip Kotler, "Atmospherics as a Marketing Tool," *Journal of Retailing*, Vol. 49, no. 4 (Winter 1973–1974), p. 50.

[5] For more discussion on atmospherics, see Bernard Wysocki, Jr., "Sight, Smell, Sound: They're All Arms in Retailer's Arsenal," *The Wall Street Journal*, Vol. 193, no. 75 (April 17, 1979), pp. 1, 35.

[6] Faber Birrens, *Color Psychology and Color Therapy* (New York: University Books, Inc., 1961), p. 143. Published by arrangement with Lyle Stuart.

[7] "Consumer Behavior in the Supermarket," *Progressive Grocer*, Vol. 54, no. 10 (October 1975), pp. 56–57.

[8] Gilbert D. Harrell and Michael D. Hutt, "Crowding in a Retail Store," *MSU Business Topics*, Vol. 24, no. 1 (Winter 1976), p. 36.

[9] Montrose S. Sommers and Jerome B. Kernan, "A Behavioral Approach to Planning, Layout, and Display," *Journal of Retailing*, Vol. 41, no. 4 (Winter 1965–1966), p. 26.

[10] Most trade publications include these data sometime during a publication year. For example, *The Discount Merchandiser* provides various sales-per-square-foot figures for various departments in a discount store in its "Annual Study on the State of the Discount Industry."

[11] *Financial and Operating Results of Department and Specialty Stores of 1974*, pp. 58, 62, 71; and *Financial and Operating Results of Department and Specialty Stores of 1979*, pp. 104, 108, 114 (New York: Financial Executives Division, National Retail Merchants Association, 1975, 1980).

[12] *Financial and Operating Results of Department and Specialty Stores of 1979* (New York: Financial Executive Division, National Retail Merchants Association, 1980), p. 11.

[13] For more information on waiting-line analysis, see Harold Bierman, Jr., Lawrence Fouraker, and Robert Jaedicke, *Quantitative Analysis for Business Decisions* (Homewood, Ill.: Richard D. Irwin, Inc., 1961), pp. 189–192.

[14] Leonard J. Konopa, "Are Work Simplification Systems Adaptable to Retailing?" *Journal of Retailing*, Vol. 38, no. 4 (Winter 1962–1963), pp. 45 ff.

[15] For more information on store planning, see *Stores*, March 1979, pp. 24–29; and March 1980, pp. 23–32.

CHAPTER 8

Store
Organization

FRANK & ERNEST

Reprinted by permission. © 1978 NEA, Inc.

Retailing was defined in Chapter 1 as the summation of all activities that result in the offering for sale of goods and/or services to individuals and/or organizations for purposes of ultimate consumption. In addition, a business firm whose predominant function is retailing was referred to as a retailer. For the retailer to be successful in fulfilling the task of performing the various activities called for in retailing, a good store organization is a necessary requirement.

The word "organization" has two distinct meanings, one of which refers to an organization as an entity in itself and the other of which refers to organization as a process. As an entity, an organization is defined as a group of people bound together in a formal relationship to achieve organizational goals. As a process, organization is concerned with structuring or arranging the parts of the organization, a meaning exemplified by the phrase, "What this place needs is more organization."[1] A retail store needs both a structure and a planned process for operating.

To develop a store organization effectively, the retail decision maker must have an understanding of management principles, formal organization structures, informal organization, and objectives, policies, and procedures, as well as retailing know-how. A well-thought-out, up-to-date management organization is just as important as a good location or store layout to retail success. Special effort should be made by the retailer to develop a good organization when starting the business. Equal care should also be taken to keep the organization up-to-date over time. Continuous evaluation of all aspects of an organization is essential to a well-managed retail operation.

MANAGEMENT PRINCIPLES

Developing a solid store organization requires, first of all, an understanding of management principles. It should be noted at this point that this book cannot, in the space allocated to this topic, attempt to cover the subject of management. Many good management principles texts[2] are available for this purpose. Five management principles are selected for discussion that are particularly applicable to retailing. Violation of these principles causes many problems in the retail store.

Principle of Unity of Command

Each subordinate should have only **one** *immediate superior.*

A retail employee serving more than one master cannot function properly. Confusion, low morale, and inefficiency result in such a situation. Remember when your father told you one thing to do and your mother told you something else. Both wanted it done *now*. How did you feel knowing that regardless of what you did you were going to be in trouble? The retail employee can feel the same way. He or she can be just as unhappy as you were in such a situation. The retail organization should develop relationships that are consistent with the principle of unity of command.

Principle of Span of Control

The number of subordinates reporting to an immediate superior should be in relation to the complexity of the task and the need for direct communication.

Various rules of thumb are found in the literature that quote different maximum spans, the most common maximum being in the range of 6 to 8 employees. The greatest problem with span of control in retailing is found in the owner-operated store that has grown over time so that 20 to 30 employees are still directly under the owner. Unless that person is quite exceptional, and most are not, that span of control can cause many unnecessary problems for the store as many important decisions will be made hastily or not made at all.

Principle of Authority and Responsibility

The subordinate who is assigned the responsibility for a task should also be given the necessary authority to perform the task.

A retail employee is given the assignment of improving the layout of the store. Was the employee also given the necessary authority to perform the task? If not, the employee cannot really be held accountable for the performance of that task.

Principle of Orderly Change

A managerial organization should promote an orderly change in positions as the company continues to change.

People get accustomed to an organization. As a firm grows, an organization structure that continues to have radical changes confuses employees and destroys morale. Orderly expansion reduces the problem through planned growth. As the store grows, the development of logical spin-offs will cause minimal problems. For example, the promotion department can have departments of advertising and public relations created under it, or the women's department could be divided into ready-to-wear, shoes, and intimate apparel. If, for some reason, the firm is reducing its organization, the idea of orderly change also holds true. In either case, the impact of the proposed change on the organization should be studied to determine if the effect of the change will have the desired result.

Principle of Specialization

When the size of the organization permits, reducing an employee's span of work will normally improve the quality of the decision making.

A retail fashion buyer who buys both men's and women's clothes cannot spend as much time on women's fashions as one who buys nothing else. A retail credit manager can study credit legislation to determine how it should affect the store. A person who is credit manager and advertising manager may not have the time to study the laws. A "jack of all trades—expert in none" and a buyer who deals only in "left-handed garden rakes" are the extremes of specialization. In developing the retail organization, realistic specialization should be the goal.

In developing the store organization, care should be taken to apply the various management concepts to ensure that the store will have a structurally sound management setup. To assist the retailer in this task, a visual presentation of the organization (organizational chart) should be developed that will show who is responsible for the various tasks in a company. By presenting the organization graphically, obvious problems can be corrected before any damage is done to the firm.

The organization structure should reflect the conditions under which the company operates. A prestige store will generally have more sales personnel per square-foot-of-selling-space than will a cut-rate bargain store. Such additional personnel may require additional levels of supervisory management in the organization structure. A multi-unit operation may require duplication of management positions in its various stores if it is spread out geographically. If all stores are located in the same town, that may not be the case. A store that does much advertising will require several positions in the organization to be committed to this task. On the other hand, a store that does little or no advertising has no need for a separate advertising department. For these and many other possible reasons, it is impossible for a retailer to effectively copy someone else's organization. Other store organizations should be studied to obtain ideas. Examining various organizational plans may bring to light something that might otherwise have been overlooked. It is the retailer's task to take these various ideas and mold them into an organization structure that will best serve the particular retail store's set of circumstances.

To assist the retailer in this decision-making process, several retail organization structures are given that should provide the starting framework for the development of a viable organization structure for a firm.

Small-Store Organization

The small store (up to approximately six to eight employees) is usually a very simple organization. All employees report to the store owner/manager on a one-to-one basis. Due to its size, employees generally have varied tasks. Very little specialization is possible. Regardless of other duties, all employees, including the owner, will usually work the sales floor. Much customer contact with management is possible under this organization structure. A typical organization for a clothing store, "The Clothes Tree," with five full-time employees would be as shown in Figure 8–1. Under each employee, the tasks assigned to that person should be listed. If the list for one employee is too long and for others too short, adjustments in work assignments should be made.

Intermediate-Store Organization

As the store cited in the earlier illustration continues to grow, by necessity, the organization must change. It is very difficult to put a number on how many employees make up a medium-sized store. Essentially such a store requires enough employees to necessitate two or more levels of supervisory management while not being large enough to permit large-scale specialization. A typical intermediate-store organization

Figure 8-1

Small-store organization.

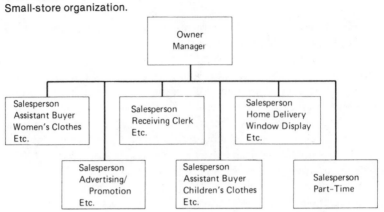

would be as seen in Figure 8-2. In such an organization, the owner/manager will generally retain under his or her direct control those functions in which he or she has the greatest interest—usually the merchandising function of the store. Personnel functions also are generally retained by the manager. Accounting and other operations that the retailer usually views as a necessary burden will be the first to emerge as a separate department under a retailer's plan of orderly change.

Large-Store Organization

Continuing prosperity of "The Clothes Tree" places additional burdens on the retail owner/manager. As the store reaches an employee level somewhere between 50 and 100 persons, additional organization changes are necessitated to relieve the owner/

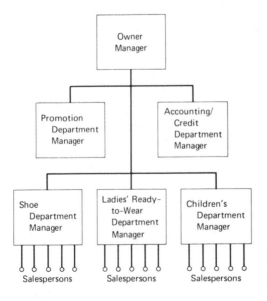

Figure 8-2

Intermediate-store organization.

Figure 8-3

Large-store organization.

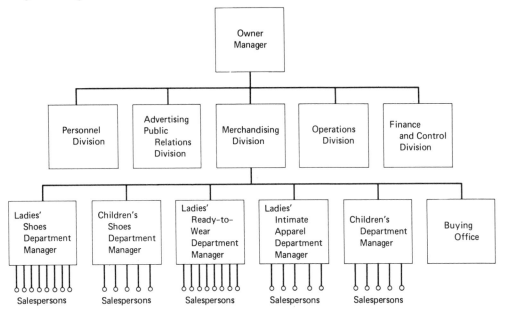

manager of much detail work. Such changes may be made earlier or later than the figures cited, depending on conditions. An organization structure for this size store could be as shown in Figure 8-3.

This organizational pattern has its origin in the Mazur Plan,[3] the result of a study conducted by Paul Mazur, an investment banker in the 1920s. The Mazur Four Functional Plan organized the store around four divisions: Merchandising, Publicity, Store Management (Operations), and Finance and Control. Later adaptations have taken personnel out of store management and have made it a separate division. This five-function organization structure is the basic ingredient in most large retail organizations today.

The organization plan that removes the owner/manager from the day-to-day operation of the merchandising function is a significant change in the organization. The so-called heart of the business is now, for the first time, under the direct supervision of someone other than the owner. Since it is such a major shift, many owners put it off too long with costly consequences for the retail store.

To better understand the five functional areas, each is discussed briefly concerning its makeup.

1. *Merchandising division.* The merchandising division is considered by many to be first among equals as compared with the other divisions in a store. In this division are found the buying functions, merchandising planning and control, and the general line management for the store—department managers, assistant managers, and sales personnel.

2. *Operations division.* Customer service, delivery, maintenance, receiving and mark-

ing of goods, and general housekeeping chores are commonly found in the operations division. Responsibility for general stockrooms and warehouses as well as store security is also given to this area of the organization.

3. *Advertising/public relations division.* The purpose of this division is to get the customer into the store so that the merchandising division can sell them the merchandise. Included in this area are all forms of advertising, interior, exterior, and window displays, and all types of sales promotion including everything from a fashion show to selecting the store Santa Claus. As for public relations, the division would handle all news releases and work for a favorable impression in the community.

4. *Finance and control division.* Accounting, credit management, and financial analysis are the responsibility of this division. Finance and control also serve as a check and balance on the remainder of the organization. Without its audit function, the retail store could not be as strong organizationally speaking as it should be.

5. *Personnel division.* Personnel deals with the hiring, training, and compensation of people employed by the store. Record keeping on each employee is also carried out by this division. Good employee morale is a goal of the personnel division.

Branch-Store Organization

At some stage in the development of "The Clothes Tree," a second store will be added to serve the market better. When this happens, another major organization change is in the making. When an organization begins to expand, the tendency is for the old store to assume a "motherhood" position. As noted in the organization chart (Figure 8–4), little autonomy is given the branch store.

Under this organizational structure, the branch manager is given the responsibility for the operation and selling functions of the store. All merchandising decisions are kept at the main unit. The *main* store does all the buying, makes the decisions concerning promotion and finance, and is responsible for all inventory decisions for the branch operation. Department managers from the main store will visit the branch operation to supervise its operations. Under this arrangement, the branch store is truly a satellite of the main store.

Multi-Unit Organization

As growth continues through the addition of more branches, the relative importance of branch operations as compared with that of the *main* store continues to increase. Through an evolutionary process, the "parent" store and the branch stores become equal. There is no longer a main store. From an organizational standpoint the management structure would be similar to the multi-unit structure presented in Figure 8–5. The central organization (personnel, finance, etc.) would serve all stores equally.

A rule of thumb is that if the organization has six branches it should shift to a multi-unit structure. A better approach is to consider factors such as size of the stores, management capability, and geographic dispersion in deciding when to go to a multi-unit type organization.

In the organization structures shown in this chapter, buying and selling were presented as moving apart from each other as the retail organization increased in size. Such a trend is found to be typical among retail stores. The basic organizational ques-

Figure 8-4

Branch-store organization.

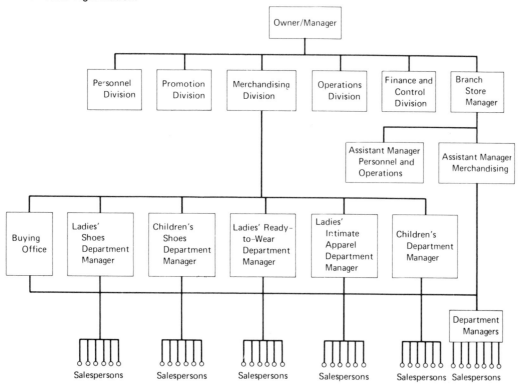

tion about this point is which is better—specialization or accountability? To put buying by itself under merchandising permits a high level of expertise to develop within the buying function. At the same time, however, this person may become too far removed from the customer. This disadvantage of separate buying and selling illustrates the advantage of having both done by the same individual. The seller does have customer contact. Another factor in favor of having the two together is accountability. The person who buys an item must also sell the item. If successful, all are aware of the responsible person who made it happen. If not successful, the same is also true. Which is best for a particular retail organization is an individual management decision. Specialization and accountability in buying are both important. The choice is a difficult managerial decision.

Another point of discussion about the organization structures as presented is that the organizations, as they grow, become structured along three lines: functions, products, and geography. The functions (personnel, finance, promotion, etc.) emerge in the earliest stages of development. The same is true for product areas. In even the smallest store presented, a distinction between women's and children's clothes was made. When branch operations began, geography entered as a decision variable. If the hypothetical organization, "The Clothes Tree," grows into a 500-unit chain, the basic organizational components of functions, products, and geography will remain the

Figure 8-5

Multi-unit organization.

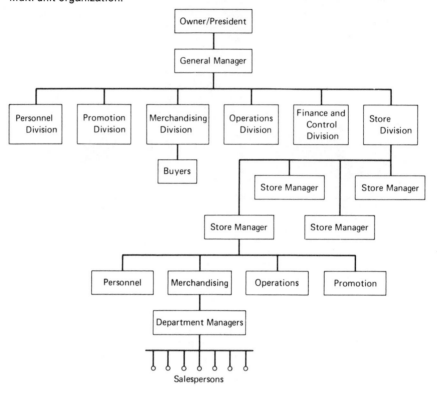

same. More supervisory levels will evolve as the geographic divisions of the company are set up. Functions at the central management level will become more specialized. Interest in more defined product categories will probably also be found. The *basic* management structure will not, however, undergo much change as the organization goes from a 20-store operation to a 500-store chain.

INFORMAL ORGANIZATION

The retailer must not only be concerned with the development of the formal organization structure over time: equally important is the informal organization. Informal organization is defined as a network of informal personal and social relations that exist in any organization.[4] Such relationships *will* develop. It is the task of the retailer to understand these relationships and to use them to the store's advantage.

If an employee has been with the store a long time, certain status has developed with that position. New employees will look up to this person. They will seek his or her advice. If management makes a major change in store policies or procedures, it may be wise to consult this long-time employee for two reasons. First, the employee may have good ideas about the proposed change. Second, the "informal leader" will be in on the decision, thereby making it more readily acceptable to the other employees.

The role of status in the informal organization should not be overlooked. Many insignificant things take on great importance in an informal organization. Which employees get the larger lockers in an employee lounge? Who gets to eat lunch every day from 12 to 1? Who has to wear a name tag and who does not? Who wears a yellow coat versus a blue coat? Who floats from department to department versus those who sell in only one area? These and many other status elements are found in the store every day. Removing such status will cause a drop in employee morale and almost always a decline in employee productivity. On the other hand, the proper application of status through a program of employee recognition for outstanding achievement, as well as appreciation by management of the subtle symbols of status, can provide the store with highly motivated employees.

The communication channel of the informal organization is the grapevine. On this wavelength will flow much information from "informed sources" ranging from the manager's secretary in the large organization to the person who had lunch with "the boss" in the small operation. Some employees are more inclined to "talk" than are others. Management can disseminate much information quickly to all employees by letting these particular employees know of some event in a subtle manner. Also, by tuning in to the grapevine, management can learn of the concerns of its employees. Will employees have to work on Christmas Eve night? Have vacation rotations been determined? Who will be the new ladies' department buyer? Will the manager's son "work" again this summer in the store? These and other questions reflect the concerns and desires of employees in a situation of uncertainty. With good communication through both formal and informal means, much of this uncertainty can be eliminated.

OBJECTIVES, POLICIES, AND PROCEDURES

For a firm to be effectively organized, the people in the organization must have guidelines to follow in order for their activities to be coordinated. To achieve this goal, each employee needs to have a clear understanding of the firm's objectives, policies, and procedures. If such is not the case, the informal organization may determine its own set of objectives, policies, and procedures which will not necessarily be the same as those desired by management.

An objective is defined as something toward which effort is directed, an aim, a goal.[5] Goals will differ with different stores. Although all stores should have a general objective to serve a target market, the prestige store will attempt to sell to the higher demographic group, whereas the cut-rate store will promote itself to the lower end of the demographic continuum. In each case, the particular store has a clearly defined measure of performance within the broad objective of defining the target market.

A policy is a guide to thinking, whereas a procedure is a guide to action. Policies and procedures are what implement the objectives of the firm as far as the store organization is concerned. Such policies and procedures are also a major tool for coordination of activities in the larger multi-store organization. To illustrate the relationship among objectives, policies, and procedures, a store may have an objective to sell a product of desired quality to the customer. A policy enacted to meet this objective may be "customers should be questioned as to what they desire in terms of product quality." The procedure decided upon to obtain this information could be a questionnaire to be returned when the customer pays his or her bill. Another example would be a policy dealing with credit that may state that only good credit risks will be accepted. The credit procedure will spell out how a good credit risk is determined. The policy and the procedure will be helpful in meeting the objective of a sound retail credit organization.

It is important to stress that the retailer should put all objectives, policies, and procedures of the store in writing. This can be a planning aid as well as a device to encourage everyone in the organization to know just what the objectives, policies, and procedures are for the store. In the small store, in particular, with little or no formal training program, employees have a hard time finding out the procedures under which they operate. If the retailer will write down the firm's objectives, policies, and procedures, everyone will know or should know what is expected of them from the first day.

By writing down the goals, policies, and procedures, coordination is also enhanced. A careful examination of the policies of the store may reveal that particular policies are in conflict with each other. In other words, there may be two guides for thinking that are focusing attention in opposing directions. The time to find this out is before a store is opened, or if the store is operating, to discover the problem as soon as possible and resolve it. The same is true for objectives and, even more so, with procedures. Organizational conflicts can be minimized if each objective, policy, and procedure is structured carefully in terms of its individual contribution to the firm as well as in terms of how it fits in with all other objectives, policies, and procedures.

SUMMARY

The organization is the framework in which the store operates to serve its target market. To develop a sound organization requires a good understanding of management principles. The development of a formal organization structure that will serve the needs of the present store, while providing for orderly change over time, is also essential. A knowledge of informal relationships, status, and the grapevine can be of great assistance to the retail manager in developing a workable store organization. Finally, objectives (goals), policies (guides to thinking), and procedures (guides to action) provide the means of coordinating the various parts of the organization for the good of the store. A sound store organization combined with good retailing know-how is a good formula for retail success.

DISCUSSION QUESTIONS

1. What is meant by the term organization?
2. Why is a knowledge of management principles important to a retail store operator?
3. Discuss various management principles that may be applicable to a retail situation.

4. Discuss how an organization might evolve over time from an organizational viewpoint. Use organization charts to illustrate the store's development.
5. How does a formal organization structure differ from an informal structure?
6. What is meant by the term status? "grapevine"? Are these two concepts interrelated? How are these concepts applied to the retail situation?
7. A store objective, store policy, and store procedure are all terms that describe the same thing. Comment on this statement.
8. Go to two retail stores in your area and examine their organizational structures. Attempt to ascertain from each retailer why the organization is set up as it is.

NOTES

[1] Henry L. Sisk and J. Clifton Williams, *Management & Organization*, 4th ed. (Cincinnati, Ohio: South-Western Publishing Company, 1981), p. 153.

[2] Among the many possible sources are Harold Koontz, Cyril O'Donnell, and Heinz Weihrich, *Management*, 7th ed. (New York: McGraw-Hill Book Company, 1980), and Stephen P. Robbins, *The Administrative Process*, 2nd ed. (Englewood Cliffs, N.J.: Prentice-Hall, Inc., 1980).

[3] Paul M. Mazur, *Principles of Organization Applied to Modern Retailing* (New York: Harper & Row, Publishers, 1927).

[4] Dale S. Beach, *Personnel: The Management of People at Work*, 3rd ed. (New York: Macmillan Publishing Co., Inc., 1975), p. 483.

[5] By permission. From *Webster's New Collegiate Dictionary* © 1980 by G. & C. Merriam Co., Publishers of the Merriam-Webster Dictionaries.

Planning for Opening Day

WINTHROP

Reprinted by permission. © *1979 NEA, Inc.*

While riding around one Saturday afternoon, you find that a new gift shop has appeared on the corner of Fifth Avenue and Elm Street. When someone asks you if you have been to the new discount store on the southside, your answer is "What store?" These and similar incidents illustrate the fact that many stores just appear and begin selling merchandise. No effort has been made to tell the public that the store is on the way. No effort has been made to build public interest in the new store. No effort has been made to obtain the various kinds of free publicity available to a new business. In other words, no effort has been made to plan for opening day.

In preparing for opening day, the retailer should actually build a plan around several key events: initial announcement, groundbreaking, construction, grand opening, and after grand opening. To aid in getting the appropriate message to the public during these various stages, a press kit should be developed for distribution to all news media and other appropriate individuals. Since the kit would be distributed at the initial announcement, its development will be the first topic for discussion (Figure 9-1). A word of caution is given to the reader. Some of these suggestions may not be appropriate for a given store. Store image, target market, and local conditions should all be considered along with the information presented in this chapter when planning for opening day.

PRESS KIT

For the retailer, the press kit can be either simple or elaborate. For definition purposes, the kit is a collection of facts and figures, photographs, and other information that will make the task of telling about the store a very easy one. Free publicity is the purpose of the kit. Any "news story" that results from the kit can be viewed as free advertising while having the added credibility of a news item.

Items for the press kit would include the following:

Written news articles. Articles on every phase of the project as well as background articles about the company and its management should be written so that the media will only have to use the items, not write them. The article in Figure 9-2, for example, is one that gives general background informa-

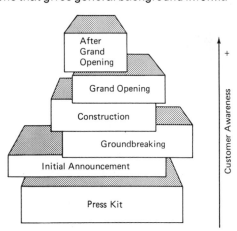

Figure 9-1

Building blocks for a successful store opening plan.

Figure 9-2

Background article prepared for news media.

Orange Julius.

Orange Julius Of America 3219 Wilshire Boulevard Santa Monica, California 90403 213/829 7611	Dateline. January 21, 1980

For immediate release

For further information contact:
Renee M. Sherr - Director/Public Relations

    ORANGE JULIUS: FROM CORNER STAND
           TO INTERNATIONAL FOOD CHAIN

There was little indication back in 1926 that the corner
soda fountain-like stand in downtown Los Angeles would
become anything more than that. Little indication
except for its unique offering: a fresh juice drink
called Orange Julius.

Quite a few things have changed since those humble, soda
jerk beginnings. Orange Julius International, Inc. is
now a major franchise food service corporation which, by
the end of 1980, will operate 620 units spanning four
continents. Since 1926, a carefully planned program of
expansion has been taking place, each year witnessing a
greater push towards upgrading and refining store
operations.

The Orange Julius drink -- a blend of fresh orange juice
ice and "secret" pure food ingredients -- is the corner-
stone of the company's success and the reason for its
new growth.

Orange Julius of America was purchased in 1967 by International Industries, Inc. In 1975, it was sold to 44 franchise owners at a cost of $4.2 million. The new owner-
ship group organized an investment company named Orange
Julius International, Inc., a private owned corporation
and holding company. Since 1975, the corporation's total
sales volume is now more than $85 million annually.

                                              (MORE)

news release

(Courtesy of Orange Julius of America.)

tion about the retailer. This type of release can be used on a continuing basis by an organization with numerous openings during the year. Articles may also be written for specific stores. One article might read as follows: "It was announced today that the 'Big D' Discount Store chain will open a store in Summerville. Mr. Dan Driggers, president of 'Big D,' stated that the new unit, which is to be located on South Main, will offer the finest selection of merchandise to be found in the area. He went on to say that . . .". By writing the article for use by the media, there is a good chance that the article will appear as written

The company is organized into five separate entities:
Orange Julius International, Inc., the parent holding
company; Orange Julius of America, handling corporate
franchising and operations; Orange Julius Canada Ltd.,
overseeing all Canadian franchising operations; Orange
Julius Proprietary Ltd., managing Australian and foreign
operations; and Julius Food Corporation, a sourcing and
distribution unit.

In 1977 Orange Julius began redesigning its stores and
expanding its menu in keeping with the company philosophy
of "giving the customer more than he expects for his
money." Orange Julius stores, primarily located in
shopping centers, enclosed malls and downtown locations,
needed a design which would be visually pleasing to
customers as well as functional. A vibrant new store
decor, emphasizing shades of yellow and orange and
featuring the use of natural wood paneling and promotional displays, was developed for existing and new
franchise stores. Along with the famous Orange Julius
drink and its successor Julius drinks in strawberry,
peach, pineapple and banana flavors, the Orange Julius
system added hot dogs, corndogs, hamburgers, fish
sandwiches and french fries to their menus.

The management of Orange Julius, responsible for the
revitalization that has included store redesign and menu
expansion, is dedicated to the standardization of
operating procedures and the maintenance of quality
control for store locations throughout the world. In
an effort to provide the customer with the best possible
service and beverage/food quality at the most reasonable
price possible, management continues to develop programs
and systems designed to meet consumer demands and gain
the competitive edge.

Orange Julius International, Inc. headquarters are located
in Santa Monica, Calif. with operational offices located
in Lakewood, Colorado; Pennsauken, N.J., Santa Monica,
Calif.; Vancouver, Canada; and Sydney, Australia. A new
regional office is scheduled to open in Indianapolis, Ind.

# # # #

by the retailer. If it does not appear exactly as written, there is still a better
chance that the facts included in the prepared article will be given.

Photographs. "A picture is worth a thousand words." This cliché illustrates picture power. A photograph of the architect's drawing of the store's exterior
and/or interior will be of interest (Figure 9-3). Stock photographs of various
lines to be carried by the store along with pictures of the people involved in the
project are also of value to the press kit. Always provide a choice of pictures. A
variety of pictures tends to promote the use of several of them. If the media
can choose a picture to be used rather than have the feeling they were told
which picture to run, more pictures will be used.

Fact sheet. As its name implies, a fact sheet is a presentation in outline form
of all the pertinent facts about the project. Items that may be included are:

1. Name of store
2. Location

Figure 9-3

An architects drawing of a new shopping mall or store can be used to create interest even before construction has begun.

(Courtesy of Homart Development Company, a division of Sears, Roebuck and Co.)

3. Date of planned opening
4. Size of store
5. Unusual features of the store
6. Name of architect
7. Name of construction company
8. Type of store
9. Lines to be carried
10. Background of principal owners
11. Other appropriate items that the retailer feels will generate interest

The purpose of the fact sheet is to present the store data to media representatives in a compact format so they can write their own stories if they wish to do so. By providing the facts in written form rather than just verbally, the probability of such facts being used is increased. The probability of the facts being correct is greatly increased since the danger of misrepresentation of information is minimized (Figure 9-4).

The means of presenting the information in the press kit to appropriate individuals will vary depending on the size of the project and the financial capability of the developer. A very elaborate four-color brochure may be used to introduce the data. At the other extreme, the typed news stories and other pertinent material simply may be contained in an envelope. Although the method of presentation in the kit is important, the most significant measure of success for the press kit will be how easy it makes the job of telling about the store. For the busy media representative, easy news material results in news copy. A good press kit provides this easy news material.

Figure 9-4

Fact sheet for Orange Julius.

January 21, 1980

ORANGE JULIUS FACT SHEET

DESCRIPTION OF CORPORATION	Privately held, major international franchise food service corporation
DESCRIPTION OF BUSINESS OPERATION	Retail, quick service beverage and food take-away industry
PHILOSOPHY	"Give the customer more than he expects for his money"
DATE FOUNDED AND LOCATION	1926; Los Angeles, California
SHORT HISTORICAL BACKGROUND	Purchased in 1967 by International Industries, Inc. Sold in 1975 to 44 franchisee owners who formed Orange Julius International, Inc., the parent holding company Major program of expansion and improvement begun in 1979
PRIMARY PRODUCT	Orange Julius drink; a blend of fresh orange juice, ice and "secret pure food ingredients
SECONDARY PRODUCTS	Strawberry, peach, pineapple, banana Julius drinks, hot dogs, corndogs, fish sandwiches, hamburgers, french fries
LOCATION OF STORE UNITS	Dense walk-by traffic areas: shopping centers, enclosed malls
NUMBER OF STORE UNITS PROJECTED FOR END OF 1980	620
CORPORATE STRUCTURE	Orange Julius International, Inc. Orange Julius of America Orange Julius Canada Ltd. Orange Julius Proprietary, Ltd. Julius Foods, Inc.
CHAIRMAN, CHIEF EXECUTIVE OFFICER/ PRESIDENT	William E. Mapes
DIRECTOR/PUBLIC RELATIONS	Renee M. Sherr
LOCATION OF CORPORATE HEADQUARTERS	Orange Julius International, Inc. 3219 Wilshire Boulevard Santa Monica, California 90403

(Courtesy of Orange Julius of America.)

After the initial press kit has been provided, the retailer needs to remember to furnish updated information continually as the store progresses.

INITIAL ANNOUNCEMENT

When the decision is made to open a new store, planning should begin for opening day. Just as store location, store design, store organization, and financial planning are crucial to the new store, so is the initial success of the store in attracting customers.

Work on customer awareness should begin as soon as possible. The first opportunity to talk about the new store is the initial announcement. The retailer should not forgo this chance to begin building customer awareness at this earliest date.

To have a successful initial announcement, the retailer should examine the situation to see how attention can be focused on the new store. For the large store, a press conference is a good device. If free lunch is provided, attendance by the news media at the press conference will be encouraged. For the smaller store, a press conference will work if the media people will come. In large cities, attendance will be a problem. A better approach may be to use a captive audience. Have the initial announcement at the Chamber of Commerce Board of Directors meeting or at a Merchants Association meeting. Choose a place where the media people will already be in attendance.

Regardless of how the audience is obtained, the initial announcement should be made dramatically. An architect's drawing of the store should be unveiled at the appropriate point. The presence of representatives of potential suppliers and company officials will lend importance to the announcement as well as add to the crowd. A local beauty queen to stand by the architect's plans will promote interest. As mentioned earlier, the distribution of the press kit should also be done at this time. If handled well, the initial announcement can get the store started off in the right direction.

GROUNDBREAKING

The groundbreaking for the new store can be developed into a publicity-oriented event. Whether the proposed location of the store is in a vacant lot or in the middle of a shopping mall, a "groundbreaking ceremony" should be held. Invite elected officials to participate. Invite a high school band to play. If it is a children shop, invite a grammar school rhythm band or singing group to participate. This will make the mothers aware of the new shop. A color guard made up of Scouts is always a crowd pleaser. Invite potential customers to the ceremony. Work to ensure a crowd. It is good psychology.

For the ceremony, use a public address system. This will allow those attending the ceremony and those not in attendance to hear the event. Always break up the ground ahead of time so the earth is easy to shovel. The retailer does not wish for "Miss Springtime," or the mayor, or whoever is doing the honors to not be able to break through the hard ground. If such is the case, the groundbreaking ceremony becomes a joke. The shovel or shovels to be used should have a fresh and clean appearance. If funds are no problem, a chrome-plated or gold-plated shovel adds class to the event. If the ceremony is held inside, such as in a shopping mall, a box of dirt can be used. The box containing the dirt should be deep enough to permit a healthy shovelful for the benefit of the cameras and large enough to allow the person to stand on the dirt when shoveling. To top off the event, "gold" letter openers in the shape of a shovel, or other items imprinted with the store name, should be passed out to the crowd as souvenirs.

To ensure publicity for this event, the media should be invited. The retailer should have his or her own camera on the scene to take pictures in case the media do not show up at all. Pictures and other pertinent data about the event should be provided for addition to the press kit. Such pictures may also be used by the retailer in advertisements promoting the new store. As stated before, make it easy for the news media. A little effort in this direction should result in better news coverage of this most important event.

CONSTRUCTION

The new store that is under construction can be a point of interest for the customers. Even an existing building can be given the appearance of construction that will attract the attention of the potential market. To begin with, a sign should be placed in front of the job site telling about the new store. If the project involves major construction, an architect's drawing of how the store will look might be included on the sign. The sign has two functions: to attract attention and to tell about the store. Such a sign may serve as the focal point for the groundbreaking ceremony or may be constructed later as the situation warrants.

The customer who is attracted to the site can be given an opportunity to get involved with the new store. A table or booth might be set up out front where customers could apply for a charge account with the new store. Another idea is to let these potential customers suggest names for certain departments in the store. The winning name or names would be announced with appropriate fanfare as the opening day approached. Special coupons may also be given out to these passers-by for purchase of items at reduced prices during grand-opening week.

The period of construction or renovation is a critical time as far as news media coverage is concerned. The new store should continue to provide news copy in final form for use by the media. The retailer should provide copy about store personnel assignments such as department managers. The public is interested in who will be moving to town as well as the local people who will hold positions of responsibility. Another news release might contain information such as "Summerville's new 'Big D' Discount Store disclosed today that it will carry the complete line of Buster Brown children's wear. Mrs. Mary Livingston, Department Manager for children's wear, indicated she was pleased to be associated . . .". Such news copy will usually be run if it is written and presented in a concise manner. A slow news day can result in several of these announcement/news stories being used. Provide the media with long and short articles. As stated earlier, more "news stories" will generally result if the retailer gives the media a choice of articles and pictures to use.

GRAND OPENING

Opening day is a special day in the life of a store. If a store remains in business for 200 years, it can only have one grand-opening day. So this important event should be handled with care. All activities up to this point have been designed to build customer interest in the new store. Customer awareness that the new store is coming is the main objective of the opening-day plan up to the grand-opening stage. At this point, the task is to turn awareness into desire in the several weeks prior to opening. On opening day, the objective is to turn customer desire into action—come to the grand opening.

In the several weeks (two to four weeks) prior to grand opening, a step-up plan of action is developed that will culminate with the arrival of opening day. During this time, advertisements are run starting with teaser copy that will begin to zero in on the date of the grand opening. Examples of teaser copy for the "Big D" Discount Store are shown in Figure 9-5.

If the store has display windows, they should be covered over with paper during this period before the opening day. The opening-day date should be put on the paper so that the windows might read in six-foot letters, "Grand Opening—September 12—Don't Miss It!" Covering over the windows will create customer curiosity. The same impact is seen in new car retailing. A car for the new model year can sit on the lot several weeks in August and attract little interest. Cover the car with a tarpaulin so no one can see anything but its shape, and see what happens. People will make a special effort to stop and take a look. For the store, the same is true. Leave the windows uncovered and few will bother to look in. Cover them up and people will go out of their way to try to see in the store.

In the week preceding the opening date, the development of interest in the grand opening should reach its climax. For example, advertisements to the effect that the ribbon cutting will be held at 10 A.M. on Thursday, September 12, should be run. Promotional items should be selected that will draw a crowd to the event. Some big-ticket items should be literally given away on a first-come basis. For example, an advertisement for the "Big D" Discount Store might read, "RCA Color Console, Retail Value—Over $500, One Set At This Price, $1.00." Several items of this nature spread throughout the store will guarantee a crowd for the opening. In fact, it is possible that such a promotion will begin to attract a crowd several days before the big event. People may show up with sleeping bags to get a good position. The chances of this happening are great in a college town. Fraternity pledges are usually found to be well qualified for staying up all night so that the TV set can be obtained for the fraternity house. People who come early are, naturally, newsworthy items. Broadcast media may conduct on-the-scene interviews of this human interest story. Newspapers will generally run a picture of the customers waiting outside. The retailer should take a picture and provide it to the news media for their use in case they do not make it to the scene. Using the picture in an advertisement on the morning of the big event also has possibilities.

Figure 9-5

Examples of teaser advertising copy.

?	?	!
"D"	What's	Sept. 12
Day	Happening	is
Are You Ready	Sept. 12	"D"
		Day
(a)	(b)	(c)

Another way in which to create interest in the new store is to hold a cocktail party and reception at the store within several days of the grand opening for a selected group of public officials, members of the target market, and members of the press. For a new mall, such a party may include 5,000 guests with a 500 foot-long bar in the center of the mall area. For a small dress shop, 50 guests and an 8-foot bar can be set up for the evening. The purpose of the party is twofold: first, a "thank you" to those who aided in putting the store together and, second, an opportunity to let a selected group see what the store will be like so the word will get around about "how great the new store is." Once again, the party can generate "newsworthy" comments. The mayor might say for the media, "I have seen the inside of the new 'Big D' Discount Store. Needless to say, I am impressed. It will make a great addition to . . .". Taped interviews at the party will usually result in favorable comments about the store.

During the night before the big day, the paper will come off the windows to reveal the new store. Flags and pennants will go up in the parking lot. The public address system will be installed. Crowd-control barriers may also be installed during this time. Last but not least, the ribbon will be placed across the door.

The grand-opening day arrives for the retailer. For the ceremony, the retailer wants a good crowd. To have a crowd is not an accident. The TV set for $1.00 will attract a certain percentage of people. Invite a band to play. Invite a grammar school chorus to sing. The singing group will draw one mother and several relatives per child to the event. Have the winners of the contest(s) that were run appear at the ceremony. Invite the mayor and other officials to take part. Select a person to cut the ribbon who will attract interest. A sports hero or movie celebrity might be available for such purposes for less than the retailer might think, particularly if the celebrity is under a promotion contract with one of the retailer's suppliers. Beauty queens are also good traffic builders. A remote broadcast by one or more radio stations in the area that serve the target market will attract customers to the scene on the morning of the event.

As the time for the ceremony draws near, news media should be admitted to the store to position themselves to witness the "mad dash for values." Any ground rules for acquiring the super bargains should be handed out to the crowd and explained over the public address system. Other bargains may be announced to the assembled group from time to time with the band playing in between.

The ceremony should start on time. Do not keep the crowd waiting. Use a master of ceremonies who will keep the festivities moving to a quick conclusion. An invocation, introduction of special guests (six at the most), a welcome by the mayor, and the ribbon cutting (Figure 9–6) is all that is needed. Keep it short so customers can spend more time in the store.

When the ribbon is cut, a slight delay in opening the door is necessary to move the program participants out of the way of the door. When this is done, a bell set up for this purpose can be rung that will officially ring into business the new store. When the bell rings, the mad dash is on. If the store is full of customers shortly after opening, planning for opening day has been a success.

News coverage of such an event would normally consist of just saying that the new store opened on Main Street. On the other hand, if a large crowd is present, pictures of this crowd may be used by the media. The customer who bought the TV set for $1.00 may also be interviewed by the press after showing the crowd running into the

Figure 9-6

A ribbon-cutting ceremony can get the new store off to a good start.

(Courtesy of F. W. Woolworth Co.)

store for the bargains. Other potential customers who see such news reports may wish to come see for themselves. Pictures of the grand opening may also be used in store advertisements to help create interest in the new retail organization.

If the grand-opening celebration is designed to run for more than one day, effort should be made to maintain the momentum of the grand-opening ceremony. Prizes should be given out each day. One shopping mall gave away high-quality used cars each day during the week-long festivities. At the end of the period, all names were put in the hat and the winner of a new car was selected. By having a new contest each day, customers were encouraged to return each day, thereby adding to the crowd and the sales volume.

AFTER THE GRAND OPENING

For many stores, the grand opening creates great momentum. The successful store does not lose this momentum. Unfortunately, for others this momentum is lost. Just as the grand opening was planned with great care, a continuous plan of action should be developed to keep the store name before the public. *Planning is continuous.* Even before the store opens, the promotion plan for the time beyond the grand opening should be formulated and made ready for implementation. To not plan for the post-grand-opening period is poor retail management.

SUMMARY

Proper planning for opening day should provide the store with a good foundation for future success. To take advantage of the free publicity possibilities available to a new store, a press kit consisting of news stories, photographs, and fact sheets should be compiled for distribution to the news media and other appropriate individuals. Initial plans for the store should be announced with appropriate fanfare. A groundbreaking ceremony should also be held. For both events, efforts should be made to create a crowd by selecting a good place and by inviting groups such as politicians, bands, and the target market. During construction, interest in the store can be created by contests, distribution of coupons good for use during the grand opening, and other means. Interest in the grand opening itself can be achieved through the use of teaser advertising, paper over the store windows, product give-aways, and various social events held at the new store. The new store that has a good turn out for the grand-opening ceremony, and is full of customers shortly thereafter, has a good start. To maintain this momentum, planning for the after-grand-opening period is required even before the store is opened.

DISCUSSION QUESTIONS

1. Why should a store go to the trouble to plan for opening day in the context of this chapter?
2. What is a press kit? What is usually found in such a kit? What is its purpose from a retailing standpoint?
3. Discuss the key events around which the retailer will develop the opening day plan.
4. What might a retailer do to have a good groundbreaking ceremony? What is the reason for having such a ceremony?
5. As the day of the grand opening approaches, what might be done to create interest in the store and its grand opening?
6. Why is after-grand-opening planning mentioned in a discussion on planning for opening day?
7. For a store in your community, develop an opening-day plan. Develop a press kit including news articles and fact sheets on the store. How would the key elements (initial announcement, groundbreaking, construction, grand opening, and after grand opening) be handled for the store?
8. List the stores in your area that have opened in the last six months. Did these stores have a planned opening? Why or why not? In developing your answer, talk to the retailers, the media, and the customers of the stores in question.

SECTION

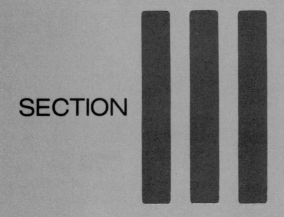

Merchandising

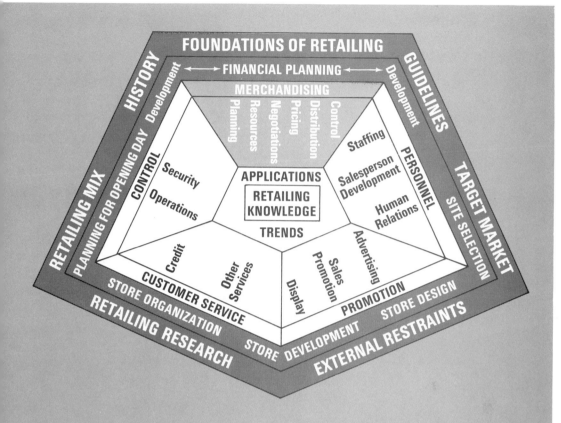

Merchandising encompasses the areas of merchandise planning, merchandise resources, negotiating for merchandise, pricing of merchandise, merchandise distribution, and merchandise control.

"Merchandise Planning" includes methods of estimating demand, determining the merchandise budget, and developing a model stock.

"Merchandise Resources" examines various potential sources of supply and how to select such resources.

"Negotiating for Merchandise" encompasses the various points that should be considered in dealing with suppliers.

"Pricing of Merchandise" studies the factors that influence price, the mathematics of pricing, and the causes of markdowns.

"Merchandise Distribution" involves the study of external traffic management, receiving, marking, and internal traffic management.

"Merchandise Control" covers the areas of inventory turnover, dollar control, and unit control.

CHAPTER 10

Merchandise Planning

"Whattya mean, do I have a different style?
They're the first shoes ever invented."

"Goods well bought are half sold." Such a statement denotes that the firm understands and has available the goods and services that its customers want and are willing to buy.[1] To buy goods well requires sound merchandise planning. Merchandise planning is a process that involves estimating demand, determining the merchandise budget, and developing a model stock so that the retailer will make the correct buying decision.*

ESTIMATING DEMAND

Estimating demand for a product is not an easy task, but forecasting is essential if the right merchandise in the right amount is to be purchased at the right time. Before attempting to estimate demand by various means, the retailer should be aware of the target market to be served and should have knowledge of both the product life cycle and the fashion cycle.

Target Market

The target market, as discussed in Chapter 2, is defined as those customers for whom the store will place primary emphasis in developing its marketing program. Age, income, education, occupation, race, religion, national origin, place of residence, marital status, sex, life-style, consumption patterns, and reasons for purchase are all variables that influence the needs and desires of the target market. These variables, in turn, determine the products and services that the customer will buy.

Product Life Cycle

The product life cycle may also affect the retailer's buying decision concerning a product or service.[2] Basically, the product life cycle is a marketing model that illustrates the selling duration of a product or service (Figure 10–1). The first stage in the life cycle is the introduction. In this stage, for example, the retailer will promote heavily to obtain customer acceptance of the new idea. No profit is expected. All expenditures are viewed as an investment in the future of the product.

The second stage in the product cycle is the market growth stage. In this stage, the retail innovator will make more profit than will be made at any future time since the item is now becoming popular and few substitutes, if any, are available. In the latter stages of market growth, similar stores and/or products will begin to enter the market. What was the new boutique on the block will now begin to experience competition.

This competition leads to the market maturity stage, which finds many competitors in the marketplace with profits on the decline. Products and services differ only slightly if at all. Due to this amount of sameness, great effort is made to differen-

*The terms "merchandise budget" and "model stock" are defined later in the chapter.

Figure 10–1

Product life cycle.

Source: E. Jerome McCarthy, *Basic Marketing*, 6th ed. (Homewood, Ill.: Richard D. Irwin, Inc., 1978), p. 241.

tiate in any way possible on the basis of product, price, promotion, and place. Such efforts make substantial cuts into profit.

The sales decline stage is what its name implies. In this stage of the product life cycle, the market for the product or service is on the decline. As a general rule, the retailer would not buy merchandise that was thought to be in the sales decline stage since new products are beginning to take away the market. To buy miniskirts or pet rocks after the majority of the target market has changed to more current items would be a tragic mistake for a retail buyer.

To use the product life cycle effectively, the retailer must have an understanding of the characteristics of the target market. Is the market made up of innovators who would buy only in the early stages of the product cycle or is the market made up of the latecomers who buy only after the product is an established commodity? A retailer who buys too soon can have just as much difficulty in merchandising a product as one who buys too late.

Fashion Cycle

Like the product life cycle, the fashion cycle is a model that illustrates how potential customers may react to a product. In this case fashion (what is currently popular) is the key.[3] As shown in Figure 10–2, the fashion cycle is thought to have three stages:

1. Distinctiveness stage
2. Emulation stage
3. Mass emulation stage

In the distinctiveness stage, the product attracts a very few individuals who are drawn to something different. With clothing, for example, it may be the beginning of a new style such as the narrow-lapel suit or "mid-calf length" skirt. The customers in this

Figure 10-2

Fashion cycle.

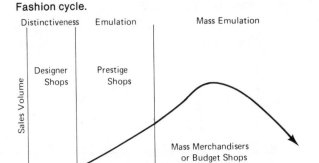

stage are usually found in the higher demographic categories since such people are thought to have enough self-confidence to risk being different.

The emulation stage occurs when the fashion good is found in high-prestige stores. Such stores serve a group who wish to emulate the "jet set" in order to be fashionable but do not wish to or cannot buy original designs. Prestige is important. A very low price will hurt the marketability of the item. At this stage, a sense of exclusiveness for the product is very important.

The mass emulation stage occurs when the item has reached the mass merchandising outlets and budget stores. At this stage the item is sold on the basis of price. No pretense of exclusiveness exists when 25 dresses just alike are found on the same rack. When the item reaches the mass emulation stage, those customers served in the distinctiveness stage begin to search out new products. This consumer reaction is what perpetuates the fashion cycle.

For years the fashion cycle, as presented in Figure 10–2, was thought to be just a "trickle-down" theory where one stage led to the next. In more recent times, advertising and customer mobility among other things have created a customer awareness that may make a fashion be accepted at both the emulation or prestige level and mass emulation or mass merchandising level at somewhat the same time. Under these new conditions the fashion cycle has the potential of being very short lived. As noted by Charles King,[4] the contemporary fashion cycle may find all levels of demographic customers all accepting the product at essentially the same time. Such possible rapid acceptance of a fashion has made merchandise planning more difficult for the retailer.

Still another way to view the fashion cycle is to see it as a "trickle-up" cycle. When a product or store is first popular with the lower-income demographic groups and then gains in popularity among higher-income individuals, the opposite effect of the traditional fashion cycle is found to occur. Blue jeans, T-shirts, musical preferences, and various foods are all examples of the "trickle-up" approach.

From this discussion, it would appear that the fashion cycle is very unpredictable. Although true, it is a factor that must be considered by the smart retailer. To ignore it is to invite trouble. Of course, estimating demand (Figure 10–3) is difficult even

Figure 10-3

Estimating what young customers will want is just one of many tasks faced by the store when it estimates demand.

(Courtesy of Gold Circle Discount Stores.)

with an understanding of the target market, product life cycle, and fashion cycle. Some of the common tools that are used to assist the retailer in estimating demand are now discussed (Figure 10-4).

Want Slips/Books

When a customer comes into the store and asks for something that is not carried by the store, a note should be made of this request. Several customers making such a request may indicate a demand for the item. The want slip or book should include the item requested and who requested it. The phone number of the customer is most helpful since the customer can be called when the merchandise is received. As shown in Figure 10-5, the want slip does not have to be elaborate. The main purpose of such a system is to get such needs in writing rather than depend on memory when the plans for buying are developed. A word of caution is necessary when want slips/books are in use. A supplier may make an effort to generate an impression of demand by sending people into a store to request an item. A new supplier who just happens to call shortly after several requests for his or her product have been received from nonregular store customers may have attempted to set the store up. On the other hand, it could be a coincidence.

Another consideration in using want slips/books information to estimate demand would be the length of time it would take to obtain the merchandise. By the time the product is received, would the customer have obtained it elsewhere or simply no longer be interested?

Figure 10-4

Tools for use in estimating demand.

Trade Publications

From *Progressive Grocer* to *Chain Store Age*, trade publications assist the retailer in determining what products are available and what may sell. In addition, many trade ads will point out what type of consumer advertising is in use or is planned for a product. If the retailer reads, for example (Figure 10-6), that Van Camp's Beans will be

Figure 10-5

Want slip.

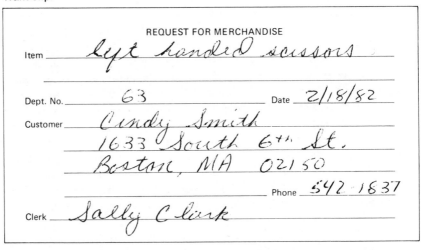

Figure 10-6

Example of trade advertisement.

(Courtesy of Stokely-Van Camp, Inc.)

advertised in major Sunday supplements, the retailer can gain insight concerning the potential demand for the product. As for a fashion item, *Body Fashions* and *Men's Wear* are two of many trade publications serving the industry. Estimating demand in this case may be aided by determining if the fashions will be advertised to the consumer through publications such as *Mademoiselle, Seventeen,* and *Vogue* for women or, for example, *Playboy* or *Esquire* for men.

Suppliers' Information

Suppliers may be of assistance by revealing information about what is or is not selling in other parts of the country. In addition, their own estimates of demand can be of interest to the retailer. How reliable this source of data is to the retailer is in direct proportion to the confidence of the retailer in that supplier. It is obvious that the supplier could put forth information that may be misleading in order to get the sale. The retailer's good judgment is essential in using this information source for estimating demand.

Comparison Shopping

Many retailers see no difference in going into a competing store during store hours to see what is selling and in breaking into that store after hours to see what is being sold. These retailers act as if comparison shopping is illegal. Not only is it not illegal, it is a sound business practice because it is a good way to determine what other stores are carrying and what they are selling. Comparison shopping is used, of course, to find out much besides what may be potential demand. Through observation, many things can be noted ranging from number of clerks to the method of display in use. Demand is best determined by making frequent comparison shopping trips on a regular basis to different stores. Making note of changes in merchandise from trip to trip can result in information that may be of great interest to the store. For example, a clothing store, "Fashions Unlimited," selling to an upper-income group may include shopping trips to the mass merchandisers and bargain basement operations in the store's trade area. By observing what is on sale at these locations, the merchandise buyers for "Fashions Unlimited" will tend to stay clear of items that have already reached the mass emulation stage of the fashion cycle, unless the "trickle-up" phenomenon is thought to be present. On the other hand, trips to very exclusive shops may indicate what may be carried next by the store. How a retailer uses comparison shopping depends on the target market.

Customer Opinion

Another source of information of aid in estimating demand is the customer. By use of panels and questionnaires, the store may learn from the "horse's mouth," so to speak, what is wanted by this group. Care should be used, however, in obtaining and using this data because many people do not really know what they want or will want several months from now—the time when the merchandise ordered may be on the retailer's shelf.

The panel probably has an advantage over the questionnaire since it provides for group interaction. Such a procedure also guarantees a response while customers may not respond to a questionnaire. The panel does have one major drawback. It is generally more expensive since panel members representing the target market are usually paid to participate. The reader will wish to review the material in Chapter 4, which deals with retail research, before making a major effort to solicit customer opinion.

Noncompeting Store

Information concerning demand can be derived from swapping ideas with similar stores in noncompeting areas that serve similar target markets. The difficulty in this approach is finding the noncompeting store with a similar target market. Census and trade data may assist the retailer in the search. Suppliers may also know of stores in similar situations in other market areas that may wish to cooperate. The advantage of this approach in estimating demand is that the retailer gets the benefit of the advice and counsel of another retailer who is faced with a somewhat similar situation.

Past Sales Performance

Additional information is available when the product under consideration has been sold in the store in the past. How did the product perform? How did customers react to it? Will reaction be the same when a reorder is placed on the shelf? Many times retailers make the mistake of assuming that if the product sold well, more should be ordered. Past performance may indicate an upward trend or point out that the market may be saturated with the product. The retailer must remember that boots or hula-hoops may sell one season and not the next. Care should be exercised when using past performance as a prediction of future demand.

Buying Office

Buying offices, as a source of supply, are discussed in the next chapter. At this point in the discussion, they are mentioned as an aid in estimating demand. Buying offices generally service many stores as they serve in their role of advisor to the retailer. In doing this, they are in a position to get the feel of the market. They also generally know what is coming out from the manufacturers and how much these products will be pushed by the manufacturers. With information of this nature, the buying office can be of great assistance to the retailer who must go through the process of estimating demand.

Sales Forecast

A sales forecast is a subjective estimate, in dollars, of the estimated demand for the products the store expects to sell. This figure represents the sum total of the information gained from want slips, trade publications, suppliers, comparison shopping, customer opinion, noncompeting stores, past sales performance of products, and buying offices combined with the good judgment of the retailer. The sales forecast is also made in light of the target market, product life cycle, and fashion cycle. Although it is just an estimate, the retailer should make every effort to make the sales forecast as accurate as possible since the merchandise budget for the store will be developed using the sales forecast.

MERCHANDISE BUDGET

The merchandise budget has been called the battle plan for the retail store. It gets this name from the fact that it is a schema or blueprint of all merchandise requirements for a store, expressed in dollars, for a particular period of time. The merchandise budget does not concern itself with individual items to be purchased. It is, instead, a financial plan to aid the store in determining the amount needed to meet purchase requirements.

The merchandise budget is developed best on a departmental basis. Therefore, in determining the sales forecast as described above, the retailer should derive an expected sales figure for each department or area of the store. The smaller the control unit the better. The sum total of all such departmental merchandise budgets will then provide the retailer with the total merchandise budget for the store.

The essential parts of the merchandise budget are:

1. Projected sales for period
2. Projected beginning-of-period inventory
3. Projected markdowns and discounts
4. Projected stock shortages
5. Projected end-of-period inventory
6. Projected purchases

One important consideration is the length of time to be covered by the merchandise budget. Such a budget will usually cover one buying season—for example, August through January for Fall and Winter clothes and February through July for Spring and Summer fashions. It should be noted that the length of time involved in the forecast has great effect on the accuracy of the budget. A merchandise budget for one month will have a greater propensity for accuracy than will one for six months. Everything else being equal, the greater the time frame, the greater the potential for error. Regardless of the total length of time, however, the merchandise budget is usually broken down into small periods such as months for control purposes.

Projected Sales for Period

The projected sales figure is the sales forecast that was determined from estimating demand as outlined earlier. The estimates are then divided into months or other planning periods for more effective use by the retailer. One difficulty with the merchandise budget is allocating the estimated sales over the period. The retailer may use past sales data for the industry plus the past sales volume for the store as a starting point. It is emphasized that these figures are just starting points. There is always the danger that what has happened before will never repeat itself. The retailer may not wish to pattern this year's activity after last year's. Why should last year's mistakes be relived? In every instance, good judgment should be included along with past sales data and estimates of future demand.

Another factor to consider in estimating sales by the month are special promotional periods. When is Easter? One year it is in March, the next year it may be in April. A college in the area may start in August one year, then change and start in September the next year. A given month may have four weekends one year, and five weekends the next year. These and other similar situations make the retailer's task of planning sales even more difficult. The secret to successful merchandise budgeting is to be aware of variables which may alter the forecasting plan from year to year. Each budget period is a new ball game. Too much reliance on the past can cause trouble for the retailer.

Projected Beginning-of-Period Inventory

How much stock should be on hand to satisfy customer demand? The amount on hand depends somewhat on the cost of being out of the item in terms of lost business, the cost of placing an order, the delivery time needed for the receipt of the item, and the amount of money tied up in inventory.

To determine the projected beginning-of-the-period inventory (BOP) or projected beginning-of-the-month (BOM) stock level, a determination is made as to how much stock will be needed to enable the store to meet its expected sales level. This determination is called the stock–sales ratio. It may be developed from past sales data in conjunction with various trade information. For example, if it is found that sales are estimated to be $20,000 for the first month of the budget period and it is determined from industry sources and past history of the store that a 4-to-1 stock–sales ratio is needed to support such sales, then the planned BOM for the month will be $80,000. Similar calculations can be made for other months using an appropriate stock–sales ratio for each period.

There is a tendency for retailers to use the stock–sales ratio method as a means of automatically determining projected BOM based on estimated sales. The stock–sales ratio procedure is only a tool to use, not a decision in itself. If sales double, an automatic merchandise budget procedure would also double inventory. As a general rule, such a large inventory increase would not be needed. If the variety of merchandise remained somewhat the same, then only the volume would increase with, perhaps, more orders placed during the period. In any event, inventory should not normally rise in the same proportion as sales. The average stock–sales ratio trade data for various size department stores substantiates the discussion. As shown in Table 10–1, the larger the store, the smaller the average stock–sales ratio.

Table 10–1

Stock–sales ratios for selected department stores, fiscal year ended January 1980

	Department Stores with Sales of		
Month	Under $1 Million	$5–10 Million	Over $20 million
February	6.55	5.98	4.99
March	5.52	4.42	4.14
April	6.33	4.92	4.01
May	6.15	5.10	4.26
June	5.75	4.89	4.64
July	5.46	5.33	4.97
August	5.67	4.98	4.59
September	6.57	5.06	4.44
October	5.42	5.28	4.01
November	3.06	4.12	3.71
December	3.07	2.55	2.25
January	7.00	5.93	5.88
Average	5.55	4.88	4.32

Source: *Department Store and Specialty Store Merchandising and Operating Results of 1979* (New York: Financial Executives Division, National Retail Merchants Association, 1980), p. XIX.

Projected Markdowns and Discounts

Because the merchandise budget reflects the dollar value of the merchandise sold at retail, it must value the merchandise at its selling price. These figures should include, therefore, all anticipated markdowns and discounts. As discussed in Chapter 13, markdowns are a fact of life for most retailing. The only question generally is, "When?" Do they come early or late in the buying season? Such decisions affect the merchandise budget. Unplanned markdowns are another matter. Few markdowns, however, are or should be completely unplanned.

As for discounts, employees are the major beneficiaries. Many stores may also participate in discount plans for students or for the elderly. Discounts may also be given for paying with cash at the time of purchase. The number and amount of discounts should be estimated for inclusion in a realistic merchandise budget.

Projected Stock Shortages

Shortages represent, in many situations, a 100 percent markdown. Shoplifting, employee theft, misweighing or mismeasuring of merchandise, damaging the item while in storage, and various forms of clerical errors make up some of the many forms of stock shortages or "shrinkage." According to the *MOR Report* of the National Retail Merchants Association, shortages in a particular department store could run in excess of 5 percent of net sales.[5] In some convenience-type stores as well as some specialty shops concentrating on the teenage market, such stock shortages may more than double the *MOR* shortage figures. At the other extreme, stores with very tight inventory procedures, for example, those specializing in fine diamonds, may have an almost nonexistent shortage problem. Of course, when these stores do have a problem, it is usually significant and very damaging to the store.

Stock shortages should be estimated for a store using past industry and store experience. If this estimate is not included in the merchandise budget, the budget will not only be unrealistic for most stores but also will be understated when viewed in the light of projected sales. To put it very simply, if shortages are not considered, there may be insufficient inventory on hand to satisfy demand.

The amount of shortage activity may differ from month to month and place to place. As a general rule, shortages increase during special buying periods such as Christmas and Back-to-School. In addition, the merchandise budget for one clothing store, for example, may reflect a higher shortage estimate than another clothing store because it is near a senior high school or a low-income housing project or any other unique situation. Once again, the judgment of the retailer is called upon to make the merchandise budget a viable, realistic document.

Projected End-of-Period Inventory

The projected end-of-period (EOP) inventory is naturally the same as the projected beginning inventory for the succeeding month or period. The figure illustrates that the merchandise budget is not just a monthly determination. It is instead a total plan with many component parts that must be coordinated. If one month gets out of kilter, the total budget will be affected. Such is the way a merchandise budget works. Much effort must be made to make each period work within the framework of the total budget.

Projected Purchases

The end product of the merchandise budget is projected purchases. The projected purchases figure represents what the store must buy at retail to meet the demands of the target market. As noted, this is a retail figure since it is based on retail sales estimates. This will later be converted to a cost figure.

The calculation of projected purchases is as follows:

$$\text{Projected Purchases at Retail} = \text{Projected Sales} + \text{Projected Markdowns \& Discounts} + \text{Projected Shortages}$$

$$+ \text{Projected EOP Stock} - \text{Projected BOP Stock}$$

A consolidated formula representing the same relationship is

$$\text{Projected Purchases at Retail} = \text{Projected Sales} + \text{Projected Reductions} \pm \text{Projected Net Change in Inventory}$$

In the shorter formula, markdowns, discounts, and shortages are grouped together under the term projected reductions. All these reductions are added to projected sales since sufficient merchandise must be purchased to cover such reductions plus the need to have sufficient merchandise on hand to meet demand.

The merchandising budget will provide a projected purchases figure for each budget period whether it be for a month or some other time frame. This figure does not, however, tell the retailer how much money is required or how much inventory needs to be purchased since some inventory is already on hand or previously ordered. To determine how much inventory needs to be purchased, the firm's open-to-buy position (OTB) must be calculated. This OTB figure represents the difference between what is in stock or ordered and what is needed.

$$\text{Open-to-Buy at Retail} = \text{Projected Purchases} - \text{Merchandise on Order} - \text{Merchandise in Stock}$$

This OTB figure is a measure of a firm's merchandising flexibility. Some flexibility is good but a very large open-to-buy, especially late in the buying season indicates that the firm may have trouble obtaining adequate merchandise for the store.

After determining the open-to-buy amount needed to meet the planned purchases level, the retailer must then convert this open-to-buy amount from a retail figure to a cost figure to know how much money is required. If, for example, open-to-buy is determined to be $10,000 and the planned initial markup is 30 percent of this retail figure, then the cost complement of 70 percent will be multiplied by the retail open-to-buy to give $7,000 as an open-to-buy figure. The $7,000 figure would be the amount the retailer should plan to spend during the period in order to acquire the needed merchandise.

$$\begin{array}{ccccc} \text{Open-to-Buy} & = & \text{Open-to-Buy} & \times & \text{Cost} \\ \text{at Cost} & & \text{at Retail} & & \text{Complement} \end{array}$$

The desired amount of open-to-buy for a store is dependent on many factors. How reliable is the demand forecast? Can orders be filled by suppliers late in the buying season? Do suppliers give advantageous price deals to those who buy early? How much open-to-buy should a retailer have? The general guideline states a need for some flexibility. Other than this guideline, it is a retail management decision.

Hank's Hardware—An Illustrative Case

To illustrate how the merchandise budget is developed, a hypothetical store, Hank's Hardware, makes use of the merchandise budget procedure to determine their financial needs in terms of inventory. A 26-week or six-month period is used for planning purposes. Using the various methods outlined in the chapter, sales for the six months were estimated as follows:

February	$12,000	May	$18,000
March	$14,000	June	$16,000
April	$16,000	July	$15,000

Markdowns were estimated to be:

February	$100	May	$2,000
March	$500	June	$2,000
April	$1,000	July	$4,000

Discounts were determined to be around 1 percent of sales while shortages were thought to be approximately 5 percent of sales.

For simplicity in Figure 10–7, the desired stock–sales ratio is assumed to be the same for each month, or three to one. In reality, as pointed out earlier in the chapter, a uniform stock–sales ratio would not always be the case.

As noted in Figure 10–7, Hank's Hardware has total projected purchases for the total budget period (February to July) of $112,060. From this amount, let us assume that the store deducts $19,205 for merchandise on order and $52,525 for merchandise in stock, leaving $40,330 for open-to-buy at retail. The store has an average markup of 40 percent on original retail. Using a 60 percent cost complement, Hank's Hardware needs to purchase at cost $24,198 of merchandise for the merchandise budget period, February–July, 19XX.

Figure 10-7

Illustrative merchandise budget.

	February	March	April	May	June	July
			HANK'S HARDWARE **MERCHANDISE BUDGET** **February–July 19XX**			
Projected Sales	$12,000	$14,000	$16,000	$18,000	$16,000	$15,000
Projected Markdowns	100	500	1,000	2,000	2,000	4,000
Projected Discounts	120	140	160	180	160	150
Projected Shortages	600	700	800	900	800	750
Projected Deductions	820	1,340	1,960	3,080	2,960	4,900
Projected BOM Inventory	36,000	42,000	48,000	54,000	48,000	45,000
Projected EOM Inventory	42,000	48,000	54,000	48,000	45,000	42,000
Net Change	6,000	6,000	6,000	<6,000>	<3,000>	<3,000>
Projected Purchases	$18,820	$21,340	$23,960	$15,080	$15,960	$16,900

MODEL STOCK

In merchandise planning, the retailer must not stop after determining demand and the merchandise budget. He or she must take these dollar figures and determine the actual physical units the store needs to purchase.

The basic ingredient of this procedure is the model stock. A model stock by definition is an ever-changing, desired assortment of merchandise carefully chosen by a store to best serve a target market. The essential element in the definition is assortment. Assortment is defined as the distribution of merchandise "in sight" (inventory in stock and merchandise on order) according to classification, subclassification, style, color, pattern, size, and price, with the quantities in each of these factors dovetailing as much as possible to fit customer demand.[6] Assortment is concerned with the variety, width, depth, consistency, balance, and flexibility of the merchandise (Figure 10–8).

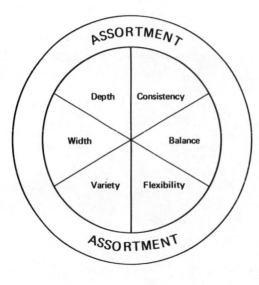

Figure 10-8

The assortment mix. Each element must be coordinated with all others if a store is to have the strongest possible merchandise assortment.

Variety

Variety is the number of lines carried in a store. A department store has a greater variety of merchandise than does a women's specialty shop. A McDonald's restaurant does not have the variety of merchandise that a Holiday Inn restaurant has to offer the customer.

Width

Width or breadth is concerned with complementary items within a merchandise line. A shoe store sells pantyhose. A store selling Atlas tires also sells Atlas batteries. A feed and seed retailer offer Rototillers for sale.

Depth

Depth stands for the number of sizes, colors, and other characteristics that are carried in a single line. A store that sells Arrow shirts in seven sizes, five sleeve lengths, four collar designs, and six colors is found to have great depth in the Arrow shirt line. Such a store would have 7X5X4X6 or 840 SKUs (stock-keeping units) in the Arrow line. Under most guidelines, the store would then carry three of each stock-keeping unit or a total shirt inventory of 2,520 units.

The term stock-keeping unit (SKU) stands for one, distinct, individual type of item carried by a store. If the store carries 12 shirts just alike in every way including size, color, style, and so on, then all 12 such shirts represent only one SKU. If, on the other hand, 6 are blue and 6 are white, two SKUs are present. Depending on the nature of the shirts, 12 of them could represent from 1 to 12 stock-keeping units. SKUs are also important to a retailer since much merchandise arrives at the store already coded as to size, color, and so on, under the National Retail Merchants Association's Universal

Vendor Marking (UVM) system. Universal Vendor Marking allows the retailer to keep track of merchandise by means of a common identifying system that can be "read" by optical scanner or manually. More discussion on UVM appears in Chapter 14 when a discussion on receiving of merchandise is presented. Mention is made of the process at this time since the basic foundation of the system is the stock-keeping unit.

Consistency

Another very important consideration in terms of assortment is consistency, or the degree to which products are related in the customer's mind. While a particular assortment may appear to be just scrambled merchandise (unrelated merchandise carried by a store) to one person, the next customer may view it as a logical combination. One example would be the gift department in a large department store. Merchandise of many types is drawn together for the benefit of the customer. Since the customer views the items as all having the same purpose—a gift, the gift department is thought to have a good breadth of merchandise from which to select. Put the same merchandise together for any other purposes and you have scrambled merchandising. The important point to note here is that how customers perceive the assortment is the only thing that counts. If it is what they want, then it is consistent.

Balance

A very important factor is stock balance. How many SKUs are needed in each line to attract a customer? Since the store has only so many square feet, it must work to achieve a balance throughout the store for maximum customer satisfaction within the space provided. The retail store also wishes to develop a balance that will be in keeping with the desired image of the store. If the store wishes to remain a men's clothing store in the minds of consumers, it must watch its stock mix to guard against adding too many nonclothing items or in some cases too many clothes for women.

Flexibility

The assortment for a store is ever changing. During a special promotion, goods not normally purchased will be added to the store. For example, in Birmingham, Alabama, as in other cities, special promotions are built around a Festival of Arts that features a different country each year. If Germany is the country for a particular year, stores in the area will buy German items for sale during the time of the festival. With few exceptions, such goods will never again be included in the assortment.

The assortment also changes due to fashion and technological obsolescence. Women's shops that used to carry a large selection of hats, purses, and shoes to match no longer do so due to changes in fashion. An example of technological change can be seen in college book stores. Where slide rules used to be part of the merchandise assortment, they have almost all been replaced by hand-held calculators.

Assortment varies with the seasons, weather, and customs of the area. A store in Miami will not vary its assortment much due to the seasons of the year. A store in Kansas will. A store located in an area where it snows may develop part of its assortment around the sport of skiing. If a community traditionally has a big St. Patrick's Day celebration, stores in the area will alter their assortment by carrying more kelly green clothes, party hats, and the like.

The model stock, as defined earlier, is a desired assortment of merchandise that is ever changing. For some items such as staple goods, the change is very slow. The amount, brands, sizes, and so on of bread needed by the store this month will be somewhat similar to those of last month, assuming no major shift in the uncontrollable variables. In such cases, the model stock is almost static in the short run. It can become almost a never-out list where a store automatically reorders to ensure never being out of high-in-demand staple items. For shopping goods, the model stock is a different story. Demand for shopping goods is dynamic. What the consumer desires now may not be true next year or even next month. For the clothing store, the retailer may know how many SKUs are needed. The question is what shirt to buy to plug into the model stock.

In developing a model stock, the retailer should write down what he or she wants the model stock to be. An illustrative page from the model stock plan for Hank's Hardware (Figure 10–9) shows how such a written presentation might look. For the retailer first starting out, the model stock plan could be the one found to work best for stores in general. For example, a retailer adds a paint department to a store. He or she may choose to use the paint supplier's suggested model stock that would call for so many cases of white, yellow, and so on. No matter if the model stock originates with the retailer or from the supplier or both, the only thing certain about a model stock is that the assortment that makes it up will usually change over time to meet ever-changing consumer demands.

SUMMARY

Merchandise planning is a process that involves estimating demand, determining the merchandise budget, and developing a model stock. To estimate demand, the retailer must be knowledgeable of the target market and how it relates to the product life cycle and fashion cycle. Information sources, which when combined with the retailer's judgment result in the sales forecast, include want slips, trade publications, suppliers, comparison shopping, customers, noncompeting stores, past sales performance, and buying offices. The merchandise budget then takes the projected sales figure (the forecast) and determines for the store the dollar amount of purchases that must be made to meet the estimated demand. A side benefit of the budget process is that the retailer is forced to study how markdowns, discounts, and shortages will affect his or her merchandise requirements. The merchandise budget also provides data that are needed to determine the open-to-buy position of the retailer and shows how much he or she is actually in a position to buy (the difference between what is on hand or ordered and what is needed). The model stock is the end product of the planning process as it turns dollar figures into physical units. Such a stock is an ever-changing assortment of merchandise carefully chosen to best serve the target market. Variety, width, depth, consis-

Figure 10-9

Illustrative model stock.

MODEL STOCK
HANK'S HARDWARE
Page 116

Item #	Name of Item	Style/Color	Size	Brand	Quantity Ordered	On Hand	Cost ($)	Retail Price ($)
73214	Step ladder	Natural	5 ft.	Saf-Step	12		8.50	14.95
73215	Step ladder	Natural	6 ft.	Saf-Step	12		9.50	17.95
73216	Step ladder	Natural	8 ft.	Saf-Step	12		12.00	19.95
73217	Step ladder	Natural	12 ft.	Saf-Step	6		16.50	28.95
73613	Paint brush	Nylon	1½"	EZ-Cote	36		.74	1.29
73614	Paint brush	Bristle	1½"	EZ-Cote	36		.79	1.29
73615	Paint brush	Nylon	3"	EZ-Cote	36		1.85	4.39
73616	Paint brush	Bristle	3"	EZ-Cote	36		2.13	4.39
73617	Paint brush	Nylon	4"	EZ-Cote	12		2.59	4.95
73618	Paint brush	Bristle	4"	EZ-Cote	12		2.88	4.95
73619	Paint roller	Paper core	7"	EZ-Cote	36		.79	1.29
73620	Paint roller	Paper core	9"	EZ-Cote	12		1.35	2.19
73816	Masking tape	2" roll	100 ft.	QK-Stic	48		.79	1.29
73816	Masking tape dispenser	Blue	2" roll	QK-Stic	6		1.29	1.89

tency, balance, and flexibility are all key elements in the development of a viable merchandise assortment for a store.

DISCUSSION QUESTIONS

1. What is meant by the term product life cycle? What significance does the product life cycle have for a retailer?
2. Is the concept of the fashion cycle important to all retailers? What is meant by a trickle-down cycle? A trickle-up cycle?
3. Discuss possible sources of information that may assist the retailer in estimating demand.
4. What is comparison shopping? Is it legal? ethical?
5. Discuss the various steps included in the development of a merchandise budget.

6. What are some considerations to keep in mind when estimating sales on a month-to-month basis for use in the merchandise budget?
7. What is meant by the term stock–sales ratio? Is there an optimum stock–sales ratio? Explain.
8. The Basket Place estimates sales to be $100,000, markdowns to be $7,500, discounts to be $500, and shortages to be 5 percent of sales. The stock–sales ratio is said to be 2.5, with no change in inventory level projected for the period. Inventory on order amounts to $23,000 and current inventory is $50,000. Average markup is 50 percent. Calculate the open-to-buy financial requirement for the Basket Place for the period.
9. "If a store has 613 SKUs in one department and 64 SKUs in a second department, the latter department is thought to be in trouble because it does not offer as wide an assortment as the first department." Comment on this statement. In your discussion explain what is meant by the term SKU.
10. Discuss with a retailer the key elements of a viable merchandise assortment for a retail store. Attempt to ascertain how the retailer determines what the assortment–model stock should be for his or her store.

NOTES

[1] Benjamin C. Butcher and James R. McAnelly, *Fundamentals of Retailing* (New York: Macmillan Publishing Co., Inc., 1973), p. 261.

[2] For more discussion on the product life cycle, see E. Jerome McCarthy, *Basic Marketing*, 6th ed. (Homewood, Ill.: Richard D. Irwin, Inc., 1978), pp. 240–245.

[3] For more discussion on the fashion cycle, see William J. Stanton, *Fundamentals of Marketing*, 5th ed. (New York: McGraw-Hill Book Company, 1978), pp. 206–211.

[4] Charles W. King, "Fashion Adoption: A Rebuttal to the 'Trickle Down' Theory," in *Toward Scientific Marketing*, ed. Stephen A. Greyser (Chicago: American Marketing Association, 1964), pp. 108–125.

[5] *Department and Specialty Store Merchandising and Operating Results of 1979* (New York: Financial Executives Division, National Retail Merchants Association, 1980).

[6] Charles G. Taylor, *Merchandise Assortment Planning* (New York: National Retail Merchants Association, 1970), p. 16.

CHAPTER 11

Merchandise
Resources

Shoe

Reprinted by permission of The Chicago Tribune-New York News Syndicate, Inc.

What is available and where to get it are the basic assignments facing a retailer when the question of merchandise resources is raised. The model stock, which was discussed in the last chapter, is just an academic exercise if the retailer cannot turn this plan into reality by knowing where to get the merchandise to fill out the model stock. To develop good merchandise resources, the retailer must be aware of available resources, should develop a file on these resources, and should analyze each resource to determine if such a resource should be used by the store.

AVAILABLE RESOURCES

A retailer determines that he or she can sell a left-handed ball-point pen. Where can such a pen be found? Contact with merchandise resources can come about in many ways. In-store sales calls, merchandise centers, trade shows, supplier advertisements and catalogs, and resident buying offices are all means of bringing the buyer and seller together. These resources provide the retailer with assistance, but the major buying decisions remain with the retailer. Central buying and full-service merchandising are also types of resources. The difference between these and those cited above is that in using these resources the individual store depends primarily on the central buying office or the service merchandiser to buy the goods needed for a viable merchandise assortment for the individual store.

In-Store Sales Calls

Much buying is done in the store. A jewelry representative will call upon a retail store bringing samples of available merchandise. A tools sales representative will call on the hardware store and invite the retailer out to the truck to look over various items. The bread representative will sell products to the store with immediate delivery. Even in the area of fashion clothing where other forms of resource contact play such an important role, in-store buying is done for reorders and late season purchases. Advantages of in-store buying are many. No travel expense in terms of either time or money is incurred by the retailer. The retailer has the undivided attention of the seller. All store records are close by in case something needs to be double checked such as the sales of a particular item for last year. Another real plus for this approach is that all appropriate store personnel may be included in the discussion if the store manager deems this appropriate. Such personnel are, after all, the people who will sell the merchandise and have the customer contact.

The smart retailer will weigh the above advantages of in-store buying against the disadvantages. First, the number of available samples may be limited due to the expense involved in carrying merchandise to the store. The in-store visit may also limit the ability of the retailer to know what other vendors will offer in terms of merchandise, prices, and so on, since other vendors are not readily accessible at the time of the in-store visit. In addition, many of the "better" vendors will not make in-store calls on smaller stores or stores in less favorable geographic locations, thereby "forcing" some retailers who rely heavily on in-store sales calls to use somewhat less desirable sources of supply.

Merchandise Centers

Merchandise centers take one of two forms: wholesale market centers and manufacturing market centers. In the garment district of New York, sales offices are a physical part of many manufacturing operations. The closeness of these garment manufacturers creates a market center. But if a New York clothing manufacturer puts an additional sales office in Dallas, it is locating in a wholesale market center—a place where there is a concentration of vendor sales offices that are not tied physically to any manufacturing facilities.

What makes a particular geographic location a merchandise or market center? Merchandise centers develop where a great number of sales offices and/or display rooms are located to serve a concentration of potential customers. These sales offices are generally located in a particular part of major cities or even in the same building in order to allow the retailer to shop and compare the available merchandise of many suppliers. In many cities, such as Dallas and Atlanta, a merchandise mart building has been constructed to help the city serve as a merchandise center. For years, New York was considered the soft-goods (apparel) market capital, whereas Chicago was considered the king of hard goods (furniture, appliances, etc.). In more recent times, the markets have dispersed. Some major American cities now considered merchandise centers, along with New York and Chicago, include Los Angeles, San Francisco, Dallas, Atlanta, Miami, and High Point, North Carolina. Why High Point, North Carolina in a list of such otherwise well-known cities? High Point is a major furniture center.

Trade Shows

Trade shows usually occur once during each buying season. The purpose of the trade show is to bring both the seller and buyer into contact with as many firms as possible. These shows are usually held in large arenas such as Chicago's McCormick Place or New York's Madison Square Garden. Various civic centers or large hotels may also be used when space requirements are not too great.

At trade shows, the vendors set up booths where the buyer can get "hands-on" experience with the merchandise. Face-to-face contact is made and merchandise orders can be taken on the spot. It is at such shows that many buying mistakes are made. The retailer who has not done his or her homework (preparation of the merchandise budget and determination of the model stock) tends to buy what is seen first. Such a practice leads to an inappropriate assortment of merchandise and a very soon depleted open-to-buy. Because of the difficulty of buying wisely at a show, due to its carnival-like atmosphere, it is best for a retailer not to buy anything during his or her first show visit. Instead, if it is possible, the retailer should go to see what goes on and then return home to begin preparations for the next show. This procedure will usually lead to more successful buying in the future.

Supplier Advertisements and Catalogs

A very important resource for last-minute or fill-in merchandise is supplier advertisements and catalogs. For the small retailer who is located in a geographically isolated area, advertisements and catalogs may serve the additional function of keeping the retailer informed between trade shows since it is probable that few sales representatives will call at the store. A word of caution about catalog buying is in order. The retailer should have some knowledge of the quality of the merchandise being ordered sight unseen. Is the catalog correct in its description? Will the vendor ship immediately or will time-consuming credit checks and other delays cause the merchandise to arrive too late to be of any use? Will the merchandise arrive at all? These problems are, of course, present with all types of vendors. Such difficulties do seem, however, to be more prevalent when nonpersonal direct sales via means of advertisements and catalogs are made. These difficulties are found to be especially true when very small retailers are involved.

Resident Buying Offices

A resident buying office can be of great assistance to a store.[1] Its entire reason for existence is to assist in the buying function. Most retail stores cannot go to the market centers every week to stay current with market trends. Stores located great distances from the market have difficulty in maintaining contact with suppliers. These and other problems can be solved through a resident buying office. Such an office will provide information about market trends, develop and maintain supplier contacts, and provide assistance to the store when the retailer does come to the market. It is noted that in most cases, the resident buying office does not actually buy merchandise. Its role is advisory in nature.

The services provided by a resident buying office are twofold: source of information and buyer assistance. As a source of information, the buying office will provide data on current and new sources of supply. This information can answer such questions as: Are quality levels being maintained by a particular supplier? Is a supplier who has been bought out by another still offering a particular item? Does a new supplier appear to be reliable? In addition to information about vendors, buying offices provide much information about the market when retailers are not at the market. Daily and weekly "newsletters" tell of new items, price deals, promotional items, and other points of interest which are happening in the market. It is noted that a resident buying office is physically located in a merchandise center. This fact alone makes it a good source of market information.

In terms of buyer assistance, a good resident buying office can be literally "worth its weight in gold" to the retailer. Small stores do not usually have much clout in the market. A resident buying office, on the other hand, which represents many stores and therefore, much potential business, does achieve preferred status for its clients. Such offices can arrange private showings of merchandise just for their member stores that may even include merchandise only shown to preferred customers. Because resident buyers are in the market at all times, they also keep abreast of all new items that are made available for sale. This enables them to have the latest and most desirable items available for viewing during the client's visit. Additional buyer assistance may be given when a store wishes to reorder merchandise. To keep from going to the market again, the retailer may request the resident buyer to make the reorder purchase. Aid may also be given in the area of merchandise adjustments, misordered merchandise, and other similar problems. Once again, the clout of the buying office can be of assistance to the retailer since the vendor may be more anxious to make an equitable settlement if a buying office is involved.

Resident buying offices fall into five basic categories depending on type of ownership and method of compensation. Such offices are either store owned or independent. Independents are divided further into salaried or broker while store-owned offices are placed in three categories: individual store, associated store, and chain store. An important distinction between the independent resident buying office and the store-owned operation is that the independent office, by its very nature, has no direct support other than that related to performance. Since it is not subsidized, many believe the independent buying office is more aggressive on behalf of its clients, thereby doing a better job than its store-owned competitors. To enable the reader to understand the possible advantages and disadvantages, each of the five types of resident buying offices are briefly outlined as to their methods of operation.

Independent Resident Buying Office—Salaried.   The salaried office gets its name from its method of compensation. Offices and stores in this category usually sign an annual contract providing for the store to pay up to approximately 1 percent of annual sales to the resident buying office in payment for services rendered. Such contract terms are quite common for the medium and larger store. For the very small store, a flat fee in place of a percentage of sales is usually the arrangement since a percentage of sales in most cases would not be sufficient compensation. Therefore, the typical contract serves as a negative inducement for a small firm to use a salaried resident buying office. The benefits may not outweigh the cost to the small store.

Independent Resident Buying Office—Merchandise Broker.   The broker is paid by the seller or vendor rather than the retailer. Since the broker makes money by selling merchandise (usually 3 to 5 percent of sales), the broker is very anxious to sell those items for which vendors offer good commissions. Little or no commission being offered by a vendor usually means that the particular line of merchandise will never be mentioned by the merchandise broker. In such situations, a good, profitable item may be missed completely by the retail buyer. With all its drawbacks, there is a positive side to the merchandise broker. For the small store, the broker arrangement means that a resident buyer is within the framework of realistic options for the store. It should be remembered, however, that the merchandise broker derives its income from the vendor. The broker's allegiance in a difficult situation will generally support the vendor or firm who helps to pay the bills.

Store-Owned Resident Buying Office—Individual.   Individual resident buying offices are owned and operated for the benefit of an individual store. At one time, such buying offices were predominant in the buying picture. Today, the economies of scale of spreading the costs of operation over many stores has tended to put individual store buying offices in an unfavorable competitive position. Marshall

Field and Neiman-Marcus are among the few retailers who still operate their own buying offices.

Store-Owned Resident Buying Office—Associated. The same economies that have discouraged the individual buying office have promoted the associated office. The associated buying office is what its name implies. It is a buying office that is owned and operated by an association or group of stores. The best known of the associated buying offices is Associated Merchandising Corporation, which represents more than 25 leading stores. Frederick Atkins, Inc. and Specialty Stores Association are other well-known group organizations. Through the group buying that this arrangement permits, more favorable arrangements with suppliers are made possible.

Store-Owned Resident Buying Office—Chain. The resident buying offices for Allied Stores and R. H. Macy serve as examples of chain-operated resident buying offices. Chain-operated buying offices should not be confused with central buying offices. A chain's resident buying office assists the buyers from each individual unit in selecting the best merchandise for each particular store. By definition, the decision to buy would rest with the local buyer while the buying office would offer advice and information. Central buying offices, on the other hand, reverse the roles of the parties. In central buying, the buying is done by the buying office after seeking advice and information from the individual store units.

Central Buying Offices

As noted, the central buying office for a group of retail stores (usually a chain) has the responsibility for actually selecting and buying the merchandise for the individual stores (Figure 11–1). What are the advantages and disadvantages of such an arrangement? Some of the "pluses" and "minuses" are presented for further discussion.

Specialization of Skills. Central buyers have the personnel to concentrate their efforts in various smaller areas of merchandise. A buyer for the central office may, for example, only work in the area of girls' clothing, sizes 3–6x, or men's outerwear, or heavy appliances. Such buyers become knowledgeable about their own products as well as those sold by the competition (Figure 11–2). Concentration of effort permits the buyer to develop a high level of expertise on the market for the product as well as on the possible resources for the item.

Better Selection of Merchandise. The fact that the central buyer usually represents many stores causes this specialized buyer to receive preferred treatment from vendors. The end result of such special treatment is generally a better choice of merchandise.

Lower Costs. The central buyer is typically buying in large quantities. Such large purchases permit the per unit cost to be lower due to quantity discounts.

Major disadvantages of central buying are believed to be twofold: market variations and the separation of buying and selling.

Figure 11-1

A national merchandise manager for sporting goods meets with part of his buying staff.

(Courtesy of Montgomery Ward.)

Figure 11-2

In search of the better product, buyers test lawn mowers that are offered for sale by the competition.

(Courtesy of Montgomery Ward.)

Market Variations. A central buying office in New York has difficulty in determining what will sell in Bangor, Maine; Omaha, Nebraska; Portland, Oregon; and Mobile, Alabama. The climates are different, the cultures are different, and the fashions are different. In short, each of the four markets mentioned and hundreds like them are unique. Some differences are obvious. For example, Sears would not have snow removal equipment for sale in its southern stores but would in its northern stores. In other cases, the differences are not as clear cut. Will double-breasted suits for men or women's wrap-around skirts sell in markets across the country? If the answer is "yes," then the question is "when?" It is generally believed that a fashion lag exists in the United States. Fashion designs accepted in the Northeast one season are thought to move to the South and West the following season. Unfortunately, even this well-known premise has been violated by the consumer from time to time. The maxi-length clothes of the mid-1970s never got any further than the Northeast, much to the dismay of many central buyers.

The success of central buying depends upon making sure that each store provides the central office with as much information as possible. What is the store's target market? What type of merchandise sells? How much is needed? Answers to these and many other questions all aid the central buyers in their task. When possible, buyers should also visit stores to see the situation firsthand. One large chain has a policy that encourages the central buyer to talk by phone to the appropriate department managers at the individual stores to promote a better flow of information. Market variations are a drawback to central buying. Minimizing this drawback is a responsibility of all persons involved in the buying function.

Separation of Buying and Selling. This disadvantage of central buying boils down to the question of what happens when the merchandise does not sell? Who is responsible? If the merchandise sells well, the retail manager has no trouble finding someone to take credit. Everyone will say it was due to them. When it does not sell, the central buyer will usually cite inadequate or incorrect information from the stores as the reason. The store manager will cite the poor decisions of the central buyer as the culprit. Central buying makes accountability for merchandise performance somewhat difficult.

Additional problems arise if the central buying office has a role in determining prices, markdowns, promotional allowances, and other retail decisions. The greater the role of the central buyer, the lesser the function of the store manager in the marketing of the product. Under these circumstances, the burden is on the central buying office to learn about and understand the selling of the product.

Specification Buying.[2] The advantages and disadvantages of central buying come into even clearer focus when the central buying office undertakes specification buying. Such an arrangement means that the central buying office creates a product to be sold exclusively by the particular group of stores. Under specification buying, the central buyer will actually determine the desired characteristics for a product with assistance from the member stores and then contract for its manufacture, usually under the brand name of the store. Sears and J. C. Penney are two examples of retail organizations that engage in specification buying. Improved quality, better product features, and lower costs through volume purchases can result from specification buying. The greatest disadvantage comes from the fact that customers of a given store may prefer a manufacturer's brand over the private label or may not like the item for any number of reasons. No matter how difficult the situation, however, the pressure within a company to sell such items is great since large quantities are normally involved in specification buying. To also look at the positive side, if specification buying results in a product that catches on, the store is the only one in the market with the item, at least in the short run. Such a situation offers much potential profit. Like all other aspects of buying, there are definite pluses and minuses to specification buying for a given market.

Full-Service Merchandising

For the retailer who is in need of or desires more than merchandise, the full-service merchandiser may be the answer. Such a resource assumes a role of co-responsibility with the retailer[3] by offering the retailer a source of merchandise plus promotional assistance, accounting systems, training programs, and/or a host of other possible services. In return, the retailer makes a commitment to purchase a significant amount of merchandise from that vendor. This type of arrangement may last for one buying season or for years. Examples of full-service merchandisers include voluntary chains, rack jobbers, leased departments, and programmed merchandisers.

Voluntary Chains.   These chains derive their name from the fact that a retail store voluntarily aligns itself with a particular wholesaler who will provide the store with all or most of the merchandise needed by the store plus various services. The store will usually take on the name of the voluntary chain such as IGA Food Stores or Ace Hardware. The arrangement places the burden of supply on the wholesaler. The retailer, in turn, generally receives a cheaper price since the benefit of quantity purchasing is present. Also, there is no need to spend a great amount of time on resource relations; thus more time is available for working with the customer. It is important to note that such benefits are great *if* the wholesaler is doing a good job. Unfortunately, there are all grades of voluntary chains in operation in the United States today. Not all provide the merchandise or managerial assistance that is of the quality it should be.

Rack Jobbers.   Another type of full-service merchandiser is a firm that provides all services for a particular type of merchandise not normally within the area of expertise of the retailer. Examples include health and beauty aids or kitchen items in a clothing or food store, or ladies' hose in a neighborhood drugstore. Jobbers may originate with a wholesaler such as for candy and tobacco products or may be direct from a manufacturer such as is the case with the L'eggs division of the Hanes Company for ladies' hose. Jobbers keep the merchandise up-to-date and well-stocked in the store. Jobbers also will rotate merchandise such as pots and pans, towels, and other items from store to store, thereby always giving the appearance of new merchandise in a particular store—something one store could not do by itself. Merchandise handled by jobbers is usually provided the store on consignment or sold with a guaranteed-return provision. Such provisions enable the retailer to assume no risk on merchandise on which he or she has admitted having little or no retailing expertise.

Leased Departments. When the retailer wants to carry health and beauty aids, he or she may lack product knowledge so a rack jobber is hired. When that item requires competent sales assistance as well, a leased department may be the answer. Shoes, jewelry, automotive supplies, food, and carpeting, when located in stores that specialize in other things, are commonly found to be leased departments. In most cases the customer does not know that he or she is buying from such a department. For years, customers bought from K mart Foods, not realizing that such stores were leased departments. The same was true for the automotive and sporting goods departments of such stores. The trend now is away from such leased departments since such operations prevent retail management from having absolute management control in a given store. The arrangement, however, will permit a store to offer jewelry and watches or shoe repair, or whatever, when the store itself has no knowledge of such things. It should be observed that if the leased department causes customer dissatisfaction for whatever reason, the offending lessees should be straightened out or the agreement should be canceled. Procrastination on the retailer's part can cause irreparable harm to the image of the store. Great care should be used when working with leased departments.

Programmed Merchandisers.[4] This arrangement is different from the others mentioned in that programmed merchandising usually involves not only merchandise but also services such as assistance in promotion and training. In this arrangement, retail management deals directly with major suppliers of resources. The agreement involves a commitment to buy particular items from a vendor for a predetermined period of time (usually one buying season) in return for the services offered by the vendor. If the relationship between the retailer and vendor is successful, the arrangement may be continued over a long period of time.

Which Resource to Use

The resources at the disposal of the retailer are numerous. A given store or organization may use all of the possibilities mentioned for various merchandise and different situations found at different stores or at different times of the year. The optimum resource mix is a management decision. The true test for success of the various possible arrangements is the end product of the buying process—the success or failure of the merchandise on the retailer's shelf.

RESOURCE FILE

To assist the retailer in determining the success or potential success of each possible resource, a resource file should be kept on all potential merchandise suppliers. The purpose of the file is to provide an orderly means for collecting data on each resource. The file is particularly important when more than one person is involved in the buying process. The file system provides a means for the various people to compare notes.

Although each file system is unique, basic ingredients found in most systems include information on:

Type of merchandise offered for sale
Quality of merchandise
Price range
Delivery performance
Terms and conditions of sale
Reliability
Name, address, and phone number of company contact

Resource file information may be kept on 3″ × 5″ cards (Figure 11–3), in a loose-leaf notebook, and/or on the store's computer.

Although important, an excellent resource file is not critical for a store that uses a full-line merchandiser or has great confidence in its resident buying office. However, for the store that has need of direct vendor contact, such a file may be one of the retailer's most guarded assets. A resource file that is developed over the years and is updated continuously can enable the retailer to locate almost any item of merchandise desired by the store. A competitive advantage may be possible for the store that knows its resources as evidenced by its resource file and uses such information wisely.

The importance of the resource file to a store should not be taken lightly. In fact, the file should be kept under lock in a fire/heatproof file or safe. Also, if an emergency of some type should occur, the store's cash money and its resource file should be at the top of the list for things to be removed to a safer place if time permits. As noted, the resource file is certainly one of the store's more important assets.

Figure 11-3

Example of resource file card.

Brand	*Norton Jenkins*
Merchandise	*Women's & Misses Coats, Jackets, Dresses, & Sportswear*
Quality	*Good to very good*
Price	*$15 – $100*
Delivery	*Within 10 days of planned date*
Terms	*2/10 net 30 - 60*
Reliability	*Marginal to good - better in off season*
Name	*Chuck Anderson*
	1900 N First Avenue
	Short Haul, Kansas 66601
	800 - 792 - 4301

Resource analysis is the ongoing process of evaluating the data in the resource file in order to determine from which vendors the store should buy or continue to buy its merchandise. To decide upon a source of supply, the retail store must determine for itself the criteria to be used in measuring the performance of a supplier. A method for comparing vendors is the next step. Finally, the retailer must decide how many vendors should be used from among those who are available. Out of these procedures will come the list of resources for a firm divided into different levels of preference. One such classification divides resources into five classes:[5]

> *Class A*—volume, prestige, and profitable resources most important to a store; these are the store's "partners."
> *Class B*—less important than A; products produce satisfactory profits for the store.
> *Class C*—resources that need watching; profit record is not good for the store.
> *Class D*—desired resources that currently will not sell to store.
> *Class E*—undesirable resources due to bad experience with store.

To use a classification system of A–E as given, the retailer must first determine how he or she wishes to analyze vendors. Items that may be included in such a criteria list are[6]

> *Merchandise salability.* Are the goods offered by the vendor of the type and quality needed and desired by the target market? Can the goods be sold at a profit for the store?
> *Price and terms of sale.* What is the actual price of the merchandise? Do price differentials occur as the result of trade, quantity, and cash discounts? Transportation charges may vary. What about special deals? Is trade credit a problem? Various terms of sale are discussed in the following chapter.
> *Alertness to new opportunities.* Is the supplier current in the field or is the firm behind the times? Which is better? The answer depends on the likes and dislikes of the target market.
> *Services.* Will the resource accept reasonable merchandise returns without difficulty? Does the vendor ship the merchandise as planned, or is the merchandise always arriving late or not at all? Is the merchandise already packaged and ready for sale when it arrives from the vendor? Does the vendor pack the merchandise so that it is not damaged in transit? Are special promotional allowances available to the retailer? Vendor services can be numerous. The checklist in Figure 11–4 shows some of the more popular services that a vendor might offer.
> *Prestige.* Is the prestige of the supplier and the brand in keeping with the image of the store? A product that is either too high class or very budget oriented can have an adverse effect on the profitability of a given store.
> *Cooperation.* Does the vendor cooperate with the retailer? Will the vendor assist the retailer in handling unforeseen difficulties such as an overburden of certain types of merchandise due to a buying error or some other reason? Will the supplier permit the return of part or all of the merchandise? It should

Figure 11–4

Checklist of vendor services.

A. Nonpersonal Promotional Aids
  1. Dealer helps
    a. Advertising cuts or mats to make it unnecessary for the retailer to prepare a suitable layout to guide the newspaper or other media
    b. Radio and TV scripts ready for use by a store commentator
    c. Blowups of manufacturer's advertisements for store display, direct-mail pieces, bill stuffers, and package inserts
    d. Samples of merchandise for display and free distribution purposes, including empty packages for display
    e. Swatches of material, sold by the yard or attached to finished articles, for similar purposes
    f. Visual displays, such as counter cards, posters, display fixtures, and window display units, ready to be set up
    g. Specially designed fixtures to contain and display the vendor's products.
    h. Sales instructional booklets (pamphlets to distribute to customers, including "stuffers" to enclose in packages and with charge statements)
    i. Motion picture and sound slide films for showing salespeople, customers, or both
    j. Unit packaging, labels, and price tickets to ready the goods for resale.
  2. Provision of supplementary attractions
    a. Special inducements for customers to buy
  3. Promotional allowances
    a. Advertising allowances
    b. Display allowances
B. Personal Selling Aids
  1. Training of store salespeople
  2. PMs and awards to salespeople for selling the particular product
  3. Provision of demonstrators
  4. Servicing the goods sold
C. Financing and Risk Taking by the Seller
  1. Extension of credit
  2. Guarantee against price decline
  3. Consignment selling and the return privilege
  4. Markdown insurance
  5. Providing warranties
D. Assumption of Inventory Responsibilities
  1. Controlling the inventory of the merchandise bought while it is in the store
  2. Warehousing purchases until needed for sale, including drop shipping
  3. Stocking the selling fixtures, displaying the goods, and doing associated housekeeping

Source: John W. Wingate and Joseph S. Friedlander, *The Management of Retail Buying*, 2nd ed., © 1978, p. 305. Reprinted by permission of Prentice-Hall, Inc., Englewood Cliffs, New Jersey.

be pointed out that cooperation is a two-way street. The retailer in turn must cooperate with the supplier. Payment of bills on time, communication concerning potential demands, and the willingness to permit the vendor to present new product ideas to the store are among the necessary ingredients of a two-sided effort that should result in better retail/vendor cooperation.

Reliability. Can the supplier be depended on to consistently meet the desired performance standards of the various criteria cited? Although it is a very subjective criterion, reliability is considered by many to be the most important of them all. Reliability involves the firm's reputation. It attempts to measure the dependability of the firm. Reliability has been found to be a very fragile commodity since it is subject to change at a moment's notice. For example, changes in a vendor's top management should be studied to determine how the firm's reliability may be affected. Changes in economic conditions have also been known to alter a firm's level of reliability. Too much cannot be said on the topic of reliability since without it the supplier is an automatic Class E resource—one that should be avoided unless no other alternative is available.

Comparison of Resources

After the criteria have been determined for resource analysis, procedures should then be developed to systematically compare the various suppliers so as to determine from which firms the merchandise should be purchased. Procedures for comparing such resources were introduced by Gist[7] and refined by Berens.[8] Building on Gist's methodology, Berens suggested the use of a six-step decision matrix approach using paired comparison procedures (Figure 11-5). The six steps were

Figure 11-5

A sample of the decision matrix approach to vendor selection.

	Criteria Weight (Step 2)	Supplier A	Supplier B	Supplier C	Supplier D	Supplier E
Criterion 1: Supplier can Fill Reorders	6	3 / 18	2 / 12	4 / 24	1 / 6	0 / 0
Criterion 2: Markup is Adequate	4	2 / 8	4 / 16	3 / 12	0 / 0	1 / 4
Criterion 3: Customers Ask for the Line	1	1 / 1	2 / 2	4 / 4	3 / 3	0 / 0
Criterion 4: Supplier's Line has Significant Changes from Season to Season	2	3 / 6	4 / 8	2 / 4	1 / 2	0 / 0
Criterion 5: Supplier's Line Contributes to Fashion Leadership	5	2 / 10	1 / 5	0 / 0	3 / 15	4 / 20
Criterion 6: Supplier's Line is Cut to Fit Customers Well	2	1 / 2	0 / 0	3 / 6	4 / 8	2 / 4
Criterion 7: Supplier Advertises Line in Local Media	1	0 / 0	1 / 1	2 / 2	4 / 4	3 / 3
Supplier TOTAL SCORES		45	44	52	38	31

Source: John S. Berens, "*A Decision Matrix Approach to Supplier Selection*", Journal of Retailing, Vol. 47, no. 4, (Winter 1971-1972), p. 52.

Step 1. Determine the relevant decision criteria for a given supplier-selection situation as discussed under vendor criteria.

Step 2. Use paired comparison procedures (comparing each criterion with every other criterion) to determine the relative weight (in numerical terms) of the decision criteria.

Step 3. Decide on the group of suppliers to be considered using the resource file.

Step 4. Compare each supplier with every other supplier by means of the paired comparison technique so as to determine how well each compares with every other (in numerical terms) relative to each rank-ordered criterion.

Step 5. Using a decision matrix (for an example, see Figure 11–5), develop a score for each supplier for each criterion by multiplying the value obtained in Step 2 by the value obtained in Step 4. The total weighted value for a supplier is found by adding the numerical values derived using the various criteria.

Step 6. Select the highest ranked supplier for inclusion in the firm's assortment. If more than one supplier is desired or the first choice is a Class D vendor (one who currently will not sell to the store), the vendor with the next highest ranking should then be considered. Such a procedure is followed until the desired number of vendors for a given line are chosen.

To aid in the self-evaluation process, the National Retail Merchants Association conducts periodic surveys that ask retailers to evaluate resources with the results being published by the Association.[9] From looking at such information, the retailer is able to learn what other merchants feel about a supplier in terms of vendor performance and product quality.

The procedures as outlined offer the retailer the opportunity to use a systematic approach for evaluating various vendors in a uniform manner. Such a methodology will, however, prove beneficial only if the retailer puts much effort into the development of the decision criteria and into an objective evaluation and ranking of the various suppliers.

Desired Number of Resources

As noted in Step 6 of the suggested procedure for selecting resources, one or more vendors may be chosen. Such a procedure does not determine how many sources of supply should be used. Should a retailer spread the store's business over many suppliers or concentrate all purchases with a few vendors? Those who favor concentration feel that such an arrangement tends to lead to lower-cost merchandise and lower expenses for buying, freight, receiving, marking, and invoice processing. Concentration is also thought to make the retailer a more important customer in the eyes of vendors, thereby making the store more eligible for preferred treatment (e.g., special allowances or assistance, earlier deliveries, and easier negotiations on returns and adjustments). The argument for concentration is essentially one that favors large economies of scale. Large shipments from few suppliers mean fewer invoices to handle as well as fewer (but larger) boxes that usually result in lower total shipping costs and more efficient receiving, marking, and general handling.[10]

The argument against concentration of resources is based on the idea that a store should "never put all its eggs in a few baskets." By spreading purchases among additional suppliers the retailer has greater assurance that salable items are not missed. Supplier complacency is also prevented. Third, insurance is provided against a decline in competence of a source of supply. Fourth, better protection is possible against the effects of strikes, fires, and acts of God that involve sources of supply.[11] Finally, in times of scarcity, the retailer who has been dealing with several suppliers seems to have access to more total merchandise during such crisis times as compared with those who buy from one source. Although not always true, it generally pays the retailer to have several sources of supply when a desired resource is scarce.

Whether or not to concentrate purchases is a question faced by all retailers. The advantages of concentration are many. Much can also be said for spreading the purchases around to many vendors. After carefully evaluating the many factors, the wise merchant will probably strike some sort of middle course. The advantages of concentration will be obtained by working very closely with a few key resources while leaving the door open to other vendors by purchasing small amounts from them. Such buying practices should encourage the less important sources to strive to improve their positions and inspire the already important sources to do their utmost to maintain their top spots.[12]

SUMMARY

A retailer who can stock his or her store with appropriate merchandise is generally ahead of the game. The secret of success, in many such situations, is knowing where to obtain such merchandise. Contact with available resources takes place in many ways. In-store sales calls, merchandise centers, trade shows, supplier advertisements and catalogs, and resident buying offices, whether company owned or independent, are all means for bringing the retailer and resource together. If the situation warrants, market contact may also be made through central buying offices, which may involve specification buying, or full-service merchandising, which includes voluntary chains, rack jobbers, and leased departments, as well as programmed merchandisers. Having examined the various sources of supply, a resource file should be developed that will contain all pertinent information about each possible supplier. Since the resource file will contain many more firms than the typical retailer will ever use, an effort should be made to evaluate each vendor. Salability of merchandise, price and terms of sale, services rendered, cooperation, and reliability are some of the proposed criteria. A systematic procedure to compare resources is also suggested in order to select with care the best possible suppliers. Finally, the question of how many resources to use must be answered. Should a firm concentrate all purchases with a few suppliers or spread the business around among many firms? As a general rule, a middle-of-the-road approach is found to be best.

1. Discuss five distinct ways in which retailer/vendor contact is achieved. Which situation is best for the retailer? For the vendor?
2. For a retailer, which is better—a trade show or a merchandise mart—for making contact with suppliers? What are the advantages and disadvantages of each?
3. What is a resident buying office? Explain how the various types serve the retailer.
4. All independent buying offices are the same. Comment on this statement.
5. What should a retail organization consider when deciding on whether to use central buying or a resident buying office?
6. Explain the term "specification buying." Under what circumstances is such a procedure desirable?
7. Explain what is meant by the terms:
   a. Voluntary chain.
   b. Rack jobber.
   c. Leased department.
   d. Programmed merchandising.
   e. Full-service merchandising.
8. Go to a retailer in your area and ask to see the store's resource file. Explain the procedure that is used by the store to develop its file.
9. What is meant by the term *vendor criteria*? What criteria might be used to analyze suppliers? Are any criteria more important than any others?
10. Explain Berens' approach for comparison of resources. Does such a procedure minimize the need for close managerial attention to the question of resource selection?
11. Should a retailer concentrate on a few resources or spread the business around among many suppliers? Discuss the pros and cons of all possible courses of action.

NOTES

[1] For more information on resident buying offices, see Robert G. Borden and Susan Hayward, "Getting the Most from the Buying Office" in *The Buyer's Manual*, ed. R. Patrick Cash (New York: National Retail Merchants Association, 1979), pp. 45–55.

[2] For an in-depth discussion of specification buying, see William T. Kelley, "Specification Buying by the Large-Scale Retailer," *Journal of Marketing*, Vol. 18, no. 3 (January 1954), pp. 255–265, published by the American Marketing Association.

[3] Louis Carrol, "The Vendor Must Have a Plan," *Stores*, Vol. 56, no. 2 (February 1974), p. 8. Copyright, National Retail Merchants Association.

[4] For additional comments on this concept, see "Programmed Merchandising," *Department Store Economist*, Vol. 27, no. 10 (October 1964), pp. 22–27. "How Stores Benefit from Programmed Merchandising," *Department Store Economist*, Vol. 29, no. 1 (January 1966), pp. 30–33.

[5] *The Buyer's Manual*, rev. ed. (New York: National Retail Merchants Association, 1965), pp. 71–74.

[6] Donald L. Belden, *The Role of the Buyer in Mass Merchandising* (New York: Chain Store Age Books, 1971), p. 19.

[7] Ronald E. Gist, *Retailing: Concepts and Decisions* (New York: John Wiley and Sons, Inc., 1968), pp. 293–295.

[8] Joseph S. Berens, "A Decision Matrix Approach to Supplier Selection," *Journal of Retailing*, Vol. 47, no. 4 (Winter 1971–1972), pp. 47–53.

[9] Results of vendor surveys have been published in *Stores*, a National Retail Merchants Association publication: Junior and Misses Sportswear Manufacturers, October 1975; Men's Sportswear Manufacturers, January 1977; Junior and Misses Dress Manufacturers, September 1978.

[10] Edwin W. Crooks, "The Case for Concentration of Purchases," *Journal of Retailing*, Vol. 42, no. 2 (Summer 1966), pp. 14–18.

[11] Belden, *The Role of the Buyer in Mass Merchandising*, p. 18.

[12] Ibid., p. 19.

CHAPTER 12

Negotiating for Merchandise

B. C.

B.C. by permission of Johnny Hart and Field Enterprises, Inc.

"How much should a retailer pay for any item?" asked a new buyer trainee. "No more than necessary," was the retail manager's reply. The answer, although an over-simplification, represents the goal of every retail store. By never paying more than necessary, the retailer is in a good position to maximize total profit from the sale of merchandise. If the retail price is the same, then every penny saved on the cost of the merchandise means more profit for the store.

In the process of negotiation, points of give and take that affect the total cost of an item include trade and other discounts, dating, transportation, price guarantees, and distribution rights. In addition, consignment buying or memorandum buying may be negotiating possibilities for new merchandise if the retailer does not wish to tie up money in the item. Negotiating often takes on an added dimension as more and more retailers import items bought in countries whose business practices differ from those found in the United States. Regardless of the factors involved in a particular retail situation, however, two underlying variables (ethics and law) appear to have an important bearing on all negotiations with vendors. Because of their importance, such variables are the logical place to begin a discussion on negotiating for merchandise.

ETHICS AND VENDORS

In his monthly publication, *Retailing Today,* Robert Kahn tells of a major retailer who sent out a letter unilaterally imposing penalty charges on vendors. The letter included a statement that defective goods returned without authorization and not accepted by the vendor will be donated to charity. One vendor wrote in reply, "We have in the past accepted merchandise from you without authorization. However, this experience has proven that you abuse the privilege you are requesting. We have received merchandise from you that is over a year old and not damaged. We have received merchandise with footprints embedded into the garments. We have received merchandise where entire leg seams have been maliciously ripped. And we have received merchandise which has been intentionally damaged."[1] If such statements are true, is this the most ethical way for a retailer to treat a vendor? Will such behavior promote the offer of a "best" price from the vendor? Probably not!

It is very important for the vendor and retailer to treat each other "right" if such firms are to have a profitable, long-term relationship. Ethics in buying involves nothing more than the Golden Rule—"Do unto the buyer or seller as you would have him do unto you." Give a "fair price" and "accept a fair price." The retailer *should not* insist on extreme price concessions from the supplier. In turn, the retailer *should* insist upon the allowances and other price considerations that are due the store. By treating the vendor in an ethical or fair manner, rewards may come to the retailer. Deliveries may be more prompt. More information on products may be forthcoming. Assistance of all types may come to those who assume a position of wishing to work with the vendor for the good of both parties.

It should be noted that, for the Golden Rule to work, both parties must be willing to pursue a commonly understood ethical business course. Since ethics are an individual decision, what is considered ethical to a particular retailer may be thought to be unethical to a particular supplier. Such problems of interpretation are multiplied when the retailer goes international. Ethics, among other things, are a function of culture. If in a country, it is considered ethical for all sellers to collude on price or to take "unfair" advantage of the buyer, if possible, then such a discussion on ethics becomes an academic exercise for the retailer. In a situation such as this, the important thing to note is the ethical position of the supplier and to remember it! In all negotiations with resources, the retailer should deal from a position of strength by making every effort to determine how ethics may affect the transaction.

LAWS AND VENDORS

Laws are said to be a minimum code of ethics. Where ethical business practices do not prevail or where strong competitive pressures cause inconsistencies in desired behavior patterns, laws have been enacted to prohibit unfair buying practices. As noted in Chapter 3, regulations at the federal level are found that place restraints on retailer/vendor negotiations. The most significant is the Robinson–Patman Act, which states, in essence, that any price differentials that cannot be justified are considered illegal. A discount must not be arbitrary unless offered to all. It is noted that price differentials given to larger stores are not illegal under the law provided that such price differences are commensurate with the savings that result from large orders. In view of the Robinson–Patman Act and other regulations, the law-abiding retailer sets as his or her negotiating goal—the lowest legal price. How laws affect the different possible discounts is discussed now as each discount is examined. [2]

POINTS OF NEGOTIATION

The goal of the lowest legal price will be achieved only if the retailer makes an assertive effort. In many situations, discounts go to those who ask. Favorable due dates go to those who request such dates. The consumer who pays the "sticker price" for a car is usually one who did not request a lower price. In all situations, the main point to remember is to request such terms before you purchase the merchandise. Also, get the terms agreed to in writing before you sign. Within the restraints of ethics and law, the retailer should not pay the "sticker price" for merchandise acquired from vendors.

Although anything can affect the price to be paid, common points of negotiation include the following (Figure 12–1):

Trade Discount

Trade discounts are given to a certain type of customer (retailer, wholesaler, etc.) to cover the cost of carrying out a particular function (credit, storage, selling, etc.). Also called functional discounts, such price reductions enable a supplier to have one price list for all firms in the channel of distribution. In some cases a supplier may use such a

Figure 12-1

Vendor/retailer points of negotiation.

price list to suggest the retail price of the item. This price list is the starting point for all discounts. Such trade discounts make price changes very easy for the supplier. Instead of having new lists printed up each time, the resource can simply change the trade discounts offered to the various firms within the channel of distribution.

Trade or functional discounts are usually quoted in a form, such as 10-10-10-5 for a particular firm, with each number representing a particular percentage off for each marketing function being performed. Such discounts mean, for example, that if an item has a suggested retail price of $395, the cost to the firm after trade discounts will be

$$
\begin{array}{ccccc}
\$395 & -\$39.50 = & \$355.50 & -\$35.55 = & \$319.95 \\
\text{x} \quad 10\% & & \text{x} \quad 10\% & & \text{x} \quad 10\% \\
\hline
\$39.50 & & \$\ 35.55 & & \$\ 32.00 \\
\end{array}
$$

$$
\begin{array}{ccccc}
 & -\$32.00 = & \$287.95 & -\$14.40 = & \$273.55 \\
 & & \text{x} \qquad 5\% & & \\
 & & \hline
 & & \$\ 14.40 & & \\
\end{array}
$$

Total cost = $273.55

Note that functional discounts are not added first and then calculated. In the example, the trade discount is not 35 percent with a resulting price of $256.75. Each is instead calculated on the declining balance.

Legally, trade discounts appear to be justified if they truly represent a savings to a supplier. If a resource sells an item to a retailer who in turn provides certain marketing functions such as the promotion of the product to the ultimate consumer, then the savings to the supplier that result from this arrangement can be reflected legally in the discount structure. From a legal standpoint, trade discounts that are offered to all in a business category are legal. When a discount is not offered to all in a business group, legal problems arise.

Quantity Discounts

Quantity discounts are a reduction in price as a result of the amount purchased. Such discounts are usually based on the total amount of all items in an order, not just the amount of one particular item ordered. The reduction takes one of three forms: noncumulative, cumulative, and special merchandise.

Noncumulative. Such a discount is a one-time consideration. For a particular order, the supplier may offer a reduction of 5 percent per case for all orders over 5 cases and 7½ percent for all orders over 10 cases. For example, if a retailer had a $225.00 order that consisted of 7 cases, the quantity discount would be $11.25 ($225.00 x 5%). This amount would be deducted from the amount of the order ($225.00) and the price to be paid would be $213.75. The amount of $11.25 is "paid" to the retailer for purchasing in larger quantities.

Cumulative. A cumulative discount can be better described as a patronage discount. Such a reduction is based on the total amount purchased during a set period as opposed to one individual purchase. For example, a discount of 5 percent may be available for all purchases over $10,000 or 5,000 units for the year. An additional 5 percent on all purchases over $20,000 or 10,000 units acquired during the period may be the next step in the discount structure. Such discounts are what their name implies. Patronage is encouraged over time in order to accumulate discount credits that will result in lower per unit prices. A word of caution is in order for users and recipients of cumulative quantity discounts. Such discounts could be considered to be restraining trade under Robinson–Patman if the supplier makes it too advantageous to buy from him or her throughout the period. The supplier must be able to show that the cumulative discount is not greater than the savings the firm will incur by having some knowledge of the demand it will have through the year.

Special Merchandise. A discount of this nature takes the form of merchandise rather than an outright price reduction. If a retailer buys eleven dozen steam and dry irons, the twelfth dozen is free. Such a "discount" will encourage the retailer who normally buys six to eight dozen to go ahead and purchase the additional merchandise so as to obtain the free merchandise. Such merchandise discounts are normally designed to encourage order sizes that are economical for the vendor to process. In some cases, for example, a pallet-sized load will be the order size to be encouraged since it can be handled much more efficiently in the distribution channel than can an order either somewhat smaller or larger in size.

Although attractive upon first examination, a closer look at special merchandise discounts reveals that they can place an extreme hardship on small retail firms. The small store may only need three dozen irons, at most, for a selling season. To buy eleven dozen to get one dozen for free puts a heavy inventory burden on the business. So great is this burden in some cases that stores have been forced to forgo the long-term savings to keep inventories at a realistic level. Special merchandise quantity discounts are not for everyone.

Quantity discounts derive their rationale from the fact that all costs incurred by a vendor are not found to be a function of the units ordered. Many costs are the same regardless of the size of the order. The salesperson who sells a $10,000 order and a $100,000 order will generally have the same out-of-pocket expenses for both. It stands to reason, therefore, that certain savings should come to those who buy in large quantities. As stated in the Robinson–Patman Act, the same quantity discounts must be given to all retailers buying the same amount of "like grade and quality" merchandise. The problem has been the meaning of "like grade and quality." Does the term imply physical characteristics or all differences (brands, package, etc.)? Court decisions have not been consistent on this point. In addition, the amount of the discount should be consistent with the savings which result from the large order. If the size of the quantity discount is greater than the savings that result to the vendor, both the vendor and the retailer can be charged with price discrimination. If a retailer, usually a large firm, puts pressure on the supplier to agree to a price that discriminates against other retailers, the firm is opening itself up to possible legal action. To restate an earlier point, the retailer should strive for the lowest legal price. The retailer should negotiate with the supplier to obtain the best possible quantity discount. To assist in the negotiations, the retailer should strive to obtain information about what the supplier is giving others in the way of discounts. Information from other stores and industry surveys of supplier trade practices are two possible sources of this type information.

Seasonal Discounts

Seasonal discounts are a means by which the supplier encourages the retailer to buy merchandise in the off season. By buying a carload lot of backyard swimming pools in October, or Christmas decorations in February, the retailer may receive a discount of from approximately 5 to 15 percent of the invoice price. In negotiating for the amount of the discount, the retailer should not take the early merchandise for a discount that is less than the cost involved in storing the merchandise plus the interest on the money tied up in that inventory. In negotiations, the retailer should remember that many benefits accrue to the vendor in an off-season purchase. Such buys help the vendor to operate more efficiently and serve to reduce warehouse requirements. As is true with other discounts, federal law requires the supplier to give the same seasonal discount to all firms in a particular business category. Seasonal discounts are permitted to fluctuate as the purchase date nears the normal buying season. The only requirement is that at a given point in time, all like firms receive a like discount.

Promotional Discounts

A supplier may wish to have advertisements for a product placed over the store name in a newspaper. To ensure that such ads will be run, a certain amount (for example, 5 percent of net invoice price or possibly $1.00 per unit) will be deducted from the cost of the merchandise.

Promotional allowances take many forms besides payment for advertising the product. A retailer may agree to feature an item in a display window in return for a discount. Preferred shelf space may go to those who pay the price. Sales personnel may be instructed to push certain items as a result of a promotional allowance provided by a supplier. These and many other possibilities make up the broad category of promotional discounts.

Under Federal Trade Commission guidelines, promotional allowances must be made available to all on a proportional basis. Such was the purpose of the "tombstone ad" cited in Chapter 3 that told of available promotional discounts for customers of Procter & Gamble. The difficulty with the guidelines is the term, "proportional." If the promotional discount is $1.00 a case, such a discount is no problem. The total promotional discount is determined by the amount purchased. If, instead, the promotional allowance is, for example, in the form of a large display case, such an allowance may not be economically justified for a small store assuming that the small store would even desire the large display case. In such a situation, the vendor and retailer must determine what would be a comparable compensation on a smaller scale. Any promotional allowance or discount not in line proportionately with promotional assistance given to other merchants has been found to be illegal. In negotiating with vendors, the merchant should insist on a proportional fair share of any promotional assistance that is made available to retailers.

Cash Discounts

A discount for paying before the due date is referred to as a cash discount. In return for the prompt payment of the invoice, the vendor will usually allow up to 4 percent off the net invoice price after other discounts. The most common discount is 2 percent, which is generally given for payment within 10 days of a 30-day obligation. Such a discount is usually shown on the invoice as 2/10–net 30.

The retailer who is wise in the ways of buying will insist on a cash discount from the vendor and then take advantage of it by using the discount. By taking the discount, the retailer achieves the goal of improving the store's credit rating in the industry by becoming known as a prompt payer. Such action also gives the retailer what many refer to as a profit cushion.[3] The idea of the profit cushion stems from the fact that some retail stores make little profit on a percentage basis. If cash discounts are not taken, profits would instead be losses. Because the impact of cash discounts on profits is so great, it will generally pay the retailer to borrow money in order to take advantage of any early payment opportunity. For example, as noted in Figure 12–2, the equivalent annual interest rate for the example of 2 percent/10 days–net 30 days is 36 percent for the 20-day period between the last day of discount and the invoice due date. Borrowing money at even the exorbitant rate of 25 percent is still a money-making proposition for the store in this example as well as in many similar situations.

The retailer can see the importance of striving for the highest possible cash discount figure. As noted in Figure 12–2, for a 30-day net payment period each additional 1 percent cash discount for the first 10 days means a difference of 18 percent interest on an annual basis. By just asking, the retailer may obtain a 1 percent increase in the discount or a 1 percent increase in the profit cushion on that particular merchandise.

On what amount should the cash discount be taken? As noted earlier, the amount is based on the net invoice price which is total invoice minus all discounts. Accepted accounting practice would stop at this point. Actual practice for many firms

Figure 12–2

Cash discounts versus annual rates of interest.

Terms	Equivalent Annual Interest Rate (%)
1/10 net 30	18
2/10 net 60	14
2/30 net 60	24
2/10 net 30	36
3/10 net 30	54
4/10 net 60	29

Computation	Net Time	Discount Time	Days Due Without Discount	360-Day Year*	Time Units in Year	Discount Rate (%)
2/10 net 30 = 36 per cent	30	− 10	= 20	÷ 360	= 18	X 2

*Common practice divides year into equal parts or 360 day year.

will go a step further and include the transportation charges in the invoice figure from which the cash discount will be taken. It is the responsibility of the buyer to ascertain if the vendor will permit transportation to be included in the base figure for purposes of calculating the cash discount.

What if the supplier desires to give no cash discount, should a discount be insisted upon anyway? What if the supplier is willing to give a discount of 1/10, should a 2 percent discount be the minimum acceptable figure? The answer to these questions is found in industry trade practices. The retail buyer must make an effort to determine if others are being permitted to take more desirable discounts. If such is the case, the smart negotiator will request such discounts, and if not granted, will consider taking such discounts anyway.

Dating

Dating is another point of negotiation between supplier and retailer. Basically, dating establishes when the retailer should pay for the merchandise. The importance to the merchant in obtaining favorable dating is just as significant as obtaining a particular discount. The longer the period before the payment is due, the longer the retailer will have the use of the money committed to that obligation. This point of negotiation is subject to much discussion since the supplier generally wants the money early while the retailer wishes to delay payment for as long as possible. If, for example, 2/10 net 30 are the terms of sale after other discounts then the 10-day discount period and the 30-day net period are both examples of dating.

Dating falls into two categories: immediate and future. Under immediate dating are the following:

Immediate—Prepayment. This requirement is generally found when a vendor is providing customized or limited-life merchandise to a questionable retailer. By questionable, the vendor feels that not enough is known about the store (usually new) or that too much is known (usually a bad credit rating). For example, a new gift shop in San Antonio, Texas, orders customized souvenir T-shirts featuring the Alamo. Such shirts are of little or no value to any other merchant. To ensure against potential loss as a result of the new store, the vendor will require payment before processing the order. Examples of limited-life merchandise include fad items and high-fashion clothing. To ship such merchandise COD to a retailer who is questionable may mean that, by the time the merchandise is reacquired by the vendor due to nonpayment, the demand for the item will be nil.

The retailer should strive to develop a good credit record as soon as possible so as not to have to accept prepayment terms. In the meantime, the buyer should ascertain if such terms will be required so money can be sent with the order. To just send the order will delay the merchandise since most suppliers will not begin the processing of such an order until payment is received.

Immediate—Cash on Delivery. For merchandise that is returnable since it is not customized or does not have a limited life, COD terms may be possible for the marginal retailer. In other words, the retailer will pay for the merchandise upon delivery. As is true for prepayment terms, efforts should be made to achieve a position where such terms will not be required.

For both prepayment and cash-on-delivery immediate dating situations, the retailer should not forget the various possible discounts that may be available. Most discounts are figured for such dating. The one that is many times left out is the cash discount. Under immediate dating, the store is paying cash for the item. Under such circumstances, the retail buyer should request a cash discount that is equivalent to those discounts being given under future dating. In many situations, cash discounts for paying cash are never mentioned unless the store brings up the subject. The smart retailer will.

As for future dating, any terms that permit a delay in payment are considered in this category. Examples of future dating include the following:

Future—Net Dating. The bill is due in a stated number of days (e.g., net 30) from invoice date. No discounts are given. The retailer is permitted to delay payment for the merchandise for the predetermined period of time. Even with no discounts, it is advantageous for the retailer to seek the longest possible net dating period. If, for example, the retailer through negotiation received net 120 as opposed to net 30 terms, the merchant now has 90 days longer before payment is due. In that additional 90 days, the retailer can use the money for other purposes or even put it in a 90-day passbook account or money market fund and earn interest on the transaction. The cash position of the retail store has been improved by the fact that the retailer has negotiated an extension in the net billing period.

Future—Cycle Dating. Cycle dating involves either end-of-month (EOM) or middle-of-month (MOM) terms. Under EOM terms, the date for beginning the determination as to when the cash discount and balance are due is automatically moved to the beginning of the month following the invoice date. For example, invoices with terms 2/10 net 30 EOM and dated July 1, July 10, and July 20, respectively, would all permit a cash discount through August 10 and call for full payment by August 30. It is noted that in actual practice, most firms treat the 25th of the month as the cut-off date. Therefore, a purchase with an invoice date of July 26 could qualify for the discount through September 10 and be due on September 30.

Middle-of-the-month (MOM) terms divide the month into two units instead of one as under EOM. Careful planning can get up to 20 days extra under this approach. For the purchase made on July 26, the invoice terms would begin on August 16. The same five-day cushion is also generally found for the middle of the month. Under such terms, the actual cut-off dates for terms are usually the 10th and the 25th of the month unless the stated dates are the 15th and the last day of the month.

By careful placement of orders, the retailer can get either an extra 35 days or 20 days to pay an obligation. For merchandise that is not critical, placing the order on October 26 instead of October 23 with a supplier using cycle dating will improve the position of the store by delaying payment. More time is given to sell the merchandise before the obligation comes due.

Future—Receipt-of-Goods. Under these terms, the determination of date due is dependent upon the receipt of the goods by the retailer. For an invoice of 2/10 net 30 ROG dated March 12, the important date is June 17, the date of arrival for the merchandise. Under such terms the last date for discount is June 27. ROG or AOG (arrival-of-goods) terms are especially important to a retailer who is some distance from a supplier. If ordinary dating is used, the discount period may be up before the goods even arrive. In such situations, the retailer is forced to decide between taking a cash discount by paying for unseen merchandise or delaying payment and losing the discount. Such is not a problem with ROG. It is advantageous for the merchant to seek ROG terms in the purchase agreement. Even if the vendor is close by, terms that start only after the goods have arrived are in favor of the buyer. Such terms tend to make the supplier more anxious to accomplish delivery. The terms also keep the leverage of payment in favor of the retailer until after the goods have been inspected by the retailer upon arrival.

Future—Extended Dating. Extended dating takes two general forms. Terms that state 2/10 net 30–60 give the retailer 60 extra days or what amounts to a 70-day discount period and 90 days in which to complete payment on the invoice. Extended dating of this type may be given by a seller of slow-moving items who is trying to encourage fewer but larger orders as opposed to several smaller orders from a retailer.

Another form of extended dating is not contingent on the invoice date for determination of the terms. For example, 2/10 net 30 as of January 1 would call for a discount period of up to January 10 and due date of January 30 regardless of whether the invoice was dated June 15, August 6, or October 27. The retailer should request such terms when buying well in advance of the selling season. Merchandise bought by the retailer in May for sale during the Christmas season would be an example of a situation that would warrant such terms. The retailer may take delivery of the merchandise in July, which will aid the supplier's warehouse situation. In return for this assistance, the retailer should request extended terms. From the retailer's viewpoint, under such terms, the invoice due date should not precede the selling season of the merchandise covered by the invoice.

Anticipation

An additional point of negotiation is referred to as anticipation. For the retailer who has successfully obtained terms of 2/10–net 30–60 for an invoice dated September 1, what happens if the retailer wishes to pay the invoice on September 10 rather than waiting until November 10 to pay the invoice with discount? Do any additional savings result from such an early payment? With anticipation, the answer is "yes."

Anticipation is calculated in the following manner:

1. Determine the number of days remaining in the discount period. In the example given, assume 30-day months:

70 days in discount period	(September 1 to November 10)
−10 days into period	(September 1 to September 10)
60 days remaining in discount period	

2. Determine the interest rate for purposes of anticipation. The rate may be a point of negotiation. In other cases, it is the prime rate (rate of interest given to major business customers by large financial institutions) or it may be quoted at 6 percent, a somewhat standard figure in many industries. As a general rule, use 6 percent unless otherwise stated.

3. Adjust annual interest rate for anticipation to proportion of year involved in the transaction. In the example, 60 days remain in the discount period. Using the standard 360-day year results in a determination of an anticipation rate of 1 percent:

$$\frac{60}{360} = \frac{1}{6} \times 6\% = 1\%$$

4. Take cash discount in normal manner. Assuming a $1,000 invoice cost, terms of 2 percent yield a net invoice price of $980.

5. Take anticipation from invoice after all discounts. In the example, $980 x 1% = $9.80 anticipation or a net amount due of $970.20 if paid on September 10. Note that it is common in some industries to combine the cash discount rate and the anticipation rate before figuring the discount. Using the example given, the retailer would deduct 3 percent (2% cash discount plus 1% anticipation) from the $1,000 invoice cost or pay $970 on September 10.

Anticipation is a practice followed faithfully by large stores since it can result in a significant reduction in price. Such an arrangement is obviously more advantageous the higher the rate of anticipation permitted. If the anticipation rate is less than the market rate of return on short-term money, the use of anticipation may not be desirable on the part of the retailer.

How does the retailer know if anticipation can be taken? Invoices may state that anticipation is allowed or not permitted. The rate of anticipation may also be given, if applicable. In many cases, however, anticipation will be permitted but will not be shown on the invoice or be mentioned by the seller during the negotiations. Industry practice or custom may permit anticipation by only those firms who know of the practice or custom. The good retailer makes an effort to learn of such business practices. If all else fails, the retailer may wish to anticipate all invoices that do not state otherwise. By so doing, the retailer will be performing a firsthand test of business practices. For suppliers who accept the anticipated payments, indications are that such firms will permit anticipation on a continuous basis. Information of this nature should be recorded in the retailer's resource file (see Chapter 11) for future reference.

Transportation

As far as the retailer is concerned, the cost of the item includes the cost of getting the merchandise to the store. In addition, negotiations should also deal with how and when the merchandise will be shipped. Most merchandise is shipped FOB (Free On Board) Shipping Point or Point of Origin. Such terms mean that the buyer (retailer) has ownership of the merchandise during shipment and, therefore, can determine the method of transportation. Under these conditions, transportation would not be included in the purchase price. It is also important to note that should the merchandise be lost in transit, the retailer must pay the vendor and settle any claims with the transport company since ownership did pass at the shipping point. Such would not be the case if the negotiated terms were FOB Destination. See Figure 12–3 for six different ways in which to quote transportation in the terms of sale and their effect on the buyer and seller.

In comparing prices of vendors, care should be taken to equate prices where transportation is a factor. For example, if one vendor quotes a price of $1,000 FOB Shipping Point and a second vendor prices an order at $1,050 FOB Destination, the only way to equate the order costs is to determine the transportation cost for vendor A. When such analysis is made, it may be determined that what appeared to be the cheaper vendor may not result in the cheaper total for the order.

Type of Cost	Vendor A	Vendor B
Merchandise cost	$1,000	$1,050
Transportation cost	65	—
Order cost	$1,065	$1,050

Since so many orders are quoted other than FOB Destination, the retailer should make every effort to keep transportation costs to a minimum. For the small retailer, a freight consolidation service may be of assistance. Such a firm combines many small shipments to achieve the lower-cost carload and full truck rates. Usually the result is lower transportation cost for the retailer. Special care should also be taken in analyzing the freight bills to ensure that the retailer has not been overcharged. Auditing of such freight charges by a knowledgeable person many times will result in much savings for the store.

Figure 12-3

Selected transportation terms and their effect on buyer and seller.

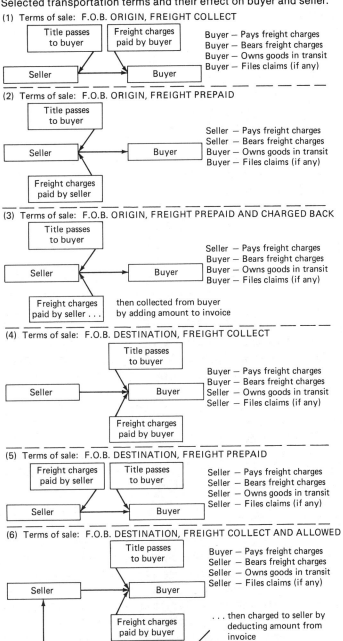

(1) Terms of sale: F.O.B. ORIGIN, FREIGHT COLLECT

Buyer — Pays freight charges
Buyer — Bears freight charges
Buyer — Owns goods in transit
Buyer — Files claims (if any)

(2) Terms of sale: F.O.B. ORIGIN, FREIGHT PREPAID

Seller — Pays freight charges
Seller — Bears freight charges
Buyer — Owns goods in transit
Buyer — Files claims (if any)

(3) Terms of sale: F.O.B. ORIGIN, FREIGHT PREPAID AND CHARGED BACK

Seller — Pays freight charges
Buyer — Bears freight charges
Buyer — Owns goods in transit
Buyer — Files claims (if any)

Freight charges paid by seller . . . then collected from buyer by adding amount to invoice

(4) Terms of sale: F.O.B. DESTINATION, FREIGHT COLLECT

Buyer — Pays freight charges
Buyer — Bears freight charges
Seller — Owns goods in transit
Seller — Files claims (if any)

(5) Terms of sale: F.O.B. DESTINATION, FREIGHT PREPAID

Seller — Pays freight charges
Seller — Bears freight charges
Seller — Owns goods in transit
Seller — Files claims (if any)

(6) Terms of sale: F.O.B. DESTINATION, FREIGHT COLLECT AND ALLOWED

Buyer — Pays freight charges
Seller — Bears freight charges
Seller — Owns goods in transit
Seller — Files claims (if any)

. . . then charged to seller by deducting amount from invoice

Source: John W. Wingate and Joseph S. Friedlander, *The Management of Retail Buying,* 2nd ed., © 1978, p. 295. Reprinted by permission of Prentice-Hall, Inc., Englewood Cliffs, New Jersey.

Another problem to be mentioned, and the most important for many retailers, is the method of shipment. Many vendors like to ship all merchandise to all buyers in the same manner via truck or UPS or whatever regardless of the instructions of the buyer who purchased the order under terms of FOB Shipping Point. When negotiating with such vendors for future merchandise, care should be taken to obtain an understanding as to how such orders will be handled. The retailer has the right to choose since the goods belong to the store while in transit.

One last point to consider is the relationship between transportation costs and cash discounts. Simply put, should retailers take the cash discount on the invoice cost or invoice cost plus transportation when both are shown on the invoice? Textbook accounting procedures permit the discount to be taken only on the invoice cost. Industry practice may, however, permit the cash discount to be taken on the transportation charges as well. As mentioned before, the retailer should make an effort to ascertain what are the trade practices for the industry, as this knowledge can result in a more profitable business for the retailer.

Price Guarantees

Merchandise purchased well in advance of the selling season will usually result in some advantage to the seller. Under such conditions, the retailer will normally seek various discounts as noted earlier. In addition, a price guarantee may be requested. Such a guarantee means that should the market price for the merchandise fall between the date of purchase and the normal purchase period, any savings that result from the lower price will be passed on to the retailer. If such an arrangement is agreed upon, the retailer has covered the store against any negative effects of a price change. If prices fall, a rebate is received. If prices rise, the retailer pays no more. In such negotiations, the merchant should attempt to stay away from an escalator clause. Such a clause is a price guarantee in favor of the vendor since it generally calls for the merchant to pay more if the market price should rise. Under conditions of inflation, the escalator clause is very popular with vendors. Retailers should be aware of the open-ended nature of prices under such an agreement. As a general rule merchants should consider price escalator clauses only as a last resort.

Distribution Rights

Can the retailer obtain exclusive rights to a product in an area in return for buying a substantial amount of an item or for adding the product to the store? Does the retailer have to give up anything to achieve this exclusive right? Can competing items be sold? Are certain levels of inventory for the exclusive merchandise required by the vendor? Are suggested retail prices strongly encouraged by the supplier? How large will the exclusive geographic area be for purposes of distribution? Answers to such questions may result in the merchant having no desire to have exclusive distribution rights to a product. The retailer should, however, examine the possibilities of such an arrangement. It may be that in a given set of circumstances, exclusive rights to a product much in demand may be the most important point in the vendor negotiations. Distribution rights should be studied with great care. It is a point rarely given to retailers unless requested.

Consignment Buying

If a retailer wants to carry an item in the store without buying it, the solution may be consignment buying. Under such an arrangement, ownership of the goods is retained by the supplier. Price is also usually determined solely by the resource. For each item sold, the retailer will deduct an agreed percentage from the selling price and remit the balance to the vendor. No money changes hands until the item is sold.

Consignment buying is popular whenever the retailer is dealing with an item of unknown demand. The first order for a particular product may be handled in this manner. Some gift shops accept homemade items for sale in this way. Student-operated book exchanges use consignment buying. The student (supplier) puts a price on a used book that is then placed in the book exchange. If the book is sold, a percentage is deducted with the balance going to the student. If it is not sold, the retailer has only lost the value of the shelf space taken up by the book. The book itself is not owned by the store so the store has no money tied up in inventory.

In examining the consignment option, the retailer should satisfy in his or her own mind why the firm (supplier) is willing to accept such terms. Since such terms are naturally not thought to be desirable to the vendor, why is the vendor willing to accept consignment buying or even push such an arrangement? The merchandise may be inferior or the vendor may just be trying to get such merchandise accepted by a cautious retailer. A question to ask is, "Will the vendor willingly accept merchandise previously delivered on consignment when it is returned, or claim some is damaged thereby stating that payment is due on such items?" Many problems can develop from a consignment arrangement. Before negotiating on such a point, the retailer should determine how cooperative the vendor will be in such a situation. Only through cooperation will consignment buying work.

Memorandum Buying

For those retailers concerned with the pricing aspect of consignment buying, memorandum buying permits the title to pass to the merchant with the resulting price flexibility while not giving up the right to return unsold items or paying for items only after they are sold. Memorandum buying is found to be quite common for some very expensive, one-of-a-kind items. Under this arrangement, most of the risk still rests with the supplier. As is true with consignment buying, the heart of any such arrangement is cooperation. Without cooperation, memorandum buying can be a major hassle for a retailer.

International Buying

When merchandise is purchased from outside the country, additional points of negotiation come into play. Freight terms may be quoted FAS (Free Along Side) Vessel, which means the supplier is quoting a price that includes getting the merchandise to the ocean-going vessel's dock. The buyer (retailer) must arrange for passage, pay all export and import tariffs as well as insurance, storage, and all expenses incurred at the dock. If the terms read CIF Port of Destination, the supplier assumes all the risk of shipment and pays all taxes related to the export of the item. The buyer takes over all obligations for the merchandise at the port of destination. CIF stands for cost, marine insurance, and all transportation charges (freight). Under such terms, all charges incurred up to the port of destination are paid by the supplier. As is true for FOB terms, the retailer should consider all prices after they are adjusted so that all include all charges to the same destination point whether it be dock-side or delivered to the store. Only then can an intelligent comparison of prices be made.

Aside from the additional freight terms, negotiating with foreign suppliers forces the retailer to become knowledgeable about foreign business practices and international monetary exchange rates. Various documents such as letters of credit and straight bills of lading also play an important role in international buying. A letter of credit simply defined is a letter written on a bank that states that a firm is good for the stated amount in the letter. The bill of lading is a transport carrier's document that serves as a document of title. A straight bill of lading is a transportation document only. A "to order" bill of lading requires the carrier to not deliver the merchandise until payment is received. Although bills of lading are also used in domestic shipping, their importance in international business is much greater due to the typical distances involved in such purchases. Since international buying is different, it is recommended that a firm seek out expert advice in the field before becoming involved in such activities. Such a store might wish to use resident buying offices which specialize in foreign buying. If the retailer knows of suppliers but is concerned with the mechanics of foreign trade, then major banks and other types of firms that have international departments can provide much advice and assistance.

SUMMARY

Negotiating for merchandise is a difficult but rewarding task for a retail store. Any time such efforts result in savings not otherwise available to a store, negotiations have been a success. Within the framework of ethics and law, points of negotiation include trade, quantity, seasonal, promotional, and cash discounts. Dating, anticipation, transportation charges, price guarantees, and distribution rights are additional factors that should be considered. Consignment and memorandum buying are particularly significant when acquiring products with unknown demand, since the risk for such purchases remains essentially with the supplier. With cultural, monetary, and transportation considerations all playing an important role, international buying requires an especially high level of expertise for the retail negotiator. The lowest legal price is the retailer's goal. Such a goal is not achieved without continuous effort on the retailer's part. Every purchase price should represent all the possible savings due the store. Anything else should still be open for further negotiations. The retailer must remember that the store has an ethical and legal right to a fair and just price.

---

1. How much should a store pay for an item? Include all variables that should be taken into consideration in commenting on this question.
2. Why are ethics a factor in negotiating for merchandise?
3. What is meant by the terms:
   a. Trade discount
   b. Quantity discount
   c. Seasonal discount
   d. Promotional discount
   e. Price guarantees
   f. Cash discount
   g. Consignment buying
   h. Distribution rights
   Cite examples of each.
4. An invoice reads: $2,500, 2/10 net 30 AOG, dated August 13. The goods were shipped on September 14 and arrived at the store on September 23.
   a. What is the last date for payment with discount?
   b. What is the amount due on date determined in part a?
   c. What is the last date for payment of account?
   d. What is the amount due on date determined in part c?
5. What is anticipation? By means of an example, explain how it is calculated.
6. An invoice reads: $1,000, 2/10 net 30–90, dated June 6. If the retailer pays the invoice on June 16, what would be the amount paid, assuming that 6 percent anticipation is allowed?
7. Gifts and Things, a gift shop located in a regional shopping mall, has just purchased a shipment of Christmas decorations from Santa Works, Inc. with a suggested list price for the shipment of $5,000. Trade discounts permitted by the vendor were 30–15–10. In addition, since the merchandise was delivered in the off season, a 10 percent seasonal discount was also provided. Also, as is normally the case for this supplier, a 5 percent quantity discount was given for purchases in the $5,000 category. Other terms were 2/30 net 90–90 as of March 1. The invoice date was January 14, and the goods were delivered on February 27. Note that Santa Works allowed anticipation to be figured at the 8 percent level.
   a. What would be the amount due on March 1?
   b. What is the last date for payment with cash discount?
   c. What is the last date for payment of the account?
   d. What is the amount due on date determined in part c?
8. Contempo Fashions has a practice of offering retailers the choice of either 3/20 net 60 or 2/20 net 30–60 terms on its invoice. Either choice permits anticipation at an 8 percent level. If the retailer pays the invoice within 10 days of the invoice date, which set of terms should the retailer select?
9. If the retailer has a cash flow problem, taking cash discounts may require the firm to borrow money to pay its obligations within the cash discount period. If the terms of sale are 2/20 net 60, with a 360-day year, what would be the maximum annual rate of interest that the retailer could borrow at and still break even on the transaction?

10. Why is international buying any different from domestic buying? What problems, if any, are encountered in international buying that affect the negotiating performance of the retailer?

NOTES

[1] Robert Kahn, *Retailing Today*, Vol. 15, no. 12 (December 1980), p. 4.

[2] For a closer look at questionable retail buying practices, see Jeffrey H. Birnbaum, "Major Department Stores are the Focus of an FTC Probe over Buying Practices," *The Wall Street Journal*, Vol. 196, no. 101 (November 20, 1980), p. 4.

[3] *The Buyer's Manual*, rev. ed. (New York: National Retail Merchants Association, 1965), p. 88.

CHAPTER 13

Pricing of Merchandise

Jim's Record Shop sells a popular album for $10.95 while Gibson's sells it for $6.95. An oil change at Sam's Service Station costs $9.50, $2.00 more than the price at Terry's Texaco. The same brand of boy's tennis shoes may sell for $17.95 at one store and $27.95 at another. These examples serve to illustrate that there is much variation in prices for the same item at the retail level. This chapter will examine reasons for these price differentials. In addition, the mathematics of pricing is presented. Finally, the causes and timing of markdowns are discussed.

FACTORS INFLUENCING PRICE

What should an item sell for? What is the service worth? The answers to these and similar questions depend on many factors. Who is the target market? What about competition? What types of costs and how much costs are involved? What is the role of price in the retailing mix? Does the item or service have any unique characteristics? Are there any legal points to be considered? Although the pricing of an item is in many respects a judgment decision on the part of the retailer, such judgment will be enhanced if the factors which influence price are taken into consideration (Figure 13–1).

Target Market

What price will the market accept? The demographics of the market will have a bearing on what the market can pay and/or will be willing to pay for an item. Does the particular target market, for example, equate quality and price? Research has confirmed the tendency for some consumers to view price as a communication of quality and related product attributes from the pricemaker.[1] If this is so, a higher price within a tolerable price range may be in order provided that such is the desired image. The other side of the issue is also important. What influences, if any, will a lower price have on the market? Will such a price convey an image of poor quality to the target market? These and similar concerns can be answered somewhat by examining the price elas-

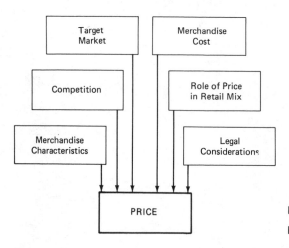

Figure 13–1

Factors influencing retail price.

ticity of demand for the item. In other words, what will be the consumer demand for the item at different price levels?

Simply put, price elasticity of demand[2] is a concept that determines the effect of a given price change on demand. It is computed by dividing the percentage change in quantity demanded by the percentage change in price:

$$\text{Coefficient of Price Elasticity} = \frac{\dfrac{\text{Quantity 1} - \text{Quantity 2}}{\text{Quantity 1} + \text{Quantity 2}}}{\dfrac{\text{Price 1} - \text{Price 2}}{\text{Price 1} + \text{Price 2}}} \quad \text{or} \quad \frac{\%\ \text{Change (Quantity)}}{\%\ \text{Change (Price)}}$$

Under normal circumstances, the coefficient of price elasticity is negative because price and quantity are inversely related (a lower price means greater quantity demanded, and vice versa). If an item is price elastic, the coefficient will be greater than plus or minus one. An inelastic coefficient will be less than one.

If an item is price elastic, a change in price will influence consumer demand. An inelastic situation would find a change in price having little or no influence on demand. The amount of the price shift can also influence consumer reaction. A slight change in price may have little influence on the target market. A price that represents a significant change from the market price will result in some change in consumer demand if the item's price adjustment is thought to be significant when measured against the consumer's purchasing power. The availability of substitutes is also an influence on elasticity. Products with many substitutes tend to have a high level of elasticity (a change in price results in a significant change in demand). The one-of-a-kind item, having no substitute, does not find its demand being affected as greatly by a change in the price.

For items that have no established price, it is hard to determine the "right" price and to establish the degree of elasticity that the price might have for use in developing the original price and future markdowns. In addition, care must be given not to price the item too low or too high. As noted, customers do tend to equate quality and price.

Competition

Consumers do tend to compare stores. Although compared in many ways, price appears to be a very popular measure of comparison. Such a situation does not, however, require the store to match the competitor's price dollar for dollar. Instead, the store may choose to price above the going price or below. The going price may not be the price that should be followed for optimum sales and profits.

Pricing Above the Competition. Needless to say, the store that prices above the market must offer the customer something in return for the higher price. The something extra must be clear in the customer's mind even if such a store differential does not actually exist. For example, if a customer feels that service is better at the more expensive store, that is what counts.

A store that is trying to convey a prestige image will wish to price above the general market for many items as part of that image. On the other hand, a prestige store that has a 1 cent sale will develop an image problem. High prices and prestige are very much related.

Location may also permit the retailer to go above the market. The only gasoline service station at a busy but isolated interstate interchange may be able to charge more for gasoline than its counterpart in a city surrounded by competition. The Dairy Queen located adjacent to the dormitories of a major university will generally be able to charge more for various products in exchange for the convenience enjoyed by the students. The customers of the neighborhood drugstore have for years exchanged location convenience for higher prices.

Services also permit higher prices. The 7–11 type of convenience store offers the customer the opportunity to buy at times when others are closed at the expense of higher prices. The store that gives "free" coffee or gift wrap or alterations or delivery to all customers must cover these expenses in some way. The way is typically higher prices. The list of possible services is endless. The important question for the merchant is whether or not the customer views the respective services as warranting a higher price. One service that was once found on the list of items in this category is credit. Today, credit is viewed by most customers as a cost of doing business rather than as something special. Most customers could not or would not justify in their own mind a firm charging higher prices as a result of granting credit. They would reason that any cost of credit would be covered by the interest rate. A firm that prices above the market and offers nothing extra but credit would be in difficulty in today's market.

In addition, the store's merchandise assortment may permit the retailer to price above the market. If the retailer places an emphasis on a broad merchandise assortment as compared with a narrow assortment, the customer may be willing to pay more in order to have all types of merchandise under one roof. Also, if the assortment contains many items or lines that are handled exclusively by the store, then direct price comparisons on the part of the customer will be difficult. This will permit the store to price such items higher than would otherwise be possible.

It is important to reiterate that successful pricing above the market entails conveying to the customer some feeling of value received for the money spent. Whether it be service, location, prestige, or whatever, the target market must be in agreement that the additional considerations are worth the price. If such is not the case, pricing above the market will not be successful.

Pricing Below the Competition.   In situations in which the retail prices are below the market, the question always asked is, "Why is the store below the market?" What benefits are derived from such a situation? Assuming a good degree of price elasticity, are too many goods being sold for too little profit? Is the low price actually scaring off some customers in the target group? A retailer must remember that a low price will not always sell a product.

One factor that influences the impact of pricing below the market is whether such a market position was obtained by an aggressive pricing strategy or by default. In the first instance, the lower-than-market price was achieved by actually dropping price or entering a market with a lower price. Such a strategy tends to draw attention to the situation with the result being a high degree of interest in the product and/or store. The situation of default, on the other hand, results when others raise prices and the retailer in question retains the status quo. Very little attention is generated for this retailer. To advertise that the store is holding the line on prices is fine. The impact of such a pricing decision, however, is nowhere near the impression on the consumer that results from an aggressive price move. In some situations, it may be better to raise the price along with competitors and then after a period of time retreat to the prices of the good old days. The impact of such a move will generally be more positive than achieving the same position by default, particularly if price is highly elastic.

Pricing with the Competition.   Pricing with the competition implies selling at the going price. It should not imply followership. When pricing at the going rate, the retailer is making the decision to remove price from the list of variables that gives the store its uniqueness when compared with the competition. Care should be taken not to price merchandise at the going rate just because it is the easiest course to follow. The missed opportunities for a store that result from management's failure to consider pricing other than at the going rate should not go unnoticed.

Cost of Merchandise

Cost is important in determining price, but it does not alone determine price.[3] It is obvious that long-run considerations require the retailer to consider the cost of the item since all costs must be paid for at some time. However, promotional considerations, for example, may justify selling a particular item at cost or even below cost if such an item is to be used to attract customers to the store. Perhaps the greatest danger to a retailer in considering cost as a determinant of price is that such a system makes cost an indication of retail value. As far as a retailer is concerned, what an item is worth is what it sells for, not its cost. A merchant who is too cost conscious may refuse to sell below cost since he or she desires to recover such costs on a per product basis. The merchant may also not price a particular item high enough, since a going price may be three times the cost. To take the cost of the item and add to it an arbitrary percentage markup is a very simple but foolish thing to do. What such a retailer is doing is basing the retail price partially on how good a negotiator the retailer is with suppliers. There is no direct relationship between what the customer perceives as retail value and the cost of the item. Only if costs continually exceed retail value will a problem develop. It is important to note that some retailers do use a pricing technique called "keystoning" (keystone markup) where price is determined by doubling the cost of the item. Such an automatic method of pricing is an easy way to determine price but, as noted, keystoning is not thought to be a sound pricing procedure.

Since a retailer uses cost as *one of the factors* in determining price, the overall merchandise cost, not just the invoice price, should be considered. Trade, quantity, cash and other discounts, as well as workroom (alterations, carpet installation, etc.) and transportation charges are all involved. To put this data in formula form yields the following:

$$\binom{\text{Merchandise}}{\text{Cost}} = \binom{\text{Invoice}}{\text{Price}}_{\text{(List)}} - \binom{\text{Trade, Quantity,}}{\text{etc., Discounts}} - \binom{\text{Cash}}{\text{Discounts}}$$
$$+ \binom{\text{Workroom}}{\text{Expenses}} + \binom{\text{Transportation}}{\text{Charges}}$$

These components make up the typical variables that determine merchandise cost. Note that workroom expenses and transportation charges are part of the cost even though they may appear on a different invoice for transportation or on no statement such as is usually true with workroom expenses. The inclusion of these expenses is essential if the true cost of the item is to be determined.

Of concern in today's market system is the replacement cost of merchandise. With costs on the increase as a result of higher invoice prices, transportation charges, and so on, and fewer discounts on certain items, merchants who do use cost as a price determinant may continually find it necessary to change the price of items on the shelf to keep up with the replacement cost. It is due to such a system that a given food store may change the price on a slow-moving item five or six times before it is sold. Evidence of six price changes on a product does not do much to satisfy the target market. If pricing had been done instead in terms of retail value, the original price may not have had to be changed to reflect changing costs. To repeat the idea presented at the beginning of the section, the merchant should not and cannot always ignore the cost of the merchandise. Such costs should not, however, be the sole determinant of price.

Role of Price in Retailing Mix

It will be recalled that the retailing mix consists of five "P's" (product, place, promotion, personality, and price). As a mix, price should be coordinated with the other variables. The influence of place on price, such as the case with the Dairy Queen near the campus, has been mentioned. The personality of the store is also influenced through price since, among other things, the typical consumer equates higher prices with a higher-class or prestige store. Product and promotion also work hand-in-hand with price in many ways. Price lines, psychological pricing, loss leader pricing, bait-and-switch pricing, and flexible versus rigid pricing are all examples of means of coordinating price with these other variables.

Price Lines. A price line is a particular price level or price point that is set for merchandise that would normally sell around that price (price zone). Such a pricing setup will eliminate the infinite number of prices in the store or department and replace them with a series of prices set at certain intervals. Instead of having shoes that sell at $22.95, $23.05, $23.69, $24.16, $24.77, $25.15, and so on, all shoes in this price zone may sell for $23.95. The next higher price zone may be a price line of $29.95.

The use of price lines, in place of infinite prices with little difference between them, offers many advantages.

1. *The decision-making process for customers is simplified.* Price lines aid the customer in making a choice since they offer the customer a clear-cut choice—$23.95 versus $29.95—instead of $23.74 for pair A and $23.87 for pair B. The latter situation may confuse the customer enough to lose the sale because the customer cannot make up his or her mind.
2. *Sales people work well with price lines.* Sales personnel seem to feel more confident when working with price lines. They are more sure of the price and use the price lines in suggesting merchandise to customers.
3. *Advertising and sales promotion is more effective.* For example, the impact of placing all shoes in a price line "on sale" is greater than featuring one particular item.

4. *Greater depth and better assortment are possible.* By having three price lines as opposed to 300 different prices, greater concentration on the optimum assortment of merchandise is possible. Elimination of items no longer thought to be necessary due to price lining will permit greater depth in the popular items given the same amount in the merchandise budget.

5. *Trading-up of the customer is made easier.* Price lines that set up the feeling of good—better—best may serve as an encouragement for the customer to trade up if the price differential is not too great. Price lines in many retail stores provide a fighting or low price line, a better line, and a prestige line. The retail tire dealer will run an advertisement featuring the lowest price line. When the customer comes to the store, efforts are made to move the customer up to the middle price line, which will generally be a better value but will cost more. Not to be confused with bait and switch as discussed later in the chapter, the retailer does plan to sell all three price lines. Efforts will be made, however, to trade up the customer to the next line. Such efforts will have much success if the price differences between the price lines are not too great.

6. *Merchandise buying is simplified.* By knowing what the selling price of the merchandise will be, the merchandise buyer can concentrate on those sources of supply that sell products in the appropriate cost range. Also, the buyer can use the established price point as an initial negotiating point with buyers.

Along with the advantages of price lines are found certain disadvantages. These include the following:

1. *Price reductions are made difficult.* Price reductions are difficult unless all lines of a merchandise group are simultaneously reduced. To reduce, for example, the top line to within a few dollars or pennies of the middle line will usually shift all business to the line "on sale." The demand for the middle line will probably "dry up." If little or no merchandise had been left in the middle line, such a shift to the top line may have been desirable. The disadvantage comes if such a shift is not desired.

2. *Too few price lines may give the impression of limited offerings.* A store with the image of offering a wide and varied selection may confuse this image by going too heavily into limited price lines. Although the store may have as much merchandise, three or four price lines do not give customers the impression that the store has a wide variety. All the advantages of price lines run counter to the store's desire for an image of "we carry everything at any price you want to pay."

Psychological Pricing. Psychological pricing techniques take many forms. Multiple pricing and odd pricing are two examples of this strategy.

Multiple pricing. Four cans of peas for a dollar sounds better than 25 cents each. Most consumers are conditioned to think that a multiple-product price means a cheaper price although this may not always be the case. A store which took part in a study conducted by a group of college marketing students placed canned tomatoes on a special display in one store and sold them for 25 cents each. In a sister store in the same town, tomatoes were priced three for 89 cents in a similar display. Much higher sales resulted at three for 89 cents than at 25 cents a can even though this later price would have been three for 75 cents. Multiple-product pricing does imply a bargain to many customers.

Odd pricing. Should the store sell the item for 50 cents or 49 cents, $2.00 or $1.98, $80 or $78, or any price level that gives the impression of a cheaper price? Much study has been done on odd pricing to determine if such prices really do have an influence on the consumer. The findings generally conclude that consumers do not universally distort odd price endings downward to lower perceived prices.[4] In other words, odd pricing may not always give the impression of lower prices to a given market. It is noted that all stores do not use odd pricing. If a store has a high-fashion image, it will not wish to sell a dress for $229.95 when $230.00 would be more desirable in terms of image. Even all stores that sell at low prices do not agree on the desirability of odd pricing. Dollar General, a Kentucky-based chain of "dollar stores," prices the great majority of its merchandise at intervals of a dollar. Typical prices will read, three pairs socks for $1, men's pants—$6, drinking glasses—three for $1, and motor oil—three quarts for $2. The chain, a heavy user of multiple-product pricing, relies almost completely on even-dollar prices. Its success in the "dollar store" discount section of retailing is working proof that odd pricing is not essential to a store that wishes to sell in the "low-price" market.

For the store that chooses to use odd pricing, several rules of thumb may be applied. For even prices,

> Under 50¢: drop 1¢ (49¢, 39¢, etc.)
> Greater than 50¢ but less then $1: drop 2¢ (98¢, 88¢, etc.)
> Greater than $1 but less than $50: drop 5¢ ($1.95, $24.95, $39.95, etc.)
> Greater than $50: drop $2 ($98, $148, $163, etc.)

It is obvious that a combination of the rules may be used in a given situation such as an appliance for $197.95. Evidence indicates, however, that $197.95 or $198 will cause the same downward price distortion for a consumer. The additional 5 cents will have no real impact.

An additional consideration when examining odd pricing is that some prices can be raised upward as well without giving many consumers the impression that such is the case. Merchandise that sells for 93 cents can probably be raised to 98 cents without much change in demand. To raise the price to $1.00 is another matter, assuming that odd pricing does have a bearing on the target market. Odd pricing is psychological. The retailer should attempt to determine for the given store situation what odd price combinations, if any, work best. Starting with the rules of thumb as given, the retailer should experiment with the target market to see if the market is receptive to such pricing techniques.

Aside from the psychological considerations associated with odd pricing, many retailers like odd pricing because it almost always ensures that the salesperson will have to make change for the customer. Merchants feel that if the salesperson must make change, the likelihood of the sale being rung on the register or being written up is enhanced. Such a procedure also gives the alert salesperson enough time to do some suggestion selling. If using odd pricing for this purpose, the retail manager must not forget the impact of any sales tax on the transaction. An item that sells for $2.85 in a state with a 5 percent sales tax has a total price of $3.00. Such an even total price will defeat the purpose of odd pricing in a store if that store has selected such pricing procedures with suggestion selling and clerk control as two of its pricing goals.

Loss Leader Pricing.   To price an item below the market price, or even below cost, for purposes of generating store traffic is known as loss leader pricing or leader pricing. A firm that uses this pricing technique successfully will choose well-known branded merchandise that have a high level of demand among the store's target customers. The food store that features bread, soft drinks, coffee, and sugar as loss leader items hopes to use such items to draw people to the store so that they will buy other items. Loss leader items should be placed strategically throughout the store so that the customer is exposed to many other items while taking advantage of the bargains. A store that places all leaders at the front of the store reduces the probability that such leaders will "pay for themselves" by generating sales of other items. If customers come in and buy the leader and leave without other items, the leader for that particular customer has only done half the job. It got the customer to the store so the store has now been exposed to the customer, but the leader did not generate sales of additional items. To overcome this problem, some stores offer leaders to customers with a minimum purchase (for example, oil for 50 cents a quart with a minimum $7.50 purchase of gasoline). Such a requirement has been found to irritate customers who come in and find that their car only needs $7.00 worth of gas. The food shopper, whose bill totals $9.75, may buy something else to meet the $10.00 minimum requirement for a special. Such a situation may cause the customer not to return. Dollar minimums do force customers to buy items to take advantage of the loss leader. The question to be answered by the retailer is whether the cost versus the benefit of the minimum requirement is worthwhile. Is the loss leader in this case generating business or running off business?

Bait-and-Switch Pricing.   The advertisement featuring bait-and-switch pricing will be identical to a loss leader ad. Both emphasize great savings to the consumer. Where the two pricing practices differ is that, with bait-and-switch pricing, the retailer has no intention of selling the featured product. The entire purpose of bait and switch is to get the customer to the store so that the customer can be traded up to a more expensive item. There is nothing legally wrong with this concept. The legal difficulty lies with the retailer who is not content with trying to trade up the customer but, instead, insists upon it if the sale is to be made. Under such circumstances, bait-and-switch pricing is considered deceptive pricing. Such a practice is not only thought to be unethical but also is subject to prosecution under federal or state statute or regulation as noted in Chapter 3.

An example of an illegal bait-and-switch practice would be a firm who advertised riding lawn mowers for $298. The first customer through the door is told that the shipment never arrived and will be canceled since it was late, but they have this much better model (which looks identical to the one pictured in the ad) for only $798. Or the customer may be told that only three are left, and they are already promised to someone else, but. . . . Or the salesperson tells the customer that he can see the customer is smart enough to know that the $798 mower is a much better buy. He goes on to say that the $298 mower is really not worth the money, and he could not sleep well if he were to sell that mower to the customer. Other situations can be cited, but they all have the same result—the store is not going to sell the $298 mower under any circumstances. Its whole purpose was to get the customer to the store in order to be switched to a more expensive item.

Flexible versus Rigid Pricing. Flexible pricing entails selling an item for different prices under different circumstances. Such is an almost necessary pricing strategy in certain forms of retailing because consumers expect it. The operator of the antique shop will "negotiate" with the customer on the price. The automobile dealer will give a customer "a good deal." In automobile retailing and similar situations, the trade-in is usually the means of achieving a flexible price. Whereas the retailer may never want to be well-known as a price cutter off the already reduced retail price, the firm may "wheel and deal" all day on the trade-in value as a promotional tool for selling the merchandise. A flexible price will also be found to exist when the clothing retailer agrees to a sale after the customer says, "I'll take the suit if you include the blue tie in the deal for free." Needless to say, flexible pricing does not make for a quick transaction. It also requires highly trained sales personnel. Sales personnel must be trained so as to know when a transaction price is satisfactory or unsatisfactory. In a store dealing with many customers, if all transactions have to be approved by the owner/manager, chaos will prevail. For flexible pricing to work, sales personnel must be given the necessary training and authority to handle the situation.

A rigid price on the other hand is what its name implies—fixed. A prestige store may have such a policy for image purposes. Many merchants follow the practice of rigid prices due to its simplicity. No time is spent in haggling over the price. Sales personnel are not required to make pricing decisions. Self-service is also possible along with its accompanying possible reduction in needed sales personnel.

The value of the item itself may tend to encourage one or the other of the pricing methods. A can of soup for 49 cents is thought to be rigid by most consumers. The $498 stove upon which to cook the soup is generally considered to be flexible. The more expensive the item, the more consumers will attempt to bargain on the item.

Merchandise Characteristics

As has already been noted, the merchandise itself can affect the method of pricing an item. Christmas decorations are worth more to consumers in December than they are in February. Bathing suits sell better in the Spring than they do in the Fall. In other words, seasonal merchandise must be priced according to the season and reduced in price in order to sell before the end of the season unless storage of the merchandise is planned. Such pricing considerations also hold true for fashion and fad items. When the fashion is "in," a premium price may be called for. When the fashion is on the way out, pricing should change to relieve the retailer of the merchandise. As for fads, a hot seller today cannot be given away tomorrow. A careful day-to-day check on pricing should be implemented for fad items. Since a fad is something in fashion for only one group, care should be taken not to buy more merchandise than needed to serve that market. A pet rock or skateboard, at any price, is of no interest to most people. Price reductions for a fad item will only sell the item to people who are aware of the fad. A mistake in pricing a fad item can be disastrous. By hesitating too long in dropping a price, for example, the retailer may end up with a warehouse full of disco fashions. By waiting too long to raise a price on such an item, all may sell out in two days, only to find the retailer down the street selling the same items for three times as much.

Aside from the characteristics mentioned, the physical characteristics of the product can also have a bearing on price. The produce market receives a truckload of watermelons that are priced at $3.00 each. The fact that the watermelons that remain on hand at the end of 30 days have zero value has a bearing on price. A vision of rotten melons keeps the initial price from being too high in order to keep from scaring off too many customers. A regular price reduction schedule is also planned to maximize the sales of the product.

For many items, several of the product features combine to influence price. Live Christmas trees, for example, are a seasonal item that may "die" if held too long. Such a product is the classic example of what happens if the retailing mix of a store does not sell a product within a given period of time. What is the value of Christmas trees on December 26? The retailer cannot give them away—not even the good ones.

One other characteristic that affects price is the uniqueness or scarcity of the product in the market. For example, if the watermelons mentioned earlier are among the first melons of the year to reach the New York City market, a premium price may be obtained because of their uniqueness. Another truckload of melons arriving in late June will not bring a premium price. Any item whose uniqueness causes demand to exceed supply will sell at a premium price provided the price is not so great as to cancel demand.

Legal Considerations

Many of the laws and regulations affecting retailing either directly or indirectly influence price. As was noted in Chapter 3, federal regulations ranging from the Robinson–Patman Act to the various trade rules of the Federal Trade Commission all have a bearing on the price that can be charged to a consumer. State and local governmental bodies have also had an impact in many areas and municipalities.

One area of particular legal concern is unit pricing. Such regulations, where in effect, require a price to be quoted in particular ways that are felt by some to hinder the merchandising of the product. For example,

> *4 for $1.00 must also show 25¢ for each can*
> *49¢ for a 1/2 bag must also show a price of 98¢ per lb*

The idea behind unit pricing is to make it easier for the customer to comparison shop by quoting the price in common units of measure.[5] When in use, unit pricing can have a definite impact on the effect of psychological pricing on the consumer.

Price reduction sales have also been of concern to many governmental agencies. Price reductions that are fictitious are now scrutinized by the Federal Trade Commission and various states agencies. The well-known Rexall 1 cent sale is perfectly legal under the regulations since, during such a sale, items that normally sell for 69 cents can be purchased for 69 cents with a second identical item being acquired for 1 cent. Such a sale agrees with the Federal Trade Commission guideline that states that a price reduction sale is not a sale unless the price of the merchandise being offered for sale constitutes a reduction, in an amount not so insignificant as to be meaningless, from the actual bona fide price at which such merchandise was sold or offered for sale to the public on a regular basis by respondents (firms) for a reasonably substantial period of time in the recent regular course of their business.[6]

Prepriced merchandise with "sale" tags already attached when received at the store are also now prohibited unless the "original" retail on the item is a legitimate price for the item. Once again, the test of legitimacy is whether or not the item has sold for that price in the market area within a reasonable period of time.[7] Such regulations have had a great effect not only on prepriced merchandise but also on the so-called catalog showroom "wholesalers." Such stores had traditionally shown an inflated "retail" price for merchandise along with their coded "secret" price which may be half of the "retail" price. No pretense can now be made that the "retail" price is as stated unless evidence can be shown that such is the case. In fact, most catalog retail prices are now called "reference prices." In addition, carefully worded disclaimer statements relating to the retail/reference price are found in the front of catalog showroom catalogs.

Legal factors cannot be ignored when determining the price of an item and how it will be presented to the target market. From the discussion on the various other factors that influence price, the same can be said for all. Choosing the "appropriate price" for an item is a skill not easily acquired by a retailer. A combination of good judgment, experience, and a conscientious effort to consider the impact of the various factors, as discussed, in any pricing decision should result in sound pricing practices for the retail store.

MATHEMATICS OF PRICING

The mathematics of pricing involves understanding the relationship between the retail price of an item and its cost.[8] Dollar markup or markon (the difference between the cost of an item and what it sells for) is generally converted to a percentage figure for storewide analysis and other forms of application. The question from a retail math standpoint is whether or not to develop this percentage based on cost or retail.

To illustrate the various relationships, assume that a store sells an item for $1.00. The cost of the item is 80 cents. The percentage relationships would be

	Dollar Amount	Percentage of Cost	Percentage of Retail
Retail selling price	$1.00	125%	100%
Markup	0.20	25	20
Merchandise Cost	0.80	100	80

From the figures given, percentage markup (mu) can be either 20 percent or 25 percent, depending on whether it is based on cost or retail (see Table 13–1 for selected markup percentages for cost and retail).

Table 13-1

Markup Percentage—Retail versus Cost

Markup % (Retail)		Markup % (Cost)
10.0%	=	11.1%
20.0%	=	25.0%
30.0%	=	42.9%
40.0%	=	66.7%
50.0%	=	100.0%
60.0%	=	150.0%
70.0%	=	233.3%
80.0%	=	400.0%
90.0%	=	900.0%

The formulas that illustrate the relationships are as follows:

$$\text{Retail selling price} = \text{Markup in dollars} + \text{merchandise cost}$$

$$\text{Retail selling price} = \frac{\text{Markup in dollars}}{\text{Markup \% (retail)}}$$

$$\text{Retail selling price} = \frac{\text{Merchandise cost}}{100\% - \text{markup \% (retail)}}$$

$$\text{Markup in dollars} = \text{Retail selling price} \times \text{markup \% (retail)}$$

$$\text{Markup in dollars} = \text{Retail selling price} - \text{merchandise cost}$$

$$\text{Markup \% (retail)} = \frac{\text{Retail selling price} - \text{merchandise cost}}{\text{Retail selling price}}$$

$$\text{Markup \% (retail)} = \frac{\text{Markup in dollars}}{\text{Retail selling price}}$$

$$\text{Markup \% (retail)} = \frac{\text{Markup \% (cost)}}{100\% + \text{markup \% (cost)}}$$

$$\text{Merchandise cost} = \text{Retail selling price} - \text{markup in dollars}$$

$$\text{Merchandise cost} = \frac{\text{Markup in dollars}}{\text{Markup \% (cost)}}$$

$$\text{Merchandise cost} = \frac{\text{Retail selling price}}{100\% + \text{markup \% (cost)}}$$

$$\text{Markup in dollars} = \text{Merchandise cost} \times \text{markup \% (cost)}$$

$$\text{Markup \% (cost)} = \frac{\text{Retail selling price} - \text{merchandise cost}}{\text{Merchandise cost}}$$

$$\text{Markup \% (cost)} = \frac{\text{Markup in dollars}}{\text{Merchandise cost}}$$

$$\text{Markup \% (cost)} = \frac{\text{Markup \% (retail)}}{100\% - \text{markup \% (retail)}}$$

In pricing, should the merchant use as the basis of calculation cost or retail? Stores that tend to be modern in their approach to retailing favor the retail price as the base figure. Why?

1. Much trade data is available using this base.
2. Proper emphasis is placed on the retail price—what the item is worth.
3. Retail figures are easier to obtain than cost data on a day-to-day basis.
4. Percentage analysis of the complete income statement on the same basis is possible since many financial operating ratios are based on sales.
5. Profitability is presented in a more conservative manner.
6. Vendor pricing may use the suggested retail price as the base from which to take trade and other discounts.

As for basing the calculation on cost, most users of this system cite convenience as the key. If a retailer knows the cost of the item and the desired markup on cost, pricing becomes automatic for each item. Since retailers should not let cost alone dictate price, such a method of pricing is limited in its application.

As noted earlier in this chapter, stores tend to increase or decrease their prices over time. For this reason an additional determination is needed. Does the price represent the initial markup pecentage or is it one of several prices charged for the item over time? In the latter case, a maintained markup determination is called for. Cumulative or maintained markup or markon is a weighted average calculation. Assume that an item has an initial markup percentage of 50 percent at retail (Price $2.00 — Cost $1.00) and the sales for 50 units are as follows:

$$
\begin{array}{lll}
10 @ \$2.00 & = & \$20.00 \\
10 @ \$1.50 & = & \$15.00 \\
10 @ \$1.00 & = & \$10.00 \\
20 @ \$0.50 & = & \$10.00 \\
\hline
50 \text{ Total Sales} & = & \$55.00
\end{array}
$$

With costs for the merchandise given as $50 ($1 x 50 units), then the maintained markup would be:

$$\text{Maintained markup \%} = \frac{\text{Net sales} - \text{total merchandise cost}}{\text{Net sales}}$$

$$\text{Maintained markup \%} = \frac{\text{Maintained markup in dollars}}{\text{Net sales}}$$

$$9.1\% = \frac{\$55 \text{ (sales)} - \$50 \text{ (cost)}}{\$55}$$

With a calculated cumulative markup percentage of 9.1 percent, the retailer can evaluate the profit potential of the item in terms of its total sales performance. Note that the only real difference in the cumulative calculation as compared with the initial markup is the shift to total sales (net) and total cost as compared with unit figures.

Other maintained markup relationships are:

$$\text{Net sales} = \text{Maintained markup in dollars} + \text{total merchandise cost}$$

$$\text{Net sales} = \frac{\text{Maintained markup in dollars}}{\text{Maintained markup \%}}$$

$$\text{Maintained markup in dollars} = \text{Net sales} \times \text{maintained markup \%}$$

where net sales = total (gross) sales minus sales returns and allowances (employees discounts, etc.).

The following examples should aid in understanding the various markup or markon relationships as presented:

Example A: Shoe City has a policy of marking merchandise so as to achieve a 50 percent markup at retail. If the shoes cost the store $15 per pair, what should Shoe City set as the retail price for the shoes?

$$\text{Retail selling price} = \frac{\text{Merchandise cost}}{100\% - \text{Markup \% (retail)}}$$

$$\$30 = \frac{\$15}{100\% - 50\%} \text{ or } \frac{\$15}{50\%}$$

Example B: Sounds Unlimited, an electronics store, bought merchandise from a vendor for $300 per unit. The merchandise was then priced at $700 per unit. Calculate the initial dollar and percentage markups using both cost and retail.

$$\text{Markup in dollars} = \text{Retail selling price} - \text{merchandise cost}$$

$$\$400 = \$700 - \$300$$

$$\text{Markup \% (retail)} = \frac{\text{Retail selling price} - \text{merchandise cost}}{\text{Retail selling price}}$$

$$57\% = \frac{\$700 - \$300}{\$700}$$

$$\text{Markup \% (cost)} = \frac{\text{Retail selling price} - \text{merchandise cost}}{\text{Merchandise cost}}$$

$$133\% = \frac{\$700 - \$300}{\$300}$$

Example C: Sam's Place, a small retail flower shop, uses the cost basis for all markup calculations. A supplier of flower pots quotes a price that will allow for a

55 percent markup on the suggested retail price. What percentage markup figure does the retailer need to know for his cost system?

$$\text{Markup \% (cost)} = \frac{\text{Markup \% (retail)}}{100\% - \text{markup \% (retail)}}$$

$$122\% = \frac{55\%}{100\% - 55\%} \text{ or } \frac{55\%}{45\%}$$

Example D: A K mart buyer wishes to buy merchandise that will sell at $13 per unit. If the desired percentage markup (retail) is 40 percent, what is the planned cost of the merchandise? (Note: Many pricing problems can be solved in more than one way. No one method is more correct than any other method that will also yield the correct solution. For illustration purposes, Example D is worked using two different approaches.)

$$\text{Markup \% (cost)} = \frac{\text{Markup \% (retail)}}{100\% - \text{markup \% (retail)}}$$

$$67\% = \frac{40\%}{100\% - 40\%} \text{ or } \frac{40\%}{60\%}$$

$$\text{Merchandise cost} = \frac{\text{Retail selling price}}{100\% + \text{Markup \% (cost)}}$$

$$\$7.80 = \frac{\$13.00}{100\% + 67\%} \text{ or } \frac{\$13.00}{167\%}$$

or

$$\text{Markup in dollars} = \text{Retail selling price} \times \text{markup \% (retail)}$$

$$\$5.20 = \$13.00 \times 40\%$$

$$\text{Merchandise cost} = \text{Retail selling price} - \text{markup in dollars}$$

$$\$7.80 = \$13.00 - \$5.20$$

Example E: A retail jewelry store set as a goal to obtain a net sales volume of $5,000 for a particular type of item. If the store's merchandise cost for the item was $4,250 and its maintained markup in dollars was $750, what was its maintained percentage markup, assuming the net sales volume goal was met?

$$\text{Maintained markup \%} = \frac{\text{Maintained markup in dollars}}{\text{Net sales}}$$

$$15\% = \frac{\$750}{\$5,000}$$

As noted in the cumulative markup illustration presented earlier in the chapter, the item was reduced in price three times before being liquidated from stock. Such markdowns are a common occurrence in retailing for many reasons. Hopefully, the most common reason for such price reductions from original retail will be for promotion purposes. These markdowns are planned by the store as part of their promotional program. Loss leaders and other planned price promotions make up the bulk of this type of markdown. As part of this promotional appeal, some stores even use automatic markdown procedures that are known to the customer. A good example of this is Filene's Automatic Bargain Basement (Figure 13–2). At Filene's Bargain Basement, all merchandise is dated when placed on the sales floor. After 12 selling days, any remaining items are reduced 25 percent. If still not sold after 18 selling days, another 25 percent reduction from original retail is made. Still another 25 percent is taken from all items with a sales floor life of 24 selling days. Finally, all items still in Filene's Basement after 30 selling days are donated to charity. Such a markdown policy is by no means desirable for every store. A hardware store selling hammers and saws has no need to continue to reduce the price since such items will "keep." One thing is certain about an automatic markdown procedure, it will build store traffic. It will not, however, do much for a prestige department store unless it is used only in the budget departments. For a store of this type, individual markdown decisions are usually found to be more appropriate for its "better" departments.

A variation of the automatic markdown procedure is the gambler's sale that many stores hold on an annual or semiannual basis. Under such a sale, prices are

Figure 13–2

Filene's famous basement with automatic markdown system.

(Courtesy of Filene's.)

automatically reduced 5 percent off retail each day. If promoted well, such a sale can create much interest toward the end of the week, if not before.

As noted, planned markdowns for promotional purposes hopefully make up the majority of the markdowns experienced by a store. Markdowns can occur, however, for other reasons. Some of these are now considered.

Mistakes in Buying and Pricing

As a retailer deals on a day-to-day basis with customers, mistakes will be made. Items will be bought that customers just do not seem to want. Other items will be priced at levels that create little interest on the part of the customer. To correct these problems, a price reduction is made. In some cases, not even a price reduction will overcome a mistake in buying. For most cases, however, a low enough price will generate some volume for the item.

Bad Selling Effort

If sales personnel make little or no effort to sell a product, the result may be an unnecessary markdown. If the parts of the promotion mix are not coordinated, in many cases, a markdown will be required. An advertisement is used that features a product, but no effort is made to reinforce the ad with an in-store display. Sales personnel are also not told that replacement stock is in the stockroom. Because of this, when the shelf is empty in two hours, no effort is made to replenish it. The result is customers going away disappointed because the item is "out of stock" while 24 cases go unsold in the back room. Such items may have to be sold later at a loss. Any time the promotion mix ceases to function properly, unplanned markdowns almost always result.

Store Policies

As noted, a policy of automatic markdowns will naturally influence price reductions. A big user of loss leaders will have this decision reflected in the amount and nature of markdowns to be used. A store with a liberal merchandise-return policy will have more markdowns as a result of such a policy. A shirt that has been returned for questionable reasons, after it has obviously been worn, will have to be reduced in price in order to sell.

Weak Stock Control

The source of many markdowns is the stockroom. Dolls arriving for the Christmas season are stacked carelessly, causing the clear cellophane on some of the doll boxes to get torn. Consequently, some dolls get dirty. The store will have to ask less for them now due to stockroom negligence. Another problem is merchandise that is not rotated carefully so that some merchandise gets too old. A drugstore that sells baby formula must take care to rotate stock since the merchandise is dated. No new mother wants to buy such merchandise beyond its expiration date. A good rotation system also will begin to note slow movers in the stockroom. A slow mover can perhaps be moved with a markdown. To discover a slow mover much later in the season may necessitate a major reduction to sell the item.

Unexpected Changes in Demand

An item that is supposed to sell does not sell. A new product takes away the items' traditional customers. The retailer should make note of this demand change and adjust the price in order to sell the item to those few who will still buy at the reduced price. Unexpected fad and fashion shifts are two of the infinite reasons for such an unexpected shift in demand.

Not only do the causes of markdowns differ for given stores in given situations, but the amount of markdowns as a percentage of net sales even differs by type of merchandise sold. As illustrated in Table 13-2, markdowns as a percentage of net sales do differ considerably from department to department and from store to store. The markdowns, as shown in Table 13-2 are determined by the formula given, with net sales including sales of items reduced in price and many not reduced. The significance

$$\text{Markdown \%} = \frac{\text{Total markdown in dollars}}{\text{Net sales}}$$

of this fact can be seen in the markdown percentage in the area of personal needs. Many cosmetic items sell at original retail. Therefore, a reduction of 50 percent on a given item is more than overshadowed by the large sum of sales at original retail. Such a situation yields a low overall markdown percentage. In fashion apparel departments

Table 13-2

Median Markdowns (Including Employee Discounts) as a Percentage of
Net Retail Sales for Various Departments in Selected Stores

Departments	Department Store Sales (millions)					
	$1–5	$5–10	$10–20	$20–50	$50–100	Over $100
Adult female apparel	19.8%	22.3%	17.3%	18.9%	18.0%	17.3%
Adult female accessories and intimate apparel	7.9	8.3	6.4	7.3	6.7	6.7
Adult male apparel	17.2	14.4	13.6	14.0	12.0	12.2
Infant and boys/girls clothing and accessories	16.4	15.1	12.3	15.6	12.8	10.6
Personal needs, food, cosmetics, tobacco	4.9	3.8	3.7	3.4	2.3	2.5
Hobby, recreation, transportation, toys	10.6	7.5	6.0	7.8	7.6	7.0
Home furnishing, furniture, decorative accessories	8.0	8.1	7.8	13.2	9.3	9.2
Appliances, outdoor equipment, housewares	6.6	6.4	7.6	8.2	7.7	6.5
Domestics, draperies, white goods	8.1	10.0	9.1	8.8	8.1	7.4

Source: *Department Store and Specialty Store Merchandising and Operating Results of 1979* (New York: Financial Executives Division, National Retail Merchants Association, 1980).

where markdowns are more prevalent, the markdown percentages are noticeably higher.

Another way to determine the markdown percentage is by means of an off-retail calculation. This formula complements the other markdown formula:

$$\text{Off-retail markdown \%} = \frac{\text{Original retail price} - \text{new retail price}}{\text{Original retail price}}$$

Off-retail is the determination of the total markdown percentage for an item, whereas the earlier calculation provides for the determination of the average markdown percentage. If, for example, a store sold 10 chairs at $200 each and then sold 30 more at $100 each, the off-retail markdown percentage would be:

$$50\% = \frac{\$200 \text{ (original retail)} - \$100 \text{ (new retail)}}{\$200 \text{ (original retail)}} \text{ or } \frac{\$100}{\$200}$$

whereas the "average" markdown percentage would be:

$$60\% = \frac{\$3,000 \text{ (total markdown in dollars)}}{\$5,000 \text{ (net sales)}}$$

When used together, the two formulas furnish the retailer with information that should provide insight into the markdowns that are being taken in the store.

The markdown percentage as shown can be affected by when the markdown is taken. Should the retailer take a markdown early in the selling season or wait until later in the period? As with so many aspects of retailing, there are advantages to either course of action. Early markdowns generally require a smaller markdown than would be needed later to get the same result. Winter clothes that are reduced in January will require fewer price cuts to move the merchandise than would be true for the same merchandise in March. Early markdowns also will tend to free selling space, thereby speeding stock turnover. The retailer usually turns the store's inventory into money much sooner with this approach. Third, sales will have a more even pattern with early markdowns. By delaying the markdown, a retailer's sales may go way down and then shoot up with an end-of-the-season sale. Early markdowns will even out these sales peaks and produce more even demand.

Delayed markdowns also have their strong points. By holding to the price for a longer period, the customer develops confidence in the price. Stores who mark down too soon find customers waiting for the reduction as opposed to going ahead and buying. Another plus for delaying any reduction is that it permits the merchant to examine the real demand for the product versus the demand for a bargain. Such information can be useful in making future buying decisions. A third factor that encourages markdown delays is the personality of the store. If the store is a prestige store, its image will not or should not permit reductions in price at regular intervals. A once-a-year or twice-a-year stock reduction sale is about all such an image will permit. Even then, the amount of reduction in most cases should not be great on items to be continued in stock. A final factor in favor of delaying markdowns is that such an action will build inventories to a point where much merchandise will be available for the planned end-of-the-period extravaganza. Promotion costs can, therefore, be spread over many items. In this instance, the economies of scale come into play. The psychology of a not very frequent big sale can also generate much traffic and volume for the store. The store that has a store-wide sale every week loses some of its drawing power. To avoid having too much of a good thing, some retailers feel that a strategy of delaying mark-downs does build tremendous interest and drawing power for the time when the sale does take place.

No matter what policy the store follows concerning the timing of markdowns, the amount of the markdown at a given time should be enough to make the merchandise attractive to consumers who are not customers at the prevailing price. This amount will vary naturally from product to product and target market to target market. A rule of thumb is to drop the price at least 12 percent in order to achieve this effect. However, for most consumers, a 12 percent reduction in the price of a candy bar will not have the same effect as will a 12 percent cut in the price of a refrigerator. Each situation is different. The retailer should take special care to examine each pricing situation carefully so as to sell each type of merchandise at a price that will yield the greatest financial return to the store.[9]

SUMMARY

The pricing of merchandise is a most difficult task for the retailer because so many factors influence the decision. What price will the target market customers accept? Should the item be priced above, at, or below the market? How much bearing should the actual cost of the merchandise have on the price? What is the role of price in the retailing mix? Should price lines be used? What about multiple pricing and odd pricing? The role of loss leaders, bait-and-switch procedures, and flexible pricing should also be considered. What about the characteristics of the product itself? Does the perishability of an item, either physically or mentally (such as fashion obsolescence) affect price, and if so, how much? As always, legal considerations must also be included. Unit pricing and cents-off promotions are two of many situations in which legal factors enter into the decision.

Pricing also involves understanding of the relationship pertaining to markup percentages on retail and on cost and the application of each. Such is particularly true when prices are adjusted over time. Both markups and markdowns must be decided upon by the retail manager. The initial pricing factors have a great influence on the original markup. As for markdowns, price reductions may be planned or be caused by bad selling effort, mistakes in buying, store policies, weak stock control, and unexpected changes in demand. Since the markdowns given by a store affect the total store image as well as its distribution of sales volume, the timing of the markdowns is a major retail decision. Special care should be taken by the retailer in making all pricing decisions since these decisions have a direct impact on the profitability of the firm.

1. List and then discuss at least five factors that aid in determining the retail price for an item or service.
2. How does price elasticity of demand influence the pricing decision?
3. What factors should be considered in the decision to price merchandise above the market, at the market, or below the market? Elaborate on these factors in your answer.
4. Should the price of a TV set be determined by the cost of the TV set? "Yes" or "no"? Explain your answer.
5. Should a store use individual prices or price lines? What are the advantages and disadvantages of each?
6. What is meant by the term psychological pricing? Cite examples. Explain fully.
7. How do merchandise characteristics have a bearing on price?
8. What is unit pricing? What type of impact might it have on retail pricing decisions when it is implemented in a given location?
9. Discuss the various causes of markdowns. Cite examples in your answer.
10. Should markdowns be taken early in the selling season or should they be delayed? Explain your answer.

1. If a toy has a markup on cost of 63 percent, what is the equivalent markup percentage on retail?
2. A retailer bought left-handed widgets for $7.30 each. If a markup percentage on retail of 40 percent is desired, what would be the retail selling price for the widgets?
3. A women's clothing store purchased dresses from a vendor for $25 per unit. The retail price for these dresses is $40 each. Calculate the initial markup in dollars and the percentage markups for both cost and retail.
4. If an item, whose markup percentage (retail) is 35 percent, sells for $15, what is its merchandise cost?
5. Assume that a gift set cost the retailer $3.00 and that the original retail price is $5.00. Twenty of the gift sets were sold at $5.00, and the other 30 sets in the order were sold for $2.00. Calculate:
   a. Initial markup % (retail)
   b. Initial markup % (cost)
   c. Maintained markup %
   d. Markdown %
   e. Off-retail markdown %

[1] Benson P. Shapiro, "Price Reliance: Existence and Sources," *Journal of Marketing Research*, Vol. 10, no. 3 (August 1973), p. 293, published by the American Marketing Association.

[2] For a more in-depth discussion on price elasticity of demand, see Richard H. Leftwich, *The Price System and Resource Allocation*, 7th ed. (Hinsdale, Ill.: The Dryden Press, 1979), pp. 43–56.

[3] Arthur V. Corr, "The Role of Cost in Pricing," *Management Accounting*, NAA, Vol. 61, no. 5 (November 1974), p. 15.

[4] For additional insight into odd pricing, see Zarrel V. Lambert, "Perceived Prices as Related to Odd and Even Price Endings," *Journal of Retailing*, Vol. 51, no. 3 (Fall 1975), pp. 13–22, 78.

[5] For information on the long-term effects of unit pricing, see Bruce F. McElroy and David A. Aaker, "Unit Pricing Six Years After Introduction," *Journal of Retailing*, Vol. 55, no. 3 (Fall 1979), pp. 44–57.

[6] Federal Trade Commission consent order against Melvin S. Landow, et al., 1977, *Federal Trade Commission Decisions*, 89 (Washington, D.C.: U.S. Government Printing Office, 1978), p. 447.

[7] Federal Trade Commission order against Giant Food, Inc., 1962, *Federal Trade Commission Decisions*, 61 (Washington, D.C.: U.S. Government Printing Office, 1964), pp. 326–363.

[8] For additional information on the mathematics of pricing, see Murray Krieger, *Merchandising Math for Profit* (New York: Fairchild Publications, Inc., 1968).

[9] For an in-depth look at markdowns, see Murray Krieger, *Creative Markdown Practices for Profit* (New York: Fairchild Publications, Inc., 1971).

CHAPTER 14

Merchandise Distribution

Reprinted with permission from The Saturday Evening Post Company © 1973.

Merchandise distribution is generally defined as all those activities that result in the physical placement of merchandise near the point at which it will be sold. Under this definition are found such tasks as the routing of shipments, the auditing of freight charges, the handling of damage claims, the receiving of merchandise from shippers, the marking of merchandise, the temporary storage of merchandise, and the distribution of merchandise to various departments and/or stores if the firm is a multi-unit operation. As can be observed, merchandise distribution *can* mean the difference between a profitable year and a bad one. Careful examination of the merchandise distribution function is essential if the retailer is to be assured that maximum dollar return for the store is not being hampered by problems that are related to the distribution of merchandise (Figure 14–1).

EXTERNAL TRAFFIC MANAGEMENT[1]

The first three tasks mentioned fall under the heading of external traffic management. Traffic management is defined as the management of the movement of goods from origin to destination. Ideally, the objective is to place the merchandise at the point of sale *when needed* at the lowest possible transportation cost, commensurate with needs for protection of the merchandise and getting it in desired sizes or packages, so the merchandise division of a store may profit from goods being available for sale according to the merchandise plan.

Every effort should be made to meet the stated objective in the most efficient manner. Why? Transportation represents one of retailing's largest single expenses. Because of this fact, retailers, both large and small, should initiate the operations normally conducted by a traffic department. Notice that the suggestion is to institute the operations of a traffic department. Obviously, the small store cannot have a separate traffic department. Someone in the store, however, should make every effort to study transportation costs and to see how such costs can be reduced. Such efforts do pay off. The May Company in one recent year, for example, reduced its transportation costs by over $2 million (or 12.3 percent of total transportation charges) by carefully watching its expenditures for transportation. How does a company save this much on transportation? One way is for the company to follow the chief functions of traffic management closely so as to keep transportation expenses in line. These *functions* are the following:

1. *See that all purchase orders are routed properly.* Routing is defined as the calculated selection of the best modes of transportation to move a given shipment from a vendor

Figure 14–1

Elements of merchandise distribution system.

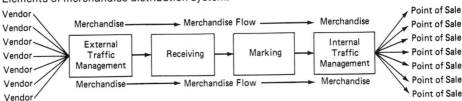

to a store. It means telling the vendor how you want the merchandise shipped, what weight shipment via what mode of transportation and via what specific carrier. It should be remembered that, since most shipments are sent FOB Shipping Point (see Chapter 12), the retailer has the right to route the shipment. Only if the terms of sale are FOB Destination does the retailer not have the right to some say in the routing of the merchandise.

The proper route helps to ensure that the store will receive the right merchandise at the desired time. At Cincinnati-headquartered Federated Department Stores, Inc., for example, it has been determined that the selling life of fashion garments is only 14 to 18 days. When such facts are considered, any shipping hours that can be saved can have a crucial impact on sales.[2] To assist the firm in selecting the proper transportation modes, McDonnell-Douglas' AFDT (Air Freight Decision Tool) program is one of the tools used by Federated. AFDT is a computer model for determining when to use air freight as the transportation mode. The procedure recognizes that there is generally a range of product values within each commodity or product line. AFDT scans a product's value spectrum for both surface and air distribution costs recognizing that as product value decreases, changing cost ratios tend to favor surface modes. Computer analysis, therefore, plots these costs to determine the crossover point or Air Potential Threshold (APT). As noted in Figure 14-2, items with product values greater than those found necessary to meet the requirements of the APT would best be sent by air.[3]

As noted, routing also involves the selection of specific carriers. If AFDT indicates that a surface mode of transportation should be used, then which carrier should be used? Cost is certainly a factor but not the only consideration. Dependability is also vital. Will the goods arrive when needed? Does a particular carrier offer an express service or overnight delivery? Does that firm appear to be willing to work with the mer-

Figure 14-2

Distribution cost comparison. Surface shipment versus air.

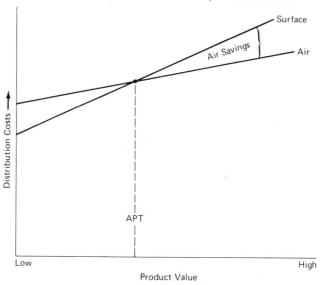

Source: Jack W. Farrell, "Faster Handling Reduces Inventory," *Traffic Management*, Vol. 15, no. 6 (June 1976), 27.

chant on lost shipments and other problems? Equally as important is how many shipments are lost by that carrier? The retailer cannot sell lost merchandise. The retailer must select the carrier with care.

As decisions are made by the retailer concerning the best way in which to route merchandise, the task then is to be sure that each vendor receives routing instructions that reflect these decisions. To accomplish this task, the retailer may attach complete routing instructions to each individual order or send a letter containing instructions to a vendor to be followed each time a shipment is made to the retail firm. The retailer must not forget this important task. The store generally has a right to select the route since the store usually owns the merchandise during transit. The routing instructions should never read "Ship Best Way" or "Ship ASAP" (As Soon As Possible). Neither "Best Way" nor "ASAP" is the name of a freight line. The retailer should not leave the choice of transportation up to the vendor. As with buying operations, the purchase of transportation should reflect the best value for the retailer.

2. *Chargeback manufacturers for excessive transportation charges resulting from manufacturer's failure to follow routing instructions.* Many believe that the most important aspect of the external traffic function is the policing of inbound shipments for possible violations of the routing instructions. If a violation should occur, the buyer may cite this in future negotiations with the vendor, as noted in Chapter 12. A stronger way to secure compliance with the requested routings is for the traffic department to charge the manufacturer back for any violations. It should be noted that the vendor may not be very happy about such chargebacks. The store, however, must remain firm in the face of such objections if it wants its routing instructions to be followed. For its efforts, the store may recover a significant amount of the store's transportation bill. Although a 4 percent recovery rate is considered excellent, some stores have recovered as much as 9 percent or even more of their transportation costs through chargeback procedures.

3. *Check freight rates charged by carriers to determine their correctness.* Carriers do make mistakes. Rate structures, rules, and regulations of freight carriers are very complex. Freight bills should be checked for their accuracy by the retail store, if such expertise is present, and then by an independent freight auditor. By checking them internally first, any savings that result will not be diminished by commissions that are paid to the independent auditor. After such checks, freight bills, as noted, should be sent to an outside auditor. [4] Commissions charged for an audit vary, although the auditor's usual fee is 50 percent of the amount of overcharges collected. Due to the commission setup, it is generally recommended that, when the outside audit is completed, the freight bills should be submitted to a second auditor to see if additional funds can be obtained. If none can be found, there is no additional "expense" to the store.

While on the subject of outside traffic auditors, a good auditor can do much more than just assist in collecting overcharges from carriers. For example, the auditors may know of better freight terms being received by other stores, possible areas of freight consolidation, and erroneous freight classifications which may be in use by particular vendors. The benefits of freight audits are many. These audits will be standard procedure in the well-managed retail operation.

4. *Furnish buyers with comparative rates and transit times from different points of origin.* As they negotiate with vendors, buyers need to have freight information. By having rates and transit times readily available, the buyer may use the data to obtain freight allowances from a supplier or even select a supplier based on freight considerations. These considerations are not possible, however, if the traffic function in the store has not provided buyers with the necessary information.

Freight allowances take many forms. Essentially, they are given to equalize transportation distance. With a freight allowance, a supplier 12 states away may absorb all or part of the freight cost in order to be competitive with a nearby supplier. It should be pointed out that buyers may obtain the allowances but the traffic department must ensure that such allowances are deducted from the invoice. Many freight allowances are not taken because of lax bookkeeping in the store. A freight allowance obtained by a buyer will serve no purpose if the store does not charge back to the vendor the allowance to which it is entitled. No chargeback means less profit for the store.

5. *Control the routing of returnables.* Returnables are a high cost, "exception" type of traffic typically representing single items rejected as defective or returned for other reasons. Moving individually, such items generate all too many expensive minimum charge shipments as they flow against the mainstream of traffic.[5] By carefully routing and, if possible, by sharing the costs with the vendor to the degree that the vendor is at fault (vendor pays all if totally at fault), returnables will not be a significant drain on profits.

6. *Arrange for consolidations, pool shipments, etc.* External traffic management works to ensure carload-lot rates and other low-cost transportation methods. As noted in Chapter 12, small shipment consolidations should be utilized by the buyer after consultation with the traffic people in the store concerning the best approach to follow for a given set of circumstances.

7. *Tracing and expediting shipments that are overdue.* Finding overdue shipments is more an art than a science. The following information is needed by the retailer for tracing and expediting purposes.[6]

> Name of shipper
> Location from which shipment originated
> Carrier's name
> Carrier's PRO number (I.D. number given by carrier to shipment)
> Number of pieces in shipment
> Weight of shipment
> Date the carrier picked up shipment

A person who is knowledgeable in the ways of traffic management begins to learn where the bottlenecks are in the system. If experience indicates that certain ports, airports, or whatever are problem points, the individual will look to these areas first as a means of finding the shipment and then expediting it. As experience will show, in some situations, expediting shipments may require additional funds to speed the delivery of the merchandise. Such payola or push money that is paid, for example, to particular dock foremen or freight forwarders is considered by some as a cost of doing business. For other retailers, expediting shipments in this manner goes against their ethics since they view such payments as bribes. Regardless of how it is done, however, expediting is important to a store since merchandise not yet delivered cannot be sold. Also, merchandise delivered late does not arrive *when needed.*

8. *File claims against carriers for merchandise that is lost or damaged in transit.* The retailer should make sure that all claims are filed with carriers and that all such claims are well documented. Emphasis is also placed on expediting such claims in order to improve the cash flow position of the company. The longer the retailer waits to settle up with the carrier, the greater the chance that problems will arise.

External traffic management is a very complex subject for most retailers but one that must be dealt with. As one aid for retailers, a traffic management consultant might be hired to assist the retailer. Or the retailer might take advantage of various traffic management seminars that are available through trade associations and other sources. Another possibility for the retailer is to seek an outside firm to handle some or all of the external traffic management functions. An advertisement for a firm of this type is shown in Figure 14–3. Whether handled within the firm or by some other means, external traffic management can play a significant role in the success or failure of the retail store.

<hr>

RECEIVING

The function of external traffic management is to get the goods to the store *when needed*. Receiving has as its function the acceptance or rejection of the goods based on whether what is received is what was ordered and whether it is damaged. Needless to say, receiving is thought by some to be the most important link in the distribution chain since it passes judgment on the fitness of all items that arrive at the receiving dock. Although some might argue that some other aspect of distribution, such as external traffic management, is more important, none would disagree with the statement that receiving is a vital part of the distribution process.

Receiving involves two operations:

1. Arrival and, if necessary, the temporary storage of the goods
2. Checking of the goods

Such operations prepare the merchandise for marking. Before discussing marking, however, a few comments are in order for each of the two receiving operations.

Arrival and Temporary Storage of Merchandise

Except in the very small store, a separate place should be set aside for the receipt of merchandise. The area, if possible, should be separate from the stockroom and everything else to reduce confusion as well as to improve control. In addition, the area in which the goods are received physically should be covered from the elements as well as be of the same height as the common means of delivery so as to speed the unloading process. Any time the physical arrangements for receiving merchandise are not well planned, problems will arise. Poor receiving facilities invite damaged merchandise. For example, if the truck driver has to throw merchandise off a truck or has other problems, such as trying to deliver goods through a receiving door that is too small, something will probably be broken or scratched. Such damage is unnecessary. Proper physical facilities for the receipt of merchandise will solve many problems.

In the ideal setup (see Figure 14–4), the receiving area in a store, which may include marking facilities as well, will be divided into straight-line sections for the orderly flow of goods. As the goods come off the truck, for example, they are placed in a holding area if a backlog exists in checking. The holding area should be physically separated from checking by doors that can be closed so that merchandise coming in

Figure 14–3

A trade ad for a firm offering external traffic management assistance to the retailer.

WALSH IS . . .

. . . A TRUCKER . . . A CONSOLIDATOR . . . A
MANAGEMENT SERVICES CONTRACTOR !

**WALSH . . . AS YOUR
MANAGEMENT SERVICES CONTRACTOR**

. . . removes the transportation and distribution responsibility from the retailer.

. . . provides flexibility of response to changing factors and costs in transportation.

. . . provides the expertise to observe and reckon with rising transportation and distribution costs and brings known, accurate and predictable costs to these vital functions.

. . . can effect savings of up to 30% in distribution costs for certain customers, plus decreases in inventory costs, more rapid turn of merchandise, decreases in pilferage and claims, standardization of procedures and uniform paperwork.

Walsh <u>specializes</u> in shipment of garments on hangers . . . consolidating garments on hangers and in cartons for shipment on the same trailer, which results in considerable savings for its customers.

(201) 330-1900

WALSH TRUCKING CO., INC.

2820 16th Street • N. Bergen, New Jersey 07047

(Courtesy of Walsh Trucking Co., Inc.)

Figure 14-4

Receiving area.

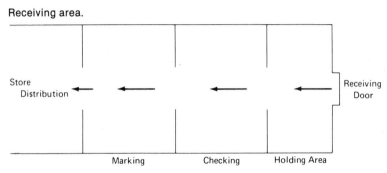

| Store Distribution | Marking | Checking | Holding Area | Receiving Door |

cannot be placed accidentally among merchandise that has already been checked. An additional advantage to this arrangement is that it minimizes the potential for theft since usually little or no store merchandise will be easily available to personnel of the carrier.

To speed the off-loading of merchandise, the use of various conveyor systems may be employed. Conveyors also reduce the probability of damage as a result of less actual handling of the merchandise. Although the initial outlay for this equipment may be great, the benefit over time may make the equipment quite beneficial to the retailer.

One other consideration at this point is the importance of noting any damaged merchandise that should come off the carrier. If damage is observed, a notation should be written to that effect on all transportation and receiving documents. Such written evidence of damage will speed the handling of damage claims by the store.

Checking of the Merchandise

As noted in Figure 14-4, checking is the second phase in the receiving process. Such action must be taken if the store is to ensure that what was ordered is what was received. To determine the correctness of the shipment, the following procedure may be followed:

1. *Compare invoice against purchase order.* The purchase order should be compared with the invoice to check the quantity of items ordered, the description of the merchandise, and the terms of sale. Any merchandise not in agreement with the purchase order will be placed in a separate holding area for special review and action by the buyer. Such goods will not move forward into the stock of the store until all discrepancies are cleared up. One well-known retailer has been known to have over $250,000 in merchandise on hold at one time waiting for action of some type.[7]
2. *Sort merchandise.* Merchandise is sorted out upon removal from containers in preparation for checking.
3. *Checking.* Merchandise is checked in terms of quantity received and, in some cases, for quality. The quantity check is usually conducted in one of two ways: direct check or blind check. In the direct check, the incoming goods are checked against the invoice. If the goods are needed on the sales floor and the invoice has not arrived, the merchandise

is generally checked against the purchase order to avoid delay. The direct check method has as its main advantages the speed and ease of the system. The primary disadvantage is lack of control over the quality of the operation. If an employee knows that 144 items are supposed to be there, he or she may make a guess and say that 144 did arrive. If in reality, only 134 actually were shipped, the checking procedure has created a shortage of 10 units on the books of the store.

The blind check is what its name implies. The checker examines the merchandise that has been received and then records a description of it, the amount received, and other items of information that the store will later check against its records. There is no doubt that the blind count overcomes most of the problems of careless checking since the checker does not know what he or she is supposed to find. Against this main advantage are placed two disadvantages—time and money. By its nature, the blind count is a slow process as each item has to be written up as well as counted. Because it is slow, blind checking costs more. The retailer, in deciding on whether to use a direct check or a blind check, must analyze the situation in terms of cost versus benefit. Does the greater accuracy of the blind check justify itself in light of its cost? For most stores, the answer is "no." It is for this reason that the direct-check method is by far the more common procedure in use in stores today.

The entire checking procedure takes on more subjective considerations when quality is considered. Some quality checks involve comparing samples received earlier with the merchandise now being received. Some of the major chains have even gone so far as to routinely take samples of merchandise received at various locations and send them to their test facilities for quality checks. For most situations, however, the responsibility for the quality check still rests with the merchandise buyer. The buyer examines the goods and then makes a quality decision based on his or her expertise in the product category.

A recent innovation in the retail industry has changed many of the procedures that have been followed in receiving for years. The innovation is UVM—Universal Vendor Marking.[8] For those stores so equipped with the necessary optical scanning devices, merchandise arriving from a growing number of vendors is premarked in such a way that an optical scanning device is able to automatically identify the manufacturer, style, color, and size of the merchandise being received as well as provide a quick count of the items. Such a system also provides a quick method for matching merchandise received more accurately against the invoice. As noted in Figure 14–5, UVM is not limited, however, to stores that have equipment to "read" the product markings. Since UVM uses OCR–A, Optical Character Recognition-Font A (a style of type that can be read by humans as well as machines), the system can be read without machines.

As seen in Figure 14–5, Universal Vendor Marking provides more data from the vendor on the ticket than does the Universal Product Code. The retailer may have the same data using a code bar system, but it must be coded at the retail level. Note that the varying width lines take up much space on the bar code ticket (which is in limited use). Under UVM, however, the numbers that are read by machine are also readable with the human eye.

The reader should not confuse UVM with UPC (Universal Product Code). The Universal Product Code is a bar code system that identifies only the manufacturer and the product. All other data such as price, date purchased, and so on are stored in a computer. When the UPC markings are "read" by an optical scanner, the other perti-

Figure 14-5

Universal Vendor Marking versus Universal Product Code or bar code marking.

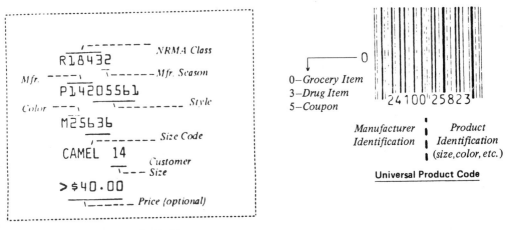

MARKING PREPARED BY VENDOR

Universal Vendor Marking

Universal Product Code

MARKING PREPARED IN STORE

Universal Vendor Marking

Bar Code Marking

nent data can be retrieved from the "memory" of the system. It is noted that, with UVM, a computer can be used, but such is not necessary as the data that is attached to the merchandise is in a form that the retailer and consumer can read with the human eye. Customers like UVM for this reason since they can see the price of the item. No readable price on the merchandise has been one of the major customer dislikes of the Universal Product Code. As shown in Figure 14–5, the retailer can put information on the merchandise by means of the bar code system accompanied by human readable type. As many as 56 digits of data may be encoded on such tickets by the store. UVM, however, makes much of this work unnecessary, thereby simplifying the work in receiving as well as in marking.

Before leaving this discussion of Universal Vendor Marking and Universal Product Code, a dilemma that is now faced by retailers should be addressed. The dilemma is that there does not exist in retailing today a truly universal marking code; instead, there are two! For some stores, the fact that there are two universal codes presents no problem. But for other retailers, like hypermarkets, the problem is real since food items, magazines, and the like are coming to the store with UPC markings, whereas soft goods such as clothing and bedding are arriving with UVM tags. The checkout equipment cannot handle both systems. Neither can the same equipment be used in receiving or in taking inventory. There is no question that retailing has a significant need for one and only one universal marking system. Unfortunately, no major effort is currently underway to create this one universal system. [9]

Once the merchandise is checked and found to be what was ordered and to be in good shape, the next step is the placing of any local store information including price, department number, cost, etc. on the item by means of a marking operation. If the store is equipped to handle UVM-OCR-A and the incoming articles have the code, then only a small quick-stick label is needed to fit on the vendor ticket. Such a ticket could be made in large batches since the ticket to be printed would not have to be broken down into the basic SKU units by style, color, or size. With UVM–OCR-A, the merchandise sort does not have to be as fine as with other marking procedures because much "readable" data are already provided by the vendor.

Whether using Universal Vendor Marking, bar code marking, or the more traditional marking methods, some of the same problem areas exist in terms of marking the merchandise for local use. For example, how much and what kinds of information are desirable on the price tag? Common information added by many stores include:

1. Date placed on sales floor or date received
2. Vendor/wholesaler identification number
3. Department number
4. Class of merchandise
5. Cost

For items such as wholesaler identification, department number, and class or type of merchandise using the National Retail Merchants Association's classification system or some other process, there is no need to disguise the data since customers do not really care about such things. Date and cost are something else again. Merchandise marked with a symbol of 3/82 may date the merchandise in the customer's mind even if 3/82 in reality means Department #3/Wholesaler #82. Not only is it important to disguise the date in some way but also to be sure that no other data on the tag might be construed to mean the date. In coding the date, some merchants use various symbols to show the various buying seasons. Others simply add 10 to the month and year and reverse their positions. For example, merchandise marked in March 1982 would show a date on the ticket of 92/13. Most customers will not perceive that 92/13 is a date. The code is, however, very easy for store employees to understand—a necessary ingredient in any marking code.

Most retailers also desire to have their cost of the item on the merchandise. To put the cost on the tag successfully requires the use of a cost code of some kind so as to conceal the cost from the customer. Cost codes take many forms. Some use any ten letters of the alphabet in sequence. Others use diagonal lines. Still others use numbers in some predetermined order so that they stand for other numbers. The best and easiest way to develop a cost code, however, is to come up with one or more words that when taken together include ten letters with no letters repeating. Why words? Words have been found to be easier to decipher than symbols or just letters given in some order. On the other hand, for the customer who does not know the code word(s), the code is as hard to figure out as any other system. Some ten-letter nonrepeating combinations for use as cost codes are

Chain Store	Blonde Hair	Stolen Card
Retail Shop	Republican	Toy Machine
Shoplifter	Bankruptcy	Rusty Chain
Milk The Cow	Blue Monday	Sour Pickle
Round Table	Cut Flowers	White Cloud

To use the cost code, bankruptcy, for example, the merchant who sells an item that cost the store $60.39 would put UYNC on the price tag to represent the cost of the item.

$$\frac{\text{B A N K R U P T C Y}}{\text{1 2 3 4 5 6 7 8 9 0}}$$

With such information on the price tag, there will be no further need to refer back to the store records when cost information is desired on the merchandise at some later time. It should be emphasized that cost codes and other data can be put in a form that can be read by machine as well as by the human eye. The dual nature of the code gives added flexibility to the system.

For the store that chooses to go with traditional marking practices or is not affected by UVM or UPC, it is still desirable to price-mark by means of machine rather than by hand. Normally, fewer errors are made with a machine and such tags are neater. As noted in Figure 14–6, machines of all types are available for use by the retailer. Even the smallest store should mark its merchandise by machine. Much data can be placed on a small tag if a machine is used. If, for any reason, a machine is not used, special care should be followed in marking merchandise by hand. Never use common ink colors such as blue, black, or red. Customers can change them too easily. Instead, use orange, purple, or some other unusual color that the customer may not have handy. The retailer is asking for trouble when pricing is done in *BIC* Blue.

Where to place the tag on the merchandise as well as how to attach it are other considerations. For the latter, the rule of thumb is to attach the tag in such a way that the tag but not the merchandise will be destroyed or noticeably altered if removed. For the merchant, this means that no tags will be placed on bottle caps that can be switched by the customer. No price tags will be of the type that peel off easily so they can be transferred to another item. Tear-away tags and plastic fasteners that must be cut to be removed aid in reducing price tag switching. For further discussion on the retail secur-

Figure 14-6

Pricemarking machines are available for every purpose as shown in this ad for Monarch.

ity aspect of marking, see Chapter 24. As for where to place the tag, the tag should be placed in a consistent manner so that both the customer and the employee can locate the tag without difficulty. If such is not done, unnecessary damage to the merchandise and its package may occur as customers search for the price. A rack of coats will stay neater when prices are on the sleeve facing the customer as opposed to being placed in the neck or inside the coat. Prices "buried" inside shirt collars will result in many shirts found partially unwrapped after the rush of the day. Except for the most exclusive shop where prices may not even be on the merchandise, the price tag should be placed where customers and employees can find it as well as read and understand it.

One additional concern with pricing is making sure that the correct price is placed on the merchandise. Once the merchandising manager or buyer or department manager determines what the price will be for an item, the head of the marking department who, in many stores, is also head of receiving, is generally the one responsible for ensuring that the correct price is placed on the item. Some stores even instruct their marking people to attach an actual tag after it has been run off on the machine to the purchase order or to the work order—a separate form found in larger stores for use in scheduling the work of the marking personnel. Random checks of the actual work produced also serve to catch errors and promote more conscientious work. In addition, some have the marker put his or her symbol on the tag thereby permitting an easy check on the markers who make mistakes and those who do not. A contest among the markers with the winner receiving some sort of prize and recognition before the other employees can also encourage more accurate production in the marking department.

Tight control is obviously the key to a successful marking operation. For this reason, if accurate marking is desired, then marking must be centralized. Stores that permit their sales personnel to mark on the sales floor are asking for errors. Distractions and confusion in the selling area promote mistakes, not to mention a messy appearance as boxes and the pricing table clog up the aisles. Also a problem are the printed price tags that are left unsupervised while the employee goes off to help a customer. Some customers in this situation help themselves to price tags that they later attach to the merchandise of their choice, thereby defeating all the security the retailer thought was in the system when tear-away tags and other procedures were adopted for use. Marking merchandise on the floor may not be the cost-cutting procedure the retailer thinks it is when compared with centralized marking. Along with the other considerations already mentioned, the retailer should ask how many sales were lost because the store personnel were too busy marking instead of selling or because customers were confronted with such a mess in the aisles that they could not obtain what they wanted or did not care to bother to try. An objective evaluation of some retail situations would find marking taking precedence over selling. In summary, if at all possible, use central marking. The benefits, in most cases, outweigh the costs.

INTERNAL TRAFFIC MANAGEMENT

The movement of goods from marking to the final point of sale and possibly even beyond to home delivery make up the area known as internal traffic management. With the growing number of multi-unit operations, this aspect of merchandise distribution is increasing in importance for many retail organizations as merchandise is moved from store to store. In addition, stores today place less and less emphasis on storage. The possibility of inventory obsolescence as well as the actual dollars tied up in inventory have made retailers' thinking move from the concept of storage to one of distribution to the point of sale. One example is Shillito's—a division of Federated Stores, Inc., that has built an in-and-out distribution system that serves the eight stores of the division with great efficiency. [10] Distribution, not storage, is where the emphasis is concentrated.

Successful internal traffic management is not something that is achieved by accident. Careful routing of the merchandise must be followed to keep down cost and to ensure that merchandise quantities are at the desired levels in the stores. Perhaps of even greater concern is shortage control as it relates to internal store distribution. Management needs to know what is in the stockroom. Much merchandise can "disappear" within the store's internal distribution system if care is not taken to ensure that the transfer system is sound. Although problem areas are many, some of the more common causes of shortages to watch for are the following: [11]

Failure to Check Seals on Transfer Trucks and to Follow Up on Reports of Broken Seals

Each truck or container (Figure 14–7) moving through the internal distribution system should be sealed at the point of origin after marking, and delivered so that the seal is broken only by the person who is supposed to receive the goods. The unbroken seal tells the recipient of the goods that the merchandise has not been tampered with during the transportation phase. If the seal is found to be broken, management should carefully examine the reasons for the damaged seal. Lax follow-up on broken seals will result in a system that ceases to have any credibility. But what about the retailer who uses no system of seals on merchandise in transit? That merchant has no idea whether goods are being lost in transit or not. Such a lack of controls can spell financial disaster for a store over time.

Moving Merchandise Through the System Without Appropriate Paper Work

The truck driver stops at store A to move some goods to store B, or store C calls the distribution center and tells them to put several items on the truck that is leaving in five minutes. Is the necessary paper work done to keep track of the merchandise? In many cases, the store personnel do plan to do the paper work tomorrow but tomorrow never comes. The result is merchandise at store B while the records show it to be at store A. Such a breakdown in the record-keeping system is uncalled for. Good retail procedures will require that paper work must move with the merchandise. Nothing should be moved without proper written documentation. Every exception that is made to this rule generally causes problems, or, at least, has the potential to cause difficulty.

NesTier.
moves
department
store
merchandise

StrapPak containers reduce handling costs and pilferage

These NesTier® plastic shipping containers are ideal for distribution of soft goods, general merchandise, auto parts, health and beauty aids, etc. They provide optimum cube and prevent unstable loads because the strapping fits flush to the top of the lid of each box, thus eliminating recessed areas. Attached flip-up lids open so StrapPaks can nest when empty, then seal easily for maximum security of contents in transit.

StrapPaks may be reused over and over again to cut per trip costs to a minimum. These tough injection molded boxes are available in two sizes: 27 x 18½ x 12″ and 27⅝ x 20¾ x 15¼″, capacities 2.4 and 4.0 cu. ft. The larger model is designed to accept garments *on hangers* (see photo above), thus simplifying and speeding handling. Carts and shelf trucks are also available. For details, ask your NesTier dealer for Bulletin 904.

When you need containers, contact THE CONTAINER PROs, NESTIER CORPORATION, Dept. NF, 10605 Chester Road, Cincinnati, Ohio 45215. *Telephone toll-free 800-543-4454 (in Ohio, 800-582-2017).*

THE SYSTEMS PROFESSIONALS

NESTIER
CORPORATION
A BUCKHORN COMPANY

Figure 14-7

A trade advertisement for internal distribution containers.

(Courtesy of Nestier Corporation.)

Failure to Check Merchandise Quantities on Transfers

Since goods are moving internally, many have a tendency not to check the merchandise when it is received at the department level in the branch store. The assumption is that if the distribution center or other store said that 12 dozen items were sent, then that is the truth. It pays to check all incoming merchandise. One chain found that a distribution center employee was shaving some merchandise quantities and selling the difference on "the street." If an order was for 24 dozen wallets, he would send 23½ dozen and write it up as 24 dozen. Since the wallets were already marked, they went immediately into existing stock at their destination. Only when the physical inventory was taken did the shortage come to light. When shortages began to reach alarming proportions, the units in the chain began to take different measures to check on the problem. One of the measures was to check quantities of goods in transfer. When this procedure was followed, the offending employee was caught. The employee confessed to having been short-changing the shipments for about ten years. The procedure used to catch the culprit was something that the store should have been doing all the time.

By setting up procedures to ensure the orderly and secure flow of merchandise to the point of sale, internal traffic management permits the merchant to keep track of the merchandise in an efficient manner until it reaches the point of sale, hopefully at the time *when needed.* With this task accomplished, the distribution function is complete unless the customer wishes the merchandise to be delivered. If delivery is desired, a whole additional set of problems must be faced by the merchant. These are discussed in Chapter 23 under Customer Service.

SUMMARY

Merchandise distribution consists of those activities that result in the physical placement of merchandise near the point where it will be sold. Under this topic area is found external traffic management, receiving, marking, and internal traffic management. External traffic management involves seeing that all shipments are routed properly, taking advantage of all possible chargebacks for failure to follow routing instructions, auditing freight charges, furnishing buyers with freight information, controlling the routing of returnables, arranging for various types of freight consolidations, tracing and expediting overdue shipments, and filing claims against carriers for lost or damaged merchandise. Receiving is concerned with the actual receipt of the merchandise and the necessary checks which must be made to determine if the proper goods were received. Marking is the placing of any additional information on the merchandise such as department number and price, keeping in mind how the process may differ when the Universal Vendor Marking system or the Universal Product Code is involved. Where to place the tag and how to attach it as well as the accuracy of the tag are additional marking considerations. Internal traffic management covers the areas of merchandise movement after marking to the point of sale. With the growing number of multi-unit operations, more and more retailers are being faced with the numerous problems associated with the internal routing of merchandise. Failure to control the merchandise distribution function can mean many unnecessary problems for the store. A good system, on the other hand, will get the right merchandise to the right place *when needed.*

DISCUSSION QUESTIONS

1. Define or explain the following terms:

   a. Traffic management   b. Routing
   c. Chargeback   d. Air potential threshold
   e. Freight allowance   f. Blind count
   g. UVM–OCR-A   h. Cost code

2. Explain how a retailer might develop an economical routing plan for merchandise received by the store. What should the retailer do if the route as developed is not followed by the vendor?
3. What services are provided by a freight auditor? Should all retailers use such an auditor? Why?
4. Why is it important to file damage claims promptly with carriers?
5. How should a receiving area be set up physically at a store or distribution center?
6. What are the procedures to follow in checking in merchandise? Be specific. Does UVM–OCR-A or UPC have any influence on these procedures?
7. Which is better—direct count or blind count? Explain the advantages and disadvantages of each.
8. In light of the discussion in the chapter, what should the retailer keep in mind when marking the merchandise? In placing the tag on the merchandise? What about accuracy?
9. Discuss some of the more common reasons for shortages that may be found in internal store distribution.
10. In examining the subject of merchandise distribution, which of the following is most important? Which is least important? Why?

    a. External traffic management   b. Receiving
    c. Marking   d. Internal traffic management

NOTES

[1] Much of the information in this section is taken from Dorothy E. Geiss, "Traffic Management," *Stores,* Vol. 58, no. 2 (February 1976), pp. 8–9, 27–28, and "How to Cut Down on Transportation Costs," *Stores,* Vol. 58, no. 4 (April 1976), pp. 34–35. Copyright, National Retail Merchants Association, 1976.

[2] Jack W. Farrell, "Faster Handling Reduces Inventory," *Traffic Management,* Vol. 15, no. 6 (June 1976), pp. 24–25.

[3] Ibid., pp. 25–27.

[4] Names of companies who perform freight bill audits may be obtained from the National Retail Merchants Association.

[5] Farrell, "Faster Handling Reduces Inventory," p. 28.

⁶ Clarence A. Randall, "Working with Traffic, Receiving, and Marking Departments," *The Buyer's Manual*, ed. R. Patrick Cash (New York: National Retail Merchants Association, 1979), p. 458.

⁷ Lewis A. Spalding, "Push for Productivity," *Stores*, Vol. 62, no. 12 (December 1980), p. 45. Copyright, National Retail Merchants Association, 1980.

⁸ Fred Lazarus, III, "Voluntary Universal Vendor Marking," *Retail Control*, Vol. 44, no. 7 (March 1976), pp. 48–52, published by the National Retail Merchants Association.

⁹ William H. Bolen, "Wanted: A Universal Marking Code," *Southern Business Review*, Vol. 3, no. 2 (Fall 1977), pp. 35–37.

¹⁰ Jack W. Farrell, "In-and-Out Distribution," *Traffic Management*, Vol. 15, no. 6 (June 1976), pp. 30–31.

¹¹ Francis P. Rieser and Joshua A. Polan, "Inventory Shortage Control," *Retail Control*, Vol. 44, no. 5 (January 1976), p. 21, published by the National Retail Merchants Association.

CHAPTER 15

Merchandise Control

Reprinted by permission. © 1979 NEA, Inc.

Planning, buying, pricing, and distribution are all vital to successful merchandising. One additional consideration that should be included is merchandise control. Merchandise control is defined as all those procedures that a retail store employs to determine the status of its inventory in light of customer demand and general economic conditions. These procedures include the analysis of inventory turnover, as well as the study of inventory in dollar terms and in physical units. If the retailer understands the store's inventory situation, the store will be well on its way to becoming a more profitable operation with a sound merchandising program.

INVENTORY TURNOVER

Is a store always out of merchandise or never out of anything? If either situation exists, the inventory of the store is usually found to be out of balance. In the first instance, sales are lost because customers cannot find what they want so they go elsewhere. In one such study of customers' reactions to retail stockouts, it was found that a particular store that had been out of an item on two previous shopping occasions may lose the customer in approximately 40 percent of the cases if the store is out of the item on the customer's next visit.[1] Needless to say, most stores cannot afford the luxury of losing such a great percentage of their customers. As for the opposite situation, can the store afford to never be out of anything? To never lose a sale due to a lack of merchandise in stock may sound desirable, but the cost of carrying the inventory necessary to ensure that no item in stock is ever below its level of demand will generally be too great for a store to successfully absorb in its pricing structure. In other words, most merchants expect to be out of certain items when such merchandise is requested. Items that are important to store traffic, however, such as bread and milk in a convenience store should be excluded from those items that the store can be out of at times. Such essential items would be on a never-out list. For these never-out items, the customer expects the store to have them in stock since that is why most customers shop at the store. A service station may lose some sales if all types of fan belts are not carried. On the other hand, to be out of gasoline is unforgivable since the lack of this item will be detrimental to the total retail operation.

To aid the reader in determining how sales and inventory relate to one another, the determination of inventory turnover should be studied in terms of the total store and, perhaps, more important, in terms of the merchandise classifications within the store. As its name implies, inventory turnover is a measure of how quickly goods are replaced by the store. It is defined as the number of times during the period (normally a year) that the average inventory of the store is replaced in order to support the store's level of sales. Formulas for determining inventory turnover are:

$$\text{Turnover (retail)} = \frac{\text{Net Sales}}{\text{Average Inventory (retail)}}$$

$$\text{Turnover (cost)} = \frac{\text{Cost of Goods Sold}}{\text{Average Inventory (cost)}}$$

$$\text{Turnover (units)} = \frac{\text{Unit Sales}}{\text{Average Inventory (units)}}$$

From an analysis of these formulas, it is observed that higher turnover can be achieved with smaller in-store merchandise requirements if suppliers are close by and are willing to accept numerous small orders from the retailer. Under such circumstances, however, the chances of being out are great since it is very difficult to always correctly estimate demand and suppliers may not always be able to supply the item on a moment's notice. Inflation may also be felt more readily by such a store since no inventory hedge is held. The retailer who seeks higher turnover through hand-to-mouth buying will feel immediately the effect of every price change in the marketplace. In addition, there are certain costs associated with placing an order that are more or less constant regardless of the size of the purchase. The store that places many small orders as compared with one large order as a means of cutting inventory expenses may be using all that may be saved on money tied up in inventory and then some on ordering, clerical, and receiving expenses. The loss in quantity discounts that can result from such an arrangement may also be a factor.

Against these points that discourage too much emphasis on stock turnover are the following considerations that favor rapid turnover. First, rapid turnover means fresher merchandise. A customer likes to come into a store and see new merchandise instead of the same old stuff. Also, fresh merchandise generally means the most up-to-date merchandise. The latest color, improvement, and so on is to be found with the latest merchandise. Second, high turnover gives a greater return on the money that is committed to inventory. The return on such funds cannot commence until the merchandise is sold. The more times the merchandise covered by such funds is sold (higher turnover), the greater the return on the inventory dollar. A third plus for lower inventory levels is the reduced expenses that result from the fewer square feet of storage that are needed. In addition, lower insurance costs and even lower taxes may result from a lower average inventory figure for the store.

To aid the reader in understanding how turnover is calculated, suppose that an office supply store sold 210 two-drawer file cabinets during the year and that the average number of file cabinets in stock at any one time was 35 units. The stock turnover for file cabinets for the store would be

$$\text{Turnover (units)} = \frac{\text{Unit Sales}}{\text{Average Inventory (units)}}$$

$$6 = \frac{210}{35}$$

It is important to note that the retailer must be careful not to combine retail, cost, and/or physical units in any one calculation. These are three distinct ways in which to determine turnover. They are not interchangeable.

In Chapter 5, inventory turnover on a cost basis was calculated by using estimated cost of goods sold for a new store. For an existing store, data can be based on fact rather than on estimate. In the same manner, if actual sales and average inventory at retail are known, turnover at retail can be easily calculated and compared to industry norms.

When a store analyzes its inventory turnover, the tendency is to desire a high turnover figure. As noted, such a high turnover figure can mean many lost sales through stockouts. The best way to state what the desired turnover rate should be is to state that "everything else being equal, the higher the turnover rate the better." The retailer must carefully analyze his or her situation to determine if the given circumstances result in too great a cost if the retailer strives for the highest possible turnover rate. A turnover figure that is good for one store may be very poor for another.

To aid the retailer in analyzing turnover calculations, the National Retail Merchants Association provides stock turn data for department and specialty stores by sales categories. As noted in Table 15–1, the data are provided for stock turns at retail at both the median and superior performance level. For purposes of analysis, a higher turnover figure is assumed to be more desirable in the data.

In using turnover figures as provided by the National Retail Merchants Association or any other trade sources, care should be taken by the retailer as store figures are compared with national norms. Each store is unique. If the store has a turnover figure that is equal to the national average, does this mean that the store is operating at the desired turnover level? The answer to this question is an obvious "no." Conditions may be such that too many sales are being lost due to a lack of breadth of merchandise in the store. Or the store may be out of merchandise too often, since it is a great distance from many of its suppliers who cannot replenish on a moment's notice. Retailers should use turnover norms for guides to thinking instead of using them for automatic operating objectives. Retailers must keep in mind that many stores that have gone out of business involuntarily have had very high turnover figures. The objective of every retailer is high turnover but only when combined with adequate inventories in order to sustain demand.

DOLLAR CONTROL OF MERCHANDISE

As noted in the formulas for inventory turnover, store inventories may be calculated at either their retail or their cost values. Either method is in use by many stores and either is accepted for tax purposes by the Internal Revenue Service. Which method should a retail store choose as it attempts to analyze its inventory for purposes of merchandise control? It is up to the retailer to decide. Each method has its advantages and disadvantages.

Retail Method of Inventory Valuation

The retail method has as one of its main selling points the fact that it makes the retailer think in terms of what the item is worth, not what was paid for it. Along with this somewhat intangible benefit of the retail method, there is the more tangible advantage that the store can determine its goods on hand and its cost of goods sold without actually taking a physical count of its inventory. This is done by subtracting sales and other deductions at retail from inventories at retail. The difference between the two figures

Table 15-1

Median and superior stock turns (times) at retail for various departments in selected stores

Departments	Department store sales (millions)											
	$1–5		$5–10		$10–20		$20–50		$50–100		Over $100	
	Med.	Sup.[1]	Med.	Sup.	Med.	Sup.	Med.	Sup.	Med.	Sup.	Med.	Sup.
Adult female apparel	3.0	3.9	3.3	3.9	3.6	5.6	3.8	4.1	4.7	5.1	4.5	4.8
Adult female accessories and intimate apparel	2.5	3.6	2.9	3.3	2.9	3.4	3.0	3.6	3.2	3.9	3.3	3.7
Adult male apparel	2.0	2.4	2.3	2.7	2.3	2.7	2.4	3.2	2.8	3.5	3.1	3.4
Infant and boys/girls clothing and accessories	2.5	2.5	2.7	3.2	2.8	3.0	2.8	3.2	3.3	3.7	3.8	4.2
Personal needs, food, cosmetics, tobacco	2.0	2.5	2.6	3.0	2.6	4.4	2.7	3.7	2.9	3.2	3.4	3.8
Hobby, recreation, transportation, toys	1.7	3.7	2.2	2.4	2.0	3.1	2.2	2.5	2.0	2.4	2.6	3.0
Home furnishings, furniture, decorative accessories	1.8	2.1	1.8	2.2	1.6	1.9	1.7	1.8	1.8	2.1	2.1	2.3
Appliances, outdoor equipment, housewares	2.1	2.5	2.4	2.6	2.1	2.8	2.0	2.4	2.4	2.7	2.7	3.2
Domestics, draperies, white goods	1.7	2.2	2.0	2.4	2.0	2.8	2.0	2.4	2.2	2.4	2.3	2.7

[1] Median (med.) is median (middle) turnover figure in sample; superior (sup.) is upper quartile turnover figure (75 percent) in sample.

SOURCE: *Department Store and Specialty Store Merchandising and Operating Results of 1979* (New York: Financial Executives Division, National Retail Merchants Association, 1980).

would represent ending inventory or goods on hand at retail. These data are then converted into cost data for the determination of cost of goods sold.

To aid in the understanding of the retail method, a step-by-step explanation of its application should be of help to the reader.

1. *Determination of value of beginning inventory at retail and cost.* The retail value is what the goods are selling for. Adjustments should be made in the retail value for any recent markups. Care should also be taken to add freight charges to the billed cost so as to include all appropriate costs in the calculations. Any recent purchases should be added to both cost and retail values to ensure that inventory values are up-to-date.
2. *Determination of cost complement.* The cost complement is found in the following manner:

$$\text{Cost Complement} = \frac{\text{Value of inventory at cost}}{\text{Value of inventory at retail}}$$

3. *Determination of inventory deductions.* All deductions should be subtracted from the value of inventory at retail at this point. Sales, markdowns, employee discounts, and an estimate of shortages—shoplifting, employee theft, damage in storage, and clerical errors are common sources of shortages—should be deducted in order to have a more realistic ending-inventory valuation.
4. *Determination of value of ending inventory at retail and cost.* Using the three steps given, a store can estimate its inventory without the necessity of a physical count. As noted in the inventory analysis example, a retailer can calculate the store's ending inventory at cost just by knowing the original retail–cost relationship and how well that store or department did at retail during the period.

Inventory Analysis—Retail Method		
	Cost	*Retail*
Beginning inventory	$68,000	$110,000
Net purchases, Billed	21,000	33,000
Markups on old merchandise		300
Freight	150	
Value of merchandise	$89,150	$143,300
Deductions		
Sales for period	$30,000	
Markdowns	7,000	
Discounts	300	
Shortage (estimate)	2,000	
Total Deductions		− 39,300
Ending inventory at retail		$104,000

$$\text{Cost complement} = \frac{\$89,150}{143,300} = 62\%$$

Ending inventory (Cost) = Ending inventory (retail) × Cost complement
$64,480 = $104,000 × 62%

The advantages of the retail method of inventory valuation are many to the retailer who wishes to make a conscientious effort in the area of inventory analysis. Some of these advantages are:

1. *Quick availability of operating data.* The store needs to know how well it is doing. Since it is not practical for a store to take a physical inventory every day, the retail method permits the store to calculate its gross margin (sales minus cost of goods sold) readily. Since profits depend on the gross margin of the store, the retailer can examine, under the retail method, what impact various markups and markdowns are having on profit. Information of this nature permits the retailer to adjust to changing market conditions while, it is hoped, maintaining the desired profit level.

2. *Evaluation tool.* The retail method permits the store to plan on even a departmental basis in terms of sales, purchases, and inventory on hand and then to keep close tabs on the plan on a week-by-week or even day-by-day basis. By studying the variances or deviations from the plan, retail management can develop insight into the operation of the store.

3. *Automatic conservative inventory valuation.* The procedure automatically values the ending inventory at cost or market, whichever is lower, without the need to change the value of individual items as a result of changes in the market. If goods increase in retail price through increased markups, the cost complement becomes less, thereby keeping inventory cost at the previous level. If, on the other hand, markdowns are taken, the retail method will automatically lower the inventory value at cost to reflect the lower market value. To illustrate how the procedure works, suppose that the inventory of a store is valued at retail at $100,000 with a cost complement of 60 percent. What happens if (assumption A) retail prices increase by 10 percent or (assumption B) decrease by 10 percent? In the first instance, A, the cost complement will decrease to 54.5 percent but the inventory valuation at cost remains the same.

Assumption A

	Cost	Retail	Cost Complement
Beginning inventory	$60,000	$100,000	
Markups on old merchandise		10,000	
Value of merchandise	$60,000	$110,000	54.5%
Ending inventory at cost = $110,000 × 54.5% = $60,000			

In the second instance, B, the drop in the retail value will be reflected in the cost inventory figure, not as a result of a change in the cost complement but instead as a direct effect of a drop in the retail value of the ending inventory. As prices fall, the value of the inventory is decreased at cost as well as retail.

Assumption B

	Cost	Retail	Cost Complement
Beginning inventory	$60,000	$100,000	
Value of merchandise	60,000	100,000	60%

(cont.)

	Cost	Retail	Cost Complement
Deductions		10,000	
Ending inventory at retail		$ 90,000	
Ending inventory at cost = $90,000 × 60% = $54,000			

4. *Claim settlements.* By virtue of the fact that the retail method carries the inventory at cost or market value, whichever is lower, and the store would have records of daily sales, the store has perpetual inventory capability. If a natural disaster should strike or even a burglary, the retail method provides an acceptable basis for determining not only the amount of loss but also its fair market value. Insurance companies find the retail method to be an acceptable procedure for the determination of such losses.

5. *Determination of shortages.* Stock shortages can be detected by comparing what should be on the shelf at retail (beginning inventory at retail minus deductions) with what is actually on the shelf at retail. Any merchandise that did not clear the register or is not otherwise accounted for will show up in the shortage figure. By making use of the retail method at the departmental level, the merchant can determine the amount of shortage on a department by department basis—a much more meaningful figure than if calculated only for the store as a total unit. It should be noted that the procedure as outlined only deals with the amount of shortage—not the cause. As was pointed out, the retailer should estimate the amount of shortage in order to value correctly the retail inventory for purposes of the retail method. When the amount is actually calculated, this figure might then be used in all further retail inventory valuations as the shortage estimate, until the next actual determination of the figure is made.

Another possible method of estimating such figures is to take a moving average of the last three or six or whatever actual shortage figures for use as an estimate. The idea behind this approach is to not permit any one unusual situation to put too much influence on the shortage figure. The average of the last three calculations for estimating purposes might, for example, compensate for any unusual circumstances which might affect shortages at a given moment. The average figure, therefore, will give more stability to the shortage estimate for purposes of inventory valuation.

Still another possible source for determining the shortage estimate is provided by industry trade groups such as the National Retail Merchants Association. As given in Table 15-2, the median shortage figures for department stores by department range from little or no shortages to almost 4 percent of sales. In other sections of the book, suggestions are given as to how to reduce damage to merchandise as well as how to cope with customer and employee theft. Efforts that reduce such sources of shortages should result in more favorable inventory valuations under the retail method.

The retail method of inventory valuation also encompasses certain disadvantages that may outweigh the advantages of the system for a given retailer. The more often cited disadvantages of the retail method include the following:

1. *Retail method cannot be applied to every situation.* The retail method will work only when the value of the merchandise at retail is known at the time the goods are received. If the merchandise is to undergo further processing which will change its value such as

Table 15-2

Median stock shortages [1] as a percentage of net retail sales for various departments in selected stores

Departments	Department store sales (millions)					
	$1–5	$5–10	$10–20	$20–50	$50–100	Over $100
Adult female apparel	1.9%	2.4%	2.5%	2.4%	3.3%	3.5%
Adult female accessories and intimate apparel	1.9	2.0	1.7	2.0	2.6	2.7
Adult male apparel	1.5	2.9	2.1	2.1	3.1	2.6
Infant and boys/girls clothing and accessories	1.7	1.8	1.8	2.0	2.6	2.1
Personal needs, food, cosmetics, tobacco	1.5	1.8	1.7	1.0	1.9	1.9
Hobby, recreation, transportation, toys	NA	2.3	2.5	2.3	3.4	2.0
Home furnishings, furniture, decorative accessories	3.1	NA	1.6	NA	1.5	1.1
Appliances, outdoor equipment, housewares	1.1	0.8	NA	NA	1.8	1.4
Domestics, draperies, white goods	2.5	1.9	1.1	NA	1.6	1.1

[1] Difference between book inventory at retail (as derived under the retail inventory method) and the physical inventory in terms of retail values.
NA—Not available.
SOURCE: *Department Store and Specialty Store Merchandising and Operating Results of 1979* (New York: Financial Executives Division, National Retail Merchants Association, 1980).

in the prescription shop, bakery department, or various installation services, then the retail method will not work. Such retail operations must be evaluated on a cost basis even when the remainder of the store is operating under the retail method of inventory valuation.

2. *Average figures create some difficulties.* Does the actual markup figure at a given point in time bear any resemblance to the average figure that was calculated at the beginning of the period for use in the retail method? If not, then the retail method may greatly overstate or understate the actual inventory situation. It is for this reason that the method normally should not be used for store-wide analysis. Even at the department level, problems can arise if certain items within the department have higher turnover rates than other items or if prices fluctuate considerably. Such activities increase the chances that the average markup will not be representative of the actual price–cost relationship.

3. *The retail method is difficult to successfully implement and maintain.* To use the retail method of inventory valuation, numerous records must be maintained on a current basis. Such efforts can encompass considerable expense for the store. Every time a price is changed, the corresponding records should be changed to include the new price. Employee discounts, merchandise returns, merchandise transfers, and new purchases at retail must also be recorded so as to keep the inventory figure up-to-date. It is easy to see how the retail method of inventory valuation could become a nightmare from a paperwork standpoint. For stores large enough to justify the acquisition of electronic data processing equipment and large enough to tie such equipment in with automated point-of-sale data collection registers, the disadvantage of paperwork is

erased and the retail method becomes a valuable tool for up-to-the-minute inventory analysis. For the smaller store, the costs of such procedures may outweigh the benefits.

Before leaving the discussion pertaining to the retail method of inventory valuation, it should be pointed out that a complete POS (Point-Of-Sale) system, with scanners that read SKUs off each item sold, could eliminate the need for the retail method in a store. So why discuss the retail method? Some stores may never use POS equipment because of their size and/or financial limitations. Other retailers may not use scanners throughout their stores. Scanner use may be limited to high-fashion and/or big-ticket departments. Still others may continue to use the retail method in addition to POS data because they like the way that the retail method depreciates the inventory and/or aids in the evaluation of departments or merchandise classifications as compared to item information. There is definitely no clear-cut feeling in retailing as to the future of the retail method of inventory valuation. Some believe it is dead. Others say that there will always be a need for it.[2] Further discussion of the role of electronic data processing equipment in merchandise control is given later in the chapter when analysis of inventory in terms of units is discussed.

Cost Method of Inventory Valuation

As its name implies, the cost method involves valuing the inventory at cost at the time the inventory is taken. It is by its nature a much simpler approach than the retail method since it requires little record keeping. It is for this reason above all others that many small retailers use the cost method of inventory analysis.

To use the cost method, a physical inventory must be taken. The cost codes that were placed on the merchandise during the marking procedure (Chapter 14) form the information base for taking inventory at cost. The personnel read and interpret the code as they record the value of the ending inventory at cost. The ending inventory at cost becomes the beginning inventory at cost for the next evaluation period. Purchases are also recorded at cost. With such data, the cost of goods sold can be calculated and the gross margin of the store (sales minus cost of goods sold) can be determined.

The main advantage of the cost method is its ease of implementation. People with little accounting or retailing experience understand the system. Such people naturally appreciate the fact that only a few records must be maintained to operate a store and evaluate its inventory under this system.

A system with such simplicity would naturally be used by all retailers if it did not also have some very important disadvantages:

1. *There is no method available to determine shortages.* Under the cost method no effort is made to determine the value of the inventory at retail. Therefore, there is no way to determine if, or more realistically, how much is being lost through the various forms of shortages. Under the cost method there is no comparable calculation for shortage determination as given under the retail method.
2. *To determine inventory calculations is time consuming.* To use the cost method, a physical inventory of the store must be taken at cost which necessitates the decoding of cost codes if not done in conjunction with a computer. Such a task is time consuming and also prone to errors on the part of store personnel.

3. *Lack of short-term operating data.* Under the cost method, many forms of reports and other information cannot be obtained except when a complete physical inventory is taken in the store (may be only once or twice a year depending on the type of merchandise carried by the store). Under such a limitation, it is extremely difficult for a retailer to use this method of inventory valuation for control purposes.

4. *Depreciation of merchandise.* As noted earlier, the retail method will adjust the cost value of the inventory as retail prices are reduced so as to keep the value of the inventory in line with market conditions. Such is not done automatically under the cost method. The retailer must continually take time to make decisions dealing with the depreciation of merchandise if the inventory valuation under the cost method is to be a realistic figure.

FIFO versus LIFO as a Basis of Inventory Valuation

No matter which method of inventory valuation is used, the actual inventory should be sold on a First-In, First-Out (FIFO) basis. The items that have been around the longest are naturally sold first. FIFO is, therefore, the logical procedure to follow in the stock room. For tax purposes, however, the retailer does have another option, Last-In, First-Out (LIFO), where the items acquired last are assumed to be sold first. The retailer will find that, during periods of inflation, LIFO offers certain tax advantages. It should be emphasized that under LIFO, the items acquired last are *assumed* to be sold first. LIFO has nothing to do with the actual flow of inventory—it is exactly opposite of what the merchant usually desires in terms of physical merchandise control. LIFO is merely an accounting exercise. The choice of FIFO or LIFO allows the retailer to use the store's merchandise as a variable that can have a direct bearing on the profits of the store. A brief comparison of the two methods should help the reader to understand them.

First-In, First-Out (FIFO). Inventory valuation under FIFO brings correct stockroom and merchandising procedures in line with the stated value of the inventory. The problem with FIFO is replacement cost. If costs are rising or falling the cost of goods sold will be understated or overstated. Only in periods of stable prices does FIFO provide a proper inventory valuation.

For example, a merchant who was opening a small shoe department bought 400 pairs of tennis shoes in July at $10 a pair and 400 more pairs in November, which were up to $15 a pair due to a price increase in raw materials. The inventory at the end of December was 200 pairs of shoes. FIFO would assume that the 200 pairs of shoes were worth $15 a pair or that all the $10 shoes were sold first. As noted in Figure 15–1, FIFO will therefore result in a lower cost of goods sold and so will give a higher profit figure.

Gross Margin = Sales − Cost of Goods Sold

Last-In, First-Out (LIFO). As seen in Figure 15–1, LIFO will, on the other hand, provide a higher cost-of-goods-sold figure and consequently a lower taxable profit than will FIFO during the period of rising wholesale prices. The only mechanical difference between FIFO and LIFO is that in the example, LIFO will assume that the 200 pairs of shoes remaining in inventory were those that were bought first when the price was $10 a pair. The cost-of-goods-sold figure is therefore assumed to better reflect the

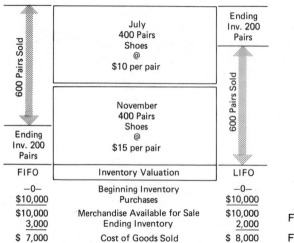

FIFO	Inventory Valuation	LIFO	
−0−	Beginning Inventory	−0−	
$10,000	Purchases	$10,000	
$10,000	Merchandise Available for Sale	$10,000	Figure 15-1
3,000	Ending Inventory	2,000	
$ 7,000	Cost of Goods Sold	$ 8,000	FIFO versus LIFO

replacement value of the merchandise and so does not overstate the profit picture for the firm.

Since most retail firms have historically used the FIFO method, should a firm switch to the LIFO method; and if so, when? Given the assumption of inflation the benefits of electing LIFO are realized essentially in improved cash flow arising from reduced income taxes in the year in which the method is adopted. Further improvements in cash flow may be realized in the following year from reduced estimated tax payments since these payments are usually based on the previous year's actual tax liability. Additional cash flow benefits will be realized in future years assuming that costs continue to increase. Essentially, the benefits are measured by the tax effect on the difference between LIFO cost and replacement cost of year-end inventories. As for the timing of the switch, select a time when minimum adverse reaction will occur as a result of a drop in profits on the earning statement—particularly if the retail operation is a publicly held company.[3] LIFO does affect earnings per share. When K mart Corporation switched to LIFO in fiscal 1980, earnings were reduced by 5 cents per share.[4] The stockholder who is unaware of how LIFO works may not react favorably to such a drop. Therefore, the best time to make the switch would be during a year when profits are good. In such a situation, the store will generally show a profit even with the adoption of LIFO. It should be noted that, once the switch is made, the store cannot switch back and forth at will. The Internal Revenue Service has established procedures that must be followed whenever a change is made in the inventory valuation procedure.

For purposes of analysis, the total store does not have to go either FIFO or LIFO. Selected product lines or departments are permitted to be treated differently for this purpose.[5] The retailer should study the situation carefully to make the most profitable decision from a tax standpoint. Merchandise control was defined as all those procedures that a retail store employs to determine the status of its inventory. If a store can affect its financial situation by means of the method employed to value inventory, such procedures should be studied in light of what would be best for the store. Merchandise control from a dollar standpoint can and does have a major influence on whether or not the operation of the store is a success.

Whereas dollar control is concerned with the inventory taken collectively, unit control deals with individual physical units. Dollar control can be used for planning and budgeting on a store-wide basis while unit control is concerned with the proper mix of merchandise to meet customer demand. In other words, good merchandise control in a store will use both dollar control and unit control. The operator of a well-managed store considers both to be important.

Before discussing the various forms that unit control may take in order to determine the physical inventory of the store, it might be of interest to point out various considerations that favor its use by the retail store. These benefits or advantages of unit control include the following:

1. *Unit control will point out popular items.* Fast sellers will be singled out under the system, thereby enabling such items to be reordered much sooner if such items are to be retained in stock by the store.
2. *Unit control permits inventory aging.* Unit control not only should reveal how many of an item are on hand but the relative age of each individual item. Aging, therefore, "discovers" slow-moving items that can perhaps be put "on sale" now to reduce a greater potential loss if discovery is not made until a later time.
3. *Unit control permits analysis of inventory by vendor.* Do items from a particular supplier sell well? Or do a high number of markdowns occur? Are items from a particular vendor delivered on time? How many returns are made to the vendor? Unit control can aid in answering the question of the importance of each vendor to the store's overall profitability.
4. *Unit control aids in the development of automatic systems for inventory reordering.* Data generated within the unit control system provides both a history of customer demand and vendor performance. For items with somewhat predictable demand, models can be developed that will tell the retailer how much should be ordered and when by using the data collected under unit control. This point will be examined further when perpetual unit control is discussed.

When one thinks of unit inventory control, three somewhat distinct forms of application come to mind:

Periodic visual count
Periodic actual count
Perpetual actual count

As will be noted, each can be applied to particular situations with satisfactory results.

Periodic Visual Count

As its name implies, this method is sometimes referred to as the "eyeball method." Used primarily by small retailers, the system can work very effectively if:

1. Depth of merchandise is high.
2. Demand is highly predictable.

3. Merchandise is of low unit value (more can be carried in stock per inventory dollar).
4. Replacement goods are readily available.
5. Goods are arranged in the store in a manner that permits visual inspection.
6. Merchant knows the stock well enough to maintain the proper mix of merchandise without elaborate inventory records.

If these factors are met, the periodic visual count can be a very inexpensive, simple to understand, and easy to use method of unit control. In its application, it takes many forms. The two-bin system, for example, is quite popular. In a hardware department, two kegs of nails are purchased, then one is placed on the sales floor and one in storage. When the one on the sales floor is empty, the one in storage is put on the sales floor and another one is ordered. This simple example illustrates perhaps the greatest problem with this system. Will demand for the item continue to be predictable? If not, the store may "get stuck" with nails it cannot sell or be out of nails too often if such an item has increased in demand. A retailer who carefully studies patterns of demand can usually overcome this problem in the majority of situations.

Periodic Actual Count

Before discussing the mechanics of the periodic actual count, care should be taken to distinguish between inventory counting for unit control purposes and that conducted for dollar control purposes. As noted earlier, dollar control requires the interpretation of cost codes and the reading of various cost information that is found on the merchandise. Unit control is much easier and quicker since no cost data are involved. The number of physical units is the only concern. Dollar control will involve all the data necessary for unit control. The reverse is not true.

The actual counting of merchandise on a regular basis for unit control purposes provides the retailer with information for making needed purchases. The interval between such counts may range from once or twice a year to once a week or even more often. It is obvious that the longer the interval, the less useful will be the data for control purposes. Since no count is made between the periodic checks, merchandise could be depleted, or not be selling as well as expected, without management's learning of it from unit control until the next periodic count. Another problem with the system is that the actual taking of the inventory is time-consuming and error prone since it is usually taken by sales personnel during store hours. If such a system is used, store personnel must not let their sales efforts suffer as they take the periodic unit count.

To speed the inventory work, certain areas of a store will be counted each week, others every two weeks, some once a month, and so on. By spreading the work, all the inventory counts do not come due at any one time. Scheduling of the work in this manner eases somewhat the inventory burden on the store employees. In order to select which departments or areas of the store that need to be checked more often and which need only be checked occasionally, certain factors should be considered:

1. Desired Depth
2. Demand Predictability
3. Number of Transactions

A department with limited depth, unpredictable demand, and numerous transactions should probably be analyzed quite often. The reverse would naturally be true if great depth and known demand were found to be present in a department with an expected low transaction level.

When would a store use a periodic actual counting system as opposed to some other approach? When a store wants better control than is provided under the visual system but does not want to put forth the effort and/or money required to implement a perpetual count. The periodic actual count is a type of middle-of-the-road solution to the problem of unit control. For the merchant who understands its weaknesses, and who is in a situation where the procedure can realistically be implemented, this system can provide much useful data at a fraction of the cost of a perpetual system.

Perpetual Actual Count

An up-to-the-minute record of the physical units on hand is the goal of a perpetual unit control system. As noted, one of the weaknesses of the periodic actual count was what could take place between counts. With the perpetual system, any changes which are made in the units in inventory are immediately reflected in the data collected for purposes of unit control.

When should a retailer adopt a perpetual unit control system? When:

1. Merchandise is of sufficient value to justify the cost of the system.
2. Merchandise is of sufficient value to make it desirable to minimize inventory levels—especially when the store is in close proximity to suppliers.
3. Demand is highly unpredictable.
4. Merchandise is a fashion or seasonal item.
5. Merchandise available for sale is removed physically from the customer and salesperson who only view a floor sample or catalog (a common situation in appliance, furniture, and building supply retailing).

The perpetual system can be carried out manually or it can be put on various forms of electronic data processing equipment.

Manual Perpetual Count. If done manually, special care should be taken never to let the system falter, even for a minute. Lapses in record keeping are quite common where the retailer does not insist on the recording of information at almost the moment of sale to ensure that the perpetual count retains its accuracy. To aid in the success of the manual count, many retailers have found it to be far better for someone other than the salesclerk to record the data. Several methods or procedures in use are outlined.

Sales slip. The salesperson writes on the sales slip the necessary information—one copy of which goes to the person or department charged with the responsibility of unit control. Information from the sales slips is posted on the inventory cards for each item carried in stock. Inventory cards need not be elaborate. Many stores use 3″ × 5″ index cards to keep track of the merchandise. As shown in Figure 15–2, only four items of information are needed for

Figure 15-2

Inventory control card.

Item:	BASKETBALL - WILSON ALL-AMERICAN							
Date	Rec	Sold	Bal	X	Date	Rec	Sold	Bal
10/1	100	4	96	X				
10/3		11	85	X				
10/4		2	83	X				
10/5		6	77	X				
10/6		4	73	X				
10/8		15	58	X				
10/9		1	57	X				
10/12		7	50	X				
10/15		1	49	X				
10/16		8	41	X				
10/20		12	29	X				
10/21	72	5	96	X				
10/22		7	89	X				
				X				
				X				
				X				

the system to work—amount received, number sold, date of inventory adjustment, and balance on hand. More elaborate cards can, of course, be used if the retailer chooses to do so.

Ticket stub. A ticket is attached to the merchandise. When the item is sold, the stub is removed from the merchandise and given to unit control. Information from the stub is posted on the inventory control cards as illustrated in Figure 15-2.

Point-of-purchase stubs. As items are sold, employees check off the items on an inventory control card that may be attached to a point-of-purchase display, on the merchandise itself, as in the case of major appliances, or in a location available to sales personnel such as might be found in new car retailing. In each instance, the sales personnel check off the items as they are sold. Since this method is generally used for big-ticket items, the accuracy level is much higher than would be true for the same system in areas such as ladies' ready-to-wear.

Automated Perpetual Count. The ultimate in retail unit control is the automated perpetual count. Such a system has the capability to provide almost any kind of information in the area of merchandise control which can be of use to the retailer. Its only real drawback is cost. Although completely automated perpetual inventory systems are coming down in price, they are still financially out of the reach of many small retailers if an in-house operation is desired. One hope for many small stores is an outside service bureau that in return for a fee amounting to approximately 1 percent of sales will provide various weekly and monthly reports that are developed from data provided by the store. The actual price of such an outside service will generally depend on the number of transactions processed, size of the master files, size and frequency of reports, and the type of transmission and delivery service provided. [6]

Before discussing the completely computerized system, which includes point-of-sale recorder systems, another form of automated counting will be mentioned. This system, punched or magnetic price ticket, is being used by many retailers, and is more financially realistic to many retailers than the completely automated system.

Punched or magnetic price ticket. This system operates by automatically reading code-punched tickets or magnetic tags, which are removed from items when sold. At different times during the day, the tags are collected and fed into a tag converter system. Depending on the capability of the system, reports of various types are generated for use by management as well as a perpetual count of the inventory. One type of punched tag that is used for this purpose is shown in Figure 15–3.

Point Of Sale (POS). The use of point-of-sale recorders closes the last possible hole in the perpetual inventory system. With punched or magnetic price tickets, there is always the possibility that the salesperson will forget to remove the coded price tag. Under POS, the register automatically records the information as the sale transaction is placed on the machine. Such systems may require the salesperson to record the unit control data on the machine

Figure 15–3

Manual punching of sales data into a point of sale recorder. Also note the punched inventory ticket.

(Courtesy of Montgomery Ward.)

Figure 15-4

Built-in reader for recording point-of-sale data. Register identifies
product and puts price on ticket.

(Courtesy of Giant Food, Inc.)

(Figure 15-3) or may use an optical scanning device, either built-in (Figure
15-4) or hand-held (Figure 15-5), to perform the procedure automatically.
Either way, the chances of not having a record of the transaction from a unit
control standpoint are minimal. If the clerk is required to put in the data, the
registers are usually programmed in such a way that they will insist that the
inventory data be placed in the machine before the cash drawer will open.
Under such conditions, even the absent-minded employee will remember to
include the data needed for unit control.[7]

Many of the point-of-sale recorders in use today are much more than fancy cash
register. They are in essence, on-line computer terminals that provide the
store with the capability to determine sales of particular items and/or departments or whatever by the hour, day, or any other time frame. These machines
may also give the retailer the capability to run credit checks through the
register as well as to conduct price audits (price of the item as shown on the

Figure 15–5

A trade ad for a major supplier of hand-held scanning equipment which points out many of the benefits of POS equipment.

OCR WAND READERS RING UP PROFITS.

Recognition's OCR WAND readers lead to better profits through improved merchandise management and substantially reduced underrings.

With over 85,000 units delivered and with operating hours in excess of 100 million, Recognition's OCR WAND® readers are a thoroughly tested technological dream-come-true.

More than 200 retail companies worldwide — department stores, dress shops, hardware stores, and others — are now using OCR (optical character recognition) technology with Recognition's readers to capture price and merchandise information. Instantaneously. Accurately. Effortlessly.

Recognition's OCR WAND readers have proven themselves the ideal tool for POS transactions in multi-unit or chain store operations.

OCR WAND readers record pricing and merchandise data with accuracy and completeness of better than 99%. Underrings are virtually eliminated. In fact, OCR WAND readers can pay for themselves in less than one year based on the underring reduction alone.

OCR WAND readers improve merchandise management because the accurate, up-to-the-minute sales data they provide makes sure only the right merchandise is at the right place at the right time. And, at the right price. As a result, markdowns are reduced, sales increase, and inventory turns improve.

But ... the OCR WAND reader is only part of the Recognition story. Recognition will design an entire system utilizing OCR and tailored to the specific needs of your retail chain operation. Recognition sales representatives and systems analysts provide consultation on OCR system design and installation, tag and document preparation, personnel training, and maintenance back-up.

Recognition's OCR WAND reader and a broad line of other innovative products are helping businesses the world over improve productivity and reduce costs. Virtually all major oil companies, many of the largest banks, and several credit card companies utilize Recognition's equipment to process documents from bank checks to claim forms; from credit card slips to utility bills; from currency to consumer coupons; from sales tags to letter mail. Just what you'd expect from a leader in OCR technology with offices throughout the United States, Canada, Europe, and Japan.

For more information on OCR systems and OCR WAND readers, call or write us today. Find out how Recognition's OCR WAND readers can ring up profits for you. Write to: Eldon Rindels, Manager, Marketing Services, Recognition Equipment Incorporated, P.O. Box 222307, Dallas, Texas 75222.

OCR WAND is a U.S. Registered Trademark of Recognition Equipment Incorporated.

See Recognition's OCR WAND Reader demonstrated at the 70th Annual Convention and Retailers Business & Equipment Exposition, Jan. 11-14, New York City, in the Madison Suite, New York Hilton Hotel.

RECOGNITION: THE ORIGINATOR OF THE OCR WAND READER

(Courtesy of Recognition Equipment, Incorporated.)

price ticket is compared with the price of the item as recorded in the computer).

With the advent of the Universal Product Code and Universal Vendor Marking with its use of Optical Character Recognition, retailers can, if the economies of scale warrant, tie their ordering, receiving, marking, and control activities into a single system. Such is already in use in many stores as automatic order points have been developed for items with somewhat predictable demand. After considering lead time requirements for delivery and the cost of being out of an item or being overstocked, order points can be determined. As for how much to order, the economic order quantity has been found to be a function of inventory carrying cost, demand predictability, and ordering costs (usually about the same regardless of the size of the order).[8] The determination of the order point and order quantity coupled with the closed-loop automated perpetual inventory system provides a procedure for automatic order placement when quantities fall to a certain level in terms of physical units.

When the predetermined order point is reached, the system automatically places a reorder. It then records the reorder with dollar and unit control and provides receiving and marking with a copy of the purchase order. When the goods arrive they are checked, marked, and distributed, and the system records where the items have been sent. Point-of-sale recorders then make day-by-day reports of sales to unit and dollar control. When the merchandise level is reduced to its reorder point, the system starts the entire process once more (Figure 15–6).

Notice that, at all stages, dollar control can also use the data generated by the system. The form of the data, however, is quite different. Dollar control is concerned with cost and retail figures whereas unit control is only concerned with physical units of merchandise. As noted earlier, both systems are important to merchandise control. Both are necessary ingredients of a good control procedure. Both dollar control and unit control can be aided by an automated information system for merchandise control.[9]

SUMMARY

Merchandise control is defined as all those procedures that a retail store employs to determine the status of its inventory in light of customer demand and general economic conditions. One tool used in such control is the determination of inventory turnover. The higher the turnover (the number of times during a period that net sales in dollars or units exceed average inventory), the better, everything else being equal, is usually the retailer's goal. Care should be taken, however, not to forget that high turnover may mean excessive stockouts, an always dangerous situation for a retail store. Along with turnover, the use of dollar control and its companion, unit control, form the nucleus of an inventory information system which tells the retailer the status of his merchandise. Dollar control may be by the retail method which enables the store to have access to quick reports, have an evaluation tool, have an automatic inventory valuation adjustment, and have a determination of shortages, or by the cost method which offers simplicity. Tax considerations also enter the picture as the retailer considers First-In,

Figure 15-6

Closed-loop automated perpetual inventory system.

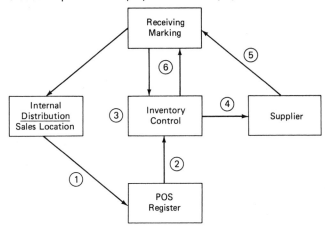

1. Customer takes merchandise to checkout from Sales Location.

2. POS Register informs Inventory Control by means of SKU number or UPC code that item has been removed from inventory.

3. Inventory Control checks to see if item inventory is sufficient. If reorder point is reached, order will be sent to supplier.

4. Supplier received computer — generated order via mail or electronic purchase order system.

5. Supplier ships merchandise to Receiving.

6. Receiving receives copy of purchase order from Inventory Control. Also informs Control when goods arrive and where goods will be sent internally (Sales Location).

First-Out (FIFO), or Last-In, First-Out (LIFO) as a means of valuing inventory. There is, of course, no relation between Last-In, First-Out and what actually takes place in the stock room. Unit control, the companion of dollar control, is concerned with the analysis of physical units rather than dollars. Functions of unit control include pointing out fast- or slow-moving items, analyzing vendors, and examining the status of the inventory for purposes of reordering. Unit control may be performed on a periodic visual count basis, periodic actual count basis, or perpetual actual count (manual or automated) basis. A good merchandise control system can assist the retailer in understanding the status of the store's inventory—a necessary ingredient in the successful implementation of the merchandising function in a retail store.

DISCUSSION QUESTIONS

1. Define or explain the following terms:

    a. Merchandise control   b. Inventory turnover

    c. Dollar control   d. Unit control

e. LIFO
g. Shortage
i. Visual inventory count

f. FIFO
h. POS recorders
j. Demand predictability

2. Joe's TV Sales and Service has a turnover rate of 2.5 while Smith's Television City has a 4.6 turnover figure. Joe is upset because Television City is doing better than he is. Is Television City doing better? Why or why not?

3. Bill's Bicycle Shop sold 120 Thomas Bond bicycles at $100 each. Average gross margin is 50 percent. A periodic actual count system of unit control is used by Bill's. The results of the count for last year were:

Jan.1	12 units
April 1	27 units
July 1	32 units
Oct. 1	63 units
Jan. 1	18 units

Calculate the inventory turnover by three different methods:

a. Turnover (retail)
b. Turnover (cost)
c. Turnover (units)

4. Compare the advantages and disadvantages of the retail method of dollar control and the cost method of dollar control. Which is better?

5. By use of an example, explain how the retail method of dollar control provides for an automatic conservative inventory valuation.

6. Super G Stores found that the beginning inventory for its men's department was $150,000 at retail. At the same time, average gross margin was determined to be 40 percent. During the six-month period under study, freight on new merchandise was $600 and markups on old merchandise amounted to $300. Billed purchases for the period were $40,000. Sales for the period were $50,000. Markdowns were 5 percent, discounts were 1 percent, and shortages were 2 percent (all are percentages of sales). Determine the value of ending inventory at cost by using the retail method of inventory analysis.

7. The Electric Connection, an electronics shop, purchased 15 units of a new line of stereo equipment at $200 each on October 15. Additional shipments of this new equipment were received on November 30 (10 units at $250 each) and January 12 (25 units at $300 each). During the accounting period the Electric Connection sold 40 units at $500 each. Calculate the cost of goods sold figure for the store using both LIFO and FIFO. What are the advantages and disadvantages of each method?

8. Dollar control or unit control—which is more important? Defend your answer.

9. When is the periodic visual count method of unit control a realistic alternative for the retailer?

10. Distinguish between the taking of inventory for the purpose of determining inventory under the cost method of dollar control and the periodic actual count under unit control.

11. When should a merchant adopt a perpetual unit control system?

12. Interview a retailer who uses a complete POS system in his or her stores. Also interview a retailer who uses a mechanical register system. Ask each of these

retailers about their system in terms of its advantages and disadvantages. Ascertain why they use their particular system. Conduct a detailed comparison of their comments.

NOTES

[1] C. K. Walter and John R. Grabner, "Stockout Cost Models: Empirical Tests in a Retail Situation," *Journal of Marketing*, Vol. 39, no. 3 (July 1975), p. 52, published by the American Marketing Association.

[2] For additional ideas on the future of the retail method, see James T. Powers and Arthur Ullman, "Will Increased POS Result in the Demise of the Retail Accounting Method?" *Retail Control*, Vol. 45, no. 11 (September 1977), pp. 2–16, published by the National Retail Merchants Association.

[3] Louis C. Moscarello, "The Pros & Cons of LIFO," *Retail Control*, Vol. 43, no. 10 (August 1975), pp. 13–14, published by the National Retail Merchants Association.

[4] "K mart Net Climbed 4.2% in Fiscal 1980 on 8.9% Sales Rise," *The Wall Street Journal*, Vol. 195, no. 55 (March 19, 1980), p. 16.

[5] Moscarello, "The Pros & Cons of LIFO," p. 14.

[6] Edward A. Strobin, "P.O.S. in the Independent Small Store," *Retail Control*, Vol. 43, no. 7 (March 1975), pp. 37–38, published by the National Retail Merchants Association.

[7] For information on how POS can help a retailer, see Marian Rothman, "New Uses, Threats, and Solutions via POS," *Stores*, Vol. 61, no. 6 (June 1979), pp. 41–43, published by the National Retail Merchants Association.

[8] For additional information on how to calculate the automatic order point and economic order quantity, see Harold Bierman, Jr., Lawrence Fouraker, and Robert Jaedicke, *Quantitative Analysis for Business Decisions* (Homewood, Ill.: Richard D. Irwin, Inc., 1961), pp. 70–80.

[9] For more information on POS and inventory management, see Anthony Joseph, "Operating and Control Benefits and Limitations of POS for the Small Store," *Retail Control*, Vol. 48, no. 8 (April–May 1980), pp. 2–21, published by the National Retail Merchants Association; C. Kleinman, "Major Operating and Control Benefits," *Retail Control*, Vol. 48, no. 1 (September 1979), pp. 36–48, published by the National Retail Merchants Association; Joseph A. Nagy, "P.O.S.: The New Tool of the Market," *Retail Control*, Vol. 48, no. 1 (September 1979), pp. 19–26, published by the National Retail Merchants Association; Marian Rothman, "Expanding the Concept of Inventory Management," *Stores*, Vol. 61, no. 6 (June 1979), pp. 31–34, published by the National Retail Merchants Association; and Bernard Rotsky, "The Electronic Purchase Order System (E.P.O.)," *Retail Control*, Vol. 48, no. 10 (August 1980), pp. 2–9, published by the National Retail Merchants Association.

Retail Personnel

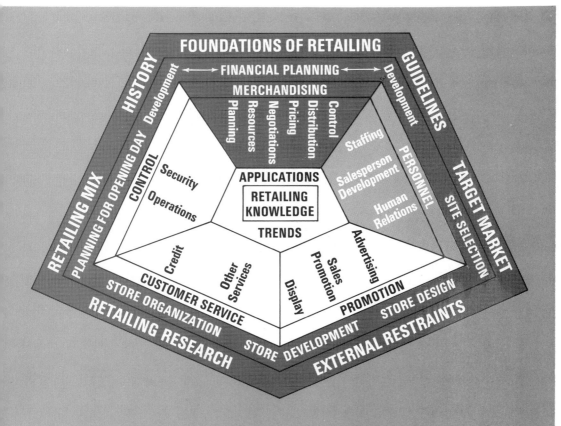

Staffing the retail store, salesperson development, and human relations in retailing are all important topics in the area of retail personnel.

"Staffing the Retail Store" is concerned with determination of need, recruitment, selection, orientation, training, compensation, and performance evaluation.

"Salesperson Development" looks at the retail selling process and examines various categories of salespersons. This chapter is also concerned with the mental and physical attributes of salespersons.

"Human Relations in Retailing" deals with motivation, leadership, communications, and disciplinary action as they relate to the retail situation.

Staffing the Retail Store

"I know I'm overqualified, but I promise
to use only half my ability."

"I really like Sheron's Place. The people who work there are so nice." "I always shop there when I can because those people know what they are talking about." "I don't know where that store finds its employees, but I sure wish a few other stores would use the same source." Comments such as these are heard from time to time as shoppers describe the nice experiences they have had with the staffs of retail stores. Such comments are, unfortunately, not commonplace. In many stores, retail personnel are a problem! To guard against this situation, a retailer should make a careful examination of the entire staffing function to see if improvements can be made for the good of the store.

The staffing function in a store is rather complex. Staffing is concerned with determination of need, recruitment, selection, orientation, training, compensation, and performance evaluation (Figure 16-1). Successful implementation of all seven staffing areas by retail management increases the probability that the retail organization will be staffed by individuals who perform their tasks in an efficient and effective manner. If a manager or owner worked for anything less than to have the best retail staff possible, the probable reward would be less than desirable store performance. The retailer must never forget that, to most customers, the staff is the store.

DETERMINATION OF NEED

In staffing a store, the success or failure of the entire staffing operation may depend on determining what type of staff is desired. What will be the responsibilities of the position to be filled? What qualifications should a prospective employee have to meet these needs? A successful determination of need lays a solid foundation for the remaining aspects of staffing.

Figure 16-1

Elements of retail staffing.

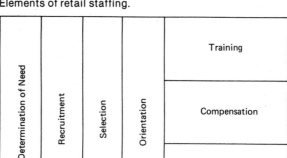

Determination of the Position's Responsibilities

Before a store can search for a particular employee, it must know something about the job to be filled. To aid in this process, a job description of the tasks to be performed by the position holder, Figure 16-2, should be prepared. The written job description lets the prospective job applicants, as well as the current store personnel, know exactly what are the duties and responsibilities of the position. The job description can also be quite valuable in setting the compensation level of the position as well as in evaluating the performance of the position holder over time.

Many retailers in small stores do not write up job descriptions because they feel that their store size makes such written descriptions unnecessary. This is not so. Regardless of size, written job descriptions help management to analyze each position in relation to the others in the store. By simply putting down what each person does and/or should be doing on the job, a comparison of the various positions can be made. By studying such descriptions, overlapping tasks can be eliminated while overlooked tasks can be assigned.

Determination of the Qualifications of the
Person Who Will Fill the Position (Job Specifications)

By knowing what the job really consists of, retail management has a better idea of the qualifications a person should have to fill the position. A person who is overqualified will generally not be happy in a position that offers little challenge. On the other hand, a person in a position "over his or her head" will usually not succeed. As a retailer sets

Figure 16-2

Example of a job description.

POSITION:	Head Clerk – Ladies' Ready-To-Wear
RESPONSIBILITIES:	(1) Perform duties of department manager in his/her absence
	(2) Assist the department manager with his/her recordkeeping responsibilities
	(3) Other responsibilities as may be assigned by the department manager
SPECIFIC DUTIES:	(1) Sell merchandise in such as way as to promote customer satisfaction
	(2) Handle all layaways
	(3) Assist in the training of all employees
	(4) Assist in the preparation of displays as well as general housekeeping duties
	(5) Conduct a morning inspection prior to the time of opening
	(6) Other specific duties as may be assigned by the department manager

forth the type of person who will be sought for the retail position, certain characteristics of retail employment should be kept in mind:

Long and Wrong Hours. Most customers like to shop at night, on Saturday, and where possible, on Sunday. These same customers, for the most part, would not like to work during these times. As for long hours, management in particular does not limit itself to a 40-hour workweek. The person who is successful in retailing must be one who has no major reservations about working under both long and wrong hours.

Many Part-Time Workers. Stores have little need for a full complement of personnel during every selling hour of the week. It is for this reason that stores are forced to search for quite a few personnel who are willing to work on a part-time basis. In many cases the desired characteristics are modified to match those persons who are more likely to be willing to work part time at the "wrong" time.

Low Pay. For years, retailing has been a low wage payer. Although retail management, in most cases, has been paid a competitive salary, the retail clerk has received somewhere near the minimum wage. Without a monetary incentive, obtaining and retaining employees who are qualified is sometimes difficult.

Women. Historically, the majority of the retail sales force has been women. In addition, many of these women have not been the primary breadwinner in the household. Their loyalty to the job, therefore, may not be what it might if the job were crucial to the financial survival of the family unit.

Little Work Experience. The people who enter retailing are generally found to have little or no work experience. Therefore, their success on the job is very hard to predict. Equally as difficult is the attempted matching of the job description to the individual with no "track record."

High Turnover. As a result of the conditions cited, high employee turnover is found in retailing. Many change from job to job while others exit from the retailing profession after only a short period of time. High turnover is the reason given for limited training programs in many retail stores. Actually, lack of training may be a cause of the turnover. Likewise, many retailers cite high turnover as a reason why wages cannot be greater. Why pay more to a person who will be gone tomorrow? The argument can also be viewed in the opposite manner. Higher wages could reduce turnover by attracting a more stable employee who would view the position in a more permanent manner.

The job specifications should spell out any qualifications that a person must have to carry out the requirements of the position. For example, a prospective employee in a cosmetic department might need any or all of the following qualifications:

1. Must have completed two years of college.
2. Must have at least two years of work experience.
3. Must be capable of making decisions under stress.
4. Must have specific product knowledge.
5. Must have attractive appearance (see Chapter 17 for more discussion on desired personal characteristics).

Another qualification that may be important is whether or not the salesperson should have anything in common with the customers of the store. Researchers such as O'Shaughnessy[1] and Churchill, Collins, and Strang[2] have pointed out that retail salespersons who are similar to their customers *may* do a better job than salespersons who are dissimilar to their customers. The latter authors do stress, however, that the evidence is such that salespersons should not be considered solely on the basis of how their characteristics match those of the store's customers. From the evidence, it would appear that, everything else being equal, it would be better for employees to have something in common with their customers. Such does not, however, appear to be a necessary ingredient for retail success.

One other consideration that must be dealt with when developing job specifications is the Civil Rights Act of 1964 as amended. Any job specification that excludes minorities from job consideration either directly or indirectly because they are a minority may be challenged. This is especially true if the store employs 25 or more persons, as these stores are under the jurisdiction of the Equal Employment Opportunity Commission (EEOC). Any time that such a firm's minority employment percentage is significantly lower than the minority's percentage makeup relative to the total population of the area, the EEOC may take legal steps to correct the imbalance.

Having taken into account the general aspects of retail employment and the specific personnel requirements of the position as guided by the job description, the retail manager should now be in a position to know what type of personnel are needed or preferred and can probably be obtained by the store. By conducting a realistic and well-thought-out determination of what is really needed by the store in the way of personnel, the merchant is ready to proceed with the next phases of the staffing of the store which are the recruitment and selection of personnel.

RECRUITMENT AND SELECTION

Recruitment is the bringing together of potential job applicants and the store. Selection is the determination of which one of the applicants, if any, would be best suited for the job. Why are these two important elements of retail staffing presented together? Recruitment when taken by itself can generate many bodies. The real question is "How many of these bodies are potential employees?" The use of selection procedures is the only way to answer the question.

Recruitment

Recruiting for a position is similar to prospecting for gold. It is simple if you look in the right place. Knowing where to look is the heart of the recruitment effort.

Current Employees.   Present employees have one advantage over all other recruits—they are known quantities. Another advantage of considering current employees is the improvement in morale that usually results when employees feel that they have a chance for advancement. Care should be taken, however, to sincerely consider employees for advancement if such employees are recruited for the position. The impression of a half-hearted effort simply for show can mean nothing but problems for the store.

Position Advertisements.   A large retail chain that is looking for a major executive may wish to advertise the position in the Tuesday edition of *The Wall Street Journal.* The Tuesday paper, more than any other, has become known as the job issue. The Sunday editions of many metropolitan newspapers have similar reputations on a regional basis. Position advertisements may also be placed in the appropriate trade journals. Such advertisements serve to attract people from other retail operations. Still another advertising possibility is those media which are aimed toward potential employee groups. College newspapers along with the *College Placement Annual,* which is available at college placement offices, are examples of media that could reach the college market.

Care should be taken if position advertisements are used when no effort is being made to recruit from within. Present employees will see the advertisements and discontentment will begin. If current employees are not aware of the recruitment effort (the author believes they should be aware of the effort and also be under consideration for the position if qualified), a blind advertisement should be run that does not identify the store. Most papers and trade publications will provide a blind address for such purposes. It is always interesting when the position ad for the store receives inquiries from the store's own employees who are not aware that the source of the advertisement is their own employer.

Employment Agencies.   Another way in which to maintain an anonymous role during initial recruitment, if such is desired, is the use of a private or public employment agency. For a fee, which is paid by the employer or employee or together, a private agency will advertise the position without store identification and do any level of screening of applicants as may be desired by the employer. Care should be taken in the selection of a private agency if one is used by the firm. There are some very reputable employment firms and there are others that the store would be better off without. Government employment agencies may also be a possibility if the position is of a type that can be filled by people who tend to use such public agencies. A retailer should check with public employment agencies to determine if an agency of this type is a realistic source.

Educational Institutions.   Various programs at schools and colleges have proven to be a good source of prospective employees. As a source of sales personnel, the distributive-education students in the high schools have proven to be of great value to stores. For low-level supervisory positions, vocational schools and junior colleges offer recruiting possibilities. For the various management programs, senior colleges and universities may hold the key to recruitment success.

Referrals.   Current employees, friends, relatives, and so on may direct interested persons to the store. This source may be good and bad. Good from the standpoint that the prospective employees are recommended by someone who knows them. Bad from the standpoint that recruitment of this nature encompasses many of the problems associated with nepotism. Too many lifelong friends working together on the sales floor may mean too much talking and not enough working.

Unsolicited Applicants. The most popular recruitment source for many stores when recruiting new sales personnel is the unsolicited walk-in or write-in candidate. Care should be taken not to rely on this source too much, as other recruitment sources that require more effort on the part of the retailer could yield stronger candidates. On the other hand, a walk-in should not be considered a second-rate applicant. By being an unsolicited applicant, the person may be exhibiting the kind of aggressive behavior that could translate into desirable behavior on the job.

Selection

Recruitment having done its job, the selection of the best applicant, if any, is a procedure that should not be taken lightly. Selection procedures generally make use of one or more of the following:

Application Form. After recruitment locates a potential employee, an application form is usually completed by the applicant. This form, in conjunction with any personal contact already made with the applicant, forms the foundation of the first screening step in the selection process. There is no need to waste either time or money on those who are obviously not qualified. To aid in this screening phase, the application form should be detailed enough to bring out the various pertinent data that are needed by management. Information to be sought on the application form (Figure 16–3) may include a complete history of previous employment with level of compensation and reason for leaving each position, educational history, military history, and general demographic data. References may also be requested on the application for employment. If so, no relatives, pastors, or close friends should be permitted as references since it is difficult for these people to be candid when asked about a prospective employee's character and willingness to work. It should be noted that every question on the application form should be designed so as not to violate the Civil Rights Act of 1964 as amended or EEOC guidelines.

Tests. Testing may take the form of psychological testing or tests which measure achievement. Even though these tests are subject to error, they still are considered useful as a screening device.

1. *Psychological tests.* Is the worker's interest of a nature that he or she will like the particular job? Does the worker have the aptitude to handle the work? What about the personality of the applicant? Can the individual, for example, handle stress situations such as a complaining customer right in the middle of the Christmas rush? Many tests have been devised to measure various points of concern that fall under the heading of psychological testing.
2. *Achievement tests.* Whether the applicant can add, make change, or comprehend written instructions can be determined by achievement tests. Such tests for first-level retail clerks may consist of nothing more than several simple math problems and an English question or two that will check on the literacy level of the candidate. Achievement tests for potential management trainees may, on the other hand, include complex pricing

Figure 16-3

Application form designed for college market.

GIANT CAREER DEVELOPMENT TRAINING PROGRAM

COMPLETE AND MAIL TO GIANT FOOD INC., P.O. BOX 1804, Washington, D.C. 20013
AN EQUAL OPPORTUNITY EMPLOYER

PERSONAL BACKGROUND

NAME _____   SOCIAL SECURITY NUMBER _____
       LAST   FIRST   MIDDLE

_____
       PRESENT STREET ADDRESS

_____
       CITY   STATE   ZIP CODE

BIRTH DATE _____ TELEPHONE NUMBER (DAY) _____ (EVENINGS) _____

Why are you selecting a career as a manager in a Retail Food Business? _____
_____
_____

Why do you feel you would be an asset to Giant Food? _____
_____
_____

EDUCATIONAL BACKGROUND

Prep or high school and town _____ Year Graduated _____ Course _____
Are you presently enrolled in school?_____ Anticipated Graduation Date _____

Colleges Attended	Years Attended	Date Graduated or to be Graduated	Degree	Major Subject
1.				
2.				
3.				

Courses Enjoyed Most in College 1. _____ 2. _____ 3. _____
Cumulative Grade Point Average Overall _____Out of a possible _____
Cumulative Grade Point Average in Major _____ Minor_____
College Honors (including scholarships and honorary societies) _____
College Activities (athletics, publications, class organization offices and other student functions) _____
_____

My outside interests, hobbies and recreations are _____
Special Work Skills _____

EMPLOYMENT HISTORY

LIST JOB HISTORY FOR THE PAST FIVE YEARS. ACCOUNT FOR ALL PERIODS OF THE TIME (INC. MILITARY, PERIODS OF UNEMPLOYMENT, ETC.) LIST ALL RETAIL EXPERIENCE AND MILITARY SERVICE REGARDLESS OF YEAR. IF ADDITIONAL SPACE IS REQUIRED, ATTACH SEPARATE PAGE.

ITEM	PRESENT OR LAST EMPLOYER	NEXT TO LAST EMPLOYER	2ND TO LAST EMPLOYER	3RD TO LAST EMPLOYER	4TH FROM LAST EMPLOYER
COMPANY NAME					
COMPANY ADDRESS					
CITY & STATE					
JOB TITLE					
FULL-TIME/PART-TIME	F/T ☐ P/T ☐	F/T ☐ P/T ☐	F/T ☐ P/T ☐	F/T ☐ P/T ☐	F/T ☐ P/T ☐
DATE STARTED					
DATE TERMINATED					
STARTING SALARY	per	per	per	per	per
LAST SALARY	per	per	per	per	per
SUPERVISOR'S NAME					
REASON FOR LEAVING					
IF MILITARY SHOW TYPE OF DISCHARGE					

HAVE YOU EVER BEEN DISCHARGED BY ANY EMPLOYER? ☐ YES ☐ NO   IF YES, STATE EMPLOYER, DATE, REASON _____

FORM 8179

(Courtesy of Giant Food, Inc.)

problems as well as an assortment of questions that seeks to determine if the candidate has a working knowledge of the various subjects that make up the area known as retail management.

In using tests as a selection device, care should be taken to ensure that any test used is in compliance with the 1978 Federal Uniform Guidelines on Employee Selection Procedures.[3] To be used, a test question must have been validated against job success as measured in terms of work output (production rate, error rate, etc.). To overcome the legal problems of testing, some retailers have ceased all testing. A better approach is to do good validation studies for the tests in use. These studies will satisfy EEOC standards while they give the retailer confidence in what can be a very effective employee selection tool.

Physical Exam.   Most stores have group medical insurance that requires a physical examination of all new employees. Many of these stores, however, administer a modified version of the physical exam to all prospective employees who have successfully passed through several screening stages. Blood pressure check, chest X-ray, and other general medical procedures are used on the applicant. Physical exams at this stage are, for the most part, limited to potential managerial applicants and those who will be involved in jobs that include physical stress.

Interview.   Depending on the position to be filled, at various points in the selection process interviews may be held with the applicants. Obviously, in the small store, only one interview will probably take place between the applicant and the owner. If the operation is larger, more people may become involved in the interview process. Although interview procedures can get carried away, having the applicant meet with several different people in a large organization is good for all concerned. It permits several different people who might be working with the person to have a chance to be in on the evaluation process. It also allows the applicant to meet some of the people with whom he or she will be working and gives the applicant some idea as to whether or not he or she will like his or her associates if the position is taken.

If interviews are used as a method of selection, care should be taken to learn as much as possible from such interview sessions. If more than one person interviews an applicant, the answers given by the applicant should be checked for consistency. If the applicant is destined to work in a stress situation such as at the customer service desk (main recipient of complaints in a store), an interviewer may even test the applicant by saying unpleasant things about the school the person went to or where the person is from. If the person offers a tactful defense of the school or town in the interview, the assumption is that the person may also be able to tactfully defend the store when approached by an irate customer. In this instance, the interview procedure is used to see how the person reacts to a situation instead of just asking how they would act given the particular set of circumstances. If interviews are used, each interview should have a purpose. Each person who is involved should write down their comments and rate each applicant. As a result of multiple interviews, a good cross section of opinion can prove to be useful to the selection process.

Information Follow-Up.   The information brought together on an applicant by the various means cited should be checked out in all cases for its correctness. Is the reason given for leaving a particular position a valid one? The person could have been fired from the position for pilferage. Did the person even hold that position? What do the references really say about the individual? For factual information a phone call usually yields more correct information than do formal letters of recommendation. Does a person's achievement test score match his or her educational level? A low score may just mean it was a bad day for the applicant. Has the applicant had unusual medical problems in the past? In other words, is the applicant just looking for a good health insurance package or does he or she really want a job? These and other points of concern should be checked out by the retailer. Such follow-up may be conducted by the company itself or by an outside firm. One widely used firm for such checks is Equifax, Inc. (formerly known as the Retail Credit Company) of Atlanta, Georgia. By using a national firm like Equifax, the retailer may also learn of things that have not been brought out before that might have a bearing on the personnel decision. Any person in the store who will handle any significant amount of money or will play a major role in the operation of the store should be checked out thoroughly. Such a statement should not be interpreted to mean that it is not important to check other employees. The only distinction is the thoroughness of the work. It is simply a matter of cost versus benefit.

Which Selection Procedures Should Be Used? Of the many information sources available for use in the selection process, the results of a study by Hollon and Gable[4] indicate that the interview is the most widely used information source for selection purposes (Table 16–1). Other popular tools are application blanks and business and personal references. No other information source was used by as many as 40 percent of the retail respondents in the study. The study results should not be used to infer that a retailer *should use* the more popular tools and maybe *not use* handwriting analysis, or even a technique not even listed in the table and/or in the discussion in the text. Within the legal constraints mentioned earlier, the retailer should use those procedures that yield good results for that retailer. If the information source appears to be useful in the selection of good employees, the smart retailer will use that information source regardless of whether it is used by others.

Offer of Employment. After using the various tools of selection, a decision must be made. Whether the decision for a particular applicant is *yes* or *no*, the applicant should be told promptly after the selection has been made. To wait too long before extending an offer may mean that the applicant, if any good, will probably already have another position. On the other hand, it is not fair to have an applicant who is no longer under consideration believe that he or she is still in the running.

The job offer should be extended in writing. Any conditions of employment should be stated in the letter. When the applicant should start work and what, if anything, the applicant should do before that time should be spelled out. The amount and method of compensation should also be included so as to minimize any misunderstandings at a later time. Finally, the method and time limit for acceptance should be provided the applicant. For management personnel, the letter may be a letter tailored to each situation. For retail salespersons, the letter may be a form letter with places to fill in the blanks. In any case, it is wise management to put it in writing. Many future problems can be eliminated by following this simple procedure.

Table 16-1

Information sources used in the retail employee
selection process (percentage reporting usage)

Technique	Exempt Employees[1]	Full-Time Nonexempt Employees[2]	Part-Time Nonexempt Employees[2]
Interview	82.3%	95.2%	93.4%
Application blank	77.8	92.3	90.2
Business references	70.4	74.9	66.4
Personal references	55.6	62.4	58.5
Credit report	33.3	27.0	19.6
Police check	19.0	21.7	19.8
Physical exam	13.8	14.0	9.5
Testing	9.0	16.4	13.5
Polygraph[3]	4.5	7.1	5.8
Assessment Center[4]	3.4	1.3	0.3
Handwriting Analysis[5]	0.0	1.1	1.1

$N = 378$.

[1] Not covered by minimum wage and overtime provisions of the Federal Labor Standards Act (managers, other executives).

[2] Covered by minimum wage and overtime provisions of the Federal Labor Standards Act (full-time or part-time: sales clerks, office workers, etc.).

[3] "Lie-Detector" Test.

[4] Pooled judgments of specially trained managers who use various criteria to evaluate a prospective employee.

[5] Graphologist infers certain personality traits from the shapes of letters, location of words, and use of words.

Source: Charles J. Hollon and Myron Gable, "Information Sources in Retail Employment Decision-Making Process," *Journal of Retailing*, Vol. 55, no. 3 (Fall 1979), p. 62.

ORIENTATION

The employee takes the job and reports to work full of enthusiasm and willingness. At the end of the day, the same person tells the manager to find someone else. What made the employee quit after one day on the job? Obviously, anything could be the cause. The problem most of the time, however, is lack of new employee orientation on the part of mangement.

Orientation should begin before the employee starts to work. When the person is hired, a copy of the store's employee handbook should be given to the new employee to read. The handbook (see Chapter 18 for information on what it should contain) should help to answer many of the questions that the new employee might have. It should be emphasized that every store regardless of size should have such a handbook.

When the new employee does report for work, he or she should not be told to "go to work." Management should, instead, take the person around and introduce the new employee to the personnel of the store. One particular employee should also be assigned the task of working closely with the person for the first several days. The employee assigned to the new person should make sure that coffee breaks, lunch periods, and slack times are not lonely times for the new person. Such times can be used effectively to answer the numerous questions that a new employee will usually have. Management should also make it a point to personally check on the person during the first day in particular and to praise the new employee at the end of the first day on the job if such praise has merit.

For many employees, it is also good to give them material to take home and work on that first night. Such "homework," if not carried to an extreme, will give status to the employee among his or her family and friends in a way very similar to the great feeling that a first-grader has when doing those first few "homework" assignments. Such take-home work helps to stress the importance of the job. Care should be taken not to overburden the new person with too much homework particularly if it is a part-time salesperson. Management trainees should, of course, expect such work.

Orientation includes anything to help the new employee become accustomed to the new environment. Everything from the location of the employee lounge to how to work the time clock should be covered. A checklist of items of interest to a new employee should be developed and followed by management to ensure that nothing is overlooked. A good orientation program for new employees can be the first building block in a successful employer–employee relationship that can reap benefits for the store for years to come.

TRAINING

As observed in Figure 16–1, orientation is a process that is geared to the first few days on the job, whereas training is a continuous process. New employees need training; old employees need training. There is always room for additional learning.

The Act of Learning

All learning involves three almost simultaneous processes.[5] First, there is the *acquisition* of new information—often information that runs counter to or is a replacement for what the person has previously known either implicitly or explicitly. Training may, for example, involve teaching an older salesperson a new method of selling. Second, *transformation*, the process of manipulating knowledge to fit new tasks, must take place. The older salesperson may adjust to the new method of selling by mentally using the old method as a base to improve on rather than repudiating the old method. The end result is the same. The third aspect of learning is *evaluation*, that is, checking whether the manipulated information is adequate to the task. Does the new selling method work better than the old one? If the answer is "yes," learning has taken place. Training programs should be designed with these three processes (acquisition, transformation, and evaluation) in mind.

Benefits of Training

"Training is a lot of trouble." This managerial attitude may spell trouble for the store. A store with a viable training program (such as the one for developing salespersons outlined in the next chapter) should reap many benefits from its efforts. The first and foremost benefit is more qualified employees. Other benefits as a result of better qualified or trained employees are less need for employee supervision, higher pay since employees are more productive, and lower turnover as a result of all the reasons cited. Morale and motivation are also good in an environment in which people see a means of improving themselves both mentally and financially through training.

Methods of Training

The choice of training methods depends on the situation. Common methods in use include the following:

Go Get'em "Method." The employee is only told to "Go Get'em." An approach such as this is certainly *no method* at all. It is included, however, since it is in wide use. Management simply assumes that the employee knows what to do. When learning does take place under this procedure, what is learned is often wrong. Although no training costs are involved in this approach, the cost over time to the store will probably be quite high.

Sponsor Method. As noted under orientation, an experienced employee should be made responsible for seeing that a new person becomes accustomed to the store and its people. This experienced employee may have a role to play in addition to helping orient the new person—he or she may also be assigned as the sponsor for the new employee. The sponsor is given the task of training the new employee on the job on a one-to-one basis. It should be apparent that much of the success or failure of the sponsor method of training rests with the proper selection of the sponsor. Does the sponsor teach the new person the correct way to do things or the way to do things that is simply the easiest way? To encourage the sponsor to do a good job, recognition of the important role that the sponsor is playing for the store should be made evident to the sponsor through extra compensation or extra days off or something of that nature. To be a success, the person assigned to be a sponsor should not look upon the task as an unnecessary burden. If viewed in this manner, the sponsor system will be a failure.

Programmed Learning Method. Training can be an individual concept under programmed learning. The approach uses the idea of repetition to encourage learning. Repetition can be developed through written exercises, or it can be developed through the use of teaching machines, a computer application of the concept of programmed learning. The written exercise is the more inexpensive approach to this learning technique. Under this idea, the reader is given a short section of information that is then followed by either objective or fill-in-the-blank questions about the material. The next section then builds on the first and again asks questions about the material. Many written programmed learning aids are available for use by the retailer who wishes to use this approach.[6]

More elaborate applications of programmed learning can be found with the use of teaching machines. Whether using an on-line computer terminal or individual units, such machines allow the employee to interact with the machine. When the student makes a mistake, the error is pointed out to the person and the person is given an explanation as to why such is the case. Teaching machines can perform all the tasks of written programmed learning plus provide simulations for all types of situations. The drawback to the automated approach is cost. For the on-line terminal system, a given variable must be that the firm already has computer capability—a problem for the small store.

Programmed learning, in its many forms, allows the trainee to move through material at his or her own speed as it promotes learning through mental repetition. Programmed learning, however, is not always the answer. It cannot measure progress in a skill area such as sewing. In its present state, the quality of a seam cannot be judged correctly by machine. Subjective matters run into difficulty when attempts are made to teach such material solely by the use of programmed learning.

Group Method.   A store holds a two-hour session on shoplifting prevention for all its employees. Employees are briefed on new store procedures at five ten-minute sessions prior to each shift change. These and many other situations make up the very popular approach to training known as the group method (Figure 16-4). The advantages of the group method are many. Management knows that all employees are told the same thing. Having one or two training sessions is less expensive. Group training can also reach all employees in a very short period of time. The main drawback of this method is the lack of individual attention. Under the group method, it is almost impossible, particularly if the group is large, to give the individual attention that helps to promote good learning.

The group method is often used to train new employees in stores where the number of new people warrants the group approach. Training employees prior to the

Figure 16-4

The group method of training can be used for both new or old employees as management attempts to disseminate information.

(Courtesy of J. C. Penney Company.)

opening of a new store is also usually done as a group. As noted, the group method is generally used when the economies of scale dictate its application.

Progression Method. The progression method is a step-by-step training method that moves the trainee from position to position as a means of learning various tasks in the store. Training procedures like this are found more commonly in management training programs. Progression can be applied to sales personnel, however, as a means of making employees more knowledgeable about all aspects of the store's operation.

A typical management training program using the progression method might consist of six parts. Such a program would carry the trainee through the following phases on the way to becoming a store manager:

1. Stockroom and Basic Store Operations (three months)
2. Sales Assistant (selling to customers) (three months)
3. Junior Assistant Manager (merchandising, promotion, customer service) (twelve months)
4. Assistant Manager (buying, merchandising, promotion, control, personnel) (twelve months)
5. Senior Assistant Manager (overall store operations with emphasis on planning) (twelve months)
6. Probationary Manager (responsible for operation of store under supervision) (six months)

Step-by-step plans are designed to give the trainee exposure to all aspects of the store. Upon completion of a well-planned progression program of training, the store employee should be well prepared to play an important role in the future success of the retail operation.

COMPENSATION

Regardless of the method of training, the incentive to learn can be advanced by a well-planned method of compensation that rewards the employee for a job well done. All employees, new or old, like to feel that they are getting a fair day's pay for a fair day's work.

Characteristics of a Good Compensation Plan

A good plan includes the following characteristics:

1. *It should provide incentive.* The harder-working employee will be rewarded for his or her efforts by means of a commission, bonus, merit raise, and the like.
2. *It should be simple.* The employee should be able to understand the system and figure out what his or her compensation will be.
3. *It should be easy to administer.* The compensation plan in use should not be an administrative nightmare. Simple record-keeping should be the only requirement.

4. *It should provide a "living wage."* Compensation must be enough to justify the efforts of the employee if good work is the objective. Without a "living wage," low employee satisfaction can cause problems for a store.
5. *It should provide regular and prompt payment.* Compensation plans work better when they can be depended upon. Employee motivation is also generally higher when prompt payment follows good work.
6. *It should be fair.* This characteristic plays a significant role in the effectiveness of a compensation plan. Of importance here is not only the question of whether the plan is fair or not. Of equal importance is the question of whether the employees think it is a fair plan. If employees do not believe that the compensation plan is fair to all, it really makes no difference if it is or is not.

Selected Compensation Plans

Store managers are normally paid a salary plus a negotiated percentage of the store's sales or profit. As for other store employees, four different compensation plans are generally used for the determination of wages: (1) straight salary, (2) straight commission, (3) salary plus commission, and (4) quota-bonus.

Straight Salary.   Straight salary provides a sense of monetary stability to the employee. A manager gives an employee $200 for a 40-hour week regardless of any external considerations. This plan is easy to understand and to administer while at the same time giving the employee prior knowledge of what his or her salary is going to be. Since the employee gets just as much when engaged in nonselling activities such as going to a training session, employees do not feel that they are being penalized for doing such activities. Employees also tend to feel more professional since their income is not related directly to sales. They can think of themselves as counselors instead of salespersons. Weighing against these advantages is the fact that some employees do not do their best without direct monetary encouragement. In addition, the downward inflexibility of the straight salary plan makes it very difficult to lower wages when conditions merit such action.

Straight Commission.   In application, straight commission is the opposite of straight salary. Under straight commission, the amount of compensation is directly related to the amount of sales made by the individual. If a salesperson receives an 8 percent commission, he or she must sell $2,500 worth of merchandise in a 40-hour week to match the $200 payment cited in the discussion under straight salary. Of course, under straight commission, if the salesperson sells $3,000 worth of items, the pay is $40 more or $240 for the week. It can also work the other way since, if only $2,000 is sold, the compensation will be $160. Straight commission is a compensation plan that is easy to understand. It also provides the financial incentive to work harder. There are, however, disadvantages to the plan. The competition among employees can get out of control. Shoppers have been run off by personnel who "fight" over customers on the sales floor or by over-aggressive salespersons who "attack" potential customers as they come in the store. Another problem is that sales in the store may be down through no fault of the salesperson. Even if a drawing account (salesperson borrows against future earnings) is used, the psychology of the situation does not promote good employee morale if no sales are being made. A third disadvantage is that it is very difficult to get employees to do anything else but sell under this plan. For example, it is very hard to get a person on commission to be a good sponsor for a new employee and to orient that person into the ways of the store. For the most part, such an arrangement will just not work under straight commission. Another personnel difficulty with straight commission is moving employees around from department to department or store to store. The new department or store may be less desirable from the commission standpoint or at least in the eyes of the employee. One other point to be discussed is the problem that is created when a customer returns merchandise upon which a commission has already been paid. Most stores obtain the excess commission back from the salesperson over a period of several months as opposed to a lump-sum reimbursement. This approach minimizes the hardship that is placed on the individual salesperson. In any event, however, it is not a happy situation.

The straight commission plan is popular in retailing whenever big-ticket items (cars, furniture, appliances, encyclopedias, etc.) are involved. For other forms of retailing the drawbacks of straight commission will generally outweigh the importance of the incentive to sell, which is the main point in favor of the straight commission method of employee compensation.

Salary Plus Commission. The best of the two previously discussed plans come together under this approach. Assume, for example, that a salesperson makes $150 in salary for a 40-hour week plus a 2 percent commission on all sales for the period. In a week when sales total $2,500, the salesperson's total compensation will be $200. In most cases, salary is the major part of the total wage, but the reverse could certainly be true if more incentive is desired in the plan. Salary plus commission gives the employee the security of the straight salary plus the incentive feature of straight commission. It is, however, more difficult to understand than the first two plans particularly if compensation rates are not uniform. Stores should examine how they might initiate this form of compensation plan if they are currently using either straight salary or straight commission. Such a change in method of compensation could be quite beneficial.

Quota-Bonus. Another combination of straight salary and straight commission is the quota-bonus plan. This approach differs from salary plus commission in that commissions are paid only on sales in excess of the quota instead of on all sales as would be true under a salary plus commission plan. For example, the salesperson could receive $150 per 40-hour week plus 5 percent on all sales over $1,500. With $2,500 in sales for the week, the salesperson would make $200 for the week. The success or failure of the plan rests on the determination of the quota. If the quota is too low, sales personnel may view themselves as commission employees with all the problems that go with such arrangements. On the other hand, if the quota is so high as to be almost unobtainable, the incentive aspect of the plan is no longer present. Quotas are generally based on historical sales data that are updated to reflect projected conditions of the upcoming selling season. As for the amount of the bonus, larger bonuses simply mean more incentive for the worker. Perhaps the greatest problem with the quota-bonus plan is its complexity when viewed through the eyes of the worker. Many plans are much more complex than the one just cited. When this is so, the employee has a hard time really understanding the incentive aspects of the plan. Because employees do

Figure 16-5

Methods of compensation in relation to sales productivity.

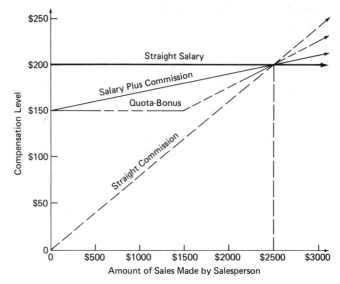

not understand many quota-bonus arrangements, feelings of mistrust can develop between management and worker as to how the compensation should be figured.

Which of the four compensation plans is the best one to use? Figure 16-5 looks at the four plans as they relate to sales productivity in terms of the examples used in the text. A retailer should do such an analysis when deciding on which plan to use and on what figures to use in a plan.

Of course, in making the compensation decision, management should also take into consideration any fringe benefits provided employees. They are a part of the total compensation package and may have a bearing on which plan is selected. Fringe benefits that are provided by various stores are almost infinite in number. Some of the most popular ones are:

Employee Discount	Paid Vacation
Pension Plan	Profit Sharing Plan
Health Insurance	Life Insurance
Sick Leave	Disability Insurance
Christmas/Birthday Bonus	Free Parking

As a general rule, it can be said that as more fringe benefits are made available to the retail employee, more store loyalty will likely be present on the employee's part. It is important to note that fringe benefits do not overshadow the importance of direct remuneration. Fringe benefits can, however, be an integral part of a total compensation package that is designed to meet the needs of the store and its employees.

"It is company policy to appraise the job performance of each employee on a periodic basis. The purposes of reviews are to maintain and improve each employee's job satisfaction and morale, improve job performance, provide a basis for job promotions and transfers, and discuss job problems and interests."[7] This statement is the recommended store policy for performance evaluations as provided in the National Retail Merchants Association's *Independent Store Policy Manual.* The policy as given will be implemented by better retailers with special emphasis on the periodic review. Where possible, quarterly reviews are desirable, especially for persons with short tenure. At the other extreme, all employees should undergo at least an annual performance evaluation.

It should be remembered that performance evaluation is not a pure science. Even in certain of the quantitative evaluation methods, subjectivity is the source of the quantitative data. Given the problems inherent in the procedure, every effort should be made to use as many of the various evaluation techniques as possible. This should improve on the chances of obtaining a valid appraisal of an employee's efforts in relation to his or her job. Both quantitative and qualitative procedures will be examined for possible consideration.[8]

Quantitative Measures

As in other areas of sales, many quantitative measures can be applied to the salesperson. The retailer can look at such statistics as sales returns as a percentage of sales, number of returns as a percentage of total transactions, compensation as a percentage of sales, and net sales per hour worked. These and numerous other calculations yield interesting data when determined for each employee in the store. Such data may reveal, for example, that a given employee makes many small sales but cannot seem to make the more expensive, high-margin sale. As a result of the evaluation, management may wish to work with the salesperson to overcome this weakness. These quantitative evaluations also point out salespersons who are doing extremely well in certain areas.

Qualitative Techniques

Even a good evaluation procedure cannot quantify things like loyalty, creativity, and appearance. To study these aspects of the retail job, the store should have several managerial personnel, if the size of the store permits, evaluate the employee in a more or less qualitative manner. Many stores use various rating procedures such as a weighted scale in an attempt to quantify the end result for ease of comparison. Another qualitative possibility is the use of a shopping service. This outside firm will send people in to "shop" the store. From their observations will come detailed reports on the sales personnel as seen through the eyes of the "customer." Such shoppers may discover that a certain clerk is not loyal to the store but is quite helpful to customers. Shopping services will generally yield both good and bad information about employees. It is up to management to interpret the results.

Employees should be told that they are going to be evaluated. Just as students work harder if they know they will be tested over the material, store employees will work equally as hard to obtain a good "score" in the performance rating. If employees discover, and they will, that the store is secretly being shopped, morale will fall because they feel they are being spied upon. On the other hand, if they are told in a straightforward manner that shoppers will be in the store to check on them, many of the negative feelings that stem from using shopper services will be eliminated. It should be emphasized to the employees that performance evaluations are not done simply to catch wrongdoers. These evaluations also point out achievers so they may be rewarded for their efforts. In other words, performance evaluation should be presented to the store employees in a positive manner.

Performance Review

By means of rating forms (Figure 16–6) and other analysis tools, the quantitative and qualitative methods of performance evaluation reveal much to management about an employee.[9] When management reviews this information, does this mean that the performance evaluation is complete? No! To finish the process, the retail manager should schedule a review session with the employee where he or she will be allowed to learn what was found during the evaluation process and how his or her performance ranks relative to the firm's expected norms of behavior.

For the performance review session, it is suggested that the manager (interviewer) keep certain points in mind:

Allow sufficient time for interview.
Minimize interruptions; restrict incoming phone calls.
Be relaxed; the employee will not relax if the interviewer appears uncomfortable.
Speak simply; never talk down to an employee.
Be straightforward; tell it like it is, be candid.
Meet employee on his or her level; do not pull rank.
Take your time; do not seem impatient.
Keep your feelings to yourself; do not argue with employee.
Praise strong points; be sincere.
Obtain employee's point of view about job situation.
Accept responsibility for helping the employee to improve.
Upon completion, make a written record of interview.

Employees like to know where they stand. A performance evaluation procedure with provisions for periodic review will accomplish this desire. Performance evaluation also helps management by providing an inventory of the staff of the organization and how that staff is performing in relation to the store's stated objectives. Since retailing is a labor-intensive industry, it makes good sense to evaluate this most important element in the retail organization.

1 line short

Figure 16-6

Performance review form.

```
                        Performance Review Form

    Employee Name _____  Date Hired _____

    Department _____ Supervisor _____ Last Review Date _____

    1. (s) Alertness to customer service...   ☐ Good   ☐ Average   ☐ Needs Improvement

       Comments: _____

       _____

    2. (s) Manner in dealing with customers..  ☐ Good   ☐ Average   ☐ Needs Improvement

       Comments: _____

       _____

    3. (s) Merchandise Knowledge............   ☐ Good   ☐ Average   ☐ Needs Improvement

       Comments: _____

       _____

    4. (s) Selling Ability..................   ☐ Good   ☐ Average   ☐ Needs Improvement

       Comments: _____

       _____

    5. (s) Stock keeping....................   ☐ Good   ☐ Average   ☐ Needs Improvement

       Comments: _____

       _____

    6. Knowledge of store systems...........   ☐ Good   ☐ Average   ☐ Needs Improvement

       Comments: _____

       _____

    7. Cooperativeness......................   ☐ Good   ☐ Average   ☐ Needs Improvement

       Comments: _____

       _____

    8. Reliability..........................   ☐ Good   ☐ Average   ☐ Needs Improvement

       Comments: _____

       _____

    9. Flexibility..............            ☐ Good   ☐ Average   ☐ Needs Improvement

       Comments: _____

       _____

    10. (Personal) Appearance & Grooming..   ☐ Good   ☐ Average   ☐ Needs Improvement

       Comments: _____

       _____

                                    (1)
```

(continued)

Figure 16–6 (*continued*)

```
                              Performance Review Form, Cont'd.

11. Creativity.......................      □ Good    □ Average    □ Needs Improvement

    Comments: _____

    _____


12. Loyalty..........................      □ Good    □ Average    □ Needs Improvement

    Comments: _____

    _____


13. Attendance & Punctuality.........      □ Good    □ Average    □ Needs Improvement

    List number of days absent & time period, plus any other comments: _____

    _____

    _____


14. Selling Cost compared to area average:    YTD Area _____   YTD Employee _____


    General Comments: _____

    _____


    Rated by: _____    Review Conference by: _____

    Date: _____    Date: _____


                                        (2)
```

SUMMARY

Staffing is concerned with determination of need, recruitment, selection, orientation, training, compensation, and performance evaluation. Determination of need involves management decisions dealing with the responsibilities of a position and the qualifications that are needed for a person to successfully fill that job. Recruitment and selection deal with finding the right candidates by using sources such as current employees, position advertisements, employment agencies, educational institutions, and referrals and then making a choice with the aid of application forms, tests, interviews, and background checks. Orientation entails getting the newly selected employee off to a good start. Training for both new and old employees can take many forms (sponsor method, programmed learning method, group method, progression method). Any form that is selected should consider the three processes of learning—acquisition, transformation, and evaluation—in its presentation to the employees. As for compensation plans, they should provide incentive, be simple, be easy to administer, provide for regular and prompt payment, and provide a "living wage" while being fair to all concerned. Four common compensation plans are straight salary, straight commission, salary plus commission, and quota-bonus. The last aspect of staffing—performance evaluation—examines the employee both quantitatively and qualitatively for purposes of determining raises, promotions, transfers, and even terminations. A good staffing function is vital to the success of a retail operation. Managerial time and effort that is spent on the staffing function is time and effort well spent.

DISCUSSION QUESTIONS

1. Staffing is not as important in retailing as it is in other industries. Comment on this statement.
2. Go to a store in your area and develop job descriptions for a store manager, a department manager, and a salesperson. Next, determine what you think the job specifications (qualifications) should be for a person filling each position. What type of person is actually filling each position?
3. Discuss the various characteristics of retail employment with retailers in your area. Determine if they view the characteristics in a positive or negative manner.
4. You are a retail manager. Where can you look for potential employees?
5. Are referrals a good recruitment source? Explain.
6. What selection procedures can be used to screen out less desirable candidates for employment?
7. In making an offer of employment, what should be kept in mind by management to ensure that no problems will arise at some future time?
8. "An adult should be able to take care of himself or herself. That's why I say orientation is a waste of time and money." Do you agree with this comment? Why or why not?
9. Explain the three processes that when taken together constitute the act of learning.
10. Why bother with training? Explain five different training methods. Cite examples.
11. A good compensation plan should have what characteristics? List and explain.
12. Distinguish between the four major compensation plans. Develop a sales productivity graph for the four methods where all plans will be equal at the $3,500 sales level.
13. Go to a major store in your area and talk with the manager about that store's performance evaluation program. If no such stores exist in your area, develop a performance evaluation procedure for a hypothetical store using various measurement procedures that are available from various information sources.

NOTES

[1] John O'Shaughnessy, "Selling as an Interpersonal Influence Process," *Journal of Retailing*, Vol. 47, no. 4 (Winter 1971–1972), pp. 32–46.

[2] Gilbert A. Churchill, Robert H. Collins, and William A. Strang, "Should Retail Salespersons Be Similar to Their Customers?" *Journal of Retailing*, Vol. 51, no. 3 (Fall 1975), pp. 29–42.

[3] "Uniform Guidelines on Employee Selection Procedures," *Federal Register*, Vol. 43, no. 166 (August 25, 1978).

[4] Charles J. Hollon and Myron Gable, "Information Sources in Retail Employment Decision-Making Process," *Journal of Retailing*, Vol. 55, no. 3 (Fall 1979), pp. 58–74.

[5] Jerome S. Bruner, *The Process of Education* (New York: Vintage Books, 1963), p. 48.

[6] For one example of an available written programmed learning aid, see Delbert J. Duncan, *Retailing—Modern Concepts and Practices* (Homewood, Ill.: Learning Systems Company, 1970).

^{7} *The Independent Store Policy Manual* (New York: National Retail Merchants Association, 1980), p. B-99.

^{8} For an in-depth look at performance evaluation, see *Measuring Executive and Employee Performance* (New York: Personnel Division, National Retail Merchants Association, 1977).

^{9} Much of the discussion for this section is taken from Stanley Guss, "How to Conduct a Successful Employee Review," *Personnel News and Views*, Vol. 7, no. 2 (Summer 1977), pp. 8–18, published by the National Retail Merchants Association.

CHAPTER 17

Salesperson Development

Reprinted by permission. © 1978 NEA, Inc.

When a customer walks into the store and then, in a few minutes, walks out without buying, the retailer should ask, "Why?" The reason for the walkout may be merchandise-related. On the other hand, the walkout may be the result of the store's sales personnel. The customer may have been insulted by the salesclerk. The salesperson may have indicated that he or she had no idea how to make the product work. Or even worse, the shopper may not have been able to get any assistance from the employees of the store. Some walkouts may eventually be back. Others will never be seen again. The results for the store could be different if the store would make a concerted effort to develop sales personnel who through much individual effort earn the right to be called "salespersons."

To reiterate, good salespersons are the result of positive effort on the part of both the store and the employee. As was discussed in the previous chapter, great care should be taken in the selection process and the training program to ensure that the salesclerk is up to the task of serving the customer. To aid the salesperson in achieving this goal, care should be taken during the training period to teach the person how to sell. Just as much care should be given in providing refresher training to employees after they are on the job. Employees are many times blamed for most of the problems in a store. For a given situation, the accusation may be true. The important question is why? Has the salesclerk been taught what to do? Has the salesperson been trained to sell? Has the employee been told what makes a good salesclerk? The most highly motivated sales employee in the store may never achieve his or her potential due to a lack of selling knowledge. How to make such a salesperson productive is the purpose of this discussion. Topics to be covered include the categories of salespersons, the selling process, and the desired physical and mental attributes of employees.

CATEGORIES OF SALESPERSONS

The broad area of retail selling can be divided into three categories: order-taking, order-handling, and order-getting. Although different, all three categories involve dealing with the customer. All three are synonymous with the retail store as far as the customer is concerned. If, for example, the customer is angered by the clerk, he or she is angry with the store. All three can aid business or hurt it depending on how they perform their tasks.

Order-Taker

The gasoline attendant or fast-food counter person are order-takers (Figure 17–1). Their tasks are to take orders and serve the customer without delay. Very little room is available for creative selling but some is possible. The simple mention of french fries by the order-taker may result in additional sales. Order-takers usually work in highly structured situations. Personal appearance and personality are valuable attributes in this environment since first impressions are about all the customer has time for in such a short contact period.

Figure 17-1

The retail selling environment may call for an order-taker.

(Courtesy of Kentucky Fried Chicken.)

Order-Handler

No selling as such is usually called for in this situation. The cashier at Giant Food (Figure 17-2) is not expected to sell merchandise. The person is, however, expected to be efficient, pleasant, and have knowledge of store policies and procedures. In addition, if the order-handler is aware of the products available and their location, then additional sales may be generated by directing the customer to needed items. Such a person is also in a position to be the recipient of many complaints about prices, service, and so on, depending on the type of store. The good order-handler knows how to react to such complaints.

Order-Getter

The heart of many retail success stories is the order-getter (Figure 17-3). This salesperson handles transactions, takes orders, and gets orders. In performing these responsibilities, this person is aware of the sales potential of the store, attempts to serve the customer, and is not content with just selling a product. Such a person sells the product, store, and himself or herself successfully to the customer. The salesperson

Figure 17-2

The order-handler is an important retail salesperson.

(Courtesy of Giant Food, Inc.)

Figure 17-3

Many retail selling situations require an order-getter.

(Courtesy of Sears, Roebuck and Co.)

who fits into this category works to learn the merchandise. He or she also studies various ways to make the sales presentation more effective. No stone is left unturned in the quest for selling excellence.

Which Category Is Needed?

The unfortunate thing about many retail situations is that a person who would make a good order-handler holds a job that requires an order-getter if it is to be done well. If such a situation exists in a given store, management should correct the problem by dismissing the employee or, better still, by working with the employee to develop the individual into an order-getter. It should be noted that there is a place for all three types of salespersons in retailing. Also, it should be observed that all are in a position to influence the sale. It is for this reason that all employees, regardless of the category they fit into, should understand the retail selling process so that, if the situation warrants, they can get the order.

RETAIL SELLING PROCESS

The retail selling process is a step-by-step procedure that if handled correctly should result in increased sales. Steps in the process are precustomer contact, prospecting, initial store contact, presentation of merchandise, handling objections, closing the sale, suggestion selling, and sales follow-up (Figure 17-4). For given retail situations, some of the steps are more appropriate than others. Care should be taken, however, not to

Figure 17-4

Steps in retail selling process.

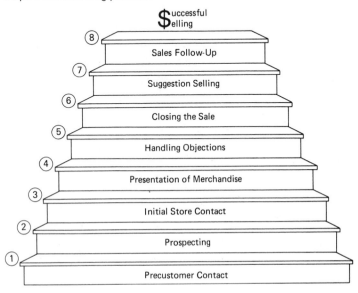

assume, for example, that prospecting or sales follow-up does not apply to a given store. It might apply very well with a little creative selling effort.[1]

Precustomer Contact

Essentially, the precustomer contact step points out the need for the salesclerk to do his or her homework before contact is made with the customer. Does the employee know the stock—what is there and where it is? Do the sales personnel know what is and is not on special? Do the salesclerks know how to fill out a merchandise ticket, work the cash register, and make change? Are store policies and procedures clear to the employee as to what to do about layaways, returns, and a hundred other things? Teaching employees about such matters is part of a training program. The real question is, "Did they remember it and is their knowledge current?" All employees must be drilled continually on store procedures to ensure a sound store operation. A clerk who misses a sale because he or she was unaware that merchandise of the type requested was in the stockroom has no excuse for such poor effort. In addition, if management failed in any way to aid the clerk in knowing that the merchandise was there, then management is even more at fault.

In addition to knowing such things as store policies, stock levels, stock locations, and what is or is not featured in a store promotion, one other very important precontact consideration is product knowledge. To be effective, sales personnel must know something about the items they are selling. Many sales are lost because the salesperson did not know enough about the product being sold.

Product knowledge takes many additional forms. The shoe salesclerk learns about quality shoes and how to fit them. The salesperson learns how to figure wallpaper requirements. A retail employee studies styles, fashions, colors, and so on so as to better assist the customer who is in the market for clothes. The person who works in kitchen utensils studies the products so as to be able to answer the inevitable question about the strawberry picker, "What is it?" Questions about product care, prices, and an infinite number of other possibilities make up the list of areas in which product knowledge is needed.

Although having complete product knowledge is literally impossible to achieve, special care should be taken to develop as much expertise as possible on the subject. The reason is simple. Many customers buy where they have confidence in the product knowledge of the sales personnel. Customers may, for example, buy their piece goods at the Yardstick Fabric Shop because they feel that the sales personnel can assist them with their sewing problems. Many customers buy all their hardware items for their do-it-yourself projects at a particular store because they feel they can get a correct answer to the question, "How much paint should I buy for a 9' × 12' room?" or anything else they need to know. The customer comes to the store to take advantage of the store personnel's product knowledge.

A salesperson who combines product knowledge with a knowledge of store procedures, promotional practices, and other pertinent variables has done his or her homework. The knowledge gained by the salesperson in the precustomer contact phase will serve as a solid foundation for the remainder of the steps in the selling process.

Prospecting

A salesclerk who does not wait for the customer to come in and ask to buy but instead searches out the potential customer becomes involved in a process called "prospecting." Prospecting takes two forms:

Finding new customers to buy the products.
Getting regular customers to buy more products.

In the first instance, the appliance representative checks the records of the repair service department of the store. If the salesperson notices that a family is having trouble with an old clothes dryer, he or she may call them and offer to sell them a new one. Another example may be a jewelry store that notes in the paper that Jane Doe is getting married. The store may contact the young bride-to-be and invite her to come in for a free gift and while there to register her bridal patterns. Bridal registers can lead to many sales besides possibly developing the bride into a long-term customer.

The second form of prospecting, getting regular customers to buy more products, is a golden opportunity that is often overlooked by many sales personnel. Such prospecting amounts to nothing more than having the salesclerk call a list of customers when a shipment of merchandise arrives or, possibly, when a special promotion is being held. The salesperson might call and say, "Mrs. Parrish, I just wanted to call and tell you that we have a new shipment of shoes that I feel sure you will like. I thought of you when I was unpacking them this morning." Such personal attention will sell lots of shoes. Or the salesperson might call to tell Mrs. Browne, "Royal Doulton is having a special promotion on their new figurines and I knew you would want to see them to add to your collection." To do this form of prospecting successfully, the salesclerk must have some idea of what the customer does like. Care should also be taken not to call the same customer too often. Doing it too much makes the process lose its psychological effect on the customer. While on the subject of psychological effect, some stores will go a step further in the prospecting process and actually send out the merchandise to the customer for his or her examination. This procedure does not always work. For some customers, however, nothing is ever returned. The secret to success of this form of prospecting is knowing your customer in terms of what effect having the actual possession of the goods will have on the purchase decision. If successful, prospecting becomes a major step in the selling process. In most cases, prospecting alone will not sell the merchandise. It may, however, get the customer to the store.

Initial Store Contact

As the name implies, initial store contact is the first actual contact that the clerk has with the customer who walks into the store. Good initial contact is vital to the sale. The salesperson cannot expect to successfully close the sale unless he or she has successfully opened it (Figure 17–5).

In retailing today, perhaps the weakest stage in the selling process is the initial contact with the customer. How many times during a given day does the following situation take place? A customer who enters the store is approached by the salesclerk.

Figure 17-5

Good initial customer contact starts the sale off right.

(Courtesy of Sears, Roebuck and Co.)

"May I help you?" asks the clerk.

"No thank you, I'm just looking," responds the customer.

The ritual is so automatic that many sales personnel and customers do not even realize that initial contact has even been made. A survey of opening remarks of 100 sales floor personnel in retail clothing stores illustrates the overuse of the opening phrase, "May I help you?" and its companion, "Can I help you?"[2] As noted in Table 17-1, the majority of clerks used these worn-out clichés.

The problem with "May I help you?" and similar phrases is not only with the fact that they are overworked. Such statements also leave no logical phrase to follow the reply, "No thank you, I'm just looking." The salesperson is left defenseless. His or her services have been offerred, and they have been turned down. If the clerk stays with the customer, he or she will probably irritate the customer. If the clerk leaves, the customer may steal the item or not buy the item because he or she could not find what was desired without the clerk's assistance.

In the survey mentioned, only 12 sales personnel opened the sales presentation with any degree of positive selling effort. Besides being different, phrases such as, "What color did you have in mind?" and "What size do you wear?" open the door for the clerk to be of assistance without asking to help. Statements such as these also flow very smoothly into the presentation of the merchandise phase of the selling process. Opening remarks even more difficult to turn away from are, "Have you seen our ad in today's paper?" or "Have you seen our sale merchandise?" Such statements generate much customer interest. Perhaps the best statement found in the survey was the clerk

Table 17-1

Opening remarks of 100 sales floor
personnel in retail clothing stores

Opening Remark	Number of Respondents
May I help you?	58
Can I help you?	19
What size do you wear?	5
May I be of assistance?	3
What can I do for you today?	2
What can I help you with today?	2
What can I show you today?	2
Can I help you, honey?	1
Can I show you something?	1
Have you seen our ad in today's paper?	1
Have you seen our sale merchandise?	1
I have something I want you to see.	1
May I show you something?	1
What color did you have in mind?	1
What size were you looking for?	1
Would you like to try it on?	1

Source: William H. Bolen, "Customer Contact: Those First Important Words," *Department Store Management*, Vol. 33, no. 3 (April 1970), p. 26.

who walked up and said, "I have something I want you to see." Why is such a statement hard to resist? For one thing, it is not a question. It is, instead, a positive statement. Besides arousing curiosity, this particular opening remark also tends to make the customer feel like someone special rather than just another customer.

Management should stress to its retail employees that good initial contact with the customer is vital to the sale. Originality must be the key. No phrase fits every situation. Sales personnel should be instructed to work on not saying "May I help you?" to every customer. In many instances, the reason why they never fluctuate from the standard clichés is that they have never been instructed to do so by management and have never considered the potential impact of such statements on their selling performance.

The discussion pertaining to initial store contact has concentrated so far on the most obvious situation that is found in a store. But what should a salesperson do if there is more than one customer to assist at the same time? The answer is certainly not to ignore one while the other is being served. The customer not being served should be told, "I'll be with you in a moment." That tells the customer that he or she has been noticed. It also helps to reduce the number of walkouts as a result of a delay in service. Then when the waiting customer can be helped, the salesperson should begin by saying, "Thank you for waiting." The same courteous treatment should also be given for telephone inquiries. If the customer calls, the store should answer promptly and if necessary put the caller on hold. Then, like the customer in the store, the caller should be told, "Thank you for waiting." It is good business to make a good first impression on the customer. A successful initial contact with the store can have a lasting impression on the customer.

Presentation of the Merchandise

The initial contact has been made and assistance is desired. Now what? How the merchandise is presented to the customer will have a major bearing on whether or not the sale is made. Although the actual presentation of the merchandise depends on the individual retail situation, general guidelines for achieving a good presentation are the following:

1. *Don't sell the steak—sell the sizzle.*[3] This guideline comes from one of the great masters of selling, Elmer Wheeler. The statement implies that a salesperson should not spend all the time in a sales presentation talking about product features, product characteristics, and so on. Care should be taken to ensure that buyer benefits are also included. For example, a customer likes to hear about the eight different wash cycles on the clothes washer. Better still, the customer likes to hear how these eight cycles will get clothes clean. Customers do not buy cold cow meat when they buy steak. They buy the steak's good taste and the good times that come with cooking out. In other words, they buy the benefits of the product along with the product. Any good presentation of merchandise will suggest buyer benefits to the customer.

2. *Obtain customer involvement.* The best way to sell many products is to obtain customer involvement by any possible means. A wristwatch placed on the customer's arm for inspection has a greater chance of staying on that arm than one that remains in the display carton. If the salesperson is in automobile retailing, the best way to sell a car is to get the customer to take a spin around the block in the car. A toy store that permits children and adults to play with the electric trains will generally sell more trains than will a place that keeps all trains in plastic-wrapped boxes. The good sales presentation attempts to get the customer to identify with the merchandise. If a customer comes into the store, sees a sport coat, tries it on, and he and his girl friend like it, the customer may no longer be satisfied without it. Such a desire would probably not have been created if the salesperson had not gotten the customer to try it on.

3. *Don't confuse the customer.* Many salespeople confuse the customer by showing too many items in the process of presenting the merchandise to the customer. A good rule to follow is to limit the number to three or four items in front of the customer at any one time. If additional items are needed to sell the customer, the previous items should be put away. If the customer has seven watches on the counter to choose from, the decision is very difficult. The good salesperson may have shown seven watches to the customer but only three will remain after the process of elimination for the customer to select from. An additional benefit in limiting items is that it reduces the chances of shoplifting. If seven watches are out of the glass case and the salesperson is distracted for a moment, only six may remain on the counter. If only three are on the counter, the chances of one disappearing into the "customer's" pocket are reduced greatly. Such a disappearance would be too obvious.

4. *Demonstrate with a flair.* The creative salesperson who sells dresses or cars or anything else should not say, in essence, "There's one and there's another one." The dress on the hanger can just be held there in front of the customer or it can be twirled around and placed before the customer with the bottom touching the floor to illustrate the fullness of the skirt or the soft draping qualities of the fabric. The diamond ring can be placed on the counter or placed on blue velvet to enhance the feeling of quality. If the vacuum cleaner is supposed to be lightweight and easy to handle, the salesperson demonstrating the vacuum should make it look easy. A good sales presentation comes with prac-

tice. During slow times in the store, the salesperson with encouragement from management might wish to practice such demonstrations to make them as flawless and as dynamic as possible.

5. *Message adaptation.* The same merchandise cannot be successfully presented to all customers in the same, identical manner. Why? Customers have different buying motives. The creative salesperson understands customer behavior and attempts to use this knowledge in adapting the sales presentation to the individual customer. As noted in Chapter 3, consumers have both rational and emotional motives that affect their buying decisions. The retail salesperson should attempt to evaluate each customer to determine how the sales presentation can be adapted to him or her. To tell customer A during the presentation that the product is just on the market may make that person want it because of a desire to be different. For a different customer, such a statement may kill the sale since that customer may be in a demographic group that only buys a product after it has become the socially correct thing to have. As the salesperson learns the clientele, message adaptation may become the factor that has the greatest bearing on the success of the presentation of the merchandise to the customer.

Handling Objections

Objections are part of selling. In fact, many people believe that customer resistance is a positive sign that progress is being made on making the sale. Many objections are nothing more than a means of procrastination. The salesclerk who learns to handle objections in a positive manner is ready to take the final step and attempt to close the sale.[4]

Customers object for various reasons. Such objections, however, normally fall into one of six categories:

Objections to forestall action. "I will come back next week." In this instance, the customer has not really been sold on the idea that he or she cannot live without the product. More buyer benefits are called for in the sales presentation.

Product objections. "I really don't like the new cars. They are just too small." For this situation, the customer must be sold on the advantages of the product. Better gas mileage, easier to park, and so on could be buyer benefits to point out to the customer.

Source objections. "I would like to buy the television here but I am concerned about what I hear about your credit deparment." In this case, the salesperson should first find out what the customer has heard and then respond to the objection. Care should be taken by the salesperson to uphold the integrity of the firm. Customers rarely appreciate the salesclerk who agrees with them and also criticizes the store and/or its management and policies. One thing is certain, agreeing with the customer will not remove the objection that rests in the way of the sale. Good salespeople will be loyal to the store. If sales personnel cannot be loyal to the store in front of the customer, they should not work there.

Service objections. "I'm afraid I can't get good service on the refrigerator if I buy it from you." Overcoming these objections simply boils down to a matter of convincing the customer that service is adequate.

Price objections. "I just can't afford it." The salesperson must answer in his or her own mind if the objection is valid or does it mean that the customer is ready to negotiate on price or does it mean that the customer wants to be convinced that he or she really needs the product. The salesperson should not be afraid of price objections. Price resistance is probably the most popular form of customer objection.

Objections to the salesperson. "Are you sure we need eight gallons of paint?" The customer is resisting the salesperson's professed product knowledge. Before selling the paint, the salesperson is going to have to sell himself or herself.

The six categories of objections illustrate that the customer will complain or object to just about anything connected with the retail operation. Such resistance is part of selling. The retail employee should develop ways to handle objections. Methods that have stood the test of time include the following:

Direct rebuttal. This approach may be used when the customer states an obvious untruth or makes a statement that represents a serious objection. For the sale to be made, the objection must be met head-on. Obviously, tact is important in any direct rebuttal. If the salesperson reacts too strongly or appears to go too much on the defensive, the sale will probably be lost.

Yes . . . but. The salesperson agrees with the customer but then adds what may amount to a rebuttal after that. In the "yes . . . but" approach, the salesclerk avoids taking an adversary position.

Counterquestion. The salesperson puts the shoe on the other foot and asks the customer, "Why?" The counterquestion approach may uncover the real reason for the objection, thereby enabling the salesperson to respond to the true problem.

Testimonial. The customer is told about a person who had a similar objection and how that person solved the problem and bought the product.

Restating the objection. By having the salesperson restate the objection, the objection may lose some of its steam in the translation. Also, if the customer hears the objection from someone else, he or she may notice that it sounds less important now than it did earlier.

Whether the objections are handled in any of these ways or in some other fashion, the salesperson should address himself or herself to the problem. Only if serious objections are overcome in the customer's mind can the sale be made.

Closing the Sale

If precustomer contact, prospecting, initial contact, and sales presentation are all handled well and most objections are handled without too much difficulty, the close should not be too difficult. The close does not, however, usually happen automatically. The salesperson must assist in even the best situations. Closing techniques that may be used include the following:

Give a choice. The customer is asked to make a small decision that implies the larger decision. "Would you like to take the brown or the blue suit?" Such a question is not conducive to a "no" answer.

Offer a special service. The customer is looking at the ceramic bird. The salesperson asks, "Shall I gift wrap it for you? Can we mail it for you?" Such an offer of service may make the difference. The customer may like the service suggestion or may now feel indebted to the salesperson since the salesperson was trying to be so helpful.

Offer inducement. "If you buy today, you get the sale price. Tomorrow, the merchandise goes back to its regular price." If the sale price is really a bargain, such a closing attempt will usually get some action.

Summarize. After the sales points have been made, the salesperson summarizes each selling point and stops to get agreement from the customer after each point. All those "yes" statements, if handled well, can lead to a positive "yes" when the customer is asked to buy.

Advise not to wait. Under this approach, the customer is told that it is the last shirt like that in that size. Any delay implies that the shirt may be sold to someone else. If the customer has been sold on the item but is planning to put off the decision, such a close may complete the sale. The salesperson should be cautioned about being honest in using this closing technique. If the customer comes to the store the next day and sees the item right where he or she bought the "last one" yesterday, the customer may have unpleasant thoughts about the store. Using the "advise not to wait" technique in a dishonest manner may make the sale but lose the customer.

Whether attempting to close the sale by one of the methods cited or by some other approach, the timing of the closing attempt is crucial to the sale. The salesperson should not rush the customer or take too long in asking for the sale. During the presentation of the merchandise, the salesperson should evaluate the customer to determine what type of close might work on that person. Each customer is different. Regardless of the difference, however, a close should be attempted in every case. It is better for a salesperson to make a mistake in attempting to close the sale than to never try to close the sale in the first place.

Suggestion Selling

Suggestion selling is the icing on the cake. As its name implies, the salesperson uses the opportunity after the sale has been made to suggest something else to the customer. Since the customer has just said "yes," suggestion selling reaches customers when they are in a positive frame of mind. Although suggestion selling is a very effective retail sales device, such selling is usually handled as poorly as the initial contact step in the selling process. Unfortunately, many salespersons feel that they do suggestion selling when in reality they do not. The clerk who says, "Will there be something else?" is not doing suggestion selling. Such a statement is as useful as "May I help you?"

Suggestion selling should be a definite suggestion. The customer buys a suit. Suggestion selling may also sell a shirt and/or tie. A customer buys paint. The salesperson asks if brushes and dropcloth are needed. A person buys shaving cream. The clerk asks if razor blades are needed. If the suggestion is not definite, the effect will be greatly diminished. The waitress who asks, "Can I get you something else?" will sell much fewer desserts than the waitress who asks, "What about some fresh strawberry shortcake?" Store management should emphasize to its employees the need to suggest particular items when doing suggestion selling. Some stores have even gone so far as to pick out an item and have everyone in the store suggest the item after every sale with accompanying badges for the personnel to wear to remind them and their customers about the item. Such a form of suggestion selling is probably not as effective as the more personal approach. The reason why such stores do follow this procedure, however, is to promote some kind of suggestion selling in the store. The feeling is that some suggestion selling is better than none at all.

Sales Follow-Up

For some sales situations, the need for sales follow-up is obvious to the salesperson. For example, the salesperson tells the customer that the fence will be installed next week. When next week comes, the salesperson should make every effort to see that what was promised is happening in the customer's backyard. If for any reason such is not possible, the salesperson should call the customer and explain why. The customer should not have to call the store and ask, "Why?" Similar situations can occur with delivery, alterations, and special orders. If a store shows concern after the sale, customers will usually show their appreciation by buying again at the store.

Less obvious to most salespersons but still very important in terms of sales follow-up is the need for the salesperson to show appreciation to the customer for the sale that has taken place. The clerk may compliment the customer's decision by saying, "I'm glad you chose that one. That was my favorite too." The salesperson should also thank the customer for buying. Like many stores, K mart encourages its personnel to say after the sale, "Thank you for shopping at K mart." Management should encourage all employees to say "Thank you!" with enthusiasm, not just, "Thank you." Customers can tell the difference.

ATTRIBUTES OF A CREATIVE SALESPERSON

The creative salesperson must naturally understand the selling process. In addition, certain mental and physical attributes play an important role in the success or failure of a salesperson in a given job (Figure 17–6). Judgment, tact, personality, and attitude are some of the desired mental attributes. As for physical attributes, personal appearance and personal hygiene are generally thought to be important to the retail salesperson.

Mental Attributes

Judgment.   The salesclerk with good judgment is a real asset in a retail store. A salesclerk who gives a candy sucker to a two-year-old as a means of being nice is using poor judgment. The parent may not want the child to have the candy. Even worse, what if the two-year-old child gets choked on the sucker?[5] Also, a salesperson with good judgment will not talk about the internal problems of the store in front of customers. Neither will that person get involved with the personal problems of

Figure 17–6

A good retail salesperson should use good judgment and tact and should have a good personality and attitude along with an attractive personal appearance.

(Courtesy of Gold Circle Discount Stores.)

customers. Good judgment obviously takes many forms. Many times it comes with maturity, but the two are not always related. In selecting sales personnel, stores should attempt to hire those with the potential for good judgment. Such people make the retail manager have an easier task.

Tact. The clerk in the store asks the proud mother as she shops with her year-old son, "What is it?"[6] The plump woman who tries on a magnolia blossom print dress is told by the salesperson, "Gad, that looks terrible. It makes you look fatter than ever." A clerk who has tact will not make such statements. In the first instance, she will talk in terms of what a beautiful baby that is or what a lovely child. She will never ask whether it is a boy or a girl. In the second instance, she may suggest other more appropriate items of merchandise without ever making a negative comment about the customer's original choice. *Webster's New Collegiate Dictionary* defines "tact" as a keen sense of what to do or say in order to maintain good relations with others or avoid offense.[7] Unfortunately, too little tact is found in retailing. Although vital, tact is difficult to instill in sales personnel who lack the instinct for it.

Personality. Too many salespeople are lethargic in their jobs. The result is a salesperson who puts forth a personality that resembles a sour lemon. On the other hand, an alive, enthusiastic personality helps to make a good salesperson. The enthusiasm of a salesclerk toward his or her job, products, and store can be contagious. If customers observe alive salespeople, this enthusiasm may be transferred to them. It is always more enjoyable to go into a store where the salesclerks are not apathetic or indifferent. A positive personality is directly related to positive sales results.

Attitude. The positive attitude of the salesperson is vital to a dynamic retail store. Is the clerk willing to accept change? Is the clerk willing to try to improve himself or herself? If a negative attitude is present, the development of the creative salesperson stops. Unless a positive attitude on the part of the salesclerk is present, nothing that has been discussed in this chapter will make any difference. In order to change a negative attitude, careful study must be done to attempt to ascertain the cause. When the cause is found, something can then be done to help the employee develop a more favorable outlook. As is true with personality, a clerk with a bad attitude can give the same feeling to customers. Something must be done. This is an area in which procrastination on the part of management can be harmful to the store.

Physical Attributes

Personal Appearance and Personal Hygiene.
The two areas mentioned in the heading join together to make a most important variable. To put it rather bluntly, the salesperson must fit into the situation physically to be a success. The fashion consultant in women's clothing cannot be a 250-pound ugly duckling and be a success on the sales floor. The woman who sells cosmetics the best is a woman who does not need most of the products she sells. The salesman in men's clothing cannot wear clothes out of fashion and expect his customers to buy the latest thing. The clerk with body odor, bad breath, dirty hair, beat up shoes, or makeup that makes her look like a witch just will not work in a retail store. As far as the customer is concerned, the salesperson is the store. Physical attributes must be correct or sales will be lost.

Obviously, care should be taken when dealing with physical problems. Tact is the order of the day. For the clerk who has makeup problems, for example, the person could be called in for a talk. Better still, as one store did, a makeup seminar was held for all female employees. At such demonstrations, a person is selected to be the subject to be worked on. As prearranged between management and the cosmetic specialist, the person "picked" was the employee with the makeup problem. The seminar, in this case, proved to be a very tactful way of getting the salesperson to learn how to fix her face. Physical attributes of employees are a vital ingredient in the total selling mix. By careful selection of sales personnel and by continuous counseling, most major difficulties pertaining to physical problems can be eliminated before they have a chance to develop to a point where customers begin to notice.

SUMMARY

To most customers, the salesperson is the store. Because of this identification, it is essential that every effort be made—regardless of whether the store has need for order-takers, order-handlers, or order-getters, or some combination of the three—to carefully evaluate such people in light of their mental and physical attributes and to instruct them in the selling process. Every step of the selling process (precustomer contact, prospecting, initial store contact, presentation of the merchandise, handling objections, closing the sale, suggestion selling, and sales follow-up) should be explained thoroughly to the sales personnel and then put into practice by them. The results of such efforts should be store personnel who are more productive on the sales floor. Developing a creative salesperson is not an easy task. If the store is successful in such development, however, the rewards to both the individual and the store can be great.

1. What are the three categories of retail salespersons? Cite examples for each category.
2. What is meant by the term retail selling process?
3. What is the salesperson concerned with in the precustomer contact step of the retail selling process?
4. What is prospecting? Is prospecting limited to new customers? Why?
5. What is meant by the term initial store contact? Why is this phase of selling so important? Go to stores in your area and observe the opening statements that are used by sales personnel. How does what you find agree with the survey in the book?
6. Discuss various guidelines that should be considered in the presentation of merchandise to the customer.
7. Explain the six categories of customer objections. Cite examples. How should such objections be handled by the salesperson? Cite examples.
8. Explain the various techniques that may be applied in closing a sale.
9. What is meant by the term suggestion selling? Cite examples.
10. List and explain the various mental and physical attributes that play an important role in the success or failure of a salesperson. Cite examples.

NOTES

[1] For more information on the retail selling process, see J. E. Lee, *Five Basic Steps in Planned Retail Selling* (Oxford: Pergamon Press, 1970), and Kenneth H. Mills and Judith E. Paul, *Successful Retail Sales* (Englewood Cliffs, N.J.: Prentice-Hall, Inc., 1979).

[2] William H. Bolen, "Customer Contact: Those First Important Words," *Department Store Management*, Vol. 33, no. 3 (April 1970), pp. 25–26.

[3] Elmer Wheeler, *Tested Sentences That Sell* (Englewood Cliffs, N.J.: Prentice-Hall, Inc., 1937). Copyright by Elmer Wheeler.

[4] The discussion in this section is based in part on David L. Kurtz, H. Robert Dodge, and Jay E. Klompmaker, "Sales Resistance and Objections," *Professional Selling*, rev. ed. (Dallas, Tex.: Business Publications, Inc., 1979), pp. 171–186.

[5] William H. Bolen, "Parent with Child: Guidelines for This Different Sales Situation," *Personnel News and Views*, Summer Edition (1971), pp. 12–15. Copyright, National Retail Merchants Association.

[6] Ibid.

[7] By permission. From *Webster's New Collegiate Dictionary* © 1981 by G. & C. Merriam Co., Publishers of the Merriam-Webster Dictionaries.

CHAPTER 18

Human Relations
in Retailing

BLONDIE

© 1977 King Features Syndicate, Inc.

In a customer survey dealing with sales personnel, 78 percent of the respondents reported that they experienced lack of attention, indifference, and abruptness "often" or "half the time" from the retail selling personnel they came in contact with in stores. [1] Although studies of this type are numerous, their findings usually "tell the same story." The typical retail store has difficulty getting and/or maintaining desired behavior on the part of its personnel.

To aid in overcoming this problem, the retailer should keep in mind that the employee of a store is a person. If management would only remember this simple fact, then such an obvious statement would not have to be made. The "human relations" aspect of retailing is crucial to the long-term success of a store. The retail operator must remember that to an employee money is not everything. In fact, in most stores, the money paid to employees is not anything more than the going rate. "Other things" besides money must help to contribute to the overall success of the store's personnel program.

Human relations is defined as the integration of people into a work environment in a manner that facilitates cooperation, creativity, and productivity. [2] How can a store achieve this cooperation, creativity, and productivity among its workers so that they will act in the desired manner? Proper motivation, effective leadership, good communications, and fair disciplinary action are all means to this end. Managerial concern in these four areas alone should result in a much stronger store from a personnel standpoint (Figure 18-1).

MOTIVATION

Motivation is defined as management's ability to get workers to act in a certain way under their own volition. The employee who makes an effort to do the job that management wants done can be said to be motivated. But how positive is the motivation? Does the person view his or her job as an *expiring task*—sees job as work to do; *perspiring task*—really tries to do a good job but still has a negative outlook; *aspiring task*—sets ambitious goals and standards for the job; or *inspiring task*—views job as one of great importance to the company and society? [3]

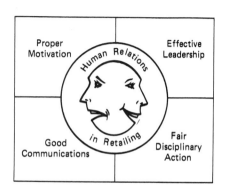

Figure 18-1

Elements of an effective human relations program.

These four ways in which employees can view a job may be the result of the managerial philosophy in effect in the store. Douglas McGregor, in his book, *The Human Side of Enterprise*,[4] sets forth two managerial philosophies that he referred to as Theory X and Theory Y. As noted in Figure 18-2, Theory X assumes that motivation occurs only at the bread and butter level. Under X, management is very authoritarian whereas Y uses a participative approach. In Theory Y, it is noted that motivation can occur in numerous ways, only one of which is money. Both theories assume that efficiency can be high under that particular approach and that workers can be motivated. The expiring and perspiring worker would be assumed to be motivated under Theory X. The aspiring and inspiring worker would best be served by Theory Y. Neither managerial philosophy is assumed to be the ultimate solution. Both approaches have

Figure 18-2

Basic assumptions of Theory X and Theory Y.

Theory X

Theory X Holds That Efficiency Will be High When:

1. Authority flows in a single stream from organization superiors to subordinates.
2. Supervision is detailed and the span of control is narrow.
3. The individual is considered to be a social absolute and his physiological properties are respected in organizing work.
4. Work is routinized.

Theory X Assumes That:

1. Work is inherently distasteful to most people.
2. Most people prefer to be directed and have little desire for responsibility and little ambition.
3. Most people have little capacity for creativity in solving organization problems.
4. Motivation occurs only at a bread and butter level.
5. Most people must be closely controlled and often coerced to achieve organization objectives.

Theory Y

Theory Y Holds That Efficiency Will Be High When:

1. Authority flows from formal and informal sources up and down and across the organization—which are oriented in the same direction.
2. Supervision is general and the span of control is wide.
3. The individual can behave as a social and psychological being as well as a physiological being—that is, when work does not ignore the fullness of man.
4. The task is a meaningful whole, providing some variety and requiring some skill and judgment.

Theory Y Assumes That:

1. Work is natural provided the conditions are bearable.
2. Self-control is often indispensable in achieving organization goals.
3. Self-control in line with organization objectives is a combination of rewards which satisfy ego and social needs, as well as bread-and-butter needs.
4. The capacity for creativity in solving organizational problems is widely distributed in the population.
5. This capacity for creativity is underutilized in organizations.

Source: Robert T. Golembiewski, "Organizing Work: Theories and Techniques," *Advanced Management-Office Executive*, Vol. 1, no. 6 (June 1962) pp. 26–27.

their places in different retailing situations. The approach in use will, however, affect the form that motivation takes as it influences employee behavior. Where possible the trend does tend to favor a move toward a Theory Y or participative philosophy of management. In view of this fact it is important to know how people in business motivate others. The results of a study done to find this out showed that among other things good motivators:[5]

> *Set moderate goals.* Such action fosters self-confidence. As each goal is achieved, a more difficult one is set. Telling employees that their performance must increase by 20 percent may have a negative effect. Breaking down the 20 percent into small increments that appear obtainable is a good strategy to follow.
>
> *Have confidence in their own ability.* A manager who believes that his or her subordinates can succeed through his or her help can give this feeling to the employees. Confidence is contagious.
>
> *Delegate authority.* When a store manager delegates authority, confidence is shown in others with a corresponding increase in morale.
>
> *Think positive.* Much has been said about the power of positive thinking. A positive thinking retail manager will have a greater chance of having employees who think positive and act that way.
>
> *Build new upon old.* Using accepted methods of operation to build on reduces resistance to change. The transformation of old into new does not attempt to degrade the old methods.
>
> *Have a sense of humor.* The ability to laugh with workers, not at them, introduces a human quality into motivation.
>
> *Listen.* Listening as opposed to talking may give the manager the insight needed to properly motivate.
>
> *Be people-oriented.* This catchall statement implies that, to be a good manager, the retail operator must not just think like a merchandising manager. In addition, he or she must also be a people manager. One without the other will not yield the results desired by the store.

Being people-oriented also entails understanding employees. A good motivator learns what employees seek in their jobs. Do they seek belonging? Do they seek status? What do they seek? As noted earlier, money is not everything for most people. In Chapter 3, Maslow's hierarchy of needs was discussed in terms of consumer behavior. This same idea can be used in motivating employees. For example, if the employee makes a "living wage," has some feeling of job security, and is accepted by co-workers (Maslow's first three steps in the hierarchy), then status as defined by the informal organization (see Chapter 8) becomes a powerful motivator. Status is measured in many ways. A different name badge or no name badge can be a symbol of status, just like wearing a different color smock or no smock. Shift work, break times, lunch times, work schedules, and a host of other things take on an enormous importance to workers in a store. By the judicious use of these various measures of status, management can get workers to put forth much effort. If those who sell more get the best work schedules, for example, then management by its action will motivate others to do likewise. If the best work schedule is simply passed around, however, as opposed to being earned, it has no status and something else will be the motivator. It is the task

Figure 18–3

Continuum of leadership.

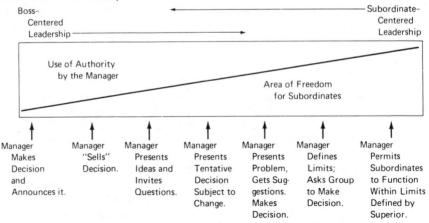

of management to tune in to its employees to determine what they view as status symbols. Each store is different. In store A, being a sponsor is sought after, whereas in store B it is disliked. Motivation is an individual concept that is influenced by group interaction within the particular store. Effectively motivating workers is not an easy task.

LEADERSHIP

Along with motivation, another very important tool of human relations is modeling—this is behavior change as it reflects the example of the leadership.[6] Although hard to define, leadership can be said to be the directing of workers in such a way that the objectives of the store are met. From the top down in the organization, the type of leadership sets the tone for the operation of the store. Leadership styles can vary considerably relative to the application of Theory X or Y in the organization. Tannenbaum and Schmidt[7] in their leadership continuum, Figure 18–3, presented seven different leadership styles that can be successful depending on the leader, the subordinates, and the nature of the situation. In other words, a successful leader is one who knows one's own self, understands one's subordinates, and uses this knowledge to lead in a given situation. With the trend toward Theory Y, the trend in leadership style is toward the right-hand side of the continuum. Care should be taken, however, not to go too far to the right. If the retail manager is not careful, participative management can lead to chaos and no leadership. The reader will note that the far right position on the continuum still has limits as defined by the worker's superior. Remember—the leader must lead. The only question is how.

The retail manager, department manager, or whoever is in a position of leadership within the store should keep in mind that leading people is not the same as being their boss. In comparing the two, a boss generally lacks maturity while a leader will be mature in the handling of employees. Every person in any position of leadership in retailing should attempt to objectively decide which of the two terms more realistically describes his or her leadership style (Table 18–1).[8] It is easy enough being a boss. Being a good leader is hard work.

Table 18–1

Traits of "The Boss" versus "The Leader"

"The Boss"	"The Leader"
Indecisive	Decisive
Subjective (self-centered)	Objective
Argumentative	Persuasive
Dogmatic	Flexible
Insecure	Confident
Difficulty in working with others	Works well on a team
Does not try to communicate	Communicates well
Apathetic	Goal oriented
Impulsive and expedient	Patient

Another way in which to view leadership is the approach that The Goodyear Tire and Rubber Company takes in its *Mini Retail Management Guide*.[9] The *Guide* emphasizes the importance of modeling as it states that leadership begins with the leader. For a leader, an ounce of example is worth a ton of talk. The *Guide* goes on to define the successful leader in the following manner:

1. *The successful leader puts peopel first.* Instead of making people work, he inspires people to want to work.
2. *The successful leader does not merely buy the time and energy of people.* He taps their hidden power through recognition, incentives, and appreciation.
3. *The successful leader is a team builder.* He doesn't carry the ball on every play. He gives the other players a chance to score points.
4. *The successful leader is a self-starter.* He creates plans and sets them in motion.
5. *The successful leader can be led.* He is interested in the best way—not in having his way.
6. *The successful leader is not a stuffed shirt.* He can laugh at himself.
7. *The successful leader looks up.* He lifts the minds of people and stimulates positive, constructive, and optimistic thinking.
8. *The successful leader is both the head and the heart of his organization.* The leader sets the tone of operation for the store.
9. *The successful leader has vision.* He refuses to let difficulties or losses interfere with long-range goals. He holds to his main course with poise and faith.

From the discussion on leadership it is observed that more emphasis is being placed on getting the worker to feel that he or she is part of the team. Given the competitive nature of the business, the management of the retail store must make every effort to obtain and keep the best possible employees. Good leadership is vital to this goal along with proper motivation, effective communications, and fair disciplinary action. The importance of good communications is examined next.

Communication is the mutual interchange of ideas by any effective means. [10] How does this process called communication operate? As observed in Figure 18-4, the process is a closed-loop system. The communicator sends a message to an audience by the use of some channel with a hoped for desired effect. It should be emphasized that feedback is essential to good communications.

Applied to retailing, communication is a mutual interchange between retailer and employee. The retail manager as communicator sends messages to the employees. The manager must make every effort to determine if the messages are received and understood by examining the effect that the communications have on the audience (employees). The retailer must also remember that communication is a "mutual interchange"; thus he or she is not always the communicator but should be the audience to messages being sent to him or her by the employees. Employees will be watching to see what effects their communications have and their attitude will be greatly affected by whether or not they feel like they are being "heard."

As noted in the discussion on motivation and leadership, good communication is important to both of these aspects of human relations. People like to feel that they are "in the know." In order to make employees "in the know," many channels are available for management to use in getting the message to the store's employees. These channels include the following: [11]

> *Posters and bulletin boards.* Posters and bulletin boards are very inexpensive channels for communications. They are also thought by many to be very ineffective because people will not read the information. But this does not have to be the case. One way to overcome this problem with posters is to saturate all employee areas with the message so that repetition will get the message across. As for bulletin boards, keep them current by changing them frequently. Unless a board is kept up-to-date, it loses its communications credibility very fast. The most effective way to get people to read the board is to put something on it that is of personal interest to employees. Posting work schedules, vacation times, and even the results of the weekly football pool

Figure 18-4

The communication process.

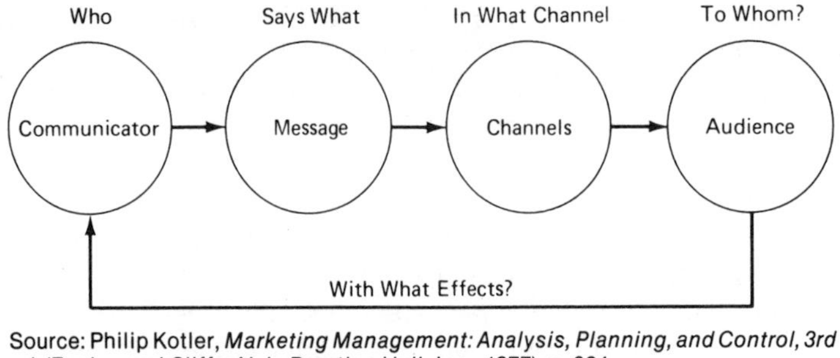

Source: Philip Kotler, *Marketing Management: Analysis, Planning, and Control, 3rd ed.* (Englewood Cliffs, N.J.: Prentice-Hall, Inc., 1977), p. 324.

can create reader interest. Newspaper clippings that tell of the marriage of one of the employees or how the softball team that is sponsored by the store won the state championship can generate much interest in the board. A sometimes overlooked advantage of the bulletin board stems from an environmental factor. When several employees gather at a bulletin board, their group interaction relating to posted information can have the effect of stimulating their interest in the information.[12]

Employee handbook. As noted in Chapter 16, the new employee should be given an employee handbook to read even before reporting for work. Handbooks are useful for purposes of orientation. Their use, however, should not be limited to this purpose. All employees, new and old, should be aware of what is in the handbook. Topics found in handbooks may include the philosophy of the company, company history, job regulations, policies, procedures, fringe benefits, dress code, and even how to act in the store if shopping there on your day off. This handbook should be kept up-to-date and be given to all employees each time it is revised. It is important to note that the employee handbook does not have to be an elaborate, expensive undertaking. The retailer can use a spirit duplicator (probably what most people are used to seeing when tests are given in college) to run off a few copies of the rules and regulations for a store. Every store should have a handbook. It is a good investment and a good communication channel.[13]

House organ. Whether newspaper, magazine, or a one-page handout, the house organ can disseminate much information to employees. To gain readership, features such as personal items about employees (weddings, retirements, achievements, etc.), jokes, and even pictures of the Christmas party can be used. House organs vary in their method of distribution. Although most are given out at the store, more and more are being mailed to the employee's home so the whole family can take an interest in what is happening at the store. There is no such thing as a typical house organ. They usually come out approximately once a month and what they contain is, of course, up to management. Probably the greatest problem with house organs is that, when stores implement these publications, they have no idea how much work is involved in putting out a good house organ. The result is that the house organ comes out with much fanfare only to die a graceful death after a few issues. Unless there is a definite managerial commitment to have a house organ, one should never be started.

Letters and pay inserts. If a message is placed in the pay envelope, it will probably get the attention of the worker. Likewise, letters sent to the employee's home should obtain recognition. Care should be taken, however, not to overuse these communication channels. An insert with every paycheck or an average of one letter every week can destroy the impact of this approach. The good communicator saves this approach for "important" communications.

Person-to-person communication. By use of the chain of command, information is passed in either written or verbal form. Person to person is the channel most frequently used and is appropriate on either an individual or group basis. It is also the channel used for the informal organization. As noted in Chapter 8, the grapevine can be used to disseminate information rather quickly to all employees. Just by telling the "right" people, the desired message can be given out whether it be information that will quell a rumor or news about the health of one of the employees.

In communicating with workers, the retailer should remember that the English language is not very explicit. Words can mean different things to different people. The clerk may not be aware of terminology, abbreviations, or internal management expressions that are being used by the manager. And workers may also be afraid to ask what they mean. The result is that the communication has little effect on the worker. A careful choice of words aids in getting the message across.

Another potential communications problem relates to the existence of unworded messages known as metacommunications. A metacommunication is a message that, although not expressed in words, accompanies a message that is expressed in words. [14] The manager may ask the worker who is returning from lunch, "Did you enjoy your lunch?" The hidden message in that statement may communicate the idea that, "I see you are late getting back from lunch again." Did the manager wish to send the hidden message? It matters little whether the hidden message was intended or not—the fact is that the message was sent.

Retailers may also find themselves sending kinesic messages to their employees. Kinesic communications are ideas that are expressed in strictly nonverbal ways. [15] Such messages are just as important as what is spoken or written. The retail operator should communicate interest and concern in the workers by his or her actions. A supervisor who is always too busy to show interest in an employee is still communicating with the employee. The message being sent, however, is not one that is conducive to encouraging a productive worker. Employees usually interpret any slight on the part of management in a negative way.

As mentioned earlier, employees also act as the communicator sending messages to the retailer. Most of their communications would be on a person-to-person basis. The retailer should be aware that this form of communication will not only be verbal or written but also nonverbal. Understanding employees in this way is vital. Some retailers also provide more formal channels of communication for their employees. Examples of these channels range from a simple suggestion box to a complex hearings procedure. Communications must be a mutual interchange if good human relations are to exist in a store.

DISCIPLINARY ACTION

In spite of efforts aimed at good communications, leadership, and motivation, a worker will sometimes not do the work as instructed or will display conduct that is not conducive to good store operations. When such a situation arises, disciplinary action may be called for. Disciplinary action, if needed, serves to create discipline among workers. For purposes of this discussion, discipline is defined as worker self-control in accordance with store policies, procedures, and rules. Without discipline, a store cannot function.

Disciplinary action is any corrective action taken by management to promote employee conformity with the policies, procedures, and rules of the store. It is by no means the only way to achieve discipline. Training is another more positive approach. Good communications are also an asset. But discipline will not usually exist without the implied threat of disciplinary action. The typical child may have more enthusiasm to do certain things like clean up the yard if the idea of disciplinary action is possible as a "reward" for inadequate effort. Workers are no different.

It is important for the merchant to realize that failure to require discipline on the part of a worker tells not only that worker but also the rest of the employees that something that was thought to be wrong is okay. The lack of disciplinary action against an offending employee cannot be treated by management as an isolated case. Other workers will be watching to see if disciplinary action is taken against the offender and whether or not the action taken is thought to be fair. A program of disciplinary action that employees think is fair and just can give a real boost to the morale of the workers.

Developing a fair and just program of disciplinary action is not an easy task. Some principal ingredients of a sound disciplinary system are the following: [16]

Definite policies and procedures. Retail management should have definite policies and procedures that spell out what type of discipline is desired by the company. These policies and procedures should be known and understood by all within the company.

Communication of rules. Employees must have some idea of what they should or should not do before they can be held accountable for their actions. As noted in the communication section, employee handbooks and bulletin boards as well as other methods (channels) can be used to disseminate information to employees. It is certainly the employee's responsibility to know the rules. Management should, however, make every effort to assist the employee in becoming knowledgeable of the rules.

Burden of proof. The employee is assumed not to have committed the infraction unless it is proven otherwise. Under this premise, for example, Sally is thought to have punched in her friend on the time clock, which is a major offense under most stores' disciplinary systems. But Sally should be considered innocent until the evidence can show otherwise. The burden of proof is on the store in disciplinary cases.

Consistency of treatment. One of the more difficult aspects of a system of disciplinary action is consistency. Are all employees who are caught for similar infractions treated in the same manner? Two employees fail to ring a sale. Nothing is said to one while the other is reprimanded. Is such inconsistency fair? Obviously not! Poor morale can easily result from inconsistent disciplinary action. Each department manager must make an effort to act in a manner that is consistent with overall store policy. With so many people in a large store being involved with developing discipline, consistency becomes quite difficult.

Consideration of the circumstances of the case. The need for consistency requires that all employees who break a rule be told by management that they broke the rule. The individuals' reasons for the violation, however, may make the severity of the disciplinary action differ. For example, suppose that two workers get to work late. Disciplinary action for one worker may mean dismissal since that worker has been late many times before. For the other worker, an oral reprimand may be all that is needed since in that case the worker's car wouldn't start and the person had never been late before. Flexible justice with justification is in most cases fair justice.

Progressive penalties. Where possible, it is good to set up penalty steps for handling disciplinary action. These steps are:

1. Simple oral warning
2. Oral warning with notation in personnel file
3. Written warning with notation in personnel file
4. Suspension
5. Dismissal

For minor offenses, the steps are followed as the behavior is repeated. For a major offense such as theft, misuse of the time clock, or being intoxicated on the job, a first offense may call for dismissal. Since most employees get the message after one or two incidents, it is recommended that past offenses be removed from the record after a period of time—one to two years. Giving the worker who has reformed a clean slate can do much to improve the morale of the worker.

Reasonable rules and standards. What if the store requires the employee to keep the sales floor in view at all times. But on the other hand, the store also prohibits the employee from marking merchandise on the sales floor yet the layout of the store prohibits the employee from seeing the sales floor when marking in the stockroom. It is impossible to comply with the two rules—one must be broken. Unreasonable rules are obviously difficult to enforce. If the regulation is not practical, the regulation should be changed in order to maintain the integrity of the disciplinary program. The retailer should not ignore the situation. If ignored, disciplinary matters will become a frustration for all concerned.

Right of appeal. In a store of any size, the right to appeal the disciplinary action should be available. Even in a small store where the owner has probably made the initial disciplinary decision and there is no one else to appeal to, the employee should be given an opportunity to present his or her side of the case. It is obvious that the right to appeal a disciplinary decision is basic to our system of justice. An appeal system should be available, if possible, since employees like the idea of right of appeal if needed. Also, it is always possible that the worker is right and that the department manager or whoever was in error. Managers who administer disciplinary action that is justified should never be overly concerned with appeal procedures.

Since most offenses are minor, disciplinary action in the retail store is made up mostly of reprimands or expressing verbal disapproval for some action. The purpose of the reprimand is to secure desirable behavior from the employee without creating unnecessary dissatisfaction. To achieve this purpose, things to remember in giving a reprimand include [17]

Have just cause. Before any form of disciplinary action is taken, remember that the burden of proof rests with management. A reprimand without foundation can be very embarrassing to the retailer.

Make it a private matter. A reprimand in public can cause more problems than most offenses that call for a reprimand. Other employees usually feel sympathetic toward the offending employee under such circumstances instead of being concerned about the offense. It is also possible that a public reprimand for a particular offense may cause the employee to lose face with fellow employees—a penalty far greater than the infraction of the rules might call for.

Observe the common rules of courtesy. Avoid making broad accusations. Be businesslike. "Call a spade a spade." Tell the employee what has been done wrong so that he or she can do better in the future. Always be positive and helpful when reprimanding, never petty or vindictive.

Match reprimand to fit the situation. People are different—reprimand accordingly. Some are a little hardheaded thereby necessitating a stronger reprimand in order for the message to be impressed on the person. In addition, the manager's action should be affected by whether it is a first offense or a repeated offense.

Close the case when the problem is solved. "Don't beat a dead horse." There is no need to keep reopening the wound on an offense long corrected. If the reprimand did achieve better performance, it has done its job. The manager should now "forget it."

Positive follow-up. Once the reprimand has done its job, work to give the employee the impression that there are no bad feelings. Follow up in a short time with a casual contact with the employee to show that all is forgiven.

Reprimanding an employee successfully is not easy. By considering the six points that were given, the retailer should improve not only the giving of reprimands but the entire disciplinary system. The end product should be a more efficient, well-run store. The retailer must never forget that there is no inconsistency between efficiency and human relations.[18]

SUMMARY

Human relations is defined as the integration of people into a work environment in a manner that facilitates cooperation, creativity, and productivity. To aid in meeting these objectives, a store should strive for proper motivation, effective leadership, good communications, and fair disciplinary action when dealing with its workers. To motivate the worker, the retailer must understand the employee's view of the job, the philosophy of management within the firm, the techniques that motivate people, and the hierarchy of employee needs. As for leadership, various styles of leadership are possible. Regardless of the method, however, a careful distinction should be made between being the leader and being the boss. In addition to considering what makes a successful leader, the retailer should never forget that, due to modeling, leadership begins with the leader. When striving for good communications, the merchant should attempt to understand the various communication channels (poster and bulletin boards, employee handbook, house organ, letters and pay inserts, person-to-person, etc.) that deliver the message to the audience (employee). By means of feedback, the store operator learns of the effect that the message has had on his or her audience, a necessary part of good communications. The employees also act as communicators with the intended audience being the retailer. The fourth aspect of human relations to be considered is fair disciplinary action. A firm must have disciplined workers.

Although not easy to develop, a good disciplinary action program must build on a good communications system that tells the worker what should and should not be done. Whether dealing with a reprimand or with a necessary dismissal for a serious offense, important considerations in developing a good disciplinary action system are definite policies and procedures, communication of rules, burden of proof, consistency of treatment, circumstances of the case, progressive penalties, reasonable rules and standards, and right of appeal. Managerial concern in these four areas (motivation, leadership, communication, disciplinary action) should result in a much stronger store from a personnel standpoint.

DISCUSSION QUESTIONS

1. Define or explain the following terms:

   a. Human relations
   c. Leadership
   e. Modeling
   g. Theory X

   b. Motivation
   d. Disciplinary action
   f . Metacommunication
   h. Theory Y

2. What are some things that people might do to make themselves good motivators?
3. Should status be used as a tool of motivation? Why or why not?
4. Present and explain Tannenbaum and Schmidt's leadership continuum. Why should a retailer be concerned with such a model?
5. "There is no difference between being the boss and being the leader." Comment on this statement.
6. Present and explain the model dealing with the communication process.
7. In the communication process, what is meant by channels? Cite examples.
8. List and discuss the principal ingredients of a sound disciplinary system.
9. What should be considered when giving a reprimand?
10. "The retailer must never forget that there is no inconsistency between efficiency and human relations." Comment on this statement.

NOTES

[1] Lucille H. Blum, "Customer Response to Sales Personnel," *Personnel News & Views* (Spring–Summer 1980), p. 33, published by the National Retail Merchants Association.

[2] Edwin P. Flippo, *Management: A Behavioral Approach*, 2nd ed. (Boston: Allyn & Bacon, Inc., 1970), p. 12.

[3] The four levels of motivation are adapted from Charles L. Lapp's four levels of living as cited in the article by Raymond L. Hilgert, "Positive Personal Motivation: The Manager's Guide to Influencing Others," *Personnel Journal*, Vol. 53, no. 11 (November 1974), p. 833.

[4] For additional information on the concept of Theory X and Theory Y, see Douglas McGregor, *The Human Side of Enterprise* (New York: McGraw-Hill Book Company, 1960).

[5] Jack C. Staehle, "How to Motivate Others," *Administrative Management*, Vol. 35, no. 5 (May 1974), pp. 57–58.

[6] Henry A. Singer, "Human Resources and Retailing Management," *Retail Control*, Vol. 44, no. 8 (April–May 1976), pp. 11–12, published by the National Retail Merchants Association.

[7] Robert Tannenbaum and Warren H. Schmidt, "How to Choose a Leadership Pattern," *Harvard Business Review*, Vol. 36, no. 2 (March–April 1958), pp. 95–101. Copyright © 1958 by the President and Fellows of Harvard College; all rights reserved.

[8] Adapted from Frank Goble, *Excellence in Leadership* (New York: American Management Association, 1972), p. 136.

[9] The Goodyear Tire and Rubber Company, *Mini Retail Management Guide* (Akron, Ohio: Training Manual), p. 19.

[10] Ted J. McLaughlin, Lawrence P. Blum, and David M. Robinson, *Communication* (Columbus, Ohio: Charles E. Merrill Publishing Company, 1964), p. 21.

[11] Edwin B. Flippo and Gary M. Munsinger, *Management*, 3rd ed. (Boston: Allyn & Bacon, Inc., 1975), p. 388.

[12] McLaughlin, *Communication*, p. 393.

[13] For additional information on how to prepare an employee handbook, see Frank M. Cruger, "Pointers on Preparing an Employee Handbook," *Management Aids for Small Manufacturers*, 197 (Washington, D.C.: Small Business Administration, 1968).

[14] William C. Himstreet and Wayne M. Baty, *Business Communications: Principles and Methods*, 6th ed. (Boston: Kent Publishing Company, 1981), p. 18.

[15] Ibid., p. 19.

[16] Dole S. Beach, *Personnel: The Management of People at Work*, 3rd ed. (New York: Macmillan Publishing Co., Inc., 1975), pp. 605–609.

[17] Taken in part from McLaughlin, *Communication*, pp. 244–247.

[18] *The Buyer's Manual*, rev. ed. (New York: National Retail Merchants Association, 1965), p. 43.

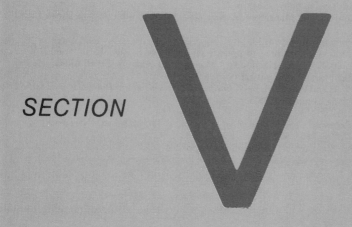

SECTION V

Retail

Promotion

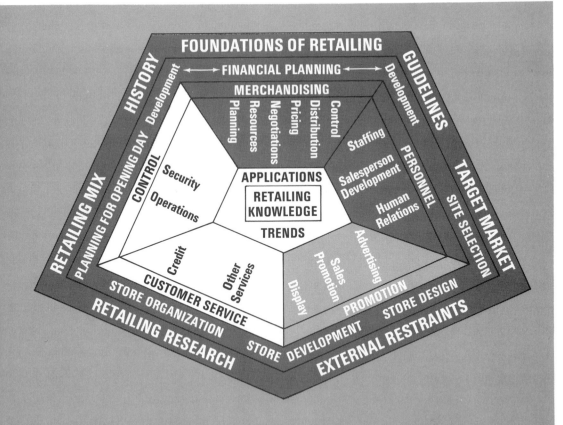

Retail promotion includes advertising, sales promotion, and retail display.

"Advertising" deals with retail image, objectives, characteristics of media, budgeting, scheduling, cumulative effect, and coordination.

"Sales Promotion" looks at trading stamps, contests, coupons, demonstrations, sampling, special events, and premiums along with solicitations, theme promotions, traveling displays, classes and schools, and co-op promotions.

"Retail Display" discusses the advantages of display, what to display, what makes a good display, types of display (window, interior, and point-of-purchase), and display management.

"That's right—last gas for one hundred meters."

In today's market, a retailer must do everything possible to reach as many potential customers as possible with the store's limited funds. The most efficient method of reaching these potential customers for most retailers is the marketing tool known as advertising.[1] For purposes of definition,

> Advertising is any controlled form of nonpersonal presentation and promotion of ideas, goods, or services by an identified sponsor that is used to inform and persuade the selected market.[2]

The definition points out the true role of advertising in the promotional mix of a store.

1. *Advertising is a controlled form of promotion.* By paying for the ad, the retailer can control the placement and content of the advertising for the store.
2. *Advertising is nonpersonal.* The retailer cannot expect advertising to do all the selling. It will not replace personal selling effort where it is needed. Advertising and personal selling must complement one another.
3. *Advertising can sell something besides a product.* The retailer should use advertising to sell the services of the store. For many retailers, service is their only differential advantage. For some retailers, selling ideas is also significant. If a retailer is trying to promote a civic cause or a unique or different retailing image, this idea may be presented through the store's advertising.
4. *Advertising requires an identified sponsor.* The retailer wants to be sure the store is identified. A retailer should take extra care to ensure that a potential customer has no doubt as to the name of the store and where the store is located.
5. *Advertising should inform.* Advertising should aid in the search process of the customer. How can a store inform customers about the "Annual White Sale"? Advertise the sale!
6. *Advertising should persuade.* Persuasion is the heart of advertising. Customers do procrastinate. Advertising attempts to overcome this problem by encouraging the customer to "shop early while the supply lasts."
7. *Advertising should aim for the selected market.* Good advertisements should zero in on the store's target market. Both message and media decisions should be made with the target market in mind.

As a retailer studies the store's advertising program, factors to be considered include advertising's effect on the retail image, objectives of advertising, characteristics of available media, and advertising budget. Additional factors are advertising schedule, cumulative effect of advertising, and coordination of advertising with the other parts of the marketing program. By examining these key factors, a retailer can improve upon his or her understanding of the role and capabilities of advertising. Although advertising's effect on the retail image will be discussed first, none of the seven advertising areas is any stronger than any other in the chain of advertising success (Figure 19–1).

ADVERTISING AND THE RETAIL IMAGE

As noted in Chapter 2, a retail image is how a person perceives a store in his or her own mind. The retailer needs to be aware that a customer will visualize the store by what he or she sees in an ad. If an advertisement is cluttered in that it has many items set off in

Figure 19-1

Factors in the chain of advertising success.

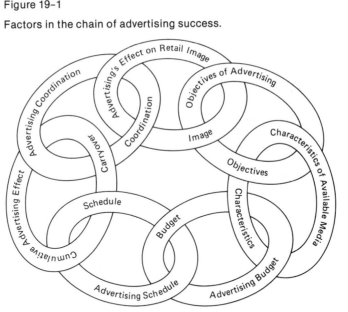

little blocks, the customer will generally see the store as a budget or discount operation. On the other hand, if the ad features one item and includes much white or unused space, the customer will usually assume that it is a prestige, status, or high-fashion operation. The retailer must use extra care to ensure that the ads are conveying the correct image. Research procedures can be utilized to determine if the appropriate image is being presented. In a less formal and inexpensive manner, the retailer can take copies of the store's newspaper ads, for example, to a town outside its trade area. The merchant can go to the local coffee shop or stop people on the street, show them the ads, and let them describe the store from what they see in these ads. This informal test may reveal to the retailer that the ads convey the idea that his or her expensive dress shop is a budget store. Such a finding would tell the retailer that changes (more white space, less emphasis on price, etc.) need to be made in the advertising copy and layout.

The retail image is not only affected by the actual ads for the store. Where the retailer places ads is also important. An ad in a high-quality magazine means quality to a customer. An ad on a particular radio station can be interpreted to mean a discount operation. An ad on another radio station, possibly an FM station, can be translated into a feeling of prestige. The retailer must remember that the advertising vehicles used as well as the ads themselves create an image that represents the store to many people. Presenting the correct retail image is a vital part of any effective advertising program.

DEVELOPING ADVERTISING OBJECTIVES

Another essential ingredient that is necessary for a sound advertising program is a retailer who knows exactly what he or she wants to accomplish with the store's advertising. To do this, objectives must be developed.

An objective is something toward which effort is directed, an aim, a goal.[3]

In other words, a retailer should have a goal for the store's ads. A retailer should know what he or she wants the ads to accomplish. It is important to note that an objective—such as to increase sales—is not sufficient to meet the test of a good advertising objective. To have such a general objective is to say that the retailer is in favor of "Motherhood" and "Apple Pie."

Instead, the retailer must strive for specific objectives. An objective that states that the retailer wants a 5 percent increase in sales is better than just wanting an increase in sales. An objective that indicates that an increase of 5 percent in the sales of the record department is desired is better than to state that a 5 percent increase is the goal of the advertising program. In other words, the more specific the goal or objective, the better.

There are many possible objectives for a retail advertising program. Does the retailer want:

> *Sales leads.* If sales leads are the goal, then each ad should provide copy to encourage sales inquiry by the reader either by providing a coupon or a phone number for instant response.
>
> *Increased per capita consumption.* If the objective is increased per capita consumption, then the retailer will want to be sure that each advertisement points out new ways to use the products in the store.
>
> *Increased store traffic.* If the aim is more traffic, the ads may feature carefully selected items with large price reductions (loss leaders) in order to attract customers to the store.
>
> *Increased awareness of a new product line.* If this is the objective, advertising should feature this line in greater proportion to other lines carried by the store.
>
> *Combination of objectives.* The retailer might want to accomplish several objectives with the store's advertising program. If this is the case, a priority list should be developed and adhered to in the development of advertisements. It is quite common for retailers to have more than one objective for their advertising. But the retailer must guard against having too many objectives and achieving none because of a lack of priorities among them.

When a list of objectives is developed for the store's advertising, the retailer should then use these objectives to develop specific goals for each particular ad to be run by the store. In other words, each ad is developed with the overall objectives of the firm in mind. If a flow chart of objectives were developed for a store, it might look something like that shown in Figure 19–2. When the advertisements are run, the results will flow in reverse on the flow chart. If the objectives of the individual advertisements are accomplished, then broadcast and print advertising objectives will be met. This, in turn, will achieve the overall advertising objectives for the store. Finally, advertising objectives must be developed within the framework of overall promotional goals and objectives. A retailer must decide what role advertising will play in the overall promotion strategy. It is upon the basis of this decision that the overall advertising objectives of the firm are developed.

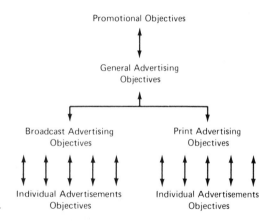

Figure 19-2

Flow chart of advertising objectives.

A knowledge of the various available advertising media and their various methods of application for retail situations is vital to a well-planned, successful advertising program. For a given situation, there are particular media that would be appropriate for a retailer to use. For purposes of discussion, the more common media which include newspapers, magazines, radio, television, and outdoor advertising will be examined. Transit, specialty, direct mail, and "donation" advertising are also analyzed for retail applications.

Newspaper Advertising

Newspaper advertising (Figure 19-3) is the principal advertising resource for most retailers. The newspaper offers the opportunity to reach many customers with minimum expense. Short lead time between ad preparation and appearance of the ad in print is a point in favor of the newspaper. Newspapers also usually cover a particular geographic area thereby making them well suited for general-line retailers. Newspapers generally fall into one of two classes:

> *Weekly newspaper—one to three issues per week*
> *Daily newspaper—four or more issues per week*

The advantages of the weekly paper are the disadvantages of a daily paper, and vice versa. The ad in the weekly paper will have a longer life whereas the repetitive effect of ads in the daily paper will be greater. A retailer who uses a weekly paper must gear promotions around the day or days of the week on which the paper comes out. A daily paper eliminates this problem.

The retailer should be aware of certain preferred positions in a newspaper and request these positions when placing ads. The retailer may even pay extra if it is important enough to ensure such ad placement. Newspaper layout is usually developed with news copy starting in the upper-left-hand corner and ad copy starting in the lower-

Figure 19–3

Newspaper advertising may be just a small ad or an eight-page insert that can also be mailed out as a direct-mail piece by the store.

(Courtesy of The Grand Union Company.)

right-hand corner. Such a layout approach results in most newspaper ads on a given page being placed together. With this in mind, the advertiser should strive to make the ads more effective. This may be accomplished by the use of ad placement, ad layout, or both.

In terms of ad placement (Figure 19–4), the full position (next-to-and-following news copy or upper-right-corner) is most desirable since the reader follows the news copy right into the ad. A less desirable but still preferred position is the next-to-reading position. The idea here is that the reader will see the ad while reading the column next to the ad. Still another preferred position but one that is seldom available is the island position, which is supported by editorial copy on at least three sides. A preferred position may also mean placing the ad for the dress shop in the women's section or placement of the ad on the first or last page of a newspaper section or above the fold on the newspaper page. Regardless of the preferred position desired, the retailer should always make it a practice to request preferred positions (position request) whenever advertising space is bought. This is true even when no special rate may be charged. Those retailers who ask increase the chances of their ads being run in preferred positions.

Ad layout can also result in more advertising value per dollar. Extra effort should be taken to make each ad special so it will stand out from the other ads on the page.

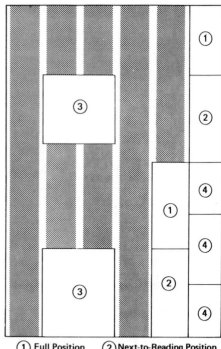

Figure 19-4

Typical ad placements on newspaper page.

① Full Position ② Next-to-Reading Position
③ Island Position ④ Buried Position

Reverse printing (white-on-black), special borders, white space, unique type (printing), and anything else that makes the ad different from the others on the page will be to the advantage of the retailer's ad (Figure 19-5).

Magazine Advertising

Magazine advertising for retailers is limited primarily to large retailers such as Sears or Penney. Regional retailers can, however, make use of the regional and/or metropolitan editions of many magazines such as *Time* and *Newsweek*. For example, a New York–based operation could advertise in the New York edition of *Time* as a means of reaching its market. In addition, many cities have a city magazine that could be appropriate for many retailers to use in their promotion mix.

When compared with newspapers, magazines are considered to be geared demographically to a particular market whereas newspapers divide up the market geographically. In other words, readers of a particular magazine generally have common interests, incomes, ages, and so on as opposed to the common bond of location for newspaper readers. This fact permits the magazine advertisement to zero in more closely on its target market. The other major comparison between magazines and newspapers is the lead time required for ad placement. The time required for magazine advertisements is usually much longer than the one or two days required for most newspapers.

Figure 19-5

Examples of suggested newspaper layouts for local advertising by a national retail chain.

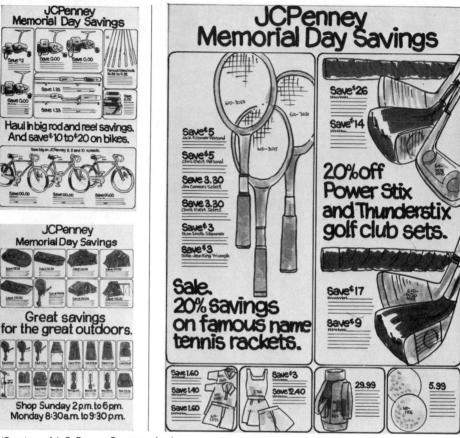

(Courtesy of J. C. Penney Company, Inc.)

Radio Advertising

After newspapers, radio is the most popular advertising medium for most retailers. As with newspapers, radio gives much flexibility. Assuming available time, the retailer can contract for a radio ad and have it on the air the same day. Copy changes can also be made just as quickly.

The effectiveness of a radio ad can be aided by placing it on the right radio station. In larger cities with multiple stations, the retailer should study the market and determine which stations, if any, the store's customers listen to so that ads can be placed on those stations. The retailer should guard against placing an ad on a station just because he or she listens to that station. Only when the retailer as an individual is part of the store's target market will such reasoning have any validity.

For the small town with one radio station, the retailer should determine if the target market listens to the radio. If the answer is "yes," the retailer should determine what time of day they listen since stations in towns by themselves generally try to serve all markets by different program formats during the day. For example, if the store is selling to the farm market, the retailer will wish to place an ad on the air between 6 A.M. and 7 A.M. and 11:30 A.M. and 12 noon. These are typical times for farm programming in a one-station town.

An additional consideration for the retailer is to be aware that most radio stations today are automatic in that all ads are placed on tape cassettes and placed on the air by machine. What this means for the retailer is that there is no longer a lag between back-to-back ads. If a listener is not careful, he or she may not notice that a different ad is now being aired. To guard against an ad being lost in a series of ads, a distinct voice different from the station personnel may be desirable, assuming, of course, that it is a good voice. Different music, a jingle, or anything to make the ad stand out from the crowd is desirable.

The copy for a radio ad should be developed carefully in order to keep copy points to a minimum. The retailer should guard against saying too much in one ad. Repetition of one or two points in an ad will greatly increase the possibility that the ad message will register with the listener. Such repetition within an ad and the repetition of the same ad being used over a period of time will work to overcome the generally recognized main disadvantage of broadcast advertising—the short life of the actual message.

Television Advertising

Television advertising has the advantage of combining sight, sound, and movement to present the message to the market. "Seeing Is Believing" is the hallmark of effectiveness for television advertising. It is noted that the retailer who does not take advantage of this television characteristic is wasting advertising dollars. For example, a retailer states in an ad that the store is a beautiful store with a wide selection of merchandise. Instead of talking about it—show it! In developing television ads, the retailer should remember the old cliché—*A picture is worth a thousand words.*

When compared with radio in the larger town, television advertising does not give the market selectivity that radio provides. Also, the out-of-pocket cost of television can be significantly higher than that for radio. The retailer pays for the ability to "show" the product. Another factor is that television generally covers a wider geographic area than most radio stations. This fact will result in wasted advertising exposure for a store serving only a very small market area.

Outdoor Advertising

Outdoor advertising consists primarily of outdoor posters (billboards), bulletins, and roadside signs (Figure 19–6). The use of outdoor advertising is particularly important to those retailers who appeal to the transient or traveling customer—restaurants, service stations, motels, and the like. Careful placement of outdoor advertising can result in an appreciable increase in business for such retailers.

In developing the outdoor ad, brevity is extremely important. For example, such an ad should probably have no more than five to seven words. The copy should also be

Figure 19–6

Outdoor advertising has helped a retailer like the *Sizzler* build a market share.

(Courtesy of Collins Foods International, Inc.)

quite large and of a style that is easy to read. The illustration and colors should also be eye-catching. Black on yellow and blue on white are two of several effective contrasting color combinations for use in outdoor advertising. In developing an outdoor ad, the retailer should make every effort to design an ad that can be completely understood by a customer in 5 seconds as the customer speeds along at 55 miles per hour or faster.

Transit Advertising

Transit advertising is made up of advertisements outside and inside of public transportation vehicles (bus, train, etc.) and advertisements in close proximity to bus stops, subway stations, and so on. Transit advertising is typically a larger-city medium since mass transit vehicles are generally not in use in small towns.

By using transit advertising, the retailer can place outdoor advertising in areas of town that do not permit outdoor signs. This is possible by placing an ad on the outside of a bus or taxi that goes to that area.

By using transit advertising, a store's advertising message can be aimed at persons who are possibly riding in the direction of the store advertised. Therefore, there is little time lag between the prospective customer reading the ad and being at the retail location.

Copy considerations for transit advertising are very similar to those for outdoor media. In fact, transit ads on the outside of vehicles are actually nothing more than "moving billboards." As for ads inside vehicles, the retailer may use longer copy if necessary since this form of advertisement has a somewhat captive audience.

Specialty Advertising

By definition, specialty advertising includes all useful items that carry an advertising imprint and are given without obligation to customers or prospective customers. Common imprinted items include pens, pencils, matchbooks, calendars, key chains, and rulers.

When using advertising specialties, the retailer should make a special effort to select items that are unique to the market area yet useful. For example, an auto parts store in Florida may give out ice scrapers in the area that makes the item unique. But, is it useful? It could be—if it features a soft rubber edge for removing moisture from car windows on a spring morning.

Advertising specialties are particularly well-suited for the limited advertising budget found in the typical small retail establishment. For example, an inexpensive ball-point pen distributed to students within a market area may result in increased store traffic if free refills are provided for the pens given out. Also, each pen can bear a "Lucky Number" that can win prizes for the recipient of that pen. Again, store traffic will probably increase as customers check the new numbers each week. Much advertising impact can result from a few dollars when the retailer uses specialty advertising in a creative manner.

Direct-Mail Advertising

In terms of flexibility, the most versatile of all advertising media is direct mail. Direct mail can be sent to as many or as few people as desired. Its size is limited only by postal regulations, not page size as is true for newspaper ads. If well-planned, direct mail can be an integral part of a retailer's advertising program.

Direct mail takes many forms. Perhaps the most popular is the "personal letter." The more "personal" it appears to be, the greater its effectiveness—and its cost. Circulars are less expensive but do not have the impact of the personal letter. Catalogs are another possibility. Even the small retailer can put out an attractive catalog at minimum expense by purchasing a standard catalog from a supplier and having the store's name imprinted on the catalog. In other words, a retailer does not have to be a Sears or a Montgomery Ward to have a catalog.

The ultimate success of the direct-mail advertising effort depends on who receives the direct-mail piece. For such purposes mailing lists can be purchased or generated internally. If the latter approach is used, every effort should be made to develop a sound mailing list. The retailer might develop a list of customers by starting with the store's own credit files. Names and addresses from checks that are passed in the store can then be added to the list. A contest can also be run where customers must register to win a prize. Careful tabulation of these entry blanks after the contest is over can provide additional names of customers or potential customers who have been in the store.

But what about a list of potential customers who might not have been in the store? One possibility is to use a cross-reference directory that enables the retailer to pick certain areas of town that match the appropriate demographic characteristics of the target market. The retailer can then select names and addresses from these areas for the mailing list.

Another way in which to develop a mailing list is to keep up with news events that might affect one's business. For example, if a retail florist reads that a certain girl is engaged and will be married in several months, a special mail piece could be sent to her inviting her to come by the florist for a free gift. These efforts would probably result in several additional weddings per year for the florist. Creativity and ingenuity are the keys to developing a prospective customer mail promotion.

Direct mail does get the recipient's attention when it is received, but special effort by the retailer can increase the chances of it being opened and read. Sending the direct-mail piece first class instead of third class is a step in that direction. Addressing the mail to a person instead of occupant is also desirable. If the mail piece bears a special-issue stamp as opposed to a postage-meter stamp, its attention value will be increased. Finally, if it is addressed by hand, its effectiveness is enhanced. All these suggestions are not appropriate for the 10,000-piece direct-mail promotion. If the scale of operation permits, however, the more personal touches introduced to the mail piece, the more effective the mail piece.

"Donation" Advertising

"Donation" advertising includes all advertising by retailers in high school annuals, dance recital programs, and other nonbusiness-related places. Such advertising should not be considered advertising and, therefore, should not come out of the advertising budget. This advertising is just what its name implies—it is a financial donation by a firm to a group—and no advertising return should be expected.

If the retailer feels that it is not possible to get out of doing such advertisements, or if he or she wants to support certain school organizations in this way, the best thing to do is to prepare camera-ready copy for the annual, program, and so on. With this work done, the retailer need only pull the ad copy out of the file and give the ready copy to the "donation" advertising salesperson.

Other Media

The list of possible media is almost unlimited. The choices range from sky-writing to projecting a 12-stories-tall advertisement on the side of a building. A more down-to-earth choice is theater advertising. A retailer should examine who goes to a particular theater before deciding on whether to use this advertising vehicle. In addition, up-to-date slides or movie footage should be used in the theater advertising. Ancient film footage cannot do a retailer much good. The cost for such advertising is usually a set number of dollars per 1,000 movie goers. Contracts usually run for one week or the usual length of a movie run. This enables the retailer to advertise only during the time when the movie being run matches the retailer's target market.

Another form of advertising is Yellow Pages advertising. Whether or not to place an advertisement in the Yellow Pages, which would be in addition to the firm's listing, is a matter of choice. One consideration is the importance of the phone as a source of business. The florist receives much business requesting flowers for sickness or funerals over the phone. The service station with road service should receive calls from stranded motorists as the result of Yellow Pages advertising. On the other hand, a high-priced, high-status dress shop would probably derive no benefit from an advertisement in the Yellow Pages. Such an ad may even be detrimental to the store in that it might cheapen the store in the eyes of its target market.

DEVELOPING THE ADVERTISING BUDGET

As noted at the beginning of this chapter, each element in the development of an advertising program is interdependent. In this regard, the advertising budget is dependent upon the advertising objectives, which in turn should have been developed with a realistic understanding of how much it would cost to meet specific objectives. And it should be emphasized that advertising does cost dollars. Table 19-1 shows the amount spent on advertising in 1979 by selected major retailers. Taken as a group, the 25 firms listed in the table had annual expenditures for advertising in excess of $3.1 billion. No

Table 19-1

1979 Advertising Expenditures for Selected Retailers

Company	Advertising Expenditures
Sears, Roebuck and Co.	$ 709,312,000
K mart Corporation	287,095,000
J. C. Penney Co.	278,000,000
Montgomery Ward & Co.	200,000,000
Federated Department Stores	174,000,000
F. W. Woolworth Co.	157,560,000
Safeway Stores	136,625,000
R. H. Macy & Co.	128,480,000
Associated Dry Goods Corp.	118,000,000
Kroger Co.	108,000,000
Allied Stores Corp.	103,807,000
May Department Stores	84,000,000
Great Atlantic & Pacific Tea Co.	77,000,000
Dayton-Hudson Corp.	71,000,000
American Stores Co.	67,000,000
Carter Hawley Hale Stores	62,824,000
Zayre Corp.	53,000,000
Grand Union Co.	47,000,000
Jewel Cos.	43,113,000
Levitz Furniture Corp.	43,000,000
Lucky Stores	43,000,000
Winn-Dixie Stores	41,260,000
City Products Corp.	40,000,000
Walgreen Co.	37,000,000
Supermarkets General Corp.	30,000,000
Total	$3,140,076,000

Source: Reprinted with permission from the November 3, 1980 issue of *Advertising Age.* Copyright 1980 by Crain Communications, Inc.

matter whether the firm is large or small, however, careful development of the advertising budget is extremely important to the firm.

The advertising budget should be developed with several criteria in mind:

1. *Develop budget in relation to need.* Many times the retailer will develop the advertising budget based on what was sold the previous year or will use trade data.[4] This data may tell the retailer, for example, that for last year a particular type of store spent on the average an amount equal to 2 percent of sales on advertising. To base a budget on a given percentage of sales of the past sales period is fine if it works. The problem is that it will work only through the luck of the retailer. Under the percentage method more funds may be allocated to advertising than is necessary or less money than is required to do the appropriate job. The needs of the retailer should determine the budget. The budget should not determine what advertising is needed.

2. *Develop budget considering total coverage time.* A retailer should budget the advertising funds in such a way that money will last throughout the advertising period. It is essential that the retailer plan for continuous advertising coverage while setting aside certain funds for special sales and promotions. If the budget is for a year the retailer may set up a program as follows:

12(1 unit per month)	(for advertising continuity)
2 units	(for Easter)
2 units	(for Back-to-School)
6 units	(for Christmas)
22 units	(Total advertising budget)

The retailer will then allocate the advertising funds into 22 parts for planning purposes (Figure 19–7). This system will provide the retailer with continuous promotion while giving proper support to those special periods of the year. It is noted that each retailer should determine where the promotional emphasis should be placed. It is for this reason that one retailer may put more than six units at Christmas while another retailer

Figure 19-7

Budget allocation procedure that ensures continuous advertising effort throughout the period.

	Jan	Feb	Mar	Apr	May	Jun	Jul	Aug	Sep	Oct	Nov	Dec
Monthly Allocations	1	1	1	1	1	1	1	1	1	1	1	1
Special Allocations			Easter (2)					Back to School (2)		Christmas (6)		
Total Monthly Allocations	1	1	2	2	1	1	1	2	2	1	4	4

Assume an annual advertising budget appropriation of $110,000
One Allocation Unit = $5,000 ($110,000 ÷ 22 units)
Monthly Budget Allocation for Advertising

January	$5,000	April	$10,000	July	$5,000	October	$5,000
February	$5,000	May	$5,000	August	$10,000	November	$20,000.
March	$10,000	June	$5,000	September	$10,000	December	$20,000

might not put any additional advertising support during the Christmas season. Advertising objectives are a key element in making this decision. If Christmas is significant in terms of the objectives, then more advertising units will be assigned to this period. If not significant, then fewer units or no additional units will be assigned to Christmas promotions.

3. *Develop a contingency within the budget.* As a rule of thumb, the longer the budget period, the greater the contingency amount, everything else being equal. This built-in flexibility allows the retailer to react to changing economic and competitive pressures during the budget period. A word of caution is in order. A budget with all contingency is no budget. The retailer must guard against establishing large contingencies just to avoid making difficult budget decisions. Experience will teach a retailer how much contingency is needed for each situation. If no information is available, a rule of thumb is 10 percent of the advertising budget for contingencies. This rule should be adjusted as soon as experience dictates.

As the retailer develops and uses the store's advertising budget, he or she should evaluate on a continuous basis its advertising needs. For a retailer, budgeting should not be a once- or a twice-a-year occurrence. The retailer who works for effective budgeting is always comparing budgets with actual experience so that the next budgeting period will reap the benefit of the past budgeting periods. To have an accurate and effective advertising budget requires effort on the part of the retailer.

DEVELOPING THE ADVERTISING SCHEDULE

While the advertising budget is being developed, the retailer must schedule advertising in order to plan when and where the advertisements should be run. To aid in the scheduling process, a scheduling chart should be developed (see Figure 19–8).

If a store has an advertising schedule such as the one shown in Figure 19–8, then the retailer is using an alternating media schedule. The idea behind such an alternating plan is to have continuous advertising exposure without the expense of everyday advertising use. One particular type of alternating plan would go one step further and alternate the size of the ads. For example, as shown in Figure 19–8, if every third newspaper ad is one-quarter page while the other two are one-eighth page ads, the alternating plan with staggered ads would be in use.

Another benefit of scheduling besides the ability to set up an effective staggered plan is that, through proper planning of the schedule, the retailer can determine what advertising media he or she wishes to use during the period. This knowledge enables the merchant to then go to the newspaper or radio station, for example, and buy what is needed well in advance of the actual ad date. The buying of advertising in advance will permit the retailer to get desired ad placement. It will also enable the merchant to get a favorable price for the advertisements through quantity discounts and "horse trading" with the media. If a retailer offers the advertising medium sufficient ad placements at one time with little effort on the medium's part, the cost of advertising may be much less than even the lowest price shown on the rate card. To ensure this, the retailer should secure a rate card from each radio station and/or other advertising media for comparison with the rates quoted by the representative.

Figure 19-8

Example of media schedule.

January, 19XX

1	2	3	4	5	6	7
	Radio —					
	20 Ten-Second Ads Per Day					
		Newspaper		Newspaper		Newspaper
8	9	10	11	12	13	14
	Newspaper		Newspaper		Newspaper	
15	16	17	18	19	20	21
	Radio —					
	20 Ten-Second Ads Per Day					
		Newspaper		Newspaper		Newspaper
22	23	24	25	26	27	28
	Newspaper		Newspaper		Newspaper	
29	30	31				
See February Schedule Chart						

THE CUMULATIVE EFFECT OF ADVERTISING

Another key element in the development of an effective advertising program is the retailer's understanding of the possible cumulative effect of advertising. What is meant by the cumulative effect of advertising or advertising carryover? Cumulative effect or advertising carryover is the length of time that an advertisement or a series of advertisements affects a store after the advertisement or series of advertisements have been run.

As noted earlier, it is important in both budgeting and scheduling of advertising for the carryover effect to be considered. In terms of budgeting, the funds should be allocated in such a way as to ensure that a series of ads be run on a regular basis to reinforce the cumulative effect. The way to accomplish this budgeting effectively is to schedule the advertisements carefully.

Another way for the retailer to view the cumulative effect of advertising is to look at advertising as an investment as opposed to a short-term expense. If viewed in this manner, each ad that is run is an investment in all future ads that will be run. The cumulative effect of one ad will make the next ad have greater impact. As the pattern of impact builds up over time, the result is more advertising impact per dollar of advertising expense.

Such carryover effect can only be achieved with a regular advertising program.

A retailer who runs one ad and then waits a month before running another ad is not achieving maximum effect from the store's advertising dollars. The effect of carryover is easy for the retailer to see if he or she will take a lesson from major product advertisers. If a major manufacturer ran one ad on television per month that stated that "our headache remedy is best," very little impact would result. Instead, a well-planned advertising program is developed to present the advertising idea in a repetitive manner. The net result of their efforts is positive advertising impact on the market with good recall of the advertisements for the product. This net result can be the same for retailers if they will schedule advertisements to take advantage of the investment characteristic or the carryover effect of advertising.

One important consideration for the retailer to remember is that advertising will carry over to the next period but that its impact will decay rapidly without additional advertising to "feed" the cumulative impact. The rate of decay appears to vary with the type of advertising. Sale price advertising decays rapidly, whereas institutional advertising declines more slowly. For example, a consumer might forget very quickly that a store featured a certain price in its ad, but they would remember that the store ran the ad for a much longer period of time. How long does carryover last? For almost any situation, the cumulative effect is minimal after three months from date of ad placement for institutional effect while the effect is quite small for sale price advertising even after one month.[5]

COORDINATING THE ADVERTISING PROGRAM

Advertising is supportive of the rest of the promotional mix of a store. In return, all parts of the promotional mix should work in conjunction with advertising. For example, suppose that a store ran a newspaper advertisement for men's shirts that resulted in much customer interest. But the store employees were not told of the ad and, therefore, told all customers who came in that they were in error. The result is that the store would sell no shirts. Also, potential customers would be lost because they would not appreciate what appeared to them to be a bait advertisement. How can this situation be avoided? *Coordination!* The salesclerks should have been told of the advertisement and shown the shirts in question. They should also have been instructed as to where replacement merchandise might be located in the stockroom. If these procedures had been followed, the results of the newspaper ad would have been quite different.

Another example of the result of good advertising coordination concerns the retailer who uses various advertising methods. Good coordination will ensure that all advertisements are presenting the same advertising idea. Coordination will result in all store displays being developed in conjunction with store advertising. Coordination will also result in the appropriate merchandise being on hand for the sale.

A third example of coordination is working with vendors for the mutual benefit of all concerned. The retailer should coordinate the store's advertising effort with that of suppliers so that the maximum effect will be derived from the advertising effort. In addition, the retailer may receive financial assistance for advertising purposes (generally 50 percent of cost) if the store will cooperate with the vendor in running ads of a particular nature at a particular time.[6] Coordination of advertising with other promotional variables is difficult. Successful coordination is essential, however, to an effective advertising program.

SUMMARY

Advertising is any controlled form of nonpersonal presentation and promotion of ideas, goods, or services by an identified sponsor that is used to inform and persuade the selected market. To achieve the most effective use of advertising, the retailer must make special effort to ensure that the advertising program is presenting the desired image for the store. The merchant must also develop advertising objectives. Third, a knowledge of the various media available to the retailer (newspaper, radio, television, direct mail, etc.) and how to best use them to meet the advertising objectives is helpful. Sound budgeting is also essential. An advertising schedule that will show the retailer how to get the best coverage for a set time period is important. The retailer must also understand the idea of the cumulative effect of advertising for best advertising results. Last, but equally important with the other considerations, is coordination. To get the most out of the store's advertising, the retailer must coordinate all advertising with the store's overall marketing program. A good retail advertising program does not happen by accident.

DISCUSSION QUESTIONS

1. Define advertising. Explain your answer.
2. Why is the image created by advertising important to a retailer?
3. What would be some possible advertising objectives for a store of your choice?
4. Discuss the advantages of five different advertising media. What media choices are best suited for various types of retailers?
5. Select a store in your area that advertises by means of various media. Conduct a personal interview with the store's manager to determine how the various media were chosen.
6. How might a retailer go about developing an advertising budget?
7. "Developing an advertising schedule is too much trouble." Do you agree or disagree with this statement? Why?
8. Develop an advertising budget and advertising schedule for a shoe store assuming the retailer plans to spend $3,000 per year on advertising; $10,000 per year on advertising; $25,000 per year on advertising.
9. What is meant by the cumulative effect of advertising?
10. Is coordination of advertising with other parts of the marketing program important? Why?

[1] For a more complete look at the subject of advertising, see William H. Bolen, *Advertising* (New York: John Wiley & Sons, Inc., 1981).

[2] Ibid., p. 6.

[3] By permission. From *Webster's New Collegiate Dictionary* © 1980 by G. & C. Merriam Co., Publishers of the Merriam-Webster Dictionaries.

[4] For estimates of 1979 advertising to sales and advertising to gross profit margin for various types of retail operations, see *Advertising Age*, Vol. 51, no. 30 (July 14, 1980), p. 72.

[5] Alfred A. Kuehn, "How Advertising Performance Depends on Other Marketing Factors," *Journal of Advertising Research*, Vol. 2, no. 1 (March 1962), pp. 2–10.

[6] For examples of manufacturer–retailer co-op plans, see the current edition of *Co-Op Profiles: The Money Book*, published by the Radio Advertising Bureau, 485 Lexington Avenue, New York, N.Y. 10017.

CHAPTER 20

Sales Promotion

"...I get 50 extra trading stamps for that...that's on sale...I have a coupon for a dime off on that...I get a little one free with the big one...That didn't have a price on it...That's half price because it's a day old...That I get for..."

Advertising, personal selling, and sales promotion all join to sell the store and its contents to the target market. As noted earlier, advertising attempts to build traffic for the store whereas personal selling attempts to turn this traffic into buyers. Sales promotion, on the other hand, includes all those activities, either nonrecurring or continuous, that supplement the store's advertising and personal selling by creating additional traffic and sales. Sales promotion includes trading stamps, contests, coupons, demonstrations, sampling, special events, and premiums along with solicitations, theme promotions, traveling displays, classes and schools, and co-op promotions (Figure 20–1). Although the number of items that can be included under sales promotion appears to be infinite, the items as given are those most commonly associated with sales promotion in a retail situation.

TRADING STAMPS

Trading stamps as a promotional tool have seen good times and bad. In 1969 trading stamp volume rose to a record $821 million, only to fall to a level of under $300 million just six years later (Figure 20–2). Since that time, stamp volume is once again on the increase but with no signs of rapid growth.[1]

The reader should make note of the fact that trading stamps are not a new marketing phenomenon. In fact, the earliest records of trading stamps in the United States date from the 1890s when Schuster's Department Store of Milwaukee instituted a plan called the Blue Trading Stamp System. In contrast to this user-issuer, the Sperry and Hutchinson Company (S & H) started in 1896 as an independent issuer. After the turn of the century, stamp plans spread across the land. Since those early days, such plans have changed little. The only difference is that originally stamps were given only on cash sales or upon payment within a specified time.[2] Such restrictions are not generally in use today. Trading stamps are defined as fractional certificates that are redeemable for merchandise and/or cash. Such certificates are given out to customers as a means of attracting business, usually at the rate of one stamp unit for every 10 cents of the amount of the purchase. The idea behind stamps is to get customers to come into the store time after time so that they may collect enough stamps to receive their "free" merchandise. If these repeat visits actually take place then stamps are thought to have been successful.

Should a retailer use trading stamps as a tool of sales promotion? Several factors should be taken into consideration when one attempts to answer this question.

Figure 20–1

Forms of sales promotions.

Sales Promotion (Trading Stamps, Contests, Coupons, Demonstrations, Sampling, Special Events, Premiums, Solicitations, Theme Promotions, Traveling Displays, Classes & Schools, Co-Op Promotions)

Figure 20-2

Annual trading stamp volume in millions of dollars, 1969–1980.

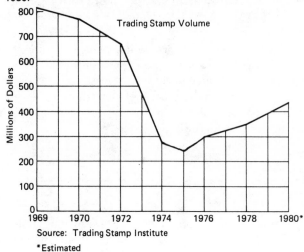

Source: Trading Stamp Institute

*Estimated

Source: Trading Stamp Institute of America.

Does the store's target market already have the stamp habit? If "yes," stamps may be a good idea for the store. The idea of stamps will not have to be sold to the market.

Is there a stamp redemption center in the town? If "yes," the stamp with the redemption center will tend to be much more popular than the stamp which must be mailed off to be redeemed. People like to see before they "buy."

Does the store sell to a local as opposed to a transient target market? If "yes," stamps may be more beneficial to the store. Stamps help to build repeat business in the local market.

Is the store located in a rural area as opposed to an urban area? If "yes," stamps may have a greater effect on traffic. People will drive across a "small" town to buy at a certain store to get stamps. Most people will not, however, drive across New York City or even Manhattan just to receive them.

Is the target market of the store 25 years of age or older? If "yes," stamps have a better chance. Younger people as a group do not appear to be as interested in stamps.

Is a strong stamp family available to the retailer? If "yes," the store will be able to benefit from the business attracted to these other noncompetitive firms. A stamp family consists of those firms, usually noncompeting, in an area that give a particular stamp. If the best food store, gasoline station, and bakery, for example, give a certain stamp and the merchant who is considering stamps does not compete directly with these firms, the store has available a strong stamp family it can join in case the decision is made to add stamps.

Is the average sale to a customer $5 or more? If "yes," then the average sale will be large enough to justify the effort. There is also a psychological advantage in giving many stamps to a customer at the time of purchase as opposed to a few stamps for a small purchase. The customer gets the impression that he or she is really getting something extra.

Is the store operating with excess capacity? If "yes," then sales can increase without greatly increasing operating cost. If stamps do increase sales and traffic as they should and the store cannot absorb this increase, then any benefits that the store receives will be counterbalanced by the additional expenses that result.

These eight factors should be weighed very carefully by the retailer before adding stamps, since once added to the promotion mix, stamps are costly to drop. It is very expensive to discontinue stamps since customers feel that stamps are figured in the prices of the merchandise. If stamps are dropped by a store, most consumers expect that store to drop prices to compensate for the loss of stamps. It has been found that a price cut, to be effective, must be a minimum of 4 to 5 percent. A stamp dropper must lower prices accordingly and retain the price cut for several months for the action to be successful.[3]

As noted, many people feel that stamps cause costs and, therefore, prices to rise. Is such a feeling correct? The answer depends on the success of the stamp program in use in the store. If the store increases its volume after adding stamps by 10–15 percent, then the increased volume will generally pay for the stamps. Problems arise, however, when volume does not rise by any appreciable amount after the addition of stamps. In this case, stamps do cost the merchant, but prices may not rise accordingly due to competitive factors. It should be noted that stamps in most all cases also cost the merchant in terms of time required at the checkout. Unless the retailer has invested in costly automatic dispensing equipment, the checkout process is delayed by stamps. One additional problem with stamps is theft. Many employees would never think of stealing money from the register but will "acquire" stamps for their personal use. Stamps are "money." They cost the merchant on the average one fifth of a cent or an amount that is equivalent to 2 percent of sales. Personnel should be held accountable for the stamps in their possession just as they are for the money in their cash drawer. Failure to control stamps can be very costly. Do such costs outweigh the benefits? It is difficult to draw any general conclusion. The effectiveness of trading stamps varies substantially, even among settings that are superficially similar.[4]

CONTESTS

A contest with prizes that interest the target market will generate traffic. Like trading stamps, the decision to use contests is an individual one. If the store has a prestige image, using a contest could make the customer feel uneasy about the store. In addition, if every store in town is in the midst of a contest, then the user of a contest loses any differential advantage that might have accrued to that store in a less saturated market.

If contests are not overused and are compatible with the store image, then such devices may be feasible. But what kind of game or contest should be used? Which is better—skill or chance?

Skill

A contest or game involving skill should be studied carefully before its application to ensure that the game is not so hard that there will not be a winner. In addition, all entry blanks in a game or contest involving skill must be checked and checked thoroughly. Unless the checking procedure is well thought out, a skill game may turn out to be quite a burden for the retailer. Imagine a store with 5,000 one-page essays on "Why I Love America." Picking a winner without making someone mad is almost impossible. Or what about a contest to see how many English words of four letters or more can be made out of a phrase or slogan. Lorillard, the makers of *Kent* cigarettes, ran such a contest that asked the participant to make as many words as possible out of the phrase, *"Kent Micronite Filter Cigarettes."* Since a potential winner could send in over 9,000 words, the entry blanks were checked against a particular word list that was later found not to have included all possible choices. The end result was a Consent Order from the Federal Trade Commission that ordered Lorillard to rejudge the contest to determine the true winners of its "Kent Castle Contest."[5] What started out as a sales promotion vehicle for the firm ended in a promotional nightmare.

Before discussing games of chance, it should be pointed out that there are certain games that give the appearance of requiring skill but are primarily games of chance. Such contests are sometimes aggravating to customers. Suppose that the store hands out word lists to customers who are directed to match words to definitions and return the list on their next visit. A shopper goes home and works for hours on the entry only to find out later that the official answers for the contest are half serious and half humorous. Customers may not appreciate being misled into thinking the game was truly a measure of skill. Games should be fun. Much work, with the reward having no correlation to effort, can turn the customer off to the store as well as the contest.

Chance

As a general rule, games of chance are better to use than games of skill. They are easier for the consumer to understand and are generally easier to administer. The various horse and dog racing games are examples of games of chance. Putting one's name in a box from which a winner will be drawn is also an example of a chance contest. The customer usually receives a chance to win or an entry blank when a purchase is made. It should be noted that in states with laws that prohibit a lottery, stores must give away game chances or entry blanks without requiring a purchase. To make a customer buy merchandise in order to receive a game ticket or entry blank constitutes the act of buying a lottery ticket. It is for this same reason that contests that ask the respondent to include a label with the entry blank also permit the contestant to simply print the name on a 3" × 5" card or do something similar so as not to require a purchase to participate. After receiving the game ticket, token, or the like, the customer then compares the winning combination with what is on her or his ticket or drops the completed entry blank into the contest box. Traffic for the store usually goes up as people come again to get additional chances to win.

Most people look at a list of winners in a national sweepstakes to see if someone in their part of the country won something. If none is shown, most begin to have doubts about the game. A local winner gives credibility to a contest. It also generates interest. The reaction of most people is that if Lesley Smith, a neighbor, can win $100 or a 5-minute shopping spree, or whatever, then so can I. Local winners in each individual store in an area make for a better promotion.

The retailer with ten stores may wish to set up a contest to ensure that there will be winners in each store. Contest "rigging" is perfectly legitimate so long as the odds of winning at each store are stated correctly. As noted in a Federal Trade Commission Consent Order involving a retailer of sewing machines and other products, the approximate numerical odds of winning each prize must be given in a contest. In addition, the total number of prizes to be awarded must be provided, the value of the prizes as stated must be in line with the prizes' actual market value in the trade area, and all conditions, terms, and obligations with which individuals will be asked to or must comply with to receive a prize must be spelled out in advance to the contest participants.[6] Because of these and other legal requirements along with the administrative burden of running a contest, large retailers in particular will want to look into the possibility of having an outside firm develop and operate their contests. The D. L. Blair Corporation is one of several firms that specialize in this type of service.

COUPONS

Should a store accept coupons as a means of building traffic for a store? The answer is "yes" even though such coupons do create additional paperwork at times. Coupons may be either from a manufacturer or vendor that are redeemable at many different stores or from a particular retailer that can be used only at that store. In cases where the manufacturer is involved, the industry trade practice calls for a 7 cent handling charge to be paid to the retailer for each coupon handled by the store. In other words, if the coupon is for 10 cents off on any tube of Crest toothpaste, the retailer upon submitting the coupon to Procter and Gamble, maker of Crest, would receive 17 cents from the firm for accepting and handling the coupon.

One acute problem facing the coupon promotion program of a manufacturer is misredemption. It is difficult to guarantee that the Crest coupon was redeemed on a tube of Crest. A quick check used by manufacturing concerns is to compare the number of coupons redeemed with the amount of merchandise ordered by the retailer. If more coupons are redeemed than could have been covered by inventory, the retailer can be in for legal difficulties for committing fraud.

The problem of coupon misredemption sometimes finds the retailer in the middle of a bad situation. For example, a supermarket manager knows that misredemption constitutes fraud. The manager also knows that a customer who has shopped at the store for 20 years has a tendency to use coupons for which he or she has not purchased the appropriate item. Should the retailer tell the customer that this is illegal, thereby running the risk of losing a faithful customer? If the retailer's noncoupon sales of the items are quite significant, chances are good that knowledge of the misredemption will never go beyond the store. What the retailer should do and what is done may not be the same in situations of this nature. Coupons can create many problems for a merchant.

If coupons are such a problem, why do retailers put up with them? The answer is quite simple—*customers like them.* In 1980, more than 60 million U.S. households (or 76 percent) used manufacturer cents-off coupons. Why were so many joining the "coupon craze"? Important factors were

Inflation
Coupons were accessible to more people
More manufacturers were using coupons

Who are the consumers who use coupons? The findings of the Research Department of the Nielsen Clearing House reveal household coupon usage by race to be as follows:

White	79%
Nonwhite	57%
Hispanic/other	70%

In addition, medium- and upper-income families were more active coupon users than were lower-income families. But even lower-income families seem to be getting the coupon habit. In 1980, lower-income family coupon usage amounted to 60 percent of all such families, up from 51 percent in 1975.

It should be pointed out that coupon usage in many stores has moved a step beyond being just a retailer who accepts coupons. These stores have turned coupons into a major promotional device for the store by offering to redeem all manufacturer coupons at double or even triple their face value. "Double coupon days" provide the store with a differential advantage in the eyes of many customers since the 25 cent coupon for Tide is now worth 50 cents at one store and only 25 cents at other stores. Such promotions do build traffic but at a price. The 25 cent coupon for Tide on a "double day" means that the store will lose 18 cents on the transaction (Figure 20-3).

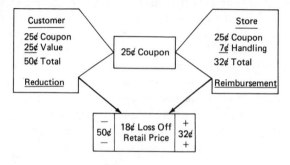

Figure 20-3

Impact of "double" coupon promotion on item purchased with 25 cent coupon.

If the store attracts shoppers who also buy other items or will continue to attract the customer after the store quits having the "double day," then the promotion will pay for itself. On the other hand, if a particular store is located in an area where many people have become coupon enthusiasts, then "double coupon days" may prove to be costly. In such situations, shoppers may come to the checkout with coupons for almost everything in the shopping basket—a very expensive experience for the retailer as illustrated in Figure 20–3. For these coupon shoppers, if the store drops the promotion, most will stop shopping at the store. Should a store use a double-coupon promotion? There is obviously no one best answer. A careful analysis of the marketplace will play a major role in providing an answer to this question.

It should be emphasized that as long as manufacturers distribute coupons, and 90 billion were distributed in 1980, most retail stores will be almost required to accept coupons. And with 76 percent of all U.S. households using coupons, the store's target market likely has the coupon habit. With such popularity, retail stores should make every effort to feature coupons in their ads and to ensure that merchandise is on the shelf to back up the coupons in the hands of the target market. Actions of this nature on the part of the retailer should result in increased sales for the store or at least will not give a competitor a differential advantage by allowing that store to more effectively accommodate coupon users.[7]

DEMONSTRATIONS

"Seeing is believing. Believing is wanting." If the retailer can show the customer something of interest, the customer may decide to buy. Demonstrating a product for sale is one type of demonstration. The other type is a demonstration that may not be related directly to the store such as square dancing, karate, magic, or even how to play tennis. These demonstrations have as their purpose building traffic for the store.

The retailer should use special care to select both product and general-interest demonstrations that will appeal to the store's target market. A karate demonstration may draw a crowd. The question to be asked by the merchant is, "Do I want that particular group of people to be drawn to my store?" "Will this crowd scare off the real target market?" "Will the demonstration actually result in reduced sales?" If such is the case, then the demonstration has had less than desirable results.

The possible number and types of demonstrations that can be used are almost infinite. For example, the best way to sell a pan for making crepes is to demonstrate how to use it in the store by making crepes. A good demonstration will make it look easy. Furniture refinishing and cleaning are popular areas for using demonstrations. Sewing is another. Demonstrations of all types serve to attract attention. Even a HO-gauge train that is demonstrated every 10 minutes in the toy department will serve to build traffic as children come and bring their parents to see the train.

It should be pointed out that demonstrations in a store do not have to be elaborate. They should, however, be planned and executed carefully. A crepe that does not turn out right or a fashion show that seems to drag on forever, or square dancers who take up so much room that shoppers cannot get in the store are demonstrations headed for trouble. A retailer should do his or her homework *before* conducting or allowing a demonstration. *No* demonstration is better than a disastrous one.

SAMPLING

Just as many manufacturers use product samples to generate business, retail firms can, likewise, use samples as a means of generating sales volume. *Hickory Farms*, a retail operation that specializes in various meats and cheeses, offers free samples to its customers. Many a cheese ball has probably been sold after a free taste. A bakery shop that gives out free samples, especially to children, will probably have children bring their parents in the store more often than would be the case without free samples. A store that sells relatively inexpensive items with high repeat purchase potential has a good setup for sampling.

Sampling of another variety involves giving out items such as cloth or wallpaper swatches or paint chips. The idea is to get the customer involved with the product in a setting away from the store. Customers have come to expect such samples to be available. If these samples are not made available, most customers will take samples anyway. A wallpaper book or bolts of cloth can suffer great damage if samples are taken in a haphazard manner. The smart retailer will encourage free samples but will make every effort to provide these samples in a systematic manner.

SPECIAL EVENTS

The purpose of a special event is to draw many people to the shopping area. Because of the scope of such an event, individual stores, unless they are quite large, would not normally conduct one by themselves. A shopping center, mall, or merchants association is more likely to become involved in such an event due to the size of the undertaking. Special events should be given careful consideration by retailers since they do provide opportunities for:

Dramatizing a retailer's move into a new market.
Providing new services that focus on problems that customers are facing such as coping with the problems of aging.
Establishing the store or mall as an "entertainment center," while helping to increase traffic and sales.
Creating a trend—or speeding up its arrival (Sanger-Harris' Great Skate event created a demand for roller skates before roller fever hit the Dallas market).
Bringing the customs, culture, and merchandise of other countries to the attention of local customers (Figure 20–4).
Creating a differentiated image for a store or center that may have basically the same merchandise assortment as its neighbors.[8]

Figure 20-4

Special promotions can include any event that attracts the attention of the target market. Shown here is a special promotion of gift items from the Peoples Republic of China at Broadway Plaza, Los Angeles.

(Courtesy of The Broadway.)

Special events are transforming stores and/or malls into entertainment, information, and service centers. The options available to the merchant are numerous. Some of the more popular special events that are used by retailers are now examined.

Special events range from a circus to an automobile show. For a circus, the merchants must pay to get the circus to come while car dealers may pay the merchants for the privilege of displaying their cars. Singing events are also quite popular. Having all the local churches furnish choirs during Christmas helps to build the Christmas spirit, not to mention shopper traffic as family and friends alike come to hear the music. Music for hire is also available as various country and western and rock groups travel throughout the country. Merchants should, of course, select groups based on the musical likes of the target market, not the likes of the merchant.

Special events can also involve charity and politics. Having a fish-o-thon for the March of Dimes is a possibility. A water tank is set up and stocked with fish. For a contribution of $1.00 or more, the customer gets a chance to drown a worm for 15 minutes. All fish that are caught can be taken home. As for politics, one of the favorite stopping places for candidates for president on down is a shopping area. Many merchant groups have taken advantage of this fact by sponsoring political debates and forums on various issues. The League of Women Voters, Jaycees, or other civic groups are usually invited to take part and to serve as moderators for such events. The selection of an independent moderator removes the merchant from any direct involvement with the event beyond providing a place for the program. Under such a setup, those for and against certain issues can be equally happy shopping in the stores before and after the special event.

Parades are another possibility for a special event. Thanksgiving Day means parades like those sponsored by Macy's and J. L. Hudson, which are truly special events in New York and Detroit as well as throughout the country thanks to television. Parades do much to build spirit and sales at Christmastime. On a much smaller scale, the day after Thanksgiving is ushered in with many Christmas parades across the country in various central business districts as well as malls of all sizes. Although Thanksgiving weekend probably could be called parade time in America, other events in various locations can give rise to a parade. A high Irish population may result in a St. Patrick's Day parade while an Armed Forces Day parade can be quite successful when a large military installation is nearby. In small town America, a parade honoring fair week or the high school football team can be a big event. A parade every weekend can become a joke. For a given locale, however, there are probably several events during the year that can be honored successfully with a parade. Almost everyone loves a parade. It is for this reason more than any other that parades are a good promotional tool. Parades, simply put, attract people.

Another example of a special event is an art display for ages 3–12. Each school, nursery, kindergarten, and so on, is asked to display the artwork of its young students. Donations are made to those schools that participate. The artwork may then be judged or not as the case may be and prizes given. Such judging is irrelevant to the promotion. The idea is that little Sally, aged 6, will bring Mom, Dad, sister, and brother, not to mention grandparents and no telling who else to see her artwork that has been displayed. While there, it is quite possible that something will be purchased, especially for the young artist. Such art shows can be a very effective, yet inexpensive promotion. Special events that involve children in some way are very successful for most retail situations (Figure 20–5).

PREMIUMS

A premium is something that is sold, usually at cost (self-liquidator), or is given without charge to the shopper only after the customer performs some task such as the buying of at least $5.00 worth of groceries or the taking of a test drive in a new car. Many such premiums are designed to build traffic over time. For example, a 24-volume set of encyclopedias is made available at 1 volume per week at cost. The encyclopedia is written to encourage the purchase of later volumes. It may show a listing for "America" in Volume 1 that will refer the reader to "United States." Since there is little use for half of a set of such books, the shopper will tend to come back week after week to complete the set once the first several volumes have been purchased.

Premiums may also be a one-time promotion that are used to build traffic. For years, Goodyear has used a Christmas record that was made available for under $2.00 as a means of stimulating in-store traffic during the Christmas season. Goodyear also has used a toy blimp for the same purpose.

The success of a premium promotion depends greatly on the careful selection of the premium. Dishes, flatware, towels, books, records, toys, and house plants have all been very effective for given retailers. Choose a premium that will have desirability in

Figure 20-5

A special event for children in progress at Woodfield Mall, Schaumburg, Illinois.

(Courtesy of The Taubman Company, Inc., Woodfield developer.)

the eyes of the target market. If the market has need for an inertia nutcracker, then such a premium has potential. If people in the area eat few nuts, a premium of this type will not be a good idea. A good premium is something people want.

SOLICITATIONS

Another form of sales promotion is personal, telephone, and mail-order solicitations. A retail store employee may call all new arrivals in town (such lists can possibly be obtained from the power company) and invite them to come to the store for a free gift. Some stores that like this idea choose to use Welcome Wagon or a similar service for this purpose. This type of firm will call on new arrivals for a group of noncompeting merchants and explain the products and services that are offered by these merchants. Another idea is to call all the people in the store's target market and invite them to come in and participate in a sale and/or contest. A restaurant sends all students arriving on campus a "welcome" letter that is good for one free hamburger. It is observed that solicitations include some prospecting, samples, gifts, and various other inducements to attempt to get the customer to come to the store. These solicitations try to tell enough about the store so as to make the store appear to be desirable to the target customer. As with some other forms of sales promotion, the main purpose of the solicitation is to achieve that initial store visit on the part of the customer. If the customer comes for his or her one free hamburger and is never seen again, the solicitation was good. Obviously, the hamburger was not.

THEME PROMOTIONS

A good promotion has a theme. The most successful theme promotion for almost any type of retail store is Christmas. Easter probably ranks second and Back-to-School is close behind in position number three. Other popular themes include dog days, Washington's Birthday, and inventory clearance (Figure 20–6). Not only should store displays follow up on the theme, as will be discussed in the next chapter, but everything in the store should be coordinated with the theme of the promotion.

The theme to use is one that can be promoted easily and can be applied through-

Figure 20–6

A theme promotion—inventory clearance.

(Courtesy of Radio Shack.)

out the store. A little thinking on the retailer's part will generate many possible themes for use during the year (Figure 20–7). A food chain may make use of Dairy Month as a promotional theme while a farm supply store may build a promotion based around Ground Hog Day. Historical events, local happenings, and even arbitrary ideas like "dynamite days—where high prices are blasted away" can be used as a theme. In most cases, what the theme is is not as important as the fact that there is a theme. A well-planned theme promotion generally results in a well-coordinated promotion that usually makes money for the store.

Figure 20–7

Possible theme promotions.

JANUARY	White Sale After Christmas Sale Super Bowl Sale	JULY	Dog Days Sale Firecracker Sale Christmas-in-July Sale
FEBRUARY	Washington's Birthday Sale Valentine's Sale Early Bird Spring Sale	AUGUST	Back to School Sale Football Sale Summer Clearance Sale
MARCH	Easter Sale Windy Sale Winter Clearance Sale	SEPTEMBER	Labor Day Sale Autumn Sale Stay Warm Sale
APRIL	Shower of Values Sale Get Ready for Summer Sale After Easter Sale	OCTOBER	Ghost and Goblin Sale World Series Sale Columbus Day Sale
MAY	Mother's Day Sale Graduation Day Sale Bridal Sale	NOVEMBER	Turkey Day Sale Election Day Sale Christmas Layaway Sale
JUNE	Father's Day Sale Vacation Sale. Picnic Sale	DECEMBER	End of Year Clearance Sale Santa Claus Sale Exchange-It Sale

TRAVELING DISPLAYS

People like to see a "real" racing car or Hitler's bullet-proof car or President Kennedy's limousine. Crowds will line up to see a picturerama of the Lord's Supper or the signing of the Declaration of Independence. Military displays of planes, tanks, and various other equipment also attract many people. Displays of these and other types are available to stores as they tour the country. In some cases, the displays are free. Some charge admission or seek a donation but are free to the merchant while some will cost the merchants who sponsor the traveling display. The number and variety of such displays is quite large. By careful evaluation and advanced scheduling, merchants should be able to obtain traveling displays that will be of interest to the target market. Even small towns may be able to obtain many of these displays by scheduling them between their big-city stops while they are in the geographic area. Advanced planning is the key to obtaining such displays in this manner.

Charm school, cooking classes, and sewing instruction are just three of the many possibilities for retailers in the area of instruction for promotional purposes. Charm classes for little girls include everything from modeling to table manners (Figure 20–8). Cooking instruction for the newlywed may include the basics of cooking while other courses may specialize in fondue or the art of making bread. Other possible classes for the retailer to consider are:

Furniture refinishing	Tennis	Budgeting
Makeup	Pool	Home repair
Slimnastics	Driving	Houseplants
Auto maintenance	Table tennis	Dancing
Tax preparation	Hair care	Découpage
Interior decorating	Karate	Guitar
Gardening	Painting	Landscaping

Classes of all types may sell merchandise directly, as when a store conducts a course on houseplants. Students are shown how to care for plants by using products sold by the store. Most participants will buy such products for use at home. In the case of the driving school, the student comes to the store for each lesson. Since the room

Figure 20–8

"Wendy Ward" charm course for little girls.

(Courtesy of Montgomery Ward.)

that is set aside for such instruction is usually in the back of the store or on the second floor or whatever, the student must pass through the store for each lesson. Chances are good that something will be purchased during some of these trips. Of course, the driving school will usually charge a fee so that it may be self-supporting. Other schools or classes may be free or not completely self-sufficient. In all cases, however, sales should be aided by classes since participation in such programs gets the customer into the store.

CO-OP PROMOTIONS

Sales promotion, as has been noted in this chapter, takes many forms. In using sales promotion the retailer may decide to develop an independent promotion or may choose to tie in with a manufacturer or vendor. In the latter case, all or part of the cost of the promotion may be carried by the supplier or other participant. In return for such economies, the retailer may, of course, lose some flexibility in the setting up and execution of the promotional vehicle.

Co-op promotions take many forms. A travel agency may wish to tie in with a promotion of cruise clothes. The firm may pay for all or part of the advertising associated with the promotion in return for the privilege of setting up a sales desk in the clothing store for the duration of the promotion. The question to be answered by the clothing store retailer is whether such an arrangement is in the best interest of the store. Does the retailer desire to have an element operating within the store over which it does not have complete control? In most cases, the answer is "no."

In another, more common form of co-op, a manufacturer or vendor supplies sales assistance in the form of displays, sales advisors, or whatever, which usually ties in with a national or regional promotion by that supplier. Del Monte, for example, has provided food retailers with such a promotion for several years that is backed by national advertising support. Stores that participate are provided with various promotional materials to place throughout the store in order to give the store the same appearance as the one that is featured in ads run by Del Monte. These promotions are good, but an individual retailer will not normally receive exclusive use of such material in a market area since product lines like Del Monte are usually carried by most stores. Competing stores in a given area can usually be found to be taking part in such promotions, thereby eliminating any chance of a differential advantage being given to a store as a result of the co-op arrangement. As was noted in Chapter 3, co-op promotions must be offered to all to avoid charges of discrimination. Chances are very good, therefore, that a well-planned and well-promoted co-op promotion will be used by more than one retailer in a given area. For this reason, co-op promotions that originate with manufacturers and vendors are used by the retailers in most cases as a means of staying competitive rather than as a means of obtaining a differential advantage in the marketplace. The only tie-in promotion that offers uniqueness is probably one that originates with the retailer. Even here, this uniqueness may be short lived if the promotion is a success. Successful tie-ins have a way of being copied and even improved on by competitors within a short period of time. This is one of the many reasons that make retailing such a dynamic form of business enterprise.

Sales promotion includes all those activities, either nonrecurring or continuous, that supplement the store's advertising and personal selling by creating additional traffic and sales. Included under this topic are trading stamps, contests dealing with skill and/or chance, coupons originating with either the supplier or retailer, demonstrations of both a product nature and of general interest, and sampling, which runs the gamut from a free cookie to a cloth swatch. In addition, sales promotion encompasses special events (fashion shows, parades, political debates, singing groups, and even an art show for children), premiums (items that are given away or are sold to customers only after the customer fulfills a predetermined obligation), and solicitations (personal, phone, mail) where a direct appeal is made to a customer to come and shop. The topic area also includes theme promotions that range from a Dog Days Sale to a Columbus Day Sale, traveling displays that vary from pictureramas to a jet plane, classes and schools that offer training in everything from how to drive to how to budget, and co-op promotions that can offer the retailer a tie-in with a national campaign or even another local firm. A good sales promotion program is no accident. Care should be taken in choosing its components so that the sales promotion program that is used will be successful in building traffic and sales for the given store in its particular environment.

DISCUSSION QUESTIONS

1. Should a store use trading stamps? What are some factors to consider in deciding on this question? Talk to retailers who use stamps and those who do not. Use their ideas to help formulate your answer.
2. Do trading stamps mean higher prices? Why or why not?
3. What information must be disclosed to contestants of a game or contest?
4. Should a store have a "double coupon day"? Discuss that question with retailers in your area. What is your opinion concerning this question? Does it agree with that of area merchants?
5. Cite at least three examples of stores in your area who use demonstrations and/or sampling as a means of sales promotion. In your opinion, are they effective? Why or why not?
6. A store decides to use a special event as a traffic builder. What are some ideas that it might use? What should be considered in selecting the event?
7. What is a premium? Go to two stores in your area and determine if premiums are in use. Interviews with the store managers should then be conducted to determine why premiums are either in use or not in use in each store.
8. Develop lists of possible theme promotions for a clothing store, hardware store, auto parts store, and a full-line department store.
9. Discuss the pros and cons of a co-op promotion. As a retailer, would you participate in such an arrangement?
10. Of all the methods of sales promotion, which one is the most effective and least effective for a clothing store, hardware store, auto parts store, and a full-line department store? Give reasons for your choices.

[1] For additional information on trading stamps, see Jeffrey H. Birnbaum, "Industry Blues Fail to Deter S & H Stamps," *The Wall Street Journal*, Vol. 196, no. 25 (August 5, 1980), p. 29.

[2] Harold W. Fox, *The Economics of Trading Stamps* (Washington, D.C.: Public Affairs Press, 1968), p. 1.

[3] F. E. Brown, "Price Movements Following the Discontinuance of Trading Stamps," *Journal of Retailing*, Vol. 43, no. 3 (Fall 1967), p. 13.

[4] Harold W. Fox, *The Economics of Trading Stamps*, p. 153.

[5] Federal Trade Commission Order Against Lorillard et al., 1974, *Federal Trade Commission Decisions*, 83 (Washington, D.C.: U.S. Government Printing Office, 1975), pp. 1195–1203.

[6] Federal Trade Commission Order Against Oden Distributing Co., Inc. et al., 1974, *Federal Trade Commission Decisions*, 84 (Washington, D.C.: U.S. Government Printing Office, 1975), pp. 1125–1133.

[7] Information for this discussion taken in part from Mary Ann Linsen, "High-Flying Coupons Soar to the Skies," *Progressive Grocer*, Vol. 60, no. 2 (February 1981), pp. 65–76.

[8] Pam Phillips, "On Stage," *Stores*, Vol. 62, no. 3 (March 1980), p. 47. Copyright, National Retail Merchants Association, 1980.

CHAPTER 21

Retail Display

Reprinted with permission from The Saturday Evening Post Company © 1980.

"The value of a good display is far-reaching—appearance is improved, sales increased, a new interest has developed and stimulated the minds of salespeople, and the whole store moves forward to a higher level."[1] Such a statement by Winthrop Frye in the April 1933 issue of the *Journal of Retailing* illustrates the fact that retailers have long been aware of the value of a good retail display.

A retail display is a nonpersonal presentation of merchandise and/or information to the target market that takes place within the physical environment of the store. The worth of a good display is as obvious now as in the past. An effective display enhances the appeal of the product at the point of sale, takes advantage of existing traffic without the extra cost of advertising to attract more, and provides new interest to the buying public as well as the selling staff. A minor rearrangement of a display will sometimes give a fresh, more interesting look to a merchandise grouping, a department, and even to an entire store.[2]

Additional advantages of display include:[3]

1. *Displays involve little merchandise risk.* The merchandise in most displays can be sold as new following its use. This advantage is only found when displays are changed often enough to prevent merchandise from becoming shopworn. Of course, some merchandise can be and is sold right from a display. The L'eggs point-of-purchase display rack is an example of such a situation.
2. *Displays operate at point of sale.* If the customer sees something appealing, the customer can react by buying the item without delay. With advertising, the consumer learns of an item but must wait to buy it at some future time. There is little procrastination when the promotional tool is display. Good displays get positive action now.
3. *Displays present merchandise live.* A picture, which is said to be worth a thousand words, is normally nothing compared with the real thing. When a person sees a picture of merchandise, it usually generates more interest than just reading about it. This interest is enhanced further by seeing the actual merchandise. Displays provide this opportunity to see the "real thing."
4. *Displays can attract many viewers at little or no cost.* Many magazines figure their charges on the basis of cost per thousand readers. If displays were figured in like manner, a window display at Five Points in Atlanta, Georgia—the heart of the Atlanta central retail district—would be, for example, so inexpensive as to make the computation a little ridiculous. At the same time, the merchant must always remember that there is no true correlation between the quality of the display and the price of such a display. Many good displays cost little or nothing. Creativity, not dollars, is the key that attracts many viewers—potential customers.

Besides the advantages of retail display, what makes a good display, what are the types of display (window, interior, point-of-purchase), and what are the managerial considerations that pertain to display?[4] What the retailer should display is the first area of discussion.

WHAT TO DISPLAY

More retailers are becoming involved with display. G. Fox and Company of Hartford, Connecticut, for example, has developed the following formula for its display program:

where M.A.S.S. stands for *Make A Strong Statement*.[5] Every display should be designed to make a strong, powerful presentation to attract the shopper's attention. Displays are not thought to be passive. They, instead, project the merchandise in the direction of the shopper. Of all possible items to project, merchandise selected for such purposes normally falls into one of five categories:

> *Advertised merchandise.* Feature in the display the items that have been singled out in other media. Such displays add emphasis to the newspaper's pulling power, for example, and make it easier for the customer to buy advertised items.
>
> *Fashion merchandise.* A fashion display not only tells the customer what is "in," it also promotes a fashion image for the retailer.
>
> *Impulse merchandise.* A favorable projection of an impulse item is essential to the sale of such merchandise. Good point-of-purchase effort places such items in the right place in the store layout in a form that has attention-getting characteristics.
>
> *High-margin merchandise.* Displays, by their nature, place special emphasis on items. Such special emphasis can naturally lead to sales. If the unit sales of high-margin or high-profit items can be increased through the use of displays, the profit margin of the store can be enhanced greatly. The smart retailer displays these more profitable items whenever it is practical to do so (Figure 21-1).
>
> *Best-selling merchandise.* To further increase the sale of a winner, the retailer

Figure 21-1

Merchandise selected for display may be high-margin merchandise or even best selling merchandise.

(Courtesy of Radio Shack.)

should call it to the customer's attention, remind the customer that he or she needs to buy, and make it easy to do so. As is pointed out by G. Fox and Company, good judgment is the rule to follow in determining what items to use for display purposes. Even if common white diapers are the best seller in the infant's department, it is difficult to *make a strong statement* for common baby diapers. A window display of diapers or an elaborate interior display featuring such a product would be almost impossible to make into an attention-getter. It would certainly be a mind-boggling experience for the person who is held responsible for creating such a display.

In addition to the considerations noted, merchandise selected for display should have, if possible, visual attractiveness. For example, diapers sell but do not have visual attractiveness. In a store of any size, there are possibly other things besides diapers that sell well. The retailer will probably want to feature these other items in the store's various displays. To obtain visual appeal, the merchant may even feature some items just for their attention-getting value. A department store may feature fur coats in several of its window displays with little expectation of selling out of such coats. Such a display will instead attract attention and will probably result in the sale of many cloth coats. The same idea is used in tire retailing. Most major tire manufacturers have a "super X-12 radial with six steel belts and rubber dripping off the tread." Such tires sell for $200 plus and are featured prominently in retail displays. Very few units are sold, but the tire display results in the sale of many cheaper tires. The visual attractiveness of that "super tire" display makes consumers feel that the tires they can afford must be pretty good too.

One other factor to consider in deciding on what to display is the interest of the target market. A smart retailer will develop displays that, it is hoped, will strike the "fancy" of the market. This may involve displaying some things that the store does not even sell along with the marketable items. A display of 1920 fashions or old toys or antique furniture or whatever may serve to draw attention to the display. Another application of this idea is for the retailer to feature an item that is the latest thing as shown on television and in the latest fashion magazines. If the target market has heard or read about it, the display will say, "here it is—now come see it and buy it." Still another idea to use in getting the attention of the target market is to integrate current events or happenings into the display. If it is raining outside—a display featuring umbrellas is good. When a heat wave hits the market area, bathing suits and air conditioners can be great sellers if displayed in a prominent manner. When Ronald Reagan was elected President of the United States in 1980, many retailers found a way to sell crystal candy jars. How? By filling the jars on display with jelly beans. If it interests the target market in a positive way, any everyday event can be used as an integral part of a retail display. Obtaining customer interest in the display in this manner helps the display to project its merchandise to the customer. A word of caution is in order on this point. A good display has as its number one function to project merchandise in a manner that attracts the customer's attention. The display should not overpower the product. For example, customers should never feel that they would love to have the rack that a product is displayed on but not the product. Displays sell products—not displays.

A good display makes a strong statement as it achieves the goal of merchandise projection. People stop at such a display and may even buy the product. But what makes people stop? How can a display effectively project merchandise? How can a display make a strong statement to the customer? What makes a good display? Developing good displays is not easy. The following ten guidelines should assist the merchant in developing effective displays (Figure 21-2):

1. A good display should have a theme.   As discussed in the previous chapter, theme promotions that coordinate all areas of the store generally make for successful promotions. In terms of display, such theme promotions mean that the various displays throughout the store make an effort to tie in with the theme. If the theme is graduation, various tie-ins can even be made in areas not normally related to graduation. For example, a display of major appliances may present the idea "Congratulations Mom and Dad—Reward Yourself With A Microwave Oven. You Deserve It!" In hardware, the display may suggest, "Graduation = More Room. With that son or daughter moving out—it's time you had a room." In most cases the theme is simply the device that ties all the displays together. It helps to build continuity throughout the store while providing the vehicle that will assist the merchant in making a strong statement about the products offered for sale by the store.

2. A good display should be distinctive.   A window display like all the others in the area does not attract attention. A mannequin just standing there with a sign at its feet that reads "Sale" has accomplished little. In theory, everything in the store is for sale. Few retailers give away much merchandise so what does the display hope to accomplish? Distinctive or striking displays help to build a particular image

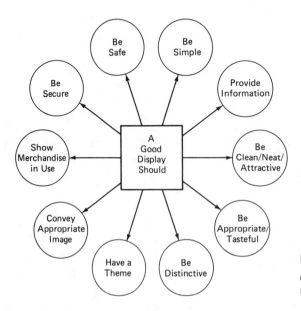

Figure 21-2

Guidelines for developing effective retail displays.

for a store. It should be noted that a retailer in seeking distinctive displays is not necessarily seeking displays that will give an expensive appearance. In some cases, prestige is important, but a distinctive display of hammers, bath towels, or mops and brooms can also aid in the selling of these products. What is distinctive is determined by the market situation. Customers compare in their own mind the displays of each store. If a store follows a "me-too" approach, the displays in that store will probably suffer in attention-getting potential.

It should be noted that any display, no matter how distinctive, can lose its distinctiveness over time as the same people see it again and again. Distinctiveness is, therefore, promoted by a retailer who has a policy of changing displays as often as necessary or at least every two weeks. Even during the Christmas season when many displays may go up right after Thanksgiving and stay up about a month, minor changes as well as some significant adjustments within the displays should be made. This will help the displays to continually attract customers back to the store and to areas within it.

Distinctiveness can be achieved many times by doing something unusual. In a store that caters to college women, a display may consist of a model showing the current fashions of the day. What makes this display a model instead of a mannequin is the fact that the model in the display *is* a college student. Every 15 minutes, a new model relieves the other one and the live display continues. A mannequin that breathes is an attention-getter. The reactions of people are quite humorous as they try to figure out if they really did see that mannequin move. Such a display idea can receive attention from local news media, especially if the retailer contacts the media ahead of time. A display of this type can get much free publicity. Live models and many other ideas are distinctive but should not be overused. The quest for distinctiveness is never ending.[6]

3. A good display should be appropriate and tasteful.   The display card for the deodorant display reads "No Sweat—Buy Now." Displays that use "cute" messages turn many people off. Realistic mannequins wearing see-through blouses may be quite distinctive but in poor taste if the display is in plain view of the general public. What is considered appropriate and tasteful is, of course, changing to a more liberal viewpoint. For example, a current examination of displays will reveal the use of mannequins of both sexes in the same underwear display. Such a display was an unheard of idea just a few short years ago.

For many target markets, tasteful and appropriate would now include being careful not to depict only so-called traditional situations. Displays should also show, for example, men in the kitchen and women in work situations. For those in favor of planned parenthood, a display that features a family with more than two children is thought to be in bad taste. A target market that is involved with the environment and the balance of nature may not appreciate a display of fox fur coats or alligator shoes. A display that features "Saturday Night Specials" may sell some pistols but will probably do more harm than good to the total store in terms of general customer reaction. Tasteful and appropriate are in the eyes of the beholder. The retailer's task is made easier if the store's target market is known and understood.

4. A good display should be clean, neat, and attractive.   There is no excuse for a messy display. Dirty windows, stained carpets, dusty props with paint peeling off, and mannequins with broken fingers all add up to a less than desirable display. For displays that customers can touch, the retailer should plan to straighten and otherwise repair the display two or three times a day. You can see the results of such effort in the attractive display shown in Figure 21–3.

Changing displays frequently reduces the problem of cleanliness but does not eliminate it. All displays should be checked at least once a day to ensure that none are in need of repair or adjustment. There is nothing attractive about a display in disarray.

5. A good display should provide information. What is the item? Where can I find it? What is it used for? What is its price? A large department store may put in the corner of each window where the displayed items can be found in the store. In most cases, however, the display itself should provide most of the information in a visual manner.

Perhaps the most controversial question about information in displays is whether price should be included. The same rules apply to display that apply to other forms of promotion. The prestige store does not use price in any display other than, perhaps, point-of-purchase. The discount retailer, on the other hand, uses price at every opportunity. As with most situations, the final decision on whether to use price in a display is a managerial one based on the expectations of the target market.

Figure 21–3

A good display should be neat, clean, and attractive.

(Courtesy of Schwinn Bicycle Company.)

6. A good display should be simple. A display has some similarities to a billboard or outdoor ad. The customer who is walking by the display window will be exposed to the display for only a few seconds unless the person stops to look more closely. The person going up the escalator will have only a short time to view the merchandise which has been placed on a ledge near the moving customer. In light of the time factor, a display should not be too complex. A good display will not feature too many different items. Instead it will zero in on coats, perfume, auto polish, or whatever the product category may be. A good display does not use the shotgun approach.

Another consideration that has a bearing on the simplicity of the display is that good displays do not have to be fancy. A display with the sun shining in one corner and a waterfall with a pool of goldfish at the bottom in the other may be nice, but there is so much to look at. The customer may not see the merchandise among all the splendor of the display. Having only one focal point in the display is the best way to ensure simplicity. A good display will use one thing or item to catch the eye. The arrangement of the display will then encourage eye movement in a particular manner. Displays with more than one focal point reduce their effectiveness by confusing customers.

7. A good display should show merchandise in use. Whenever possible, a display should not just show a product. It should also show the product as it will be used. Ladies' hosiery laid on the counter is not as effective as showing them being worn. A bathing suit being worn in a beach setting is better than just displaying a bathing suit. Instead of a display of boxes of outdoor grills, open one up, set it up, and, if the store has a patio, light it up and cook hot dogs. These hot dogs could be sold or given away depending on the financial condition and desires of the store. Seeing the grill in use will sell grills. By showing the merchandise in use, the retailer is suggesting a possible reason for purchase for those who need a reason. At the same time, a product displayed in its natural setting makes it seem more desirable to all customers.

8. A good display should convey the appropriate store image. The importance of atmospherics and image has been stressed throughout the book. The area of display is no exception. Displays help to give the store its personality (Figure 21–4). When the customer first comes near the store, what is seen? The display windows. What if the windows are filled with numerous unrelated items with sale prices on everything? A big sign also proclaims that great savings are available every day. The image conveyed by such display windows is generally one of a store with low prices. It is for this reason that such windows are many times referred to as dime-store windows. At the other extreme, a window features a high-fashion item in a dramatic setting. No price is mentioned. The window looks expensive. That is its projected image. Once inside, a store through the medium of display can change its mood and appearance quite rapidly. A store can transfer itself into a winter wonderland for the Christmas season or a college campus for back-to-school. In some cases, customers will come just to see the displays. As a general rule, the more elaborate the display, the more expensive the image portrayed by it.

Colors that are used in a display along with the physical arrangement of the display also contribute to the store image. As was noted in Chapter 7, colors mean different things to people. For example, a store that desires a conservative image will

Figure 21–4

Displays should fit the image of the store. Budget shoes, for example, should be displayed in such a way that customers can get to them and try them on.

(Courtesy of Venture Stores.)

feature soft colors instead of bright red and orange in its various displays. As for the physical arrangement of merchandise, a display with formal or symmetrical balance projects prestige more so than a display with no physical balance. What is wanted are uncluttered displays with plenty of free open space and one focal point. The focal point should occur approximately one-third down the display and in the center (Figure 21–5). This display will, from a balance standpoint, project an image of quality or prestige. In examining the area of image and display, the retailer must first decide what type of image is desired. The dime store should use a dime-store window but a high-fashion store should not. The question boils down to what are the desires of the target market? What do they expect? The retailer must make every effort not to confuse the customer by the use of inconsistent displays. If the customer expects dime-store displays, then that is what is appropriate and proper for that particular store. As stated earlier, know your target market.

9. A good display should be safe.   A creative in-store display that falls over on a child who is playing on it is no award winner. Displays can be dangerous. Retail stores should take special care not to develop displays which have the potential to hurt shoppers. A display of electric shop tools should have no provision for plugging in such tools. A six-year-old may plug in a saw and proceed to cut his finger off. Knives should be displayed only in a locked case for the same reason. Safety also is concerned with the materials used in the display. Avoid glass if at all possible. A woman was going through a store with a shopping cart when her cart hit a very futuristic looking glass case. The results were disastrous. Fortunately, no one was hurt seriously. The display case should have been made of shatterproof glass or even plastic to avoid the problem. Many stands for mannequins are found to be made of glass. What if two children get

Figure 21–5

Balance is an important aspect of display.

Formal Balance

No Balance

on such a stand and begin to jump up and down? The retailer is taking a gamble when it is assumed that the glass will not break.

Safety problems also stem from the fact that displays by their nature are not very sturdy. The retailer should work on this problem. If a mannequin is near a traffic area, chances are good that the mannequin is going to be hit. In designing the display, the retailer should plan for this. One answer would be to attach the mannequin to the ceiling with the use of monofilament fishing line. If this is done then the mannequin should only wobble slightly when hit instead of falling over.

One other area of concern is the point-of-purchase display. Is the display safe? Can the customer get the item without difficulty? In a china department, for example, the plate and cup and saucer of many patterns are displayed on little stands on a shelf around the department. A customer comes to buy and in the process wants to see several patterns up close. Can the customer or the salesclerk reach them without a high level of risk that something will get broken? The china display may be attractive and distinctive from a distance, but is it practical from a safety standpoint? Merchandise that is stacked too high or in a haphazard manner can also be a problem. Even the home appliance display that features a microwave oven can be dangerous if someone attempts to operate it in an improper manner or to pick it up only to drop it on the customer's foot. The potential for danger is great in a store. Even more so if the store is of a self-service variety. The retailer must be alert to the problem of safety. No one can probably eliminate display-related accidents in a store, but conscientious effort in this area should result in a reduction of such incidents.

10. A good display should be secure.   A display puts merchandise in its best light in order to make the customer want the item. Of course, the idea is for the customer to buy the item not to steal it. Several ideas that have been used to achieve an attractive display with minimum security problems are the following:

(a) When displaying shoes, gloves, and other items that come in pairs display only one. Most people have little need for one shoe.

(b) Display merchandise in a set pattern. It will be obvious to all if something is missing. For example, perfume can be displayed in a fan shape on the counter. If something is removed, the fan pattern will reveal it. Many "shoppers" will put back the item once they observe that it will be obvious to the store personnel that the item is missing.

(c) Never use expensive items when cheap merchandise will do the job. Putting $50 cufflinks on a mannequin when cheap ones or even buttons will do is not being security conscious.

(d) Never drape things on chairs or on the arms of mannequins without attaching them firmly to the display. More than one display has been rearranged by a "shopper" who was trying to lift a coat off the mannequin's arm only to find that the coat was pinned to the rest of the display.

(e) Use enclosed cases in less secure areas. A store would not put a display in a window that has no glass on the outside to make it secure. Displays in stairwells, near and in elevators, and other similar areas should likewise be developed within enclosed cases. It is too easy for a customer to steal if it is felt that he or she has privacy. A stairwell may give this privacy. Displays in less secure areas should be planned with great care.

TYPES OF DISPLAY

Throughout this chapter mention has been made of displays of various types. These displays fall into three categories: window, interior, and point-of-purchase. Each of these categories will be discussed in terms of their own particular characteristics.

Window Displays

Display windows, whether open or closed back, are an integral part of the exterior of the store.[7] If such windows are available, they should be used with great care. Window displays are generally of one of three types: promotional, institutional, or public service.

Promotional windows sell merchandise. Institutional windows sell the store. Public service windows sell items and ideas not related to the store. A promotional window is what most people think of when they think of a window display (Figure 21-6). A dress in the window of a clothing store or various hand tools in a hardware store window are two examples of a promotional display. Santa Claus in the window during the Christmas season would be an institutional display. Several times during the day Santa Claus would demonstrate toys and other items and then invite all to come into the store and see him. A public service display would be a window that features the Girl Scout program or the American Red Cross blood donor program or other things of this nature. Stores with numerous windows have been known to devote one window completely to public service purposes. Each new two-week period finds a different organization featured in the window.

The design of any one window should be developed in light of the rest of the window displays. It is amazing what the effect can be if, for example, all the windows of a clothing store feature the same color. For purposes of illustration, imagine a store that has 12 windows across the front featuring a different bright yellow spring dress in each. The visual impact of seeing these windows at a distance is perhaps even greater than seeing the windows up close. For these same 12 windows during the Christmas season, each could feature one of the 12 days of Christmas as sung about in the popular song of the same name. Other uses of the 12 windows taken as a group are infinite. In developing window displays, the retailer should consider the total visual impact of all the windows taken collectively as well as the individual requirements of each window.

Figure 21-6

A promotional window display telling the public that Filene's has Neiman-Marcus merchandise in its famous Bargain Basement.

(Courtesy of Filene's)

Interior Displays

Whenever practical, interior displays should reflect stocks that cannot be seen—the countless items that are hidden in warehouses, stockrooms, or in drawers of the departments of the store.[8] Other functions of interior display include departmental identification, direct promotion of merchandise, and the presentation of the store's personality. Depending on their application, interior displays may, therefore, also have a promotional, institutional, or public service function in the same manner as window displays. To achieve these functions, interior displays are set up in different places. Some of the common places are:

> Wall displays/wall signs—*common in large, one-floor stores (Figure 21-7).*
> Aisle displays—*mannequin at end of each aisle of clothing.*
> Ledge displays—*near escalator or behind counters in "O" arrangement.*
> Post displays/post signs—*common in stores with many posts that support the roof.*

Figure 21–7

The customer search process is aided by interior displays such as wall displays/wall signs.

(Courtesy of Giant Food, Inc.)

Interior displays may feature products from many different departments if located in a major traffic location within the store or may just involve the products of one department if found at the entrance to that department. No matter where they are located, interior displays help to develop a particular atmosphere or personality within the store. Many stores sell essentially the same merchandise, so why do customers prefer one store over another? One very common response to such a question is that the customer just likes the looks of that store. Such an answer reflects a successful program of interior display.

Point-of-Purchase Displays

Along with interior displays, point-of-purchase displays are considered to be in-store displays. The distinction between the two is the amount of direct customer involvement. Point-of-purchase displays are just what their name implies. The display is on or near the point of sale. In many cases, it will even physically hold the merchandise that is being presented to the customer. The difference between an interior display and a point-of-purchase display can be illustrated with the following example. A display at the entrance to the hosiery department featuring several mannequins wearing Hanes pantyhose is an interior display. The counter where Hanes pantyhose are sold with its boxes, signs, and so on is the point-of-purchase display.

By virtue of their location, point-of-purchase displays are the last chance to influence consumer behavior. It is for this reason that so many vendors make every effort to get retailers to use promotional material for point-of-purchase purposes that feature their products. The stakes are high since studies show that point-of-purchase displays do sell products. For example, in one such study, conducted by *Progressive Grocer*, the use of a display featuring a drain cleaner (Sani-Flush) resulted in 170 percent more sales for participating stores as compared with stores where the point-of-purchase display was not used. A Campbell soup display resulted in sales of 125 percent above normal in the same study.[9] In another study conducted by the Point-of-Purchase Advertising Institute and the Du Pont Company, it was found that almost one out of two purchases in supermarkets are unplanned or impulse purchases.[10] The message for the retailer should be clear. By presenting items in a favorable manner at the point of sale, the retailer should improve upon the store's performance. Why? A good point-of-purchase display will aid in projecting the merchandise in front of the customer.

Point-of-purchase displays take many forms (Figure 21–8). Some of these forms are the following:

Cutouts. A cutout is a manufacturer-supplied point-of-purchase display that is usually made out of cardboard or some other nonpermanent material. As a display, it will have to be put together by the vendor representative or by the store's own personnel. In some cases, the cutout is the same as the shipping carton. In these cases, in

Figure 21–8

Point-of-purchase displays feature products at the point of decision. A point-of-purchase display may be a display, as on right, that features many products. Or it may be a display like the L'eggs display on the left that features only one product line.

(Courtesy of Gold Circle Discount Stores.)

particular, the store's personnel should be instructed to follow directions on the box very carefully so that the display will not be destroyed in the process of getting to the merchandise.

Dump Displays.   When merchandise is "thrown" into a bin or box or even a cutout, so that the merchandise appears to be laying in a pile, this is a dump display. An expensive shoe store may choose to use a dump display for its end-of-the-year clearance sale. All sale shoes will be taken out of boxes and "dumped" on a table or on the floor. Some of the area's most prominent women will be seen digging into the pile for the best savings of the year. Because it projects a bargain image, a dump display is a very popular display technique for sale merchandise.

Merchandise Racks.   Racks may be permanent (L'eggs hosiery, Ever-Ready batteries, General Electric light bulbs) or disposable (chewing gum or candy boxes at checkout). Many manufacturers strongly encourage the use of racks in stores because racks make the vendor's merchandise stand out from the competition. In fact, some vendors want merchandise racks in stores so much that they will pay the retailer in cash and/or merchandise for their use. Although such offers can be attractive, the retailer should guard against accepting every offer that comes along. A store with too many merchandise racks looks like a store that sells merchandise racks.

Audiovisual Displays.   The shopper in men's wear learns that a particular brand of pants fits better because of a new type of fabric. How? By watching and listening to an audiovisual display. Clothing, appliances, and sporting goods are three areas where such displays are popular. Although in most cases the audiovisual displays are manufacturer-supplied, the retailer should be careful not to accept too many of them for use in the store. Too many can overpower the background music of the store as well as become only baby-sitters for children. Also, most customers are less likely to stand there and watch the sales message if other displays are also operating close by.

Signs.   The importance of signs as a point-of-purchase promotional device should not be underestimated just because they are quite easy to work with as compared with other forms of display. A good sign can help to close the sale. A poor sign can turn the customer off at the last minute. When talking about the quality of a point-of-purchase sign or any display sign, it should be noted that a sign's impact on the customer is influenced by the number of signs that are placed before the customer. If a customer walks down a merchandise aisle and sees 25 signs, does the customer really see any of them? Too many signs hurt the quality of any sign as a promotional tool. In addition, two other aspects of signing should be considered: physical quality and message quality. Both are vital to a good sign.

Physical Quality of Sign.   What does the sign look like? Does it look professional or does it look like it was prepared by a six-year-old in a hurry? Most people do not print or write very well. For this reason, a "homemade" sign usually leaves something to be desired from both readability and store image standpoints. For a retailer there is really no excuse for such ill-prepared signs. Sign machines such as those made available under the names Showcard and Printasign[11] provide the retailer with a means to produce quality signs at a reasonable price (Figure 21–9). For stores that do not wish to purchase such sign machines, sign-making kits, stick-on and rub-on

Figure 21-9

Signs for a display can be made by machine.

(Courtesy of Reynolds Printasign Company.)

letters, stencils, and even free-lance artists are available. Signs are important. They should be neat, clean, and fresh in their appearance. The retailer should take whatever measures are necessary to ensure that the physical quality of the sign does not detract from the message of the display.

Message Quality of Sign. What does the sign say? Does it read:

Shoes	or	Back-to-School Fashions
Sale	or	Save Now for Fall
Diamonds	or	Give a Gift of Love
Save	or	10 Cents Off Regular Price

The message on a display sign should be viewed as reason-to-buy copy. The display caught the customer's attention. The sign now takes over in an attempt to close the sale. The merchant should remember that the message does not have to be long. It might tie in with the theme promotion in use in the store. It might tie in with the advertising copy currently being run by the store. The message can be developed in many ways. For any situation, however, the message should not be developed in a haphazard manner. Just remember that the sign on the display may influence a sale.

Anything that can do that is important. Time spent on improving the message quality of display signs is time well spent.

Products. The various point-of-purchase display forms discussed all serve to draw attention to the product that is for sale. The merchandise rack or dump display, for example, holds the item while the sign above the display tells about it. But what does the product itself look like? In a dump display, part of the eye appeal is the pile of merchandise. In other words, the retailer wants the display to look like the merchandise was dumped in the bin or in a pile. On the other hand, if the point-of-purchase display is supposed to be neat with all labels lined up in a particular way, then that display will also have eye appeal and will attract attention in its own way. A look at Figure 21–10 reveals the eye-catching attractiveness of a display that is not unusual in any way except that it is straight and orderly. The retailer must realize that orderly displays of merchandise do not happen without encouragement from management. Such displays will also have to be put back in order over time as customers "mess them up" as they pick up merchandise and examine products. A good display program will direct employees to use their "free" time to straighten the store's merchandise displays. There is no question that orderly displays are pleasing to the eye. There is also little doubt that displays that are pleasing to the eye promote sales.

Figure 21–10

A point-of-purchase display that consists primarily of the product itself can have impact due to the fact that it is straight and orderly.

(Courtesy of Safeway)

Four "I's" of Point-of-Purchase Advertising. From the discussion, it becomes clear that a good point-of-purchase display is no accident. To provide guidance to the retailer who wishes to strive for excellence in point-of-purchase displays, the four "I's" or elements of point-of-purchase advertising that should be a part of every retail display are presented for consideration.

Impact. The point-of-purchase display should grab the shopper's attention.
Identification. The point-of-purchase display should provide bold, vivid evidence as to what the product is.
Information. The point-of-purchase display should tell the customer what is needed and wanted in terms of information.
Imagery. The point-of-purchase display should provide the impression that what is being sold is relevant to the customer as it says, "Buy me!"[12]

It is unfortunate but most retail point-of-purchase displays neither *M*ake *A S*trong *S*tatement as talked about earlier in the chapter nor fulfill the requirements for the four "I's" of point-of-purchase advertising. What that means, of course, is that the impact of those that do is great. It will pay the retailer to work on having good point-of-purchase displays. Why? The result of such efforts should be reflected in increased sales.

DISPLAY MANAGEMENT

Proper management of the display function is essential if a store is to get the most out of its display program. All displays should be coordinated with each other and with the other parts of the promotional program. Funds must be budgeted to ensure that display plans can become a reality. Budgeting procedures that are similar to those discussed in the advertising chapter should be instituted to accomplish this objective. Personnel who are properly trained in the area of display should be hired. If size does not permit such specialization, every effort should be made to have a current employee take courses or do some special reading in the area of display. A good display program requires the commitment of everyone in the store from owner and manager on down. Good displays do not just happen.

SUMMARY

A retail display is a nonpersonal presentation of merchandise and/or information to the target market that takes place within the physical environment of the store. Advantages of display include the fact that it involves little risk, operates at the point of sale, presents merchandise "live," and attracts viewers at little or no cost. As for what to display, the retailer should remember to *M*ake *A S*trong *S*tatement with whatever is chosen to ensure proper merchandise projection. Advertised merchandise, fashion items, impulse products, high-margin items, and best-selling merchandise are possibilities along with items that have visual attractiveness as well as those that hold the interest of the target market. A good display has a theme, is distinctive, is appropriate, is neat, provides information, is simple, shows merchandise in use, conveys the appropriate store image, is safe, and is secure. Types of displays include window displays (promotional, institutional, and public service), interior displays (wall, aisle, ledge, and post), and point-of-purchase (cutouts, dumps, merchandise racks, audiovisuals, signs, and the product itself). The importance of signs is emphasized since both the physical quality and the message quality of the display sign play such important roles in the success or failure of all types of display. Getting displays created, funded, and coordinated is the job of the retail manager. A good display program is no accident.

DISCUSSION QUESTIONS

1. Why is display used in the retail store? Cite at least five reasons in your answer.
2. Explain M.A.S.S. and merchandise projection.
3. What types of merchandise might be considered for use in a retail display?
4. List and explain briefly the ten guidelines to follow in determining what makes a good display. Cite local display examples that illustrate or violate each of the guidelines.
5. Are retailers concerned with having displays that are safe and secure? Talk to local retailers about their efforts, if any, to accomplish this goal.
6. What are the three types of window display? Cite examples of each type from your own experience.
7. What is meant by physical quality of a sign? message quality of a sign? Why are such things important to a retailer?
8. Go to a small store and a large store in your area and determine if they have ongoing programs of display management. What differences do you observe between the two organizations?
9. In your opinion, are local point-of-purchase displays effective as measured by the four "I's" of point-of-purchase advertising? Cite examples to explain your answer.
10. What is display? How does it rank in terms of importance with other parts of the store's promotional program?

NOTES

[1] Winthrop B. Frye, "Better Displays—A Sales Stimulant," *Journal of Retailing*, Vol. 9, no. 1 (April 1933), p. 15.

[2] Donald L. Belden, *The Role of the Buyer in Mass Merchandising* (New York: Chain Store Publishing Corporation, 1971), p. 142.

[3] *The Buyer's Manual*, rev. ed. (New York: National Retail Merchants Association, 1965), p. 353.

[4] For additional information on retail display, see *Visual Merchandising* (New York: National Retail Merchants Association, 1976).

[5] Discussion based in part on display program in use by G. Fox and Company, Hartford, Connecticut.

[6] For examples of distinctive displays, see Emily M. Mauger, *Modern Display Techniques* (New York: Fairchild Publications, Inc., 1964), pp. 85–117.

[7] For window display ideas, see Shirley Joel, *Fairchild's Book of Window Display* (New York: Fairchild Publications, Inc., 1973).

[8] *The Buyer's Manual*, p. 321.

[9] "How to Make Displays More Sales Productive," *Progressive Grocer*, Vol. 50, no. 2 (February 1971), p. 38.

[10] Louis J. Haugh, "Buying-Habits Study Update: Average Purchase Up 121%," *Advertising Age*, Vol. 48, no. 26 (June 27, 1977), p. 58.

[11] *Showcard*—Showcard Machine Company, Chicago, Illinois. *Printasign*—Reynolds Printasign Company, Pacoima, California.

[12] Orville C. Ottow, remarks at awards presentation, Point-of-Purchase Advertising Institute, Chicago, Illinois, February 15, 1977. Mr. Ottow is past chairman of the Point-of-Purchase Advertising Institute and is vice president of Tri-Pack Corporation, Chicago, Illinois.

SECTION **VI**

Customer Service

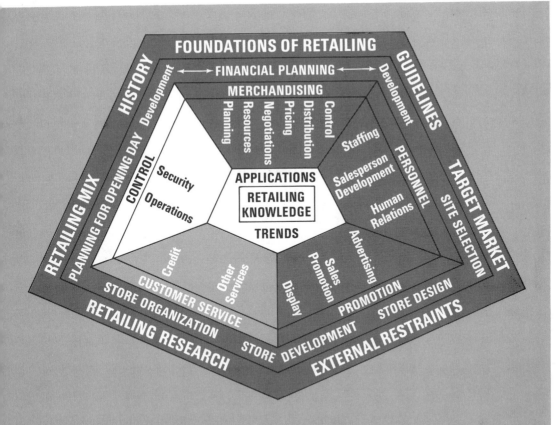

Customer service encompasses the area of retail credit along with other forms of customer service.

"Retail Credit" asks the question, "Should a store offer credit?" Credit laws and regulations, forms of credit, credit as a selling tool, collection, and various aspects of credit management are also examined.

"Other Forms of Customer Service" studies service objectives, factors that determine the type of service to be offered, and whether the service should be for free or fee. Delivery, alterations, package wrap, and the handling of complaints and adjustments are among the services discussed.

CHAPTER 22

Retail Credit

BUGS BUNNY

Reprinted by permission of NEA. © 1978 by Warner Bros. Inc.

"Will that be cash or charge?" "Charge." "Fine, now will you be using Master Card, Visa, American Express, or our own card?" "I think I will use the 30-day charge plan or maybe even put it on layaway." In the modern retail store credit is a way of life. For most stores, it is not a question of whether or not to offer credit. The only question is what kind. As in the situation given, some stores have so many different plans that it is difficult at times to keep them all straight. Why do stores offer so many credit options? Customers expect it. Most customers today even require it if they are going to be able to buy the things they want and need. In today's world, credit is not considered a differential advantage. It is, instead, viewed by most as a necessity.

Credit is defined as a medium of exchange of limited acceptance.[1] Credit or a promise to pay is exchanged by the customer for the product or service that is offered by the store. Do stores give credit? Not really. Stores actually accept credit. Such acceptance is by necessity accompanied by risks. It is for this reason that the acceptance of credit is limited. A person's *character*, *capital* (assets), and *capacity* (earning power) along with the market *conditions* surrounding the transaction all influence the amount of credit to be accepted by the store. These so-called four "C's" of Credit are by their nature quite dynamic. The amount of credit to be accepted is, thereby, also very flexible. Credit is intangible. A consumer may have much credit one minute and none the next due to many reasons that can range from the customer losing his or her job to a change in a store's credit policy.

Should a particular store offer credit? How do laws and regulations affect retail credit? What different forms of credit can the retailer make available to the consumer? Can credit be a selling tool? What about the problem of collection? Credit Management—How can the operation of the credit function be improved? Answers to these questions should provide the merchant with the information needed to build a strong credit operation within the store—a desirable asset in any retail organization.

SHOULD A STORE OFFER CREDIT?

Offering credit in the retail store is not a recent phenomenon. Records have been found of credit transactions entered on clay tablets in the Biblical city of Ur that date back to 2000 B.C.[2] As noted in Chapter 1, the early general store in the United States also accepted credit as a means of carrying the farmer until harvest time. Although history shows that credit has been a part of retailing for a long time, such a history does not require the modern store to offer all forms of credit or even offer credit. Every store should examine very carefully its target market to determine how they view credit. In addition, the impact of credit on the store's overall operation should be studied.[3]

Target Market

What about the target market? Do they want credit? Why do customers use credit? Reasons that customers have given for using credit include:[4]

> *Makes shopping easier and more convenient.*
> *Enables one to establish a credit rating.*

Allows one to buy without readily available funds.
Eliminates the need to carry cash.
Makes it easier to exchange or return merchandise.
Provides a record of purchases and payments for budget purposes.
Makes telephone and mail-order shopping easier.
Is a status symbol.
Enables one to be identified as a regular customer.
Enables one to receive advance notices of sales and other promotional infor-
mation.

On the other hand, customers who do not like credit cite many reasons for not using it including:[5]

Makes buying too easy.
Is wrong to go into debt.
Is better to wait and pay cash.
Is expensive.
Is dangerous since someone else may put an item on your account.
Is only for those with full-time work or substantial income.
Is difficult to carry a wallet full of credit cards.
Limits bargain hunting since credit customers tend to buy only at stores that
offer credit.

Because customers' views on the use of credit do differ widely, understanding the feelings of the store's target market is important in deciding on whether to offer credit. Can or will a customer buy if the store does not offer credit? This difficult question must be answered by the retailer.

Competition

Do other stores offer credit? If "yes," what kind? If all other competing stores offer credit, the retailer must normally also offer credit unless some other factor such as lower prices or better merchandise assortment can outweigh the importance of credit in the consumer's mind. In most cases, credit of some type will be required to be competitive.

Type of Goods

The more expensive the item, the more important credit is to the customer. "Big-ticket" items almost require credit. Few cars or appliances could be sold without it. Other types of goods are also finding a use for credit. Even food stores, the last major holdout against bank cards, are now using such a credit plan. Because food stores have experienced much trouble with checks (some checks have turned out to be long-term loans), many are now accepting bank cards as a means of reducing the financial and administrative burden of personal checks.[6]

Size and Type of Community

The smaller the community the more personal will be the relationship between customer and store. That is not always good. The retailer must remember that it is just as hard to collect from friends. Is the community a union town with the possibility of a strike? Strikes affect one's ability to pay. Agricultural communities have good years and bad years. If the orange trees in Florida are damaged due to cold weather, the grower has few oranges to sell. He, in turn, has little money with which to pay bills.

Effect on Sales and Profits

Unless competition requires it, no store would normally offer credit to customers just to increase sales. Profits should also rise. Credit creates administrative problems. A profitable reward is, it is hoped, in the offing for those who develop such a program.

Cost of Operation

Any generalization about the cost of various credit alternatives can be dangerous. Such costs should not, however, be overlooked because they are not readily ascertained.[7] Items for possible consideration in examining credit cost include the cost of credit investigations, capital invested in accounts receivable, bad-debt expense, as well as out-of-pocket expenses associated with running the credit department. Although the credit function may generate some income through the collection of finance charges, only in rare instances will the direct revenue from credit exceed the direct costs. Credit pays its way through increased sales and the profits that result.

CREDIT LAWS AND REGULATIONS

The period beginning in the late 1960s up to the present will probably go down in history as the era of the consumer. This feeling is reflected in many ways, one of which is the various laws and regulations that have been passed pertaining to consumer credit. Some of these laws and regulations are (Figure 22–1):

Figure 22–1

Federal credit laws and regulations.

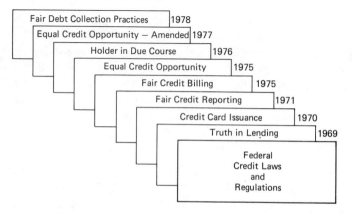

Truth in Lending (1969)[8]

The purpose of Truth in Lending, which went into effect on July 1, 1969, was to assure a meaningful disclosure of credit terms so that the consumer would be able to compare more readily the various credit terms available and to avoid the uninformed use of credit. For the retailer, Truth in Lending means many things. For example:

All credit terms and conditions must be disclosed to the consumer before an account is opened.
Interest rates must be quoted at the annual rate, not just a nominal rate. For an example, see Figure 22-2.
All credit terms must be disclosed in an ad or none disclosed at all.

It should be noted that Truth in Lending does not require that interest be charged or determine the amount if interest is charged. Its only concern is disclosure. Some retailers are under the impression that they must charge a certain percentage due to Truth in Lending. Such is not the case. Another misconception some retailers have is that because of Truth in Lending consumers now shop for credit. Studies reveal little credit consciousness in the marketplace.[9]

Credit Card Issuance (1970)[10]

For those retailers who wish to issue their own credit cards, Title V of the Consumer Credit Protection Act states "that no credit card shall be issued except in response to a request or application therefor." Retailers can no longer send out unsolicited credit cards to prospective customers. Also affected is the credit liability of the cardholder. If the card is lost or stolen, the customer's liability is limited to the first $50 of unauthor-

Figure 22-2

Interest rate calculations.

Situation – $400 Oven Purchase with $24 Service Charge to be Paid in 6 Monthly Payments

$$\text{Nominal Rate} = \frac{\text{Service Charge}}{\text{Amount to be Financed}}$$

$$6\% = \frac{\$24}{\$400}$$

$$\text{Nominal Annual Rate} = \frac{\text{Nominal Rate}}{\text{Time Involved in Units}} \times \text{Time Units in Year}$$

$$12\% = \frac{6\%}{6 \text{ Months}} \times 12 \text{ Months in a Year}$$

$${}^*\text{True Annual Rate} = \frac{\text{Nominal Annual Rate} \times 2 \text{ (number of installments)}}{\text{Number of Installments} + 1}$$

$$20.57\% = \frac{12\% \times 2 (6)}{6 + 1}$$

*Disclosure required by Truth in Lending Law.

ized purchases. In addition, if the retailer does not provide the customer with a postage paid card or other means to notify the store in writing in case of loss of the card, the customer has no liability for such card misuse. In such a situation the retailer must assume the total liability.

Fair Credit Reporting (1971)[11]

A retailer may not procure or cause to be prepared a consumer report on a consumer unless it is clearly and accurately disclosed to the consumer that an investigative consumer report including information as to the customer's character, general reputation, personal characteristics, and mode of living, whichever are applicable, may be made. Such disclosure must be made in writing no later than three days after the date it was first requested. This type of investigative report should not be confused with a routine credit request that relies primarily on the ledger experience of creditors. A retailer who sells big-ticket items will probably have greater concern for this Act than will other merchants due to the need for more in-depth credit information before a credit decision can be made.

Fair Credit Billing (1975)[12]

The purpose of this act is to protect the consumer against inaccurate and unfair billing and credit card practices. Provisions of the Act include:

> Within 60 days of the receipt of an account statement, a customer has the right to notify a retailer in writing that an error exists in the statement. The retailer has 30 days in which to respond and an additional 60 days in which to make any corrections in the statement if errors are, in fact, present or to inform the customer that the statement is correct. During the 90-day period no legal steps may be taken against the customer for nonpayment. Failure to follow this procedure may result in the retailer not being able to collect all or part of the bill even if the retailer's records turn out to be correct.
> Payments on account must be posted promptly when received to avoid billing for unnecessary finance charges.
> Returns on account must be handled promptly by all parties to avoid billing for unnecessary finance charges.
> Discounts for paying with cash given by a retailer to a customer cannot be prohibited by third-party credit card issuers such as bank card firms.
> A bank cannot require a retail store to have a bank account in that particular bank to have the use of that bank's credit card.

Equal Credit Opportunity (1975)[13]

Simply put, the Act makes it unlawful for any retailer to discriminate against any credit applicant on the basis of sex or marital status with respect to any aspect of a credit transaction. Provisions of the Act and its accompanying Regulation B include:

> If each marriage partner requests a separate account, such accounts may not be treated as one for any purpose.

> *Joint accounts (husband and wife) must be maintained in the names of both husband and wife.*
>
> *A credit evaluation system in use by a store may not automatically give more value to a particular sex or favor married people over single credit applicants or vice versa.*
>
> *A creditor can no longer ask the female credit applicant about her plans for a family or her method of birth control.*
>
> *Alimony and child support payments must be considered as income for credit purposes by the retail store if the applicant wishes to reveal such facts. The applicant is not required to disclose such information.*
>
> *A creditor shall provide each person who is denied credit or whose account is terminated the reasons for such actions, if the applicant so requests.*

Equal Credit Opportunity as Amended (1977)[14]

As amended, the Equal Credit Opportunity Act went on to prohibit credit discrimination due to race, color, religion, national origin, or age in addition to marital status and sex. Extreme care should be taken by the retailer not to make any arbitrary use of demographic information in the determination of credit worthiness. Each person is an individual. Both Equal Credit Opportunity Acts make it illegal for the retailer, or for any business for that matter, to use automatic credit decision rules that are based on group data.

Fair Debt Collection Practices (1978)[15]

The purpose of this law is to protect the consumer against the use of abusive, deceptive, and/or unfair debt collection practices. In an attempt to accomplish this objective, the Act prohibits such actions as:

> *Any collection effort between the hours of 9 P.M. and 8 A.M.*
>
> *The public publication of any list of customers who allegedly refuse to pay debts.*
>
> *The advertisement for sale of any debt to coerce payment of the debt.*
>
> *The use of obscene or profane language during the collection process.*
>
> *The use or threat of use of violence during the collection process.*
>
> *The use of postcards as a method of communicating with the consumer regarding any debt.*
>
> *The false representation that any individual is an attorney or that any communication is from an attorney.*
>
> *The collection of any special fees or charges unless such amounts are authorized by the agreement creating the debt or are permitted by law.*

Holder in Due Course (1976)

In addition to the various laws in the area of consumer credit, numerous regulations have also been put into effect that have had an influence on the retailer. Of all such provisions that have been instituted at either the state or federal level, the one with possibly the greatest impact for many retailers has been the adoption of the Holder in

Due Course rule by the Federal Trade Commission. Up until the adoption of this regulation, which became effective on May 14, 1976, a consumer had to honor his or her obligation to a creditor (for example—a finance company) regardless of any dispute with the seller (for example—the automobile retailer). For illustration purposes, assume that a consumer bought a car on credit from a retailer, only to find out later that the retailer had sold the note to a bank or other sales financing organization. If the car failed to operate the day after purchase, the consumer would react by just not paying for the car as a means of leverage to get the car fixed. Up until May 14, 1976, such leverage was not possible since the retailer no longer was financially involved. The rule is intended to ensure consumers of a continuing right to raise claims and defenses based on misconduct by sellers including breach of contract, breach of warranty, misrepresentation, or fraud.[16] Any third-party contract holder is now subject to all claims and defenses that the debtor could assert against the seller. What this provision means for the retailer is that the risks of the third-party lender have now increased. With higher risks, the discount (the difference between the face value of the note and the amount received by the retailer) for such loans will tend to be higher, thereby cutting into the profit margin of the store.

FORMS OF CREDIT

Due to the various possible combinations of the several types of credit, the actual number of forms of credit available to a retailer are infinite. By separating these plans into categories, however, five distinct credit arrangements (charge, revolving, layaway, installment, third party) are found for possible use in a retail store.

Charge Account Plan

With no interest or carrying charge, the charge account plan is popular with most customers. The period of payment is generally 30 days, but some stores offer up to 90 days or even longer before the bill becomes due. For the retailer, the drawback to this plan is that no income is derived from the credit operation and no financial incentive (carrying charge) is given the customer to pay even when due. Stores that seek a prestige image often use a charge account plan since such a plan is becoming less common in stores that seek mass appeal. Many small stores also use such a plan as a differential advantage over their competitors. Customers really like charge account plans when the date is 60 days away or more. The 30-day charge has no unique attraction since almost any credit plan permits full payment within 30 days without penalty.

Revolving Charge Plan

Revolving charge plans have evolved from a plan that originated with Wanamaker's of Philadelphia in 1938. The plan called for four monthly payments to pay off any amount. No interest or service charges were incurred. Building on this idea, J. L. Hudson's Department Store in Detroit in May 1956 first introduced the revolving plan with an option to pay in full within 30 days without a finance charge or to pay a set amount and extend the balance with a finance charge being added to the amount.[17] The revolving plan with option terms is probably the most popular form of retail credit in use today. Both Sears and J. C. Penney, for example, conduct most of their credit business with the use of such a plan.

Customers seem to like the idea of the revolving charge plan because it, as its name implies, gives them an option. In a tight month, the customer can pay a minimum amount (usually a sliding scale that averages about 10 percent of the balance) while in a good month, the customer can pay off the balance without penalty. The customer only pays finance charges when he or she opts to extend the payments. For a store the revolving plan can be a revenue producer by means of service charges. A revolving plan's greatest asset, however, is that it "makes" the customer buy more since it is set up to spread the payments over time. A customer who has run up a $1,000 balance, only owes $100 at the end of the month under a typical revolving plan. The customer can pay $1,000 as under a 30-day charge plan but under revolving charge, only $100 is actually owed at that time. Such plans do wonders during the Christmas season and other peak times to aid in the selling of merchandise. One other consideration for the retailer is the cash flow situation that is set up whenever revolving credit plans are utilized. Under most plans, the $1,000 amount mentioned in the example may be paid off as agreed over a ten-month period. Can the retailer afford to carry this credit for ten months? Most can, and want to, to earn the interest charges and to get the customer to add on more as the initial balance is reduced. For some, however, a financial hardship may occur. Such problems are more common with small stores but even the large store is not immune. One of the many reasons for the failure of the W. T. Grant Company is thought to have been the cash flow problem that occurred as a result of the amount owed to the chain under its revolving charge plan. Extended terms coupled with bad-debt losses can cause severe financial problems for a firm.

Layaway Plan

For the store that sells to a target market with a high credit risk, the layaway credit plan serves to reduce the risk to the store since the merchandise is held by the store until it is paid for. On the surface, it would appear that there are no risks to the retailer under such a plan. Unfortunately, risks are present. The greatest risk is the lost sales potential of the merchandise. A dress is put on layaway at the beginning of the selling season. Three months later, the customer decides she does not want it. Can the dress now be sold to someone else? Probably—but at a substantial markdown. Because of such risks, a down payment that is not refundable should be required for each item that is placed on layaway. Set amounts should be due on the item at intervals that correspond to the pay periods of the customer to encourage the purchase of the item. Many stores also add a monthly service charge to encourage the purchase of the item by the customer as soon as possible. Layaways can be a real problem for a store. A secure and sometimes large storage area is a necessity. Good records must also be kept in order to remove merchandise from layaway and put it back on sale as promptly as possible if the customer fails to make a payment. Keeping accurate records of payments can also eliminate many problems with customers who say they have made a payment while the store's records indicate they have not. A good layaway department is not handled in a haphazard manner. Layaways are a good marketing tool for selling to certain markets (for example, teenage and low income). For some situations, the layaway plan of credit may, in fact, be the *only* credit offered by the store. Even where other forms of credit are available layaways have their place and not always just for credit purposes. A father may buy a bicycle in October for his child for Christmas with the understanding that the merchant will store it by means of layaway until December 24. No retailer should automatically discount the possibility of using the layaway credit plan. It has many possible applications.

Installment Plan

The installment form of credit is the type of credit more commonly used by the retailer for the sale of big-ticket, durable items. It is an agreement for the purchase of a particular item with a predetermined number of payments and a finance charge added to the amount. Automobiles, appliances, and similar items are usually financed in this manner. Because the car or appliance or whatever generally serves as collateral under such an agreement, the amount of interest charged is usually not as great as under a revolving charge plan. In instituting an installment plan, adherence to the following installment credit principles will successfully serve the retailer and the customer alike.[18]

1. Installment sales should be limited to goods of high unit value that are consumed over a relatively long period.
2. The amount of the down payment should be sufficient to create a sense of ownership on the part of the consumer as well as large enough to provide for the initial depreciation of the item.
3. The amount of the regular payment must be relative to the financial condition of the consumer.
4. At no time should the unpaid balance be greater than the resale value of the item.
5. Time of payment should correlate with the consumer's pay period.
6. The length of the installment terms should be as short as possible.
7. Finance charges should be adequate so as to defray the costs of the installment transaction.
8. Security for the transaction in some form should be established (usually the item being purchased).
9. The customer should always be allowed to prepay in full the unpaid balance at any time without penalty.
10. Because of the typically large dollar amount and the length of time involved, the retailer should investigate the credit worthiness of the customer.

Under an installment sales agreement, repossesion of the goods as a result of nonpayment is possible. Few retailers gain much or win friends by having to perform such an unpleasant task. To get around this problem, many stores sell their installment contracts without recourse to sales finance companies at a discount—the rate being not as favorable as before the adoption of the Holder in Due Course Rule by the Federal Trade Commission.

Should a store accept Visa, Master Card, American Express, and the various other third-party credit plans as a supplement to in-house credit or even as a replacement for it? To make an intelligent decision, the retailer must first understand the operation of such third-party plans. Under a typical third-party agreement, the retailer will agree to:

1. Date each sales draft and to use the proper imprinter.
2. Not complete a transaction for an expired or stolen card.
3. Obtain credit authorization for any charge over a predetermined minimum amount.
4. Fill out legibly the sales draft by writing in a description of the merchandise—not just "miscellaneous merchandise."
5. Turn in to the third party all sales drafts within three business days.

Failure to follow these and other procedures will void the third party's obligation to pay the retailer for the sale. In practice most firms honor a sales draft, for example, with "miscellaneous merchandise" written on it, but the important thing for the merchant to know is that they do not have to do so. The typical third-party agreement is usually written in favor of the third party.

Along with the fine print in the agreement, another very important point of concern is the amount of discount that the third party will take for providing the card. The discount rate can run as high as 10 percent or more. Usual determinates of the discount schedule are:

1. Number of third-party credit transactions in store.
2. Average dollar value of third-party credit transactions in store.
3. Competition among third-party credit plans.
4. Use of third-party credit plan by target market.

In major market areas, for example, where competition among bank cards is heavy, the discount for a particular card may be as low as 2 or 3 percent or even lower. In other words, for each dollar charged on that card, the retailer receives 97 cents if the rate is 3 percent. The smart retailer will negotiate on the discount rate. Regardless of what the retailer may be told, there is no set rate.

In analyzing the cost versus benefit aspect of third party credit plans, stores in the past have assumed that the addition of bank cards, for example, would erode in-house credit sales. Some erosion is present, but studies indicate that bank card shoppers, in department stores at least, represent a different population since many do not carry an in-house card. Bank card users are found to be younger and more mobile than are their in-house counterparts. A store serving a transient or tourist market may reap great benefits from the acceptance of national bank cards.[19]

The retailer should also not forget the travel and entertainment cards. How does the average American Express ticket, for example, stack up against those of the bank card and store card? "Although bank card purchases tend to be higher than those charged on in-house accounts, the American Express ticket averages even higher," reports the vice president and treasurer of Thalhimer's department store.[20] Many stores feel that it pays to accept both bank and travel and entertainment cards.[21] The answer for a given store rests with the target market.

In order to examine all possibilities, one other third-party credit plan should be examined. This is a third-party plan where the store appears to be its own credit issuer as far as the customer is concerned but is in reality using a third-party plan. In addition to banks like Citibank that offer this private-label program, other firms, such as the General Electric Credit Corporation (GECC), also perform this credit service for numerous retailers. The GECC plan, for example, allows the retailer to set up a credit program that will fit the needs of that particular organization. As noted in Figure 22–3, some of the services offered are processing of credit applications, handling statement

Figure 22–3

A trade ad for a private-label credit plan.

(Courtesy of General Electric Credit Corporation.)

billings, and providing credit promotions to help the store build traffic and sales. If the retailer desires, even the people who work in the store's credit department will actually be employees of the "third party." Under this type of credit program, the entire credit operation can be assumed by the third party or only selected aspects of the program may be taken over.[22]

Statements and studies such as those cited make it appear that every store should accept a third-party credit plan of some type. The truth of the matter is that it is very difficult to really determine how much new incremental business and/or profit actually results from the adoption of a third-party credit plan. The use of a decision matrix for evaluating such an adoption (Figure 22–4) reveals that both gains and losses will probably result from such a decision. Is the adoption of a third-party plan in the long-run best interest of the retailer? Each retailer should answer this question only after a careful evaluation of the variables that interact in that particular retailing environment.[23]

USING CREDIT TO SELL

Credit is a tool of selling. The credit program of a store can be used to solicit more sales by encouraging new customers to buy on credit while at the same time giving reasons to present customers as to why they should buy more.

Figure 22–4

Decision matrix for evaluating the adoption of a third-party credit plan.

CURRENT CUSTOMER TYPE	CUSTOMER OUTCOMES				
	Cash Customer	Obtains Retailer Charge Card	Has or Obtains Third Party Card for Use Only at Retailer	Has or Obtains Third Party Card for Use at Retailer and Elsewhere	Converts to a Noncustomer
Cash Customer		(1) No Gain	(2) No Gain	(3) Possible Loss	(4) Loss
Retailer Charge Card User	(5) No Gain		(6) No Gain	(7) Possible Loss	(8) Loss
Noncustomer	(9) Gain	(10) Gain	(11) Gain	(12) Gain	

Adapted from J. Patrick Kelly and Paul J, Solomon, "A Decision Matrix for Adoption of Bank Credit Cards," *Retail Control*, Vol. 44 no. 3 (November 1975), p. 20.

New Customers

Why should a store make an effort to solicit new credit accounts? Soliciting credit customers can increase sales volume because as a group they are closely tied to those stores at which an active account is maintained, have less resistance to price, and have a tendency to buy a higher quality of merchandise.[24] Such solicitations can take many forms. Some of these are:

In-store booth where each passing customer is asked, "Do you have an account with us?"

Solicitation letter to each graduating senior, newlywed, new resident, or other potential customer groups.

Present customers are asked to recommend new customers. The present customers are given $5.00 in script to be applied against future purchases in the store for each name that results in an active account.

As noted earlier in the chapter, a store can no longer send out unsolicited credit cards. Therefore, all new account solicitations are aimed at getting the signed credit application. In most cases, the credit card will not be far behind.

Existing Customers

One of the greatest assets a store can have is a good paying credit customer. A store with many such customers has no need for third-party credit plans. Such a store also has a real gold mine for generating sales. Ways to encourage sales from good credit customers include:

Stuffers with the monthly statement that feature merchandise ideas (suggestion selling).

Private sales just for "preferred" customers.

Presale promotion aimed at giving first choice on sale merchandise to credit customers.

Discount certificate to be used during a slow month (for example—January) as a means of generating sales while making the credit customers feel goodwill toward the store.

It should be noted that firms lose some of the direct sales-generating power of credit when third-party credit of the type that is known to the customer is introduced to the store. For example, customers may lose part of their identity with the store when the bill comes from Visa as opposed to coming from the store where the merchandise was purchased. Statement stuffers cannot be sent with such a bill. A list of all customers who buy on credit at the store is also not available when customers use most third-party plans. On the other hand, collection is no problem for the store with a third-party plan. In addition, as mentioned earlier, third-party plans like Master Card and Diners Club may attract a different target market than may the store's in-house credit program. Although offering credit does create some risks, it can be used to create sales. Smart retailers view credit as a sales tool.

No sale is complete until the cash is in the drawer.[25] Collection is a necessary part of a good credit program. The ideal collection system would be one that solves the problem of the volume of work by being largely routine in operation. Such a system must also encourage promptness and regularity of payment. The reason for this is fourfold:

1. Possible correlation between length of time debts are unpaid and resulting volume of bad debt loss.
2. Slow collections result in the loss of future sales since people who owe will not or cannot buy more.
3. Lax collections give customers a bad image of the store.
4. Weak collections make customers buy beyond their means since they know the firm will probably not make an effort to collect.[26]

A routine collection system can take many forms. A suggested sequence to follow is given in Table 22-1. The four stages (impersonal routine, impersonal appeals, personalized appeals, and drastic or legal action) put teeth in the system yet give the customer ample opportunity to pay the debt. The retailer must never forget that along with a formal collection system a priceless ingredient is needed in collections. That ingredient is the personality of the credit worker.[27] If the customer is in temporary financial trouble, the merchant does not wish to lose the customer forever. Harsh collection procedures *will* lose the customer. The good credit worker makes an effort to sweeten a difficult situation. The employee attempts to work with the problem customer. Stores gain little when a customer is forced into bankruptcy. It will pay the store in most cases to be understanding of the customer's problem and to work on this problem *early*. A store with many accounts in stage 4 of the collection system has a credit and collection system in great difficulty.

CREDIT MANAGEMENT

A well-managed retail credit system does not just happen. Making the credit decision, setting credit limits, credit authorization, credit billing, and credit system evaluation are all decision areas that must be faced successfully if the credit system is to work.

Making the Credit Decision

The first step in making the credit decision is to collect information from the prospective credit customer using an application form that is in compliance with the various regulations as given earlier in the chapter (see Figure 22-5 for such a form). The local credit bureau may then be called. References may be checked. The credit decision is made on the basis of such information. Some stores, in a move to reduce the administrative workload of making the decision, use an automatic decision if the purchase is less than, for example, $25. The rule is—sell on credit up to $25; anything over

Table 22-1

General Collection System

Stage of System	Collection Devices Available for Use	Debtors Involved
Impersonal routine	Statements—1st, 2d, 3d, etc. Statement inserts and stickers Notes on statements Form letters of reminder type (Note: These refer only to devices used after expiration of credit period.)	Those awaiting notice Honestly overlooked Temporarily financially embarrassed Careless or procrastinating debtor
Impersonal appeals	Form letters appealing to: "Anything wrong" tone "Tell us your story" tone Pride in credit responsibilities Sense of fair play Seeking reply from debtor: Telephone Telegram Special letters: Registered Special delivery Trick reply	Honestly overlooked Careless or procrastinator Temporarily embarrassed Overbought Accident or misfortune Disputed account
Personalized appeals	Personal collector: Telephone Personal interview Personal letters to: Debtor Employer Credit bureau	Overbought Eventual insolvents Accident or misfortune Frauds—no intent to pay Disputed account
Drastic or legal action	Extension agreement Composition arrangement Collection agency Garnishment or wage assignment Repossession Attorney Suit Other actions	Same as debtors shown in the *personalized appeals* stage (all should have assets)

Source: Robert H. Cole, *Consumer and Commercial Credit Management,* 6th ed. (Homewood, Ill.: Richard D. Irwin, Inc., 1980), p. 342.

$25 is checked. If possible, a rapid credit decision is the best course to follow. It does not leave the customer waiting in the wings too long. In some cases, by the time the retailer decides on "Yes," the customer has decided on "No, I don't want the merchandise." Haste makes waste, but do not take forever to make a credit decision.

Setting Credit Limits

For an active account, how much can the customer charge? The answer is that account's credit limit. Most credit systems have a two-stage limit plan. The first is the automatic limit. For example, an account has a limit of $300. That limit does not mean that the customer cannot buy more than $300. It only means that the credit manager will have to evaluate the customer's situation before allowing this limit to be exceeded.

Figure 22-5

A credit application for a retail store.

JCPenney Charge Application

Signature				For Office Use Only		
Your Signature(s) mean(s) that you have read and agree to the terms of our Charge Account Agreement.	Applicant's Signature		Date	Store Number	**940869**	
	Co-Applicant's Signature		Date	Account Number		

General Information — (Please Print All Information)

					FLC	RI
Type Of Account You Want (Check One) □ Individual □ Joint	Have You Applied For An Account Before? Applicant □ Yes □ No Where When	Co-Applicant □ Yes □ No Where When			CBC	
					JCP-12	
Name Of Applicant To Whom Our Billing Statements Should Be Sent (First) (Initial) (Last)		Social Security Number	Date Of Birth / /	No. Of Dependent Children	J	I
Name of Co-Applicant (If Joint Account Requested) (First) (Initial) (Last)		Social Security Number	Date Of Birth / /	Relationship To Applicant	CL	Audit Code
Name And Relationship(s) To Applicant(s) Of Any Other Person(s) You Will Allow To Charge Purchases To Your Account (First) (Initial) (Last) (Relationship)					CBSC	

Information About Applicant To Whom Our Billing Statements Should Be Sent	**Information About Co-Applicant (If Joint Account Requested)**	Date	TB
Present Residence Address—Street	Present Residence Address—Street	CCID	
City, State Zip	City, State Zip	CCA	
Area Code & Phone Number ( )	How Long At This Address Yrs. Mos.	Monthly Mtge./Rent	Area Code & Phone Number ( )	How Long At This Address Yrs. Mos.	Monthly Mtge./Rent	CCAB	Date
Do You □ Own □ Rent □ Own Mobile Home □ Live With Parents □ Other (Please Specify)	Do You □ Own □ Rent □ Own Mobile Home □ Live With Parents □ Other (Please Specify)		
Former Address — Street How Long	Former Address — Street How Long		
City, State Zip	City, State Zip		
Employer's Name (Give Firm's Full Name) How Long	Employer's Name (Give Firm's Full Name) How Long		
Employer's Address Business Telephone	Employer's Address Business Telephone		
Type Of Business Present Position Monthly Salary	Type Of Business Present Position Monthly Salary		

You Need Not Furnish Alimony, Child Support Or Separate Maintenance Income Information If You Do Not Want Us To Consider It In Evaluating Your Application

Other Income — Source(s)	Amount (Monthly)	Other Income — Source(s)	Amount (Monthly)

Bank Accounts (Include Cp-Applicant's, If Joint Account Requested)

Bank — Branch	Account In The Name Of	Checking & Savings □	Checking □	Savings □	Loan □
1.					
Bank — Branch	Account In The Name Of	Checking & Savings □	Checking □	Savings □	Loan □
2.					

Credit References (Include Co-Applicant's, If Joint Account Requested)

Credit Cards (Include Loan Or Finance Companies)

Firm Name	Location	Account/Loan Number	Account/Loan In The Name Of
1.			
2.			
3.			

Personal Reference

Name Of Person Not Living At Address Of Applicant Or Co-Applicant	Relationship To Applicant	Present Residence Address

JCP-9500 (Rev. 10/80)   After completing application, detach at perforation, fold down from top, moisten flap, fold and seal. Postage paid by JCPenney.

(Courtesy of J. C. Penney Company, Inc.)

The second credit limit is the real limit. It is the amount, whatever it may be, that the customer cannot go over. The second and higher limit is usually not an automatic figure. The judgment of the credit manager determines the limit.

One decision for credit managers concerns the customer's knowledge of the credit limit. Should the store tell the customer what his or her credit limit is? Visa tells the limit. Many other credit plans do not. A store probably should not tell a customer the amount of credit that will be permitted. The reason is that many customers resent being told that they have limited credit. Most customers also do not understand that most such limits are first stage limits rather than their actual credit limit. In addition, it is difficult once you tell a customer that the credit limit is $300 to later lower that limit.

Retail Credit 423

There appears to be more advantages to not disclosing the credit limit than to revealing it to the customer.

Credit Authorization

The clerk makes the credit sale. How long does it take to get credit approval? Many stores have a floor limit of $25 to $50 meaning that any purchase made by a customer with proper identification that is under the limit does not have to be approved. Other stores with automated POS systems have the computer register automatically record the credit sale and authorize the sale after checking the customer's record. For other situations, an employee in the credit department will check the records when called from the sales floor. Two methods are used. The quicker method is to have a "bad file." If the customer is not listed, the charge is approved. The customer's file is not checked. The slower method is to check each file each time. Whether using an automated system or a manual one, speed and accuracy are important. A malfunctioning system that takes ten minutes for an authorization can lose a sale. Customers do not like waiting around while the store decides whether to sell to them or not.

Credit Billing

There are basically two ways to bill a customer. These are country club billing and descriptive billing. In the case of country club billing, the store sends along with the statement each month a copy of each sales ticket for examination by the customer. Such a procedure helps to reduce questions about the bill since the sales tickets refresh the memory of the customer. Descriptive billing does away with the practice of sending sales tickets. A description of each transaction is instead printed on the statement that is sent to the customer. Such a system requires less paperwork and saves on postage since no statement will probably cost more than the minimum postage for that type of mailing. Either system can be computerized for faster billing at less cost.[28]

The other major idea dealing with credit billing is the concept of cycle billing. Most retail stores use this approach. Basically, cycle billing involves spreading the work of the credit department throughout the month instead of mailing all statements on the first of each month. Cycle billing usually results in a more efficient credit operation.

Evaluation

Is a firm with no credit losses performing its credit function? What about a firm with a high bad-debt loss? In either case, a careful evaluation should be made to determine if the credit function is being carried out in a proper manner. It should be noted that an overly tight credit policy can hurt profits just as much as can an open-door policy. Credit should involve some risks. Since credit sales account for over half of all retail sales in department and specialty stores, and in other types of stores as well, and with the typical bad-debt loss being in the area of 0.5 percent of sales, it is estimated that at least $1 out of every $100 in credit sales will be uncollectible if a store's performance conforms to industry norms.[29] Considering the profit margin of many stores, the significance of a sound credit operation to the successful operation of a store becomes obvious. A careful study of credit should be undertaken by the retailer.

SUMMARY

Credit is defined as a medium of exchange of limited acceptance. In deciding whether or not to offer credit, a store should examine carefully its target market to determine how they view credit. In addition, the impact of credit on the store's overall operation should be studied. Credit laws and regulations dealing with Truth in Lending, credit cards, credit reporting, credit billing, equal credit opportunity, debt collection practices, and the Holder in Due Course clause all affect how the retail store will operate its credit department. The merchant should become familiar with such documents. Charge account, revolving charge, layaway, installment, and third party are all credit options that are available to the retailer. It is to the advantage of the retailer to know the characteristics of each. Moreover, the importance of credit availability should not be overlooked as a selling tool for new or current customers. Care should be exercised, however, in the granting of credit so that collection does not become the major part of the credit operation. A general collection system should in any event be designed to encourage early payment as a means of assisting with this problem. Other areas of concern to the credit department involve billing, credit limits, and credit authorizations along with making the credit decision. In all cases, the credit function should be evaluated to determine if the credit and collection operation is being conducted in a sound manner. Retail credit does cause the retailer many problems, but many sales are made possible by its use.

DISCUSSION QUESTIONS

1. Define credit. Explain your definition.
2. Should a store offer credit? Include in your discussion the ideas of retailers in your market area concerning this question.
3. How were the following credit areas affected by federal law?

   a. Credit billing   c. Credit cards
   b. Credit reporting   d. Equal credit

4. What was the purpose of Truth in Lending? Does the Law affect all retailers? How?
5. What is meant by the term Holder in Due Course? How did the 1976 Federal Trade Commission decision pertaining to the Holder in Due Course clause affect credit operations at the retail level?
6. Compare these forms of credit: charge account plan, revolving plan, and installment plan. Which plan is the best one for use in a retail store?
7. Layaways—why is this retail procedure considered a form of credit?

8. "Credit sells." Comment.
9. Go to a store in your area and determine what form of collection system is in use in the credit department. Compare it with the general collection system given in the chapter. Which is better?
10. Should credit limits be disclosed to the customer?
11. Country club billing versus descriptive billing—which is better?

NOTES

[1] Robert H. Cole, *Consumer and Commercial Credit Management*, 6th ed. (Homewood, Ill.: Richard D. Irwin, Inc., 1980), p. 5.

[2] *The Buyer's Manual*, rev. ed. (New York: National Retail Merchants Association, 1965), p. 370.

[3] Discussion taken in part from Robert H. Cole, *Consumer and Commercial Credit Management*, 6th ed., pp. 68–71.

[4] *The Buyer's Manual*, p. 372.

[5] Ibid., p. 373.

[6] "Using Credit Cards to Buy the Groceries," *Business Week*, 2356 (November 9, 1974), p. 50.

[7] Michael J. Etzel, "How Much Does Credit Cost the Small Merchant?", *Journal of Retailing*, Vol. 47, no. 2 (Summer 1971), pp. 59, 92.

[8] For more information, see U.S. Congress, *Consumer Credit Protection Act*, Public Law 321, 90th Cong., 2nd sess., 1968, and Board of Governors of the Federal Reserve System, *Truth in Lending—Regulation Z with amendments*, 1969 to the present.

[9] For further information on consumer credit awareness and Truth in Lending, see William H. Bolen, "The Impact of Truth in Lending on Revolving Credit Use," *The Credit World*, Vol. 61, no. 6 (March 1973), pp. 7–11, and "Consumer Awareness of Truth in Lending," *Business Ideas and Facts*, Vol. 7, no. 2 (Fall 1974), pp. 37–41.

[10] For more information, see U.S. Congress, *Consumer Credit Protection Act* (amendment), Public Law 508, 91st Cong., 2nd sess., 1970.

[11] Ibid.

[12] For more information, see U.S. Congress, *Consumer Credit Protection Act* (amendment), Public Law 495, 93rd Cong., 2nd sess., 1974.

[13] Ibid., and Board of Governors of the Federal Reserve System, *Equal Credit Opportunity—Regulation B with amendments*, 1975 to the present.

[14] U.S. Congress, *Consumer Credit Protection Act* (amendment), Public Law 239, 94th Cong., 2nd sess., 1976.

[15] For more information, see U.S. Congress, *Consumer Credit Protection Act* (amendment), Public Law 109, 95th Cong., 1st sess., 1977.

[16] Board of Commissioners, Federal Trade Commission, "FTC Adopts Holder in Due Course Rule," *The Credit World*, Vol. 64, no. 3 (December–January 1976), pp. 10–11.

[17] Robert H. Cole, *Consumer and Commercial Credit Management*, p. 72.

[18] Ibid., pp. 103–108.

[19] Marian Rothman, "Bicentennial Ruboff? More Department Stores and Bank Cards Are Coming to Terms for the 200th," *Stores*, Vol. 58, no. 8 (August 1976), p. 22. Copyright, National Retail Merchants Association, 1976.

[20] "American Express Bids for Male Transient Trade," *Stores*, Vol. 58, no. 8 (August 1976), p. 24. Copyright, National Retail Merchants Association, 1976.

[21] For comments of various retail executives concerning how they view third-party credit, see Marian B. Rothman, "Third-Party Credit Gaining in Big Stores," *Stores*, Vol. 61, no. 9 (September 1979), pp. 31 ff. Copyright, National Retail Merchants Association, 1979.

[22] For an in-depth look at third-party credit, see William T. Thornhill, "Credit Cards—A Time of Change," *The Credit World*, Part 1, Vol. 68, no. 5 (April–May 1980), pp. 14–18; Part 2, Vol. 68, no. 6 (June–July 1980), pp. 8–12; Part 3, Vol. 69, no. 1 (August–September 1980), pp. 8–12.

[23] For more discussion, see J. Patrick Kelly and Paul J. Solomon, "A Decision Matrix for Adoption of Bank Credit Cards," *Retail Control*, Vol. 44, no. 3 (November 1975), pp. 15–25, published by the National Retail Merchants Association.

[24] Robert H. Cole, *Consumer and Commercial Credit Management*, p. 226.

[25] Dean Ashby, "The Priceless Ingredient in Collections," *The Credit World*, Vol. 65, no. 2 (November 1976), p. 14.

[26] Robert H. Cole, *Consumer and Commercial Credit Management*, pp. 340–341.

[27] Dean Ashby, "The Priceless Ingredient in Collections," *The Credit World*, p. 14.

[28] For more information see W. C. Brock, "Faster Billing at Less Cost," *The Credit World*, Vol. 65, no. 2 (November 1976), pp. 16–17.

[29] *Financial and Operating Results of Department and Specialty Stores of 1979* (New York: Financial Executives Division, National Retail Merchants Association, 1980), pp. 28, 35, 39, 43, 49, 55, 65, 75, 85, 95, 105, 109, 115.

CHAPTER 23

Other Forms of Customer Service

"Remember, the customer is always right—but she has to prove it."

As noted in Chapter 22, retail credit is in demand by customers. It also tends to affect the buying decision. The question that the retailer should ask is, "Are there other forms of customer service that are in demand and that, therefore, have a tendency to affect the buying decision?" If the answer is "yes," then a decision must be made about offering such services.

Customer service is defined as all those "fringe benefits" that are made available by the store for the purpose of further inducing the customer to purchase merchandise. Examples of customer service in addition to credit range from delivery service to providing a water fountain. For most forms of service, it is quite difficult to determine the incremental sales that have been generated as a result of such services being offered. For example, it is hard to measure what effect providing pay telephones or restrooms for the use of customers has on sales.

Customer service is generally not the reason the retail store is in business. It is, instead, a way of promoting the desired goal of more sales of merchandise. Customer service is, by its nature, a supportive function. Being supportive, however, should not be construed to mean not necessary. For many stores, the only differential advantage is found in their customer service mix.

Should a retailer offer various services for his or her customers? The decision-making process that is needed to answer this question properly is quite involved. As noted in Figure 23-1, the retailer must decide on the store's customer service objectives, must study the various factors for determining what types of services should be offered, and must decide who will pay for each service (free or fee). For each service listed in the model and for numerous others as well, the retailer must then make difficult decisions concerning which services will be added now, considered for later use, and not considered feasible at all under current circumstances. And it should be stressed that these are difficult decisions. Customer services do cost money—some more than others. Any unnecessary customer service can place an unnecessary burden on the profit picture of the store.

Figure 23-1

Customer service decision model.

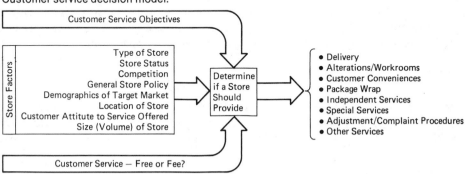

OBJECTIVES

In an attempt to determine if a firm should offer various forms of customer service, the retailer should examine the store's reasons for offering such services. Why offer customer service? Possible objectives include:[1]

> *To increase the form utility of the product sold—examples include clothing alterations, engraving, carpet installations, wallpaper hanging.*
>
> *To provide comfort and convenience for shoppers—examples include restrooms, chairs, telephones, bulletin boards.*
>
> *To pull additional traffic to the store—examples include utility paying facility, ticket office, post office branch.*

FACTORS DETERMINING TYPE OF SERVICE

If such objectives are desirable, the next task of the retailer is to examine the various factors that have a bearing on the customer service decision. The importance of these factors naturally varies from store to store. Because of this variation, the optimum customer service mix can be different for different stores. Factors that have a bearing on the type of services to be offered include the following:[2]

Type of Store

Is the store a full-service department store or a limited-service discounter? Does the store sell furniture and heavy appliances or lightweight easy-carry products? The type of store helps to dictate the services to be offered. A jewelry store may fix watches and set rings. Alterations are common in clothing stores. Stores that sell home furnishings (Figure 23–2) may offer help with interior decorating. Some services are more or less standard in certain types of stores.

Store Status

Is the store a prestige store? Does the image of the store require the offering of many services? Is the store attempting to establish a place for itself in a crowded retail market? A store that offers coffee and doughnuts to all shoppers, or even cocktails, or offers tickets to the symphony or for a Caribbean cruise is offering services that would be inappropriate in a discount store. Generally, the more status-conscious store will offer more in the way of customer services than the mass appeal store.

Competition

Stores cannot ignore the services that are offered by competition. The retailer should be aware of what services are offered but should not always follow and add every possible service. The real question is whether or not the customer really wants that particular service.

General Store Policy

Does the store follow a promotional policy that generates store traffic? Or is it very conservative in its promotional approach, thereby limiting efforts to the promotion of merchandise? In the latter case, the minimum level of customer service will be utilized

Figure 23-2

Interior decorating service can be of great assistance to customers and can help to in-crease sales.

decorator studio

(Courtesy of Montgomery Ward.)

(alterations, deliveries, etc.). In the first instance, however, any service whether it be check cashing, day care, or you-name-it will be considered along with all merchan-dise-related services. The name of the game is traffic. Any service with promotional possibilities will be considered for possible adoption by the store.

Demographics of Target Market

What is the income level of the target market? the age level? the education level? Answers to these and other demographic questions will help to determine the kinds of services that should be offered. A high income level may allow or require home delivery at higher prices or offer a market for cruise or symphony tickets. The older customer is accustomed to free alterations so a store serving the older market may wish to offer this service without a quoted charge. The younger customer, on the other hand, has grown accustomed to such charges so charging for alterations is no problem.

Location of Store

Is the store located in the central business district, shopping center, or neighborhood? A store in a central business location may offer parking as a service. Outlying stores do too, but such is not considered as significant to these store locations. The neighborhood store may offer immediate area (12-block) delivery. The shopping center location may offer the only clean restrooms in the center. Almost any store location can offer unique possibilities for customer service. It is the retailer's responsibility to determine the various forms of customer service that will complement the particular store location so that the objectives of customer service can be met.

Customer Attitude to Service Offered

Is the service essential, expected, or optional in the opinion of the customer.[3] Essential services range from parking to bagging for a supermarket. For a high-fashion clothing store, everything from "free" alterations to fancy chairs is considered necessary. For a new car dealer, a "service" department may be more important to the sale of a new car than the new car itself. Other services are expected but are not essential for many customers. A store that sells paint may rent a paint sprayer at cost to its customers. Customers may expect the availability of alterations and even dressing rooms, but are they essential to the sale of merchandise? In most cases, such services are expected but are not crucial to the success or failure of the store. As for optional services, is a free car wash expected when a customer fills up with gas at the local service station? Do

Figure 23-3

Is the providing of consumer information booklets an essential, expected, or optional customer service?

(Courtesy of Safeway)

customers expect the store to take back for refund any and all merchandise in any condition with no questions asked? Since optional implies not required, a retailer could probably do without the free car wash or whatever. The merchant must decide if optional services are providing the store with a differential advantage and, consequently, more sales (Figure 23-3).

Size (Volume) of Store

Can a store support a particular service economically? Can a store financially afford to offer a kind of service? A retailer wishes to offer delivery service for the store's appliance department. Sales of *heavy* appliances average about six a week. Such a store cannot justify a delivery truck on the basis of sales compensating for the cost of the service. In some cases, a store may choose to offer a service even when a loss occurs to build traffic for the store. Check cashing is a service that can cost the merchant. Even though the smaller store may know that check cashing is good business, such an operation may not be able to withstand the financial risk. If a store can't afford the service, offering it anyway may jeopardize the entire store operation. Care should be taken, however, with the word—"can't." Imaginative management may figure out a way if the reward potential is high.

SERVICE—FREE OR FEE

The question the retailer must address is whether all customers will pay the cost for various services, or only those who use the service, or will the store absorb the cost? For example, "free" alterations may be subsidized by all customers through higher prices whereas a fee for alterations has those who use the service paying all or part of its cost. The third choice is to have the store pay all costs with no influence on price.

The question of free or fee raises its head at every turn for the retailer. Should a charge be made for delivery? Should that cup of coffee be free or for sale? Are the toilets free or pay in the restroom? What about gift wrap or the telephone? Even parking can be free, free only with a purchase, a reduced rate for shoppers, or even the going rate.

Customer expectations and competition are certainly crucial to the question of "free or fee." Another major consideration is the cost of the service to be provided. As noted in Table 23-1, the cost of just two common categories of customer service (wrapping and delivery) represent over 1 percent of total company sales for department stores. If a store could pass these costs on to the customer who uses such services, the store would by this action increase its profit margin by more than 1 percent of sales. Such a rationale makes fee services quite a popular concept. Unfortunately, if customers have other ideas, problems are in the offing for the store.

One other aspect of the free versus fee question deals with charging some customers for a service and not others. For example, traditionally, men's alterations have been free whereas women's alterations have been charged to the customer. But this is now changing as a result of a 1980 suit brought by a young woman against

Table 23-1

Customer services (wrapping and delivery) as a percentage of sales

Customer Service	Department Store Sales (millions)				
	$5–10	$10–20	$20–50	$50–100	Over $100
Central wrapping and packing	.69%	.80%	.72%	.61%	.55%
Delivery	.59	.57	.32	.48	.59
Total	1.28%	1.37%	1.04%	1.09%	1.14%

Source: *Financial and Operating Results of Department and Specialty Stores of 1979* (New York: Financial Executives Division, National Retail Merchants Association, 1980), pp. 61, 62, 71, 72, 81, 82, 91, 92, 101, 102.

Macy's of New York. In that suit, the woman claimed that she was discriminated against because she was charged an alteration charge on a pair of slacks while her male friend got his altered for free. After the New York State Human Rights Commission ruled in her favor, retailers across the country began the task of examining their store policies dealing with how they charge for services.[4]

FORMS OF CUSTOMER SERVICE

As was noted in Figure 23–1, the forms of customer service that a store uses are dependent upon the objectives of the store, factors in the marketplace, and whether the store follows a philosophy of fee or free. Although infinite in number, common forms of customer service include delivery, alterations/workrooms, customer conveniences, package wrap, independent services, special services, and complaints and adjustments. Delivery will be examined first.

Delivery

"When in doubt, discourage delivery." "The package you take with you gets home today." The first slogan is for the benefit of sales personnel. The second is for customers. Their common bond is that they are attempting to discourage delivery. Why? Home delivery is beset with problems. For example, most customers want the item now. If it cannot be delivered in a reasonable length of time, sales will be lost due to customer unhappiness. Another difficulty stems from the problem of not-at-homes. A clothing store leaves the clothes hanging on the front door of the not-at-home customers. Do the clothes remain there or does someone come along and enhance their wardrobe? Leaving a package with a neighbor is also full of problems since neighbors do not even speak to each other in many cases, much less take care of packages. In more than one instance a neighbor has denied receiving a package even when they are shown where they signed for it. Of course, making call-back trips to a home is very expensive. But which is better? It's a matter of taking a risk or spending extra time and money to call back later.

Still another problem is damage in transit. A customer who lives three flights up a set of narrow stairs in an apartment building buys a piano. Although the customer is not directly concerned with delivery, the thing the customer wants is an undamaged piano in the living room. Anything less will be unsatisfactory. It is the store's responsibility to get it there undamaged if the sale is to be made. A fourth problem area stems from the fact that delivery demands fluctuate greatly. A furniture store needs to deliver numerous reclining chairs on December 24 but has little demand in January. To invest in the capacity to meet December demand is wasteful since it will be idle a great part of the time. But a retailer who can say that we will deliver on December 24 can get the sale if such a delivery is desired by the customer. The real question is how important is delivery to the customer?

Can a store charge for delivery? Many stores do. A common method is to require a minimum purchase of, for example, $25, or a "service charge" for delivery will be made. Another procedure is to offer two-zone delivery. Within 5 miles of the store, a delivery fee will only be charged for items that cost less than $25. All deliveries within an area of 5 to 50 miles will be charged a fee. No deliveries will be made beyond 50 miles. The two-zone system should be set up to conform to the population concentrations in the area. The zones should not be determined in an arbitrary manner.

The assumption up to this point in the discussion has been that the store is operating its own in-house delivery system. There are advantages to this arrangement. The vehicle used for such purposes may have advertising value. The prestige furniture store with the "fancy" truck tells all the neighbors of a customer that a purchase has been made at that store. Others may buy there also so that the truck can be seen in their driveways as well. In addition, delivery personnel under the store's control can be trained to present a good impression for the store. They can also be taught to prospect. The delivery person has the rare chance to see inside a customer's home. Such access is so important in some situations that the salesperson will assist with the delivery. Perhaps the greatest advantage of the store-owned delivery system, however, is control of its operation. If a store promises delivery on Wednesday afternoon, chances are good it will be delivered at that time if the store operates its own system. If the store is the boss, its commitments should be met whenever possible. With these advantages, every store would have its own delivery system if this delivery form did not have one major drawback—cost. Due to delivery's high dollar requirements, many stores cannot afford their own system. The alternatives are a consolidated system, United Parcel Service or Parcel Post, or no delivery offered by the store.

Consolidated delivery system. This type of system is generally operated by an independent firm that offers to deliver the items for many firms on a regularly scheduled basis. It works in the following manner. A company truck comes by each store and picks up all the packages to be delivered. The fee for such services is normally based on the number of packages and their weight. The items are then delivered according to the firm's delivery routes and the retailer is billed for the services rendered. Does such a firm make a second or third attempt to find the customer at home? Yes—in most cases. Since the volume of deliveries usually merits going to each area on the schedule on a regular basis, the cost of a callback is not as great for the consolidated firm as it is for the firm that would have to go out of its way to attempt a delivery. Weighed against these advantages would be disadvantages such as no control over the personnel making the delivery or the exact delivery time. In other words, the advantages of the store-owned system would be the disadvantages of this system.

United Parcel Service (UPS) or Parcel Post (PP). As for United Parcel Service (UPS) or Parcel Post (PP), major use of this approach is made by stores such as J.C. Penney to handle catalog orders. Where possible, the retailer will probably prefer UPS over PP since service is usually quicker as well as cheaper. Automatic insurance in the amount of $100 is also offered without extra charge by United Parcel Service. The retailer should look into UPS as a delivery option. Parcel Post is, of course, a standby option when needed to serve areas not reached by UPS. UPS or PP can be the answer when shipping small packages (less than 50 pounds) to customers who are outside the normal delivery zones for the store.

No deliveries. The last option is, of course, no delivery. For small items, such a solution may work. For large items, it can be a problem. A furniture store has a customer who wishes to buy a sofa but the store does not offer delivery. Due to the lack of delivery the customer may lose interest in the sofa. Some stores who have followed this approach have minimized the problem by offering so-called lower prices to compensate for no delivery. Such stores also provide the customer with the name of a person who can deliver the item for them. The difficulty with this setup is that if the merchandise is damaged, most customers will blame the store even though the store really has nothing to do with the particular delivery arrangement. One thing is certain: no matter which system is used, delivery is a point of potential customer irritation in all sales in which it is involved.

Alterations/Workrooms

A customer buys a pair of pants that needs adjustment in the length. A rug is purchased but needs to be cut to a certain size. Drapes are ordered to fit a window. In these and many other situations, the customer wants two things. First, the work to be done correctly. Second, the work to be done on time as promised. A well-run workroom (Figure 23–4) can help to accomplish both goals as well as to keep costs to a minimum.

Work Done Correctly. The workroom is a great source of potential waste for a store if work is done incorrectly. A window shade that has been cut too short by accident may lose all its value and have to be written off. Mistakes do happen but it should not become a habit. In some cases, a form can be devised that shows clearly what needs to be done. For cutting floor covering, a form may be set up like graph paper where the salesperson can actually draw the rug or linoleum in the shape desired. For clothing alterations, numerous operations can be listed so the salesperson need only check that the waist needs taking up one inch instead of writing it out. Any method to simplify the communication process is a step toward getting the job done without waste.

The other factor in getting it done right is the person doing the job. Can that person sew or whatever? Does the person really understand what needs to be done? The retailer should select personnel for this task very carefully. A good workroom operation can be a real asset to a store but only if it is staffed with competent people.

Work Done on Time. A customer is told that the coat will be ready at noon on Friday. At noon on Friday, the customer is told that it will be ready at noon on Mon-

Figure 23-4

Workrooms are important to a customer. In this instance, will the work on the bicycle be done correctly and completed on time?

(Courtesy of Schwinn Bicycle Company.)

day. Monday comes and goes and it is still not ready. Needless to say, the sale may be canceled or all future sales may be lost or both as a result of such a situation. Work promised at noon on Friday should be ready at noon on Friday. No "ifs" or "maybes." For that rare situation where the workroom person got sick or the store had a power failure or whatever, the customer should be called and told the situation. In *no* instance should the customer make a special trip to the store only to learn that the item is not ready. To permit such a thing is poor retailing.

How can a backlog of work be prevented so that the items are ready when promised? The best possible solution is a unit of measure system in which the day is divided into units with each unit being worth, for example, five minutes. Twelve units are in an hour and 96 units are in an eight-hour workday. Time studies are then done in the store to determine how long it takes to perform a certain function such as putting cuffs on a pair of pants. If such an operation is found to take ten minutes, a value of 2 units is given to this particular operation. All other procedures are also analyzed in a similar manner. The results of such an analysis determine how much work can be done in a given day. As the various jobs are turned in, a tabulation is made of the units required to do each job. Assuming that one person works in the workroom, when the units reach 90 the next work is then scheduled for the following day and the time promised is adjusted as well. It is important to stop at 90 to keep some units (6) free for special jobs that may come up or for unexpected problems. Such a procedure promotes quality work and minimizes customer unhappiness.

Costs. As noted, a firm should attempt to have correct work done on time at minimum cost. It is found that alterations/workroom expenses are a function of the cost per productive hour, the efficiency or rate of output for the workroom, and the amount of work per job. Cost per hour represents wages paid to the workroom staff. As for rate of output, anything that improves productivity improves efficiency. The amount of alteration per job also influences cost. A chalk-happy salesperson in a clothing store, for example, can cause unnecessary work to be performed. The three cost elements are interrelated yet independent.[5] A retailer should strive to get good work at a reduced cost. Such is the case no matter if the customer or the store or both are paying for the work.

Another way that some stores with multi-unit operations are keeping costs down is to go with a centralized alterations/workroom operation. Wallach's of New York, for example, currently services 28 stores out of its Long Island City central shop. Since it opened the first centralized workroom in 1954, Wallach's has been joined by numerous other retailers who see centralization as a way to cut costs, improve efficiency, and enhance the quality of the work. Against these advantages are problems that seem to go with centralization. Centralization generally takes longer for the work to be done, the fitter at the store and the tailor at the workroom do not always communicate in the same manner as when all were at the store, and the excessive handling of merchandise tends to give some merchandise a shopworn look.[6] There is no concensus among retailers as to whether alterations/workrooms should be centralized or handled at the individual stores.

Customer Conveniences

The area of customer convenience runs the gamut from check cashing to restrooms. Such services are rarely considered essential in every situation but are expected by many customers. The need for such services is naturally based on various factors such as the type of store and the expectations of the target market. Some possible ways to provide customer convenience include the following:

Chairs.   In almost any store where shopping could last at least five minutes, a place to sit down is a welcomed benefit to a tired customer. Chairs by the fitting room, in the corner, and/or other locations throughout the store will actually help to build traffic for the store. The shopper may say to a tired companion, "Come on. Let's go in here. They have a place where you can sit down." Many a sale has been made in a dress shop while the tired husband tries out one of the store's chairs.

Restrooms.   For a store that caters to shoppers with children, a restroom is essential. Pregnant women also require frequent trips to the lounge. For this reason, a store that sells maternity fashions needs such a facility. A store of some size, 50,000 square feet or more, will find the shopper staying in the store long enough to have a need for a restroom. One thing is certain: a store without public restrooms will on occasion lose a shopper prematurely. Why do stores not have restrooms? They are hard to keep clean. They may attract many nonshoppers. Restrooms are also a haven for shoplifters. To solve this problem, some stores control entrance by means of electric locks. As noted in Chapter 7, other stores are now placing the restrooms outside the shopping area of the store by placing the facility in the lobby area. The shopper in this case actually leaves the store to use the restroom. Although this setup is better from a store security standpoint, it may not be as convenient for the customer who has not completed his or her shopping.

Telephone. A place where a customer can call a cab or make other local calls free of charge is welcomed by the customer. Time restraints must be placed on such calls, but most customers understand the necessity for such an arrangement. Pay telephones should also be provided in a larger store for those customers who do not wish to have a time limitation.

Check Cashing. A retailer who cashes checks on Saturday in a town with no Saturday banking is usually a popular place. Such stores may cash checks far in excess of their sales volume for the day. On Saturday or any other day, there are certain risks involved for a store offering this service. The store is required to absorb a few bad checks, but it also results in many sales since customers may buy things at the store while there. A store that provides this service is also increasing its chances of armed robbery since it has such a large sum of money on hand to serve the needs of the customers.

Bulletin Board. A message board where customers can post items for sale, jobs wanted, announcements, and so on can be a traffic builder for a store with a neighborhood target market. For a large market, the bulletin board idea becomes too impersonal to be as effective. In any case, however, the universal problem is how to keep the board up-to-date. The best policy to follow is to remove all notices after one week. If the customer wishes to put up another note, that is fine.

Parcel Pickup. Parcel pickup is a very important service for stores in congested areas where customers park some distance from the store. Upon leaving the store the customer leaves his or her package at a particular location and is given a number. When the customer drives back to the store, the customer gives the number to the store employee who matches numbers and puts the merchandise in the customer's car. Care should be taken not to give the wrong merchandise to a customer. It can be embarrassing as well as expensive.

Carts. Shopping carts have the advantage of promoting shopping by all customers. If the customer is holding several items, he or she will tire quickly and head to the checkout. A cart frees the customer's hands so they can be used to select items for purchase. A study should be undertaken to determine how many carts, if any, should be in service in the store. A grocery store needs a cart for almost every customer. A department store may need six or eight baby buggies. The individual situation will dictate how many are required.

Personal Shopping Service. Shopping services run the gamut from shopping with the customer to shopping for the customer. New York's Saks Fifth Avenue offers a multilingual shopping staff that is fluent in six languages to assist its customers. Marie Leavell of Dallas keeps extensive files on regular customers so that they can know each customer well. Whether through the use of phone, mail, and/or personal contact, personal shopping services seem to be growing in popularity as many people appear to want to spend less of their time shopping for goods and services.[7]

Other Services.   Other possible services for the convenience of the customer range from free coffee to a water fountain with cups. Many people take pills at various times during the day. Cups let them use the store's water to take their medication. While in the store, of course, they are in a good position to see something and buy it. Another example of service could be a roll of paper towels by the meat counter in the supermarket. If a customer gets her hands wet touching the meat, she can dry them off. In analyzing customer convenience services, it is the little things that sometimes mean so much to a customer.

Package Wrap

Wrapping a package takes one of three forms: customer wrap, mail wrap, and gift wrap.

Customer Wrap.   Preparing a package so that a customer can take it with her is the most popular form of package wrap and a real source of irritation to many customers. A store employee who puts the bread in the bottom of the sack and canned goods on top does not win friends for a store. The customer who, after buying motor oil and a white shirt, finds oil on the shirt when he takes it out of the bag becomes irate. The bag of canned goods that tears in the middle of the parking lot or in the driveway of the customer's house makes the customer have censored thoughts about the store. A dress becomes very wrinkled because it is forced into a box that is too small. Almost all customers have experienced situations where customer wrap has been a point of irritation. Beyond knowing certain fundamental rules such as put heavy things on bottom and use a big enough box, the greatest way in which to improve customer wrap is to use common sense. Store employees should be instructed to "think" instead of treating every wrapping situation in the same way.

Another way to improve on customer wrap is the appearance of the bag or box itself that is used for this purpose. A prestige store should not use brown kraft paper bags (grocery bags) for customer wrap. A dollar store may not wish to use bags with its name in bold letters since some customers may not wish to walk down the street advertising the fact that they have shopped at a dollar store. Some customers may even buy something at a particular store just to get the box with the store's name on it so they can impress their friends. Retailers should not underestimate the importance of the appearance of their customer wrap.[8]

Mail Wrap.   Stores that mail items for customers or to customers should procure strong boxes and good packing material. The customer who opens up a box of dishes and finds them broken is unhappy. It is possible that more care in preparing the package for mailing could have prevented the breakage. Also, the appearance of the package when it arrives is representative of the store's image.

Gift Wrap.   The gift package can identify, add prestige, and offer that extra service that brings customers to the store.[9] Neiman-Marcus, for example, knows the status of a Neiman-Marcus gift extends to the package. Special interest is taken in each package Neiman-Marcus puts together to make sure it upholds the prestigious image of the store.[10]

A good gift wrap service must make every effort to minimize waiting on the customer's part. Standard boxes with paper already cut to fit and bows ready to stick on add up to a quick yet effective operation. Preparation in advance can really pay off. The store might become known as the place to buy Christmas presents since customers do not grow old waiting to get the items wrapped with Christmas paper.

Stores may also choose to offer "fancy" gift wrap for a fee. By offering free gift wrapping as well, customers do not seem to mind paying for a "special" wrap that they want. Many customers decide at the last minute to pay several dollars extra for such special wrapping. If extra money is involved, the retailer should be sure that the store personnel can make the customer's package look as good as the sample. Of course, all gift wrapping should be done well. A short course in how to gift wrap might be conducted for all store personnel who might be involved with this service.

One last consideration involves the question of central wrap. During busy seasons such as Christmas, Mother's Day, and Father's Day, a central location might be utilized for such purposes. Slack times may permit gift wrapping to take place within each department or at each register. Some stores, during slack periods, combine layaways with gift wrapping and have the same person perform both functions along with dressing room monitor or some other task. Multiple duties for this person must cease, however, during the store's peak periods or customer service will suffer.

Independent Services

Independent services are typically things that a store offers a customer that do not relate directly to the primary merchandising effort of the store. Examples include (1) a place where the customer can buy tickets to a baseball game or rock concert, (2) a place to rent items such as rug shampoo machines or electrical hand tools, (3) a tax service on the premises during the tax season, (4) a watch and jewelry repair facility that can fix items not even bought at the store, (5) and a dental clinic where customers can have teeth filled, dentures fitted, and mouths X-rayed. The idea behind such services is twofold. First, a service is rendered. Second, it brings customers into the store. Such services are usually placed in areas that require the customer to go through the store to get to the service location. The customer is exposed to much merchandise along the way and hopefully will stop and buy.

One point of concern when considering services is that a place for customers to come, for example, and pay their bills takes up "X" number of square feet of selling space. Can the store put that space to more productive use? Also, for certain services, the store's sales staff may use valuable time selling tickets or explaining to customers how to work rental equipment. Is this time well spent? The cost of services should be scrutinized very carefully. The primary function of the store—selling merchandise—should not suffer because the store is too involved with services which are independent of the store.[11] Of course, if the retailer's "merchandise" is service, as discussed in Chapter 26, then the situation will be viewed quite differently.

Special Services

The progressive retailer will want to serve the "special needs" customer. Ramps, wide aisles, curbside parking, fitting room and restroom accessibility, and elevator buttons in Braille are some of the numerous ways in which stores can physically aid the 36

Figure 23-5

A prescription counter in a major food store offers the customer a service that is somewhat independent of the rest of the store.

(Courtesy of Giant Food, Inc.)

million disabled consumers who have the potential to be shoppers. The store's employees, likewise, should be prepared to assist these customers. Sensitivity training, sign language courses, as well as finger spelling and personal shopping assistance by appointment are all ways to provide this customer with a special type of customer service. A barrier-free shopping environment coupled with employees who have an understanding of the needs of disabled customers can be a real plus in attracting the handicapped shopper as well as his or her friends and family to a particular store.[12]

Complaints/Adjustments

Stanley J. Fenvessy, a consultant whose specialty is customer service, states, "present customers are and always will be our best prospects."[13] To keep customers coming back, customer complaints must be heard and corrected to their satisfaction. Stores must make it easy for a customer to complain, to seek an adjustment, or to obtain some other form of satisfaction. To do anything less will drive away the customer and the customer's friends as well. The wise retailer may provide a service desk at the front of the store (Figure 23–6), may solicit written comments from customers (Figure 23–7), or may call customers at random to ask their opinion of the store. The retailer should at-

442   CUSTOMER SERVICE

Figure 23-6

A customer service desk at a Woolco store in Great Britain.

(Courtesy of F. W. Woolworth Co.)

Figure 23-7

Store owners can find out what customers think of their store by giving out cards that solicit the customer's opinions.

- • Pleasing you is Rich's business - we'd appreciate your comments on the quality of our service.
- • Place card in Dear Store boxes throughout Rich's or return by mail.

Dear Store...

DATE   RICH'S STORE VISITED   DEPARTMENT   SALESPERSON'S NAME

	YES	NO
Did salesperson greet you promptly?	☐	☐
Did salesperson make your shopping at Rich's pleasant?	☐	☐
Did salesperson know department merchandise?	☐	☐
Would you like this salesperson to help you again?	☐	☐

ADDITIONAL COMMENTS: _____

_____

OPTIONAL:

NAME _____

ADDRESS _____

PHONE _____

(Courtesy of Rich's)

tempt to discover what the store's problems are so they can be corrected while they are still insignificant to the successful operation of the total store.

It is appropriate to talk of complaints and adjustments as the last topic in a section on customer service. Why? Customer service is a major source of problems for a store. A customer is billed for an item that has already been paid for. An alteration was done incorrectly in the store's workroom. Delivery was not made as promised. Eggs are broken in a grocery bag due to improper bagging. Closely tied to customer service is the personal selling effort of the store. Rude, incompetent, or pushy salespeople are just three of the many reasons why a customer might complain about the sales personnel of a store. Merchandise can also be a problem. Inferior quality may be the cause, or the customer may not know how to work the product or wear it or whatever. On the other hand, there may be nothing wrong with the product other than that the customer has just changed his or her mind.

Whether the problem be merchandise or service or both, the retailer wants the customer, if possible, to leave the store as a friend.[14] To accomplish this task, an 11-step procedure should be adopted for use in handling complaints and adjustments. As shown in Figure 23-8, the retailer should be pleasant and businesslike. Every effort should be made to assure the customer that satisfaction will be the end result. The retailer should encourage the customer to talk by listening, not interrupting and not arguing. Many times customers will talk themselves out of a complaint or adjustment if the retailer will let them. The merchant should also make an effort to please the customer. In other words, make an effort to see it as the customer sees it if at all possible. Finally, seek suggestions from the customer and then take action quickly. Do not put the customer off. Say what the store will do; then do it. The procedure should not stop here. The store should naturally thank the customer for the interest shown in the store. Of greater significance, however, is the effort made to correct the problem so it will not occur again. Whatever the problem, it should be corrected without delay.

It should be emphasized that records should be kept of all complaints and adjustments that are made. Such records help to point out weak areas in the store. Such files also help to single out chronic complainers so they can be given special treatment by the store. It is noted that the keeping of records on complaints can be made easier if the store uses a centralized adjustment system where all customers are sent to one loca-

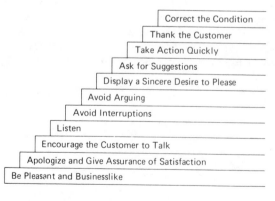

Figure 23-8

Steps for handling complaints/adjustments.

Source: Lloyd W. Moseley, *Customer Service: The Road to Greater Profits* (New York: Chain Store Publishing Corporation, 1972), p. 166.

tion for purposes of adjustment or complaint. At this centralized location, employees who are trained in handling problems can serve the customer in a more objective manner than can the salesclerk in the department who might have made the original sale. On the other hand, a decentralized system where problems are handled by each department is favored by some since it allows the clerk to perhaps switch the customer to another product while providing face-to-face feedback from the customer concerning the problem.

It is important in closing this discussion to note that more and more stores are moving to a policy of "Satisfaction Guaranteed or Your Money Back." The only exception to this policy being the chronic complainer. The thinking behind this move is that an unhappy customer provides the store with bad word-of-mouth "advertising" that costs more than the amount lost in an unjust adjustment. The idea also assumes that the customer will later have a fit of conscience and come into the store and buy many things to make up for past misdeeds. Added to this is the feeling that customers will buy more if they feel they can return it without a hassle. Of course, most goods are never returned so the net result is an increase in sales. Therefore, a policy that is designed to minimize complaints and encourages adjustments in the customer's favor may in turn be having a positive effect on sales. Such is the goal of all forms of customer service.

SUMMARY

Customer services are all those "fringe benefits" that are made available by the store for the purpose of further inducing the customer to purchase merchandise. Being supportive in nature, customer services attempt to increase the form utility of the product sold, provide comfort and convenience for shoppers, and/or pull additional traffic to the store. Factors that determine what type of services a particular store will offer include type of store, status of store, competition, store policies, demographics of target market, store location, customer attitude to services offered, and size (volume) of store. The question of free or fee must also be answered. Customer expectations, competition, and the cost of the service to be provided are all factors to be considered in determining whether to charge for a particular customer service. Common forms of customer service include delivery (in-house, consolidated, UPS or PP), alterations (goal is correct work on time at lowest cost), and customer conveniences (chairs, restrooms, telephone, check cashing, bulletin board, parcel pickup, carts, personal shopping service, and other services). Others forms are package wrap (customer, mail, and gift), independent services (ticket booth, repairs, and rentals), special services (ramps, wide aisles, and employees who can "speak" sign language), and complaints and adjustments (service and merchandise). "Satisfaction Guaranteed" is the goal of most stores today. All forms of customer service work to achieve a positive effect on sales.

1. List possible objectives or goals of customer service for a retail store. Then go to several retail stores in your area that offer various services and determine what their objectives are. Compare the various objectives. Do they appear to be similar or different? Explain your answer.
2. What factors are thought to influence the selection of various customer services to be offered by a given store?
3. "Free or Fee"—which is better? How can a retailer decide which way to go?
4. A retailer is toying with the idea of dropping in-house delivery service. He wants to know what he will possibly gain and lose by taking such action. He also wishes to know what other delivery options he might consider. Provide him with answers to his questions.
5. What can a retailer do to improve the chances that a pair of pants needing alterations will be ready when promised? Be specific.
6. List as many forms of customer service in the customer convenience category as possible. For given stores in your area, are such services essential, expected, or optional?
7. Should a store offer independent services? Special services? Discuss these services with retailers in your area. How do they feel about such services?
8. Explain the 11-step approach to handling complaints and adjustments.
9. Do you agree with the idea that the customer is always right? Explain your answer.
10. Is customer service a necessary part of retailing? Why not eliminate it?

NOTES

[1] William R. Davidson, Alton F. Doody, and Daniel J. Sweeny, *Retailing Management*, 4th ed. (New York: The Ronald Press Company, 1975), p. 459.

[2] Bernard W. Smith, "Customer Service," in *Operations Manual for Smaller Stores*, Volume 1, ed. Seymour Helfant (New York: National Retail Merchants Association, 1960), p. 207.

[3] Classification system for customer service discussed in Carl M. Larson, Robert E. Weigand, and John S. Wright, *Basic Retailing* (Englewood Cliffs, N.J.: Prentice-Hall, Inc., 1976), p. 364.

[4] "Alterations: Finding the Answers to More Equal Pricing for Men and Women," *Stores*, Vol. 62, no. 11 (November 1980), p. 34. Copyright, National Retail Merchants Association, 1980.

[5] G. J. Marder, "The Alteration Problem," in *Operations Manual for Smaller Stores*, Volume 2, ed. Seymour Helfant (New York: National Retail Merchants Association, 1960), pp. 443–449.

[6] "Alterations," *Stores*, Vol. 62, no. 11 (November 1980), pp. 30–35. Copyright, National Retail Merchants Association, 1980.

[7] Marian B. Rothman, "New Needs, New Tactics," *Stores*, Vol. 61, no. 11 (November 1979), pp. 38–42. Copyright, National Retail Merchants Association, 1979.

[8] For more information on package wrap, see Maryann Ondovcsik, "How They Wrap It!" *Stores*, Vol. 62, no. 9 (September 1980), pp. 60–65. Copyright, National Retail Merchants Association, 1980.

[9] H. L. Greilsheim and Helen Snyder, "Gift-Wrapping," in *Operations Manual for Smaller Stores*, Volume 2, p. 583.

[10] Edward S. Dubbs, "Gift Wrap," *Stores*, Vol. 58, no. 8 (August 1976), p. 15. Copyright, National Retail Merchants Association, 1976.

[11] For more information on independent services, see Marian B. Rothman, "A New Look at Services," *Stores*, Vol. 62, no. 5 (May 1980), pp. 56–58, and "Hot New Services? Health Care!" *Stores*, Vol. 62, no. 6 (June 1980), pp. 52–53. Copyright, National Retail Merchants Association, 1980.

[12] For more information, see Marian B. Rothman, "The Customer with Special Needs," *Stores*, Vol. 61, no. 10 (October 1979), pp. 54–57. Copyright, National Retail Merchants Association, 1979.

[13] Stanley J. Fenvessy, *Keep Your Customers (And Keep Them Happy)* (Homewood, Ill.: Dow Jones-Irwin, 1976), p. 1.

[14] Lloyd W. Moseley, *Customer Service: The Road to Greater Profits* (New York: Chain Store Publishing Corporation, 1972), p. 166.

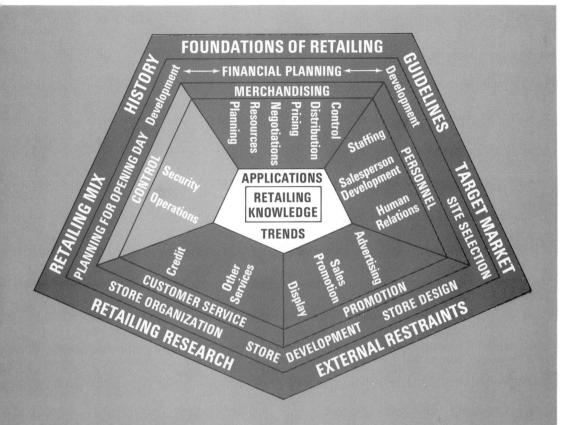

Retail security and operations control make up the area known as retail control.

"Retail Security" looks at shoplifting, employee theft, bad checks, and bad credit cards, as well as other problem areas.

"Operations Control" covers the areas of expense control, which includes the classification and allocation of expenses along with budgeting and work simplification, and performance control, which analyzes the store from both a financial and managerial standpoint.

"Getting pretty cocky, aren't they?"

Reprinted with permission from The Saturday Evening Post Company © 1979.

Effective retail security is essential to a retailer who wishes to have a profitable operation. Most store owners today cannot afford the luxury of lax security when dealing with customers or employees. For purposes of definition,

> Retail security is defined as awareness, prevention, and detection of merchandise and money shortages.

The definition of retail security illustrates the proper approach to the subject. The retailer must first be aware of security problems. The merchant who says that the store has no security problem is making a foolish statement. This is an expensive attitude to have. Awareness involves not only being conscious of actual incidents of theft; it also is concerned with an understanding of potential security problems.

Awareness of security needs must come first, but prevention is equally important in handling the problem. By prevention, you stop shortages before they happen rather than catching possibly only half of the guilty parties after the fact. The retailer should remember that even though he or she may reclaim some merchandise, many other items may be lost by not being diligent in the prevention area.

Detection is the "court of last resort" in any retail security system. Mr. Joseph Bernstein, a shortage control consultant, summed up the role of detection when he wrote,

> It is far less expensive to prevent and minimize theft and shortages than it is to detect it. This not only applies to the cost in money, but also the distasteful emotional and human experience of thievery and its results within an organization.[1]

Detection procedures are essential to a system of retail security, but the main thrust of effort should be aimed in the direction of awareness and prevention of the retail security problem.

It should be emphasized that good retail security does not come cheap. It is estimated that stores spend billions on various security programs on an annual basis. In terms of security as a percentage of sales, Table 24–1 shows that such expenses range

Table 24–1

Median costs of security operations of
department stores by sales volume, 1979

Sales Volume (millions)	Cost of Security[1] as a Percentage of Sales
$5–10	.19%
10–20	.29
20–50	.42
50–100	.72
Over $100	.62

[1]Cost of security includes payroll expenses for guards, fitting room checkers, and employee purchase checkers. Other items included are fire extinguishers, alarms, sprinklers, polygraph tests, outside detectives, honesty shoppers, and security consultants.

Source: *Financial and Operating Results of Department and Specialty Stores of 1979* (New York: Financial Executives Division, National Retail Merchants Association, 1980), pp. 59, 69, 79, 89, 99.

from .19 percent to .72 percent for department stores, with larger stores spending more on security per sales dollar than smaller stores.

An effective security system should concern itself with shoplifting. Employee theft should also be studied. A store's policies and procedures for handling checks and credit cards, as well as fires, robberies, civil disorders, power failures, natural disasters, and burglaries should also be examined from a security standpoint. A successful retail security program must be a total commitment to be aware of the possibility of shortages, to prevent these shortages, and, if necessary, to detect various forms of theft so as to give the store a better profit picture (Figure 24–1).

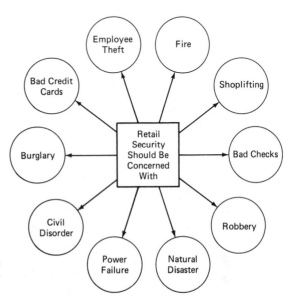

Figure 24–1

Ten areas of concern that must be addressed by a store's retail security program.

SHOPLIFTING—METHODS

A customer just like you is a potential shoplifter. Although there are some professionals in the business, most shoplifters (approximately 80 percent) are amateurs who were given the opportunity to steal by a store's weak program of shoplifting prevention and detection. "Customers" shoplift in two ways:

1. Steal merchandise.
2. Pay less than the stated price for merchandise.

Both methods of shoplifting are destructive to a firm's profit picture. How? It is estimated that the average value of a shoplifting loss for a store is $32. When that figure is multiplied by the 4 million shoplifters that are apprehended each year, the loss adds up to $128 million. But if you consider the fact that industry sources claim that only 1 in 35 shoplifters is caught, the loss figure grows to an estimated level of $4.5 billion in shoplifting losses.[2] And if that figure seems high, other studies estimate store losses due to shoplifting to be in excess of $10 billion annually.[3] But no matter which study a retailer chooses to read and/or believe, the conclusion is the same: shoplifting is expensive.

To understand shoplifting better is to understand that everyone is a potential shoplifter and that the methods they will use are almost unlimited. To protect the store's merchandise, the retailer must become aware of the various methods of shoplifting and devise means of prevention and, if necessary, means of detection.

Booster Box

The booster box derives its name from the "on-the-street" name for a shoplifter. The "booster" or shoplifter will design a box with a trap door or other device so the box can be opened and closed very quickly. The booster will carefully wrap the box and tie it with twine so that it appears to be tightly wrapped even though it will open. To the merchant, the box is a package ready for mailing. To the shoplifter, the box is an open invitation to steal.

Coat

A coat draped over the arm provides a visual barrier thereby preventing the retailer from seeing what is going on behind it. A coat can have a pillow case or other holder pinned or sewed inside the lining in order to have a place to put merchandise. A coat is very effective, for example, when the customer runs into a display with a shopping cart. The customer will naturally kneel down to pick up the overturned items. When this happens, the coat being worn falls to the floor around the customer. Again, a visual barrier has been created. Retailers should also watch for a customer wearing a heavy coat out of season. Another indication is a raincoat being worn by a mother on a sunny day while her daughter wears a sun dress. Check for consistent clothing. As is true with most shoplifting devices, a coat being worn or carried by a customer may only indicate, for example, that the person has low blood pressure. It is not illegal for a customer to have a coat—only to use it for illegal purposes.

Purse

A purse is a natural item for a person to carry, but the retailer can watch for several things. First, be careful to note that each customer who leaves with a purse came in with one. The same holds true for belts, socks, shoes, and other clothing items. Big purses are a "flagwaver" for the retailer to watch, but if current fashion calls for big purses, the store owner will have to react accordingly. One particular problem for purse-related shoplifting is the shopping cart with baby seat. A purse left open on the baby seat can acquire a stolen item and be closed very quickly. Some retailers are, in fact, eliminating the baby seat from their shopping carts for this reason.

Booster Bloomers

These are very baggy pants worn under a dress or coat with tight elastic around the legs. The shoplifter or accomplice drops merchandise into the bloomers and they walk out of the store. Much merchandise can be carried out in one trip using this method.

Crotch

The crotch method is perhaps the pinnacle of professional shoplifting. As its name implies, it simply involves placing merchandise between the legs and walking out of the store. Due to their methods of dress, women are naturally the greater users of this method but a man wearing an overcoat will also use this approach. The retailer must realize that almost any item can be carried out in this manner. TV sets, typewriters, cartons of cigarettes, and even a frozen turkey are actual items that have been stolen with the crotch method. To guard against this approach, the retailer should watch for slow-walking customers who are pigeon-toed. This may or may not be an amateur shoplifter who is using this method. For the professional who has built up the thigh muscles, it is almost impossible to detect the theft unless the retailer actually sees the item being placed between the legs. One cannot help but be impressed at the professionalism of the shoplifter who will place a 12-pound frozen turkey between her legs and walk nonchalantly through the checkout to her car parked around the corner.

Bag

The store shopping bag is a handy shoplifting tool. The customer can easily rake merchandise off the counter into the bag. The retailer should also watch for a wrinkled bag. It could be wrinkled because it was in the shoplifter's pocket when he or she entered the store. It may now have the retailer's merchandise in it as it leaves the store.

Along the same lines of thought, a retailer who sells magazines should be careful to ensure that these magazines are not becoming "bags" for items placed in the pages. The same holds true for newspapers, record covers, and other possible "bags." A retailer should make a habit of checking items to guard against things being concealed inside. Checking items will be effective only if the retailer looks in everything. For example, the checker will not only open the lunch box being purchased to see what, if anything, is inside but will also open the thermos in the lunch box to check its contents as well.

Fitting Room

The fitting or dressing room creates many problems for the security-minded retailer. First, the retailer must decide if the store is going to have a fitting room. If one is needed, then it must be used for no other purpose. To store items in a dressing room is to ask for trouble. For many customers, the temptation will be too great. The customer who wants to steal might wear old clothes into the dressing room and new clothes out. An alert employee will many times notice the change. A customer may wear the new clothes out under the old clothes. The way to guard against this approach is to limit the number of items to go into the dressing room. A check-in-out system to show, for example, if the customer took one, two, or three items into the fitting room and brought out the same amount is a suggested system. Care should also be used in the physical design of the fitting rooms. Curtains that hang at least 18 inches off the floor instead of doors are just one suggestion that can reduce theft by not giving the customer "too much privacy."

Diverting Attention

To divert attention, a customer may request an unusual item that would require a trip to the stockroom. In a well-managed store, another clerk would be on the floor to observe while the salesperson goes to look for the item. Such an attention-diverting method cannot always be thwarted, particularly in the small store, but the retailer should be aware of the possible implications when a customer requests the clerk to leave the sales floor. For the poorly-manned store, there is something to be said for moving all merchandise to the sales floor, thereby eliminating the need for anyone to leave the customer.

Another attention-diverting method is to cause some sort of disturbance to take place in the store. Fainting, falling, or fighting are sure-fire ways to disrupt a store. When a customer faints, it is natural for all to want to help. A clerk who leaves her work station may invite shoplifting by those who knew the fainting was going to happen and by those who were not expecting it. A similar reaction will usually occur for a fall or a fight. In some cases, however, the reaction to a fight may be the reverse as many people may look the other way while a "husband and wife" have an argument about something. The retailer must remember that, while they are fighting, their hands could be stealing.

Still another method of diversion involves the cash register. As the operator places change in a customer's hand, the customer may spread his or her fingers causing the money to fall on the floor behind the register. While the register operator leans over to get the money, all those items around the register that were placed there to guard against being stolen are now fair game. The retailer should instruct sales personnel to give more change out of the register and pick up the other money when no customer is at the register.

Price Changing

This method of shoplifting results in the customer paying for the item but paying a cheaper price. The customer may switch bottle caps if prices are placed on the caps. Since the same top fits many containers, putting the price somewhere other than on the cap is a solution. If the retailer is using stick-on labels that come off easily and can be reapplied, price tags end up meaning nothing at the checkout. Tear-away tickets that are destroyed when taken off are an answer. String tags are another problem. Plastic string tabs that must be cut to be removed are a possibility.

Price changing is also quite popular when prices are written on the price tag by hand. Instead of switching tickets, the ticket is actually altered. The best way to guard against this problem is to have printed price tickets. If this is not considered feasible, unusual ink colors are a solution. Never write a price in blue or black. Do not make it too easy for the customer to change 1.33 to $.83 by changing the "1" to a dollar sign and the "3" to and "8."

SHOPLIFTING—DETECTION AND PREVENTION

The various methods cited are by no means all the methods of shoplifting in use, but they do give an idea of the task facing the store owner as he or she attempts to do something about customer theft. One possible way to prevent shoplifting is to have obvious methods of shoplifting detection. Included in this category are mirrors, closed-circuit television, electronic article surveillance, elevated office/sales/observation areas, and combinations of those listed.

Mirrors

Mirrors are a common detection device. Convex mirrors placed at strategic locations in a store can give good visual coverage for the retailer. Unfortunately, it also gives good visual coverage for the shoplifter. If mirrors are installed, be sure that someone is watching when the shoplifter looks at the mirror.

One-way mirrors are another possibility for observing the sales floor. The only drawback to this tool is that the area behind the one-way glass must be dark to give the appearance of a mirror. This darkness is not always practical.

Closed-Circuit Television

Television cameras do appear to attract interest and discourage shoplifting. But an effective system must give an indication that the system is working. Movement of the camera or placement of a TV set for all to see that shows what is being televised are two ways to get believability into the system.

The retailer must guard against the fake camera that looks fake. Dummy cameras have been observed where the camera had one wire running from it to an electrical wall socket for all to see. Some have an inch of dust on the lens or they have been moved accidentally where they are now pointing at the wall. Care must be taken to ensure that dummy cameras get the same upkeep as a real one.

Electronic Article Surveillance

Electronic Article Surveillance (EAS)[4] devices are being used by more and more stores. An electronic wafer, disc, soft tag, or similar device is attached to the merchandise when it is placed in the store. When the merchandise is purchased, the wafer or other device is removed or desensitized at the register. If it is not removed or neutralized in some way, the EAS device will set off an alarm when the merchandise to which it is attached is carried through the door of the store. Obvious care should be exercised to make sure that electronic devices are removed or desensitized by store personnel when items are purchased to guard against, at the least, an embarrassing situation. Since EAS can cause problems if employees forget to remove or desensitize EAS devices, why use them? Because they do seem to work. Marshall Field and Company of Chicago, for example, found that apprehensions for theft fell 60 percent after EAS was installed. The deterrent effect does appear to be obvious. EAS does seem to have a positive effect on shrinkage.[5]

Raised Office/Sales/Observation Areas

A raised observation tower or area where employees are always located can provide a place from which the entire sales area can be observed. The office of a supermarket should be above ground level. A raised prescription counter of a drugstore is another ideal observation post. Employees do not have to observe the sales floor at all times for a raised area to be effective as a prevention device. The fact that they might detect something is enough to reduce the shoplifting problem.

Combination of Methods

Detecting shoplifters in a store may require and probably should require a combination of methods. For example, a drugstore may have a raised area for prescriptions, make use of convex mirrors, and use a TV camera (Figure 24–2). The retailer must continually analyze his or her store to ensure that its security system is what it should be.

Obvious detection efforts do aid in shoplifting prevention. Other things that the retailer might do in the area are:

1. Greet customers when they come in the store or a department. This indicates that the sales force is alert.
2. Display signs that warn against shoplifting.
3. Keep small and/or expensive items under glass and key or behind the counter out of the reach of customers. This way the merchandise can easily be seen, but it cannot easily be stolen (Figure 24–3).
4. Keep merchandise levels low on counters.

Figure 24–2

A possible security system for a drugstore.

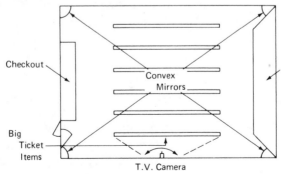

Figure 24-3

An attractive yet simple display that is secured by being under glass and/or out of the reach of customers.

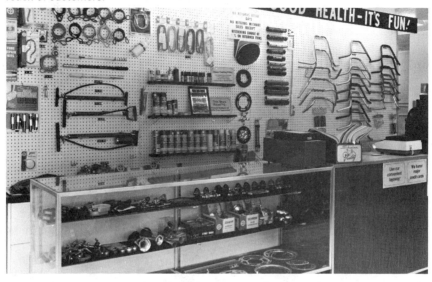

(Courtesy of Schwinn Bicycle Company.)

5. Have visual contact between aisles.
6. Keep sales floor well-lighted.
7. Keep completed sales tickets and tags off sales floor. Shoplifters may use these to show proof of purchase.
8. Where possible, use security fixtures that help protect merchandise from theft while permitting the customer to have a "hands-on" experience with the item (Figure 24-4).
9. Play a subliminal message over the store's background music system that states, "I will not steal. If I steal, I will go to jail." Needless to say, this preventive device is quite controversial since the customer does not realize he or she is hearing that message. But a New Orleans supermarket, for example, reduced pilferage from $50,000 to $13,000 for a six-month period after installing the subliminal message system. Cashier shortages also dropped from $125 to less than $10 per week.[6]

EMPLOYEE THEFT—METHODS[7]

As bad as shoplifting losses are, employee theft may be an even greater problem. In its "1980 Annual Census of American Chain Stores," *Chain Store Age Executive* cited various studies that concluded that employee theft accounts for as much as 50 to 65 percent of all shrinkage with employees being involved in 70–85 percent of all thefts involving $500 or more in merchandise.[8] Because of the magnitude of the problem, awareness of possible employee theft should be an objective of a sound security system. As is true with shoplifting, one of the best ways to understand employee theft is to be aware of the various methods put to use by employees in stealing from a store.

Figure 24-4

Anti-theft displays play an important role in overall store security.

Anti-Theft Display Systems That Won't Stand Out In A Crowd.

(Trade Ad Courtesy of Securax, Inc.)

Throwing Merchandise Away

Many employees will "throw away" merchandise and then return to the store at night to retrieve it from the trash. The only way to eliminate this possibility is to compact or incinerate the trash as it is discarded. If such is not possible, random unannounced checks of the trash by store management should prevent this situation.

Failure to Ring a Sale

An employee may make a sale to a customer but pocket the money rather than ring it up on the cash register. Efforts should be made to ensure that employees do ring all sales. One aid would be to odd price merchandise. For example, if there is a 5 percent sales tax in the state, an item should not cost 95 cents. The $1.00 price for the item will not encourage use of the register since the employee would not have to make change. Other ways to have the register used center around the customer. Some stores offer the purchase free if a register receipt is not given the customer. Others offer free prizes if a "star" appears on their receipt. Still other firms insist on a receipt if something is to be returned. Such policies encourage the customer to ask for a receipt which ensures that the clerk will register the sale.

Vendor Kickbacks

Vendor collusion is a problem of major proportions for retailing. A receiving clerk at a department store signs that he has received six dozen boxes of an item when, in reality, only five dozen are taken from the truck. The deliveryman then sells the other dozen and splits the take with the receiving clerk. The store is out a dozen items it paid for. Random checks, blind counts (clerk does not know what was ordered), and other auditing procedures can help to alleviate the problem.

Discount Selling and Free Merchandise

Selling merchandise at less than retail or actually giving it away to family and friends without prior authorization cost retailers literally millions of dollars per year. A clerk may have her sister come through the checkout each day where she "buys" $20 worth of merchandise for $10 or less. Another possibility is for a clerk to ring up a sale for one shirt and then put three shirts in the bag. The exchange of "free" gifts among employees is another approach to this method. If allowed to continue unchecked, employee "discounts" of this nature can become financially damaging. On the floor observation by management and close checking of employee purchases can aid in minimizing this so-called "Christmas spirit" among employees.

Fraudulent Refunds

An employee who has a refund book and authority to get to the cash box can be dangerous for a retail store. Such an employee can easily write up a fraudulent refund and then pay himself or herself out of the register for the items supposedly returned. If it is not possible to separate the two functions of writing a refund and giving the money, the store should get the name and address of the person getting the refund with the intent of writing them. Not only would such a letter be a goodwill gesture, it would also serve to determine if the refund was given to a real person and that the amount of refund given was correct. If many of these letters are returned with addressee unknown, this should indicate to management that further investigation of the refund procedure is warranted.

Coming Early and Staying Late

An employee who comes to the store an hour early and roams around the store may be stealing small items and putting them in his or her pockets, or the employee may come early, pick out the coat he or she wants, take the tags off, and wear it home at the end of the day. An employee who stays late may be doing the same thing. Employees should not be permitted to be in the store without supervision. All employees should be told that they will not be permitted in the store before a certain time and will not be allowed in the store after a certain time.

Night cleanup and stocking present special problems for the security-minded retailer. One solution is to remain open for business while stocking and cleaning are going on. The chance that a customer may come at any time may keep the employees honest. This solution, of course, makes the store subject to customer theft during this period. Random visits by store management, closed-circuit television, and uniformed guards may be other ways to minimize after-hour employee theft. The best solution, considering the cost of electricity and employee theft, is to be closed to all when closed and do all cleaning and stocking during regular store hours.

Fake Employee Discounts

A fake employee discount occurs when a salesclerk makes a sale but then writes up an employee purchase for the same item and takes the 20 percent employee discount. She gets the money from the customer and pays the store for the merchandise. The store is the loser, of course, because the clerk pockets the 20 percent discount. Sound store procedures should prevent this scheme from being successful. If the clerk has to give a receipt to the customer, a record of the customer sale will be on the register. Also, if all employee purchases have to be approved by a supervisor, with the merchandise then turned over to the supervisor until the employee leaves the store, such theft problems will remain at a minimum.

Key Duplication

A key that is stolen for only ten minutes can mean bankruptcy for a store. In that ten-minute period, a dishonest employee can go and have the key duplicated. He can then return at night with a truck and several accomplices and clean out the store. Special care should be taken to restrict the number of keys in circulation. Also, these keys should have "Do Not Duplicate" stamped on them. Any key that is "misplaced" for a short period of time should be reported to management so that the situation can be analyzed and lock changes made if necessary. In addition, any time an employee who has had access to a key quits or leaves the employ of the store for any reason, all locks should be changed at the store.

EMPLOYEE THEFT—DETECTION AND PREVENTION

Detection and prevention of employee theft are important in minimizing the problem. As is true with shoplifting, obvious detection procedures can serve as a preventive tool.

Honesty Shoppers

Shopping service firms or "honesty shoppers" can be hired by the retailer to check on the honesty of the store's employees.[9] The shopping service employee will make a purchase to see if the store employee performs according to store policies and procedures. They will check to see if a receipt is given, if correct change is made, and so on. Employees should be told that shopping services will be in the store unannounced from time to time. Under such circumstances, every customer is suspect, thereby promoting better, more honest employee performance.

Uniformed Guards

The presence of uniformed guards at store entrances and exits will tend to make employees use the correct door and to carry only paid-for merchandise out of the store. Employees should be made aware they are subject to search by these guards upon leaving the store. Such checks should be made on a random basis for all employees. The older employees should not be exempt from such random searches. There is much evidence to show that long-time employees may be greater security risks than new employees. Many long-term employees "know the ropes" and thus feel free to steal from the store.

Polygraph

Where permitted by law, the polygraph or lie-detector test is a means of theft detection but an even greater means of theft prevention. Some stores are now requiring all employees to take the test every six months to check on theft. To install such a system requires that *all* employees from manager on down be subject to the polygraph examination. All past thefts must also be forgiven to prevent a mass resignation and/or firing of employees due to past activities. The polygraph test is an emotional issue with many people. Special care must be taken in selling the polygraph as an employee theft prevention device. To just announce that "lie detector tests will begin at 9 A.M. tomorrow" will probably cause more problems than it will solve.

Prevention of employee theft goes beyond detection methods if the store is to have a good security program. Management should set up additional preventive measures such as:

Check Employee Records

A check should be made of employee references and past work experience to determine the honesty of the employee. It may be determined that an employee had been fired from his previous position due to questionable circumstances. Such a finding may not indicate that the employee should not be hired, but it might be of interest should similar circumstances occur in the manager's store.

Remove Temptation

Store management should work to eliminate the easy theft. One possibility could be a separate cash drawer for each employee at a register. Uniforms for all employees with no or very shallow pockets will reduce the pocketing of merchandise. Procedures for handling employee coats and handbags that keep them off the sales floor will reduce temptation. Management, by giving the appearance of being on its toes, will deter temptation for many employees.

Prompt Action When Caught

When an employee is caught, prompt dismissal and legal action should not be far behind. An employee should be told the consequences of taking merchandise or money from a store and should then observe that prompt action is taken when an employee theft is discovered. Knowing and seeing the consequences act as great deterrents.

WHAT TO DO WHEN A THEFT IS DETECTED

When employee theft is involved, the retailer normally has time to be cautious and deliberate before confronting the employee with the facts of the situation. But in shoplifting cases, prompt action is essential in order to catch the "customer."

A retail store should set up step-by-step procedures to follow when a shoplifter is spotted. These procedures should be similar to the following:[10]

1. *Notify store management but keep shoplifter in sight at all times.* The latter is essential in some court jurisdictions to prove concealment.
2. *Have store management approach the suspect.* Management is usually told the situation by use of the store intercom. It might say, "Mr. Sherrell, go to Department 19." Department 19 is where the theft took place. Mr. Sherrell is fictitious. Any time his name is used, it alerts the whole store that shoplifting is in progress. It is best to have management approach the suspect since they should be aware of the procedures to follow. No threats or undue force should be used. The employee should take the merchandise from the suspect immediately. If the suspect has left the store, he or she should be asked to return to the store with the store employee. Note: Most court cases indicate that letting the customer leave the store before apprehension improves the chances of conviction. If the customer should break away and run, do not give chase. The suspect may have several friends waiting around the corner to back him or her up as soon as the employee doing the chasing gets near.
3. *Bring the customer to the office of the store.* Be polite. Have a store employee who is the same sex as the suspect in the office at all times to avoid possible trouble. The police should also be called at this time. Be empathetic with the suspect. Work to obtain a written statement that is then signed and witnessed.

The procedure stops at step 3 if the retailer is not going to take legal action. A warning to the suspect and notification to other stores in the area of the situation may be as far as management might wish to go. Generally, however, store owners should proceed to step 4 and go to court. Court action is the same for shoplifting or employee theft.

4. *Go to court.* If legal action is to be taken, all evidence should be noted carefully by the retailer. Mark items that were stolen so, in later court action, the marked items can be identified without doubt. The retailer should also make notes about the event or record the facts on tape for later use. Such recording of facts is important since the actual trial may not come for months. On the day of the trial, the retailer should read over the notes or play the tapes to refresh his or her memory for a better performance at the trial. Such a procedure should result in a higher conviction rate for a store—a preventive measure in itself.

BAD CHECKS[11]

For purposes of definition,

A bad check is any check that is not honored for payment by the bank it is drawn on within the normal course of business operations.

Since accepting checks is necessary for most retailers, the acceptor of checks should satisfy himself or herself on two counts with regard to every check offered:

1. *The checkwriter is the person named on the check.* The retailer can determine this by asking for a driver's license or for any other form of official identification card. I.D. cards that include a picture of the individual are particularly useful for identification purposes. Please note that a retailer should not accept a Social Security card for use in identifying a customer, as these cards are too easy to obtain under false conditions.
2. *The checkwriter has sufficient money in his or her account to cover the check.* There is no way to correctly ascertain this information since outstanding checks prevent even the bank from knowing for sure. The retailer can, however, ask to see major company credit cards that the customer might have in order to use them as a measure of financial responsibility. The assumption is that, if the customer has credit with major companies, he or she is probably a person who would not write a bad check.

The retailer should also set up certain rules to guard against the potential of bad-check loss. Some of the more common rules are:

1. No second-party checks.
2. No counter checks.
3. No check in excess of amount of purchase.

There are, of course, certain situations where the retailer will want to alter these rules and, for example, accept counter checks. The retailer must remember that if the store is going to offer these extra services for checkwriters, extra risks are inherent in the decision.

In the case of bad checks, the retailer may want to install special equipment or use procedures aimed at curtailing the problem. Examples include the following:

Camera systems. The various camera systems include dual cameras that take a picture of the checkwriter, the check, and pertinent identification such as a driver's license. Such a system can provide all the evidence needed to catch and convict a bad-check passer.

Dry thumb prints. The system is similar in concept to the camera system. Under the system check-cashing customers are asked to press their right thumb on the back of their checks. The check is then inserted into a machine that develops a visible thumbprint that can be used later for identification purposes. Compared with the camera system, this method is quicker and is done by a machine small enough to be set up at all checkout counters.

Check guarantee program. Under this approach, particular companies become co-makers of checks for approved customers. For a fee, the company reimburses the store for a check written by one of its approved checkwriters. The problem with this situation is that most approved customers are regular customers with a low level of risk. The check guarantee program does not usually work for new customers, transients, or infrequent customers. These higher-risk checkwriters do not fall under the protection of the guarantee and must be handled in the conventional manner by the retailer.

File system. A file system is similar to the check guarantee system as far as the customer is concerned. In both systems, the customer may be given an I.D. card to show that his or her checks are approved (Figure 24–5). In the latter case, however, the approval to cash the check is strictly a store decision. Records may be kept to provide a check record of the customer. In addition, if there is doubt about who the checkwriter really is, he or she can be asked pertinent information that can be compared with the information in the file.

The merchant should examine his or her check-cashing policies to determine if he or she should install special equipment or procedures. The merchant should also examine the human element to determine if too strict procedures for check cashing may, in fact, be driving away more business than would be lost through bad checks. The retailer must always remember: Bad Checks = Bad Profits.

BAD CREDIT CARDS

Another solution to the problem of bad checks as presented is to honor credit cards. As noted in the chapter on "Retail Credit," stores generally honor bank cards (Visa, etc.), travel and entertainment cards (American Express, etc.), their own credit cards, or some combination of the three.

For bank cards and travel and entertainment cards, retail security involves ensuring that all store personnel are aware of and are following the prescribed procedures set forth by the card companies for handling cards. Such procedures generally include:

1. Check the "hot" card list so that a stolen card is not honored.
2. Date the sales draft (card form).

Figure 24-5

Some stores are using a check-cashing card to reduce their losses from bad checks.

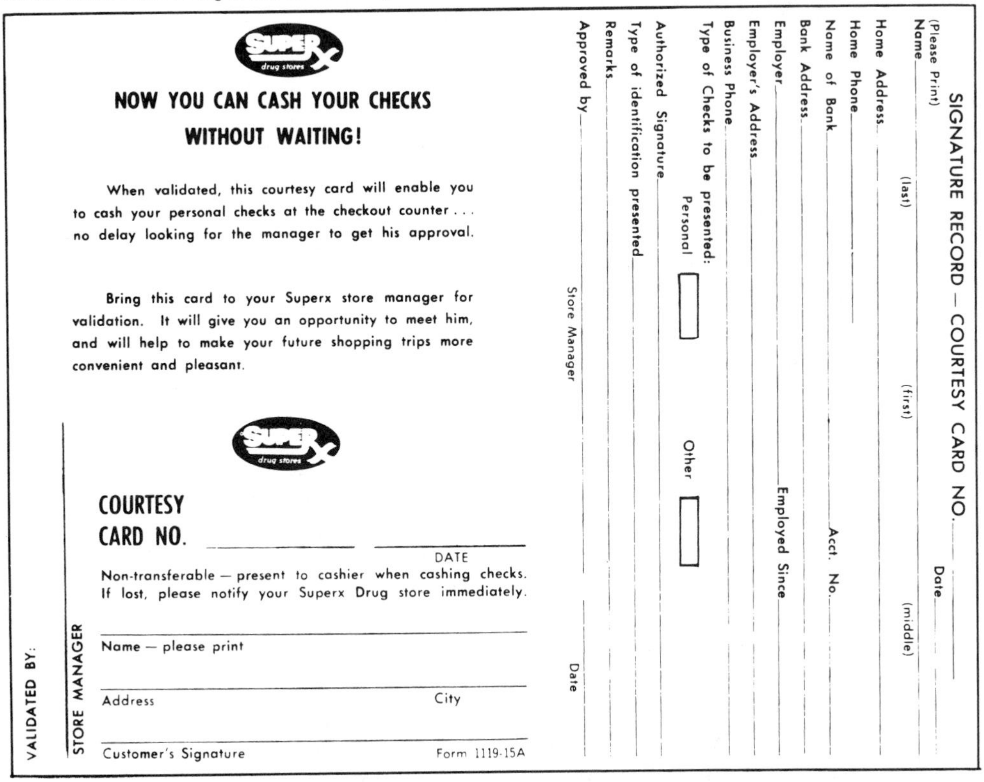

NOW YOU CAN CASH YOUR CHECKS WITHOUT WAITING!

When validated, this courtesy card will enable you to cash your personal checks at the checkout counter . . . no delay looking for the manager to get his approval.

Bring this card to your Superx store manager for validation. It will give you an opportunity to meet him, and will help to make your future shopping trips more convenient and pleasant.

COURTESY CARD NO. _____ _____

DATE

Non-transferable — present to cashier when cashing checks. If lost, please notify your Superx Drug store immediately.

Name — please print

Address   City

Customer's Signature   Form 1119-15A

VALIDATED BY: STORE MANAGER

SIGNATURE RECORD — COURTESY CARD NO. _____

(Please Print)
Name _____ (last) _____ (first) _____ (middle)   Date _____
Home Address _____
Home Phone _____
Name of Bank _____
Bank Address _____   Acct. No. _____
Employer _____   Employed Since _____
Employer's Address _____
Business Phone _____
Type of Checks to be presented: Personal ☐   Other ☐
Authorized Signature _____
Type of identification presented _____
Remarks _____
Approved by _____   Store Manager   Date _____

(Courtesy of SuperX Drugs.)

3. Completely fill in the sales draft.
4. Have the customer sign sales draft and compare signatures on the sales draft and the card.
5. Get approval for all sales over the predetermined limit.
6. Have all sales drafts turned in promptly for processing.

If the procedures cited are followed, the store will get its money and the credit company must worry about collecting from the customer. If these procedures are not followed, the credit card company may have up to 135 days recourse against the merchant if the customer does not pay. If the card is on the bad-card list, of course, the merchant loses that money just as he or she would a bad check.

If a firm has its own credit card, procedures such as those listed should be followed. In addition, care should be taken in the distribution of the cards. Tight security should be maintained during the printing of the cards and their distribution. If a card is messed up in printing, it should not be discarded until management has made note of it. At that time, the card should be cut up as opposed to just being thrown away. If cards are mailed to customers, a nonidentifying envelope should be used to guard against theft in the mail system and at the customer's mail box. If a retailer is going to have an independent credit card system, he or she should study how Master Card, American Express, and others set up their security system. Everything the big card firms do will not be applicable to the smaller retail operation. Many useful things, however, can be learned from these firms that specialize in the business of credit cards.

OTHER AREAS OF RETAIL SECURITY

Retail security is made up of additional aspects beyond the commonly identified areas of shoplifting, employee theft, and bad checks and credit cards. A good security system will have procedures set up for fire, robbery, civil disorder, power failure, natural disaster, burglary, and any other situation that may leave the store open to theft of any kind. An examination of what should be done in each of these situations should be given special attention by the retailer.[12]

Fire[13]

There are numerous retail fires in a given year. People are injured and, in some cases, killed. Damage is many times great. The probability of a fire happening in a store is great enough to warrant planning for this unfortunate event. Good planning may not always prevent a fire, but it could result in reduced property loss and, perhaps, save a life.

Fire prevention consists of many things. Stores should have fire extinguishers placed strategically throughout the store. These extinguishers should be checked on a regular basis for proper pressure. It is also good to have employees try out an extinguisher to see how it works as part of their training so that, in the event of a fire, precious time will not be spent learning how to work it. In addition to extinguishers, the store should be equipped with automatic sprinklers at the recommended level of one sprinkler head per 130 square feet of selling space and 100 square feet of stockroom space. Smoke alarms should also be used since their reaction time to a fire is about 10–15 seconds whereas sprinkler systems may take up to 3 minutes to sound the alarm. All equipment should be checked on a regular basis to ensure that all is in working order. The New York flagship store for Macy's sustained $10 million in damages in a major fire—a loss much greater than necessary—because the store's sprinkler system did not function due to a valve that was left shut by mistake.

Store employees should be organized for a fire. They should know what to do if a fire starts. Each sales area should have fire marshals who will get customers out while others will be charged with calling the fire department, fighting the fire if it is a small one, and securing the area. Of course, if the fire is large, cash and store records should be saved, if possible, by the store employees before leaving the store.

Robbery[14]

The threat of robbery can be minimized through various procedures that reduce accumulations of large amounts of cash. Money should be removed from active registers several times during the selling day. In addition, bank deposits should be made frequently instead of once a day. The retailer may also wish to balance the registers at times other than closing. Finally, at least two employees should make each trip to the bank using various routes and various times.

The most vulnerable time for a robbery attempt is at opening and closing time. At least two employees should be present at these times since the presence of more than one person tends to discourage a robber. But if that does not work and a robbery is attempted, store employees should be instructed to forget all the heroics they have seen on television. While the employees cooperate with the robber, they should be instructed to observe the criminal's physical characteristics (height, weight, age, color of hair, race, build, voice, clothing, and mannerisms) so that the police can later be given a good description of the robber.

Civil Disorder

From time to time riots have taken place in various cities, especially during the summer months. Although civil disorders have been the result of various causes, they all seem to have one thing in common—retail stores are looted! Some stores have handled the problem by ignoring it. Other retailers have stood in the doorway of their stores with gun in hand with varying degrees of success. In many situations, a show of strength has effectively discouraged looting. But this show of strength should be ready to be implemented during the early stages of the crisis before things get out of hand. The local merchants association should develop a contingency plan in cooperation with the police department and any private security firms that may be employed by the various stores. These plans should provide for the removal of all money and records at the first indication of trouble along with a show of organized force that will discourage looters. It must be remembered that, at such times, there will not be enough police to handle all situations. Retailers, organized as a group, may have to fill the void until state police, National Guard, and others arrive—which is usually 12 to 24 hours after the public disorder has begun. It should be emphasized again that all plans should be coordinated with the various police organizations. They need to have knowledge of what the merchants will do in such a situation and the merchants need to know what the police plan to do as well.

Power Failure

No matter if it is day or night, if the lights go out in today's modern retail store, the result is, in most cases, total darkness. Some customers as well as employees will panic. Some will use the opportunity to steal. Some may even get hurt as they attempt to get out of the store. These problems can be prevented by proper planning. A good security program and many laws as well will require that a retailer install backup lighting throughout the store that will come on *automatically* if the electricity goes off. Some larger stores may even go so far as to have their own backup generators that run the lights, computers, and the various security systems when normal electric service is interrupted. With blackouts and brownouts becoming more common in many areas of the country, power failure is no longer a rare occurrence for merchants. The retailer should plan properly for this very likely event.

Natural Disaster

Snowstorm, tornado, hurricane, flood, and other acts of Mother Nature can play havoc with a store. Proper planning for these events is different from planning for some other security problems because there is usually some time at least between the warning that the event will take place and the event. The one exception being a tornado, which may strike without warning but usually does so only when conditions have caused a tornado watch to be issued. For a tornado, employees should be instructed where to go in the store with assignments made previously as to who will direct customers to safe areas until the warning is over.

As for a snowstorm, hurricane, flood, and other more predictable acts of nature, security procedures will generally involve closing the store, securing it, and maintaining a skeleton crew to operate its vital functions and keep it secure. The first thing a retailer should do is arrange with the media a code name that will tell the media that the phone call informing them that the store is closing at a certain time or is closed is valid. This is particularly crucial in larger cities where many prank calls to the media make it necessary for the media to not accept any messages for broadcast without the use of verification codes—no matter what the content of the message. At times of impending natural disaster, stores may also wish to board up their windows or tape them if high wind is expected or place sand bags at strategic locations if water is going to be the problem. As for snow, if the store has a flat roof, the use of a snow blower on the roof at regular intervals could prevent a roof collapse during a period of heavy snowfall. Finally, the fact that people are in the store during this time of natural disaster will reduce or eliminate the problem of looting. It is unfortunate but true that an unattended store during a time of natural disaster is inviting to criminals since law enforcement officials are usually busy with the problems related to the natural disaster itself.

Burglary

Can a store prevent a burglary? As in all other security areas, the answer is "no!" But the threat can be minimized. How? Leave a light on in the store when closed so that people outside can see as much of the store as possible. Leave all cash register drawers open to show that they are empty. Place strong deadbolt locks on strong doors at all entrances of the store. A regular household lock can be opened by a trained burglar quicker than a person can open it using the key. Remove all attractive merchandise from the window and near the door at night to discourage the burglar who will break the glass, grab the merchandise, and run. A person will often have second thoughts if he or she has to actually enter the store to reach the goods. Place movement detectors at appropriate locations throughout the store that will notify the police if motion is detected. Other stores use "electronic eyes" that sound the alarm if an electronic beam is broken. This system works but can be overcome by a smart burglar. Because of this, most new burglar systems are of the type that detect motion.

Retail security is defined as awareness, prevention, and detection of merchandise and money shortages. An effective security system must concern itself with shoplifting. Common methods of shoplifting of which the retailer should be aware fall into categories such as the booster box, use of a coat or purse, bag, and fitting or dressing room irregularities. Methods of detection include TV cameras, electronic devices, and convex mirrors. Some methods of prevention are to display warning signs, keep sales floor well-lighted, and have salesclerks who are "on the ball." Employee theft involves many methods such as vendor kickbacks, throwing merchandise away, and fraudulent refunds. Methods of detection include honesty shoppers and polygraph. Removing temptation, checking employee records, and taking prompt action when an employee is caught are all methods of employee theft prevention. To aid in stopping customer and employee theft, the store should set up step-by-step procedures to handle the thief. Special care should be taken not to threaten or use undue force when apprehending a suspect. Bad checks are another problem for the retailer. If the retailer is to accept checks, then bad checks are a cost of doing business. The merchant must work, however, to minimize this cost by the use of established procedures and possibly by the use of specially designed cameras or fingerprint machines to aid in customer identification. Credit cards are also a concern for the retailer. Special care should be taken to match the credit card with its user. Retail security also involves planning for the unexpected such as fire, public disturbance, or power loss. Effective retail security is a complex, ever-changing, full-time task for the retailer. A task the merchant must perform. The retailer cannot afford to do otherwise.

DISCUSSION QUESTIONS

1. Define retail security. Why is it important to a retailer?
2. Discuss five methods of shoplifting.
3. Discuss five methods of employee theft.
4. Select a store in your area and ascertain how it attempts to prevent and/or detect shoplifting and employee theft.
5. Set up a step-by-step procedure for handling a shoplifter from the time the theft takes place until the day in court. Do retailers in your area have such a procedure?
6. What is a bad check? What can a retailer do to help prevent bad checks from being accepted in his or her store?
7. What are some common procedures to follow in handling credit cards?
8. Is planning for a fire worth the trouble in the modern store? Why or why not?
9. Ask a retailer to explain his or her procedures for handling a fire, robbery, public disorder, and natural disaster. If the store has contingency plans for such occasions, determine if the employees are aware of such plans. If the store has no such plans, attempt to determine why this is the case. Finally, write a proposal for the retailer that outlines various things that should be considered in handling these security areas.

[1] Joseph E. Bernstein, "The Prevention and Detection of Internal Theft," *Retail Control*, Vol. 43, no. 4 (December 1974), p. 56, published by the National Retail Merchants Association.

[2] Marian B. Rothman, "Internal and External Theft, What It Costs," *Stores*, Vol. 60, no. 1 (January 1978), p. 44. Copyright, National Retail Merchants Association, 1978.

[3] "Trying to Get the Jump on Theft," *Chain Store Age Executive*, Vol. 56, no. 8 (August 1980), p. 145.

[4] For a detailed look at electronic article surveillance (EAS), see Marian B. Rothman, "EAS for All?" *Stores*, Vol. 62, no. 6 (June 1980), pp. 31–38. Copyright, National Retail Merchants Association, 1980.

[5] Robert A. Rupe, "Formula for Loss Prevention," *Retail Control*, Vol. 48, no. 7 (March 1980), p. 13. Copyright, Financial Executives Division, National Retail Merchants Association, 1980.

[6] Reprinted by permission of *The Wall Street Journal*. © Dow Jones & Company, Inc., 1980. All Rights Reserved.

[7] Discussion taken in part from Bob Curtis, "Methods of Employee Theft," *Security Control: Internal Theft* (New York: Chain Store Age Books, 1973), pp. 47–72.

[8] Reprinted by permission from *Chain Store Age Executive*, August 1980, © Copyright Lebhar-Friedman, Inc., 425 Park Avenue, New York, N.Y. 10022.

[9] For information, see S. J. Curtis, *Modern Retail Security* (Springfield, Ill.: Charles C. Thomas, Publisher, 1960), pp. 255–258, 915–920.

[10] Discussion taken in part from Bob Vereen, "Store Security Problems," *Hardware Retailer* (June 1968), p. 59.

[11] Discussion taken in part from William H. Bolen and Anthony J. Faria, "Bad Checks = Bad Profits," *Retail Control*, Vol. 43, no. 6 (February 1975), pp. 20–31, published by the National Retail Merchants Association.

[12] Discussion for this section taken in part from Marian B. Rothman, "So Losses Don't Mount, Handling Disasters," *Stores*, Vol. 60, no. 4 (April 1978), pp. 41–44. Copyright, National Retail Merchants Association, 1978.

[13] Reprinted by permission from *Chain Store Age Executive*, February 1981, © Copyright Lebhar-Friedman, Inc., 425 Park Avenue, New York, N.Y. 10022.

[14] Discussion taken in part from "Crime Knows No Season," *Stores*, Vol. 60, no. 2 (February 1978), pp. 53–54. Copyright, National Retail Merchants Association, 1978.

CHAPTER 25

Operations Control

"Don't look now, but there goes 'PROFIT'!"

"Last year our store made a profit of $100,000!" Such a statement by a retailer may sound great, but does it mean that the store did as well as it could have? Should that store have made $200,000? The control function is called upon by management to answer this question. As the reader will recall, merchandise and security control areas have already been discussed. As noted in Chapter 15, merchandise control is concerned with determining the status of a store's inventory. Is the turnover as planned? Both dollar control and unit control are employed to ensure that the merchandise on hand is appropriate to the needs of the store. As for security control, the prevention of lost profits as a result of shoplifting, employee theft, bad checks, and other forms of criminal as well as noncriminal activity is vital to the continued operation of the store. But what about the control of day-to-day expenses? What about the overall control of store performance? Operations control serves these needs of a store.

Operations control is defined as the evaluation of store operations for the purpose of improving overall store performance. As indicated, operations control is concerned with the store's expenses as well as its overall performance. Hence, operations control can be divided into two main elements: expense control and performance control (Figure 25–1). The discussion that follows will examine the elements as shown in the figure.

EXPENSE CONTROL[1]

A store spends an amount equal to 3 percent of sales on receiving and marking. Is such an expense necessary? Is the amount spent appropriate to the need? How does that expense compare with the industry average? The answers to these and other questions

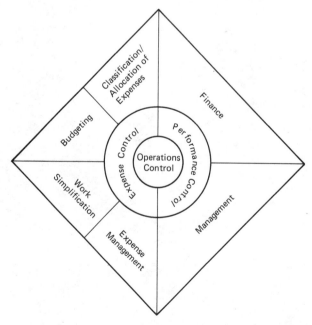

Figure 25–1

Elements of operations control.

are made possible by the procedures that encompass expense control. These procedures include classification of expenses, allocation of expenses, budgeting, work simplification, and expense management. A store that follows these procedures as outlined will be in a better position to judge the efficiency of its operation.

Classification of Expenses

Due to the numerous expenses that are incurred by a store, the wise retailer will search for a classification system that can be used to study the expenditures that have been made. Such a system will improve the chances that no expense area will go undetected and, therefore, not be evaluated. Numerous standard classification systems are available from various trade groups. The one to be included in this discussion is the system provided by the National Retail Merchants Association. It is noted that other systems are similar in scope.

To control expenses, the retailer must first determine what his or her expenses are. To aid in this task, the National Retail Merchants Association provides a suggested breakdown of expenses with 17 categories or natural divisions. By using such a system, the retailer will be able to compare company performance with published industry standards. The suggested breakdown of expenses also provides a starting point for firms who have no set ideas about how to classify expenses. The 17 standard natural divisions of expense as suggested by NRMA are:[2]

01 – Payroll. *Includes salaries, wages, commissions, bonuses. Does not include alterations or service departments.*

03 – Media costs. *Includes space cost for print media and time cost for broadcast media. Does not include internal production costs.*

04 – Taxes. *Includes all taxes paid or accrued other than taxes based on income.*

06 – Supplies. *Includes cost of items consumed in the operation of the business.*

07 – Services purchased. *Includes delivery, collection, cleaning, and/or other nonprofessional services rendered by outsiders.*

08 – Unclassified. *Includes all charges that do not fit anywhere else. Traffic fines and donations to charities are two examples.*

09 – Travel. *Includes all travel on business.*

10 – Communications. *Includes telephones, postage, and other forms of communications.*

11 – Pensions. *Includes money set aside for pension purposes.*

12 – Insurance. *Includes the cost of all insurance.*

13 – Depreciation. *Includes depreciation on capital accounts.*

14 – Professional services. *Includes fees for accounting purposes, legal assistance, and special surveys and audits.*

16 – Bad debts. *Includes the actual debts that have been written off.*

17 – Equipment rental. *Includes all long-term rental or lease items.*

18 – Outside maintenance and equipment service contracts. *Includes all maintenance contracts on equipment.*

20 – Real property rentals. *Includes expenses incurred or rent paid for real estate used in the operation of the business.*

92 – Credits and outside revenues. *Includes any credit to expense that may result from the receipt of outside revenue or from a charge to accounts outside the framework of the expense centers.*

The reader will note that the natural classification system of 17 categories has four digits missing in the order of numbers. Versions prior to 1976 had 05 as an interest account, 15 as donations, and 19 as a transfer account. The first two have been moved to 08, and 19 has been changed to a 90 series for several transfer situations that are unusual or are not always related directly to store operations. The 02 account, allocated fringe benefits, on the other hand, is still used, but it is treated like a 90 transfer account for purposes of expense classification. It should be noted that the number system itself was not changed as many retailers already had their classification system set up. The new is designed to fit in with the old.

Allocation of Expenses

For the small store, a classification of expenses is equivalent to an allocation of expenses. For the larger operation, there is need to determine in more detail just how the money was spent or how it will be spent for payroll or equipment rental or any other of the natural expense divisions. To accomplish this task, the operations of a store can be divided into ten areas of responsibility. Each of these areas in turn can be broken down into smaller areas and even subareas of responsibility so that operations control can determine with a good degree of accuracy just where (expense center) the money is being spent within the store.

Expense Centers.   The ten major areas of store operation are divided into 44 expense centers under the National Retail Merchants Association Retail Accounting System. The ten areas and 44 expense centers are:[3]

*010   *Property and equipment*
020   *Real estate, buildings, and building equipment*
030   *Furniture, fixtures, and non-building equipment*

100   *Company management*
110   *Executive office*
130   *Branch management*
140   *Internal audit*
150   *Legal and consumer activities*

200   *Accounting and management information*
210   *Control management, general accounting, and statistical*
220   *Sales audit*
230   *Accounts payable*
240   *Payroll and timekeeping department*
280   *Data processing*

* The Property and Equipment Summary Account is numbered 010 instead of 000 to accommodate EDP programming techniques.

300   Credit and accounts receivable
    310   Credit management
    330   Collection
    340   Accounts receivable and bill adjustment
    350   Cash office
    360   Branch/store selling location offices

400   Sales promotion
    410   Sales promotion management
    420   Advertising
    430   Shows, special events, and exhibits
    440   Display

500   Service and operations
    510   Service and operations management
    530   Security
    550   Telephones and communications
    560   Utilities
    570   Housekeepng
    580   Maintenance and repairs

600   Personnel
    610   Personnel management
    620   Employment
    640   Training
    660   Medical and other employee services
    670   Supplementary benefits

700   Merchandise receiving, storage, and distribution
    710   Management of merchandise receiving, storage, and distribution
    720   Receiving and marking
    730   Reserve stock storage
    750   Shuttle services

800   Selling and supporting services
    810   Selling supervision
    820   Direct selling
    830   Customer services
    840   Selling support services
    860   Central wrapping and packing
    880   Delivery

900   Merchandising
    910   Merchandising management
    920   Buying
    930   Merchandise control

When thought desirable, an even finer breakdown can be obtained. For example, the 720 account, receiving and marking, can be divided up as follows:[4]

720   Receiving and Marking
    721   Receiving
    723   Checking

Expense data for the industry, which are classified by sales volume, are available from NRMA for purposes of evaluation. Data for 10 divisions, 44 subdivisions, and 22 minisubdivisions are made available to stores on an annual basis so that performance can be compared with industry figures.[5] These comparison figures are useful to the retailer as decisions are made dealing with store performance. For example, suppose that a department store with annual sales of $12 million is spending 30 percent of sales for payroll expenses. Is 30 percent similar to that of other stores? A check of the *FOR Report*, Table 25-1, reveals that department stores in that sales range typically (median) spend less than 20 percent of sales on payroll. Such data indicate that the retailer should look further for the reason(s) why the store is spending such a large pro-portional share of sales on payroll. It is for reasons such as this that the retailer should use an expense classification system and an allocation system similar to the standard system in use for that particular type of retail operation. The results of the many pos-sible comparisons can be quite interesting.

Selling Centers.   The allocation of expenses to the various expense centers tells the retailer how much is being spent in each phase of the store's operation. The data do not, however, indicate the profitability of the store or any of its departments. To determine profitability, it is necessary to allocate expenses on the basis of income-

Table 25-1

Median Gross Margin and Expenses by Natural Division as a Percentage of
Total Sales for Selected Department Stores, 1979.

Variable	Sales (millions)					
	$2–5	$5–10	$10–20	$20–50	$50–100	Over $100
Gross margin	37.48%	39.05%	37.47%	39.30%	39.43%	40.89%
01 Payroll	19.96	19.22	16.95	18.00	17.10	17.84
03 Media costs	2.83	3.12	3.31	3.14	3.19	2.39
04 Taxes	2.23	2.08	2.17	2.09	2.16	2.54
06 Supplies	3.09	2.76	2.93	.3.08	2.93	2.28
07 Services purchased	1.90	1.59	1.78	1.65	2.44	2.57
08 Unclassified	0.97	0.62	0.65	0.65	0.58	0.98
09 Travel	0.51	0.48	0.40	0.43	0.37	0.33
10 Communications	0.82	0.78	0.86	0.78	0.95	0.86
11 Pensions	0.38	0.57	0.39	0.61	0.81	0.71
12 Insurance	1.31	1.08	0.82	0.86	0.87	0.95
13 Depreciation	1.06	1.35	1.46	1.46	1.44	1.43
14 Professional services	0.27	0.25	0.23	0.22	0.20	0.13
16 Bad debts	0.26	0.27	0.37	0.39	0.53	0.54
17 Equipment rentals	0.21	0.15	0.33	0.56	0.29	0.29
18 Outside maintenance/ equipment service contracts	0.00	0.40	0.18	0.32	0.28	0.10
20 Real property rentals	2.49	3.14	3.00	2.72	3.23	2.57
92 Credit and outside revenues	−0.28	−0.62	−1.00	−0.87	−0.70	−1.07

Source: *Financial and Operating Results of Department and Specialty Stores of 1979* (New York: Financial Executives Division, National Retail Merchants Association, 1980).

producing departments. The expenses of the store must be deducted from the gross margin (sales minus cost of goods sold) figures of the selling departments, as such is the only true measure of profitability for the store. This expense allocation should not be a problem, but it usually is. The difficulty lies with the allocation of expenses that are not related directly to a department. For example, a men's wear department has payroll expenses, travel expenses, and expenditures for equipment and displays. Everyone agrees that such expenses are a part of that department and naturally should be allocated to men's wear. But what about the salary of the store manager, building rent, utilities, and numerous other items? Assuming that the store stays in business, these costs will continue even if the men's department does not. How can these expenses be allocated to the selling departments of the store for purposes of analysis? Is this expense allocation fair to a department manager who has no control over the manager's salary and other variables? Controversy on this point has led to two methods of expense allocation: contribution margin and net profit. Each approach will be examined as to its method of application and its advantages and disadvantages:

Contribution margin method. The idea behind this method is that each selling department is a responsibility center. Using this premise, a department manager and the department are evaluated using only those expenses over which that department has control. All direct expenses are charged against the department. Indirect expenses, on the other hand, are considered for accounting purposes to be general expenses for the store and are used only when analyzing the total store. For example, suppose that a department had sales of $90,000 with a cost of goods sold of $40,000. From the gross margin of $50,000 would come the $20,000 of direct expenses (payroll, travel, etc.) leaving a balance of $30,000. The $30,000 figure is considered to be the contribution margin of the department—$30,000 is what the department is contributing to overhead. It is emphasized that for purposes of analysis, only direct expenses are allocated to the department.

Sales		$90,000
Cost of goods sold		40,000
Gross margin		$50,000
Direct expenses		
Payroll	$10,000	
Travel	2,000	
Advertising	5,000	
Supplies	3,000	
Total		$20,000
Contribution margin		$30,000

The advantages of the contribution margin method are thought to be twofold. First, each department can be compared with every other department to see how each is contributing to the support of the total store. Second, each department manager's performance can be measured in terms of how well he or she has generated income while controlling expenses. In other words, the method measures somewhat the efficiency of each department.

The disadvantages are also twofold. First, the departments do enjoy the benefits of delivery, credit, and so on. Therefore, a true picture of a selling department cannot ignore such expenses. Can a department function without such services? The second and related disadvantage is that, if the department is not charged in some way for indirect expenses, excessive use of such services may result. For example, under a contribution margin plan, a department is not charged for delivery. The personnel of that department may therefore encourage its use as a means of generating some additional sales. The department is making money, but the store may be losing money. Charging deliveries to the department originating such requests will usually reduce such requests. It is felt that a department naturally watches more closely those expenses for which it is in some way held accountable.

Net profit method. The net profit method solves the accountability problem by allocating *all* expenses to the selling departments. Direct expenses are allocated in the same way as under the contribution margin approach. The allocation of indirect expenses may be determined on the basis of a formula using either the department's square feet of selling area or the department's sales as a percentage of the total store figures. Other suggested allocation procedures are shown in Table 25–2. Herein lies the greatest problem with the net profit method. It is extremely difficult to make an equitable distribution of all indirect expenses. An even greater difficulty is getting the various department managers to agree on any such allocation of expenses. Still another disadvantage is the fact that the evaluation of the department manager is based on figures over which he or she does not have total control. Such should always be kept in mind by the upper management levels when measuring the performance of the department. As for advantages, the net profit approach does give a net profit figure for a department, does promote more concern in the various departments for controlling indirect expenses, and does encourage an analysis of all expenses at all levels of the organization. Under the net profit approach, using the previous example, a department with a gross

Table 25–2

Suggested Expense Allocation Procedures for Use in
Net Profit Method for Selected Expense Centers[1]

Expense Center		Selling Center Allocation Procedure
110	Executive office	Net sales
230	Accounts payable	Number of vendor invoices
240	Payroll and timekeeping department	Number of employees
330	Collection	Credit sales volume
340	Accounts receivable	Number of credit transactions
420	Advertising	Number of advertising inches/minutes
570	Housekeeping	Square feet of selling/nonselling floor space
610	Personnel management	Number of employees
720	Receiving and marking	Number of units received
880	Delivery	Number of units delivered
920	Buying	Planned purchases

[1] For example, if a selling center's number of deliveries makes up 5 percent of all deliveries made by the store, then 5 percent of the expenses for expense center 880 will be allocated to that particular selling center.

margin of $50,000 would have the $20,000 of direct expenses but would also have indirect expenses charged against it (for illustration purposes—$20,000). Therefore, the department would show a net profit of $10,000.

Gross margin		*$50,000*
Direct expenses	*$20,000*	
Indirect expenses	*20,000*	
Total expenses		*40,000*
Net profit		*$10,000*

It should be noted that, depending on how the indirect expenses are allocated, the department could show a loss, break even, or make profit.

Regardless of the approach used for allocation of expenses, good managers should remember that either method has its strong and weak points. Making an arbitrary allocation of indirect expenses can cause problems. Ignoring indirect expenses can also cause problems. Perhaps a better approach than either is a combination of the two methods. Such a procedure provides a contribution margin figure for use in analyzing accountability while the net profit figure is used to measure profitability.

Budgeting

The next step in expense control calls for the development of on-going expense plans. These plans take into consideration the past, present, and future. In other words, the retailer should develop budgets for each expense center and for each selling center as a means of reflecting what the needs of the store are and will be in the future. Such plans are generally for a period of one year but are usually divided into units of time—usually one month—within the budget period.

In its simplest sense, a budget is last year's history adjusted to reflect:[6]

Changes in the level of economic activity
Changes in the state of the art
Changes in policy or practice (e.g., level of service)

However, a budget can, and should be, a good deal more creative. The budgeting procedure should include:

Intelligent innovation
Prudent risk-taking
Elimination of frills
Reasonable return on investment
Absorption of functions
Old-fashioned just making do and, sometimes, radical thinking and challenges to the axioms of the retailing business

Zero-Base Budgeting. Zero-base budgeting is a process requiring the justification of every dollar of an organization's projected expenditures for a forthcoming fiscal year. It places previously authorized expenditures on an equal basis with requests for new funds.[7] Starting with a clean slate or zero base forces each expense center and/or selling center to justify all its expense needs. The dialogue that results from this situation tends to encourage the elimination of frills, intelligent innovation, and the other desired results of creative budgeting as well. To base a control device solely on history is poor retail management. Need should be the primary consideration.

Fixed-Base Budgeting.   After need has been evaluated, budgets for expense centers can be determined on a fixed-budget basis. The fixed budget requires the establishment of a specific, predetermined amount. For example, expense center 530, security, should have budget requirements that can be predicted if related to need. The monthly budget form for the department might be as in Figure 25–2. Note that there is a provision for a determination of the variance between actual and planned performance. As each period of time passes, the discrepancy, if any, between the budgeted or planned amount and the actual amount spent is carefully scrutinized. Some stores will use a 5 percent variance rule. A difference under 5 percent is no problem. Five percent or more means that the department manager is asked for an explanation. Such a procedure makes budgeting an effective control device.

Care should be taken in any system of expense control, however, to ensure that a budget does not become too rigid. A budget made months in advance cannot always anticipate all events that will take place. Some provisions should be made for flexibility. A procedure that automatically penalizes a department for going over the budget is wrong. On the other hand, a budget that is too flexible with no concern by management if the budget is not met is really no budget at all. Budget figures should be adjusted only for unexpected, unpredictable, legitimate reasons. To do anything less is to not have a budget system of expense control.

Productivity-Base Budgeting.   A possible solution to the need for a flexible budget is to develop the budgets for the store and its various departments on the basis of various levels of productivity. Such budgets are often actually referred to as flexible budgets. Since budgets must be built upon sales forecasts and other predicting techniques, a certain level of uncertainty is found in every forecast and in every budget. A

Figure 25–2

Expense center 530—security (budgeted expenses in dollars).

| NATURAL DIVISION | CURRENT PERIOD | | | | YEAR-TO-DATE | | | |
	Actual	Budget	Variance Amount	Variance Per Cent	Actual	Budget	Variance Amount	Variance Per Cent
01 Payroll	2426	2500	74	3.0	7639	7500	(139)	(1.8)
06 Supplies	512	450	(62)	(13.8)	1364	1350	(14)	(1.0)
07 Services Purchased	400	400	00	—	1300	1200	(100)	(8.3)
08 Unclassified	53	50	(3)	(6.0)	162	150	(12)	(8.0)
Total	3391	3400	9	.3	10465	10200	(265)	(2.6)

budget based on various levels of productivity tends to put a degree of certainty into an uncertain situation. For example, a flexible monthly budget, as in Figure 25-3, for Department 860, Central Wrapping, shows the projected expenses for various levels of demand as measured in units of sale. Under the system, the department manager knows how he or she stands as demand or whatever other measure of productivity fluctuates. There is no need to explain as many variances for excess expenses over budget under this system. Excess money in the budget is also minimized since the budget is tied more to current need as opposed to projected need as would be true under the fixed-base plan. Once the budget level is known, variance analysis can be conducted in the same way as for a fixed-base budget. Flexible budgeting allocates money according to need as the need arises as measured by some unit of productivity.

Work Simplification

Another aspect of expense control is concerned with going beyond the dollars expended and looking at what is being done to create the expense. Productivity-base budgeting equates expenses to given productivity, but can productivity per dollar be measured? Any change that can reduce the time and effort expended to perform a task reduces expense. Such changes are the goal of work simplification. Work simplification takes many forms. For example, a store required its sales personnel to fill out a three-part form for layaways. Although each part contained the same information, the salesperson had to write it all three different times. By switching to a form that permitted the material to be written only once, time was saved on each transaction along with an accompanying increase in accuracy since the employee tended to make fewer mistakes when writing the information just once.

Another example of work simplification is inventory taking by means of a portable device that puts the data on magnetic tape. The store employee determines the quantity of the item on the shelf and records the product number and amount into a magnetic tape recorder in a manner very similar to operating a ten-key adding machine. The store then calls its distribution center and plays the tape over the phone to a computer that records the data, compares the data with desired stock norms, and prepares an order for shipment to the store the following morning. Many man-hours are saved when using this procedure. No time-consuming orders need to be written up.

Figure 25-3

Expense center 860—central wrapping.

NATURAL DIVISION	UNIT OF MEASURE—UNITS OF SALE					
	LEVEL OF SALES IN UNITS					
	100	200	300	400	500	600
	Budgeted Expenses in Dollars					
01 Payroll	$414	$414	$621	$621	$ 828	$ 828
06 Supplies	45	90	135	180	225	270
08 Unclassified	25	30	35	40	45	50
Total	$484	$534	$791	$841	$1098	$1148

An additional benefit is that few errors appear since the data are not handled several times. The initial investment in equipment is substantial, but the savings that result in increased productivity may more than compensate for such expenditures.

Work simplification is not easy since it involves asking "why?" to every procedure in use in the store. For example:

Why are new credit accounts handled by four different people?
Why do receiving personnel check all goods twice?
Why do goods go to forward storage areas instead of straight to the sales floor?
Why are two different forms needed to transfer merchandise from one department to another?
Why is the stockroom located so far away from many selling stations?

Such questions can tread on sacred territory. People resist change. For many situations, the real reason for performing a task in a particular way is that it has always been done that way. The fact does not in itself make it bad, but it does not automatically make it good either. Work simplification is simply an effort to increase the productivity level in the store so that more work will result from a given dollar outlay. The retailer who follows a systematic plan of work simplification should have a better run as well as a more profitable store because of it.

Expense Management

Using the information gathered as a result of the process of expense allocation, budgeting, and work simplification, expense management attempts to determine if the proper amount has been allocated to perform a particular task. It is noted that expense management is not synonymous with cost cutting. Expense management is instead a procedure or a way of thinking that ensures that the expense needs of the store are provided for. Such a procedure may even make use of various forms to ensure that a systematic approach is followed (Figure 25–4). If the various procedures of expense control indicate that more money might be needed for security, or central wrapping, or other areas, then it is the task of expense management to evaluate the need in relation to the total store and all its financial requirements. Such an evaluation may result in more funds being allocated to the department in question or less. The individuals within a company who are given the task of expense management must be people who have a complete understanding of the store and its goals and objectives. No one else will be able to perform this most crucial managerial task in a successful manner. It should be emphasized that weak expense management means weak expense control. Expense control is only as strong as its weakest component. A firm with weak expense control is a retail store that is asking for trouble.

PERFORMANCE CONTROL

Just as expense control places a heavy emphasis on the performance of the store's expense centers, performance control is concerned with the operation of the total store. Total store control concentrates on two areas: finance and management.

Figure 25–4

Forecasting and controlling costs help to ensure profits. Many forms can be used to help accomplish this task.

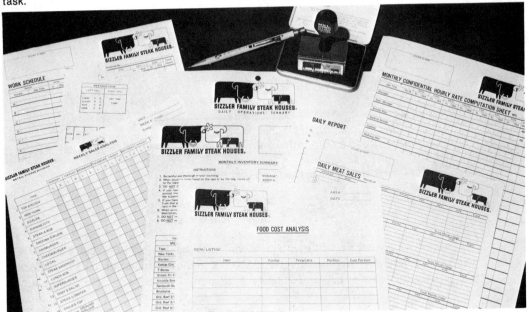

(Courtesy of Collins Foods International, Inc.)

Finance

Did the store provide an adequate return on investment (ROI)? Did net profits as a percentage of net sales increase over last year? Is the current ratio (current assets to current liabilities) at a desired level (2 to 1 is desirable for most operations)? These and similar questions can be answered if the store operation is evaluated from a financial standpoint.

Return on Investment (ROI). One very important financial measure that deserves special mention is return on investment. By using data from the store's financial statements[8] and other sources, the retailer should make an effort to determine exactly what is the store's rate of return. If such a figure is very low when compared with other financial opportunities, the retailer should either improve the store's performance or shift the financial resources to some other venture. Although ROI is not a day-to-day calculation for use in making merchandising decisions, it is useful in evaluating:[9]

The use of capital in existing units and their contribution to profit.

The potential of new ventures and their contribution to profit.

The effect on profits of additional investment relating to the expansion of existing store units, replacement of existing units with new facilities, and elimination of units that are performing poorly.

Depending on the desires of the store, return on investment can be calculated in several different ways. The investment base may be:[10]

Total company
Selling location
Merchandise division or department
Operating and/or service division or department

whereas the profitability level can be:

Net profit
Contribution before corporate overhead
Contribution before corporate overhead plus departmental fixed expenses

The formula for return on investment is, therefore,

$$\text{ROI} = \frac{\text{Profitability Level}}{\text{Investment Base}}$$

For example, if a store's income statement indicates that the profit level for the store was $25,000, a retailer who has invested $300,000 in the business would have a return of 8.3 percent on his or her investment for the period. There are, of course, many

$$8.3\% \text{ (ROI)} = \frac{\$\ 25,000}{\$300,000}$$

available investments that yield more than 8.3 percent. If the future does not appear to hold any promise for improvement, hard decisions will be called for from a performance control standpoint.

Ratios.　Along with return on investment, other popular financial measures that reveal useful information about a store are presented in "The Ratios of Retailing" as compiled every year by Dun & Bradstreet (Figure 25–5). These 14 calculations reveal much about a store. The compiled data also make possible the comparison of the store's performance with median industry performance as well as with upper- and lower-quartile results. Financial norms are also provided by various trade groups and trade publications on an annual basis. The retailer should use this information where appropriate. Judgment is needed, however, since a given store may not be "typical," therefore, its performance may not be "typical." To assume that a store is doing well or badly when the *only* basis is a financial comparison with industry data is a very weak system of control. Financial data are, however, a good tool of evaluation if used properly.[11]

Management

Operations control should also include a complete audit of all aspects of store management. Such an analysis of managerial performance involves an evaluation of all policies and procedures that are followed by the management group. In terms of this

Figure 25–5

Ratios for retailing.

How the Ratios Are Figured

To the economist and the statistician, terms such as "median" and "quartile" are everyday working language, no more mysterious than "gross markup" to the retail store proprietor. But though they involve precious dollars and cents, their precise meaning is foggy at best to many business executives.

In the ratio table, three figures appear under each ratio heading for each retail line. The center figure, in bold type, is the median; the figures immediately above and below the median, are respectively, the upper and lower quartiles. To understand their use, the executive must also know how they are calculated.

First, year-end financial statements from concerns covered by the survey are analyzed by **Dun & Bradstreet** statisticians, who calculate each ratio individually for each concern in the sample.

The individual ratio figures, entered on data processing cards and segregated by line of business, are then arranged in order of magnitude—the best ratio figure at the top, the weakest at the bottom. The figure that falls just in the middle of this series becomes the median for the ratio in that line of business. The figure halfway between the median and the highest terms of the series is the **upper quartile;** the term halfway between the median and the bottom of the series is the **lower quartile.**

In a strictly statistical sense, then, each median is the **typical ratio figure** for all the concerns studied in a given retail line. The upper and lower quartiles, in turn, typify the experience of the firms in the top half and the bottom half of the sample, respectively.

Definitions of Terms

Collection Period—The number of days that the total of trade accounts and notes receivable (including assigned accounts and discounted notes, if any), less reserves for bad debts, represents when compared with annual net credit sales. Formula: divide the annual net credit sales by 365 days to obtain the average credit sales per day. Then divide the total of accounts and notes receivable (plus any discounted notes receivable) by the average credit sales per day to obtain the average collection period.

Current Assets—Total of cash, accounts and notes receivable for the sales of merchandise in regular trade quarters, less any reserves for bad debts, advances on merchandise, inventory less any reserves, listed securities when not in excess of market, state and municipal bonds not in excess of market, and U.S. government securities.

Current Debt—Total of all liabilities due within one year from statement date including current payments on serial notes, mortgages, debentures, or other funded debts. This item also includes current reserves, such as gross reserves for federal in-

come and excess profit taxes, reserves for contingencies set up for specific purposes but does not include reserves for depreciation.

Fixed Assets—The sum of the cost value of land and the depreciated book values of buildings, leasehold improvements, fixtures, furniture, machinery, tools, and equipment.

Funded Debt—Mortgages, bonds, debentures, gold notes, serial notes, or other obligations with maturity of more than one year from the statement date.

Inventory—The sum of raw material, material in process and finished merchandise. It does not include supplies.

Net Profits—Profit after full depreciation on buildings, machinery, equipment, furniture, and other assets of a fixed nature; after reserves for federal income and excess profit taxes; after reduction in the value of inventory to cost or market, whichever is lower; after charge-offs for bad debts; after miscellaneous reserves and adjustments; but before dividends or withdrawals.

Net Sales—The dollar volume of business transacted for 365 days net after deductions

for returns, allowances and discounts from gross sales.

Net Sales to Inventory—The quotient obtained by dividing the annual net sales by the statement inventory. This quotient does not represent the actual physical turnover, which would be determined by reducing the annual net sales to the cost of goods sold and then dividing the resulting figure by the statement inventory.

Net Working Capital—The excess of the current assets over the current debt.

Tangible Net Worth—The sum of all outstanding preferred or preference stocks (if any) and outstanding common stocks, surplus and undivided profits, less any intangible items in the assets, such as goodwill, trademarks, patents, copyrights, leaseholds, mailing list, treasury stock, organizational expenses, and underwriting discounts and expenses.

Turnover of New Working Capital—The quotient obtained by dividing annual net sales by net working capital.

Turnover of Tangible Net Worth—The quotient obtained by dividing annual net sales by tangible net worth.

(continued)

Figure 25–5 (continued)

Retailing

Line of Business (and number of concerns reporting)	Current assets to current debt — Times	Net profits on net sales — Percent	Net profits on tangible net worth — Percent	Net profits on net working capital — Percent	Net sales to tangible net worth — Times	Net sales to net working capital — Times	Collection period — Days	Net sales to inventory — Times	Fixed assets to tangible net worth — Percent	Current debt to tangible net worth — Percent	Total debt to tangible net worth — Percent	Inventory to net working capital — Percent	Current debt to inventory — Percent	Funded debts to net working capital — Percent
5531* Auto and home supply stores (3,041)	4.66	8.26	41.56	48.63	8.60	9.79	41	8.0	63.0	147.3	214.4	145.1	121.3	106.0
	2.33	4.26	21.64	24.03	4.85	5.05	22	5.1	27.2	61.8	94.1	94.5	73.3	53.5
	1.45	1.86	10.37	8.51	2.58	2.82	10	3.5	12.5	20.5	33.2	62.5	33.7	19.5
5641 Children's and infants' wear stores (1,688)	7.21	10.32	37.72	41.10	5.67	5.84	19	5.2	39.6	87.4	152.7	138.2	77.5	115.0
	3.20	4.84	18.03	19.58	3.37	3.52	9	3.5	16.4	35.2	58.1	99.2	43.0	64.1
	1.83	1.47	6.23	5.55	1.77	2.05	3	2.3	6.4	12.2	17.7	71.4	19.8	24.6
5611 Clothing and furnishings, men's and boy's (5,652)	5.89	9.11	34.70	38.50	6.21	6.26	33	5.3	38.7	104.2	153.8	149.1	81.1	90.2
	2.91	4.05	16.60	18.04	3.53	3.75	15	3.6	16.4	45.3	62.4	101.7	49.8	46.6
	1.81	1.48	6.19	6.00	2.16	2.38	5	2.6	6.5	16.7	22.8	70.9	25.1	18.6
5311 Department stores (847)	5.44	4.09	16.77	19.78	5.98	6.08	51	6.3	46.7	81.5	147.3	127.9	86.7	72.4
	3.09	2.00	8.78	10.25	3.75	4.06	25	4.6	23.5	42.7	62.3	86.6	56.9	36.7
	2.02	.66	2.58	2.93	2.37	2.66	8	3.3	8.8	19.0	26.4	60.2	31.0	11.4
5651 Family clothing stores (2,171)	8.79	10.29	32.90	39.97	5.09	5.42	30	5.4	37.6	76.1	127.6	131.8	72.1	94.6
	3.80	5.09	15.97	19.21	2.87	3.15	11	3.3	16.3	30.8	50.6	94.9	37.5	52.1
	2.06	1.78	6.24	7.05	1.57	1.91	4	2.2	6.0	9.9	15.7	66.4	16.6	19.9
5712 Furniture stores (6,941)	6.18	9.02	34.95	38.57	6.59	7.02	72	6.9	39.2	108.1	161.0	130.7	102.7	90.4
	2.98	4.42	16.16	17.45	3.48	3.76	32	4.4	15.1	41.9	65.7	83.2	61.7	44.3
	1.74	1.73	6.76	6.17	1.81	2.04	13	3.1	5.6	15.5	24.6	45.6	31.2	16.7
5541 Gasoline service stations (3,062)	6.90	6.00	59.23	100.68	16.89	28.57	18	39.3	81.4	83.5	132.4	100.4	151.5	207.2
	2.79	2.95	25.05	39.53	8.44	12.54	7	22.2	44.5	29.6	50.2	67.5	71.6	75.1
	1.42	.93	9.26	10.30	3.62	5.00	2	11.4	19.4	9.3	16.2	36.8	27.2	20.1
5411 Grocery stores (4,197)	6.36	4.27	39.68	68.37	17.39	24.88	6	22.0	92.2	92.0	166.3	129.0	104.6	197.2
	2.70	1.79	20.17	33.21	9.18	13.07	2	15.4	45.6	35.9	64.5	89.4	55.3	87.4
	1.43	.74	9.32	11.89	4.52	6.37	0	10.4	20.8	11.5	19.6	59.5	22.2	28.0
5251 Hardware stores (3,036)	8.39	9.18	29.72	34.24	5.43	5.40	31	4.7	42.2	88.0	153.9	129.4	71.6	104.6
	3.81	4.47	15.81	18.06	3.12	3.36	17	3.3	16.6	33.1	57.3	95.4	36.6	58.2
	2.00	1.60	6.12	6.33	1.80	2.18	8	2.3	6.7	10.6	16.9	72.9	16.9	23.9
5722 Household appliance stores (2,168)	4.44	8.56	43.63	56.79	8.70	11.02	34	8.3	47.4	155.5	204.6	167.9	115.9	111.9
	2.20	3.62	19.71	24.59	4.50	5.43	19	5.1	21.3	55.6	77.2	93.3	78.1	50.5
	1.37	1.37	7.60	7.71	2.22	2.92	9	3.6	8.2	17.7	26.2	53.2	40.0	16.2

SIC*	Store type														
5944	Jewelry stores (2,051)	7.17	14.61	35.87	38.00	4.23	4.12	54	3.6	32.0	105.0	145.6	138.9	75.0	71.8
		3.26	7.71	19.74	19.88	2.38	2.47	26	2.4	14.0	42.8	57.9	97.3	44.4	36.2
		1.93	3.29	9.50	9.23	1.38	1.54	10	1.6	5.8	13.8	20.2	70.6	18.7	15.1
5211	Lumber and other building materials dealers (3,699)	4.51	6.00	34.28	37.93	8.07	8.64	53	10.0	56.8	123.7	185.2	115.2	137.1	94.1
		2.49	3.46	17.73	19.14	4.59	5.01	37	6.2	25.5	55.6	80.0	78.4	78.3	45.4
		1.60	1.74	8.66	8.74	2.64	3.00	23	4.1	11.3	20.9	30.8	50.8	41.6	15.2
5399	Miscellaneous general merchandise stores (2,444)	10.29	9.18	26.88	36.92	5.69	6.89	26	6.9	38.4	68.4	109.3	123.3	64.7	107.9
		4.20	4.06	13.96	17.86	3.02	3.77	10	4.0	15.1	24.4	40.6	90.6	33.3	49.9
		2.15	1.48	6.00	6.58	1.65	2.06	3	2.5	5.8	7.9	12.3	62.5	14.2	19.0
5511	Motor vehicle dealers (7,162)	1.76	2.27	30.51	37.65	21.28	24.62	10	8.6	46.8	313.9	364.4	363.7	102.3	86.1
		1.42	1.24	17.28	20.70	13.81	15.80	5	6.6	23.3	191.4	217.4	234.9	89.3	41.5
		1.24	.57	8.12	8.57	8.64	9.46	3	4.9	11.1	108.3	120.9	140.3	75.3	16.1
5231	Paint, glass, and wallpaper stores (913)	5.98	10.81	52.37	61.20	7.50	8.82	41	10.3	51.8	94.5	149.1	115.2	116.9	138.6
		2.77	5.47	24.55	31.65	4.26	5.06	27	6.1	23.4	39.7	62.7	82.7	65.7	63.4
		1.66	2.04	8.55	9.70	2.23	3.03	14	4.0	10.2	13.0	20.9	51.3	28.1	27.1
5732	Radio and television stores (2,396)	4.28	10.00	50.01	73.85	9.36	12.05	20	7.5	55.5	162.2	207.8	191.3	105.6	122.6
		2.09	4.01	22.20	29.72	4.71	5.99	9	4.9	26.1	60.1	84.2	106.8	72.6	54.2
		1.36	1.36	7.84	8.03	2.23	3.14	4	3.3	11.7	17.5	30.4	67.4	37.0	18.9
5261	Retail nurseries, lawn and garden supply stores (1,135)	4.62	9.55	41.24	64.74	7.35	10.26	30	10.2	80.8	119.2	188.5	152.1	131.7	169.1
		2.08	4.49	19.29	27.23	3.69	5.09	14	5.6	38.3	47.7	72.5	90.4	75.0	70.9
		1.27	1.34	7.62	7.66	1.68	2.26	6	3.2	15.6	14.1	24.9	44.5	33.9	19.6
5661	Shoe stores (2,866)	6.07	10.71	41.66	47.05	6.40	6.47	16	4.9	36.0	100.3	152.5	158.0	72.1	101.3
		3.01	5.16	19.97	21.52	3.67	3.91	6	3.3	14.3	42.3	60.6	108.1	43.8	54.4
		1.81	1.85	7.90	7.61	2.18	2.44	2	2.4	5.6	14.5	20.5	82.1	21.8	21.8
5331	Variety stores (726)	8.68	8.23	29.78	36.49	6.43	6.03	11	4.4	48.5	88.3	168.9	145.1	64.6	98.5
		3.75	3.74	13.19	17.04	3.60	3.71	3	3.2	21.0	32.1	53.5	103.4	33.2	58.5
		1.93	1.16	5.41	6.18	1.74	2.32	1	2.4	8.7	9.1	16.5	83.1	14.3	24.7
5621	Women's ready-to-wear stores (9,558)	7.08	10.71	40.62	45.64	6.11	6.49	34	6.9	43.1	84.6	131.7	124.3	89.8	108.1
		3.32	5.00	18.77	21.73	3.42	3.86	15	4.5	19.8	34.0	52.0	87.8	50.0	56.6
		1.88	1.68	6.72	6.96	1.95	2.33	5	3.0	7.6	12.0	17.5	57.8	23.0	21.8

Reprinted with the special permission of *Dun's Review*, October 1979, Copyright 1979, Dun & Bradstreet Publications Corporation.
* Standard Industrial Classification (SIC) code number.

book, for example, is management meeting all guidelines for effective retailing as outlined in Chapter 2? Is management following the techniques and procedures for a sound retailing operation as given in Chapters 5 through 25? Such an audit is an ongoing process that should be conducted by the management of the store. But where does management begin? A suggested audit outline is given by Wingate and Schaller in their *Management Audit for Small Retailers* (available from the Small Business Administration as part of its Small Business Management Series).

It is also suggested that the management of the store should have an outside consultant come in at least once every five years and determine the overall state of the store. An audit would naturally include all areas of performance control in addition to merchandise control and security control. Although the outside auditor may be viewed as an unnecessary expense by some people, an impartial third person making an examination of the store's operation can result in a very worthwhile epxenditure. Retail owners and managers may be too involved with problems to see them in their right perspective. A good retail auditor on the other hand will probably be able to see both "the forest and the trees." An occasional outside audit is best, but the use of internal audits alone is much better than none at all. Every effort should be made to make the store as sound as possible. A store whose operations are under close control is a store with greater potential for profit.

SUMMARY

Operations control is defined as the evaluation of store operations for the purpose of improving overall store performance. To achieve this purpose, procedures dealing with expense control and performance control should be instituted. Expense control involves several areas. First, the expenses of the store must be classified into their natural divisions. For cost purposes, expenses are then classified by expense centers as a measure of efficiency. For purposes of profitability, such expenses must be allocated solely to the selling departments. Contribution margin or net profit or a combination of the two are the allocation procedures which are followed by most stores. Budgeting also plays a key role in expense control. For best results, a clean slate each budget period (zero-base) is best. Fixed-base and productivity-base are two other approaches to budgeting. The latter is more difficult but does provide more flexibility within the budgeting procedure. Any procedure of expense control would not be complete if efforts were not made to improve on the tasks that were generating the expenses. Work simplification examines every situation to see if it can be made more efficient. Expense control is not just cost cutting in nature. Its goal is the effective management of expenses so that the needs of the store will be met effectively and efficiently.

As for performance control, its concern is the total store with special emphasis on the financial and managerial areas. Return on investment as well as other financial ratios reveal much about a store's operation. When dealing with the management area, performance control examines all aspects of the store's managerial effort. Although conducted internally on a continuous basis, it is also wise to have an outside audit conducted at least once every five years. The procedures that make up both expense control and performance control should, if followed, result in a better managed, more profitable store.

DISCUSSION QUESTIONS

1. Define operations control. Explain your definition.
2. Expenses are said to fall into 17 natural divisions. What are they? How is such a classification system helpful to the retailer?
3. What procedure does the National Retail Merchants Association provide for the allocation of expenses to expense centers?
4. Select a large store and a small shop in your area. Go to these retailers and ascertain how they classify and allocate expenses. Comment (pro and con) on what you have found.
5. Why is the use of the contribution margin method or net profit method essential to a store? Why not just use the expense center approach to expense control?
6. Should a firm use zero-base or productivity-base budgeting?
7. "A firm with a good procedure for cutting costs is a firm with a good expense control system." Comment on this statement.
8. Ascertain if stores in your area believe in performance control. Do you agree with their thinking on the subject?
9. By using financial statements for the last three years for a given retailer, conduct a ratio analysis. How does the store compare with the most appropriate set of ratios as given in Figure 25-7?
10. Performance control is concerned with the performance of the managerial team. Since management must be the group to conduct a continuing audit of the firm, what can be done to ensure that management is meeting all of its goals and objectives? Be specific in your suggestions.

NOTES

[1] Information in this section is taken in part from *Retail Accounting Manual*, rev. ed. (New York: Financial Executives Division, National Retail Merchants Association, 1976).

[2] Ibid., pp. II–6, 7, 8, 9.

[3] Ibid., p. III–3.

[4] Ibid., p. III–5.

[5] Ibid., p. II–1.

[6] Jack Kivetz, "An Imaginative Approach to Budgeting & Expense Control," *Retail Control*, Vol. 44, no. 3 (November 1975), pp. 37–38. Copyright 1975, Financial Executives Division, National Retail Merchants Association.

[7] William U. Westerfield, "The Retailer and Zero-Based Budgeting," *Retail Control*, Vol. 45, no. 9 (June–July 1977), p. 38. Copyright 1977, Financial Executives Division, National Retail Merchants Association.

[8] For information on accounting statements and procedures, see Horace Brock and Charles Palmer, *Accounting: Principles and Applications*, 4th ed. (New York: McGraw-Hill Book Company, 1981); Glenn L. Johnson and James A. Gentry, Jr., *Finney and Miller's Principles of Accounting—Introductory*, 8th ed. (Englewood Cliffs, N.J.: Prentice-Hall, Inc., 1980); and Jeffrey Slater, *Practical Accounting Procedures* (Englewood Cliffs, N.J.: Prentice-Hall, Inc., 1979).

[9] *Retail Accounting Manual*, p. XI–1.

[10] Ibid., p. XI–2.

[11] For additional ideas on profit improvement, see Louis C. Moscarello, "Profit Improvement Programs in the Retail Environment," *Retail Control*, Vol. 48, no. 1 (September 1979), pp. 2–18. Copyright 1979, Financial Executives Division, National Retail Merchants Association.

SECTION VIII

Retailing
Applications
and Trends

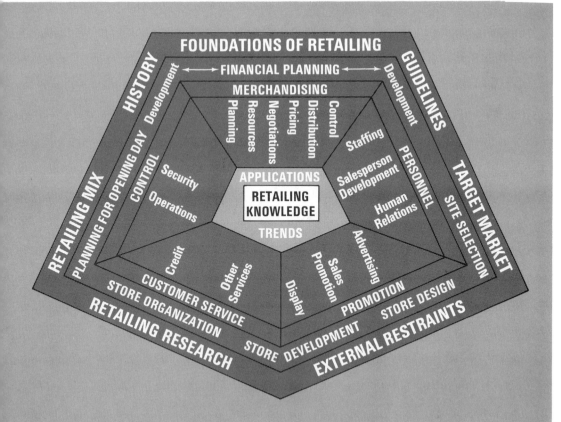

There are various retailing applications and trends that merit the attention of the reader.

"Retailing Applications" examines both service retailing and non-store retailing and how each relates to the other and to in-store product retailing.

"Retailing Trends" looks at the future of retailing in terms of market, store development, merchandising, personnel, promotion, customer service, and control. Career opportunities are also analyzed.

CHAPTER 26

Retailing Applications

"How did you know I sell door-to-door?"

What do movie theaters, street vendors, hair stylists, commercial airlines, and vending machines have in common? Give up? The common bond among these various business categories is that they are all forms of retailing. As is true with any introductory retailing text, *Contemporary Retailing* has examined the various aspects of the subject of retailing with a heavy emphasis on the traditional retail setting that consists of a physical building, inside of which is sold a physical product. Yet, a careful review of the definition of retailing (the summation of all activities that result in the offering for sale of goods and/or services to individuals and/or organizations for purposes of ultimate consumption) reveals that it says nothing about retailing having to be conducted in a building or that a tangible product must be sold. It is noted that most stores offer services, but their primary reason for being in business is to sell products. It is also observed that most retailers will, from time to time, make sales over the phone or as a result of a catalog but that the majority of the firm's sales volume will be the result of customers coming to the store. There is little doubt that the traditional application of retailing knowledge is for the situation in which a firm's primary mode of operation is to sell a physical product within the physical environs of a building. And it should be since this is the situation that is most common in retailing today.

But what about other retailing applications? What about the retailer whose primary product is service, not a physical product? What about the retailer who has no physical store where a customer can come and shop? How does that retailer sell a product? To answer questions such as these, this chapter examines both service retailing and nonstore retailing. It is good business to know and understand these nontraditional segments of the retailing industry since every retailer will probably be involved in one or both of these areas at one time or another. It is also possible that the retailer will be competing against a service and/or nonstore retailer. Or the retailer himself or herself will be a service and/or nonstore retailer. As illustrated in Figure 26–1, all stores will be involved in one or more of the three elements of the retailing applications triad. A store may be a pure service retailer, a pure nonstore retailer, a pure in-store product retailer, or any combination of the three. Only one thing is certain. Every retailer should have knowledge of all three application areas. In-store product retailing has already been examined in detail. Service retailing is now discussed, followed by nonstore retailing.

SERVICE RETAILING

Services are defined as activities, benefits, or satisfactions that are offered for sale.[1] What types of firms may be considered service retailers? The answer is any firm where the customer buys—yet there is no transfer of ownership. All repair shops are service retailers as are places where things can be rented. In addition, there is the pure service retailer. A hair stylist, tax return preparer, and weight reducing specialist are all retailers who sell a skill, not a physical product. Ask a hair stylist to show you the product. Only when the service is performed will any evidence be available as to what the "product" was that was offered for sale.

In Chapter 23, independent services were discussed as part of customer service.

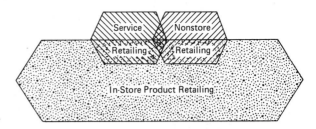

Figure 26-1

Retailing applications triad.

Such services are supplemental to a store's merchandising efforts as are other services such as package wrap or delivery. A service retailer, on the other hand, may offer certain products, such as picture tubes and tuners in a TV repair shop, but these would be supplemental to the retailer's primary reason for being in business—which is service. The following are some of the common types of service retailers.

Air travel	Hotel
Appliance repair	Jewelry/watch repair
Bank	Lawn service
Beauty shop	Movie theater
Dance studio	Photographer
Equipment rental	Restaurant
Funeral home	Shoe repair
Health spa/gym	Travel agency
Home security	Vehicle rental

To understand service retailing better, a look at such a firm's target market and retailing mix is crucial. Just as the service retailer's target market may be unique, so may its retailing mix. These elements merit further discussion.

Target Market

Who buys a service? Almost everyone. But more services are marketed to the higher demographic group than to any other. Why? Such people have a life-style that promotes interest in services. These people also have more discretionary income (earnings after all essentials have been purchased) and have a willingness to spend it. Research by New York's Monroe Mendelsohn Research reveals that there were 15.8 million adults in 1980 who lived in households with incomes of at least $40,000. These "affluents," which represent about 10 percent of the U.S. population, had annual discretionary income in excess of $15,000 whereas households with incomes below $40,000 had an average annual discretionary income of only $1,400. [2]

Day care, interior decorating, laundry, and lawn care are some of the services that have increased in recent years to serve another distinct target market—the working family. Although some of these husband–wife working families are in the affluent category as a result of two salaries, many other working families are not, but they need various services to continue their work. Some services are essential (e.g., day care), others make life less hectic (e.g., laundry and lawn care). Still others are thought to be nice to use (e.g., interior decorating services) but are justified on the basis that "because of work, there are not enough hours in the day to get things done like decorating the house."

It should be emphasized that all people have the potential to be customers for a service retailer. But it does appear that some customer groups are more prone than others to use various services. Remember, if the customer sees no need for the service, the service retailer who is providing that service will fail. Or if the customer wants a particular service but does not have the ability to pay for it, then the service retailer will still fail. Just as is true in all other forms of retailing, the target market should be clearly defined and understood before the service retailer makes a major commitment to offer a service.

Retailing Mix—Product

The "product" that the service retailer sells is intangible, perishable, nonstandardized, and personal. If the retailer understands these characteristics, there is a greater probability that the services of that retailer can be sold.

Intangible. Services are sold and then produced. A customer cannot see the service that he or she is buying. A customer wants to take a trip. The first step is at a travel agency where the customer is told, "Don't worry. We will handle everything." Or a photographer is hired to take pictures at a wedding. If the pictures do not turn out, there will be no retakes. The bride-to-be puts much faith in the photogapher. When a person buys a picture already taken, he or she sees the product before the purchase. But when the wedding pictures are "purchased," the only thing bought is the skill of the photographer, which, it is hoped, will result in good pictures.

What can the retailer do to market an intangible product? Make it tangible whenever possible. G. Lynn Shostack, writing in the *Journal of Marketing*, suggests that the more intangible the "product," the more tangible should be anything that is related to the "product."[3] For the photographer, mentioned earlier, what this translates into is a nice studio, appropriate car, good-looking equipment, and even printed picture contracts that look well thought out and complete—just like the bride-to-be wants her pictures.

To promise fast service is an intangible. But to give a "fast service" card to customers that guarantees fast service is something that is tangible. Written warranties are another tangible device. The repair shop "says" that the car is fixed. Such an intangible promise is more convincing if it is in writing. Appearances are important. How would you like to do business with a bank that looked like it would go broke any minute? Or with a lawn care service business whose own lawn could use some work? Or rent a dirty car? Although services are intangible, customers will search out any tangible evidence that is related to that service. Service retailers should provide this tangible evidence. It will make easier the job of selling the service.

Perishable. Many types of service retailers are forced to work with the problem of perishability. A motel in Florida may give cheaper rates in the summer to use some of the excess capacity that it does not seem to have enough of in the winter. A restaurant may have a busy lunch time but no business at night, while another experiences the reverse situation. Each may run specials during the slack periods to encourage customers to come at those times. Motel rooms or restaurant tables or whatever, when not used for the particular time frame, are lost forever. Due to this fact, every effort should be made by the service retailer to level out demand as much as possible. Fluctuations will exist. But efforts should be taken to reduce these fluctuations.

Nonstandardized. One visit to the hair salon may result in an excellent haircut. The next visit may leave something to be desired. The repair shop may have five repair teams out making calls. Some will do better than others. The personality of each person involved results in nonstandardization. Customers also differ over time. The customer may be happy with one dance lesson and not happy with the next lesson when, in reality, there is no difference between the two lessons other than the customer's attitude.

What the service retailer can learn from this product characteristic is that many customers will request adjustments as well as register complaints after buying a service. Due to the intangible nature of the "product," it is many times difficult to objectively decide on the validity of a customer's complaint about service. Because of this difficulty, many service retailers attempt to go along with most customers. To do otherwise is to give tangible evidence to a customer and his or her friends that the retailer is not providing "proper service."

Personal. Due to the intangible nature of a service, the person performing the service and the service itself many times become interchangeable in the mind of the customer. A customer may wish to take parachute lessons from a particular person because of the confidence that the customer has in the skill of that instructor. Or a person may select a certain auto mechanic or jeweler because it is felt that that individual will fix the car or the necklace right and do it on time.

From the discussion of the four "product" characteristics of services, it becomes clear that a particular service will involve all four characteristics to some degree. The importance of each characteristic relative to a particular service will, of course, vary. For example, a particular hairdresser may be very much concerned with the personal aspect while not being overly concerned with peaks of demand. A restaurant with fluctuating demand may be most interested in perishability whereas a fortune-teller may feel that the best way to market the service is to concentrate on the personal "product" characteristic. Of course, not all restaurants will view it the same way nor will all fortune-tellers. Are all four characteristics ever of equal importance in terms of a retailing service? It is possible, but not very likely. The retailer is encouraged to study the market and the service carefully. If the relative importance of the various "product" characteristics can be determined, this type of information can be very helpful as the rest of the retailing mix is developed.

Retailing Mix—Place

The importance of place is obviously a function of the type of service retailer. A firm that operates a garbage collection service brings its service to its customers after the customer uses the telephone to buy the service. Needless to say, the physical location of the business or its appearance has little importance. The same is true for a plumber. But for the photographer, restaurant, or bank, place is very important. Where these businesses are located and how they look can help or hinder their operation.

If a brokerage firm's office is located in the "financial district" of a town, this gives the customer tangible evidence that the firm knows what it is doing. Equally important, customers who buy stocks are probably already accustomed to coming to that particular part of town to do business. Therefore, the location is viewed as being convenient by the appropriate target market. For other retailers, service locations may be placed all over town in order to be convenient to the customer. An equipment rental firm may have several locations around town whereas a film-developing service may have a location in the parking lot of every shopping center in the city. Still another location consideration is to place a store service unit near the point of major demand. Why do most car rental firms have "stores" at major airports? Airports are the point of major demand for the car rental business.

Retailing Mix—Promotion

How does one advertise an intangible? How about having the football hero "fly" through an airport on the way to obtaining a rental car without a hassle? Or how about showing people having fun at a restaurant, amusement park, or movie theater? As is true with all advertising, buyer benefits are crucial to the successful service advertisement. "At Holiday Inn, the best surprise is no surprise." To the experienced traveler who has had unpleasant surprises, the Holiday Inn promotion says much. It emphasizes a buyer benefit.

No matter what type of service the retailer offers, the advertising for that service should stress such intangible things as dependability, competence, and the ability of the firm to meet the needs of the customer. The fact that the firm has been in business for fifty years also might be used to imply that "if we were not doing it right, we wouldn't be around that long."

Another way in which to promote most services is through the use of testimonial advertisements. Testimonials from local people help new customers to overcome uncertainty. For example, a customer has a very expensive oriental rug that needs cleaning. Will the rug come clean? Will it be ruined in the process of cleaning it? Will the cleaning firm pick up the rug and then take "forever" to return it? These are obvious concerns of a potential customer. A good testimonial from a satisfied customer in an advertisement should bring up these concerns and meet them head on.

As for the advertising media that might be used by service retailers, car rental firms, banks, and savings and loan associations are typical examples of service retailing that use television, newspapers, and other major media. But these media are much too expensive for the many service retailers that fall into the category of small business. For these firms, direct mail offers a possible answer as do specialty advertising and throwaways. A car wash operator may go through a parking lot near the business and place a coupon for "$1 off on a car wash" on the windshield of every dirty car in the lot. Or a local health spa may send out a mail piece to all households living in the high-income areas of town near the firm's location offering a free visit or some other type of incentive.

For most service firms, word-of-mouth "advertising" is very important to the firm. Of course, by definition word-of-mouth "advertising" is not advertising since it is an uncontrolled form of unpaid testimonial. A retailer may, however, want to encourage customers to talk up a service with their friends. One way to do this is used by a furniture upholstery firm that gives cards to customers to give to their friends. If the friend has work done by the firm within 60 days of the date on the card and presents the card to the upholstery firm at the time of purchase, the original customer will receive a $5 check. Should all service retailers use this type of system to encourage word-of-mouth "advertising"? No. But it does appear to work for some service retailers. The type of service offered and the target market will have a major influence on how much control the service retailer might be able to have over the word-of-mouth "advertising" that is being transmitted about the business.

Retailing Mix—Price

How much should a retailer charge for a service? Some typical pricing tactics for service retailers are the following:

1. *Cost-plus pricing.* A painting contractor may cost out a job including paint, labor, and so on and then add a fee of 10 percent for supervision and finder's fee. The obvious disadvantage of this tactic is that it discourages cost control. A service retailer who is not careful can price oneself out of the market.
2. *Fixed minimum pricing.* A TV repair call may never cost less than $30. No matter if the repairperson finds that the set was just unplugged or needed a new part, the minimum service charge is the same—a point of irritation for many customers.
3. *Discretionary pricing.* "What the traffic will bear" is sometimes the name given to this pricing approach. For the same amount of work the lawn service charges more to a well-to-do customer than to someone else with less capability to pay.
4. *Loss leader pricing.* "Rent a new car for $10 a day." "Clean your living room carpet for just $15." Although ad headlines like these are sometimes illegal because they are bait-and-switch in nature, others are quite legitimate. Their purpose is to generate interest in the service for future use as is the case with the car rental special. As for the carpet cleaner, the end result may be that other rooms are cleaned at the regular rate or spot preventive chemicals are added for a fee or even carpet is sold to replace worn carpets if the carpet cleaner is associated with a seller of carpet.
5. *Prestige pricing.* As was noted in Chapter 13, customers have a tendency to equate price and quality. For some people, getting a haircut that costs more than the going rate makes the haircut better. For that service retailer who has provided the tangible evidence that the service is worth more, customers in the target market are usually willing to, and even expect to, pay more. When a target market's ego is involved, prestige pricing is a valid pricing tactic.
6. *Discount pricing.* The opposite of prestige pricing is the approach known as discount pricing. This pricing technique may be used only at times such as for encouraging business during slack periods (weekend rental rates for cars). It may also be used on a continuing basis as a means of building volume. A formal wear rental service may charge below normal rates with the idea that more volume times less per unit profit will exceed the amount that would be earned by having less volume times greater per unit profit.

Retailing Mix—Personality

The personality of a service retailer is how that retailer is perceived by the customer. As was discussed in Chapter 2, for any retailer, the target market and the other parts of the retailing mix join together to create the retail personality or image. It is observed that, due to the intangible nature of what is being sold by a service retailer, it may be that the personality element in the retailing mix is even more important for a service retailer than it is for an in-store product retailer.

"Fly the friendly skies of United." "Orkin, We're number one." "Avis—We try harder." Slogans such as these for national service retailers project a positive personality for an intangible element known as service. Just as a service is intangible, so is a retailer's image. The retailer should find out what that image is and work to either retain the established image or make desired changes in it over time.

Or the service retailer may acquire a personality by means of a franchise. Helen's Real Estate Service has an image, but can it be enhanced if Helen becomes a Century 21 "neighborhood professional"? If Century 21 has a good image among the people in the market area, then Helen will be helped. Likewise, if a motel becomes a Quality Inn or an appliance repair center that fixes General Electric appliances becomes a franchised General Electric Repair Center, the personality of the business will be altered. Depending on the target market's view of the image of the local business and the image of the planned franchise affiliation, the change may be good or bad. Regardless of the approach that is followed concerning image, one thing is certain. A service retailer without a positive personality or image in the eyes of the target market is in serious trouble regardless of the status of the other elements in the retailing mix. Having an appropriate retail image is crucial to a service retailer.[4]

NONSTORE RETAILING

When the retail buying decision takes place at a location other than the conventional place of business of the retailer (seller), the process is known as nonstore retailing. Mail-order, catalog, telephone, in-house, and vending, along with other forms of activity as well, make up an area of retailing that is growing in importance relative to the total retailing industry. As might be expected, there is overlap among the various types of nonstore activity. For example, many catalogs are used as a mail-order promotion. Likewise, the telephone may be used to call customers who had received within the last few days a mail-order promotion or a catalog. For purposes of discussion, however, the different types of nonstore retailing will be treated as separate entities.

Mail-Order Retailing

By definition, mail order is a form of direct marketing that attempts to make the sale without outside assistance. The mail-order selling effort stands alone. If *Reader's Digest* desires to sell its latest fix-it book, a mail-order effort, usually with a sweepstakes, will be sent to appropriate potential customers including, in most cases, those who have already purchased books from *Reader's Digest.*

The successful mail-order promotion has two important ingredients: mail piece and mailing list. The mail piece, like any other type of advertising, should stress buyer benefits. If the ad is for the fix-it book mentioned earlier, the benefits to be stressed may be the money to be saved on the service call, the convenience of not having to wait for the serviceperson, and the self-satisfaction of fixing the problem yourself.

As for who to mail to, one good source is the firm's own customers. Because they have already bought from that retailer, they are good prospects for new business. Two other potential sources are people who are something and people who have done something (Figure 26–2). A compiled list (people who are something) contains names that are grouped in a meaningful manner (zip code, church membership, age of car owned, etc.). Reuben H. Donnelley Corporation uses telephone directories and auto purchases to create lists that represent over 80 percent of all U.S. households. R. L. Polk & Company's *Polk Family Census* provides a demographic breakdown of almost all metropolitan homes. Along with firms that compile lists by characteristic, another group from whom retailers can get names are suppliers of rented lists (people who have done something). The names of people who have an American Express card, bought

Figure 26–2

Want a list of names of people who *are* something or *have done* something? They are available from firms like Addresses Unlimited and Market Compilation and Research Bureau.

(Courtesy of Addresses Unlimited and MCRB.)

from Sunset House, or subscribe to *Time* are all available as rented lists. For a mail-order retailer who sells cheese, the best rented list would be people who have bought similar products by mail. The greater the similarities between the retailer's target market and the rented list, the greater the probability of success for the mail-order promotion.[5]

Catalog Retailing

The catalog concept in retailing is not new. As noted in Chapter 1, Montgomery Ward issued its first catalog in 1872. Today, catalog retailing has come a long way in terms of development. The modern catalog retailer may be one of several things. First, the firm may be a general merchandise retailer like Sears or J. C. Penney, a specialty retailer like L. L. Bean or Horchow, or a seasonal retailer like the Godbee Pecan Company that only sells by catalog during the Christmas season. Second, the firm may have no store outlets (Horchow), or one/few outlets (L. L. Bean), or numerous retail outlets (Sears). Third, the catalog orders may be received by the firm by phone, mail, in-store, separate catalog outlet, or not identifiable as a catalog sale.

The last category cited points out another major distinction among catalog retailers: Is the main purpose of the catalog external sales or in-store sales or both? The catalog showroom retailer uses catalogs but usually has limited catalog sales. The Broadway, a California retailer, mails out 700,000 catalogs at a time, but all go to families within five miles of a store location. Like Broadway, Dayton's of Minneapolis uses catalogs with the purpose of getting people into the store. Although both Broadway and Dayton's do include order blanks and telephone order numbers in their catalogs, some retailers have gone so far as to leave them out, therefore forcing all catalog customers to come to the store to buy.[6] Of course, for those retailers who have no outlets, the nonstore operation is its only business. But the third part of the catalog business is those retailers who go after both in-store sales for catalog users close to home and pure mail-order sales for catalog users in outlying areas. Bloomingdale's is one retailer who has moved to a two-pronged direct-mail effort. With its 13 catalogs a year, it hopes to reach its traffic area that is defined as within 50 miles of a store location and a larger outside market whose customers may never have been to a Bloomingdale's store.[7]

Some recent trends in catalog retailing are that (1) more stores are going to the use of catalogs and those that have been using catalogs are expanding their catalog coverage beyond their trade area. (2) More stores are using catalogs throughout the year as opposed to using them just at Christmas. (3) More stores are letting others share the cost of the catalog either by selling it to customers (Neiman-Marcus and Horchow) or by selling space advertising in the catalog (Montgomery Ward). (4) Catalog sales are up due to factors such as working women, older population, rising energy costs, and fear of being out alone.

Using these trends as a foundation, it would seem that the future of catalog retailing is positive. The big five catalogers (Alden, Penney, Spiegel, Sears, and Ward) are all doing well. And why not! Maxwell Sroge, a mail-order specialist, cites one good reason. He finds that the average profit margin in a traditional store is 2.5 percent compared with 7.0 percent for a mail-order catalog operation. Another figure for Horchow tells the same story. The Dallas retailer did $422 per gross square foot in 1978 or $38 million in sales with 90,000 square feet.[8] Needless to say, not very many retailers obtain those kind of figures.

Telephone Retailing

Like other forms of nonstore retailing, telephone retailing can take several forms. It may exist only when a salesperson calls a customer for prospecting purposes. It may exist only when a customer calls a retailer to place an order for flowers, prescription drugs, chicken-to-go, or merchandise from a catalog (Figure 26–3). Or it may exist when the customer buys from an ad for a Bearcat scanner in *The Wall Street Journal* that directs the customer to call a toll-free number to order the radio. In these instances, it does not matter who places the call. What does matter is that the retailer should have a knowledgeable and pleasant person representing the firm on the phone. A discourteous person, a frequent busy signal, or a person who forgets to obtain all required information can make a nightmare out of telephone retailing.

Another form of telephone retailing is what some people refer to as "junk calls." Under this approach, an automatic dialing device calls numbers in a selected order depending on the target market that is being sold. A "real" person begins the conversa-

Figure 26–3

A center for receiving telephone orders.

(Courtesy of Sears, Roebuck and Co.)

tion and then the call is turned over to a taped message to which the customer is directed to listen. The tape makes the sales pitch and then asks questions. At the end, the tape asks for the order. At no time does a "real" person come back on the line. Since one person can handle many calls with this type of system, why is it not in wide use? It appears that "junk calls" irritate many target customers.

One last aspect of telephone retailing deals with the unethical techniques that are used by some to sell over the phone. "Hello, we are conducting a marketing research study on . . .". Too many telephone retailers begin their sales calls in this fashion. It is done so frequently that a legitimate telephone survey is not possible in many market areas because customers want to know what the gimmick is instead of answering the survey questions. Although it is done by many firms, using a false cover to begin a telephone sales presentation is not a business practice that should be followed.[9]

In-Home Retailing

A person's home is a place where the customer is in charge. This fact makes selling there easier or more difficult, depending on what is being sold. As is true for most forms of retailing, there are several types of in-home retailing, some of which create more problems than do others. The four types are cold canvass selling, route selling, service selling, and party selling, each of which merit discussion.

Cold Canvass Selling.   As one of the most difficult forms of selling for most people, cold canvass selling requires the salesperson to call on the customer without a prior indication of interest on the part of the customer. It is noted that many excellent products are sold in this manner (Electrolux, Avon, Fuller Brush, and *World Book* to name several). If an item can be demonstrated as a means to promote the sale, then an in-home sales call will permit the product to be demonstrated in its actual surroundings. The customer will not have to worry about if the vacuum cleaner, for example, will work on the rug in the living room—the customer can try it out and see.

Route Selling.   Milk, eggs, soft drinks, bread, bottled water, and even potato chips are delivered on a regular basis or on an "as requested" basis to many households by route salespeople. Laundry and dry cleaning and diaper pickup are examples of services that fit into the same category. As a selling method with high costs, route selling is not as popular as it once was. In fact, it tends to be limited more and more to higher demographic neighborhoods where people have the financial ability to pay the premium price that is often charged.

Service Selling.   Service selling takes place when the retailer comes to the customer's home and performs a service. Lawn care, heating and air conditioning installation and/or repair, interior decorating, and house painting are just some of the possibilities under this form of in-home selling. As will be noted, much of this falls in the category of service retailing as discussed earlier in the chapter. For a retailer to sell a service in the home, in-home solicitation (cold canvassing), referrals, and traditional forms of promotion (newspaper, radio, etc.) may all be used to initiate the customer contact.

Party Selling. What do Tupperware, Sarah Coventry, and Stanley Home Products have in common? They all sell using the party plan. With this approach, a hostess agrees to have a "party" in her home. Friends are invited. Games are played. Refreshments are provided. And products are demonstrated and orders are taken. The hostess usually receives a free gift for having the party. Also, she may receive additional gifts if she has a set number of guests at her party, if those at the party buy a certain amount of merchandise, and if someone who came to the party will have a party. Party selling does work. People who attend usually buy something just to help out the hostess. The party retailer is cautioned about planning too many parties for the same circle of friends. There is just so much Tupperware that a person needs at any given time. Too many parties with the same people will result in poor attendance and few sales. The successful party retailer will strive to have at least 50 percent of the guests at any party be people who have not been to a similar party within the last six months to a year, depending on the nature of the products being sold.

Vending[10]

For most people, a vending machine is a place where a customer can buy a soft drink and a package of crackers 24 hours a day, 7 days a week. But many other items can be merchandised in vending machines. Cigarettes, ice cream, stamps, sandwiches, pantyhose, candy, paper, toothpaste, combs, water, and, it would seem, an almost infinite number of other items, can be found in vending machines. So many items, in fact, that less than half of all machines sell beverages and that less than half of all dollar sales come from beverages.

For the nonstore retailer who is involved in vending, one obvious factor in the success of this type of business is machine location. If the machine is in the wrong place, it will not succeed. The target market for the products in the machine must be in close proximity to the machine location. A lighted machine will attract more customers as will a machine that is in a cluster with others. But these factors are only important after the machine is in a location that will serve the target market.

Vending is not without its problems. Equipment maintenance, vandalism, location commissions and fees, equipment cost, and personnel retention all give the vending retailer cause for concern. Location fees and commissions by themselves can be enough to make some retailers want to get out of vending. Commissions of from 5 to 10 percent of sales with guaranteed minimums in some cases make vending much less attractive for marginal operations.

Other Forms of Nonstore Retailing

It goes without saying that nonstore retailing can include almost anything that takes place in the noncommercial sector of the economy. Church bazaars, garage sales, and the lemonade stand set up at the bus stop by the neighborhood children might all be classified as nonstore retailing. But in addition to these noncommercial ventures, other less conventional forms of nonstore retailing should be mentioned. These include consumer shows, motel selling, and street vendors.

Consumer Shows. A local civic club may sponsor an antique show and sale at the local civic center. An antique dealer will pay a fee to use a booth at the show and, sometimes, will give the sponsor a commission on what was sold as well. Much of the success for this type of retailing venture rests with the work of the sponsoring group whose responsibility it is to promote the show and provide the target market.

Motel Selling. Clothing, jewelry, and appliances are just three of many things that are sold in this manner. The retailer will promote the motel sale in advance of the visit by means of the mass media and/or direct mail depending on the target market to be served. For used TV sets, cheap prices may be stressed in both TV and newspaper ads that appeal to the lower demographic groups. On the other hand, Mr. Chu from Hong Kong who visits the city once a year to take orders for custom-made lace table cloths and other expensive items may use only direct mail that is sent to the area's most well-to-do customers announcing his visit. When people think of motel selling, most think of the first example, but are not aware of the second possibility. Both situations do work. Motel selling is a way for a retailer to expand his or her market to other cities without making an investment in a store. In some cases, when motel selling is an unqualified success, a traditional store in that town is the next step.

Street Vendors. There are two types of street vendors: licensed and not licensed. In the first case, a furniture store may have a fleet of trucks that it will fill with merchandise and send to surrounding small towns for the purpose of parking on the courthouse square. Customers learn to expect the truck, so they buy their furniture in this manner. More conventional items like ice cream and hot dogs are also sold by this method as are fruits and vegetables.

The second type of street vendor is one that is nontax-paying, usually part-time, and illegal. In New York City alone, for example, annual dollar sales volume for itinerant street vendors is estimated to be in the area of $112.5 million.[11] For legitimate retailers, what this figure means is lost sales. For customers, it can mean bargains, and it can mean being cheated. For cities, it means lost revenues because no business fees are collected. Itinerant retailers are a problem in major cities. But it is not a new problem. The person selling fruit or pencils on the street has been a part of the American street scene for many years. The street vendor is just as much a retailing institution as was the peddler. In fact, perhaps, the term street vendor may be just a modern term for the same thing.

SUMMARY

"Retailing Applications" looks at two forms of retailing that are different from traditional in-store product retailing. The first—service retailing—deals with selling activities, benefits, or satisfactions to the ultimate consumer. As for the target market for a service, it is typically higher demographic groups or working families. Product characteristics (intangible, perishable, nonstandardized, personal), place considerations (does customer come to service or does service go to customer), promotion factors (dependability and competence as shown in tangible ways like testimonials), pricing tactics (cost plus, fixed minimum, discretionary, loss leader, prestige, discount), and personality (the sum total of all other elements plus image building tools like slogans and well-known affiliations) all join together to give the service retailer a retailing mix that will serve the target market. As for the second form of retailing discussed, nonstore retailing is viewed in terms of mail-order, catalog, telephone, in-home (cold canvass, route, service, and party selling), vending, and other forms (consumer show, motel selling, and street vendor). In all forms of nonstore retailing, the retail buying decision takes place at a location other than the conventional place of business of the retailer (seller). It is noted that both forms of retailing (service and nonstore) may be conducted independently, together, and/or in conjunction with in-store product retailing.

DISCUSSION QUESTIONS

1. Select various types of stores in your area that operate as in-store product retailers. Ascertain how these firms feel about service retailing and nonstore retailing. Are they involved in either category in any way? If yes, how?
2. It is said that a service is intangible. Does that cause the retailer any problems? Does it offer any benefits?
3. For your town, develop a list of service retailers by type. Attempt to limit your list to firms that sell service as their primary product.
4. Explain how the development of a retail strategy differs for an in-store product retailer and a service retailer.
5. How are services priced? Answer this question by talking to service retailers and customers of service retailers. How does your list compare with the pricing tactics given in the chapter?
6. Catalog, mail order, or telephone—which is the best form of nonstore retailing?
7. Junk calls! Conduct a search of the literature to ascertain current opinion (legal and marketing) concerning this retailing tool.
8. Conduct a survey in your area concerning the feasibility of selling various items by means of route selling. Can soft drinks, bread, and bottled water be marketed in this fashion? How much would customers be willing to pay for this service?
9. Party selling! Is it limited to jewelry and kitchen aids? Develop an in-home party selling plan for a product that never (as far as you know) has been sold in this manner.
10. Discuss with retailers, police, government officials, and itinerant street vendors the local situation as it pertains to street vending. What do you feel should be done? Explain your answer.

NOTES

[1] Philip Kotler, *Marketing Management*, 4th ed. (Englewood Cliffs, N.J.: Prentice-Hall, Inc., 1980), p. 133.
[2] Reprinted by permission of *The Wall Street Journal*, © Dow Jones & Company, Inc., 1981. All Rights Reserved.

[3] G. Lynn Shostack, "Breaking Free from Product Marketing," *Journal of Marketing*, Vol. 41, no. 2 (April 1977), pp. 77–79. Published by the American Marketing Association.

[4] For additional reading on service retailing, see Lee Adler and James D. Hlavacek, "Key Repair Service Factors for Consumer Durable Goods," *Journal of Marketing Research*, Vol. 15, no. 4 (November 1978), pp. 634–638. Published by the American Marketing Association; Stanley C. Hollander, "Is There a Generic Demand for Services?" *MSU Business Topics*, Vol. 27, no. 2 (Spring 1979), pp. 41–46; John M. Rathmell, *Marketing in the Service Sector* (Cambridge, Mass.: Winthrop Publishers, Inc., 1974); Martin R. Schlissel, "Pricing in a Service Industry," *MSU Business Topics*, Vol. 25, no. 2 (Spring 1977), pp. 37–48; and Gregory D. Upah, "Mass Marketing in Service Retailing: A Review and Synthesis of Major Methods," *Journal of Retailing*, Vol. 56, no. 3 (Fall 1980), pp. 59–76.

[5] For additional information on mail-order retailing, see William H. Bolen, *Advertising* (New York: John Wiley & Sons, Inc., 1981), pp. 259–277.

[6] Lewis A. Spalding, "B(U)Y the Book," *Stores*, Vol. 62, no. 5 (May 1980), p. 11. Copyright, National Retail Merchants Association, 1980.

[7] Larry Kofsky, "Bloomingdale's Makes the Move to Mail Order," *Direct Marketing*, Vol. 43, no. 5 (September 1980), pp. 64–71.

[8] Spalding, "B(U)Y the Book," p. 13.

[9] For more information, see Stan Crock, If the Phone Rings and It's Zsa Zsa, Don't Be Surprised," *The Wall Street Journal*, Vol. 194, no. 32 (August 15, 1979), pp. 1, 28.

[10] For more information, see "Census of the Industry, 1980," *Vending Times*, Vol. 20, no. 6–A (June 1980).

[11] Jerome Greenberg, Martin T. Topel, Elaine Sherman, and Kenneth Cooperman, "The Itinerant Street Vendor: A Form of Nonstore Retailing," *Journal of Retailing*, Vol. 56, no. 2 (Summer 1980), pp. 68, 70.

Reprinted by permission of the Chicago Tribune-New York News Syndicate, Inc.

Throughout this book various topics have been presented that reflect the current state of the art and science of retailing. To look beyond the present to what it will be like in 10, 15, or more years is a difficult endeavor at best. It is important, however, for retailers to look to the future since the store that plans for the future increases its chances of being in business at that time.

In examining the future, a careful study of trends can be quite helpful. Trends pertaining to the market, store development, merchandising, personnel, promotion, customer service, and retail control are examined. Career opportunities in retailing are also studied. It should be noted that retailing is dynamic. Predicting its future is no easy assignment.

MARKET TRENDS

It is estimated that in the year 2000, there will be 264 million people in the United States, up from 247 million in 1990. As shown in Table 27–1, the age mix of the population will undergo change as the population continues to mature.[1]

As for income, the trend appears to be in the direction of higher incomes. Even with double-digit inflation, real income is still on the rise for many consumers. It is thought that by 1985, more than half of all U.S. families will have incomes in excess of $25,000. This income trend literally reverses the income pyramid of just a few short years ago when few families were in the higher income brackets, Table 27–2.

Other demographic projections include:

Nonfamily households will move from 26 percent to 30 percent of the total market by 1990.

Unmarried couples, although increasing at a rapid rate, still will represent less than 2 percent of all households.

Over half of all households will be two-income households.

Total households are expected to expand at two times the rate of the population.[2]

These and other demographic trends illustrate the growth potential that is present for some retailers and not available for others. Working wives and more singles means fewer children per household, which means that children's shops will offer limited opportunities in all but the major market centers in the years to come. On the other hand, the retailer who caters to the over-65 set may be in for much growth in the next few years (Figure 27–1). This is especially true if the store is located in the warmer parts of the United States. Consumers in general will also probably continue the trend of movement toward the South and/or West. The Sunbelt area has been and will certainly continue to experience a growth in population. Such a trend should be considered when deciding on expansion. A store in the Northeast might have second thoughts about its ability to maintain its market if its customers are leaving the area.

Movement will also continue in terms of short-term mobility. Stores should offer the services necessary to continue to attract the transient customer. More leisure time means more time for travel.

Table 27-1

Population Shifts in the United States, 1960–2000[1]

Age	Population (millions)					Percentage change			
	1960	1970	1980	1990	2000	1960–1970	1970–1980	1980–1990	1990–2000
Under 20	69	77	73	77	81	+11.1%	−5.2%	+ 5.7%	+ 4.3%
20–24	11	17	21	18	19	+54.3	+22.6	−15.4	+7.8
25–34	23	26	37	42	36	+10.4	+46.1	+13.1	−14.6
35–44	24	23	26	37	41	−4.5	+9.6	+45.5	+13.0
45–54	21	23	22	25	36	+13.3	−3.9	+9.9	+45.1
55–64	16	19	21	20	22	+19.4	+13.0	−3.4	+10.6
65 and over	17	20	24	28	29	+20.4	+19.8	+15.4	+3.9
Total	181	205	224	247	264	+13.4	+9.4	+10.0	+7.2

[1] Based on data from Bureau of the Census, *Current Population Reports*, Series P-25, using Series E for projection purposes.

Source: William Lazer, "The 1980s and Beyond: A Perspective," pp. 21-35, *MSU Business Topics*, Spring 1977. Reprinted by permission of the publisher, Division of Research, Graduate School of Business Administration, Michigan State University.

Table 27-2

Changing Distribution of Family Income in 1975 Dollars

Family Income Category	Percentage of Family Income	
	1975	1985
$35,000 and over	16	28
$25,000 to $35,000	16	26
$20,000 to $25,000	17	16
$15,000 to $20,000	21	14
$10,000 to $15,000	18	10
Under $10,000	12	6

Source: Fabian Linden, "Age and Income—1985," *Conference Board Record*, 13 (June 1976).

Figure 27-1

The number of older consumers is increasing. The retailer who serves this market can expect many new opportunities.

(Courtesy of Venture Stores.)

The trend is clear. Customers of the future will be mobile, will be adults with adequate financial resources, and will be many in number.

Where will the stores of the future be located? What type of stores will they be? One trend that is taking place is a move back to the central business district. In many large cities, an increasing interest is being seen in the downtown areas as good retail locations in the suburbs become harder to find. In Miami, it is the Omni Center; in Chicago, Water Tower Place; in New York, the Market at Citicorp Center; in Philadelphia, the Gallery at Market East; and in Boston, Faneuil Hall Marketplace. Each is an example of a downtown shopping center that has put new life into a central city. These new intercity developments serve both transient and traditional downtown customers.[3] Retailing is certainly an evolutionary business. Retailing got its start in the central business district. For many cities, the future may find a rebirth for retailing in the downtown area.

Another trend will find that bigger may not always be better. The super store will have success, but the smaller store will also have its place. This trend can already be seen with K mart stores. K mart is building smaller, some as little as 30,000 square feet, stores for many areas as opposed to the large traditional K mart store. In the past, if the area could not support a large K mart, nothing was built. Shopping malls have also promoted this idea. The small, personal shop or boutique with service to match may be the predominant store of the future.[4] A paradox is found in this trend, because the small shop went to the mall to live off the big store and its promotion program.

Store development will also be influenced in the future by developments in the energy area. The regional shopping center must draw people from a large geographic area. If the gasoline supply does decrease and/or becomes too expensive, such centers will suffer as shoppers will be forced to buy closer to home. The large center serving a 100-square-mile trade area could become a thing of the past if the means to transport customers to the center becomes too expensive or nonexistent.

The interior of the store should become more flexible in the years to come. Modern buildings will find all interior walls to be free standing and quite mobile. New materials will open up new avenues for the retailer to pursue in terms of wall, floor, and ceiling treatments. As for layout, more use of free-flow patterns should result as retailers continue the present trend to personalize their stores and the departments within them.

As for trends in the area of organizational development, the trend should be toward both large and small. Fewer middle-sized operations will exist. Just as Rich's became a part of Federated Department Stores and Neiman-Marcus became a division of Carter Hawley Hale, other private retailers will join large organizations for buying power and other reasons related to economies of scale. The small unit, independent in every way, should, however, continue to operate as it has in the past.

Merchandising in the future will become more streamlined, as well as automated, but still will be as unpredictable as ever. Assortments in stores will become even more simplified than is now true. In clothing, for example, more average sizes will be used in place of specific sizes like 15–33. Buying should become more regionalized as it becomes more tailored to regional needs. Computer terminals with TV screens attached may even permit buying to take place without even leaving the store. The buyer, along with other store personnel, may sit in front of the equipment to see the latest items on the market.

A merchandising prediction that could cause major shifts in all areas of merchandising is the suggestion that retailers will change from life-style merchandising back to classification of merchandise by price line. This idea, as expressed by Lasker Meyer, chairman of Abraham & Strauss, at the January 1981 meeting of the National Retail Merchants Association, is one that will bear fruit if the necessity of poor business forces retailers to act. For as Mr. Meyer stated, "Retailers continue to stress higher-priced and life-style departments despite studies that show that these areas produce the poorest results. In terms of gross margin and operating profit, Budget Departments are best, Moderate second, and Better poorest."[5] Although egos are involved, retailers will make the change if the survival of the store requires it.

As for what the future holds for UPC and UVM, it is anyone's guess. It is safe to assume that these systems, or some other system, will be in use in 1985 or 2000 and beyond. The advantages of vendor coding are too numerous to see its demise. Careful study of the coding situation is important to the retailer who wants to ensure that he or she has the appropriate equipment or that he or she can obtain it to utilize the codes that will be found on merchandise. The savings to the store in using such codes should outweigh the cost involved in procuring equipment to "read" the information.

Unit pricing, along with other forms of pricing that are tied to the consumer movement, should gain in popularity. A more price-conscious public will find the retailer, as a general rule, being more careful in the pricing of merchandise by checking competitors' prices and by making the effort necessary not to violate various pricing rules and regulations that will be enacted at the state and federal level in the years to come.

As for the distribution of merchandise, more use of containers and air freight will find the retailer of the future keeping lower levels of merchandise in stock since inventory replenishment should be faster as well as more reliable. Speed and reliability will result from the automated ordering that the retailer's own system will provide along with the automated warehouse operation that will be in existence at the supplier level. These innovations coupled with jumbo jets and container trucks will bring the goods to the store without unnecessary delay.

Merchandise control in the future will be much like that found in some larger stores today. Even the small store of the future, thanks to its minicomputer, will be able to have up-to-the-minute data on all aspects of its merchandise program. Such a capability will not replace the human element in making decisions. Such information as provided by the system should, instead, improve the quality of the decisions that affect the merchandise program within the store.

Where will future retail management come from? This most difficult question was analyzed in *Stores,* a publication of the National Retail Merchants Association.[6] The consensus appears to be that upper management will continue to come from within the company from people who are college trained and have retail experience, as has been the case in the past. The trend for middle management, however, will find more openings for high school graduates who have worked up through the ranks, especially among women and other minority employees. It is believed that such employees have a closer identification with the needs of customers since they have served them on the sales floor. It is also being realized that good department managers do not always need to be college trained. A college trained person may not take such a job seriously enough—viewing it instead as a temporary assignment before moving to bigger and better things. The future in personnel will find a greater emphasis on serving the customer. Those who do it best will be on their way to successful retailing careers. Even management trainees will get more time on the sales floor in an attempt to get the pulse of the customer. Therefore, the future will find a return to the basics of retailing. Such is a foregone conclusion since retailing is and always will be a "people business."

Other personnel trends will find more unionization in the Sunbelt, more use of part-time salespeople, particularly older people, who will work more on Sundays and holidays, and more training programs for such salespeople, as the costs for employees go up, in an effort to increase productivity. Such trends are full of potential problems for the retailer. A significant cost to any store is the cost of selling. Training part-time people is expensive. Paying an ever-increasing living wage is costly. Motivating people who must work on Sundays, holidays, and/or nights is difficult; therefore, productivity may suffer with a corresponding increase in cost. So great are these problems for some stores that they have already adopted a policy of next-to-no sales help. These stores rely on signs and displays to sell products. Even Sears is moving away from service as it shifts cash registers from each department to area cashiering arrangements. Of course, still other stores emphasize service and will continue to do so.[7] Although the trends are mixed, one thing is certain: the retailer of the future will continue to have difficulties in the personnel area. The merchant who can minimize these problems may create for the store a differential advantage in the marketplace.

PROMOTION TRENDS

Advertising, sales promotion, and retail display are areas where much improvement is possible for many stores. For the major chains and large independents, more use of television including cable will be seen. Catalogs and telephone sales will also become more popular as stores seek to serve fringe areas in a more efficient manner. Displays will continue the trend already set where they reflect the thinking of the target market, whether that thinking be traditional or unconventional.

For the smaller store, the greatest change will be found in taking promotion more seriously. The smaller store, due to necessity, will begin to budget its promotional effort, will become more aware of the need for continuity in promotion, and will begin to view promotion as a necessary part of its total marketing program—things that are already done by the larger stores.

Another interesting development to watch in the years to come will be the shift that is expected to take place in the media mix of stores. Robert Coen, writing in *Advertising Age*, predicts a slight shift away from newspapers as retailers in general move to television and other forms of electronic media.[8] It is interesting that radio's share of the total advertising budget will remain constant as predicted by Coen (Table 27–3).

One of the real question marks in studying future promotional trends is the category of electronic media. Will it replace print media? This is not likely in the near future. Will it become a significant form of direct media? Such is very likely. Many see "teleshopping" as the way of the future. In one such experiment conducted in Coral Gables, Florida, in 1980–1981, 150 homes were put on a system using a TV set, terminal, and telephone coupler. Consumers were able to shop from the Sears, Penney, and Service Merchandise catalogs simply by using the terminal keyboard to make information and/or illustrations appear on the screen. If desired, customers could also order directly by use of the Viewtron System.[9] Because of the apparent success of experiments like the one in Florida, it is believed that one fourth of all homes will have video terminals of either the telephone type or of the type that makes use of a cable TV system[10] by 1990. If one fourth of all homes do have this type of ordering capability by 1990, then retailers will by necessity become involved with the electronic media.

More promotional creativity should also be found in the future since it is believed that the competitive situation will be more keen as time goes on. Necessity will breed creativity. Such necessity will also call for more funds as a percentage of sales to be spent on the promotional needs of the store. The future will also find more promotional emphasis being placed on the store as compared with the product. As products become available at more stores, a store's promotional program will place less emphasis on the products sold and more emphasis on store image.

Table 27–3

Dollars Invested in Local Advertising Media, 1980 versus 2000

	1980		2000	
Media	Dollars (millions)	As a % of Total	Dollars (millions)	As a % of Total
Newspaper	$13,525	54.3%	$75,300	51.1°
Television	3,100	12.4	23,200	15.8
Radio	2,840	11.4	16,000	10.9
Magazines	—	—	1,000	.7
Electronic media	—	—	2,100	1.4
Other	5,435	21.9	29,600	20.1
Total	$24,900	100.0%	$147,200	100.0%

Source: Robert J. Coen, McCann-Erickson. Reprinted by permission from the November 13, 1980 issue of *Advertising Age*. Copyright © 1980 by Crain Communications, Inc.

Since customer service is so dependent on the type of retail situation, trends in customer service reflect a mixed picture. As has been true in the past, a retailer's position in the wheel of retailing may influence the store's use of customer service. One overall trend does appear. Customer service, in terms of both quality and quantity, will grow in the future. Competition will see to that. Just as J.C. Penney decided in the 1950s that it should add credit to retain its market share, stores now and in the future will add to and improve on the services that are offered the customer as a means of maintaining a competitive position or even, perhaps, of obtaining a differential advantage.

The future will also find EFTS (Electronic Funds Transfer System) in use in stores as customers learn to accept the idea.[11] Such a service will reduce bad-check losses for retailers while providing the equivalent of branch banking within the store for the customer. More leisure-time services such as classes and schools to teach everything from charm to cooking will be offered as a means of building traffic. One-stop shopping with an emphasis on total service will be more the rule rather than the exception for many stores in the future.

At the other extreme, some stores will feature bare-bone prices with little or no customer service. Such stores will appeal to a particular market segment who will be willing to rough it if the price is right. Such a trend can already be observed in the form of warehouse stores as discussed in Chapter 1.

In the future, more and more emphasis will be placed on retail control as a means of improving the profitability of the store. The problem of bad checks and bad credit cards may be overcome thanks to EFTS. As for customer and employee theft, techniques will be borrowed from space age technology to use in this area. Electronic Article Surveillance (EAS) will continue to become more sophisticated (and effective) while detracting less from the merchandising aspects of the product. Not only will merchandise be sensitized, but boxes and other containers will be used in a broader security effort. Although more difficult to control, employee theft will also come under closer scrutiny. Items that can be desensitized only when being rung on the register will reduce theft. Wider use of polygraph (lie-dectector) and other forms of honesty tests is also seen as a continuing trend that will help to curb the amount of employee theft.

As for security efforts in the area of fire, civil disorder, natural disaster, and the like, the trend is one of extremes. For example, stores near a store that just experienced a fire will have great interest in fire control. Others will not. Legislation requiring more retailer interest in coping with various areas of retail security will be the answer if one or two major stores should experience a major catastrophe. The trend is not positive in the area of retail security if all security efforts remain voluntary.

Operations control (expense control and performance control) may be the area that holds the most promise for the future of retailing. There is a growing realization among all types of retailers that sales gains can be generated internally through increased productivity and that this may be a more important—as well as more profitable—means of growth than expansion through physical growth.[12] The store of the future will be more cost-conscious. Widespread use of computers in conjunction with point-of-sale registers will provide the store's management with the necessary data to more tightly control its operation. The closed-loop system, as mentioned in Chapter 15, is the answer to automatic ordering of merchandise. The system will also provide better accounting for inventory and improve the flow of merchandise. Such a system, however, goes beyond merchandise control. It should also improve cost control and budgeting as well. Closed-loop systems will grow in popularity among retailers. In fact, in five to ten years, people may wonder how they ran the store without the new system.[13]

Another trend that is already being felt in the area of operations control is the control of energy. More stores in the future will concern themselves with energy management. From store design to burning lights at night, energy conservation will become very crucial to a profit-minded store. The retailer of the future will be, by necessity, more knowledgeable about energy and the latest available techniques dealing with how to restrict its use.[14] The alternative will be forced closings by various governmental bodies during periods when fuel, gas, and/or electricity are in short supply. Needless to say, a closed store is not productive.

One other trend worth noting is that retailers will be more responsive to change than has been true in the past. Consumerism, competition, and regulation have joined forces to make the retailer more receptive to the needs of the marketplace. Greater use of retail auditing procedures (internal and external) will be seen in the years to come as retailers strive to make their operations serve the needs of the consumer in the most efficient way possible. A store that meets this objective should be around when the future becomes the present.

RETAILING AS A CAREER

A close analysis of the various retailing trends reveals that retailing as a business form should offer many challenges in the years to come. And with these challenges will come career opportunities for those who have an interest in this exciting field. What are some of these opportunities? How does one prepare for a career in retailing? How does one obtain that first retailing job? Is a retailing career right for you? As the final points of discussion in this book, let us now examine these questions as a means of looking at retailing as a career.

Careers in Retailing

With over 15 million people working in retailing, there is almost any type of job being performed by someone for some retailer. Some of these numerous jobs are:

Credit manager   Promotion director
Customer service representative   Receiving clerk

Display manager	Sales associate (clerk)
Fashion buyer	Security director
Merchandise manager	Store owner

Although each job differs from store to store, it might be interesting to look at just one career path and get a brief description of the job responsibilities that are associated with each job on the career ladder. In Figure 27–2, the career path from trainee to senior vice president for merchandising for R. H. Macy & Co. is given for your examination.

Of all the career paths listed, store owner is one that is the goal of many people. Many who have reached this goal have done so with great success. An equal number have lost everything in a store that turned into a disaster. To operate a successful store requires a working knowledge of the information discussed in the first 26 chapters of this book. Retailing is not so easy or simple as some are inclined to think. Much knowledge is required if a profit is to be a realistic expectation. A business degree and some retail experience will be assets to a person but will not guarantee success. Stick-to-itiveness is also required. Just how badly the owner wants to succeed may make the difference between success and failure given the existence of the other attributes. Store ownership is a career opportunity that is full of risks so great that there is a better than 50:50 chance of failure. In making the decision on store ownership, the psyche income variable is important. Is it worth the risk to be your own boss? For many, the answer is "yes." Many successful retailers will later make the financial income that comes with a profitable store. Some will, however, just get by. In those instances, psyche income will continue to be the store owner's only reward.

Career Preparation

How do you prepare for a career in retailing? From an academic standpoint, a college degree is almost essential for any type of higher retail management position; whereas a two-year degree is appropriate for the department manager position. For sales associates, a high school degree is usually the minimum requirement, with more education being required for certain selling situations. As for what to major in, a degree in something is better than nothing, but a degree in marketing/retailing/fashion is best of all.

Along with a degree, outside work experience is very helpful in obtaining a retail job. Any kind of experience is good, but retail experience is the best of all possible alternatives. Retailing jobs at Christmas, vacation time, or after school tell the prospective retail employer that you had the initiative to get yourself a job, that you apparently liked working with customers since you are still interested in retailing, and that you have experience "under fire."

Getting That First Retailing Job

Career preparation is important, but that alone will not get you any job. The job applicant must sell himself or herself to the prospective employer. How?

1. *A Good Resumé.* A good resumé is not one that just says that the applicant is alive and well. A good resumé will stress those things that will be of benefit to a retailing career.

Figure 27-2

From trainee to senior vice president at R. H. Macy & Co. A career opportunity in retailing.

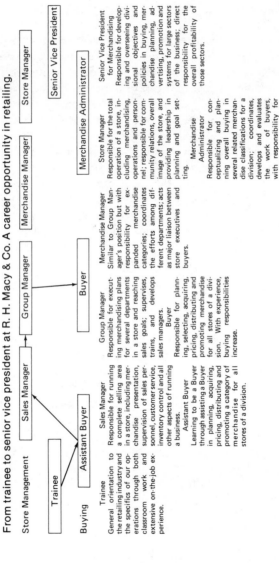

Store Management

Trainee → Sales Manager → Group Manager → Merchandise Manager → Store Manager → Senior Vice President

Buying

Trainee → Assistant Buyer → Buyer → Merchandise Administrator → Senior Vice President

Trainee
General orientation to the retailing industry and the specifics of our operations through both classroom work and extensive on-the-job experience.

Sales Manager
Responsible for running a complete selling area in a store, including merchandise presentation, supervision of sales personnel, customer service, inventory control and all other aspects of running a business.

Assistant Buyer
Learning to be a Buyer through assisting a Buyer in planning, acquiring, pricing, distributing and promoting a category of merchandise for all stores of a division.

Group Manager
Responsible for executing merchandising plans for several departments in a store and reaching sales goals; supervises, trains, and develops sales managers.

Buyer
Responsible for planning, selecting, acquiring, pricing, distributing and promoting merchandise for all stores of a division. With experience, buying responsibilities increase.

Merchandise Manager
Similar to Group Manager's position but with responsibility for expanded merchandise categories; coordinates the efforts among different departments; acts as major liaison between store executives and buyers.

Store Manager
Responsible for the total operation of a store, including merchandising, operations and personnel; responsible for community relations, overall image of the store, and providing leadership in planning and goal setting.

Merchandise Administrator
Responsible for conceptualizing and planning overall buying in several related merchandise classifications for a division; coordinates, develops and evaluates the work of buyers, with responsibility for profits.

Senior Vice President for Merchandising
Responsible for developing and overseeing divisional objectives and policies in buying, merchandise planning, advertising, promotion and systems for large sectors of the business; direct responsibility for the overall profitability of those sectors.

(Courtesy of R. H. Macy & Co., Inc.)

In other words, the resumé should tell the employer why John Jones would be a good person to check out for further consideration (Figure 27–3).

2. *Send Resumé to Correct Place.* An applicant should do his or her homework. Names and addresses of firms can be obtained through the *College Placement Annual,* annual reports, and various directories. It is recommended that you do not wait for a firm to interview at your college or university before taking action. Even if the firm only tells you to sign up for its visit in its response to your application, you have made the potential employer take notice of you before the visit to campus.

3. *Send a "Personal" Letter.* With each resumé, send a personalized letter. In the letter, the smart applicant will write, for example, "I am interested in going to work for K mart because I know . . . ". Several personal references should be made to show the reader that time and thought have been put into the letter.

4. *Interview.* The face-to-face meeting with a prospective employer is always an exciting time for a job applicant. Dress is important. Unless instructed otherwise, a business suit or tailored dress is appropriate. Personal hygiene is also crucial as is being on time. The purpose of the interview is twofold. The store is selling itself to you, and you are selling yourself to the store. If you want the job, it is recommended that you review the section in the book on staffing and salesperson development. This will give you an idea of what the store is looking for and how you can sell yourself to the store. Remember—before you will have an opportunity to sell to others in a retailing environment, you will have to sell yourself to the retail employer.

Is a Career in Retailing for You?

IF you enjoy a challenge . . .
IF you like facing new situations every work day . . .
IF you like working with all types of people . . .
IF you are not afraid to assume responsibility for business decisions . . .
IF you enjoy the various topics as discussed in this book . . .
. . . then consider a career in retailing.

SUMMARY

Although predicting the future of something as dynamic as retailing is difficult, it would appear that its future is bright even when all its problems are considered. Market trends find the population to be growing although not at every age level. Mobility is also on the increase. Trends in store development include a move to the downtown area along with an increase in super stores and smaller stores alike. As for merchandising trends, automation will play a significant role. Buying will also become more regional, pricing will become more cautious, and distribution will be more efficient. Personnel trends will find more opportunities for noncollege graduates. Personnel costs will unfortunately also continue to be a major problem. Trends in promotion will find more emphasis on this area. Stores, both large and small, will work to increase the efficiency of their promotion dollars. More emphasis will also be placed on store promotion as opposed to product promotion. Electronic funds transfer, store-sponsored leisure-time activities, and stores that offer all services or no services will all be a part of the customer service picture in years to come. Finally, due to its nature,

Figure 27-3

Suggested one-page resumé format.

```
                                JOHN L. JONES
                                1234 South Dollar Street
                                Anywhere, Kansas  64123
                                Telephone:  (913) 765-4321


OBJECTIVE:                      Career in Retail Management


ACADEMIC TRAINING:              B.B.A.  Mid-America University, 1982
                                        (Retailing Option)

                                A.S.    Simmons Community College, 1980


RETAILING COURSEWORK:           Retail Store Management
                                Retail Merchandising and Control
                                Retail Case Problems
                                Retail Advertising
                                Retail Internship - Sullivan Stores


RETAILING-RELATED EXPERIENCE:   Sullivan Stores - Internship
                                    Worked in all areas of store, 1982

                                J. C. Penney - Men's Wear Sales Associate
                                    Weekends, Summers, Holidays, 1980-1982

                                McDonald's Inc. - Counter Sales
                                    Summers, 1978-1980


HONORS:                         Alpha Mu Alpha
                                Beta Gamma Sigma


MEMBERSHIPS:                    American Marketing Association
                                Pi Sigma Epsilon - Sales and Marketing
                                    Fraternity
                                Sigma Chi Social Fraternity
                                Methodist Church


PERSONAL:                       22 Years Old, Single, No Location Preference


REFERENCES:                     Furnished Upon Request
```

retail control will play a more important role in the future of retailing than has been true in the past since it is an area where profit can be generated without the need for increased sales. The chapter also looks at retailing as a career. Careers in retailing, career preparation, and how to get that first retailing job are all points that are examined along with the question, "Is a career in retailing for you?"

DISCUSSION QUESTIONS

1. After talking to retailers in your area and examining the various periodicals available to you, what trends do you see for the future of retailing? Do they agree with the trends given in this chapter? What differences are found? What about similarities?
2. By various means, determine the career opportunities in retailing in your area. You might wish to talk to retailers, job placement firms, high school counselors, college placement officials, and others who might have information on this subject area.

NOTES

[1] William Lazer, "The 1980s and Beyond: A Perspective," *MSU Business Topics*, Vol. 25, no. 2 (Spring 1977), pp. 21–35.

[2] Reprinted by permission from *Chain Store Age Executive*, March 1981, © Copyright Lebhar-Friedman, Inc., 425 Park Avenue, New York, N.Y. 10022.

[3] For more information, see Morton S. Stark, "Shopping Center Futures: Tide Turning," *Stores*, Vol. 62, no. 3 (March 1980), pp. 20–22. Copyright, National Retail Merchants Association, 1980, and "Tomorrow's Towns," *Grey Matter*, Vol. 51, no. 2 (1980). Copyright 1980, Grey Advertising, Inc.

[4] Malcolm P. McNair and Eleanor G. May, "The Next Revolution of the Retailing Wheel," *Harvard Business Review*, Vol. 56, no. 5 (September–October 1978), p. 86. Copyright 1978 by the President and Fellows of Harvard College. All rights reserved.

[5] Reprinted by permission from *Chain Store Age Executive*, March 1981, © Copyright Lebhar-Friedman, Inc., 425 Park Avenue, New York, N.Y. 10022.

[6] "This People Business," *Stores*, Vol. 59, no. 1 (January 1977), pp. 26 ff. Copyright, National Retail Merchants Association, 1977.

[7] Reprinted by permission of *The Wall Street Journal*, © Dow Jones & Company, Inc., 1981. All Rights Reserved.

[8] Robert J. Coen, "Vast U.S. and Worldwide Advertising Expenditures Predicted," *Advertising Age*, Vol. 51, no. 49 (November 13, 1980), pp. 10–16.

[9] "Electronic Shopping," *Stores*, Vol. 63, no. 2 (February 1981), p. 37. Copyright, National Retail Merchants Association, 1981.

[10] Linda A. Gluck, "How Cable TV Provides Instant Answers," *Stores*, Vol. 60, no. 7 (July 1978), pp. 44–45. Copyright, National Retail Merchants Association, 1978.

[11] For more information, see John C. Marsh, "The Retailer and the Development of EFTS," *Retail Control*, Vol. 45, no. 1 (September 1976), pp. 43–53, published by the National Retail Merchants Association.

[12] Edward S. Dubbs, "Expansion into the 1980s," *Stores*, Vol. 58, no. 9 (September 1976), p. 3. Copyright, National Retail Merchants Association, 1976.

[13] Charles R. Braley, "Retailing in '80s: One EDP System to Do Everything," *Women's Wear Daily*, Vol. 134, no. 4 (January 6, 1977), pp. 1 ff.

[14] For more information, see "Energy: Escalating Costs Lead to New Ideas," *Stores*, Vol. 61, no. 2 (February 1979), p. 47. Copyright, National Retail Merchants Association, 1979; "Energy Management: The Slingshot vs. The Heavy Armor," *Stores*, Vol. 58, no. 4 (April 1976), pp. 13–14. Copyright, National Retail Merchants Association, 1976; Robin W. Lanier, "Rising Energy Prices and Retailing's Response: Some Thoughts on Savings and Conservation," *Stores*, Vol. 62, no. 3 (March 1980), p. 71. Copyright, National Retail Merchants Association, 1980; and M. F. Line, Jr., "Does the Retailer Have an Energy Crisis?" *Retail Control*, Vol. 45, no. 5 (January 1977), pp. 43–48, published by the National Retail Merchants Association.

APPENDIXES

APPENDIX A

Cases

Experiential Learning Exercises

LET'S TALK ABOUT RETAILING

As a member of a junior executive training program, you have been directed to prepare a speech entitled "Retailing: Past and Present." You are told to develop an outline of your talk, which is scheduled to last about 10 minutes. The leader of the training program points out that a member of the group will be selected at random to actually give his or her speech.

Develop the outline for the talk and be prepared to actually give your talk if you are the lucky one to be selected. Why would a retail store make an assignment of this nature in its executive training program?

THE COAT HANGER

The Coat Hanger is a clothing store that has operated at the same location in your town for 20 years. In the past, it has sold both men's and women's clothes with about a 15:85 assortment. Because of this merchandise imbalance, *The Coat Hanger* was considered by most to be a women's shop.

Very recently, Mary and Fred Brown bought the shop. From the start, their problem was what to do with their purchase. Mary wished to make the store into a complete young women's shop while Fred wanted to add older men's clothing so as to make it about 50 percent men's fashions. Both had very strong opinions about their ideas. Needless to say, this problem was causing the business to operate in a precarious manner. Finally, they agreed to sell to everybody. As Mary put it, "Our target market will be Mr. & Mrs. Anybody. Our goal will be to serve John Q. Public and his wife."

Do you agree with their choice of a target market? Since the store is located in your town, analyze the target market in terms of demographics. What do you determine to be a good potential target market for this store?

SUPER Z DISCOUNT STORES

Super Z Discount Stores is a multi-unit operation with stores in 35 states. The chain has, through the years, prided itself on keeping up-to-date on those activities both in and out of government that affect its operation. Unfortunately, in recent weeks through deaths, retirements, and resignations, the people who were directly responsible for such activities are no longer with the company. While the search for replacements goes on, so must the operation of the stores. To serve as a guide during the interim, and for later as well, *Super Z* requested a position paper that dealt with the uncontrollable variables that should be faced by the chain. The position paper analyzed the Sherman Act and Truth in Lending. No other uncontrollable variables were mentioned by the firm that was hired to do the job.

Did the firm include all the uncontrollable variables in its analysis? Assume that you were given the assignment. What would you include in your position paper dealing with external retail restraints?

Case 4

THE DOG HOUSE

An enterprising young college graduate, Fred Gaines, has come up with what he considers to be a million-dollar idea: hot dogs by the inch. A person would, for example, come into his restaurant and order a 3-inch dog, a 9-inch dog, and a 36-inch dog. Yes, it would be possible to buy a hot dog 36 inches long from *The Dog House*. Fred went to the bank with his idea in order to obtain a loan for his new business. Needless to say, the bank was less than enthusiastic about the idea after it found out that it was just an idea. What the bank wanted was facts that show that the idea has possibilities.

Assume that Fred Gaines lives in your town. Develop a feasibility study for his idea. If time permits, run an actual survey and determine if hot dogs by the inch would sell in your town. Do people view such hot dogs as being superior in any way to regular hot dogs? What price would they be willing to pay per inch? Answer these and other pertinent questions in your examination of the facts.

Case 5

SWEETS AND GOODIES

For seven years, Mary Jenkins has operated *Sweets and Goodies*, a bakery shop, in a Gulf Coast town of 25,000 people. In each of those seven years, she has made a profit as well as paid herself a salary. Last month she read in *The Wall Street Journal* that the Southern Flour Company was setting up franchise outlets to sell bakery products under the name *Yum Yum Tree*. Since what she read was of interest to her, she has contacted the Southern Flour Company and asked them for more details.

What does Mary Jenkins need to ask Southern Flour? What does she need to ask herself? Do you feel that she should seriously consider becoming a member of the *Yum Yum Tree* franchise system?

Case 6

MOORE'S STORES

Jeff Moore, owner of a chain of warehouse furniture stores, is giving some thought to locating a store in your town. In discussing his decision parameters, he stated that he would be interested in knowing the trade area of the town for his kind of store as well as the Index of Retail Saturation. Any other factors that could aid him in his decision are also requested.

Can you help out Mr. Moore? Calculate the trade area for your town by means of Reilly's Law and the Index of Retail Saturation. Also determine other factors that might have a bearing on the selection process.

Case 7

A & P FOOD STORE

For many years *A&P* customers came in the front door to shop. Then traffic problems forced management to place a parking lot behind the building. The resulting layout is believed to be satisfactory during busy times but not very good during slack times. "Although the layout has many problems," the manager said, "the greatest problem is the checkout stations. We need only one set of registers. Yet I do not want to close either set of doors. We still get a lot of traffic coming in both the front and back doors."

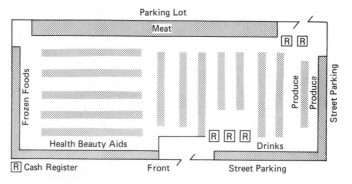

Develop a new layout for the store that will improve the flow of traffic in the store while solving the register station problem.

Case 8

BRIDGES ENTERPRISES

Bridges Enterprises, a Delaware corporation, has just bought from its originator the idea and name for a new kind of clothing store. *Just Kid'n* is a children's shop that considers children and grandmothers as well as mothers as primary customers. Store layout, promotion, and the like all follow this approach. The store currently has one shop with the originator as manager. Four people are under the manager. *Bridges Enterprises* plans to grow from this one store by first enlarging it and then developing a chain of *Just Kid'n* stores that may someday total 500 units. A plan of managerial organization is needed to permit growth with a minimum of organizational difficulties. To assist in the planning, principles of organization will be applied. A Modified Mazur Plan will also be adopted. Orderly growth is the goal.

Do you agree with the approach to be followed by *Bridges Enterprises*? Develop and chart a step-by-step plan for organizational growth for the *Just Kid'n* store group. Explain and justify your organization charts.

HAMBURGER HAVEN

Bill King quit his job with a major hamburger chain after deciding to go it alone in the hamburger business. His restaurant, *Hamburger Haven,* was to be located on one of the main streets in a southern town of 100,000 people. On a vacant lot that he bought, Bill constructed a prefab building. During the construction phase, a sign announcing the new restaurant was placed at the site since Bill wanted to generate some interest in his business. On opening day, he took the sign down early, put up a "now open" sign, prepared many hamburgers and other foods, and braced himself for the opening-day crowd. As he was later to say, "That opening day was the greatest disappointment of my life. It was as if nobody knew we were there."

What could Bill King have done to get his restaurant off to a better start? Develop a press kit for *Hamburger Haven.*

MOTHERS AND OTHERS

Pregnant women and full-figured (large) women are the target groups for *Mothers and Others.* For a store with limited sales space, special care must be taken in estimating demand and in development of the merchandise budget and model stock. *Mothers and Others* estimates demand by studying birth trends and marriage rates and by observing the number of large women in the area. Bertha Grimes, store manager, also does some comparison shopping. As for the merchandise budget, Ms. Grimes, along with her two assistants, takes the estimate of demand for the period and determines from it the amount needed to be bought. The sales estimate for the last six-month budget was $60,000, with the percentage of sales for each month as follows:

February	15%	May	20%
March	20%	June	10%
April	25%	July	10%

Assuming a stock–sales ratio of 3.0, shortages to be 2 percent of sales, markdowns to be 10 percent of sales, and discounts to be 3 percent of sales, determine the open-to-buy financial requirement for *Mothers and Others* if $5,000 of inventory is on order and $10,000 is the amount of inventory on hand. Average markup is 40 percent at retail. As for model stock, the rule of three is considered to be valid in all cases. Ms. Grimes states that, "We wouldn't have as good an assortment if we didn't follow the rule of three. It gives a customer a better selection from which to make a choice."

What are your reactions to the merchandise planning procedure of *Mothers and Others*? What is your reaction to its merchandise budget? What is your reaction to the statements of Ms. Grimes?

CONSOLIDATED STORES

Consolidated Stores is a chain of 20 retail units serving the northeastern part of the United States as well as Canada. In its buying of soft goods through the years, it has relied heavily on a salaried resident buying office for advice and service. That resident buying office has now been bought by a different organization that plans to make major changes within its operation. As a result, *Consolidated Stores* is now considering the possibility of opening its own resident buying office, switching to a system of central buying, or moving to another independent resident buyer. Top management is favoring a move to central buying due to the specialization that such an arrangement might provide. Of course, the individual stores favor the continuation of a resident buying office since this idea typically provides the individual store with more flexibility. A decision is needed soon since the buying season begins within the month.

What would you recommend to *Consolidated Stores*?

PAINTS AND THINGS

Paints and Things is a shop aimed at the do-it-yourselfer. In buying for his store, Dewey Briarcliff, the owner, did everything possible to negotiate the best deals with his suppliers. On one purchase of hardware supplies that cost him $7,000, he received trade discounts of 10–10–5. In addition, he received a 5 percent quantity discount and a cash discount of 3/10. Invoice date was July 12. Other terms were EOM–60 with 8 percent anticipation allowed. He paid the invoice on August 22.

What amount did Mr. Briarcliff pay on August 22 according to the terms of sale? Are there other points of negotiation that should have been asked about when Mr. Briarcliff talked with the supplier?

BILL'S DOLLAR STORE

Bill's Dollar Store, owned by Bill Graham, has been a part of Brooklet, Kansas, since 1953. From the very beginning, the store has followed a policy of even-dollar pricing (3 for $1.00, 2 for $3.00, etc.). A one-price policy with no price lines has also been the rule. Since the early days of the store, seconds and distressed merchandise has been the source of most of the inventory. Recently, Mr. Graham has begun to carry first-grade merchandise as well. Because many carry the same brand as the old merchandise, the owner is seeking a way to distinguish the two grades of merchandise. The idea of price lines has been considered. The idea of pricing based on cost is also under consideration. In addition, some thought has been given to introducing psychological pricing into the store. After looking at his options, Mr. Graham stated, "There are so many pricing alternatives, I really don't know which way to go."

What do you recommend to Mr. Graham? What various pricing options should be considered for use by *Bill's Dollar Store*?

Case 14

SMITH'S

In Alabama, when the name *Smith's* is mentioned, customers all over the state think of fine-quality clothing. In the past several months, the retailer has started taking his product to the people, as evidenced by the opening of the store's first two branch operations. The new locations are strong, but the new stores appear to have a problem —shrinkage. In commenting on the difficulty, Henry Smith the second-generation owner, stated, "Someone is causing us problems. I don't know where the problem is but we are getting ripped off. We never had this problem when we had only one store."

Can you give Henry Smith some ideas about how to curb his loss problem? Suggest specific procedures that should be implemented to help reduce or possibly even eliminate *Smith's* shrinkage problem.

Case 15

QUIK-SAVER STORES

A convenience-store chain, *Quik-Saver Stores*, has units throughout California. In its various stores, inventory is taken by means of a physical count every six months. Between periods, inventory is ordered by means of observation. If an item is running low, the condition of the stock is observed and an order for the item is placed. The management of the store is concerned about the taking of inventory. Is the process accurate? Since they are on the cost system, some concern is also expressed about shortages and whether the inventory count at cost really reflects a correct picture of the inventory situation. Due to his concern about a weak inventory system, the owner of the stores decided to look into the possibility of switching to a retail dollar control system. In addition, interest has also been expressed in point-of-sale registers as part of a complete perpetual unit control system. Before making these changes, the owner is searching for facts about the old approaches as well as the new ones.

Using an example, explain how the retail method of accounting works. How can it determine shortages? How does it differ from the cost method? What are the advantages and disadvantages of each? As for unit control, are periodic counts or perpetual counts better for a store of this type? What would be the advantages of each? What would you do if you were the owner of *Quik-Saver Stores*?

GIFTS BY GENE

As an exclusive gift shop in Houston, *Gifts by Gene* has experienced phenomenal growth in sales. Unfortunately, it has also experienced phenomenal employee turnover. The owner, Gene Bradford, in an attempt to get at the problem, began to search out people who had worked at the store in the past so that he might ask them what they thought about the store. From those who were willing to talk, he found out some interesting things. For example, one told him that she quit because, "I got paid the same thing whether I worked or goofed off." Another said that training consisted of learning how to get out of work. New employees were told by the sponsor/trainers that they had better not be "rate busters" on the job. Still another said, "after reporting to work with enthusiasm at 9, I left in disgust at 11. Not a single employee even recognized my existence during those long two hours that I tried to work there."

Assume that you are Gene Bradford. What would you do?

RIC'S RECORDS & TAPES

Ric's Records & Tapes is a small chain of record and tape shops that tries to locate near college campuses. As a company policy, the chain hires students to work in their stores since management believes that this practice is good for business. In the past, the problem has been finding people who can sell in a retail setting since most students have not had any retail experience. To overcome this problem, management has decided to develop a sales training program that will have as an ultimate goal the development of creative salespeople.

What type of sales training program would you recommend to the management of *Ric's Records & Tapes*?

TDG STORES

Joe Swindell was reprimanded in front of two customers for trying to sell one of them a pair of shoes that did not fit right. Brenda Carter was neither absent nor late for five years on the job. No one knew unless Brenda said something about her record. Sally Thigpen was "called on the carpet" for not wearing her name tag. It is observed that no one has nerve enough to ask the manager where her name tag is. Fred Page was fired for smoking on the sales floor. His only reply was, "No one ever told me not to smoke there." These or similar incidents took place at one or more of the units of *TDG Stores*, a five-store "chain" of junior department stores. Each resulted in the creation of other problems for the store. In some instances, even customers became disturbed by these events.

How could each incident have been handled differently? Is human relations important to the success or failure of the store? Why?

Case 19

THE FOOT

The Foot is a store that specializes in shoes for the sports-minded person. For example, Pony, Adidas, and Nike are carried by the store for runners, whereas golfers can choose from a large selection of Foot Joy and Green Joy shoes. "Shoes for any sport" is the store's slogan. As a specialty retailer, all store locations are near but not in regional shopping malls. The stores are placed near malls so as to benefit from the traffic but are kept out of the malls to keep down rents. For the upcoming year, the local store plans to spend $10,000 on advertising, 90 percent of which will be spent during the Christmas season.

Develop an advertising budget and advertising schedule for *The Foot* based on what you feel the store should do. Also, for each media used in the advertising program, develop two representative ads that will tell the retailer how you feel *The Foot* should be promoted.

Case 20

DAVID'S

David's is a food chain headquartered in Chicago. Within the walls of its home office, a heated debate is taking place over whether contests should be added to the store's already active coupon promotion program or whether the firm should replace in-store coupons as a traffic-building device. One group favors total use of contests on the grounds that contests build repeat business. This group feels that everybody loves contests regardless of where they live or how old they are or any other variable. The opposing group feels that coupons do help in the promotion of merchandise. They point to the number of coupons that are redeemed as solid evidence of their popularity.

How can this controversy be settled? Which way would you go if you were involved in the decision-making process? What are the pros and cons of each approach to sales promotion? Are there other tools of sales promotion that the management group might also wish to consider?

Case 21

THOMPSON'S

Thompson's is a full-line department store located in the state of Oregon. In terms of the store's merchandise mix, the soft goods versus hard goods comes out to about 80:20. And of the soft goods sold, 60 percent are women's items, 20 percent men's items, and 20 percent children's items. Because of these relationships, the store's management has set up a policy that displays should reflect the assortment mix of the store. Therefore, for example, 80 percent of all displays should be for soft goods, 60 percent of those should be for women's clothes, and so on.

You have just been hired as *Thompson's* display manager. How do you feel about the system for determining what should be displayed? Do you have a better idea?

THE CLOSET

The Closet is a boutique serving the 18- to 25-year-old woman. When it first opened three years ago, it offered bank cards as its only form of credit. Both Master Card and Visa are still accepted by the store. The store is now considering the addition of travel and entertainment cards as well as the creation of its own in-store credit plan. Since it is located in a major metropolitan area, management feels that travel and entertainment cards will be of great assistance to the store. It is also considering its own in-store plan as a means of making money by charging an 18 percent interest charge on its proposed revolving charge plan. The owner, Hal Bridges, believes that the option of three credit plans will bring in much additional business to the store. "Since each serves a different market, our sales could triple with three credit plans from which to choose," stated the owner. He went on to say, "Three times the sales with an actual decrease in cost, thanks to the interest we will receive with our in-house plan, really makes sense."

Do you agree with the owner? Should *The Closet* add all the credit plans as proposed. What about a private-label, third-party credit plan? What are the various factors to be considered in making this decision?

THE FACTORY

For many years, *The Factory* has been a clothing outlet for the excess output of several clothing plants in the area. It has always operated with the basic philosophy of low prices and no frills. Recently, several competing outlets have opened in the area. These stores offer alterations, take credit cards, and provide other services like restrooms and a water fountain. Although *The Factory* is not out of business by any means, it is beginning to see an effect in the amount of store traffic and sales. The manager of *The Factory* is not worried but she is concerned about what should be done.

Assume the role of a retail consultant who has been hired to study this question. What do you recommend that *The Factory* do about this situation?

SOUTHERN SECURITY ASSOCIATES

As the owner of *Southern Security Associates*, you have been hired by B. J. Lang's Department Store to put in a retail security program. Your first assignment is to propose to the management of the five-story department store a general overall retail security plan. From this general outline will come a detailed security plan at a later time.

As requested, provide B. J. Lang's Department Store with an overall security plan that includes all areas of retail security.

GOLDSMITH'S

Goldsmith's is a specialty store for women with annual sales of around $4 million. In an attempt to examine the expense situation in the store, the management of *Goldsmith's* had developed a plan whereby all the expenses would be allocated to the selling departments of the store. Such a plan had the general approval of most department managers. One manager, however, was very apprehensive. His comment was, "How can I and my department be evaluated when the figures used for such purposes are figures over which I have little or no control?" Other managers are now beginning to express similar concerns.

What should the management of *Goldsmith's* do now? Are there other methods of expense control that might be considered? How do they work? What are the pros and cons of each?

DOLLY'S DAY CARE CENTER

Dolly Duke has just purchased a day care center that was not doing very well. She has changed the name and now she wants to change its level of performance. She knows little about marketing other than she knows that her business sells a service.

Develop a general marketing plan for *Dolly's Day Care Center*. Assume that her target market is middle to upper-middle income.

COLLECTABLES BY SAUNDERS

Thomas Saunders wants to open a mail-order retailing operation that will sell china and porcelain figurines in the $100–1,000 price range. Although he knows much about the art of collecting, and collecting china figurines in particular, he is weak on how to market his product.

How would you propose that he market his product? What mail lists should he use if he decides to use mail order? Does he have other alternatives? Be specific.

YOUR STORE

You and a friend have decided to open up a retail store. Before you apply for a loan, there are certain decisions that your friend feels must be made. These are:

Name of store
Definition of target market
Store location
Product mix
Promotion mix
Pricing structure
Desired personality

Your instructor will provide you with information pertaining to the type of store and the geographic location. Given that information, give your friend the answers to his points of concern. Are there other points that also should be addressed at this time?

APPENDIX B

Glossary of
Retailing Terminology

—A—

Advertising   Any controlled form of nonpersonal presentation and promotion of ideas, goods, or services by an identified sponsor that is used to inform and persuade the selected market. (19)*

Air Freight Decision Tool (AFDT)   A computer model designed for determining when to use air freight as the transportation mode. (14)

Alterations/Workroom   A customer service provided by the store that assists the customer by efficiently and correctly making whatever changes or adaptations are needed on products purchased. (23)

Anticipation   A discount that is taken when the obligation is paid prior to the starting date of the stated terms of the invoice. (12)

Assortment   The distribution of merchandise "in sight" (inventory on hand and merchandise on order) according to classification, subclassification, style, color, pattern, size, and price, with the quantities in each of these factors dovetailing as much as possible to customer demand. (10)

Atmospherics   The conscious designing of space to create certain effects in buyers. These effects are created through the use of the various senses—smell, sound, touch, and sight. (7)

Attitude   A learned tendency to respond in a given manner to a particular situation. (3)

Audiovisual Display   A form of point-of-purchase display that uses both audio and visual methods of presentation. (21)

* Numbers in parentheses indicate the number of the chapter in which the term is used.

Bad Check Any check that is not honored for payment by the bank it is drawn on within the normal course of business operations. (24)

Bait-and-Switch Pricing Setting a low price on a featured product that the retailer has no intention of selling; used to get the customer to the store so that the customer can be traded up to a more expensive item. (13)

Balance The number of SKUs needed in each merchandise line to attract customers. (10)

Blind Check When merchandise is received, the checker examines the merchandise and then records a description of it, the amount received, and other items of information that the store will later check against its records. (14)

Booster Box A box with a trap door or other device so that the box can be opened and closed very quickly as merchandise is stashed in it. It derives its name from the "on-the-street" name for a shoplifter, "a booster." (24)

Breadth The availability of complimentary items within a merchandise line. (10)

Budgeting The development of on-going expense plans that should take into consideration past, present, and future needs. (25)

Buying Power Index A weighted average of each market's strength as measured in terms of its proportion of U.S. retail sales, U.S. population, and U.S. effective buying income as computed by *Sales & Marketing Management*. (6)

Cash Discount Price reduction offered for paying before the date due; most common reduction is 2 percent, which is generally given for payment within the first 10 days of a 30-day obligation. (12)

Cash on Delivery Dating Retailer is required to pay in full for merchandise when order is received. (12)

Catalog Retailing A form of nonstore retailing where the retailer attempts to make a sale as a result of a merchandise catalog display. Retailer may or may not also have conventional stores. (26)

Catalog Showroom A retail institution that allows a customer to "shop" a catalog and then come to the store and examine a "floor sample" before placing an order and picking up the merchandise at a central receiving point. (1)

Central Business District Generally the original retailing center, it remains the center of business activity in most towns but has usually lost its predominant influence on the retailing community. (6)

Central Buying Office Office for a group of retail stores (usually a chain) that has the responsibility for actually selecting and buying the merchandise for the individual stores. (11)

Chain A retail operation having 11 or more units (stores). (1)

Charge Account Plan A credit arrangement under which the customer is allowed a period of payment of generally 30 days but sometimes up to 90 days before the bill becomes due with no interest or carrying charge being incurred during that period. (22)

Chargeback The recovery of transportation charges from a vendor who has not followed the routing instructions of the retailer. (14)

Check Guarantee Program A program under which particular companies agree to become co-makers of checks for approved customers. For a fee, the company reimburses the store for a check written by one of its approved checkwriters. (24)

Closed-Back Window Display window with a wall in the back that forms a glass-enclosed display room thereby separating the display from any distracting background. (7)

Closed-Loop System An inventory system that involves the recording of data at the point of sale for use in the ordering of merchandise. When received, the merchandise is coded into the computer that places the item into the store's inventory—to be removed only by the point-of-sale register at the time of sale. (15)

* Numbers in parentheses indicate the number of the chapter in which the term is used.

Cold Canvass Selling   A form of in-home selling where the retailer goes to a customer's home to sell a product without a prior indication of interest on the part of the customer. (26)

Collection System   A plan of action used by the retailer to encourage the customer to pay a debt. The system includes four stages: impersonal routine, impersonal appeals, personalized appeals, and drastic or legal action. (22)

Combination Store   A retail institution that offers the customer one-stop shopping and customer service. Typically, the combination consists of a drugstore and a discount store or a drug store and a supermarket. (1)

Communication   The mutual interchange of ideas by any effective means. (18)

Comparison Shopping   Visiting competing stores to find out what stores are carrying, what they are selling, and such things as the number of clerks and the methods of display. (10)

Consignment Buying   An arrangement under which a retailer carries an item in the store without buying it; ownership of the goods is retained by the supplier. (12)

Consistency   The degree to which products in the assortment are related in the customer's mind. (10)

Consolidated Delivery System   Type of delivery system generally operated by an independent firm that offers to deliver the items for many firms on a regularly scheduled basis. (23)

Consumer Behavior   Behavior exhibited by people in planning, purchasing, and using economic goods and services. (3)

Consumer Show   A form of nonstore retailing where consumers come to a civic center or similar facility to see merchandise brought to that location by various retailers. Usually sponsored by a civic club but may be a private venture. (26)

Contest   Type of sales promotion that gives customers a chance to win prizes; may involve skill or chance. (20)

Contribution Margin Method   A method of expense allocation in which the department manager and the department are evaluated using only those direct expenses over which that department has control. (25)

Co-Op Promotion   A type of sales promotion where the retailer joins with a manufacturer, vendor, or similar entity to promote a product or products. Under this arrangement the cost of the promotion is usually shared. (20)

Cost Code   A procedure using letters, numbers, diagonal lines, or other means to represent numbers so that the cost of an item can be included on the price ticket but at the same time concealed from the customer. The easiest method is to use a cost code word or words that has ten nonrepeating letters. (14)

Cost Complement   Value of inventory at cost divided by value of inventory at retail. (15)

Cost Method of Inventory Valuation   A method for determining ending inventory that requires a physical count of merchandise. Very common in small stores. (15)

Country Club Billing   Type of credit billing in which the store sends along with the statement each month a copy of each sales ticket for examination by the customer. (22)

Coupons   Type of sales promotion that offers the customer items at a reduced rate. Coupons may be either from a manufacturer or vendor—in which case, they are redeemable at many different stores—or from a particular retailer—in which case, they are useful only at that store. (20)

Credit   A medium of exchange of limited acceptance. A promise to pay is exchanged by the customer for the product or service that is offered by the store. (22)

Credit Information Exchange   A credit bureau or other credit facility that provides credit information on prospective as well as current customers. (6)

Credit Limit   The amount that a customer can charge is usually established by a two-stage limit plan—first, the automatic limit, which sets an amount that the customer cannot go over without the credit manager evaluating the situation; second, the real limit, which is the amount that the customer's balance cannot exceed. (22)

Cumulative Effect (Advertising Carryover)   The length of time that an advertisement or a series of advertisements affects a store after the advertisement or series of advertisements have been run. (19)

Cumulative or Maintained Markup   A weighted average determination of markup as the result of sales of an item at various prices over time. (13)

Cumulative Quantity Discount   A reduction in price based on the total amount purchased during a set period as opposed to one individual purchase. (12)

Customer Convenience   Form of customer service that runs the gamut from cashing checks to restrooms. Many times the services are not essential but are expected by customers. (23)

Customer Service   All those "fringe benefits" that are made available by the store for the purpose of further inducing the customer to purchase merchandise. (23)

Cutout   A manufacturer-supplied point-of-purchase display that is usually made of cardboard or some other nonpermanent material. (21)

Cycle Dating   Retailer is required to pay in full for the merchandise after terms are set using a calendar rotation plan such as EOM (End-of-Month) and MOM (Middle-of-Month). (12)

—D—

Dating   Establishes when the retailer should pay for the merchandise. (12)

Delivery   The movement of goods from a store to the location desired by the customer; includes in-house, consolidated, or Parcel Post or UPS. (23)

Demonstration   Type of sales promotion that actually shows a product or activity in action. The demonstration may be of a product for sale in the store or of an activity such as square dancing, which builds traffic for the store. (20)

Department Store   A retail institution that offers the target customer a complete assortment of goods and services. (1)

Depth   The number of sizes, colors, and other characteristics that are carried in a single line of merchandise. (10)

Descriptive Billing   Type of credit billing in which a statement with a description of each transaction compiled on it is sent to the customer instead of sending all individual sales tickets. (22)

Determination of Need   In terms of staffing, the development of the job description and job specifications for a personnel position. (16)

Direct Check   The checking of incoming goods against the invoice to ensure that what was ordered is what was received. (14)

Disciplinary Action   Any corrective action taken by management to promote conformity with the policies, procedures, and rules of the store. (18)

Discipline   Worker self-control in accordance with store policies, procedures, and rules. (18)

Discount Store   A departmentalized retail establishment utilizing many self-service techniques to sell hard goods (refrigerators, television sets, etc.), health and beauty aids, apparel, and other soft goods, and other general merchandise at uniquely low margins. It has a minimum volume of $500,000 and is at least 10,000 square feet in size. (1)

Display   *See* Retail Display. (21)

Dollar Control of Merchandise   The evaluation of store inventory in terms of its value in dollars (retail or cost). (15)

Dollar Markup   The difference between the cost of an item and its selling price. (13)

"Donation" Advertising   All advertising done by retailers in nonbusiness-related places such as high school annuals, dance recital programs, and the like, which should be considered a financial donation by a firm to a group. (19)

Dump Display   A form of point-of-purchase display where merchandise is "thrown" into a bin or box or even on the floor. Projects a bargain image. (21)

—E—

Economic Motives   Buying motives that are concerned with quality of the product or service, price, and other rational considerations resulting in consumer action. (3)

Electronic Article Surveillance (EAS)   An electronic wafer, disc, soft tag, or similar

---

* *Numbers in parentheses indicate the number of the chapter in which the term is used.*

device that is attached to merchandise. If the device is not removed, an alarm will sound as the customer with the item leaves the store. (24)

Electronic Funds Transfer System (EFTS) A computerized banking system that brings branch banking to the customer within the retail store. (27)

Employee Handbook Written information including such topics as the philosophy of the company, company history, job regulations, policies, procedures, fringe benefits, and dress code, which is compiled by the store and given to all employees; especially useful for new employee orientation. (18)

Energy Management The development of store policies and procedures that promote the conservation of energy (e.g., policies that limit the use of natural gas or electricity). (25)

Expense Centers Areas of responsibility are divided up in such a way that operations control can determine where the money is being spent within a store. (25)

Expense Control Procedures that include classification of expenses, allocation of expenses, budgeting, work simplification, and expense management; a part of operations control. (25)

Expense Management A procedure or a way of thinking that attempts to determine if the proper amount has been allocated for a particular task in order to insure that the expense needs of the store are provided for. (25)

Extended Dating Retailer is permitted to delay payment of an invoice for a predetermined period of time. Terms may be quoted as 2/10 net 30–60. (12)

External Traffic Management The movement of goods from supplier to receiving. (14)

—F—

Fact Sheet A presentation in outline form of all the pertinent facts about a retail store. (9)

Fad A fashion that is currently popular with one particular market segment. (10)

Fashion What is currently popular in the retail market. (10)

Fashion Cycle A model that illustrates how potential customers may react to a product. (10)

First-In, First-Out (FIFO) A procedure for valuing inventory where the items that have been around the longest are assumed to be sold first. (15)

Fixed-Base Budgeting A budgeting procedure that bases financial need on a predetermined level of retail activity. (25)

Fixtures The various "furniture" items in a store that are used to convert so many square feet of floor space into a store. (5)

Flexible Pricing Selling an item for different prices under different circumstances. (13)

Floor Value Factor Used to equate productivity to location of selling department. Calculated by dividing distance from entrance to back of store by the distance from entrance to department. (7)

Franchising A form of marketing or distribution in which a parent company customarily grants an individual or a relatively small company the right, or privilege, to do business in a prescribed manner over a certain period of time in a specified place. (5)

Free-Flow Pattern Layout Physical arrangement of a store's fixtures that makes use of much open space while providing the shopper with many different choices in terms of direction. (This type of layout is often used in a high-fashion dress shop.) (7)

Free-Standing Location A building that is not connected to other stores in the immediate vicinity. (6)

Freight Allowance An allowance given by a supplier as a means of equalizing transportation distance from a cost standpoint. (14)

Freight Auditor One who examines freight charges for their accuracy. Usual fee is 50 percent of the amount of overcharges collected. (14)

Full-Service Merchandiser A supplier who provides the retailer with a source of merchandise plus promotional assistance, accounting systems, training programs, and/or a host of other possible services in return for a commitment from the retailer to purchase a significant amount of merchandise from that vendor. (11)

Functional Discount A price reduction given to a certain type of customer (retailer, wholesaler, etc.) to cover the cost of carrying out a particular function (credit, storage, selling, etc.). *Also known as* Trade Discount. (12)

—G—

General Store A retail institution with a basic assortment of merchandise, a stove, and a front porch that satisfied the customer's social, financial (credit), and merchandise needs. (1)

Go Get 'em Method A very popular method of training, which involves no training at all; usually has a negative effect on employees. (16)

Grapevine An informal communication channel through which flows much information from "informed sources." (8)

Grid Pattern Layout Physical arrangement of a store whereby all the counters and other fixtures are at right angles to each other thereby forming a maze for the customer to move through (e.g., food stores). (7)

Group Method A method of training that is used for large groups; good for reaching many employees in a short period of time. (16)

—H—

Honesty Shoppers Persons hired by the retailer from shopping services firms who actually come into the store and make purchases in order to evaluate the employees' performance in carrying out the store's policies and procedures. (24)

House Organ Information (personal and company related) that is compiled by the store as a means of communicating with employees; it can take the form of a newspaper, magazine, or a one-page handout either given out at the store or mailed directly to employees. (18)

Human Relations The integration of people into a work environment in a manner that facilitates cooperation, creativity, and productivity. (18)

Hypermarket A retail institution, often referred to as a "super store," which provides one-stop shopping for almost any customer need. (1)

—I—

Image In terms of retailing, the way a store is perceived by the customer. *Also known as* Personality. (2)

Impulse Good An item purchased without prior planning—usually an inexpensive convenience good. (7)

Independent Resident Buying Office—Merchandise Broker The broker is paid by the seller or vendor rather than the retailer. *See also* Resident Buying Office. (11)

Independent Resident Buying Office—Salaried Such offices and stores usually sign an annual contract providing for the store to pay up to approximately 1 percent of annual sales to the resident buying office in payment for services rendered. *See also* Resident Buying Office. (11)

Independent Services Services offered to customers that are not directly related to the product merchandising effort of the store (tax service, ticket sales, etc.). (23)

Index of Retail Saturation (IRS) A store's retail potential is a function of the number of consumers in area for the product or service, the per capita retail expenditures for product or service, and the number and size of retail stores in the area that sell the product or service. (6)

Informal Organization A network of informal personal and social relations that exist in any organization. (8)

In-Home Retailing A form of retailing where the sale takes place in a person's home. (26)

Initial Store Contact The step in the retail selling process where the clerk has the first interaction with the customer in the store. (17)

Installment Plan A credit arrangement more commonly used for large-ticket items where an agreement is made for the purchase of a particular item with a predetermined number

---

* Numbers in parentheses indicate the number of the chapter in which the term is used.

of payments and a finance charge added to the amount. The item itself usually serves as collateral. (22)

Interior Display　A display within the store that serves to show items that may not otherwise be seen, to identify the department, to directly promote merchandise, and to present the store's personality. (21)

Internal Traffic Management　The movement of goods from marking to the final point of sale and possibly even beyond to home delivery. (14)

Inventory Turnover　A measure of how quickly goods are replaced by the store. (15)

$$\text{Turnover (retail)} = \frac{\text{Net Sales}}{\text{Average Inventory (retail)}}$$

$$\text{Turnover (cost)} = \frac{\text{Cost of Goods Sold}}{\text{Average Inventory (cost)}}$$

$$\text{Turnover (units)} = \frac{\text{Unit Sales}}{\text{Average Inventory (units)}}$$

Isolated Location　A free-standing building with no other stores in the immediate vicinity. (6)

—J—

Job Description　A formal statement of the tasks to be performed by a position holder. (16)

Job Specifications　The qualifications that a person must have to carry out a job as outlined in the job description. (16)

—K—

Keystone Markup　Determining the price of an item by doubling its cost. (13)

Kinesic Communication　A message that is expressed (delivered) in strictly nonverbal ways. (18)

—L—

Last-In, First-Out (LIFO)　A procedure for valuing inventory where the items that have been around the longest are assumed to be sold last. This method is desirable from a tax standpoint in times of inflation. (15)

Layaway Plan　A credit arrangement whereby the store agrees to hold an item for a period of time until final payment is made. Terms of the arrangement will vary. Some stores may require a nonrefundable down payment whereas others may require set amounts due at certain times or an added monthly charge. (22)

Leadership　The directing of workers in such a way that the objectives of the store are met. (18)

Learning　Changes in responses and response tendencies due to the effects of experience. (3)

Learning　Involves three almost simultaneous processes—acquisition, transformation, and evaluation. (16)

Leased Department　An area within a store operated by another company. Customers of the store are usually not aware of this arrangement. (11)

Letter of Credit　A letter written on a bank that states that a firm is good for the stated amount in the letter. An important document in international buying. (12)

Line of Credit　A predetermined amount of money that a business firm can borrow from a lending institution without seeking additional approval from the lender. (5)

Loss Leader Pricing Selling an item below the market price or even below cost in order to generate store traffic. (13)

—M—

Mail-Order Retailing A form of direct marketing that attempts to make the sale without other sales assistance. (26)

Maintained Markup *See* Cumulative Markup. (13)

Markdown A reduction from the original retail price. (13)

Marketing Sum total of all business activities that result in the pricing, distribution, and promotion of products (goods, services, ideas) for the purpose of satisfying customers while obtaining a normal return (profit) on investment. (2)

Marketing Concept A state of mind in a company that results in all planning, policies, procedures, and actions of the company being customer oriented. (2)

Marketing Research Systematic gathering, recording, and analyzing of data about problems relating to the marketing of goods and services. (4)

Marketing System The process of moving an idea from conception to ultimate consumption. (1)

Marking Placing any local store information including price, department number, and cost on an item. (14)

Markup Difference between what the item costs and what it is sold for. *Also known as* Markon. (13)

Marquee Element of exterior design that provides shelter over the front of the store building such as a canopy. (7)

Mazur Four Functional Plan Store organization based around four divisions: merchandising, publicity, store management (operations), and finance and control. Personnel is a separate division under a later modified plan. (8)

Memorandum Buying An arrangement that permits the title to the goods to pass to the merchant. This arrangement allows price flexibility while giving the merchant the right to return unsold items or pay for items only after they are sold. (12)

Merchandise Budget A schema or blueprint of all merchandise requirements for a store, expressed in dollars, for a particular period of time. (10)

Merchandise Center Where retail buyer and manufacturer make contact on a regular basis—usually in organized merchandise marts (New York, Chicago, etc.). (11)

Merchandise Control All those procedures that a retail store employs to determine the status of its inventory in light of customer demand and general economic conditions. (15)

Merchandise Cost Invoice price minus discounts plus workroom expenses plus transportation charges. (13)

Merchandise Distribution All those activities that result in the physical placement of merchandise near the point at which it will be sold. (14)

Merchandise Planning A process that involves estimating demand, determining the merchandise budget, and developing a model stock so that the retailer will make the correct buying decision. (10)

Merchandise Rack A form of point-of-purchase display whose purpose is to project the manufacturer's product into the mind of the customer. May be permanent or disposable. (21)

Metacommunication A message that, although not expressed in words, accompanies a message that is expressed in words. (18)

Modeling Behavior change as a result of the example of the leadership. (18)

Model Stock An ever-changing, desired assortment of merchandise carefully chosen by a store to best serve a target market. (10)

Motel Selling A form of nonstore retailing where a retailer uses a motel room for a "store." Anything from used TV sets to expensive clothing have been sold successfully in this manner. (26)

* *Numbers in parentheses indicate the number of the chapter in which the term is used.*

Motivation Management's ability to get workers to act in a certain way under their own volition. (18)

Motive Something (need or desire) that causes a person to act. (3)

Multiple Pricing A pricing technique that makes a product appear to be cheaper. For example, four for $1. (13)

—N—

Net Dating Retailer is required to pay in full for the merchandise in a set number of days. (12)

Net Profit Method A method of expense allocation in which the department manager and the department are evaluated on the basis of both direct expenses and indirect expenses that are allocated to each department according to a predetermined formula. (25)

Net Sales Gross (total) sales minus sales returns and allowances (employee discounts, etc.). (13)

No-Back Window Type of display that uses no background wall and thus allows the interior of the store to be viewed as a part of the total display. (7)

Noncumulative Quantity Discount A reduction in price given one time on one particular order. (12)

—O—

Objective Something toward which effort is directed, an aim, a goal. (8)

Odd Pricing A pricing technique that makes a product appear to be cheaper. For example, a store using odd pricing would charge $1.98 rather than $2.00. (13)

Open Front Type of store entrance that can be used in an interior mall location. Has no physical store front. Gives the feeling of complete openness and encourages the shopper to come inside and look around. (7)

Open-to-Buy The difference between merchandise on hand or ordered and what is needed. (10)

$$\text{Open-to-Buy} = \frac{\text{Projected}}{\text{Purchases}} - \frac{\text{Merchandise}}{\text{on Order}} - \frac{\text{Merchandise}}{\text{on Hand}}$$

$$\frac{\text{Open-to-Buy}}{\text{at Cost}} = \frac{\text{Open-to-Buy}}{\text{at Retail}} \times \frac{\text{Cost}}{\text{Complement}}$$

Operations Control The evaluation of store operations for the purpose of improving overall store performance. (25)

Opinion Leader An individual who by virtue of being looked up to exerts a great influence over people in the marketplace. (3)

Opportunity Cost The difference between the money to be earned in retailing and the money to be earned in alternative opportunities. (5)

Optical Character Recognition—Font A (OCR–A) A style of type that can be read by humans as well as machines. (14)

Order-Getter The category of salesperson who handles transactions, takes orders, and gets orders. An example of an order-getter is a clothing salesperson. (17)

Order-Handler The category of salesperson who handles orders that customers have already assembled. An example of an order-handler is a food store cashier. (17)

Order-Taker The category of salesperson whose primary function is taking customer orders and serving the customer. An example of an order-taker is a gas station attendant. (17)

Organization An entity. A group of people bound together in a formal relationship to achieve organizational goals. A process that is concerned with structuring, or arranging, the parts of the organization. (8)

Orientation That aspect of store staffing dealing with getting the new employee accustomed to the work environment. (16)

Outdoor Advertising   Consists primarily of outdoor posters (billboards), bulletins, and roadside signs (nonstandardized). This type of advertising is directed at the mobile consumer. (19)

—P—

Package Wrap   The preparation of a package in a manner that is desired by the customer. Package wrap includes customer wrap, mail wrap, and gift wrap. (23)

Parcel Pickup   A system that permits the customer to leave packages at the store for later pickup by the customer. (23)

Party Selling   A form of nonstore retailing where the retailer gets a customer to agree to have a "party" in his or her home where games are played and products are demonstrated and sold. (26)

Peddler   A hawker who carried on his back the essentials to be sold to the outlying countryside. As an area developed, the peddler evolved into a wagon peddler who was the first "traveling store." (1)

Perception   How one interprets a situation as a result of various stimuli. (3)

Performance Control   A type of operations control that is concerned with the operation of the total store; concentrates on the areas of finance and management. (25)

Performance Evaluation   That aspect of store staffing that deals with how to maintain and improve each employee's job satisfaction, morale, and job performance. (16)

Periodic Actual Count   A method of unit control of inventory where the merchandise on the shelf is actually counted on a regular basis. (15)

Periodic Visual Count   A method of unit control of inventory where the retailer simply "eyeballs" the merchandise and replaces the items that are low. (15)

Perpetual Actual Count   A method of unit control of inventory where merchandise is counted on an up-to-the-minute basis. (15)

Personality   *See* Image. (2)

Personal Shopping Service   A form of customer service where the store's personnel either shop with or for the customer. (23)

Physical Barriers   In terms of site selection, an obstacle that restricts the customer's use of a particular store location. An example of a physical barrier would be a limited-access highway. (6)

Point-of-Purchase Display   A form of display that is on or near the point of sale. (21)

Point of Sale (POS)   A register that collects information at the point of sale for use in the unit control system. (15)

Policy   A guide to thinking. (8)

Polygraph   More commonly known as a lie detector. The polygraph is a means of theft detection but also serves as a deterrent to theft. (24)

Precustomer Contact   The first step in the retail selling process. During this period, the salesclerk prepares himself or herself by learning stock, store policies, sales procedures, and so on. (17)

Premium   Something that is sold, usually at cost (self-liquidator), or given without charge to the shopper only after the customer performs some task such as the buying of at least $5 worth of groceries or the test driving of a new car. (20)

Prepayment Dating   Retailer is required to pay in full for merchandise when order is placed. (12)

Press Kit   A collection of facts and figures, photographs, and other information that will simplify the task of telling people about the store. (9)

Price Audit   Procedure that compares the price of the item on the price ticket with the price of the item as shown in the store's records. (15)

Price Elasticity of Demand   A concept that determines the effect of a given price change on demand. If an item is price elastic, a change in price will influence consumer demand, whereas an inelastic situation will find a change in price having little or no influence on demand. (13)

* *Numbers in parentheses indicate the number of the chapter in which the term is used.*

Price Guarantee If the market price for the merchandise should fall between the date of purchase and the normal purchase period, any savings that result from the lower price will be passed on to the retailer. (12)

Price Line A particular price level that is set for merchandise that would normally sell around that price (price zone). A typical store might use three lines that would imply good, better, and best to the customer. (13)

Private-Label, Third-Party Plan A credit plan that is operated by a third party under the name of the store. (22)

Procedure A guide to action. (8)

Productivity-Base Budgeting A budgeting procedure that bases financial need on a flexible level of retail activity. Budget level will fluctuate in a predetermined manner. (25)

Product Life Cycle A marketing model that illustrates the selling duration of a product or service. The cycle consists of the introduction stage, the market growth stage, the market maturity stage, and the sales decline stage. (10)

Programmed Learning Method A method of training using repetitious use of written exercises or teaching machines. (16)

Programmed Merchandiser A resource that offers many services to a retailer in return for a definite commitment to buy merchandise. (11)

Progression Method A method of training that moves the trainee from position to position as a means of learning various tasks in the store. (16)

Projected Purchases Represents what the store must buy at retail to meet the demands of the target market. (10)

$$\text{Projected Purchases at Retail} = \text{Projected Sales} + \text{Projected Reductions} \pm \text{Projected Net Change in Inventory}$$

Promotional Discount A discount that is given to retailers to encourage them to promote a product or service of a vendor. (12)

Pro Number I.D. number given by freight carrier to merchandise shipment. (14)

Prospecting A step in the retail selling process in which the salesclerk does not wait for the customer to come in and ask to buy but instead searches out new customers to buy the products or stimulates regular customers to buy more products. (17)

Psychological Barriers In terms of site selection, an obstacle in the customer's mind that will restrict the customer's acceptance of a particular store location. An example of a psychological barrier to shopping at a store might be a location in a high crime area. (6)

Psychosociological Motives Buying motives that are concerned with one's own emotions and with acceptance by one's peers. (3)

—Q—

Quantity Discount A reduction in price as a result of the amount of merchandise purchased by the retailer. (12)

Quota-Bonus A compensation plan under which the employee is paid a set wage plus a certain percentage on sales that exceed a predetermined level. (16)

—R—

Rack Jobber A firm that provides all services for a particular type of merchandise not normally within the area of expertise of the retailer. (11)

Receipt-of-Goods Dating Retailer is required to pay in full for the merchandise according to the terms of sale that begin with the arrival of the goods. (12)

Receiving The part of the distribution process that has as its function the acceptance or rejection of goods based on whether what is received is what was ordered and whether it is damaged. (14)

Recessed Front   A type of store entrance that provides an area for customers to get out of the traffic flow, look in the windows, and enter the store. (7)

Recruitment   The bringing together of potential job applicants and the store. (16)

Reference Group   A group of people with a common bond that serves to establish norms of buying behavior for the individuals within the group. (3)

Reference Price   A "retail" price that is quoted in a catalog that supposedly represents the price being charged for an item at other stores in the trade area. (13)

Reilly's Law of Retail Gravitation   Two cities attract from an intermediate town in the vicinity of the breaking point approximately in direct proportion to the population of the two cities and in inverse proportion to the squares of the distances from these two cities to the intermediate town. (6)

Reprimand   A form of verbal disciplinary action for a minor infraction of the rules whose purpose is to secure desirable behavior from the employee without creating unnecessary dissatisfaction. (18)

Resident Buying Office   This office provides information about market trends, develops and maintains supplier contacts, and provides assistance to the store when the retailer comes to the market to buy merchandise. (11)

Resource Analysis   The on-going process of evaluating the data in the resource file to determine from which vendors the store should buy, or continue to buy, its merchandise. (11)

Resource File   An orderly means of collecting data on all potential merchandise suppliers. These data might pertain to the quality, reliability, or promptness of the supplier. (11)

Retail Accordion   A concept which states that, as stores develop, domination by general-line, wide-assortment retailers alternates with domination by specialized, narrow-line merchants. (1)

Retail Audit   An evaluation of the complete retailing operation for purposes of improving overall performance. (25)

Retail Display   A nonpersonal presentation of merchandise and/or information to the target market that takes place within the physical environment of the store. (21)

Retailer   A business firm whose predominant function is retailing. (1)

Retailing   The summation of all activities that result in the offering for sale of goods and/or services to individuals and/or organizations for purposes of ultimate consumption. (1)

Retailing Mix   All those elements that make the store the entity that it is in the marketplace. The five parts, or "P's," of the retailing mix are Product, Place, Promotion, Price, and Personality. (2)

Retailing Research   Systematic gathering, recording, and analyzing of data pertaining to the retailer's target market and/or retailing mix (product, place, price, promotion, and personality). (4)

Retail Method of Inventory Valuation   A method for determining ending inventory without the necessity for a physical count of merchandise. (15)

Retail Security   Awareness, prevention, and detection of merchandise and money shortages. (24)

Retail Strategy   The approach followed by a retailer that involves selecting a store's target market and then developing a retailing mix to effectively sell that market. (2)

Return on Investment (ROI)   A measure of profitability for a store or any part thereof. ROI is determined by dividing net profit by amount of investment. (25)

Revolving Charge Plan   A credit arrangement whereby the customer can pay a minimum amount (usually a sliding scale that averages about 10 percent of the balance) per month plus a finance charge. In most cases, the customer has an option to pay in full within 30 days without a finance charge. (22)

Rigid Pricing   A fixed price for an item under all circumstances. (13)

Route Selling   A form of in-home selling where the retailer delivers products on a regular basis or on an "as requested" basis to many households on a route basis. (26)

Routing   The calculated selection of the best modes of transportation to move a given shipment from a vendor to a store. (14)

---

* Numbers in parentheses indicate the number of the chapter in which the term is used.

Salary Plus Commission   A compensation plan under which employees receive a set wage plus an established percentage of their sales for a predetermined period. (16)

Sales Forecast   A subjective estimate, in dollars, of the demand for the products the store expects to sell. (10)

Sales Productivity of Department   Estimated departmental sales divided by the average amount of sales per square foot using trade data times floor value factor. (7)

Sales Promotion   Includes all those activities, either nonrecurring or continuous, that supplement the store's advertising and personal selling by creating additional traffic and sales. (20)

Sampling   A type of sales promotion whereby a customer is given a small amount of the product, a piece of the product, etc. Examples would be a taste of a food product, a small piece of a fabric, or a paint chip. (20)

Seasonal Discount   Discount offered on specific merchandise for a certain period of time to encourage the retailer to buy merchandise in the off season. (12)

Selection   That aspect of store staffing dealing with the actual determination of which one of the applicants, if any, are best suited for the job. (16)

Service   An activity, benefit, or satisfaction that is offered for sale. (26)

Service Selling   A form of nonstore retailing where the retailer comes to a customer's home and performs a service (lawn care, interior decorating, etc.). (26)

Shoplifting   The crime that occurs when a "customer" either steals merchandise or pays less for the merchandise than the stated price. (24)

Shopping Center or Mall   A group of stores with balanced tenancy—enough of one kind of store to attract traffic but not too many stores of any one type. A shopping center or mall should have adequate parking and good store visibility from the parking area along with two or more large stores to draw the customer. (6)

Shrinkage   Merchandise loss due to shoplifting, employee theft, misweighing or mismeasuring of merchandise, damage while in storage, clerical errors, and so on. (10)

Signing   The element of exterior design that identifies the store by name and by type of store. (7)

Social Class   Relatively permanent and homogeneous divisions in a society into which individuals or families sharing similar values, life-styles, interests, and behavior can be categorized. (3)

Special Event   A type of sales promotion whose purpose is to draw target customers to the shopping area. Examples are parades, shows, and seminars. (20)

Special Merchandise   A discount that takes the form of merchandise rather than an outright price reduction. (12)

Special Services   Services offered to disabled consumers (ramps, wide aisles, employees who know sign language, etc.). (23)

Specialty Advertising   Useful items that carry an advertising imprint and are given without obligation to customers or prospective customers. Common imprinted items include pens, pencils, matchbooks, calendars, key chains, and rulers. (19)

Specialty Store   A retail institution that concentrates its efforts on one merchandise line such as clothing, electronics, or appliances. (1)

Specification Buying   The central buying office creates a product to be sold exclusively by the particular group of stores. The central buyer actually determines the desired characteristics for a product with assistance from the member stores and then contracts for its manufacture. The product is usually sold under the brand name of the store. (11)

Sponsor Method   A method of training that assigns a current employee to the new employee to assist that person in becoming accustomed to the store and its people. (16)

Staffing   The function of hiring personnel for a store that includes the determination of need, recruitment and selection, orientation, training, compensation, and performance evaluation. (16)

Standard Metropolitan Statistical Area (SMSA)   A U.S. Census unit that contains one city of 50,000 or more inhabitants or "twin cities" that have a combined population of at least

50,000. The SMSA includes the county of each central city or cities and adjacent counties that are metropolitan in character and economically and socially integrated with the central city. (6)

Stock Keeping Unit (SKU) One, distinct, individual type of item carried by a store. (10)

Stock Shortage Merchandise that is unaccounted for when what should be on the shelf at retail (beginning inventory at retail minus deductions) is compared with what is actually on the shelf at retail. (15)

Stock Turnover *See* Inventory Turnover. (5)

Store Cluster A group of stores that is generally off by itself. The store cluster has off-street parking and normally serves a neighborhood. (6)

Store-Owned Resident Buying Office—Associated A buying office that is owned and operated by an association or group of stores. *See also* Resident Buying Office. (11)

Store-Owned Resident Buying Office—Chain A buying office that assists the buyers from each individual unit of the chain in selecting the best merchandise for each particular store. *See also* Resident Buying Office. (11)

Store-Owned Resident Buying Office—Individual A buying office that is owned and operated for the benefit of an individual store. *See also* Resident Buying Office. (11)

Straight Commission A compensation plan whereby the employee's wages are related directly to the amount of sales made by the individual. (16)

Straight Salary A compensation plan whereby the employee is paid a set wage for a set number of hours regardless of any external considerations. (16)

Street Vendor A form of nonstore retailing that sells merchandise from a sidewalk location. Merchandise sold can vary from hot dogs to furniture to "questionable" items of quality. (26)

String Street A number of stores located side by side along a street. (6)

Suggestion Selling A step in the retail selling process where the salesperson uses the opportunity after the sale has been made to suggest something else that the customer might also wish to purchase. (17)

Supermarket Any food store unit, chain or independent, with $1,000,000 or more in annual sales. (1)

—T—

Tact Keen sense of what to do or say in order to maintain good relations with others or avoid offense. (17)

Target Market Those customers of a retail operation on whom the store will place primary emphasis in developing its marketing program. (2)

Telephone Retailing A form of nonstore retailing where the telephone is used for solicitation purposes or in conjunction with other forms of direct marketing. (26)

Third-Party Plan A credit plan that is offered to customers by a firm other than the retailer but is accepted by the retailer. Examples of a third-party plan are Master Card and American Express. (22)

Tombstone Ad An advertisement run by a manufacturer in major trade publications that serve a particular retail market. The tombstone ad announces that one or more allowances are available to qualified retailers. (3)

Trade Area A geographically delineated region containing potential customers for whom there exists a probability greater than zero of their purchasing a given class of products and/or services offered for sale by a particular firm or a particular agglomeration of firms. (6)

Trade Credit The amount of inventory that suppliers will provide the retailer on credit. (5)

Trade Discount *See* Functional Discount. (12)

Trade Show A place where the buyer can get "hands-on" experience with the merchandise by being exposed to many vendors. (11)

Trading Post An early retail institution in the United States where settler and Indian alike would come to do business. (1)

* Numbers in parentheses indicate the number of the chapter in which the term is used.

Trading Stamps   Fractional certificates that are redeemable for merchandise and/or cash. (20)

Traffic Management   The management of the movement of goods from origin to destination. (14)

Training   That aspect of store staffing dealing with teaching employees job and human skills. (16)

Transit Advertising   Advertisements outside and inside of public transportation vehicles (bus, train, etc.) and advertisements in close proximity to bus stops, subway stations, and so on. (19)

Traveling Display   A type of sales promotion that generates traffic for a store or mall by providing something of interest that the target market would like to see. (20)

—U—

Unit Control of Merchandise   The evaluation of store inventories in terms of physical units. This involves periodic or perpetual counting of merchandise to ensure proper mix. (15)

Unit of Measure System   A procedure for allocating time for the purpose of scheduling work such as in alterations. (23)

Universal Product Code (UPC)   A bar code system that identifies only the manufacturer and the product. All other data—such as price and date purchased—are stored in a computer. When the UPC markings are "read" by an optical scanner, the other pertinent data can be retrieved from the "memory" of the system. (14)

Universal Vendor Marking (UVM)   Supplier coding of merchandise as to size, color, and so on in a common identifying manner so that it can be "read" by the retailer either manually or with an optical scanner. (14)

—V—

Variety   The number of lines carried in a store. (10)

Vending   A form of nonstore retailing that has the capability to complete the sale without the assistance of sales personnel. (26)

Voluntary Chain   A retail store voluntarily aligns itself with a particular wholesaler who will offer various services and provide the store with all or almost all the merchandise it needs. The store will usually take on the name of the voluntary chain. (11)

—W—

Warehouse Store   A retail institution that typically offers a minimum of customer services while using a no-frills merchandising approach. (1)

Wheel of Retailing   A concept which states that new types of retailers enter the market with low prices, low profit margin, low status, and little else to offer the consumer. Over time, the retailer becomes fat. Higher costs necessitating higher margins, improved status, and many services for the customer make the retailer vulnerable to new retailers who can and are willing to operate at a lower-cost—lower-margin level. (1)

Width   The availability of complementary items within a merchandise line. (10)

Window Display   An exterior display, either open or closed back, that is generally one of three types: promotional—to sell merchandise; institutional—to sell the store; public service—to sell items and ideas not related to the store. (21)

Work Simplification   Changes that reduce the time and effort expended to perform a task. (25)

—Z—

Zero-Base Budgeting   A budgeting procedure that starts with a clean slate each budget period. Past history does not determine the budget. (25)

Index